Mrs. Lincoln's Boston Cook Book

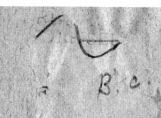

MRS. LINCOLN'S

BOSTON COOK BOOK.

MRS. LINCOLN'S

BOSTON COOK BOOK.

WHAT TO DO AND WHAT NOT TO DO IN COOKING.

BY

MRS. MARY J. LINCOLN,

FIRST PRINCIPAL OF THE BOSTON COOKING SCHOOL, AND AUTHOR OF
"CARVING AND SERVING," "BOSTON SCHOOL KITCHEN TEXT-BOOK,"
"TWENTY LESSONS IN COOKERY," "THE PEERLESS COOK BOOK,"
AND "A COOK BOOK FOR A MONTH AT A TIME."

Revised Edition.

CONTAINING OVER 250 ADDITIONAL RECIPES.

BOSTON:

LITTLE, BROWN, AND COMPANY.

1911.

710

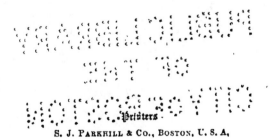

"Not to know at large of things remote
From use, obscure and subtle, but to know
That which before us lies in daily life,
Is the prime wisdom."

MILTON.

———————

"To know what you do know. and not to know what you do not know, is true knowledge."— CONFUCIUS.

PREFACE TO THE REVISED EDITION

WHEN the "Boston Cook Book" was first published, cooking schools were in their infancy, and some suggestions as to their management were included in its pages. But now, after sixteen years' dissemination of these suggestions, it seems no longer advisable to include them in a cook book. Therefore, in making this first revision of my book I have utilized the pages previously devoted to this subject and to the general index, which is superfluous, as the alphabetical index is so comprehensive, also the blank spaces at the end of some chapters, for about three hundred additional recipes, and this without increasing the size or the price.

The subject of each section forms the heading of the page.

Since granulated gelatine and baking powder are now so universally used, the proportions of each are given where needed. Recipes for many new food products are inserted, and many minor changes made in the text.

This revised edition is *not the new book* which has been in preparation for some time. Unavoidable delays in the completion of the latter and the large demand for extra copies from many persons who have worn out their first

books have led me to make this revision of the " Boston
Cook Book" now.

The new book will contain many features not practicable
here, and is designed not to *supplant* but to *supplement*
my first book.

MARY J. LINCOLN.

BOSTON, MASS., October, 1900.

PREFACE TO FIRST EDITION.

To compile a book which shall be not only a collection of receipts, given briefly for the experienced housekeeper, and with sufficient clearness for the beginner, but which shall also embody enough of physiology, and of the chemistry and philosophy of food, to make every principle intelligible to a child and interesting to the mature mind; which shall serve equally well for the cook in the kitchen, the pupil in the school-room, and the teacher in the normal class, — is a difficult task. Yet the need of a book of moderate cost, containing in a reasonably small compass all this and much more, has been seriously felt by all who are engaged in teaching cookery. Moreover, there is a special reason for the publication of this work. It is undertaken at the urgent request of the pupils of the Boston Cooking School, who have desired that the receipts and lessons given during the last four years in that institution should be arranged in a permanent form.

To one who from childhood has been trained in all details of housework, learning by observation or by actual experience much that it is impossible to receive from books, the amount of ignorance shown by many women is surprising. That a person of ordinary intelligence presiding over her household can be satisfied with only a vague conception of the common domestic methods, or that any true woman can see anything degrading in any labor necessary for the highest physical condition of her family, would be incredible if the truth of it were not daily manifest.

Happily, popular opinion now decides that no young lady's education is complete without a course of training in one or more branches of domestic work. And those who are not so fortunate as to have the best of all training — that of actual work under a wise and competent mother — gladly resort to the cooking-schools for instruction.

In compiling these receipts for use in a school and in the family, several things were demanded. In a school of pupils from every class and station in life, a great variety of receipts is desirable. They must be clear, but concise, for those who are already well grounded in first principles. They must be explained, illustrated, and reiterated for the inexperienced and the careless. They must have a word of caution for those who seem always to have the knack of doing the wrong thing. They must include the most healthful foods for those who have been made ill by improper food; the cheapest as well as the most nutritious, for the laboring class; the richest and most elaborately prepared, for those who can afford them physically as well as pecuniarily.

These receipts are not a mere compilation. A large portion have accumulated during a long period of housekeeping; and many have been received from friends who are practical housekeepers. Others have been taken from standard authorities on cooking; and all have been frequently and thoroughly tested by pupils under the eye of the author. As far as possible, acknowledgment has been made for the receipts received. Where changes and improvements have been made, or where there were many authorities for the same formula, no credit has been given.

Some cook-books presuppose the presence of an assistant; but as three fourths of the women in this country do their own work, these receipts are arranged so as to require the attention of but one person.

It is proverbial that young housekeepers are often greatly perplexed in attempting to provide little enough for only two. For their benefit many of our receipts are prepared on a scale of smaller measurements.

The materials to be used are given in the order in which they are to be put together. They are arranged in columns, where the eye may catch them readily, or in *italics* where economy of space seemed desirable.

Every caution or suggestion has been given at the request of some pupil who failed to find in other books just what she needed ; or because, in the experience of teaching, it has been shown that, unless forewarned, pupils inevitably make certain mistakes. Many subjects which in other books are omitted or given briefly, will be found to have received here an extensive treatment, because they have seemed of paramount importance.

All the chemical and physiological knowledge that is necessary for a clear understanding of the laws of health, so far as they are involved in the science of cookery, is given in this book. Nine tenths of the women who go through a scientific course in seminaries never put any of the knowledge gained into practical use. By the time they have occasion to use such knowledge in their own homes, the Chemistry and Physiology have been relegated to the attic, where they help mice to material for their nests, but help no woman to apply the principles of science upon which the health and welfare of her household largely depend.

The statement will appear incredible to most people, and yet it is true, that many women do not know what the simplest things in our daily food are ; cannot tell when water boils, or the difference between lamb and veal, lard and drippings. They cannot give the names of kitchen utensils; do not know anything about a stove, or how to pare a potato. This will explain what might otherwise seem an unnecessary minuteness of detail. The experience of such ignorance also suggested the sub-title of the " Boston Cook Book," — " What to do and what not to do in Cooking," — just *how* to hold your bowl and spoon, to use your hands, to regulate your stove, to wash your dishes; and just *how not* to fall into the errors into which so many have stumbled before you. But, more than all, it is attempted to give a reason for every step taken, and a clear answer to any questions that are likely to arise in the experience of either housekeeper or cook.

A word of grateful acknowledgment is due the many friends who have aided in this work.

First, to my mother I owe much for her excellent judgment in training me as a child to a love for all household work. Although it was often hard to " help mother " when other children were at play, the knowledge thus gained has proved invaluable. Every year's experience in teaching has made me prize more and more this early training.

Also, I am deeply indebted to Miss M. S. Devereux for the illustrations of this book. In all my work I have been greatly aided by her suggestions and generous sympathy.

And, lastly, I would not forget my obligations to a large circle of personal friends. Especially would I remember the one who, twenty years ago, aided me in making my first loaf of bread, and the many among my pupils who, out of their varied experience, have contributed much that has proved helpful.

MARY J. LINCOLN.

Wollaston, Mass., 1884.

BOOKS OF REFERENCE.

AMONG the many valuable authorities on subjects connected with food, the following have been consulted in preparing this work. The Cook Books are named, not according to their merit, but in the order in which the author has had personal knowledge of them: —

Youmans's Handbook of Household Science.
Johnston's Chemistry of Common Life.
Wells's Science of Common Things.
Lewes's Physiology of Common Life.
Gray's How Plants Grow.
Dalton's Physiology.
Webster's Dictionary.
Food. By A. H. Church.
Food for the Invalid.
Family Receipt Books without number; and Cook Books by Mrs. Henderson, Marion Harland, Mrs. Cornelius, Mrs. Beecher, Warne, Francatelli, Soyer, Mrs. Whitney, Miss Parloa, Mrs. Campbell, Miss Corson, Mrs. Beeton, and Mrs. Ewing.

CONTENTS.

LIST OF ILLUSTRATIONS.

LECTURES *and* PRACTICAL TALKS

ON

COOKERY

(*WITH DEMONSTRATION IF DESIRED*)

By MRS. LINCOLN

SUBJECTS

THE EVOLUTION OF COOKERY
ART AND SCIENCE, VERSUS DRUDGERY AND LUCK
IDEAL HOUSEKEEPING
DOMESTIC SCIENCE
ECONOMIC BUYING
RECIPROCAL DUTIES OF HOSTESS AND GUEST
LUNCHEON AND DINNER GIVING
FURNISHING A HOME
GLIMPSES OF FOREIGN HOUSEKEEPING
PRACTICAL TALKS ON THE KITCHEN
PRACTICAL TALKS ON ALL FORMS OF COOKING
EUROPEAN REMINISCENCES

Schools, Societies, and Women's Clubs desiring one or more lectures may secure Mrs. Lincoln's services by applying to her personally or by letter.

For Terms, Address —

MRS. MARY J. LINCOLN
204 Huntington Avenue, Boston, Mass.

THE BOSTON COOK BOOK.

COOKERY

COOKERY is the art of preparing food for the nourishment of the human body. When given its proper importance in the consideration of health and comfort, it must be based upon scientific principles of hygiene and what the French call the minor moralities of the household. All civilized nations cook their food, to improve its taste and digestibility. The degree of civilization is often measured by the cuisine.

Cooking (from the Latin *coquo*, to boil, bake, heat, dry, scorch, or ripen) is usually done by the direct application of heat. Fruits and some vegetables which are eaten in a natural state have really been cooked or ripened by the heat of the sun. Milk and eggs, which are types of perfect food, would be useless as food unless they came from the warm living animal. Fish, flesh, and fruits which have been dried in the sun or smoked, and are often eaten without any further preparation, have undergone a certain process of natural cooking.

Heat seems to create new flavors, and to change the odor, taste, and digestibility of nearly all articles of food. It swells and bursts the starch cells in flour, rice, and potatoes; hardens the albumen in eggs, fish, and meat; softens the fibrous substances in tough meats, hard vegetables and fruits. It develops new flavors in tea, coffee, roasted meat, crusts of bread, baked beans, etc.

1

Cold is also an important matter to be regarded in the preparation of food. Sweet dishes and certain flavors, like honey, ices, and custards ; the water, wine, or milk we drink ; our butter, fruits, and salads, — are all more palatable when cold.

Water, or some other liquid, in connection with heat is necessary in many forms of cookery. Grains, peas, beans, dried fruits which have parted with nearly all their moisture in the ripening or drying process necessary for their preservation, need a large portion of water in cooking, to soften and swell the cellulose, gluten, and starch before they can be masticated and digested. In some vegetables and fruits water draws out certain undesirable flavors ; it softens and dissolves the gelatinous portions of meat, and makes palatable and nourishing many substances which would be rendered unwholesome by a dry heat.

Air, or the free action of oxygen, upon our food while cooking develops certain flavors not otherwise to be obtained. Meat roasted or broiled has a much finer flavor than when boiled, baked, or fried. Toasted bread, thin corn cake baked before the fire, roasted apples, and many articles cooked in the open air, show the benefit of this free combined action of heat and air.

Drying in the sun was one of the earliest modes of cookery. Then came roasting before an open fire, or broiling over the coals, and baking in the hot ashes. This last was the primitive oven. As the art of making cooking-utensils developed, stewing, boiling, and frying were adopted. Then, to economize heat, portable ovens were invented ; these were originally a covered dish set over or near the fire, having sometimes a double cover filled with coals. Afterwards, stoves which kept the fire and heat in a limited space were introduced ; and improvements have been made in them so extensively that we now have them with conveniences for doing every form of cooking with wood, coal, oil, or gas.

Some one gives this distinction between man and other animals : "Man is an animal that builds a fire and uses it to cook his food." It is quite important then, as a stepping-stone to cooking, to learn the properties and management of a fire.

Fire.

Fire is heat and light produced by the combustion of inflammable substances. Combustion is a chemical operation carried on in the air, or the chemical union of the oxygen of the air with some combustible body, like hydrogen gas or the solid carbon, and is attended with the evolution of heat and light. The heat and the light come from the sun. With every particle of vegetable matter that is formed by the combined action of the sun and the carbonic acid gas in the air, a portion of the sun's heat and light is absorbed and held fast in it. And whenever this vegetable matter is decomposed, — as in burning wood, coal, or oil, which are only definite forms of vegetable matter, — this heat and light are given out. The amount of each depends upon the mode of burning.

Air is composed mainly of two elementary gases, oxygen and nitrogen (one part oxygen and four parts nitrogen), with a small amount of watery vapor and carbonic acid gas.

Pure oxygen is a gas which has a wonderful attraction for, and power of combination with, every other element. If it were everywhere present in a perfectly pure state, it would consume or burn up everything; but it is diluted or mixed (not combined) with nitrogen, another gas which is incombustible, and which lessens the combustibility of everything with which it comes in contact. Owing to this dilution, the oxygen will not unite with the carbon and hydrogen with which it is everywhere surrounded, and produce *rapid* combustion, except at a high temperature. The temperature at which this union takes place is called the burning-point, and this varies in different substances. Thus combustion is within the power and control of man; and some extra means are usually employed to increase the temperature to the burning-point, — friction, or percussion, or the use of some more highly inflammable substances, like sulphur and phosphorus. This produces heat sufficient to complete the chemical union, or, in common phrase, " kindles the fire."

The heat generated for all household purposes is produced by the chemical action of the oxygen of the air upon the hydrogen and carbon which are found in the various kinds of wood and coal. The oxygen first combines with the carbon and decomposes it, producing carbonic acid gas, which escapes into the air, from which it is absorbed by plants, or by human lungs when there is no proper ventilation. The oxygen also combines with the hydrogen gas in the fuel, and this produces the flame; the larger the amount of hydrogen in the fuel, the greater the amount of flame. Some of the products of combustion are not entirely consumed, and pass off as smoke; some are incombustible, and remain as ashes. The intensity of a fire and the amount of heat which it produces are always in proportion to the amount of oxygen with which it is supplied. There should be just air enough for perfect combustion. An excess of air projected upon a fire conveys away the heat, cools the fuel, and checks the combustion. The supply of air should be controlled by confining it in a limited space.

Fires are usually kindled at the bottom of a flue or chimney. The heated air, being lighter, rises; the colder, denser air rushes in to take its place, becomes heated, and ascends. Thus a continuous current is established, and a constant supply of fresh air secured. The chimney serves to carry off the smoke and poisonous products of combustion; the heavier, incombustible products settle in the form of ashes. The force of this current of air drawing through the chimney (a matter of great importance) is called the draught. It varies with the temperature and amount of air in the room, and the length and width of the chimney.

Fuel.

The materials generally used as fuel are wood, charcoal, coal, kerosene oil, and gas.

Soft woods, such as pine or birch, kindle quickly, produce intense heat, and are best for a quick, blazing fire.

Hard woods, like oak, ash, and hickory, burn more slowly, but produce harder coals, which retain the heat longer, and are better where long-continued heat is required.

Charcoal, which is coal made by charring or burning wood with only a limited supply of air, burns easily and produces greater heat in proportion to its weight than any other fuel. It should never be burned in a close room.

Anthracite coal is a kind of mineral charcoal derived from ancient vegetation buried in the earth, and so thoroughly pressed that nothing is left but pure carbon, a little sulphur, and the incombustible ash. It kindles slowly, yields an intense, steady heat, and burns for a longer time without replenishing than the hardest wood.

Coke, often used in cities, is the residue of coal from which illuminating gas has been manufactured. The heat is intense, but transient.

Stoves for burning *kerosene oil* and *gas* have recently been introduced, and are now so nearly perfect that the care of a fire for cooking purposes is trifling. Gas can only be used in certain localities.

The cheapest fuel is the *best* kerosene oil. There need be no waste, no superfluous heat, no vitiated air, if the fire be extinguished immediately after the work is done, and if the stove be kept perfectly clean, so as to secure a free burning and perfect combustion. With two good stoves having all the latest and best improvements, a large amount of work can be easily and satisfactorily accomplished.

The Making and Care of a Coal Fire.

If you intend to buy a new stove or range, get one simple in construction, that you may quickly learn all its parts and their uses; plain in finish, that you may easily keep it clean; and perfectly fitted part to part, with doors and dampers shutting absolutely close, so that you may control the fire and heat. This latter point is of essential importance in regulating the oven and in preventing a waste of fuel.

Become thoroughly acquainted with whatever stove you may have. If necessary, take it apart; learn how to clean it in the inside, to regulate the dampers for all the variations of wind, temperature, and fuel; and then learn how to make and keep a fire.

All stoves have a fire-box, with more or less space underneath for ashes; a slide damper under the fire, letting in the air; an outlet for the smoke; and a damper which regulates the supply of hot air, sending it around and underneath the oven, or letting it escape into the chimney. Remove the covers and brush the soot from the top of the oven into the fire-box; then clean out the grate; and if the stove have conveniences for so doing, sift the ashes in the stove and save all the old coal and cinders. Put in shavings or loose rolls of paper, then fine pine kindlings, arranged crosswise, and a layer of hard wood, leaving plenty of air space between the pieces. Be sure the wood comes out to each end of the fire-box. Put on the covers; and if the stove need cleaning, moisten some pulverized stove polish with water, and rub the stove with a paint brush dipped in the polish. When all blackened, rub with a dry polishing-brush until nearly dry. Open the direct draught and oven damper, and light the paper, as a slight heat facilitates the process of polishing. When the wood is thoroughly kindled, fill the fire-box with coal even with the top of the oven. Brush up the hearth and floor, empty the teakettle, and fill it with fresh water. Watch the fire, and push the coal down as the wood burns away, and add enough more coal to keep it even with the top of the fire bricks. When the blue flame becomes white, close the oven damper; and when the coal is burning freely, but not red, shut the direct draught. It seems impossible for some persons to understand that a coal fire is at its height as soon as well kindled, and needs only air enough to keep it burning. When it becomes bright red all through, it has parted with most of its heat, and begins to die out. Tons of coal are wasted in many kitchens, and ranges are need-lessly burned out, by filling the fire-box till the coal touches the covers, and leaving the draughts open till the coal is red.

Nearly all stoves and portable ranges have the oven at one side of and a little below the fire. In brick-set ranges the ovens are sometimes over the fire. A stove has a door on each side of the oven, with the fire-box in front. A portable range has only one oven-door, and the fire-box at the end. In ranges where the oven is over the fire, the articles to be baked are placed on a grate near the middle, as the bottom of the oven is usually very hot. In stoves or portable ranges anything which has to rise in the oven, like bread, pastry, cake, etc., is placed on the bottom of the oven, and, if the heat be too great, a small rack or grate may be placed under it. Large pieces of meat are placed on a rack in a pan; while small cuts of meat, birds, etc., which are to be baked quickly, and any dishes which are to be merely browned, like scalloped dishes, must be placed on the grate near the top. Cultivate the habit of opening and shutting the oven-door quickly but gently. Learn the hottest and coolest places in the oven. Look at things as they are baking, and turn and watch till you are sure they can be left alone. If anything bake unevenly or too fast, put a screen between it and the heat, — a pan on the grate above or underneath, or a frame of stiff paper made larger than the pan, that it may not touch the dough. When the regulating dampers are closed and the oven is still too hot, lift a cover on the top partly off, although in a stove in which the parts are perfectly adjusted this will never be necessary. When the oven is not hot enough, open the direct draught, and rake out the ashes from the grate. Keep the grate cleaned out and the fire burning freely, when a very hot oven is needed. At other times keep the draughts shut and do not waste the coal.

To keep a brisk fire for several hours or all day, it is better to add a sprinkling of coal often, rather than to let it burn nearly out, and then, by adding a larger quantity, check the fire and retard the work. In using the top of the stove remember the hottest place is over the fire and toward the middle, *not* on the front of the stove. When you have once watched the flame in its passage over the top, down the back, and under the oven, then across, out and up on the opposite side and out into the chimney, you will understand where the greatest heat must be.

Boiling.

The term "boiling" is often used erroneously in cookery. The expressions "the teakettle boils," "the rice is boiling," "boiled beef," etc., are all good illustrations of the rhetorical figure *metonymy*, but they are practically incorrect. In all cases it is only the water or liquid which boils. No solid can boil until first changed to a liquid. Solids become liquid at the melting-point. Liquids take the form of steam or vapor at the boiling-point. Boiling is the conversion of a liquid into steam by the application of heat sufficient to cause *ebullition*, or agitation of its surface. Boiling, therefore, as applied to the cooking of solids, is heating or cooking in a boiling liquid. It is one of the most generally used, and abused, forms of cooking. Boiling water, which is really cooked water, is the liquid usually employed. Water, as it is heated from below, expands into vapor. The air of the water and the steam shoot up in the form of bubbles; as they come in contact with the cold water near the surface, the bubbles collapse, the steam is condensed and descends with the cold water, making a double set of currents, which causes quite a commotion among the particles. As the whole body of water becomes hotter, these bubbles of steam rise higher and higher before collapsing, and occasion the sound which we call the "singing of the kettle." When the water is sufficiently heated, they rise and break at the surface, causing more or less agitation, according to the rapidity with which they are formed. Water is scalding hot at 150°, or when the hand cannot be borne in it. *Water simmers* when the bubbles all collapse beneath the surface, and the steam is condensed to water again, or at 185°. *Water boils* when the bubbles rise to the surface, and the steam is thrown off, as at 212°. When this boiling-point is reached, the heat escapes with the steam; and all the fire in the world cannot make the water any hotter, so long as the steam escapes. If the fire be very fierce, so that these bubbles are formed and expelled rapidly, and the water boils over, the water is no hotter; it only evaporates or boils away faster, and can only be made hotter by confining the steam, which in ordinary kettles is impossible, owing to the enormous expansive force of the steam. With a few exceptions it is a waste of fuel, time, and material to keep the water boiling at such a galloping rate that the cover has to be lifted to prevent boiling over.

A kettle should *never* be quite full, as the water expands in heating, and, in boiling over, makes needless work and injures the stove. Water will boil more quickly in a kettle with a rough surface than in one with a smooth surface, as the water adheres to a smooth surface with greater force, and this force or attraction must be overcome before boiling takes place. Small, clean gravel is sometimes kept in a smooth kettle to facilitate the boiling.

Water boils at a higher temperature when there is sugar, or salt, or anything in it to increase its density. It takes longer for it to boil; but it is hotter, when that point is reached. No one who has been burned by boiling syrup ever doubted this fact. Fresh water boils at 212°; salt water, at 224°. If we put salt with the water in the lower part of a double boiler, a greater degree of heat is obtained by which to cook the articles in the top.

Water boils at a lower temperature, that is, more quickly, when the pressure of the air upon the water is diminished. Before a rain the pressure of the air is lessened, because the air when filled with vapor is lighter. Observing housekeepers have often noticed how quickly things burn at such a time, and foretell a rain by the rapidity with which water evaporates.

The pressure of the air is less the higher we ascend above the level of the sea, since we leave much of the air below us. Cooking in boiling water requires a much longer time in mountainous regions; for the water boils so quickly that it holds less heat than in lower altitudes, where it is subject to greater pressure. Water, in boiling, loses the air or gases which give it a fresh taste and sparkling appearance. It becomes flat and tasteless. If there be any impurity in water, boiling or cooking will destroy it. Then, by cooling, and exposing to pure air again, it becomes aerated and palatable. But water for cooking, unless there are impurities to be removed, should be used when freshly boiled. This is especially important in making tea and coffee.

Soft water should be used in boiling where the object is to soften the texture, and extract the soluble parts, as in soups, broths, tea, and coffee. Hard water, or soft water salted, is better where we wish to preserve the articles whole, and retain the soluble and flavoring principles, as in most green vegetables. Beans or dried peas, which contain casein or vegetable albumen in large proportion, should be cooked in soft water, as the lime in hard water hardens the casein, and prevents the vegetables from becoming soft.

In cooking meat, fish, and vegetables in water, we should remember these two facts : —

Cold water draws out the albuminous juices, softens the fibres and gelatinous portions of meat, and holds them in solution. It draws out starch, but does not unite with it.

Boiling water hardens and toughens albumen and fibrine, bursts the starch grains, and is absorbed by the swelling starch.

Meat is cooked in water for three distinct purposes : —

First. To keep the nutriment *within the meat*, as in what is usually called *boiled meat*. To do this, we leave the meat whole, that only a little surface may be exposed. Plunge it into boiling salted water, and keep it there for five or ten minutes; this hardens the albumen over the entire surface, and makes a coating through which the juices cannot escape. Then move the kettle where the water will simmer slowly. See that the cover fits tightly, to keep in the steam. The water should be salted to raise the boiling-point, and increase the density of the water, and thus prevent the escape of the juices. A small amount of the albumen in the outer surface will be dissolved and rise as scum. This should be removed, or it will settle on the meat and render it uninviting in appearance. If the meat be put in the kettle with the bones uppermost, then the scum will not settle on the meat. In turning the meat do not pierce into it to let the juices escape. It will take a longer time to cook in this way, but the fibrine will be softened, and the meat made more tender and of better flavor, than when kept boiling furiously.

Second. Meats are cooked in water to have the nutriment *wholly in the liquid*, as in *soups* and *meat teas*. Cut the meat in small pieces; soak in cold water, the longer the better; heat gradually, and keep hot, but not boiling, until all the goodness is extracted.

Third. Meats are cooked in water to have the nutriment *partly* in the *liquid* and *partly* in the *meat*, as in *stews, fricassees*, etc. Put the meat in cold water, let the water boil quickly, then skim, and keep at the simmering-point. The cold water will draw out enough of the juices to enrich the liquid; then, as it reaches the boiling-point, the meat hardens, and retains the remainder.

Fish is usually cooked in boiling water for the purpose of keeping the juices in the fish. As the flesh of fish breaks easily, the water should never be allowed to boil rapidly. Salmon, mackerel, or any very oily fish, should be put into cold water, and brought almost to the boiling-point quickly, as they have a very strong, rich flavor. A little of this flavor can be lost without injury to the fish.

Vegetables, which are mostly starch and water, should be put into boiling water and boiled rapidly, that the small portions of albumen which they contain may be hardened on the surface; then, if the starch grains are burst quickly, they will absorb the albuminous juices within.

Milk boils at 196°. Being thicker than water, less of the steam escapes, and the whole liquid becomes hot sooner than water. The bubbles rise rapidly, and, owing to their tenacity, do not burst at the surface, but climb over one another till they run over the edge of the pan.

Milk, grains, custards, and any substances which, from their glutinous nature, would be liable to adhere to the kettle, are much more easily and safely cooked in a double boiler, or in a pail within a kettle of water. This is one form of *steaming*, or cooking over boiling water. In steaming, the water should not stop boiling until the articles are cooked. This is a convenient form of cooking many articles which it is troublesome to cook with a dry heat, and yet do not need the solvent powers of water. Watery vegetables are rendered drier by steaming; and tough pieces of meat which cannot be roasted, are first made tender by steaming, and then browned in the oven. Sometimes meat is steamed in its own juices alone; this is called *smothering*, or *pot-roasting*.

Stewing is another form of boiling or cooking in a small quantity of water, at a moderate heat, and for a long time. The word means a slow, moist, gentle heat. It is an economical mode of cooking, except where a fire has to be kept for this purpose alone. The long-continued action of a gentle heat softens the fibres; and the coarsest and cheapest kinds of meat, cooked in this way, with vegetables, may be made tender and nutritious. By judicious use of seasoning material, remnants can be made into savory and nourishing dishes. Whether we call it simply a *stew*, or *ragout*, *haricot*, or *salmi*, the principle is the same, — that of slow, steady simmering, rather than fierce boiling.

Fricasseeing (meaning "to fry") is a form of stewing. The term is usually applied to chicken, veal, or some small game, which is cut into pieces, and fried either before or after stewing, and served with a rich white or brown sauce, and without vegetables. Any meat that is quite juicy and not very tough may be first browned on the outside to keep in the juices, and improve the flavor. Coarse, tough pieces should not be browned, but dipped in vinegar to soften the fibre; and pieces containing much gristle should be put into cold water.

Braising is a form of stewing done usually in a braising-pan or kettle which has coals in the cover. Any granite or iron pan with a close cover to keep in the steam will answer the purpose. When placed in the oven, where it is surrounded by a slow, uniform heat, it needs very little attention. It is one of the most economical and satisfactory ways of cooking large pieces of tough, lean meat, pigeons, liver, fowls, heart, etc. Stock, vegetables, and bacon may be used, if a rich liquor be required; but water, herbs, and simple seasoning make it very palatable.

Baking is hardening or cooking in a dry heat, as in a close oven. Nearly all flour mixtures — bread, pastry, and some forms of pudding — are more wholesome baked than when cooked in any other way. Many forms of baking are really stewing; but the closely confined heat of the oven gives an entirely different flavor from that obtained by stewing over the fire. This is seen in the difference between stewed and baked apple-sauce, beans, etc.

Meat and fish, if baked in the right way, lose less in weight than when boiled or roasted. To bake them properly, the juices must be kept within the meat. An intense heat at first is necessary to harden the albumen; then reduce the heat, that the outside may not become too hard, and baste frequently to prevent drying. No water should be put in the pan at first, as it will then be impossible to have a greater heat than that of boiling water (212°), while for baking meat 280°, or more, is required. Put one or two tablespoonfuls of beef drippings, or some of the fat from the meat, in the pan, to use in basting, as the fat can be made much hotter than water. If the joint be very large, or the meat need thorough cooking, like poultry, veal, or pork, water can be added to check the heat as soon as the outside is cooked sufficiently to keep in the juices. This will keep the meat moist. Small cuts, and meats to be eaten rare, are better baked without water.

Many persons accustomed to meat roasted before the open fire object to the flavor of baked meat. If the oven be very hot at first, and opened every five minutes just long enough for the basting, which is an essential part of the cooking process, the smoky odor escapes. If there be no damper to check the heat underneath the oven, put the grate or another pan under the dripping-pan, as no heat is required under the meat. This will prevent the fat in the pan from burning and smoking the meat. Place the meat with the skin side down at first; then, if the juices begin to flow, the skin keeps them in; and, when turned, it brings the side which is to be up in serving next the hottest part of the oven, for the final browning. All baked meat or fish should be salted and floured all over. Salt draws out the juices; but the flour unites with them, making a paste which soon hardens, and keeps them within. Baste often, and dredge with salt and flour *after* basting. If there be no shelf attached to the stove near the oven, keep a box or frame of wood just the height of the oven, near by, and pushed up close to it; it will be found very convenient to pull the pan out upon it when basting or turning the meat.

Frying.

Frying is cooking in hot fat, — *not boiling* fat, as it is so often called, for fat can be made much hotter than the temperature required for cooking, which is 385°; the temperature for boiling fat is from 565° to 600°. Frying, when properly done, is *immersion* in smoking-hot fat. The fat should be *deep* enough to entirely cover the articles to be cooked; and as it may be used many times, it is not so extravagant as some suppose to use such a quantity. The prime secret of nice frying is to have the fat hot enough to harden instantly the albumen on the outer surface, and thus prevent the fat from soaking into the inside of whatever is to be fried. As a much higher temperature is required than that for boiling or baking, the articles are very quickly cooked; and they have a flavor quite unlike that given by any other form of cooking.

All articles to be fried should be thoroughly dried and slightly warmed. If very *moist*, or very *cold*, or *too many* articles be fried at a time, the fat becomes chilled, and the grease soaks into them. Then, as the moisture heats and boils, it causes such a commotion that the fat and water boil over, and there is great danger from the fat taking fire and spreading to your clothing, to say nothing of the trouble of cleaning the stove and floor. For this reason be careful not to let a drop of water, or of condensed steam from another kettle, fall into the hot fat.

Meat, fish, oysters, croquettes, etc., should be dried, and rolled in fine bread-crumbs, to absorb any moisture; then rolled in beaten egg, and in fine crumbs again. The hot fat hardens the albumen of the egg instantly; and that, with the crumbs, makes a fat-proof crust.

Fish balls, fritters, and fried muffin mixtures contain egg and albumen sufficient to keep them from soaking fat, if the fat be only hot enough. A Scotch bowl, or deep iron or granite kettle, and a wire basket small enough to fit down into the kettle, are best to use in frying.

The Test for Hot Fat. — When the fat begins to smoke put in a bit of bread; if it brown quickly, or while you can count sixty as the clock ticks, it is hot enough for fried potatoes, doughnuts, etc. When hot enough to brown the bread while you count forty, it will do for fish balls, croquettes, etc.

When ready to fry, plunge the basket into the hot fat to grease it, and then place in it the croquettes, or whatever you may be frying, so that they will not touch each other. Hold the handle of the basket with a long fork, and plunge it quickly into the fat, but do not drop the handle, because if the fat begin to boil up, you can then raise the basket quickly, and wait till the ebullition has subsided before plunging it in again; and thus avoid the danger of burning from the overflowing fat. The fat cools rapidly, when many articles are fried at once, and

should be reheated to the test point before frying **any**
more.

Time. — Any cooked mixture, such as fish balls and croquettes, or very small fish, oysters, scallops, etc., will be
fried brown in one minute. Thicker fish, chops, and fritters require longer cooking ; and, after plunging them into
the hot fat, the kettle should be set back from the fire to
prevent them from becoming too brown before they are
sufficiently cooked. While frying, be careful not to spill
any fat on the stove. Keep a tin plate in your left hand,
and hold it under the basket, or ladle, as you take things
from the fat.

Draining. — Thorough draining is another secret of nice
frying, and you cannot find a much hotter place than right
over the hot fat ; so hold your basket of fried food over the
hot fat, and shake slightly, till all dripping has stopped.
Then place the fried articles on soft or unglazed paper, **to**
absorb the fat, and keep them hot till ready to serve.
Never pile fried articles one on another.

Fat for Frying.

Lard, a mixture of half suet and half lard, drippings, or
oil, may be used for frying. Suet and drippings are cheapest, and are preferred by many. Suet used alone cools
very quickly and leaves a tallowy taste. Drippings should
be carefully clarified (see page 18) and freed from water,
or the articles cooked will soak fat. Lard, with a small
proportion of suet or drippings, is more generally satisfactory. There is often a very disagreeable odor to new lard,
and more or less water in it, as is shown by the froth and
ebullition as soon as it becomes hot. Before it is used for
any purpose it should be clarified with slices of raw potato
and heated until it becomes still. Olive oil is the purest fat
for frying, but it is too expensive for general use. Cotton-
seed oil has been recently introduced for cooking purposes,
and is an excellent fat for frying, though many dislike its
peculiar odor   It may be heated much hotter than lard,

without burning, and, when properly used, imparts no flavor to the food. When the fat becomes too brown for potatoes or doughnuts, use it for croquettes, etc., and then use it for nothing except fish balls and fish. When it becomes very brown, put it with the soap-grease.

If you wish to fry several kinds at the same time, begin with potatoes, following with doughnuts or flour mixtures, and crumbed articles last; otherwise the crumbs will fall off, and adhere to whatever is put in subsequently. After every frying, strain the fat through a fine wire strainer or fine strainer cloth into a tin pail, not pouring it, but dipping it from the kettle with a small long-handled dipper. Let it cool slightly before straining, as, if very hot, it will melt the strainer. Sprinkle coffee on the stove, while frying, to disguise the odor.

Sautéing.

The ordinary way of frying in a shallow pan with only a little fat, first on one side and then on the other, which the French call *sautéing*, answers very well for some purposes, —omelets, fried cakes, and many things browned in butter; but nearly everything that requires any more fat than just enough to keep it from sticking, is much better *immersed* in hot fat. Fish balls, chops, and oysters are more quickly cooked, and absorb less fat, when fried by immersion than when *sautéd*. Some people are extremely unwilling to make the change, and persist in going on in the old way of cooking in a little, half-hot fat which spatters over stove and floor, soaks into the fish or meat, and is often served as the only gravy. Upon such, dyspepsia is a fell avenger.

These directions for frying are given thus minutely not from any desire to recommend this method of cooking; but, if people *will* fry their food, they should do it in the only correct way. With the exception of salt-fish balls and small, dry, white fish, there is nothing fried, even in

2

the right way, that would not be equally good, and much more conducive to health, were it cooked otherwise. Saratoga potatoes, or chips as they are called, are really chips, for persons with weak digestion. Oysters, chops, fritters, and the materials in croquettes, muffins, and doughnuts may be cooked in many better ways.

Frying answers very well for open-air cooking, on the seashore or in camp, where appetite and digestion are strengthened. But in most modern houses, where the odors from the kitchen penetrate the remotest nook and corner, there are many serious objections, apart from the indigestibility of the food thus prepared. The acrid odors given off during the heating of fat are very irritating to the mucous membrane of the nose and throat, and they are equally so to a sensitive stomach. Some persons who can usually digest fried food cannot do so when the stomach has been irritated by the odor in frying. If all those who are so fond of croquettes, fritters, etc., were obliged to inhale the smoking fat, these dishes would seldom appear on the table.

To clarify Fat.

Any uncooked fat, such as suet, the fat from chickens, and all superfluous beef fat, should be saved and clarified, or made pure and clear. Cut the fat into small pieces, cover with cold water, and cook over a slow fire until the fat has melted, and the water nearly all evaporated. Then strain and press all the fat from the scraps. When cool, remove the cake of hard fat, or, if soft, draw it to one side and let the water underneath run off. You may put with the new fat any fat from soup stock, corned beef, drippings from roast beef, veal, fresh pork, or chicken; in fact, anything except the fat from mutton, turkey, and smoked meat. If there be any sediment adhering to the fat, add a little very cold water, and, after stirring well, pour the water off, or skim the fat from the water. Place the fat in a pan over the fire, and, when melted, add one small raw potato, cut into thin slices. Let it stand on the top of the stove or in the oven till the fat has stopped bubbling, is still, and the scraps are brown and crisp and rise to the top. Strain through a fine strainer, and keep in a cool place. Fat thus cleared will keep sweet for weeks, if melted occasionally, which should always be done when any new fat is added.

Boiling the fat causes the water in it to evaporate, and the organic matters or impurities to be decomposed, and deposited as sediment; the potato, owing to its porosity and power of absorption (being mostly starch and carbon), absorbs any odors or gases, collects the sediment, and thus cleanses the fat, very much as charcoal purifies water. Clarified fat (or dripping, as it is usually termed) answers for many purposes in cooking, — frying, sautéing, basting roast meat, greasing pans; and as shortening for bread, plain pastry, and gingerbread.

Egg and Bread Crumbing.

Hints on saving bread crusts and stale pieces, for egg and bread crumbing, are given on page 75. The crumbs should be sifted through a fine sieve. For fish or meat mix a little salt, pepper, and chopped parsley with them. Beat the eggs slightly with a fork in a shallow dish. Add one tablespoonful of water or two tablespoonfuls of milk for each egg. Add a little sugar if they are to be used for sweet dishes, and salt and pepper for all others. Sprinkle the crumbs on a board, and roll the chop, fish, or croquettes first in the crumbs; shake off all that do *not* adhere. Cover all the articles with the crumbs and let them stand till dry, then dip into the beaten egg, and be careful to have every part covered. Drain from the egg, and roll again in the crumbs. Croquettes or any soft mixture should be held on a broad knife while being placed in the egg. Then dip the egg over them, and slip the knife again lengthwise under the croquette, drain, and put it carefully into the crumbs. Scallops and very small oysters can be more easily crumbed by placing them with the crumbs in a sheet of paper, and tossing or turning till all are crumbed. Remember the order : crumbs first, then egg, then crumbs again.

Roasting.

Roasting (meaning " to heat violently ") is cooking before an open fire ; it implies the action of a much greater degree of heat than that employed in any of the previously specified methods of cooking. The heat of an open fire is about 1,000°.

In the days of open fireplaces this was the general way of cooking large pieces of meat; but now it is adopted only in large establishments, or by those who can afford the additional expense of a tin kitchen, and a range constructed especially for roasting. Baking, or roasting in a very hot oven, being a cheaper and more convenient way, is more generally used. Ovens in stoves and ranges are now well ventilated ; and meat when properly cooked in a very hot oven, and basted often, is nearly equal in flavor to that roasted before an open fire. The fire for roasting should be clear and bright, and of sufficient body to last, with only a slight sprinkling of coal, through the time for roasting.

The meat is placed on a spit, and hung in the jack in a tin kitchen, and made to revolve slowly before the fire by winding a spring in the jack, or by turning the spit at regular intervals. The meat should be rubbed with salt and flour, and placed on the spit, very near the fire at first, to harden the albumen ; then removed a little distance to prevent the meat from burning, before the inside is cooked. Place two or three spoonfuls of dripping in the pan to use in basting the meat ; baste often, and dredge two or three times with flour. When the joint is very large, place a buttered paper over it.

As the juices of meat are composed largely of water, the water will be evaporated as soon as it reaches the boiling-point, or 212°. When meat is placed in a moderate oven, the heat is not sufficient to harden the albumen on the outer surface ; the watery juices evaporate, the steam escapes, and the meat becomes dry and tasteless. But when meat is exposed to the intense heat of an open fire, or a very hot oven, the albumen hardens; and if basted frequently with hot fat, the meat is completely enveloped in a varnish of hot melted fat, which assists in communicating the heat to the inside, and checks the evaporation of the juices ; this prevents the escape of the steam, so that the inside of properly roasted meat is really cooked in the steam of its own juices. The evaporation of juices is proportionate to the amount of surface exposed. A small joint has a larger surface in proportion to its weight than a large joint weighing double or treble the amount; therefore the *smaller* the *joint* to be roasted, the *higher* the *temperature* to which its surface should be exposed, that the evaporation may be more quickly arrested.

For very thin pieces of meat, which have a still larger surface in proportion to the weight, such as steaks and chops, a greater heat is required. This is accomplished by *broiling*, which should be done near the burning-point, the highest degree of heat employed in any form of cooking.

Broiling.

Broiling (meaning " to burn ") is cooking directly over the hot coals. The degree of heat is so intense that the articles to be cooked would be very quickly burned, were they allowed to remain for any length of time over the fire. The secret of nice broiling is *frequent turning*. The fire should be bright red, and nearly to the top of the fire-box, so that the broiler may almost touch the fire. There should be no flame, as the flame from coal is due to the combustion of tarry vapors, and will cause a deposit of coal tar on the meat, giving it a smoky, nauseating flavor. When the fat from the chop or steak drips on the coals and blazes, it deposits a film of mutton or beef fat all over the meat, which has a very different flavor from that of the coal flame. When the steak has much fat, remove

part of it. A little fat will improve the flavor, baste
the meat, and keep it from becoming too dry. The
oven damper should always be opened while broiling,
that the smoke of the dripping fat may be carried into the
chimney.

Theie is nothing better for broiling than a double wire
broiler. It is well to have several sizes. Grease it well
with a bit of the fat from the meat, or with salt-pork rind.
Place the thickest part of whatever is to be broiled next
the middle of the broiler. Do not salt the meat, as salt
draws out the juice. Have the platter heating, and everything else ready, that you may not leave the broiling for
an instant. Hold the broiler firmly, with a coarse towel
wrapped around your hand to protect it from the heat.
Place it as near the fire as possible, to scar the outside
instantly ; count ten, then sear the other side. The heat
hardens the outside, and starts the flow of the juices.
They cannot escape through the hardened outer surface ;
but if the meat were cooked wholly on one side before
turning, they would soon come to the top, and then, in
turning the meat, the juices would drip into the fire. But
if the meat be turned *before* the juices reach the top, the
other surface is hardened, and they cannot escape, but flow
to the centre, and are there retained. As the juices are
converted into steam by the heat, they swell and give the
meat a puffy appearance. If the broiling be carried on
too long, these juices gradually ooze between the fibres
to the surface, and are evaporated ; and the meat becomes
dry, leathery, and indigestible.

Meat should be broiled only long enough to loosen all
the fibres, and start the flow of the juices. The meat will
spring up instantly when pressed with the knife ; and when
it ceases to do this, the juices have begun to evaporate,
and the meat shrinks. A little experience will enable one
to decide just when to remove the meat. Do not cut into
it, as this lets out the juices. It should be pink and juicy,
not raw and purple, nor brown and dry. Turn over as
often as you can count ten, and cook four minutes, if

one inch thick; six, if one inch and a half thick. The smaller and thinner the article, the hotter should be the fire; the larger the article, the more temperate the fire, or the greater the distance from the fire.

Fish should be floured to keep the skin from sticking. A large baking-pan to keep in the heat should be laid over the fish if thick, or it may be first partly cooked in the oven.

Chickens, to be thoroughly broiled but not burned or dried, require about twenty minutes. A safe way is to wrap them in buttered glazed paper; cook the inner side first, and after the first searing keep them farther from the fire, or cook them first in the oven.

Chops, bacon, birds, and dry fish are also improved by broiling in the buttered paper. Take a large sheet of white letter paper, or two small sheets. Rub them well with softened butter. This keeps out the air. Season the chop or fish with salt and pepper, place it near the centre of the paper, and fold the edges of the paper over several times and pinch them together close to the meat. The paper will char a long time before blazing, if care be taken not to break through the paper and thus let in the air and let out all the fat. The meat will be basted with its own fat and juices. A longer time will be required for the broiling; but when the paper is well browned, the chop will be done. It will be found juicy and delicious, — free from any smoky flavor.

Pan-broiling is broiling in a hissing hot spider or frying-pan. Heat the pan to a blue heat. Rub it with a bit of the beef fat, just enough to keep the meat from sticking, but do not leave any fat in the pan. Sear the meat quickly on one side, then turn without cutting into the meat, and brown the other side before any juice escapes into the pan. Cook about four minutes, turning twice, and serve very hot with salt and butter. If the pan be hot enough and no fat used, this is *not* frying, it is *broiling* on *hot iron;* and the flavor is almost equal to broiling over the coals.

Time Tables for Cooking.

Baking Bread, Cake, and Puddings.

Loaf bread	40 to 60 m.
Rolls, biscuit . . .	10 to 20 "
Graham gems . . .	30 "
Gingerbread . . .	20 to 30 "
Sponge cake . .	45 to 60 "
Plain " . . .	30 to 40 "
Fruit " . . .	2 to 3 hrs.
Cookies	10 to 15 m
Bread pudding . .	1 hr.
Rice and Tapioca . .	1 "
Indian pudding .	2 to 3 "
Plum " . .	2 to 3 "
Custards	15 to 20 m.
Steamed brown-bread	3 hrs.
Steamed puddings .	1 to 3 "
Pie-crust	about 30 m.
Potatoes	30 to 45 "
Baked beans . . .	6 to 8 hrs.
Braised meat . . .	3 to 4 "
Scalloped dishes . .	15 to 20 m.

Frying.

Croquettes, Fish Balls	1 m.
Doughnuts, Fritters .	3 to 5 m.
Bacon, Small Fish, Potatoes	2 to 5 m.
Breaded Chops and Fish	5 to 8 m.

Baking Meats.

Beef, sirloin, rare, per lb.	8 to 10 m.
Beef, sirloin well done, per lb.	12 to 15 "
Beef, rolled rib or rump, per lb.	12 to 15 "
Beef, long or short fillet	20 to 30 "
Mutton, rare, per lb.	10 "
Mutton, well done, per lb.	15 "
Lamb, " " "	15 "
Veal " " "	20 "
Pork " " "	30 "
Turkey, 10 lbs. wt. .	3 hrs.
Chickens, 3 to 4 lbs wt.	1 to 1½ "
Goose, 8 lbs . . .	2 "
Tame duck	40 to 60 m.
Game "	30 to 40 m.
Grouse	30 "
Pigeons	30 "
Small birds	15 to 20 "
Venison, per lb. . .	15 "
Fish, 6 to 8 lbs.; long, thin fish . . .	1 hr.
Fish, 4 to 6 lbs.; thick halibut	1 "
Fish, small	20 to 30 m.

Boiling.

Water, 1 qt. over gas, covered	5 m
Water, 1 qt over gas, uncovered	4 "
Coffee	3 to 5 "
Tea, steep without boiling	5 "
Corn meal	3 hrs
Hominy, fine . . .	1 hr.
Oatmeal, coarse, steamed	3 hrs.
Oatmeal, rolled . .	30 m.
Rice, steamed . . .	45 to 60 m.
Rice, boiled . . .	15 to 20 m.
Wheat Granules . .	20 to 30 m.
Eggs, soft boiled . .	3 to 6 m.
Eggs, hard boiled . .	15 to 20 m.
Eggs, coddled . . .	6 to 8 "
Fish, long, whole, per lb	6 to 10 "
Fish, cubical, per lb. .	15 "
Clams, Oysters . . .	3 to 5 "
Beef, corned and à la mode	3 to 5 hrs.
Soup Stock	3 to 6 "
Veal, Mutton . . .	2 to 3 hrs.
Tongue	3 to 4 hrs
Potted Pigeons . . .	2 "
Ham	5 "
Sweetbreads . . .	20 to 30 m.
Sweet Corn . . .	5 to 8 "
Asparagus, Tomatoes, Peas	15 to 20 "
Macaroni, Potatoes, Spinach	20 to 30 "
Squash, Celery, Cauliflower . . .	20 to 30 "
Sprouts, Greens . .	20 to 30 "
Cabbage, Beets, young	30 to 45 "
Parsnips, Turnips . .	30 to 45 "
Carrots, Onions, Salsify	30 to 60 "
Beans, String and Shell	1 to 2 hrs
Brown Bread . . .	3 "
Puddings, 1 qt., steamed	3 "
Puddings, small . .	1 hr.
Freezing Ice Cream	30 m

Broiling.

Steak, one inch thick	4 m.
Steak, one and a half inch thick	6 "
Small, thin fish	5 to 8 "
Thick fish	12 to 15 "
Chops, broiled in paper	8 to 10 "
Chickens	20 "
Liver, Tripe, Bacon	3 to 8 "

Larding.

Many kinds of meat which are very lean and dry are improved by the addition of some kind of fat. The tenderloin or fillet of beef, the thick part of the leg of veal, grouse, and liver, are often prepared in this way.

Larding is drawing small strips of fat salt pork or bacon through the surface of the meat; *daubing* is forcing strips of pork through the entire thickness of the meat. Take a piece of fat salt pork two inches wide and four inches long. Shave off the rind the long way of the pork; then cut two or three slices about a quarter of an inch thick, the same way as the rind; cut only to the membrane which lies about an inch below the rind, as this is the firmest part of the pork; then cut each slice across the width, into strips one quarter of an inch thick. This will make the lardoons one quarter of an inch wide and thick and two inches long. Insert one end of the lardoon into the end of the larding-needle, then with the point of the needle take up a stitch half an inch deep and one inch wide in the surface of the meat. Draw the needle through, and help the pork to go through by pushing until partly through, then hold the end of the pork and draw the needle out, leaving the pork in the meat, with the ends projecting at equal lengths. Take up more stitches one inch apart in parallel or alternate rows, until the whole surface is covered.

Daubing is applied to a broad, thick piece of beef or veal. Cut the pork in strips one third of an inch wide and thick, and as long as the meat is thick. Punch a hole clear through the meat with a steel, and then insert the lardoon with a large larding-needle or with the fingers. The salt and fat from the lardoons penetrate the inside of the meat, and by many are considered an improvement. Those who object to the pork will find that beef may be seasoned as well by covering the surface with nice beef suet, salted; or the pork may be laid on the meat and removed after cooking. The process is not difficult, requiring no more skill than any other kind of sewing.

Boning.

Any one who can use a sharp knife, and scrape meat or fish from a bone, without cutting her own flesh, can bone anything, from the smallest bird, chop, or fish, to a leg or forequarter of lamb, or a turkey. A small knife with a sharp, short, pointed blade, is all that is required. It is well to begin on a small scale by removing the bone from a chop or steak. The aim is to remove the flesh from the bone without cutting into the flesh, or destroying its shape more than is necessary.

To Bone a Chop or Steak. — Begin at the bone end, scrape the meat away, leaving the bone clean and the flesh unbroken. If there be a piece of tenderloin under the bone, remove it, and put it up close to the meat, which was above the bone in the original form.

Directions for boning fish are given on page 161.

To Bone a Leg of Mutton. — Cut it off at the first joint, insert the knife near the joint, and loosen the flesh from the bone, leaving all the gristle and tendons on the bone. Then begin at the tail end, and scrape the fat away from the backbone, then follow the bone (you can easily tell by the feeling, if you cannot see it) until you come to the joint; leave all the gristle and cords on the bone, and continue scraping off the flesh till the whole bone is out. One could easily cut through from the outside to the bone and remove it in that way; but the flesh would have to be sewed together, and much of the juice would escape. After removing the bone, stuff the cavity left by the bone, and sew the skin together at the smaller end. Then bring the edges together at the upper end, crowding all the flesh inside, and sew the skin together tightly. This gives a rectangular form of solid meat and stuffing. When salted and floured and exposed to a hot oven, the juices are kept inside; the meat is more conveniently served, and, when cold, does not become dry and hard.

Any other pieces of meat are boned in a similar manner.

To Bone a Bird, Fowl, or Turkey. — In this case the flesh is to be kept in the skin in order to preserve the shape. The skin should be firm and unbroken, and the bird should not be drawn. Remove the head and pin-feathers, singe and wipe carefully. Remove the tendons from the legs, and loosen the skin round the end of the drumstick. Make an incision through the skin from the neck to the middle of the back, or near the junction of the side bone. Scrape the flesh with the skin away from the backbone until you feel the end of the shoulder-blade; loosen the flesh from this, and then follow the bone to the wing joint, and down to the middle joint in the wing. The skin lies very near the bone underneath the joint, and care must be taken to avoid cutting through the skin at these places. Leave the first bone in the wing to aid in keeping the shape; it may be removed before serving. In small birds there is so little meat on the wings, that it is just as well to cut them off at the middle joint. Remove the bone from the other wing in the same way, then follow the collar bone from the wing down to the breast-bone, loosening the crop from the flesh. In removing the flesh from the breastbone, be careful not to cut through the skin on the ridge. The flesh may be pushed away with the fingers, and the fillets or pieces that are detached from the other flesh can be laid aside, and put in place afterwards. When the breastbone is bare, separate the flesh from the ribs, and be careful not to break through the membrane into the inside. Remove the flesh round the second joint, then the drumsticks, turning the flesh wrong side out as in pulling a glove from the finger.

Repeat this process on the other side. Then scrape down to the end of the backbone, and cut through the bone, leaving a part of it in the tail. Separate the membrane under the body without breaking. Thus you have the flesh in the skin, and the skeleton left entire with the contents undisturbed in the inside. Lay the stuffing in, filling out the legs and wings, then sew the skin along the back, and skewer or tie into the original shape.

An easier way of boning a fowl where it is to be rolled like a *galantine*, is to cut off the wings at the second joint, break the drumstick half-way from the joint, cut the skin down the entire length of the back, remove the flesh from the wing and second joint, turning the skin and flesh off like a glove ; then do the same on the other wing and leg, leaving the breast till the last. The wings and legs are turned inside, the stuffing is laid in the flesh, and the whole rolled over and over, and sewed on the edge of the skin and at the ends of the roll.

Measuring.

It has been said that " good cooks never measure anything." They do. They measure by judgment and experience ; and until *you* have a large share of both these essential qualities, use your spoon and cup or scales.

Measures, in preference to weights, are used in nearly all these receipts, as they are more convenient for the majority of housekeepers. When measured and estimated by the Table of Weights and Measures on page 30, the cup and spoon may be used as accurately as the scales.

Flour, meal, sugar, salt, spices, and soda should always be sifted before measuring. Any other materials that have been packed, like mustard and baking powder, if not sifted, should be stirred, and broken up lightly. One tablespoonful of solid mustard taken carelessly from the box has been found equal to three tablespoonfuls measured after sifting.

The saltspoons, teaspoons, and tablespoons used in these receipts are the silver spoons now in general use. Iron mixing-spoons vary much in size, but there is a size which holds exactly the same as a silver tablespoon. Be careful to use this size in measuring. The cup is the common kitchen cup holding half a pint. Those with handles are more convenient.

To measure a rounded teaspoonful of dry material, dip into the sifted material, and take up a heaping spoonful, shake it slightly until it is just rounded over, or convex in the same proportion as the spoon is concave. *A level teaspoonful* means the spoon filled lightly, and levelled off with a knife. *One half teaspoonful* is most accurately measured by dividing through the middle lengthwise. When divided across the width the tip is smaller than the lower half. *A heaping teaspoonful* is all the spoon will hold of any lightly sifted material. *A teaspoonful of liquid* is the spoon full to the brim.

Tablespoonfuls are measured in the same way.

A cupful of dry material should be filled and heaped lightly (not shaken down), then levelled off even with the top. A small scoop should be kept in the flour or sugar to use in filling the cup. *A heaping cupful* is all the cup will hold. *A cupful of liquid* is *not* what you can carry without spilling, but what the cup will hold without running over ; full to the brim. Place your cup in a saucer, while filling it, or in the bowl in which the liquid is to be poured. *Half a cupful* is *not* half the distance from the bottom to the rim. Most cups are smaller at the bottom, for which allowance must be made. Take two cups of the same size and shape, fill one with water, then pour the water without spilling into the other cup until it stands at the same level in both cups. This gives you the half-cupful exactly, which in the cups used here is two thirds of the height, or within an inch of the top. The *quarter* and *three-quarter* measures may be found in the same way. A *scant cupful* is within a quarter of an inch of the top.

"*Butter the size of an egg,*" is a very common expression. This equals about one quarter of a cupful, or two ounces, or one *heaping* tablespoonful, either of which is more easily written than the first expression. Place an egg in one tablespoon, then pack butter in another till it fills the spoon in the same proportion as the egg, and you will easily carry it in mind.

Have your materials measured or at hand, and all utensils ready before beginning the mixing, or putting the ingredients together. Keep a bucket or pan full of flour, freshly sifted each day, and ready for use. Measure flour first, and put it in a bowl or pan together with salt, soda, cream of tartar, and spice; measure butter and put it in the mixing-bowl: then measure the sugar, and, in scraping out the sugar, take the butter which has adhered to the cup. Break your eggs on the edge of the cup; if the white be clear, the egg is good. Put the yolks in one bowl and the whites in another; measure the milk or liquid, and, after using the beaten yolk, clean out the bowl with the milk. Or, measure all the dry ingredients, break and separate the eggs, measure the milk, add it to the beaten yolks, and measure the melted butter last. In either way you can make one cup do for all without washing. "Two eggs beaten separately" means that the yolks and whites are to be beaten separately, not each whole egg beaten separately.

A tablespoonful of *melted butter* is measured *after* melting. A tablespoonful of *butter melted* is measured *before* melting.

To economize space, in many of the receipts the abbreviations are written: one cup for one cupful, tablesp. for tablespoonful, teasp. for teaspoonful, and saltsp. for saltspoonful. All these measures mean a full measure, unless scant or heaping measures are specified.

Table of Weights and Measures.

4 saltspoonfuls of liquid	= 1 teaspoonful.
4 teaspoonfuls of liquid	= 1 tablespoonful.
3 teaspoonfuls of dry material	= 1 tablespoonful.
4 tablespoonfuls of liquid	= 1 wineglass, or ½ gill, or ¼ cup.
2 gills	= 1 cup, or ½ pint.

16 tablespoonfuls of liquid	= 1 cup.
12 tablespoonfuls of dry material	= 1 cup.
8 heaping tablespoonfuls of dry material	= 1 cup.
4 cups of liquid	= 1 quart.
4 cups of flour	= 1 pound, or 1 quart
2 cups of solid butter	= 1 pound.
½ cup of butter	= ¼ pound.
2 cups of granulated sugar	= 1 pound.
2½ cups of powdered sugar	= 1 pound.
3 cups of meal	= 1 pound.
1 pint of milk or water	= 1 pound.
1 pint of chopped meat packed solidly	= 1 pound.
9 large eggs, 10 medium eggs	= 1 pound.
1 round tablespoonful of butter	= 1 ounce.
1 heaping tablespoonful of butter	= 2 ounces, or ¼ cup
Butter the size of an egg	= 2 ounces, or ¼ cup
1 heaping tablespoonful of sugar	= 1 ounce.
2 round tablespoonfuls of flour	= 1 ounce.
2 round tablespoonfuls of coffee	= 1 ounce.
2 round tablespoonfuls of powd sugar	= 1 ounce.
1 tablespoonful of liquid	= ½ ounce.
1 bottle S. M. wine	= 3 cups, or 48 tablespoonfuls
1 bottle brandy	= 1½ cups, or 24 tablespoonfuls
1 small bottle Foss' extract	= ¼ cup scant, or 3 tablespoonfuls
1 small bottle Foss' extract	= 12 teaspoonfuls.
1 flask of olive oil	= 1⅓ cups, or 20 tablespoonfuls

Table of Proportions.

1 scant measure of liquid to 3 full measures of flour, for bread.
1 scant measure of liquid to 2 full measures of flour, for muffins.
1 scant measure of liquid to 1 full measure of flour, for batters.
½ cup of yeast, or ¼ of compressed yeastcake, to one pint of liquid.
1 level teasp. of soda and 2 full teasp. of cream tartar to 1 quart of flour.
8 level, or 2 heaped teaspoons of baking-powder to 1 quart of flour.
1 teaspoonful of soda to 1 pint of sour milk.
1 teaspoonful of soda to 1 cup of molasses.
1 saltspoonful of salt to 1 quart of milk for custards.
1 teaspoonful of extract to 1 quart of custard.
1 saltspoonful of salt to 1 loaf of sponge cake.
1 teaspoonful of extract to 1 loaf of plain cake.
1 saltspoonful of spice to 1 loaf of plain cake.
1 teaspoonful of salt to 1 quart of soup stock or 2 quarts of flour.
1 saltspoonful of white pepper to 1 quart of soup stock.
1 teaspoonful of mixed herbs to 1 quart of soup stock.
1 tablespoonful of each chopped vegetable to 1 quart of soup stock.
A speck of cayenne pepper is what you can take up on the point of a pen-knife or on a quarter-inch square surface.
A pinch of salt or spice is about a saltspoonful.
A pinch of hops is ¼ of a cup.

In these recipes, flour, sugar, and butter are measured by the rounded table-spoon.

Salt, pepper, spice, soda, and baking-powder are measured by the level tea-spoon.

The proportions of seasoning given in these receipts are not sufficient for those who like highly seasoned food. It is easier to add more, than to remove any if too highly seasoned.

Mixed Spice for Rich Cakes and Plum Puddings.

½ teaspoonful each of cloves and allspice.
1 teaspoonful each of mace and grated nutmeg.
3 teaspoonfuls of cinnamon.

Spice Salt for Soups and Stuffings.

4 ounces of salt.
2 ounces of celery salt.
1 ounce each of white pepper and ground thyme.
1 ounce each of marjoram and summer savory.
½ ounce of sage.
1 saltspoonful of cayenne pepper.
½ teaspoonful each of cloves, allspice, and mace.

Mix, sift, and keep closely covered.

Mixed Whole Herbs, for Soups and Braised Meats.

1 bunch each of whole thyme and marjoram.
1 bunch each of summer savory and sage.
¼ pound of bay leaves.

Crush and break the leaves, blossoms, and stalks, and mix thoroughly.

Mixing.

Next to care in measuring comes the manner of mixing. The most accurate measurement of the best materials is often rendered useless by a neglect to put them together properly, and the blame is usually charged to the oven or the receipt. There are three distinct ways of mixing: *Stirring*, *Beating*, and *Cutting* or *Folding*.

Stirring. — Let the bowl of the spoon rest slightly on the bottom of the mixing-bowl; then move round and round in widening circles, without lifting the spoon out of the mixture, except to scrape the sides of the bowl occasionally. Stir slowly at first, to avoid spattering; add the liquid gradually, and be sure the bowl of the spoon (not the edge nor the tip merely) touches the bottom and sides of the bowl. This is mashing as well as stirring, and the mixture soon becomes a paste. When perfectly smooth and free from lumps, add more liquid till you have the desired consistency. We *stir* flour and water together for a thickening, or butter and flour and milk for a sauce. We *stir* when we rub butter to a cream, or when we make a batter or semi-dough. When we make a stiff dough we stir at first, and then turn the whole mass over, bringing the knife or spoon round the bowl and cutting up through the dough.

Beating. — Tip the bowl slightly, and hold the spoon so that the edge scrapes the bowl, and bring it up through the mixture and over with a long quick stroke to the opposite side; under, and up through again, lifting the spoon out of the mass and cutting clear through, scraping from the bottom at every stroke. Keep the bowl of the spoon and the sides of the mixing-bowl well scraped out, that all the material may be equally beaten.

We *stir* simply to blend two or more materials; we *beat* to add all the air possible to the mixture. We beat eggs or batter or soft dough. The albumen of the eggs and the gluten of the flour, owing to their viscidity or glutinous properties, catch the air and hold it in the form of cells, something as we make soap bubbles by blowing air into soapy water. The faster we beat, and the more we bring the material up from the bowl into the air, the more bubbles we have; but one stirring motion will destroy them. Yolks of eggs should be beaten nearly as much as the whites, or till they are light or lemon-colored, and thicken perceptibly. The whites should be beaten till they are stiff and dry, or fly off in flakes, or can be turned upside down without spilling. When the two are to be put together, always plan to turn the whites into the yolks, as there is less waste than when the yolks are turned into the whites. Let the whites stand a minute, then run a palette knife round the edge close to the bowl; they will slip out easily, and leave the bowl almost clean. For beating eggs, for nearly all purposes the Dover egg-beater is the best. There should be two sizes, the larger one for the whites of eggs. Hold the beater lightly in the left hand, and move it round through the egg while turning the handle. For frosting, and snow pudding, and all beat· ing of soft dough, use a perforated wooden spoon. Bowls with slightly flaring sides, and not too deep to be clasped from bottom to rim in the left hand, are most convenient. If tipped slightly toward the right, the beating is done more effectually.

Cutting, or Folding, or Lifting. — Omelets, sponge cake, whipped cream, etc., should have the beaten white cut or folded in carefully to avoid breaking the air bubbles. Turn the mixture over with the spoon, cut through, lift up, and fold the materials together, lifting the part from below, up and over, and mixing very gently until just blended. Do not stir round and round, nor beat quickly.

All mixtures which are raised with eggs alone, should have the yolks and whites of the eggs thoroughly and separately beaten; any very thin batter, like pop-overs, pancakes, or gems made without eggs, should be beaten vigorously just before baking. And many persons are most successful when all the beating of the eggs is done in the batter.

Graham or whole-wheat flour is better than white flour for gems that are made without eggs, because it contains more gluten.

Shall we stir only one way? No; stir any way you please, so long as you blend or mix the materials. But after *beating in* air bubbles, don't break them by *stirring*, unless you wish to keep up the game of cross purposes indefinitely. Always let the last motion, before turning into the pans, be one of quick, vigorous *beating*, except in those receipts where folding instead of beating is indicated.

Table of Average Cost of Material used in Cooking.

1 cup of flour or meal . . . $0.01	1 pound of spaghetti . . . $0.16
1 " sugar 03	1 " cornstarch 10
1 " butter . . . . .15 to .20	1 can of tomatoes 15
1 egg 03	1 " salmon 18
1 cup of molasses 05	1 " lobster 15
1 " milk. 02	1 " devilled ham and tongue .30
1 tablespoonful of wine . . .02	1 tumbler of jelly 35
1 " " brandy . .04	1 jar of marmalade 25
1 teaspoonful of vanilla . . .02	1 pound of tea 75
1 " " spice 02	1 " coffee 38
1 " " soda, and 2	1 " chocolate 40
teaspoonfuls of cream-tartar .02	¼ " nutmeg 32
1 tablespoonful of butter . . .03	¼ " mace 60
Butter size of an egg 05	¼ " cloves, cassia . . .15
1 tablespoonful of olive oil . .02	¼ " ginger 10
2 tablespoonfuls of coffee . . .05	¼ " mustard 12
2 teaspoonfuls of tea 01	¼ " herbs, ground . . .10
1 quart of milkman's cream . .25	Package of whole herbs . . 8
1 " Deerfoot cream . .60	1 pound of cheese 18
1 box of gelatine 16	1 " Parmesan cheese . .50
1 lemon 02	1 peck of potatoes 25
1 orange 03	1 " apples 50
1 pound of raisins 18	1 quart of onions 10
1 " currants 10	1 carrot 02
1 " citron 18	1 turnip 05
1 " crackers 10	1 bunch of celery 20
1 " tapioca 07	1 handful of parsley 05
1 " rice 09	1 bunch of watercresses . . .05
1 " macaroni 18	1 head of lettuce 10

These prices are for the best materials, and are estimated for the season, from October to June, when butter
and eggs are higher than during the summer, and for
Boston markets, which vary greatly from the prices in
other parts of the United States.

BREAD AND BREAD MAKING.

Importance of Bread. — Bread is one of the earliest, the most generally used, and the most important forms of food adopted by mankind. Nothing in the whole range of domestic life more affects the health and happiness of the family than the quality of its daily bread. With good bread, the plainest meal is a feast in itself; without it, the most elaborately prepared and elegantly served *menu* is unsatisfactory.

Bread-making is at once the easiest and the most difficult branch of culinary science, — easy, if only sufficient interest be taken to master a few elementary principles and to follow them always, using the judgment of the best authorities, until experience furnishes a sufficient guide; difficult, if there be any neglect to use proper care and materials. It should be regarded as one of the highest accomplishments; and if one tenth part of the interest, time, and thought which are devoted to cake and pastry and fancy cooking were spent upon this most important article of food, the presence of good bread upon our tables would be invariably secured.

Origin and Meaning of "Bread." — Bread is made from a variety of substances, — roots, fruits, and the bark of trees; but more generally from certain grains. The word *bread* is derived from the verb *to bray*, or *pound*, expressive of the old method of preparing the grain. Bread is therefore made of something brayed, as brayed wheat or brayed corn. But these brayed or ground materials are not properly bread until they are mixed or moistened with water. Then the brayed grain becomes *dough*, from a word meaning *to wet*, or *moisten*. In primitive times this wetted meal or dough was baked at once in hot ashes, and made a firm, compact bread, exceedingly hard of digestion. Accidentally some one discovered that by letting the dough stand till it had fermented, and then mixing it with new dough, it raised, or lifted, the whole mass, and made it lighter and more porous. Thus we have our word *loaf,* from *lifian,* to raise, or lift up. The old dough—or leaven, as it is called—lifts up the dough. The raised ma__s is held in place by the heat in baking, and becomes the loaf of raised bread.

Bread made from Wheat.—Bread is made principally from *wheat flour.* *Rye* and *corn meal* are sometimes used, but better results are obtained when there is a mixture of wheat with one or more of these grains. Rye used alone makes a close, moist, sticky bread; while corn meal alone makes too dry and crumbly a loaf.

Wheat is an annual grass of unknown origin, cultivated more extensively in the Northern hemisphere. There are over one hundred and fifty varieties of wheat. They are classified as red or white, in reference to the color of the grains; as winter or summer,—winter wheat being sown in the autumn, and summer wheat in the spring; as soft or hard,—soft wheat being tender and floury or starchy, and hard wheat being tough, firm, and containing more gluten.

Chemical Composition of Wheat.—Wheat is the only grain which contains gluten in the proper proportion and of the desired quality essential to the making of light, spongy bread. It contains all the elements necessary for the growth of the body; but, to meet all the requirements of nutrition, the whole of the grain, with the exception of the outer husk, should be used. Wheat has several

Fig. 1. Grain of wheat, showing outer coat of silex and woody fibre.

layers of bran coats, the outer one of which is almost wholly pure silica and is perfectly indigestible. Underneath this husk lie the inner bran coats, containing *gluten,* a dark substance which is the nitrogenous or flesh-forming element,

FIG. 2 Grain of wheat with bran coat removed.

the *phosphates* and other *mineral matters* which help to make up the bony·parts of the body, and the *oil* which gives the characteristic odor to wheat grains. The centre, or heart, of the grain consists of cells filled with *starch,* a fine, white, mealy powder, which has little value as food except as a heat producer. There is also a small amount of gluten diffused among the starch cells. For convenience, these different parts of the wheat will be designated as *bran,* or the outer husk ; *gluten,* or the inner·bran coats ; and *starch,* or the *heart* of the wheat. The proportion and quality of the gluten and starch in different kinds of wheat vary according to the climate and soil in which they are grown. They are also affected by the method

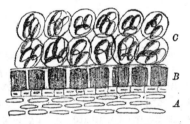

FIG. 3. Grain of wheat magnified.
A is the bran; *B* the gluten; *C* the starch.

of grinding the grain. Wheat grown in Southern or warm climates, and in the intense, though short, summer of our own Northwest, contains more nitrogen than that grown in cold, damp climates. It loses more water by evaporation, and consequently the seed is smaller and harder. In some varieties of wheat the outer *husk* is thin and smooth, and peels off readily under the stones. In others, it is thick and rough, and adheres closely to the kernel. In some, it is light-colored or brittle ; in others, dark-colored or tough. The husky portion of wheat is about fourteen or sixteen per cent of the whole weight.

The *gluten* of wheat is a gray, tough, elastic substance, consisting chiefly of vegetable fibrine. It can be examined easily by making a dough of flour and water, and working it on a sieve under a stream of water. The water will carry the starch, sugar, gum, and mineral matters into the pan below, leaving a lump of gluten on the sieve. It closely resembles a piece of animal skin, and, when dried, has a glue-like appearance; hence its name, *gluten.* The proportion of gluten varies from eleven to fifteen per cent. This tough, elastic quality of the gluten determines the quality of the flour. The more gluten and the tougher or stronger it is, the better the flour. The gluten of good flour will swell to four or five times its original bulk; while that of poor flour does not swell, but becomes watery and sticky, and sometimes gives off a disagreeable odor, owing to the deterioration of the fatty or oily element.

Preparing the Flour.

St. Louis Process. — There are several methods of converting wheat into flour. One is by *grinding* between two horizontal stones, the upper one revolving, and the lower one stationary. The surface of the stones presents an infinite number of minute cutting edges. The upper stone is convex, the lower one concave; but instead of fitting perfectly, they approach closer together from the centre outward, so that, as the grain is poured into an opening in the upper stone, it is at first rather coarsely crushed, and then cut finer and finer, as it is carried to the circumference by the centrifugal force. As the grain leaves the stones, the outer husk has been least affected; the tough, coherent gluten is divided minutely, while the brittle starch, which forms two thirds of the grain, is completely crushed. The miller then divides these products, by sifting or bolting, into *fine flour, coarse flour,* and *bran.*

The *bran* should be discarded as utterly useless for human food; but it is often mixed with an inferior quality of fine flour, and sold as Graham flour. It was at one time considered valuable as a food for those suffering from constipation, chiefly on account of its coarseness; but

science has shown us recently that minute points of glass
(and bran is nothing else) are not Nature's best agents in
removing effete matters from the system.   All of the so-
called Graham flour made by this process should be sifted
before using.

The *coarse flour* will vary in quality, according as it has
more or less of the outer bran mixed with it.   In the *soft
wheats* the husk peels off readily under the stones, and is
easily separated by bolting ; and as these soft varieties
contain the smallest proportion of gluten, they yield a *coarse
flour*, containing only an average amount of gluten, and
the *whitest fine-flour*.   But in the *hard, flinty* wheats, this
outer husk clings so closely that much of it is ground up
finely with the flour, giving it a dark color.   This flour, as
it contains a large proportion of gluten, would be more
nutritious were it not that much of the gluten adheres to
the hulls, and is lost by sifting them out, and much of the
fine, flinty bran is retained in the flour, which makes it
irritating and indigestible.

The quality of the *fine flour* depends upon the quality of
the wheat, in the first place ; also upon the number of siftings, being richer in gluten the less it is sifted ; and upon
the way in which it is stored.   The process of grinding
with the stones heats the flour ; and as it is often thrust
upon the market without being properly cooled and dried,
it spoils very rapidly.   Flour made by this process of
grinding is called the *St. Louis*, or *old-process* flour.   When
made of the very best quality of grain and carefully prepared, it makes a sweet, nutritious bread, and is excellent
in cake and pastry.   It is often designated *pastry flour.*

Haxall Process. — Another method of making flour is
by the *new*, or *Haxall* process, so called from the name of
the inventor.   By this process the outer husk is first removed, or *decorticated;* then the cleaned grain is cut by a
system of knives, which reduces it to a fine powder without the injurious effects of heating.   This flour has a
slightly granular consistency, owing to the presence of
minute particles of hard, flinty gluten.   It is usually made

from the best quality of wheat, and keeps well. It is considered by many as the best flour for bread, as it makes a whiter, nicer-looking loaf. Haxall flour swells more than that made by the old process, as it contains more of the gluten; the same measure making a greater quantity of bread than the St. Louis flour. It is, therefore, cheaper in the end, though costing more per barrel. By repeated siftings, this flour loses its gluten, as does that made by the St. Louis process, and consequently is then inferior as a food. But we can supply by other flours and other food what this flour lacks in nutritious qualities; and until the popular taste is educated to demand the amount of nutriment contained in bread rather than the whiteness of it, as a test of its quality, it is well to make our fine, white bread from this, which is the best flour, and have it as nearly perfect as possible.

There have been many variations of the Haxall process, and all are included under the term *new-process flour.*

Minnesota. — The Minnesota, or patent-process, flour is now considered one of the best grades. The Washburn, Pillsbury, and many other mills located in Minneapolis are the largest flour-mills in the world, and produce an excellent quality of flour, in which a large proportion of the gluten is retained. This Minnesota flour is made from carefully selected wheat grown in the Red River region, the best wheat-growing section in America. The first step in the process is the breaking off of the germinal point of each grain by what are called ending stones. Then it is sent through corrugated iron rollers, having shallow grooves cut spirally upon them, with rounded ridges between, and the opposing rollers grooved in an opposite direction. The grains are crushed (not ground); the starchy parts, or middlings, being quite finely powdered and easily separated from the bran or tailings. After this separation the middlings are passed through ten bolting-cloths, and then through other and finer corrugated machines, and made into the various grades of *fine, superfine,* and *fancy* flours,

Health-Food Flour. — A still better method of converting wheat into flour, and one which is indorsed by leading scientists and physicians, has been recently introduced by the Health Food Company of New York. Only the choicest kinds of wheat are used. The outer husk is first removed by moistening the grain, and subjecting it to a gentle rubbing by what is termed the "attrition process" This softens the woody fibre of the outer bran, which is easily removed by sifting, but does not affect the hard gluten coats. The grains are dried, then pulverized into various grades by a compressed cold-air blast, which dashes the grains into atoms with tremendous force. This is called *whole-wheat* flour, the name indicating that the whole of the gluten, or nutritive part of the flour, is retained. It is not sifted like other flours, but pulverized into all the varieties of *crushed wheat, coarse granulated* and *fine granulated wheat;* each variety, even the finest flour, containing all that is valuable as food. Bread made with this flour has been found, after repeated trial, to be sweet and agreeable to the taste, light and spongy in texture. with none of the objectionable features of Graham bread, and answering fully all the demands of perfect nutrition.

Cheap inferior Graham flour, made of poor flour mixed with bran, is worse than no food at all. Any flour containing much of the indigestible bran causes irritation of the digestive organs ; all the food is hurried through the alimentary canal before digestion is complete or all the nutriment can be absorbed, and thus is neither economical nor healthful. Fine flour containing the most gluten is the most nutritious, because it is all digested, and the loss of albuminous material can be supplied from other sources.

The Arlington, the Franklin, and some other brands of whole-wheat flour, are highly indorsed by those familiar with them.

The Tests of Good Flour.

The first requisite in making good bread is to use good flour. Good flour should not be pure white in color, but of a creamy, yellowish-white shade. If it feel damp, clammy, or sticky, and gradually form into lumps or cakes, it is not the best. Good flour holds together in a mass, when squeezed by the hand, and retains the impression of the fingers, and even the marks of the skin, much longer than poor flour; when made into a dough, it is elastic, easy to be kneaded, will stay in a round puffy shape, and will take up a large amount of water: while poor flour will be sticky, flatten, or spread itself over the board, and will never seem to be stiff enough to be handled, no matter how much flour is used. Haxall flour has a fine granular consistency, and runs easily through the sieve or the fingers like fine meal; while good St. Louis flour feels soft and oily. It is extravagant to buy poor or even doubtful flour. But, should it have every appearance of being good flour, and yet not make good bread, do not condemn the flour without a fair trial; and be sure the fault is nowhere else.

Every experienced cook has her own tests for flour, and some of them are amusing, if not reliable. The best way is to buy a small quantity at first, and make it into dough; then, if satisfactory, purchase whatever amount is required, and buy this same brand as long as it proves of uniform quality. The names given to flour are not a sure criterion of the quality. The flour may come from the same growth of wheat, and be ground in the same manner and at the same mill, and yet the miller or the wholesale dealers will brand it differently. And the same brand will vary in quality from year to year. Some of the varieties sold in Boston, and known to be good by personal trial, are Pillsbury's, Washburn & Crosby's, Swan's Down, Taylor's Best, Brown's Best, Marguerite, etc.; the same flour may be known in other cities under different names. There are others equally good, and every year some new brand is announced. It is estimated that one barrel of flour will last one person one year; which gives a rule of proportion by which to buy. Most good housekeepers agree that flour is not improved by long keeping, though flour dealers think differently. Flour should be kept in a cool, dry place, as the least dampness causes it to absorb moisture; the gluten loses its tenacity, becomes sticky, and the bread made from it is coarser and less light.

For small families it is better to buy whole-wheat flour by the bag or half-barrel; Haxall, for bread, by the barrel; and the best St. Louis flour for cake and pastry, by the bag, as a much smaller proportion is needed (or should be) for these indigestibles, than for the " staff of life."

Bread, Fermented and Unfermented.

Now, having discussed the subject of the flour, the next step in order is the different ways of making it into bread. These may all be included under two divisions, — those made by fermentation, and those without fermentation.

Fermentation, what is it? — Fermentation is that change in organic substances by which their sugar, starch, gluten, etc., are decomposed or recombined into new compounds. This change may be spontaneous under favorable conditions of air, moisture, and warmth; or it may be hastened by the presence of a ferment. A *ferment* is some albuminous substance in a state of decomposition, and, when introduced into any other albuminous substance, in however minute a quantity, causes a change which pervades the whole mass. These fermenting substances are in great variety, and the germs of some of them are always present in the air. There are different kinds of fermentation.

The *lactic fermentation* is the change in milk when it sours. The casein, or albuminous part of the milk, by exposure to the air and warmth, begins to decompose, becomes a ferment, and changes the sugar of the milk into an acid called lactic acid. This reacts upon the remainder of the milk, as any acid would, and causes it to coagulate or harden, and gives it a sour taste.

The *alcoholic fermentation* is that which is produced in substances rich in sugar or starch, as the fruits and grains from which wines and beer are made. Some of these ferment germs are present in the juice of grapes; and under the influence of air, moisture, and warmth, they seize upon the sugar already present in the natural fruit juices, and any that may be added, and convert it into carbonic acid gas and alcohol. In the grains, a portion of the gluten ferments and changes the starch into sugar, and then the sugar into carbonic acid and alcohol. In converting the starch into sugar there is no change evident to the eye; but as soon as the sugar is decomposed into alcohol and carbonic acid gas, large bubbles of gas appear, which swell the whole mass.

Acetic fermentation is caused by allowing alcoholic fermentation to go on beyond a certain limit, or in a temperature above 90°. A familiar illustration of this is the change of wine or cider into vinegar.

Now, bread-dough contains gluten, sugar, and starch; and if the dough be kept warm for a certain time, *lactic fermentation* will be developed *spontaneously*, and the bread made from such dough will be sour and heavy. Alcoholic fermentation can also be *spontaneously* produced in dough, by making first a batter (as the semi-fluid state is more favorable to rapid chemical change), and subjecting it to a temperature of 110° for five or six hours; then, adding more flour, allowing it to rise again, and then baking it. Bread made in this way is called *salt* or *milk-rising's bread.* But it does not keep well, and is not generally liked.

It is not always convenient to wait for dough to be raised in this manner, so we hasten the process by the addition of some active ferment. Leaven, or a piece of old dough, left to sour, and then mixed with the new dough was formerly used; this produced *lactic* as well as *alcoholic* fermentation, and though the bread was light and spongy in texture, it had an unpleasant sour taste. But since the chemistry of yeast fermentation has been understood, *yeast* has come to be considered the best ferment for producing alcoholic fermentation in bread rapidly, and with no objectionable result.

Yeast, what is it? — Yeast is a plant or germ of the fungus tribe. Under the microscope it is found to consist of numberless minute rounded or oval bodies which are true vegetable cells. Yeast is therefore one of the simplest and smallest of vegetable organisms. Each little cell consists of an enveloping skin or membrane, containing a liquid

FIG. 4.   Yeast Plant.

or sap. They grow or expand from the minutest microscopic points, and seem to bud off from each other and multiply into many millions to the cubic inch. These cells are easily propagated in any medium where they find congenial food, particularly in the juice of grapes. If grape-juice be filtered and left to stand in a warm place two or three hours, it becomes first cloudy, then thick, and gives off bubbles of gas, showing there has been some change in its composition. In a short time a grayish-yellow froth, or layer of yeast cells, collects on the surface. " Whether the germs or spores of the yeast plant exist already in the juices of the living grape, or whether they are always floating in the air, and cling to the exterior of the fruit, and only become mixed with the juice in the wine-press, is not known ;" neither is it known just how they decompose the sugar of the grape. But it is enough for our purpose to know that they grow in the juice and expand there, and that an active ferment may be dissolved out of these yeast cells, sufficient to cause alcoholic fermentation.

The natural development of yeast through the agency of plants is too slow and inconvenient a process to rely upon ; therefore we manufacture it from various substances rich in starch and sugar. Brewer's yeast is made from malt, or sprouting grain, usually barley ; home-made yeast, from flour and potatoes.

Yeast Bread the Result of Chemical Changes. — Bread properly made with yeast undergoes certain chemical changes which render it lighter, more porous, more pleasant to the taste, and more healthful, because more easily digested, and more convenient for general use. It is generally recommended by scientific and medical men as the best form of bread.

Wheat contains a larger percentage of starch than of anything else. We learn, in the chapter on Digestion, that starch as such is not absorbed into the human system. It must first be transformed into sugar. All starch that is not changed into sugar by the process of cooking or before our food is eaten, is so changed by the *ptyalin*, or ferment of the saliva, and the ferment of the pancreatic fluid. Any process which produces this change for us makes our food more digestible. "Powdered alum will dissolve in water sooner than a crystal of alum." Any fluid will penetrate more easily through a sponge than through putty, and the salivary and gastric fluids are no exception to this rule. Wheat starch in its natural state is close and compact ; and bread made simply with flour and water, and baked at once, will be close, dry, and difficult to masticate and digest. Good bread should be sufficiently soft to be easily crushed in the mouth, and of such a light, spongy texture that all the starch cells may be ruptured, and the greatest possible amount of surface be presented to the action of the digestive fluids. To obtain these qualities in bread, we try to expand the dough as much as possible without destroying its natural sweetness. Owing to the peculiar elasticity and tenacity of the wheat gluten, this is very easily accomplished by alcoholic fermentation. The flour is moistened with some warm liquid, yeast and salt are added; and it is then exposed for some hours to a temperature of about 70°. The yeast changes some of the starch of the flour into sugar, and the sugar into alcohol and carbonic acid gas. This gas, being lighter than the dough, rises, and, in its efforts to escape, expands the elastic, glutinous dough into a mass two or three times its original bulk. The toughness or elasticity of the gluten prevents the gas from escaping ; and when this expansion has reached the desired limit, —that is, before the alcoholic fermentation has changed to the acetic and soured the dough, or the tough, glutinous walls of the air cells are broken, — we check the formation of gas, and kill the ferment by baking the dough in a hot oven. The alcohol escapes into the oven; some of the starch is changed into gum, and forms the crust; and the rapid decomposition, produced by the intense heat, causes the crust to assume a brown color.

Unfermented Bread. — This is made without yeast; but the principle is the same as in fermented bread, namely, the liberation of gas within the dough. The gas escapes quickly, and all such bread must be baked as soon as possible after mixing. There are no chemical changes in the starch or sugar; the elastic, glutinous dough is simply expanded by the gas. The starch cells are ruptured by the intense heat in baking; but if the gas bubbles burst before the heat has fixed the gluten wall, the bread will be heavy. This gas is produced in the bread dough in various ways: 1st. By the gas in very cold water, and the air obtained by vigorous beating; 2d. By the introduction of water under pressure, highly charged with gas. The first method is only suitable for mixtures which are to be baked quickly in a very hot oven, and eaten immediately, like gems, puffs, etc. The latter method produces what is known as aerated bread, making a light, sweet, spongy loaf; but it is not practicable for home use. 3d. The usual method is by some gas-generating compound, as the union of an acid and an alkali; usually soda, with either sour milk, cream of tartar, or muriatic acid. This is a convenient form adopted by many people who think it hard work to make yeast bread. When the chemicals used are pure, and in such a proportion that they neutralize each other, and leave only Rochelle salt as a residue, this bread, if used only occasionally, is harmless. But Rochelle salt is a medicine, not a nutritive food; and "those who are well do not need the disturbing influence of a medicine in their daily bread," and those who are ill do not often need this particular form of medicine. Through ignorance or care-lessness this bread is often made so that there is an excess of alkali or a residue of alum ; and then, if used habitually, it is injurious, and to some extent poisonous. It is convenient to know how to make it well in an emergency, and it helps make variety. It is best, when freshly baked, in the form of small biscuit rather than in loaves, and is not as indigestible, when eaten hot, as hot yeast bread. But for a bread for general use, for bread that will keep well, for bread that will leave a sweet, clean taste in the mouth, for bread that will yield the most in bulk from a given amount of flour, for bread for promoting health, there is nothing equal to perfect, home-made yeast bread. It is not so difficult a task to make perfect bread as most young housekeepers imagine, or old housekeepers assert. It i not impossible for a young girl to succeed as well in her first attempt in this art as the mature housekeeper who counts her loaves by the thousand, provided she learns the best way of making it, and uses a reasonable amount of common-sense.

The Best Kinds of Yeast.

Who made the first yeast? and how does a young house. keeper start her own, when away from stores or friends, where she can neither buy nor borrow? are questions often asked. Simply make a thin batter with flour and water, and let it stand in a warm place till it ferments, and is full of bubbles. A pint of this ferment is equal to one cup of old yeast in starting the new.

There are three kinds of yeast in general use, — the *dry*, the *compressed*, and the *liquid*, — each of which has its peculiar merits.

Dry yeast cakes are inexpensive, always ready to use, and generally liked by those who care more for economy of time and trouble than for the quality of their bread.

Compressed yeast cakes, like "Fleischmann's" are excellent, when perfectly fresh; the best form of yeast where bread is made in large quantities. But for a small family, where only a quarter of a cake is used perhaps twice a

week, or for those living at a distance from the stores,
they are not so convenient or cheap as good home-made
yeast. They have almost entirely taken the place of baker's
yeast.

As to which is best of the many varieties of home-made
yeast, who shall decide when housekeepers disagree?
Every good cook thinks *her* way *the best*. They are all good
that make good bread; the only special advantage of one
over another being the greater ease in making or the
length of time it will keep good. People who are inclined
to shirk think it a deal of trouble to make yeast of any
kind; but there are none so independent as those who make
their own yeast.

The simplest form of liquid yeast is made with flour, salt,
and boiling hop water. To this many add potatoes and a
little sugar, and some add ginger. Chemists say that the
potato is the best form of starch for the growth of yeast.
Potato yeast rises more rapidly, and keeps longer without
souring, than flour yeast; bread made from it is sweet,
light, and does not dry quickly. As to the comparative
merits of grated raw potato or boiled potato, those who
have used them both ways with equally good results think
the grated potato has the advantage of being made in much
less time.

The really essential points are that the water shall be
boiling, so that all the cells of the flour or potato may be
ruptured. The salt and sugar assist in the fermentation,
and the hops and ginger serve to prevent the yeast from
souring by checking the fermentation before all the sugar
is converted into alcohol; they also give it an agreeably
pungent taste, if not used in too large quantities. Old
potatoes are better than new for yeast, because they contain more sugar. Porcelain or granite kettles for boiling
the hops and potatoes, and earthen bowls and wooden
spoons for mixing, are best, as iron and tin cause the yeast
to turn dark-colored.

The yeast for starting must be fresh and lively, and
never added till the boiling mixture has become lukewarm,

or the plant will be killed. It must be kep , warm, and stirred several times while rising, and the next day put away in well-scalded glass jars. Keep it in a cool place; freezing or intense heat will kill the yeast plant. Reserve a portion for the next rising in a small jar by itself, as opening the jar often causes the yeast to lose its strength. Always shake or stir well before using. Yeast is good when it is foamy or full of beads, has a brisk, pungent odor, and a good deal of snap or vim; it is poor when it has an acid odor, and looks watery or has a thin film over the top.

Making the Dough.

Flour is moistened, or made into dough, with water or with milk. This softens the gluten and starch, dissolves the sugar, and cements all the particles together. Those who prefer water claim that water bread is cheaper, has more of the natural sweet taste of the wheat, and will keep longer; while those in favor of using milk are equally sure that milk bread is more nutritious, more tender, more agreeable to the taste and the eye, more easily made, and with proper care will keep sweet and moist longer.

Proportion. — The proportion of liquid and flour varies both with the flour and the liquid. Bread made of St. Louis flour, or mixed with water, takes more flour to make the same amount, than when made of Haxall flour, or mixed with milk. The general rule is *one scant measure* of liquid, including the yeast, to *three full measures* of flour. Water bread will need about one cupful more; and milk bread, or whole-wheat bread, from one half to one cupful less of flour. Dough which is to be kneaded, or rolled and cut into special shapes, should be stiffer than that which is not kneaded, or is to be made into loaves; but in all cases it should be mixed just as soft as can be handled easily without sticking, and just as little extra flour as possible should be used. If the dough be too stiff, make several deep incisions, and work in a little more liquid. The proportion of yeast is *half a cupful of fresh home-*

made yeast to a pint of liquid: a little less in warm weather; or when mixed at night, when the dough has a longer time to rise; or when made with a "sponge," or with whole-wheat flour, as the extra amount of gluten in this flour causes it to ferment more rapidly. A larger amount of yeast can be used when it is necessary to make bread in a limited time; but great care must be taken not to allow the dough to rise beyond the desired doubling in bulk. With compressed yeast, dissolve *one fourth of a cake in half a cupful of lukewarm water*, and use as home-made yeast. It will dissolve in one tablespoonful of water; but it is important to have the half-cupful, that the proportion of liquid may be the same.

Manner of Mixing. — Many people prefer to measure the flour, and add enough of the liquid to make it the desired consistency. The better way is to measure the liquid, and add flour, using more or less according to the quality of the flour, as the measure of the liquid determines the size of the loaf. All the flour may be added at first, and the dough raised in a mass; or a drop batter may be made with about half the flour, and when this has well risen, the remainder of the flour may be added, and the whole allowed to rise again. The latter method is preferable when it is inconvenient to knead at the first mixing, as is often the case in the evening, or when there is any doubt about the quality of the yeast, as, if the yeast will not raise three cups of flour, it certainly will not raise six. This method is advisable, also, when it is necessary to hasten the process of bread-making. Dough made by "setting a sponge," as this way is called, requires less yeast, the fermentation being more rapid in a batter than in a stiff dough; and this fermented batter acts like a double portion of yeast on the fresh flour, raising it very quickly. It is the best way of making bread with milk in the summer, as it may be mixed early in the morning and baked by noon; and as it may be easily watched, it need not become sour. The question of mixing at night or in the morning is one which every housekeeper can best answer for herself.

Many old receipts read, "Make a hole in the flour, add the yeast, and then pour in the liquid." If the yeast be added to the milk or water, and well mixed with it, and the flour then stirred thoroughly into this liquid mixture, the yeast will be more evenly distributed through the dough, and less kneading will be required than when made by the old method.

The other ingredients added to the dough are *salt* and *sugar*, in the proportion of *one even teaspoonful of salt* and *one even tablespoonful of sugar* to *three pints of flour*, using a little less salt if butter is added, and a little more with compressed yeast, as that is not as salt as home-made yeast, and doubling the amount of sugar when using whole-wheat flour.

Sugar in Bread. — Many object to the use of sugar in bread. Flour in its natural state contains sugar; this sugar is changed in fermentation. Just enough sugar to restore the natural sweetness, but not enough to give a really sweet taste, is necessary in fermented bread.

Potatoes. — Potatoes are sometimes added to bread dough. Where the flour is of an inferior quality, the bread is very much improved by their use; but with good flour they are unnecessary, and the use of them increases the labor of making bread.

Shortening. — Whether bread shall be "shortened or not shortened," is another question on which there is great diversity of opinion. Those who disapprove of fat of any kind in bread claim that we eat fat enough in other forms of food, and also that the same crisp tenderness of texture may be produced by skilful kneading. Bread made with new or unskimmed milk, and kneaded well, requires no other shortening; but water bread, when shortened, is made more tender, and therefore is more easily penetrated by the digestive fluids. The latest decision of the best physicians is that fat is absolutely necessary as an element of food, and it is often given as a remedy for some diseases. The proportion which one person would receive from one tablespoonful of butter, or drippings, or lard, in two loaves of bread would not harm the most deli-cate stomach. Butter tastes best; drippings are cheap-est. Lard has for its chief merit that of making whiter bread than either of the others. The shortening may be rubbed into the flour, or, better still, melted in the warm liquid. Too much shortening clogs the glutinous cell-walls, and therefore checks the rising. Rolls, rusks, and buns, which are usually shortened more than loaf bread, should have the butter added at the last kneading.

The bread should be mixed in a deep stone-china or granite bowl; wooden bowls are difficult to keep sweet and clean. Brown earthenware is awkward in shape and clumsy to handle, while tinware, being a better conductor than china, lets the heat within the mass escape, and the tin rubs off from the constant friction. Use a wooden spoon, or a wooden-handled iron spoon, or a broad-bladed knife.

Kneading the Dough. — Kneading is the process of press-ing or working the dough in such a manner that the flour and water may be thoroughly mixed, and the yeast be so evenly distributed that the fermentation may be equal through the whole mass. It may be done by cutting or chopping, either with the hand or machinery; but there is nothing that gives the fine, even grain to bread so well as hand-kneading; and no surer test of the proper consist-ency of dough than that given by the sense of touch. There are some kinds of milk bread and rolls which are very good without it; but water bread should always be kneaded. It is often done in the mixing-bowl, by draw-ing the dough over from the side and pressing it down in the centre, turning the bowl with the other hand; but it is more effectually accomplished on a bread-board. In Spain the bakers knead the bread with such force that the palms of the hands and the second joints of the fingers are covered with corns; but strength and force are not so essential to good kneading as a peculiar and dexterous handling of the dough. The most approved process is the fo¹ ɔwing: —

Sprinkle the board with flour, and leave a little in the corner to lay your hands upon. Scrape the dough from the bowl, and toss it over with the knife that it may be well floured. Flour the hands; then, with the finger-tips, draw the dough farthest from you up and over toward the centre, letting the ball of the hand meet the dough, and then press down firmly, giving the dough somewhat of a rolling motion, that it may not stick to the board. Repeat this motion until the dough is in a long narrow shape, then turn it at right angles, and draw up, fold, and press down again; and continue this process until the dough is smooth, elastic, fine, and even-grained. Dust the board and the palms of the hands with flour often, but only slightly. Should the dough stick, lift it quickly, and always scrape off what has adhered to the board before dusting again, that the board may be kept smooth. But do not let it stick; keep it in constant motion. Do not knead hard enough to break into the dough, nor let the finger-tips pierce the smooth crust that soon forms under proper kneading. Use the fingers merely in drawing the dough over, and keep them up and out of it when pressing with the ball of the hand. Use both hands in the same manner, or draw up and press with the right, and turn the ball of dough with the left, that all parts may receive an equal pressure. When enough of this smooth, soft texture has been formed all through the dough, it can be worked for some time without even a dusting of flour. After a little experience, if care be taken in the beginning, and only a little flour added at each dusting, when the dough is sufficiently kneaded, the hands, the apron, and the board will be clean, and the dough of an even, elastic consistency, springing up instantly as you toss or pound or punch into it. The habit of mixing with the hands, and rubbing off little wads of dough from the fingers into the whole mass, should be avoided, especially toward the last of the process. There is no mechanical operation in cooking more fascinating than the deft, quick touches a natural kneader gives to a mass of dough. Young ladies

with pretty hands can display them there quite as well as with embroidery, etc. ; but the rings and bracelets should be left in the jewel-case. The stitches in tight dress sleeves are *not* " *warranted not to break* " during this process. Perfect freedom for the muscles of the arms and chest is absolutely essential to the making and kneading of bread.

Temperature and Time for the Raising of Bread. — In winter the water or milk used in mixing should be luke-warm ; and if the flour be kept in a very cold place, warm it before using. In summer the water need not be warmed, neither should it be ice-water ; the milk should be scalded (not boiled), and cooled. After the bread is kneaded sufficiently it must be made into a smooth round ball, with no dry flour left on the surface, and put back in the mixing-bowl to rise. If you have learned the knack of scraping a bowl thoroughly, it need not be washed ; otherwise it is well to wash and grease the bowl, that the dough may come out more easily after it has risen. Notice how it fills the bowl, and let it rise until it has a little more than doubled in size. Cover it, not with a cloth alone, as that serves merely to keep out the dust, but with several thicknesses of cloth, and a tightly fitting tin cover. It is important that the air be excluded, as it causes a hard crust to form, which will be difficult to mix thoroughly in the dough at the next kneading, and will also leave dark spots or streaks in the bread.

The dough should rise in a temperature of about 75°. Avoid a draught of cold air, or sudden alternations of extreme heat and cold. If it be placed on a mantel or near a stove, it must be turned frequently. When necessary to hasten the rising, place the bowl in a pan of warm (not hot) water, and keep the water at the same temperature until it begins to rise. After fermentation has been well established the temperature can be lowered without harm, provided it does not fall below 45°. In winter, bread should be mixed early in the evening ; and if the kitchen become very cold before morning, keep the dough in a warmer room; it will be risen by six or seven in the morning. In summer, mix it later at night, leave it in a cool place, and the next morning attend to it early; if possible, by five o'clock. In very hot weather mix early in the morning, and bake by noon. It should never be allowed to rise to the point of "caving in," or settling, or running over the bowl. Even if it does not become sour, it loses the natural sweet flavor of the wheat, and is tasteless and insipid. It should rise in a light, puffy, well-rounded mass; and if it half filled the bowl at first, it will be ready, when risen nearly to the top of the bowl, "to cut down," as most cooks express it. This is done by cutting it away from the sides of the bowl, and working it over into the centre with the knife. This releases some of the gas, checks the fermentation, and reduces the bulk somewhat. It will rise again very quickly, and the cutting-down process can be repeated several times, and the bread will be the better for it, provided the rising does not go too far at any time. It takes but a moment, and should always be done when the dough is risen sufficiently, if you are not ready to shape it at once into loaves. If you do not wish to bake the bread for several hours, it can be kneaded again and put in the ice-chest or cellar. When the dough rises too long, and has soured, it will have a strong, tingling acid odor as you cut into it, and it will pull away from the bowl in long threads, having a watery appearance, quite unlike the proper spongy consistency and pungent alcoholic odor when it is just right. The practice of using soda to sweeten it, when in this state, cannot be too severely condemned. Chemists say that *light* sour bread is not unhealthful, although unpalatable to most Americans. Bread in that condition is eaten largely by the Germans. Sour bread sweetened by soda *is* unhealthful, as it is very rarely that the alkali is wholly neutralized by the acetic acid. Those who boast of never having sour bread because they always keep a bottle of soda dissolved and ready for instant use, should, instead, blush at the fact of such careless housewifery. With proper care, bread, even

when made with milk, need never sour. But should the
accident ever occur, it is better to eat the bread, or dry it
for crumbs, or. throw it away even, than to use the soda.
This practice is so abominable that here it will receive
neither aid nor encouragement.

Shaping into Loaves or Biscuit. — At least an hour before the time for baking, scrape the dough from the bowl,
and turn it out upon the board, which should be dusted
with flour; knead it slightly, and divide into the proper
proportion for loaves.

The measures given in the following receipts fill two
brickloaf pans, which are eight inches long by four inches
broad and five inches deep, with nearly straight sides.
This shape gives small uniform slices. Small round pans
were formerly considered best for baking both bread and
cake; and there is some truth in the reason given, namely,
that the cells which are formed by the gas are circular in
form, and are much more uniform in a round than in an
oblong loaf, in which the corner cells are easily flat-
tened or compressed, forming heavy streaks around the
edges. But many people dislike the shape of the slices in
a round loaf, and oblong pans have been more generally
adopted. They should be greased with lard or drippings.
It is better to divide the dough into four equal parts and
put two in each pan, for several reasons: a small round
loaf is more easily shaped, and can be broken, if wanted,
while. fresh, better than a long loaf; two small loaves
rise and fill the pan more evenly than one long loaf; and
unless great care be taken in shaping to have the one
loaf of uniform thickness, it will rise more in the middle
and give uneven slices. Many make a deep cut through
the middle to prevent this; but that spoils the smooth-
round effect which adds so much to the looks of the
crust.

Use the merest dusting of flour in shaping, and knead
just enough to work out the large bubbles of gas by folding the mass over into the middle, then letting it spring
open. Pat, coax, and work it with the hand and fingers

until there are no wrinkles, and the loaves are smooth. Greasing the hands slightly with butter helps. All the flour added at this kneading rises but once, and too much will make the loaf burst out unevenly at the sides. Some careless kneaders merely fold it over, and if it look smooth on the top they think that enough; but their loaf will sometimes have a seam or crack through it, which will cause the slices to fall apart easily.

The loaves should come nearly half-way up the pan; and the same rule follows as for the first rising, namely, let it come to the top, or till the bulk is doubled. Cover with cloth and tin cover, or a large tin pan. The time for rising varies with the lightness of the dough and the temperature of the room. It is impossible to give a definite rule; but should it rise too far and stick to the cloth, or look "tumbled in," cut it down, knead, and let it rise again. Never bake it in the above state, as it will be coarse-grained, if not hollow. It is better to bake it a little too soon than to let it rise too long.

Rolls and small biscuit should rise in the pans longer and be baked in a hotter oven than the loaf, because the loaf rises in the oven until the heat has penetrated to the centre: while in the rolls the air cells are very quickly fixed by the intense heat needed to perfect the crust, and fermentation is almost immediately checked. This is contrary to the usual practice; but it is the correct way. Many people prepare biscuit for breakfast by letting them rise ten or fifteen minutes in a very hot place while the oven is heating. They are often only half baked, and then eaten smoking hot; and those who have never had anything else think them just right. The evil effects of this practice have been the occasion for much of the outcry against hot, or even fresh, biscuit. Such are entirely different from the dry, light, delicious biscuit which have had a natural, not a forced, rising, are of the proper texture, have been baked quickly, and allowed to stand at least half an hour before being eaten. The moral of the above is, never try to have raised biscuit for breakfast without

rising at least three hours before breakfast-time, unless you wish your family to become slaves to indigestion.

The Temperature for Baking. — The object of baking bread is to kill the ferment, rupture the starch grains, fix the air cells, and form a nicely flavored crust. Bread could be baked by steam, as the air cells become fixed at 212°, and the temperature of the inside of the loaf, owing to the moisture, never rises above that point; but, to give the delicious flavor of the browned crust, a much higher temperature is needed. The oven should be hot enough to brown a teaspoonful of flour in *one minute* for rolls, and in *five minutes* for loaves. This is a good rule for those who do not use a thermometer, or cannot judge of the heat by their hands. The heat should be greater at the bottom than at the top of the oven, and of sufficient strength to last through the time of baking (which is about an hour) without replenishing the fire. Divide the time into thirds; the first fifteen or twenty minutes the heat should increase, remain steady during the next, and decrease toward the last. The dough should rise, and, after fifteen minutes, begin to brown slightly. If the oven be too hot, and the loaf brown too fast, a hard crust will be formed before the heat reaches the centre, and, pressing down on the air cells, make a heavy streak; or, if removed from the oven too soon, it will be raw and doughy inside. If the heat be not sufficient to form the crust in fifteen minutes, the dough will go on rising until it becomes sour and pasty, and the air cells will run together, making a hole in the middle. The baking of bread is something that will not take care of itself. The old notion that you must not look at anything in the oven is erroneous; and until you have learned by experience just how to regulate the fire and oven, and the many tests by which every good cook determines when bread is done, look at it often, and bake according to the clock from fifty to sixty minutes. Better bake ten minutes too long, putting a paper over the top to prevent a burned crust, than not long enough. Bake it *brown*, not black, nor pale whity-brown, but *brown* all over. Rolls are often brushed with milk just before and after baking, to give them a richer brown color. Rubbing over with soft butter while still hot makes a crisp, delicious crust. When well baked, if tapped with the fingers, a hollow, empty sound will be emitted; the crust feels firm, and, if broken apart, the inside rebounds instantly on any slight pressure.

The Care of Bread after Baking. — Remove the loaves immediately from the pans, and place them where the air can circulate freely round them and thus carry off the gas which has been formed, but is no longer needed. A bread or cake cooler, made of fine wire, set in a narrow frame thirty inches long by twelve or fifteen broad, is a very useful article, as it will hold several loaves. An old wire window-screen, too small for modern windows, with cleats on the ends, to keep it two or three inches from the table, answers the purpose admirably. Many use a wire sieve; but that is small, and leaves the marks of the larger cross wires on the loaf. Never leave the bread in the pan, or on a pine table, to sweat and absorb the odor of the wood.

If you like crusts that are crisp, do not cover the loaves; but to give the soft, tender, wafer-like consistency which many prefer, wrap them, while still hot, in several thicknesses of bread cloth. When cold, put them into a stone jar or tin box; remove the cloth, as that absorbs the moisture, and gives the bread an unpleasant taste and odor. Keep the jar well covered and carefully cleansed from crumbs and stale pieces. Scald and dry it thoroughly every two or three days. A yard and a half square of coarse table linen makes the best bread cloth. Keep a good supply; keep them sweet and clean, and use them for no other purpose.

Fine white bread should be partaken of in moderation. Although the "staff of life," it is not necessary to eat bread with every kind of diet. It is most useful when taken with articles containing a large proportion of nourishment in a small bulk, as it then gives the stomach the proper degree of expansion.

Raw Potato Yeast.

¼ cup flour.	3 raw potatoes.
¼ cup sugar.	1 to 2 quarts boiling water.
1 tablespoonful salt.	1 cup yeast.

First, see that you have at least three quarts of water boiling rapidly. Pare the potatoes, and keep them covered with cold water. Mix the flour, sugar, and salt in a large bowl, and grate the potatoes as quickly as possible, not stopping to grate every scrap; mix them at once with the flour, using a wooden or silver spoon, that the mixture may not be dark-colored. Pour the boiling water directly from the teakettle over the grater, and rinse off the potato into the bowl, using perhaps a pint of water at first. Mix the water thoroughly with the potato and flour; then add, slowly, enough more boiling water to make it the consistency of thin starch. The amount of water will depend upon the quality of the flour and potatoes. If it does not thicken, pour the mixture into a double boiler or granite pan, and let it come to the boiling-point, stirring well to keep it from sticking. Strain through a squash strainer and let it cool. When lukewarm (clear through the mixture, not merely on the top), add the yeast. Cover slightly, and keep in a warm (not hot) place, until light and covered with white foam. After it begins to rise, beat it well several times, as this makes it stronger. At night, or when well risen, put it into wide-mouthed earthen or glass jars. The next morning cover tightly, and keep it in a cool place. Reserve one cupful or more in a small glass jar, and do not open it until ready for the next yeast-making. Always shake yeast well before using; take your cup to the jar instead of taking the jar to the hot kitchen; when empty, scald the jar and the cover thoroughly. This is the quickest and easiest way of making yeast, fifteen minutes being ample time for the first part of the process. It is whiter and looks more inviting than that made with hops. It keeps well two weeks, and makes delicious bread.

This receipt can be varied by using boiling hop-water.

turning and working it over until all the dry flour is well mixed with the other materials. Mix it just soft enough to be shaped into a loaf after it has risen. Scrape the dough from the sides of the bowl; smooth the top with a knife; cover and let it rise. Shape it into loaves, and when well risen bake about forty minutes.

Water Bread (with a Sponge).

1 tablespoonful butter.	1 pint water.
1 teaspoonful salt.	½ cup yeast, scant.
1 tablespoonful sugar.	About 2 quarts flour.

Put the butter, sugar, and salt in the mixing-bowl; add one fourth cup of boiling water to dissolve them; then add enough more lukewarm water to make a pint in all, half a cup of yeast, and three and a half or four cups of flour, enough to make a batter that will drop, not pour, from the spoon. Give it a vigorous beating; cover and let it rise over night. This soft mixture is called a *sponge*. In the morning add flour to make it stiff enough to knead. Knead it half an hour. Cover; let it rise in the bowl until noon, or till light and spongy; then shape it into loaves or rolls; let it rise again in the pans; bake as usual. This sponge can be divided in the morning, adding to one part of it white flour enough to knead it, and to the other part *whole-wheat* or *rye* flour and another tablespoonful of *sugar*. Make it just stiff enough to shape easily into a loaf after it is risen. Use white flour to shape it on the board, as the rye and whole-wheat flour are sticky. Or make the dough a little softer, fill gem pans two thirds full, let them rise to the top, bake in a hot oven, and you have " *raised rye* or *whole-wheat gems.*"

Milk Bread, No. 3 (with Sponge).

Pour *one pint* of *scalded milk* on *one tablespoonful each* of *butter* and *sugar*, and *one teaspoonful* of *salt;* when lukewarm, add *half a cup* of *yeast* if mixed in the *morning* or *one fourth* of *a cup* if mixed at *night*. Stir in *three cups* of

5

flour, and beat well. Let it rise over night, or, if mixed in
the morning, about three hours. Then add from *two* to
three cups of *flour*, or enough to knead it, and knead half
an hour. Let it rise in the bowl, and again after being
shaped into loaves or rolls, and bake as usual.

Whole-wheat or *rye bread* or *gems* can be made from this
sponge the same as in the preceding rule.

Whole-Wheat or Graham Bread.

1 pint milk, scalded and cooled.	5 or 6 cups fine granulated wheat flour, or
2 tablespoonfuls sugar.	
1 teaspoonful salt.	2 cups white flour, and
½ cup yeast.	3 or 3½ cups sifted Graham flour.

In the morning mix, in the order given, into a dough, a
little softer than for white bread ; let it rise till light, stir
it down, pour it into *well-greased pans*, or, if stiff enough,
shape it into loaves ; let it rise again, and bake a little
longer and in a less hot oven than white bread. Graham
or whole-wheat flour rises more rapidly than white flour,
as it contains more gluten. It is liable to become sour
if mixed over night, and then the cooks resort to the soda.
For the true remedy use less yeast, and use sugar instead
of molasses, or mix in the morning. Always sift the flour,
notwithstanding all cook-books say to the contrary. Use
a coarse sieve or squash strainer. Sift once, and, if you
observe the character of the refuse, you will be glad
to do so always. Bake part of this as biscuit or rolls.
When made with ordinary Graham flour, the bread is
much lighter if at least one third white flour be used.

Squash Bread.

1 cup squash, stewed and sifted.	1 tablespoonful butter.
2 tablespoonfuls sugar.	½ cup yeast.
1½ cups scalded milk	Flour enough to knead it.
1 teaspoonful salt.	

Mix the sugar and salt with the squash, add the butter
melted in the hot milk, and when cool add the yeast and

flour. Knead fifteen minutes. Let it rise till light. Knead and shape into loaves or biscuit. When well risen, bake

Rye Bread.

Make by rule given for Milk Bread, No. 3, adding rye flour or rye meal to the white-flour sponge.

Raised Brown Bread. (*Mrs. H. B. May.*)

1 pint yellow corn meal.	½ teaspoonful salt.
½ cup yeast.	1 saltspoonful soda.
½ cup molasses.	1 pint rye meal.

Put the corn meal in the mixing-bowl, and scald it with boiling water, just enough to wet it; let it stand ten minutes, then add cold water enough to make a soft batter. When lukewarm, add the yeast, molasses, soda, salt, and rye meal. Beat it well, and let it rise over night, or until it cracks open. Stir it down; put it in a buttered and floured tin to rise again; sprinkle flour over the top. Bake in a moderate oven two hours. Brown bread made by this rule was first tested by the writer thirty years ago, when it was a wonder and delight to watch it as it was put on a wooden shovel and placed in the great brick oven. It has been made in the same house regularly every week since then, and proves just as good now as it was in the olden time.

Thirded Bread.

1 cup white flour (St. Louis).	1 teaspoonful salt.
1 cup rye flour, or sifted rye meal.	3 tablespoonfuls sugar.
1 cup yellow corn meal.	½ cup yeast.

Mix with milk (scalded and cooled) till thick enough to be shaped. Let it rise until it cracks open. Put into a brickloaf pan, and when well risen bake it one hour.

Sour Milk Brown Bread, No. 1.   (*Mrs. Wm. B. Johnson.*)

1 pint corn meal.	1 teaspoonful salt.
1 pint Graham flour.	1 pint sour milk.
1 teaspoonful soda.	1 cup molasses.

Mix the meal with flour. Mash the soda and salt before measuring; sift and mix thoroughly with the flour; add the sour milk and molasses, and beat well. If not moist enough to pour, add a little warm water. Pour it into a well-greased mould or pail, filling it only two thirds full. Cover it with a tight cover, also greased. Steam three hours in a steamer, or set the pail in a kettle of boiling water. Keep the water boiling; and as it boils away, replenish with boiling water to keep it at the same level. Remove the cover, and place the mould in the oven fifteen minutes to dry the crust.

Sour Milk Brown Bread, No. 2.

1 cup white corn meal.	1 full teaspoonful soda.
1 cup rye flour.	½ cup molasses.
1 cup Graham flour	1 pint sour milk.
1 teaspoonful salt.	

Mix in the order given, sifting the soda, and adding more milk or water if not thin enough to pour. Steam three hours. One cup of raisins stoned and halved may be added to this, or any of the receipts for brown bread.

Raised Biscuit and Rolls.

The name "biscuit" is from the French, and means "twice baked." It was originally applied to a kind of hard, thin bread, made in that manner to deprive it of all moisture and insure its remaining in good condition for a long time. It was something like our crackers and ship bread But in America it means any kind of bread made into small, round cakes and intended to be eaten hot or fresh. *Raised biscuit* may be made from any of the doughs made by the receipts for bread; the proportions are enough for one pan of bread, and one pan of biscuit containing twelve or sixteen according to the size. They should always be made small, and shaped with the fingers, not cut with a cutter. Divide the portion of dough reserved for biscuit into halves, then into quarters, and each quarter into thirds or quarters. *To shape a biscuit,* take one of these quarters in the left hand and rest it lightly on the board. With the right thumb and forefinger draw a point of the dough up and over to the centre, and hold it down with the left thumb. Give the dough a slight turn toward the left, and repeat the drawing up and folding over until you have been all round the ball. You may roll them in the hands until all these foldings have disappeared and they are smooth and round, and call them simply *biscuit;* or you may make the folds as distinct as possible, and place them at once in the pan. The folds will spread apart in rising, and when baked they can be peeled off in layers. They are then honored with the name of *Imperial Rolls.* Put the biscuit in a shallow round pan, fitting them closely, that they may rise up, round and puffy, instead of spreading. When very light, bake in a very hot oven fifteen or twenty minutes. Keep them wrapped in a bread cloth for at least half an hour before serving. The receipts for Milk Bread are especially nice for biscuit.

Rolls.

Rolls are made by rolling the raised dough into small forms, with the hands or with a rolling-pin, and afterward cutting and folding into the desired shape; the shape and manner of manipulation giving the distinctive names. The dough for rolls should be very light, and when wanted unusually nice, more shortening should be worked into it after the second kneading. The rule for Water Bread made with a sponge is good for plain rolls; Milk Bread made with a sponge is the same as *Parker House Rolls,* which have been generally adopted by housekeepers as the stand·

ard. The following are some of the best varieties and
shapes : —

For *Finger Rolls*, make a dough by the rule for Milk
Bread, No. 2, and when risen and ready to shape, divide
the half reserved for rolls into twelve pieces. Make each
piece into a smooth ball as if for biscuit, then roll it between the palms, or with the palm of one hand on the
board, into a long roll about the size of the second finger.
Roll with buttered hands or with as little flour as possible.
Place them close together in a long, shallow pan. Let
them rise to the top of the pan, and bake in a very hot
oven for ten or fifteen minutes.

To make a *Cleft Roll*, make the dough into smooth balls, ·
then with a floured knife-handle press through the centre
but not quite through on the ends. Or make them round,
and place them some distance apart on the pan, and when
ready to bake, make a deep cut through the middle. Make
another cut at right angles with the first and you have
a *Cross Roll*.

Parker House Rolls are made after the receipt for Milk
Bread with sponge, and when well risen and ready to shape,
roll the dough on the board as you would pastry, and, if
wanted richer, spread a generous tablespoonful of softened butter all over it. Fold the dough, and roll out again
until nearly half an inch thick. Lift the rolled dough from
the board and let it shrink back all it will, and be sure it
is of uniform thickness before cutting, or the rolls will lose
their shape. Cut with a round or oval cutter; press the
thumb across the middle and fold over like a turnover,
letting the edges come together. As they rise they will
open a little, and, if folded only half-way over, they are
liable to open too far. Spread a bit of soft butter the
size of a pea on the edge before folding it, if you like
the crusty inside which that gives. Or roll the dough
thinner, and put two rounds together with a thin spreading of butter between; these are called *Twin Rolls*.

To make *Pocket-book* or *Letter Rolls*, roll the dough in a
rectangular shape one fourth of an inch thick, and cut it in

strips four inches wide and as long as the dough will allow. Spread with soft butter; fold one end of the strip over about an inch and a half, and then over again. Cut off even with the folding, and then fold another, and so on. Or cut the dough into strips two inches wide by seven long, and spread each strip with butter, and fold one third over and then again like a letter. Or roll the dough out one fourth of an inch thick, then roll up and cut pieces one inch wide from the end of the roll, turn them over on the side, and place close together in a pan to rise.

To make a *Braid*, cut the rolled dough in strips one inch wide by six inches long, and pinch three strips together at the end, then form into a braid. Or roll little balls of dough into long pieces the same as for sticks, and then braid them.

To make *Crescents*, or *Vienna Rolls*, roll the dough until only an eighth of an inch thick; cut into pieces five inches square and then into triangles. Hold the apex of the triangle in the right hand, roll the edge next the left hand over and over towards the right, stretch the point and bring it over and under the roll; bend the ends of the roll around like a horseshoe, being careful to keep in the folding. Any dough that is quite stiff may be shaped with the hands into small, oval rolls with quite tapering ends, and baked far enough apart to allow each roll to have a crust all over. These are called *French Rolls*. Any of these rolls may be rubbed with a cloth dipped in melted butter; or, better still, twist a piece of butter in a clean cloth and rub it over them just as they are taken from the oven.

Sticks.

1 cup milk, scalded.	¼ cake compressed yeast, or
¼ cup butter.	3 tablespoonfuls liquid yeast.
1 tablespoonful sugar.	White of 1 egg.
½ teaspoonful salt.	About 4 cups flour.

Melt the butter, sugar, and salt in the hot milk; when lukewarm, add the yeast (if compressed, dissolve in three

tablespoonfuls of warm milk or water), then the beaten
white and flour. Knead until smooth and fine-grained. Let
it rise over night or till light. Shape into small balls;
then roll into sticks a foot long. Let them rise slowly and
bake in a moderate oven, that they may be dried through
before browning. When shaped into large plain rolls, they
are called *White Mountain Rolls.*

Rolls designed for breakfast or dinner are better not to
be sweetened enough to taste sweet; but for tea or lunch
more sugar may be added. This brings us to another variety of rolls which are made richer by the addition of butter, sugar, eggs, and fruit, including *Swedish Rolls, Rusks,*
and *Buns.*

Swedish Rolls.

1 pint milk, scalded.	Whites of 2 eggs.
½ cup butter.	½ cup yeast
¼ cup sugar.	7 or 8 cups flour.
1 scant teaspoonful salt	

Melt the butter, and dissolve the sugar and salt in the
hot milk; when lukewarm, add the yeast and beaten whites.
Mix in flour to make a sponge or drop batter. In the
morning add the remainder of the flour, and knead twenty
minutes. Let it rise till noon or till light; then knead
again slightly, and roll out into a large, rectangular piece,
half an inch thick. Have the edges as straight as possible. Spread all over with a thin layer of *soft butter*, and
a sprinkling of *sugar, cinnamon, grated lemon rind*, and
currants. Roll up like a jelly roll, cut off slices an inch
wide, lay them with the cut side down on well-greased
pans, and when well risen bake in a hot oven fifteen or
twenty minutes. When done, glaze them with sugar dissolved in milk, and dry them a few minutes in the oven, or
rub them with soft butter. If mixed in the morning,
make a sponge with the scalded milk cooled, the eggs,
salt, sugar, and part of the flour. Place the bowl in a
pan of warm water for three or four hours; then add the
butter and the remainder of the flour. Knead, and after
it is well risen roll out as above.

Rusk, No. 1.

1 cup milk, scalded and cooled.	¼ cup yeast.
1 tablespoonful sugar	2 cups flour.
½ teaspoonful salt.	

Mix in a sponge at night or very early in the morning. When well risen, add flour enough to make a stiff dough. Knead and let it rise again, then add *one fourth* of *a cup* of *butter*, rubbed to a cream, *half a cup* of *sugar*, and *one egg*, beaten with butter and sugar. Let it rise in the bowl till light. Shape into small round biscuit; put them close together in a shallow cake pan, that they may rise very high. When ready to bake, rub the tops with sugar dissolved in milk, sprinkle with dry sugar, and bake in a moderate oven.

Rusk, No. 2.

Make a dough at night by the rule for Milk Bread, No. 1. In the morning make half the dough into a loaf for bread. Put with the remainder *half a cup* of *butter*, creamed, with *one cup* of *sugar* and *one egg*, well beaten; mix and beat well; add *half a cup* of *flour*, or enough to shape it easily. Let it rise in the bowl, shape into small rounds or into long narrow rolls, and when very light, glaze them and bake as in the preceding rule.

Rusk, No. 3. (*Miss Yandes*)

1 pint milk, scalded	1 cup potato yeast.
½ cup butter and lard, mixed.	3 eggs
¾ cup sugar.	Flour as required.

Mix early in the morning, in the order given, adding flour enough to make a thin batter. Let it rise till full of bubbles, then add flour enough to knead it. When well risen, shape into rounds, or roll out and cut them. Let them rise in the pans till very light; then bake in a hot oven about half an hour.

Dried Rusks are made after either of these receipts, and when risen are rolled thin, cut into rounds, and put two together into the pan. When baked, they are pulled apart and left in a very moderate oven to dry. Or they are cut in slices when cold, and dried until crisp and brown. They are delicious soaked in milk and eaten with butter, or used the same as bread in puddings, or soaked in a custard and *sautéd.*

Bunns.

Make a sponge over night with

1 cup milk, scalded	1 saltspoonful salt.
1 tablespoonful sugar and 1 egg beaten together.	¼ cup yeast. 2 cups flour.

Beat it well and in the morning add flour to made a stiff dough. Knead fifteen minutes. Let it rise until light, then add *one fourth* of *a cup* of *butter,* softened, *half a cup* of *currants,* and *one saltspoonful* of *cinnamon* or *nutmeg.* Let it rise in the bowl till light. Shape into small round cakes, put them close together, and when well risen bake in a moderate oven. Glaze them with sugar and milk, or with white of egg beaten stiff with sugar. Make a deep cut like a cross just before they are put into the oven, and you have *Hot Cross Bunns.* Many prefer a bit of citron put into the middle of each bunn. These are better when freshly baked. It is therefore well to make only a small quantity. They may be made from risen milk-bread dough in the same manner as Rusk, No. 2, by using the spices and the fruit and a smaller quantity of sugar. This receipt for bunns makes excellent *raised doughnuts* by omitting the currants and rolling half an inch thick and cutting with a doughnut cutter.

Raised Bread Cake, or Loaf Cake.

This is similar to rusks and bunns, only richer; and as it improves by keeping, it is well to make a large quantity.

At night mix *one pint* of *milk*, scalded and cooled, *one teaspoonful* of *salt, half a cup* of *yeast, five* or *six cups* of *flour*, enough to make a soft dough. In the morning prepare *one cup* of *butter*, creamed; add *two cups* of *brown sugar, one tablespoonful* of *mixed spices,* — *cinnamon, nutmeg*, and *allspice*, — and *four eggs*, yolks and whites beaten separately. Add this mixture to the beaten dough, and beat well. Add *two cups* of *stoned* and *chopped raisins*, or *one cup* of *raisins, one cup* of *currants* and *half a cup* of *sliced citron*. Flour the fruit. Let it rise in the bowl till light. Stir it down, and pour into two deep cake tins, making them two thirds full. Let it stand in a warm place fifteen or twenty minutes, then bake one hour or longer in a moderate oven.

Uses for Stale Bread.

All bread crumbs left on the plates or bread board or in the bread jar, any broken pieces not suitable for toast, and any crusts or trimmings of toast should be carefully collected in a pan by themselves, and dried (not browned) in the hot closet or in a moderate oven, then pounded in a mortar or rolled on an *old* bread board, sifted through a coarse sieve, and put away in a dry place. These will be useful in covering anything which is to be dipped in egg and crumbs and then fried. Bread crumbs brown better than cracker crumbs, and are much cheaper, being made from material which is usually thrown away. These are *dried bread crumbs*, and are *not* to be used for bread pudding or scalloped dishes, as they will absorb a great deal of moisture. They will keep indefinitely in a dry place *Stale bread crumbs*, which are not dried in the oven, but are made from odds and ends of stale bread, crumbled finely or grated on a coarse grater, are better for meat or fish stuffing, bread puddings, bread sauce, bread griddle-cakes, scalloped fish, etc. They should be used at once, as they soon become musty. Any whole slices of stale bread may be steamed or used for toast.

Stale Bread Steamed.

Have a large covered steamer fitting tightly over a kettle of boiling water. One with holes all over the bottom is best, as the steam condenses and runs down the sides and through the holes; while in those with holes only in the middle it forms little pools of water round the edge, which make the bread soggy. Do not put in the bread until everything else is ready, as it takes only a few minutes for it to become heated through. Arrange it all in the middle of the steamer, tilted against a small cup or dish so that the steam may pass between the slices. Do not let any of it touch the sides of the steamer, or it will become water-soaked. When ready to remove it, lift the cover quickly, turning it over instantly, that no water may drip on the bread. Spread each slice with butter as you take it out, and arrange them on a hot platter. Cover with a napkin and serve immediately. Stale biscuit may be made much nicer than new in this way. These directions may seem needlessly minute; but it is just these little things that make the difference between light, delicate, hot steamed bread, and the heavy, water-soaked stuff that is often served.

Egg Toast, or Bread Sautéd.

1 egg.	1 cup milk.
1 saltspoonful salt.	4 to 6 slices stale bread.

Beat the egg lightly with a fork in a shallow pudding-dish; add salt and milk. Soak the bread in this until soft. Turn the slices by putting those underneath on the top, and dip the custard over them, being careful not to break them. Have a griddle hot and well buttered. Brown them on one side; then put a piece of butter on the top of each slice, and turn and brown on the other side. To be eaten hot with butter, also with sugar and cinnamon if liked. This is one of the nicest ways of freshening stale bread, and is especially convenient when the fire is not in order for toasting. It is called French, Spanish, German, and Nun's Toast; but Egg Toast seems to best indicate the character of the dish. When fried in deep fat, it may be used as a pudding by serving with a sweet sauce, and is then called Italian Fritters.

Brown Bread Brewis.

Break *one pint* of *dry brown bread* and *half a cup* of *stale white bread* into inch pieces. Put a *tablespoonful* of *butter* in a large frying-pan, and when it is melted, but not brown, add the bread and cover with *one pint* or more of *milk*. Let it simmer, stirring occasionally to keep it from sticking, until the bread is soft and the milk absorbed. Salt to taste.

Brown Bread Brewis, No. 2.

Mix the same proportion of bread with *one fourth* of *a cup* of *butter* in a double boiler; add *milk* to cover, and cook over hot water without stirring until the bread has absorbed all the milk. If the bread be very dry, more milk will be needed.

Toast.

Bread is toasted, or dried and browned, before the fire to extract the moisture and make it more palatable and digestible. If the slices be cut thick and carelessly exposed to a blazing fire, the outside is blackened and made into charcoal before the heat can reach the inside; the moisture is only heated, not evaporated, making the inside doughy or clammy, and when spread with butter, which cannot penetrate the charcoal, but floats on the surface in the form of oil, it forms one of the most indigestible compounds. The correct way is to have the bread stale, and cut into thin, uniform slices about one quarter of an inch thick. The fire should be clear, red (not blazing) coals. The crusts may be removed or not according to your taste, or the purpose for which the toast is intended. If you require only one or two slices, a toasting-fork will answer; but if a larger quantity be needed, there is nothing better than a double broiler with wires about a third of an inch apart. Place the slices evenly on one side of the broiler, being careful not to put in more than can be equally exposed to the fire; close the broiler and hold it firmly, that the slices may not slip; move it gently over the fire for one or two minutes; then turn it over, that all the moisture may be drawn out; hold it nearer to the coals, and color it a delicate golden-brown. Serve at once in a toast rack or piled lightly, that it may not lose its crispness. Butter before serving, or send it dry to the table. Bread properly dried and toasted is changed from the nature of dough, which always has a tendency to sour on the stomach, into pure wheat farina. It is not so scorched as to turn the butter into oil, but absorbs the butter; and butter and farina, being easily separated, are quickly acted upon by the gastric fluid. Many persons prefer toast that is soft inside, but it should never be served to sick people in that manner. It is better to have it dry, and then moistened with milk or water, than to have it doughy. If the bread be freshly baked and you *must* make toast, dry the slices in a warm oven before toasting. Always toast over the coals, or in the oven. If toasted over a hot stove, the crumbs fall through and burn, giving it a scorched and smoky flavor.

Milk Toast.

1 pint milk, scalded.	½ teaspoonful salt.
1 tablespoonful cornstarch.	6 slices dry toast.
1 large tablespoonful butter.	

Scald the milk; put the butter in a granite saucepan; when melted, add the dry cornstarch; when well mixed, add one third of the milk. Let it boil, and stir constantly till it is a smooth paste; add the remainder of the milk gradually, stirring well; then add the salt. Put the toast in a hot deep dish; pour the thickened milk between each slice and over the whole. Keep the dish over hot water until ready to serve. If liked very soft, the slices may be first dipped in hot salted water, or in the hot milk before it is thickened.

Cream Toast.

Cream toast may be made in the same way, using a *scant tablespoonful* of *butter*, and *cream* instead of milk, or by thickening the boiling cream with *one tablespoonful* of *cornstarch* wet in a little cold milk or water; then salt to taste, and boil eight or ten minutes.

Water Toast.

Have a shallow pan with *one quart* of *boiling water* and a *teaspoonful* of *salt*. Dip each slice of dry toast quickly in the water, then pile on a hot platter. Spread evenly with *butter* and serve very hot. Do not let them soak an instant in the water.

Toast for Garnishing.

For poached eggs, cut the bread into rounds with a large cake-cutter before toasting. For small birds or asparagus, remove the crusts and cut into oblong pieces For minces and fricassees, cut into small squares or diamonds. For a border, cut, after toasting, into inch and a half squares, and then into halves diagonally, making triangles ; or cut into long pointed triangles.

Entire Wheat Bread, Made Quickly.

Put one teaspoon of butter and half a teaspoon each of sugar and salt in one cup of scalded milk. When cool, add half a cake of compressed yeast dissolved in one third of a cup of lukewarm water. Stir in fine whole-wheat flour till stiff enough to keep in shape after you stop stirring. Mix it well, but do not knead it. Let it rise to double its bulk, then knead it just enough to shape it into a long thin roll. When light and double, bake in a hot oven about thirty minutes. Mix in the morning and it will be baked before dinner.

SODA BISCUIT, MUFFINS, GEMS, ETC.

In making biscuit, etc., our grandmothers used saleratus, an alkali prepared by exposing pearlash, i. e., purified potash, to carbonic acid gas. Potash is a fixed alkali made from wood ashes. Now soda bicarbonate, made from common salt, is generally used.

Crude soda is known as sal-soda or soda-saleratus; when refined, it is carbonate and bicarbonate of soda. But the purest soda obtained to-day is that made from Kryolith, a mineral found only in Greenland. It is called Natrona Bicarbonate of Soda, and is an ingredient of the purest baking-powders.

Pure, strong alkalies are powerful corrosive poisons, eating the coats of the stomach perhaps quicker than any other poisonous agent. This caustic or burning property is somewhat weakened by the carbonic acid united with them, and is therefore less in bicarbonate of soda than in the potash compounds. The latter are now seldom used. Alkalies when properly combined with acids lose this poisonous property; the carbonic acid gas is liberated, and the compound formed by this union is called a neutral salt, being neither acid nor alkaline. When not properly combined, if the acid be stronger than the alkali, the salt is acid; and if the alkali be in excess, the salt is alkaline and still poisonous.

Soda has a great affinity for water; and when wet, a combination takes place which allows some of the carbonic acid gas to escape. This may easily be seen by the effervescence which occurs when soda is dissolved in hot water. This, the old way of using soda, was theoretically wrong, as much of the gas was lost; yet practically good results were obtained, because the saleratus formerly used was much stronger than the bicarbonate of soda of to-day, and could well be weakened.

Soda alone, when mixed with wet dough, will give off gas enough to raise the dough; but it leaves a strong alkaline taste and a greenish yellow color, and, being poisonous, must be neutralized by an acid, or else its use is not admissible. The best acid for this purpose is one which does not liberate the gas instantly on contact with the soda, before the heat can fix the air cells, and also the one which leaves no unwholesome residue.

Muriatic Acid, which is sometimes used, would be the best, as it leaves only common salt as a residue; but the gas is liberated instantly, and only a skilled hand can mix the bread and place it in the oven without losing much of the gas.

Cream of Tartar, which is tartaric acid combined with potash, and is obtained from the crystals or argols which collect in wine casks, is preferred by chemists. Being only slightly soluble in cold water, it unites with soda only when heated, and the gas is not all liberated until the mixture is in the oven. The residue from the union is Rochelle salt, which is not injurious taken *occasionally* in small quantities. The objections to cream of tartar are these: being very expensive (the price varying with the grape crop), it is often adulterated with cornstarch, flour, or other substances; and the careless cook guesses at the proportions of soda needed instead of measuring accurately. The only safe way to use these chemicals is to purchase cream of tartar of a reliable grocer, and to measure carefully *one level teaspoonful of soda* to *two slightly rounded teaspoonfuls of cream of tartar* for *one quart of flour*. It takes a trifle more than twice the quantity of cream of tartar to make the reaction complete. The soda *must* be finely pulverized before measuring; rub it on the board with a knife, measure, and then sift through the finest wire strainer into the flour. Sifting with the flour through an ordinary flour sieve is *not* enough. Cream of tartar does not become lumpy like soda; but it is better to sift it, and salt also, into the flour, and then sift all together two or three times.

6

Baking-Powders. — The most reliable and convenient quick leavening agent is a pure cream of tartar baking-powder. If pure, it will contain only soda bicarbonate and cream of tartar mixed by weight in the correct proportion, and combined with the least possible amount of cornstarch or flour necessary for its perfect keeping. Any amount of starch above this is an adulteration as truly as if some harmful substance were used. Baking-powders having their formula printed on the label of their tins, may be relied upon. Biscuits made without eggs require two level teaspoons of baking-powder for each cup of flour. Muffins and rich cakes with eggs, from one and one-half to one level teaspoon for each cup of flour or meal.

Soda is also neutralized by *sour milk* or *lactic acid*. This is economical, particularly for those who have plenty of pure milk. But milk in winter grows bitter before it sours; and the degree of acidity varies so much that the result is often failure. Sour milk is best when it sours quickly, and is thick and smooth, not separated. *One even teaspoonful* of soda to *one pint of nicely thickened* or *loppered milk* is the proportion. When the milk tastes or smells sour, but is not thick, use it as sweet milk in gingerbread or brown bread, where you have molasses to complete the acidity. Add a very little more soda if the receipt call for sweet milk, or a little less if for sour milk.

Nearly all kinds of soda biscuit, muffins, gems, etc., should have the dry ingredients mixed in one bowl, and the liquids, such as milk, eggs, melted butter, etc., in another; and when ready to bake, stir the two quickly and thoroughly together, and bake immediately in a very hot oven.

Molasses gives another acid which is combined with soda, to raise and lighten dough. Directions for its use are given under rules for brown bread and molasses gingerbread.

Soda and Cream of Tartar Biscuit.

1 quart sifted flour.	2 full teaspoonfuls cream of
1 even teaspoonful salt.	tartar.
1 even teaspoonful soda, meas-	1 large tablespoonful butter.
ured after pulverizing.	

Milk to make a very soft dough : new-process flour will take a pint or more; St. Louis flour, less.

Mix in the order given, sifting the soda, salt, and cream of tartar into the flour. Then sift all together twice. Rub in the butter with the tips of the fingers, until there are no large lumps. Mix in the milk gradually, using a broad knife and wetting only a small part of the flour with each addition of the milk. When just stiff enough to be handled (not kneaded), cut it through with the knife until barely mixed; it should look spongy in the cuts and seem full of air. Turn it out on a *well-floured* board; toss with the knife till well floured; touch it with the hands as little as possible; pat it with the rolling-pin, which must be lifted quickly that it may not stick; and when the dough is about half an inch thick, cut it into rounds and bake at once.

To make *Twin Biscuit*, roll the dough out less than half an inch thick, cut into rounds, spread with softened butter, and put two together, and bake ten or fifteen minutes.

Baking-Powder Biscuit.

These are made in the same way as the preceding, using three rounding teaspoonfuls or eight level of baking-powder in place of soda and cream of tartar.

Sour Milk Biscuit.

These should be made the same as cream of tartar biscuit, using one pint of thick sour milk instead of sweet milk, and omitting the cream of tartar. Observe the same directions as to lightness and dexterity in mixing, and vary the amount of milk according to the flour.

Whole-Wheat or Rye Biscuit (with Soda).

1 cup whole-wheat or rye flour.	1 teaspoonful cream of tartar.[1]
1 cup white flour.	1 tablespoonful sugar.
⅛ teaspoonful salt	1 teaspoonful melted butter.
⅛ teaspoonful soda.	

Milk enough to make a drop batter (about one cup). If sour milk be used, omit the cream of tartar.

Mix in the order given, and bake in hot gem pans twenty or thirty minutes.

Cream Biscuit.

When using sweet cream, make the same as cream of tartar biscuit; and when using sour cream, the same as sour-milk biscuit, omitting the butter in either case. Any of these mixtures may be baked in gem or muffin pans by using more milk, and making the dough soft enough to drop from the spoon.

Short Cakes, No. 1.

1 pint sifted flour.	1 full teaspoonful cream of tartar
½ teaspoonful salt, scant.	(omit if sour milk be used).
½ teaspoonful soda, measured	¼ cup butter.
after pulverizing	1 cup sweet or sour milk, or cold water.

Mix the salt, soda, and cream of tartar with the flour, and sift two or three times. Rub in the butter until fine like meal, or if liked very short and crisp, melt the butter and add it hot with the milk. Add the liquid gradually, mixing and cutting with a knife, and use just enough to make it of a light spongy consistency. Scrape out the dough upon a well-floured board; toss it with the knife until floured; pat into a flat cake, and roll gently, till half an inch thick; cut with a small round cutter, and bake on the griddle or in the oven. If you use a griddle, grease it well with salt pork or butter, and cook the cakes slowly; watch and turn them, that all may be browned alike.

[1] 4 level teaspoons baking-powder may be used instead of soda and cream of tartar.

When they are well puffed up, put a bit of butter on the top of each, and turn over, — or move them to one side and grease again with the pork, and turn over upon the freshly greased place. When browned on the other side and done, of which you can judge by the firmness of texture or by pulling one partly open, serve immediately. Tear them open, as cutting with a knife makes them heavy and indigestible. If to be baked in the oven, put them quite close together in a shallow pan, and bake ten or fifteen minutes.

Short Cakes, No. 2.

Make by rule No. 1, and divide into two parts; pat and roll each part into a large, round cake the size of a pie plate, and bake either in a spider or in the oven. These short cakes may be eaten hot with butter if for a simple breakfast or tea cake, or buttered and spread with sweetened fruit for dessert.

Strawberry Short Cake, No. 1.

Make a crust by rule for Dutch Apple Cake, on page 86; bake it on round tins; split, butter, and spread with sweetened berries and cream.

Strawberry Short Cake, No. 2.

Make by rule No. 1 for Short Cake, and bake on a griddle in small rounds. Tear open, and spread each half with softened butter. Put half of the cakes on a hot plate. Mash a pint of strawberries, sweeten to taste, put a large spoonful on each cake; then put another layer of cakes, and whole berries, well sugared. Serve with cream.

Peach Short Cake.

Make by either of the receipts for Strawberry Short Cake, and spread with sliced and sweetened peaches. Apricots may be used in the same way; and cream may be added if preferred.

Orange Short Cake.

The same as Strawberry, using oranges. Peel and divide the oranges, remove the seeds and thick inner skin,
and cut each section into three or four pieces. Sweeten
to taste.

Whole-Wheat or Rye Short Cakes.

1 cup white flour.	1 tablespoonful sugar.
1 cup whole-wheat or rye flour.	1 cup of sweet milk, the amount
4 level teasp baking-powder.	varying with the flour.
½ teaspoonful salt.	1 tablespoonful melted butter.

Mix in the order given, making the dough stiff enough
to be rolled. Cut into rounds and bake on a griddle; tear
open and serve with cream and salt. Or roll very thin,
cut and bake in the oven, split and pour cream thickened
as for toast over them.

Dutch Apple Cake.   (*Mrs. A. A. Lincoln.*)

1 pint flour.	¼ cup butter.
½ teaspoonful salt.	1 egg.
½ teaspoonful soda, sifted into the flour.	1 scant cup milk.
	4 sour apples.
1 teaspoonful cream of tartar.[1]	2 tablespoonfuls sugar.

Mix the dry ingredients in the order given; rub in the
butter; beat the egg and mix it with the milk; then stir
this into the dry mixture. The dough should be soft
enough to spread half an inch thick on a shallow baking-
pan. Core, pare, and cut four or five apples into eighths;
·lay them in parallel rows on top of the dough, the sharp
edge down, and press enough to make the edge penetrate
slightly. Sprinkle the sugar on the apple. Bake in a hot
oven twenty or thirty minutes. To be eaten hot with butter as a tea cake, or with lemon sauce as a pudding.

[1] 3 level teaspoons baking-powder may be used instead of soda and **cream**
of tartar.

Apple or Huckleberry Cakes.

1 pint sifted flour.	1 egg, yolk and white beaten separately.
½ teaspoonful salt.	
3 level teasp. baking-powder.	1 cup milk.
¼ cup butter.	1 heaping cup huckleberries or
½ cup sugar.	thinly sliced apples.

Mix the flour, salt, and baking-powder, and sift two or three times. Have the berries picked over, washed, dried, and sprinkled with flour. Rub the butter to a cream, add the sugar, and beat again. Add the yolk well beaten, and then the milk. Stir this into the flour and beat thoroughly; add the white beaten stiff, and, lastly, the berries, being careful not to break them. Bake in a shallow pan or in muffin pans about half an hour.

These may be made with sour milk, omitting the baking-powder, and using half a teaspoonful of soda; or leave out half a cup of flour, and substitute for it half a cup of fine white corn meal.

Huckleberry Cake, No. 2. (*Mrs. A. A. Lincoln.*)

1 pint flour.	2 tablespoons butter.
½ teaspoonful salt.	Milk or water enough to moisten.
4 level teaspoons baking-powder.	1 cup berries, washed, dried, and
¼ cup sugar.	floured.

Mix salt, baking-powder, and sugar with the flour. Rub in the butter, and moisten with milk or water to make a dough stiff enough to keep in shape when dropped from a spoon. Add the berries, which should be well floured to keep them from settling. Drop by the large spoonfuls on a well-buttered shallow pan. Bake twenty minutes.

Raised Flour Muffins or Sally Lunns (with Yeast).

1 cup milk, scalded and cooled.	1 egg, yolk and white beaten separately. –
½ teaspoonful salt, scant.	
1 teaspoonful sugar.	Flour enough to make a drop
¼ cup yeast.	batter.

If intended for tea, add *two tablespoonfuls* of *sugar*, and mix late in the forenoon. They will rise in five or six hours; then add *one large tablespoonful* of *butter* melted. When well mixed, fill muffin pans two thirds full. Let them rise fifteen or twenty minutes, and bake in a hot oven. Or they may be baked in muffin rings on a griddle, in which case it is better to add the melted butter at the first mixing. When ready to bake, have the griddle and rings well greased; contrive to take up a spoonful of the dough without stirring enough to let out the air, and fill each ring; cook until brown and well risen, then turn ring and muffin together, and brown the other side. Pull them apart, *never cut them.* This same mixture, when risen and baked in a buttered pudding-dish in which it is to be served, is the old-fashioned Sally Lunn. Cut with the point of a warm knife. If intended for breakfast, make a batter with the milk, yeast, flour, and sugar, mix late in the evening and keep in a cool place. In the morning add the egg, melted butter, and salt, and bake as usual.

Muffins or Sally Lunns, No. 2 (made quickly).

1 pint flour.	2 eggs, beaten separately.
3 level teaspoons baking-powder.	½ cup milk.
½ teaspoon salt, scant.	½ cup butter, melted.

Mix flour, baking-powder, and salt. Beat the yolks, and add the milk and melted butter. Put the two mixtures together quickly; add the whites last. Fill muffin pans two thirds full, and bake fifteen minutes in a very hot oven. This makes eight muffins. If for tea, add two tablespoonfuls of sugar to the flour. Use a scant cup of milk and one fourth of a cup of butter if you prefer.

Oatmeal Biscuit. (*Miss Barnes.*)

3 cups boiling water.	1 scant teaspoonful salt.
1 cup oatmeal	

Pour the water on the oatmeal; add the salt, and cook three hours in a double boiler. While still warm, add *one large tablespoonful* of *butter*, and *half a cup* of *sugar.*

When cool, add *half a cup* of *yeast*, and *flour* to make a stiff dough. Let it rise over night. In the morning bake in gem pans twenty minutes or till brown.

Tea Cakes.

2½ cups St. Louis flour.
½ teaspoonful soda and
1 teaspoonful cream of tartar, or
4 level teaspoons baking powder.
½ cup sugar.

½ teaspoonful salt.
1 egg
1 cup milk
1 tablespoonful butter, melted.

Mix in the order given, and bake in gem pans or cups. Add one cup of berries, and it makes a delicious berry cake.

Cream Muffins.

1 pint flour.
½ teaspoonful salt.
½ teaspoonful soda and
1 teaspoonful cream of tartar, or
3 level teaspoons baking-powder.

Yolks of 2 eggs, beaten lightly.
¾ cup cream or enough to make
a drop batter.
Whites of 2 eggs beaten stiff.

Bake in muffin pans, and serve very hot.

Tea Cake (Loaf).

1 pint flour.
½ teaspoonful soda and
1 teaspoonful cream of tartar, or
3 level teaspoons baking-powder.
½ teaspoonful salt.
3 eggs, yolks beaten and mixed with

3 tablespoonfuls sugar.
1 cup milk (mixed with the yolks
and sugar).
2 tablespoonfuls melted butter.
Whites of the eggs added last.

Bake in a brickloaf pan, in a hot oven. To be eaten hot as a tea cake.

Granulated Wheat Muffins.

1½ cups granulated wheat (Health
Food or Arlington).
½ teaspoonful salt.
2 level teaspoons baking-powder.

1 tablespoonful sugar.
1 egg.
1 scant cup milk.
½ cup water.

Mix in the order given, and bake in hissing hot gem pans twenty minutes.

Rye Muffins.   (*Miss Parloa.*)

1 cup rye flour, or sifted rye meal.	1 cup white flour.
¼ cup sugar.	1 egg.
½ teaspoonful salt.	1 cup milk.
3 level teasp. baking-powder.	

Mix rye, sugar, salt, flour, and baking-powder thoroughly. Beat the egg; add the milk, and stir quickly into the dry mixture. Bake in hot gem or muffin pans twenty-five minutes.

Corn Muffins.   (*From an unknown Friend.*)

1 cup common corn meal.	1 even tablespoonful butter.
2 tablespoonfuls sugar.	5 cups boiling water.
1 scant teaspoonful salt.	

Mix at night the meal, sugar, and salt in the top of the double boiler; add the butter and boiling water, stir until smooth, and cook an hour. Turn into a mixing-bowl, and pour over it *one fourth* of *a cup* of *water* to prevent a crust from forming. In the morning beat it up soft and smooth. Mix *one cup and a half* of *fine yellow corn flour*, *one cup and a half* of *white flour*, *two even tea-spoonfuls* of *baking-powder*, and stir them into the cooked meal. Add *one egg*, well beaten. Drop the mixture into round iron gem pans, and bake in a hot oven.

To make *corn and rye muffins*, add, in the morning,

1 cup yellow corn flour.	1 cup common flour.
1 cup rye flour.	

Or make *corn and whole-wheat muffins* by adding

1½ cups yellow corn flour.	½ cup common flour.
1 cup whole-wheat flour, Franklin or Arlington.	

These are delicious. This rule makes fifteen muffins. If fewer be desired, half of the cooked corn-meal mixture may be used, and the remainder reserved for another baking. But in this case do not forget to halve the dry mixture added in the morning, and to use one *small* egg.

Apple Johnny Cake (without Eggs). (*Mrs. Webb.*)

1 pint white meal.
2 tablespoonfuls sugar.
½ teaspoonful salt.
½ teaspoonful soda and

1 teaspoonful cream of tartar, or
4 level teasp. baking-powder.
Milk enough to mix quite soft.
3 apples, pared and sliced.

Mix in the order given. Bake in a shallow cake pan thirty minutes.

Corn Cake (thin).

1 cup yellow corn meal.
¼ cup sugar.
½ teaspoonful salt.
1 cup flour.

3 level teasp. baking-powder.
1 egg.
1 cup milk.
1 tablespoonful melted butter.

Mix in the order given, and bake in two Washington pie tins, spreading the mixture thick enough to half fill the pan.

Sponge Corn Cake (Sour Milk).

1 cup flour.
½ cup corn meal.
½ teaspoonful salt.
½ teaspoonful soda
⅓ cup sugar.

Yolks of 2 eggs.
White of 1 egg.
1 tablespoonful butter, melted.
1 cup sour milk.

Bake in a shallow round pan or in a brickloaf pan. Use the other white of egg for clearing the coffee.

Sponge Corn Cake (Sweet Milk).

1 cup meal.
½ cup flour.
½ teaspoonful salt.
½ teaspoonful soda.
1 teaspoonful cream of tartar.

1 tablespoonful melted butter.
1 tablespoonful sugar.
Yolks of 2 eggs.
White of 1 egg.
1¼ cup milk.[1]

Bake in brickloaf bread pan about half an hour.

[1] 3 level teaspoons baking-powder may be used instead of soda and cream of tartar.

Spider Corn Cake (Sour Milk). (*Miss Parloa.*)

¾ cup corn meal.	1 egg.
Flour to fill the cup	1 cup sweet milk.
1 tablespoonful sugar.	½ cup sour milk.
½ teaspoonful salt	1 tablespoonful butter.
½ teaspoonful soda, scant.	

Mix the meal, flour, sugar, salt, and soda. Beat the egg; add half of the sweet milk, and all the sour milk. Stir this into the dry mixture. Melt the butter in a hot spider, or shallow round pan, and pour the mixture into it. Pour the other half cup of sweet milk over the top, but do not stir it in. Bake twenty minutes in a hot oven.

Corn and Rice Muffins.

1 pint white corn meal.	1 pint sour milk.
1 teaspoonful salt.	1 egg.
1 tablespoonful flour.	1 tablespoonful melted butter, **or**
1 cup cold boiled rice.	drippings.
1 teaspoonful soda, scant.	

Bake in muffin pans about twenty minutes.

Hominy and Corn Meal Cakes. (*Mrs. S. S. Ropes.*)

Mix *two tablespoonfuls* of *fine, uncooked hominy, half a teaspoonful* of *salt, one tablespoonful* of *butter, half a cup* of *boiling water.* Place this over the teakettle, or on the back of the stove until the hominy absorbs all the water. Pour *one cup* of *boiling milk* on *one scant cup* of *corn meal;* add *two tablespoonfuls* of *sugar* and the *hominy.* When cooled, add *two eggs,* yolks and whites beaten separately, and *one heaping teaspoonful* of *baking-powder.* Bake in hot, buttered gem pans twenty minutes.

Maryland Corn Cakes (without Soda). (*Mrs. Upham.*)

Mix *one cup* of *fine white sifted meal, one even tablespoonful* of *butter, one teaspoonful* of *sugar, one saltspoonful* of *salt.* Add *one scant cup* of *boiling milk.* When cooled, add *one egg,* yolk and white beaten separately. Bake in stone cups about thirty minutes.

Dodgers, Dabs, or Corn Meal Puffs (without Soda).
(*Miss Alice Walcott.*)

Two cups of *fine white corn meal,* scalded with boiling water so that the meal is all wet but not soft; add *one teaspoonful* of *butter, one teaspoonful* of *sugar, half a teaspoonful* of *salt, two* or *three tablespoonfuls* of *milk;* when cold, add *two eggs,* yolks and whites beaten separately. The batter should drop easily from the spoon, not be thin enough to pour, nor 'stiff' enough to be scraped out. Have your pans greased and hissing hot, and the oven as hot as possible. Bake until brown and puffy.

Indian Bannock (without Soda). (*A. W.*)

1 cup corn meal.	1 teaspoonful salt.
1 teaspoonful sugar.	1 pint boiling milk.

When cool, add *two eggs,* beaten separately. Bake in a shallow earthen dish in a very hot oven, and serve in the dish, like a pudding.

Hoe Cake (without Soda).

1 cup white corn meal.	Boiling milk or water enough to
½ teaspoonful salt.	scald it.
1 teaspoonful sugar (if you like).	

Make it thick enough not to spread when put on the griddle. Grease the griddle with salt pork, drop the mixture on with a large spoon. Pat the cakes out till about half an inch thick; cook them slowly, and when browned put a bit of butter on the top of each cake and turn over. They cannot cook too long, provided they do not burn. Sometimes the dough is put on in one large cake, and as soon as browned underneath is turned over upon a freshly greased place; the thin, crisp crust is peeled off with a knife, laid on a hot plate, and spread with butter, and when another brown crust has formed, the cake is turned again, the crust is removed and buttered, and so on until the cake is all browned. These crisp, buttered crusts are served piled together and cut in sections.

Rice Crusts. (*Miss Ward.*)

Cook *one cup* of *cold boiled rice* in the double boiler in *milk* enough to make a thin mixture, and until the rice is very soft. Add *one tablespoonful* of *sugar*, *a little salt*, *one egg*, and *flour* enough to make it hold together. Spread on the pan, having the mixture one third of an inch thick. Bake in a hot oven. Split and eat with syrup.

Rice or Hominy Drop Cakes.

One cup of *boiled hominy* or *rice*, and *one egg*. If the hominy be cold, heat in a farina kettle with *one tablespoonful* of *water*, and stir till it is softened. Beat yolk and white separately; add *one saltspoonful* of *salt*. Drop in tablespoonfuls on a well-buttered pan, and bake brown in a hot oven.

Breakfast Puffs, or Pop-overs.

1 cup flour.	1 egg, yolk and white beaten sep-
1 saltspoonful salt.	arately.[1]
1 cup milk.	

Mix the salt with the flour; add part of the milk slowly, until a smooth paste is formed; add the remainder of the milk with the beaten yolk, and lastly the white beaten to a stiff froth. Cook in hot buttered gem pans or earthen cups in a quick oven half an hour, or until the puffs are brown and well popped over.

Rye Gems, or Shells (without Soda).

¾ cup rye meal.	2 eggs.
¼ cup flour.	1 tablespoonful sugar.
1 saltspoonful salt.	1 cup milk.

Mix the meal, flour, and salt. Beat the yolks; add the sugar and milk. Stir this into the dry mixture; add the

[1] The egg may be beaten but slightly, without separating, and then beaten well in the batter.

whites, beaten stiff. Bake in iron gem pans, or stone cups, thirty to forty minutes. *One cup* of *mixed rye meal, white corn meal,* and *whole-wheat flour,* in about equal proportions, may be used in the same way. This receipt makes six gems.

Whole-Wheat or Graham Gems, or Puffs. (*A. W.*)

2 cups of whole-wheat flour.	2 eggs, beaten separately.
½ teaspoonful salt.	1 cup milk.
1 tablespoonful sugar.	1 cup water.

Mix flour, salt, and sugar. Add the milk to the beaten yolks, then the water, and stir this into the dry mixture. Add the whites, beaten stiff, and bake in hissing hot gem pans thirty minutes.

Whole-Wheat Crisps (specially good for Children).

1 cup rich cream, sweet or sour.	2 cups fine granulated wheat flour,
¼ cup sugar.	or enough to make a stiff dough.
1 saltspoonful salt.	

Knead fifteen minutes, or till stiff enough to roll out thin as a wafer. Cut with a biscuit cutter, and bake on ungreased tins in a very hot oven. The sugar will sweeten the sour cream sufficiently.

Fine Granulated Wheat Gems (no Yeast, Soda, nor Eggs).

1 cup water.	1 saltspoonful salt.
1 cup milk.	2½ cups fine granulated wheat.

Stir the flour slowly into the liquid, until you have a drop batter. Then beat as rapidly and as long as your arm will allow. Have the iron gem pans hissing hot, and well buttered. Fill quickly, giving the batter a brisk beating several times during the filling, and bake at once in a very hot oven.

Maryland, or Beaten Biscuit. (*Mrs. Towne.*)

1 quart flour.	½ teaspoonful salt.
¼ cup lard.	1 cup cold water.

Rub the lard and salt into the flour, and mix with cold water to a very stiff dough. Knead ten minutes, or until well mixed; then beat hard with a biscuit beater or heavy rolling-pin, turning the mass over and over until it begins to blister and looks light and puffy, or "till, pulling off a piece quickly, it will give a sharp, snapping sound." When in this condition, pull off a small piece suddenly, form it into a round biscuit, then pinch off a bit from the top. Turn over and press with the thumb, leaving a hollow in the centre. Put the biscuit some distance apart in the pan. Prick with a fork. Bake twenty minutes in a quick oven. They should be light, of a fine, even grain, and crack at the edges like our crackers. In Maryland no young lady's education was formerly considered finished until she had learned the art of making beaten biscuit.

Graham Wafers.

1 pint white flour.	1 saltspoonful salt.
1 pint Graham flour.	Cold water enough to make a stiff
⅓ cup butter.	dough.
⅓ cup sugar.	

Roll out very thin, cut in squares, and bake quickly.

Wafer Biscuit (for Invalids).

1 pint flour.	White of 1 egg.
1 tablespoonful butter.	Warm new milk enough to make
1 saltspoonful salt.	a stiff dough.

Mix salt with the flour; rub in the butter; add the beaten white of egg, and milk enough to make a stiff dough. Beat half an hour with a rolling-pin, without ceasing. Break off a little piece of dough at a time, and roll it out as thin as paper. Cut into large rounds. Prick with a small wooden skewer, and bake quickly without burning.

Gluten Wafers.

Half a cup of *sweet cream* and *one saltspoonful* of *salt.*
Stir in *gluten* enough to make a stiff dough. Knead and
roll out very thin. Cut into rounds, and bake a delicate
brown on an ungreased tin. Gluten is a preparation of
wheat flour without the starch.

Waffles, Griddle-Cakes, Pancakes, etc.

The names pancakes, fritters, flap-jacks, slap-jacks,
batter-cakes, griddle-cakes, slappers, etc., are applied in-
discriminately in different localities.

Pancakes were formerly a kind of muffin mixture, made
a little stiffer than a drop batter, but not stiff enough to
roll out, and were dropped from a spoon into hot fat. and
fried like doughnuts. But, recently, the name has been
applied to a very thin batter made usually without soda,.
cooked one cake at a time on a small well-buttered frying-
pan, and turned like a griddle-cake; then buttered, and
rolled over and over, or spread with sugar and jelly, and
then rolled. In "ye olden time" good cooks were supposed to have the knack of tossing the pan so skilfully
that the cake would turn over itself; but this is now one
of the lost arts.

For convenience and clearness, the following names will
be used in this work : —

Griddle-Cakes: any kind of small, thin batter-cakes
cooked on a griddle.

Pancakes: larger, thin batter-cakes, made without soda,
and cooked in a small frying-pan.

French or *Rolled Pancakes:* the same as the preceding,
buttered, sweetened, and rolled.

Fried Drop Cakes or *Fried Muffins:* any muffin mixture,
dropped from a spoon into deep hot fat.

Fritters: a thinner mixture made without soda, either
plain or with meat, fish, or fruit, and cooked by dropping
into deep hot fat.

Waffles and Griddle-Cakes.

A waffle iron is made of two corrugated iron griddles fitted and fastened together at one side with a hinge, and revolving in an iron frame, which is to be placed over the fire. It may be either circular or oblong. Each griddle is divided into compartments, which are usually grooved into diamonds, hearts, rounds, etc.

The iron should be placed over the fire, heated on each side, and greased thoroughly, as it is very hard to clean if the cakes stick. Put a piece of salt pork on a fork, or put a small piece of butter in a clean cloth, and rub all over both griddles. The heat will melt the butter and let just enough of it go through the cloth. This is better than to put it on with a knife. Close the griddles and turn them; this causes the fat to run evenly over them. Open, and pour the waffle mixture into the centre of the half over the fire, or put a spoonful in each compartment, filling them about two thirds full. Cover, and cook one minute on one side, then turn and cook a little longer on the other. Any kind of griddle-cake mixture, with the addition of the melted butter to make them crisp, may be cooked on a waffle-iron, if one cares to take the extra trouble.

Waffles.

1 pint flour.	3 eggs.
2 level teasp baking-powder	1¼ cups milk.
½ teaspoonful salt.	1 tablespoonful butter, melted.

Mix in the order given; add the beaten yolks of the eggs with the milk, then the melted butter, and the whites last. Serve with butter, or syrup, or caramel sauce.

Lemon Syrup (served with Waffles).

1 cup sugar.	1 teaspoonful butter.
¼ cup water.	1 tablespoonful lemon juice.

Boil the sugar with the water until it thickens slightly.

Add the butter and lemon juice. Serve as soon as the butter is melted.

Raised Waffles.

Mix at night *one pint* of *milk, one third* of *a cup* of *yeast*, and *one pint* of *flour.* In the morning add *half a teaspoonful* of *salt, two eggs*, yolks and whites beaten separately, and *one tablespoonful* of *melted butter.*

Use only *one egg*, make the batter a trifle thinner, and fry on the griddle, and you have *Flannel Cakes.*

Either of these receipts may be varied by using *half* or *one third fine white corn meal* or *Graham flour* with the white flour. If intended for tea, mix in the forenoon.

To Cook Griddle-Cakes.

A soapstone griddle, which needs no greasing, is the best; but of whatever material, let it be large enough to hold seven cakes. Let it heat while you are making the cakes. If an iron griddle be used, put a piece of salt pork two inches square on a fork; and when the griddle is hot enough for the fat to sizzle, rub it all over with the pork. Just grease it; do not leave little pools of fat on the edge to burn, and smoke the cakes. Take up a tablespoonful of the mixture, and pour it from the end of the spoon. The mixture should hiss or sizzle as it touches the griddle. Put one in the centre and six around the outside. By the time you have the seventh cake on, the first one will be full of bubbles and ready to turn; and when the seventh is turned, the first will have stopped puffing and be done. Wipe the griddle with a dry cloth, and grease again after each baking. Turn your griddle often, bringing each edge of it in turn over the hottest part of the stove, that the cakes may cook evenly. Always mix waffles or griddle-cakes in a bowl with a lip, and beat up the mixture well between each baking.

Griddle-Cakes.

1 pint flour.	1 scant pint sour milk or cream.
½ teaspoonful salt.	2 eggs, well beaten.
1 teaspoonful soda.	

Crush, measure, and sift the soda and salt into the flour. Mix thoroughly. Add the milk, and beat well; then add the beaten yolks, and lastly, the whites, beaten stiff. Bake on a hot, well-greased griddle; turn when full of bubbles, and bake on the other side till they stop puffing. Use *one half* or *one third fine corn meal* or *Graham flour*, to make a variety.

To make *Huckleberry Griddle-Cakes*, add *one pint* of *berries*, picked over and rolled in flour.

Some persons prefer to mix the sour milk with the flour, and let the mixture stand over night. In the morning add the salt, soda, and eggs.

Sour milk is the best for griddle-cakes, and when thickened just right, the cakes are very good without the eggs.

Rice or Hominy Griddle-Cakes (no Soda).

1 cup sweet milk.	2 eggs, yolks and whites beaten separately.
1 cup warm boiled rice, or fine hominy.	1 tablespoonful melted butter.
½ teaspoonful salt.	Flour enough to make a thin batter

Bake either as griddle-cakes or waffles.

Bread Griddle-Cakes.

1 pint stale (not dried) bread-crumbs.	1 pint milk, scalded.
	1 tablespoonful butter.

Pour the hot milk over the crumbs, add the butter, and soak over night or till the crumbs are softened. Then rub through a squash strainer; add

2 eggs, yolks and whites beaten separately.	½ teaspoonful salt.
	2 level teasp. baking-powder.
1 cup flour.	Cold milk to thin it if needed.

Bake slowly: spread with butter and sugar, and serve *hot.*

Raised Graham Griddle-Cakes.

Mix *one pint* of *milk*, scalded and cooled, *one cup* of *whole-wheat flour*, *one cup* of *white flour*, *one fourth* of *a cup* of *liquid yeast*. Let it rise over night. In the morning add *half a teaspoonful* of *salt*, *one tablespoonful* of *molasses*, *one saltspoonful* of *soda*. If too thick, add a little *warm water*. These are more wholesome than buckwheat cakes.

Buckwheat Cakes

Pour *one pint* of *boiling water* on *half a cup* of *fine corn meal;* add *half a teaspoonful* of *salt*. Mix well, and when lukewarm add *half a cup* of *white flour*, *one cup* of *buckwheat flour*, *one fourth* of *a cup* of *yeast*. Beat vigorously. Let it rise over night. In the morning stir down, and beat again. When risen and ready to bake, add *one saltspoonful* of *soda*, sifted through a fine strainer. Beat again, and fry in large cakes.

Buckwheat cakes, even if not sour, usually require the addition of soda just before baking, to make them light and tender. But when in their best estate, they are far from perfect food. They should be eaten only in very cold weather, and but seldom even then. They are better and brown better when made with boiling milk instead of water.

Corn Meal Slappers, or Griddle-Cakes (no Soda).

1 pint corn-meal.	1 saltspoonful salt.
1 teaspoonful butter.	1 teaspoonful sugar.

Pour into this mixture *boiling milk* or *water* enough to wet the meal. When cool, add *two eggs*, well beaten, and *cold milk* enough to make a very thin batter.

Pease Griddle-Cakes.

Take *green pease* which have been boiled, but are too hard to eat as a vegetable. Drain very dry, then mash, and rub the *pulp* through the squash strainer. Or boil *one cup* of *split pease* till very tender, letting the water boil away. Drain, mash, and rub through a squash strainer, and use the same as the squash in squash griddle-cakes.

Squash Griddle-Cakes.

1 cup boiling milk.	½ teaspoonful salt.
1 cup sifted squash.	1 egg.
1 tablespoonful butter.	3 level teasp. baking-powder.
1 tablespoonful sugar.	1 cup flour.

Pour the boiling milk into the squash; add the butter, sugar, and salt. When cool, add the egg, well beaten, then the baking-powder, mixed and sifted with the flour. If too thin, use more flour; and if too thick, add a little milk. The dry mealy squash is the best.

French Pancakes (no Soda). (*Miss Parloa.*)

3 eggs.	1 teaspoonful sugar.
1 cup milk.	½ cup flour.
½ teaspoonful salt.	½ tablespoonful salad oil.

Beat the yolks and whites separately. Add the milk, salt, and sugar to the yolks. Pour one third of this mixture on the flour, and stir to a smooth paste. Add the remainder of the milk, and beat well; then add the oil. Heat and butter a small frying-pan, and pour into it enough of the mixture to cover the pan; when brown, turn and brown the other side. Spread with butter and sugar or jelly; roll up, and sprinkle with powdered sugar.

Fried Drop Cakes.

The fat for fried cakes should be clean, new fat, half lard and half clarified beef drippings. By new fat is meant fat that has not been used for meat or fish, or become browned by previous frying. The same fat may be used several times by clarifying with several thin slices of raw potato, and straining through a fine strainer after each frying. When it becomes too brown for any flour mixtures, it will answer for croquettes or fish balls. It should be very hot, and still, not bubbling; but not as hot as for mixtures which have been previously cooked. The surest way is to fry a bit of the mixture. It should rise at once to the surface, with much spluttering of the fat, swell, and begin to brown on the under side. Drop cakes will usually turn over themselves, but doughnuts and fritters should be turned. They should be cooked an even golden brown, and the fat be kept at the right temperature by moving the kettle farther from or nearer to the fire. Try them with a fork, and if it come out clean, they are done.

Drain each cake over the hot fat, and when they cease to drip, put them in a squash strainer placed in a pan on the back of the stove, or drain on soft brown paper. Change the first cooked to another pan when the next are ready to be taken out. If the fat be not hot enough, or if there be too much soda, doughnuts will absorb the fat. The alkali in them unites with the grease, as it does in making soap. The eggs will prevent the cakes from soaking in the fat, and it is healthful and more economical to use them.

Fried Flour Muffins. (*Miss I. A. Maynard.*)

1 egg.	1 saltspoonful salt.
½ cup sugar.	Flour enough to make a stiff
¾ cup milk.	batter.
3 level teasp. baking-powder.	

Mix salt and baking-powder with two cups of flour. Beat the egg very light; add the sugar, and beat again. Add the milk, then the flour, with enough more, if needed, to make a stiff batter. Drop from a spoon into hot fat.

Fried Corn Meal Cakes. (*Miss Ward.*)

One pint of *milk,* poured boiling hot upon *one cup* of *corn meal;* add *one heaping tablespoonful* of *sugar,* and *half a teaspoonful* of *salt.* Let it stand all night, or till well swollen; then add *two eggs* and *half a cup* of *flour.* Fry in hot lard.

Fried Rye Muffins.

¾ cup rye meal.	1 tablespoonful sugar.
¾ cup flour.	1 saltspoonful salt.
½ teaspoonful soda and	1 egg.
1 teaspoonful cream of tartar, or	½ cup milk.
3 level teasp. baking-powder.	

Mix in the order given, and drop from a small table-spoon into hot fat. Cook until the muffins will not stick when tried with a fork.

Fried Rye Muffins (Sour Milk).

1 pint sour milk.	1 saltspoonful cinnamon.
½ cup of molasses.	1 teaspoonful soda.
1 saltspoonful salt.	2 eggs.

Rye flour to make a stiff drop batter. Fry as in the preceding rule.

Sour Milk Doughnuts. (*Mrs. Henderson.*)

Two eggs, beaten light, *one cup* of *sugar, three even table-spoonfuls* of *melted butter, one cup* of *sour milk* (or if sweet milk be used, add *one teaspoonful* of *cream of tartar*), *four cups* of *flour,* with *half a teaspoonful* of *soda,* and *one salt-spoonful each* of *cinnamon* and *salt.* Enough more flour to make just soft enough to roll out. Mix the dough rather soft at first. Have the board well floured, and the fat heating. Roll only a large spoonful at first. Cut into rings with an open cutter. Mix the trimmings with another spoonful. Work it slightly till well floured, and roll again. Roll and cut all out before frying, as that will demand your whole attention. Remember that the fat should be hot enough for the dough to rise to the top instantly.

Doughnuts, No. 2.

1 quart flour.	1 saltspoonful cinnamon or nut-meg.
½ cup sugar.	
½ teaspoonful salt.	1 egg.
½ teaspoonful soda.	Milk enough to moisten to a stiff
1 teaspoonful cream of tartar.	dough.

Doughnuts, No. 3.

1 egg.
1 cup sugar.
1 tablespoonful melted butter.
1 cup milk.
½ teaspoonful salt.

½ teaspoonful soda and
1 teaspoonful cream of tartar, or
4 level teasp. baking-powder.
1 saltspoonful cinnamon.
Flour enough to roll out.

Raised Doughnuts.

1 pint risen milk bread dough.
1 cup sugar.
2 eggs.

1 tablespoonful melted butter.
Spice to taste.
Flour enough to roll out.

These are more wholesome than those made with soda.

Crullers. (*A. W.*)

1 tablespoonful melted butter.
2 heaping tablespoonfuls sugar.
1 egg, yolk and white beaten separately.

½ saltspoonful cinnamon or mace.
½ saltspoonful salt.
Flour enough to roll out.

Roll the dough one fourth of an inch thick. Cut in rectangular pieces, two and a half by three and a half inches; then make five incisions lengthwise, cutting to within one third of an

FIG. 5. Cruller.

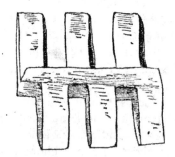

FIG. 6. Cruller after Folding.

inch at each end. Take up every other strip, fold each strip together slightly in the middle, and drop them into hot fat.

Wonders, or Cheats.

Beat *one egg ;* add *one saltspoonful* of *salt* and enough *flour* to make a very stiff batter. Roll out as thin as a wafer, cut with large round cutter, and fry one minute in hot fat. Serve with honey or syrup, or with cream and jelly, or any delicate pudding sauce.

Henriettes.

1 egg, yolk and white beaten separately.	1 saltspoonful baking-powder.
	½ saltspoonful cinnamon.
¼ cup cream.	1 teaspoonful wine or brandy.
1 saltspoonful salt.	Flour enough to roll out.

Roll as thin as a wafer, and cut with a pastry jagger into small squares or diamonds. Fry in boiling lard. Drain, and sprinkle with powdered sugar. Or add less flour, make a thick, stiff batter instead of a dough, and press the batter through a pastry tube into boiling lard, making rings or any shape preferred.

Cinci, or Rags.

1 cup flour.	¾ cup boiling water.
1 saltspoonful salt.	1 egg.

Pour the boiling water gradually upon the flour and salt, and stir to a smooth paste ; cool, add the egg, and beat well. Press through a pastry tube into hot lard. Drain, and sprinkle with sugar.

Fritter Batter (for Oysters, Clams, or Fruit).

Yolks of *two eggs,* beaten well ; add *half a cup* of *milk* or *water,* and *one tablespoonful* of *olive oil,* one saltspoonful of *salt,* and *one cup* of *flour,* or enough to make it almost a drop batter. When ready to use, add the whites of the eggs, beaten very stiff. If intended for fruit, add *a teaspoonful* of *sugar* to the batter. If for clams, tripe, or meat, add *one tablespoonful* of *lemon juice* or *vinegar*. This batter will keep several days.

Oyster Fritters. — Boil the oysters till the liquor flows freely. Drain, strain the liquor, and use it to make a batter, as in the preceding rule. Dip each oyster in the batter and fry until brown in hot fat.

Clam Fritters. — Drain the clams, and chop the hard part. Use the liquor to make a fritter batter. Add the clams and fry by small spoonfuls in hot fat. Clams in the shell should be steamed and dressed. Drain, and dip each whole clam into the batter. If large and tough, chop the hard part, and use the same as raw clams.

Apple Fritters. — Core and pare *three* or *four apples*, but do not break them. Cut them in slices one third of an inch thick, leaving the opening in the centre. Sprinkle with *sugar*, *lemon*, and *spice*. Dip each slice in the fritter batter and fry in hot fat. Drain, and sprinkle with powdered sugar.

Vegetables for fritters, such as celery, salsify, or parsnip, should be boiled till tender, then drained and cut into small pieces; then stir them into the fritter batter.

Swedish Timbale Cups. — Make one half the recipe for Fritter Batter, without separating the eggs, put the batter in a cup, heat the timbale iron in hot fat, then lower it into the batter about one inch, turn it partly over as you take it out, plunge it into deep hot fat, and when browned slightly, remove, drain, and remove cup from the iron.

Parmesan Fritters, for Soup. — Boil four tablespoons of water (or five of milk) with one rounded tablespoon of butter and a pinch of salt. Stir in quickly one third of a cup of flour; when well mixed, remove; add three tablespoons grated Parmesan; cool, and add three unbeaten eggs, reserving one white. Beat well, and drop in bean-like bits from a teaspoon into deep hot fat. Cook till a light brown, drain, and serve with cream soups.

OATMEAL, INDIAN CORN, AND OTHER GRAINS USED AS FOOD.

Oatmeal is highly nutritious, being richer in nitrogen than any other grain; but as it does not contain a tough, adhesive gluten, like wheat, it is not easily made into fermented bread. Its nitrogenous matter resembles casein more than gluten, and is called *avenin* (from *avena*, the oat). It is used as a mush or porridge, eaten with sugar and milk. It is rich in food for muscle and brain, useful for children and laboring people, but irritating to many people whose digestive powers are weak.

Groats, or *Grits*, are oats from which the outer husk and inner flinty cuticle are removed.

Indian Corn is used in many forms. Some varieties which contain a large proportion of sugar, are eaten green from the cob as a vegetable. The whole grains, hulled, are eaten as samp; broken grains of various sizes, as hominy; the ground grains, as either coarse or fine meal. Meal grows musty very quickly when ground by the old process, owing to the moisture of the corn and the heat of the stones. In the new-process, or granulated, meal the corn is first dried for two years, then ground into coarse grains like sugar. Indian corn is also used in the form of a very fine powder, called cornstarch. Corn meal, when cooked, is best made into small loaves or cakes and eaten hot. It is rich in nitrogen, and contains more fat than the other grains. This causes it to attract the oxygen from the air, and spoil rapidly. It should be purchased in small quantities. It is better adapted to strong laboring people, as it is very heating for persons with weak digestion.

Rye meal and flour are used, more especially in New England, in the form of bread and mush. Rye is sweeter than wheat, and makes a moist bread which can be kept for some time without becoming hard and unpalatable. Rye should be purchased in small quantities, kept in a cool, dry place, sifted and examined thoroughly before using.

Barley is used in soups and sometimes in gruels. It cannot be made into good bread, as it has too little gluten. It is nutritious, being rich in phosphates. It contains starch and mucilage, and, in the form of gruel, makes a soothing drink in fevers. The husk is removed, the grains are ground and polished, and then it is termed *pearl barley.* Barley crystals or flakes and granulated barley are also used.

Buckwheat has less flesh-forming and more heat-giving elements than wheat. It is therefore suitable only when used in cold weather and by those who labor hard or exercise freely. It is used principally in the form of griddle-cakes.

Rice contains very little of the flesh-forming element. It has more starch and less fat than any other grain. It is cheap, and is largely used by people in very hot climates. It should always be used with milk, eggs, or some fatty substance. Rice is easily digested.

Oatmeal Mush.

One cup of *B. B. oatmeal*, and *one teaspoonful* of *salt*, to *a scant quart* of *boiling water.* Put the meal and salt in the top of the double boiler; add the boiling water. Place the upper boiler on the stove, and boil rapidly eight or ten minutes, stirring occasionally with a fork. Then place it over the hot water, and cook from forty to sixty minutes if liked dry, from two to three hours if liked very soft. Remove the cover just before serving, and stir with a fork to let the steam escape, to dry it off. Served with *baked apples* and *sugar* and *cream.*

Oatmeal comes in three grades. B. B. is the whole oat with the outer husk removed. It is less pasty than the finer grades. The Scotch consider the coarse oatmeal the best, the finer kinds being only suitable for children and invalids.

Oatmeal, rice, or any mush that contains much starch, is more easily digested if it is masticated, and mixed with the saliva. When eaten as a soft porridge and still further thinned with milk, if it be swallowed whole, the saliva has no chance to do its part, and the whole process of the digestion of the starch is left for the intestines. The meal should be thoroughly cooked, stiff, and dry, rather than thin.

Hominy, cracked wheat, and *granulated wheat* are cooked in the same way, using only *three cups* of *boiling water* instead of one quart.

The *cracked wheat* may be poured into a mould wet with cold water, and when jellied eaten cold with sugar and cream.

Whole wheat requires *five cups* of *boiling water* to *one cup* of *wheat*, and should cook *six hours*.

Hasty Pudding, or Indian Meal Mush.

Put *one quart* of *water* on to boil. Mix *one pint* of *corn meal, one teaspoonful* of *salt*, and *one tablespoonful* of *flour* with *one pint* of *cold milk*. Stir this gradually into the boiling water and boil half an hour, stirring often. Eat it hot, with milk, and only in cold winter weather.

Fried Hasty Pudding.

Cook as above and pour it into a brickloaf pan; when cool, cut into *three-quarter inch slices*. Dip them in *flour*, and brown each side in *hot fat* in a frying-pan. Or dip in *crumbs, egg*, and again in *crumbs*, and *fry* in *deep fat*.

Any of these mushes may be fried the same way. When eaten with bacon, they make a nice relish for breakfast.

BEVERAGES.

Tea.

THERE are three varieties of the tea-plant; both black and green tea can be prepared from them all. Green tea is made from young leaves steamed, roasted, and dried quickly on copper plates. Black tea is made from leaves which have been exposed to the air ten or twelve hours before roasting. The action of the air upon the leaves during this long exposure causes the dark color. Green tea gives up less of its juices in drying, and this accounts for its energetic action on the nervous system.

The tea-leaf contains the largest amount of nutritive matter of any plant used as human food, though only a small portion of it is extracted by our common method of making tea. There is a large proportion of casein in the leaves. Many of the savage tribes of Tartary boil the leaves with soda, and eat them with salt and butter. But in our method of using tea as a beverage merely, we use such a comparatively small quantity that the amount of nutriment is very little; its chief value being the sense of warmth and comfort that it gives. It excites the brain to increased activity, and produces wakefulness; hence it is useful to students and night-workers. It retards the action of the natural functions, causes less waste, and, to a certain extent, saves food. For this reason, when not used in excess, it is suited to poor people, whose supplies of substantial food are scanty; and to old persons, whose powers of digestion and whose bodily substance have begun to fail. It should not be used early in the morning, as the body needs immediate nourishment in a larger quantity; and it should at all times be taken moderately, both as to quantity and strength.

The water should be freshly boiled. Scald and heat the teapot, which should be of earthen or china, *never* of tin. Allow *one teaspoonful* of *tea* for *one cup* of *boiling water*. Reduce the proportion of tea when several cups are required. Put the tea in a strainer, pour through it *half a cup* of *boiling water* to cleanse the grounds. Then put the tea in the teapot; pour on the *boiling* water; cover closely and place it where it will keep hot, but not boil, for five minutes. If cold or lukewarm water be used in making tea, the *thein*, or nitrogenous substance, will not be obtained.

In boiling tea or allowing the leaves to remain long in the tea, by repeated steeping, the fragrant aroma is wasted and the tannin is extracted, which may cause gastric disorders to those who drink it. Never make tea in a tin teapot, as the tannic acid acts upon the metal and produces a poisonous compound.

A slice of *lemon* is a good substitute for milk in tea. The lemon prevents the headache and sleeplessness which the tea causes in some persons.

A French chemist recommends grinding tea like coffee. It will yield nearly double the amount of its exhilarating quality. Also to put a lump of sugar into the teapot with the tea.

Iced Tea, or Russian Tea.

Make the tea by the first receipt, strain it from the grounds, and keep it cool. When ready to serve, put *two cubes* of *block sugar* in a glass, *half fill* with *broken ice*, add *a slice* of *lemon*, and fill the glass with *cold tea*.

Coffee.

Coffee grows on small trees. Mocha, the best variety, is grown in Arabia. Other choice kinds come from Java, the West Indies, and South America. The fruit of the coffee tree is something like the cherry, and contains two seeds or beans. Bruising the fruit separates the berries, which are then washed and dried. The raw berries are tough, difficult to grind, and have but little flavor. Coffee should be roasted and kept in air-tight cans, that the fine flavor may be perfectly developed and preserved. Coffee is more stimulating than tea, and, when taken very strong after a hearty meal, aids digestion. It should be made in such a way that the full strength and aroma are obtained, without developing the tannic acid. This is done by pouring boiling water upon the coffee and keeping it in a closely covered vessel just below the boiling-point, or boiling not longer than five minutes. If allowed to boil longer, or left uncovered, the volatile oil which forms the fragrant aroma is dissipated, and the tannic acid extracted. This acid, when combined with cream or milk, forms a leathery, indigestible compound which irritates the internal membranes.

The proportion of one third Mocha and two thirds Java coffee is agreeable to most people. Many prefer to roast and grind the coffee for themselves ; but in coffee-houses the arrangements for roasting are now so complete, that it is well for small families to buy coffee already roasted, and to grind it as needed, or buy it ground in a small quantity.

The coffee-pot should be of granite ware or porcelain, and kept scrupulously clean, cleansing the spout as well as the pot every time it is used. A brownish deposit is soon formed ·on the inside of the pot, if the coffee be allowed to stand in it long, or if it be not often scoured. Many a cup of ill-flavored coffee is owing to its having been made in an unclean pot.

The proportions are, *one heaping tablespoonful* of *coffee* to *one cup* of, *boiling water*, reducing the proportion slightly when several cups are required. *Half a cup* of ground coffee is enough for *one quart* of *water*, and will make sufficient for five people. It takes a greater proportion of coffee and water, and it is more difficult to make just enough for one person than for more, as the last coffee poured out is not as clear as the first. The

8

old notion of allowing extra for the pot is not without reason.

Fish glue or inferior isinglass, which can be purchased at a druggist's, is a cheap and convenient article to use in clearing coffee. Egg shells should be saved and used for the same purpose. Wipe the eggs as soon as they come from the market, and then the shells may all be used. Two or three shells contain albumen sufficient to clear a quart of coffee.

Various modifications of the biggin, or French coffee-pot, are in use, and the coffee made in them is excellent, as none of the aroma is wasted. They are generally quite expensive, and some soon get out of order, if not handled carefully. The spout of the coffee-pot should be closed with a cork, or a thimble fitted for that purpose, or a piece of soft brown paper twisted so as to form a stopper. This prevents the escape of the steam and aroma. Coffee, if allowed to boil, should stand at least ten minutes after boiling, to give it time to settle and become clear.

Roasting Coffee.

Put *one pound* of *raw coffee* in a small frying-pan. Place it on the stove, and shake and stir occasionally for fifteen minutes, or till yellow. Then cover it, and increase the heat, and shake till the kernels are all a deep cinnamon or chestnut color, and have an oily appearance. Be careful that none are burned. Keep it covered, and when still warm, not hot, add *one egg* and its shell. Beat until every kernel is coated with the egg. The egg will dry quickly. It helps to preserve the flavor, is the cheapest form in which to use egg for clearing, and does not interfere with the grinding of the coffee.

Coffee should be kept in air-tight tin cans, and ground only as required. The finer it is ground, the stronger will be the extract.

Coffee (Common Coffee-Pot).

1 heaping tablesp. ground coffee.	1 egg shell.
1 square inch isinglass, or	1 cup freshly boiling water.

Scald the coffee-pot. Put in the coffee and isinglass. Add the boiling water. Cover the spout, and boil just five minutes. Stir it well. Set the pot on the back of the stove, where it will keep hot, but not boil. Add *half a cup* of *cold water.* Pour out a little of the coffee and pour it back again to clear the grounds from the spout. Let it stand at least ten minutes. If served in the pot, be careful not to roil the coffee by shaking the pot or by careless pouring. *A tablespoonful* of *caramel* mixed with the ground coffee gives additional flavor and color.

Steamed Coffee.

The same proportions as in the preceding rule. Place the coffee-pot in a kettle of boiling water, or make the coffee in a granite double boiler kept expressly for that purpose, and steam twenty minutes. Pour it from the grounds into a hot coffee-pot for serving.

Coffee made with Cold Water.—Put the required proportion of cold water and coffee into a china or granite coffee-pot, cover closely, and let it stand over night. In the morning let it just come to the boiling-point, and serve at once. It needs no straining nor clearing. (*Miss Devereux.*)

Coffee made with an Egg.

One egg is sufficient to clear *one cup* of *ground coffee.* If a smaller quantity be desired, *half an egg* may be used, as, if fresh, the remainder will keep till the next day. Or the whole egg may be beaten with the ground coffee, and such portion of it used as is needed, keeping the remainder closely covered.

To make the coffee, add *half a cup* of *cold water* to the portion of egg to be used and *one third* of *a cup* of *coffee.*

Beat well; put it in the hot coffee-pot; add *one pint* of *boiling water* and boil five minutes. Keep it hot, but not boiling, for ten minutes. Pour out a little and pour it back to clear the spout.

Filtered Coffee.

This is made in a French biggin, or any double coffee-pot fitted with one or more strainers. The coffee, which is ground very fine, is placed in the strainer; this is put into the receptacle for holding the made coffee, the boiling water is poured in and allowed to drip slowly through the coffee. If there be only two parts to it, the coffee-pot should stand where the coffee will keep hot, but not boil. Many of the coffee-pots made on this principle are placed in another vessel containing boiling water.

To serve Coffee.

Cream, scalded milk, and *block sugar* are essential to good breakfast coffee. Put in *one tablespoonful* of *cream* and *two tablespoonfuls* of *milk,* and fill the cup three fourths full. Never fill to overflowing. Let each person add the sugar desired, unless you know the individual tastes of the family. The milk should be just hot, but never boiled, as boiled milk gives a very unpleasant flavor.

After-dinner coffee, or *black coffee,* is made by either of the receipts previously given, using double the proportion of coffee: *two heaping tablespoonfuls* of *coffee* to *one cup* of *water.* It should be very strong and perfectly clear; served in small cups, with block sugar if desired, but not with cream or milk, as the milk counteracts the purpose for which the coffee is taken.

The addition of *three tablespoonfuls* of *whipped cream* to a cup of coffee gives *Vienna Coffee.* An equal amount of boiled milk and filtered coffee is called *Café au Lait.*

Cocoa and Chocolate.

Cocoa is the fruit of a small tree which grows in Mexico, Central America, and the West Indies. The fruit is shaped like a large, thick cucumber, and contains from six to thirty beans. The beans are roasted, like coffee. The husks or shells are taken off, and used in that form as cocoa shells. They need longer boiling, and are preferred by many persons with weak digestion. They are sometimes ground with the bean, making an inferior article of cocoa. Starch is also used to adulterate cocoa. The best cocoa is made from the whole bean after the husk is removed. Cocoa nibs are the beans broken instead of ground.

Chocolate is the finely ground powder from the kernels mixed to a stiff paste with sugar, and sometimes flavored with vanilla. It is the most nutritious and convenient form of cocoa; a small cake of it will satisfy hunger. It is a very good lunch for travellers. If the oily scum which forms on the surface after boiling be removed, it is less indigestible.

Chocolate does not produce the injurious effects which render tea and coffee objectionable, and is far better for children and working-people.

Cocoa.

Put *half a cup* of *broken cocoa* into a pot with *two quarts* of *water*. Boil gently two hours, until reduced to one quart; or use *half cocoa* and *half shells*. Serve with *sugar* and *cream*, or *scalded milk*. It is more digestible if allowed to cool and the globules of fat removed, then reheated.

Prepared Cocoa.

This ground cocoa comes in many forms, and some are recommended to be prepared at the table; but all kinds are better boiled *one minute* in a very little water, the same as chocolate, and thinned with *hot milk*.

Shells.

Steep *one cup* of *shells* in *one quart* of *boiling water* three or four hours, adding more hot water as it boils away. Strain, and serve with hot milk, or cream and sugar.

Chocolate.

Put *one square* of *Baker's chocolate, two tablespoonfuls* of *sugar, two tablespoonfuls* of *hot water,* and *a pinch* of *salt* in a small saucepan, and boil until smooth; stir constantly; add gradually *one pint* of *boiling water,* and when ready to serve add *one pint* of *hot milk.* Use *all milk* and *two squares* of *chocolate,* if liked richer; or thicken with *one teaspoonful* of *cornstarch* wet in *a little cold water,* and boil five minutes before adding the milk.

German, or Sweetened Vanilla Chocolate.

Melt *two sticks* of *chocolate* in *two* or *three tablespoonfuls* of *hot water.* Stir to a smooth paste; add gradually *one pint* of *hot milk* and stir or mill it five minutes. Serve in cups three quarters full with *two* or *three tablespoonfuls* of *whipped cream* on the top. Sweeten and flavor the cream before whipping.

Hot Milk.

Heat the milk over boiling water until it is barely hot, but not scalded. Test the heat by tasting. Shake in a few grains of salt, and sip it by the teaspoonful. One of the best " nightcap drinks."

Lemonade.

Boil one cup of sugar and one pint of water ten minutes; add thin shavings of the yellow peel of one lemon, and pour it hot over the juice of three lemons. When cold, strain it, and add chipped ice and water as desired.

Fruit Punch.

Boil two cups of sugar and one quart of water twenty minutes. Pour it boiling hot over the following mixture: half a cup each of lemon and orange juice, one cup of strawberry juice, half a cup of canned cherry syrup, and one cup of chopped pineapple. When ready to serve, strain it, dilute with ice water, and add one cup of fresh strawberries quartered, one banana sliced, and half a cup stoned cherries. Dilute with Apollinaris if preferred.

SOUP.

Nothing can be easier than to make a good soup if one only *knows how* and has the *will* to do it; and if one will, it is easy to know how. Considerations of economy and healthfulness make it the duty of every housekeeper to thoroughly inform herself on the few essential points in soup-making. When these are learned it will be as simple as any other duty.

As soups are *not* made from *nothing*, a supply of materials should always be kept on hand, such as *dried sweet herbs* (which may be purchased at any city market for a trifle; twenty-five cents' worth will last a year or more); also *whole*, as well as *ground spices;* and, more particularly, fresh vegetables, — *onions, carrots*, and *turnips.* If we had access to the French market, we could buy the smallest amount whenever it might be desired; but as only a few marketmen in America will sell a single onion or a single carrot, it is well for those who cannot cultivate for themselves to purchase in large quantities. They may be kept in a cool place by covering with clean sand. *Parsley* may be grown in the house if you have a sunny window; and we can all have salt and pepper. Now, having these seasoning materials always at hand, you may easily find other material in the store-room, or from the day's supply of fresh meat, fish, etc., without buying expressly for soup; that is, if you, instead of the marketman, have the bones and trimmings.

Every pantry should have a " catch all." It is vastly more important there than in the sewing-room or on the toilet-table. The coal-hod, refuse pail, and sink *catch all* in many households. One or two large bowls — not tin, but deep earthen dishes, provided they are sweet and do not leak — will better answer the purpose After breakfast or dinner, do not put away the remnants of steaks or roasts on the platters, but look them over and put by themselves any pieces that can be used again, either cold or in what are called *made dishes.* Then put all the bones, trimmings, fat, gristle, and everything, especially the platter gravy, which usually flavors the dish-water, into the " catch all." If you have just one bone from a steak or chop, if it be not burned it is worth saving, and in cool weather will keep till you have another. If there be a tablespoonful of any vegetables, a stalk of celery, an egg, baked apple, or a bit of macaroni, put them away neatly. You will find a use for them. If you have boiled a fresh tongue, a fowl, a leg of lamb, or a cup of rice, plan to make a soup also, and thus save the water. This economy may be carried to the extreme of saving the water in which cabbages, beans, or potatoes have been boiled, or of keeping a fire several hours in a hot day only to save a few cents' worth of bone, or of spoiling all the soup by adding a spoonful of turnip already sour; but as a rule we err in the opposite practice.

Soups are made from meat, fish, and vegetables, with water or milk; seasoned or, flavored with any or every kind of vegetable, sweet herbs, spices, curry powder, catchups, aromatic sauces, and with some kinds of fruit. They are served thin and clear, or thickened with vegetables or cereals, and with or without meat.

Soups are classified and named in various ways, according to material, color, quality, etc. Soups *with stock* have meat as the basis. Soups *without stock* are made of fish, vegetables, and milk. They are sometimes called *soup maigre.* Soups are named from the principal ingredient, or an imitation of the same, as Potato, Onion, Beef, Mutton, Chicken, Gumbo, Macaroni, Okra, Ox-tail, Giblet, Cock-a-leekie, Lobster, Mock Turtle, Mock Bisque, etc. ; or from the color, as Clear, or Amber, Brown, and White ; or from the consistency, as Thin soups and Purées ; or from the quality, as simple Broths, Bouillon, and Consommé; or from the season of the year, as Julienne; or from the people who use them, as Scotch Broth, French Pot-au-feu, Indian Mullagatawney; or from the name of the makers, or in any way one's fancy and invention may suggest. But from the scores, yes, hundreds of receipts in the cook-books, which seem so bewildering to the beginner, a few simple rules may be deduced which will make the process of soup-making intelligible; and when once the foundation is laid, you may build and enlarge as you choose.

Do not be discouraged because you have not all the dozen or more ingredients mentioned in most receipts. You will find many of them may be omitted with a perfectly satisfactory result. Much depends upon *what* is omitted, though, as Potage à la Reine without chicken, or Julienne without vegetables, or Mullagatawney without curry powder, would disappoint those who think only of the name; but, called by any other name, you would find them very good soups.

Soups with Stock.

Soups made with stock include all the varieties made from beef, veal, mutton, and poultry. Perhaps a glance at the meaning of the word *stock* will make clear its application to cookery. Stock is from the Anglo-Saxon *stician*, to stick, and the idea of fixedness is expressed in all its forms. Stock in trade or business means the money or material laid by, or *stored, stocked, fixed,* as a source of supply, ready for use at any time; and in the business of soup-making, stock is the material *stored* or prepared in such a way that it may be kept or fixed for use in making different kinds of meat soup; or, more definitely, it is a liquid containing the juices and soluble parts of meat, bone, and vegetables, which have been extracted by proper cooking. This liquid is more or less solid when cold, according to the gelatinous nature of the ingredients. It varies greatly in quality, owing to the manner in which it is prepared and the material used.

Stock is usually made from the cheaper, inferior parts of meat, which yield the most nutriment when cooked in this way; also from odds and ends of cooked meat, which perhaps could not be used otherwise. The chief object in making stock is to obtain in the quickest manner the largest possible amount of nutriment from the cheapest parts of meat, and after getting it to keep and use it. This is best accomplished by observing the following rules : —

First. Cut the meat into small pieces, and soak them in *cold* water before heating, that every atom of nourishment may be extracted. Cold water draws out and dissolves the meat juices, while hot water hardens the albumen on the outside of the meat and prevents the juices from escaping into the liquid.

Second. Use a careful selection and proportion of meat, bone, and water, and season judiciously, so that no one flavor will predominate.

Third. Use a steam-tight kettle, and *simmer*, — not boil the material rapidly, — that the juices may be retained in the water, and not wasted by evaporation.

Fourth. Make stock the day before using, if possible, that the fat may be more easily removed ; but do not give up making it simply from "lack of time," for it *can* be made quickly.

A *soup digester* is the proper vessel for making stock. This is a porcelain-lined iron kettle with a bale, and having a cover fitting closely into a groove, so that no steam can escape except from the valve in the top of the cover, which at once indicates when the water is boiling rapidly. One holding six quarts, and costing three dollars, is a convenient size for a small family. If you cannot afford a digester, get a granite ironware kettle, with a tightly fitting cover. Plain ironware will do if you have nothing better ; but it rusts easily, and, if tin-lined, the tin melts in careless usage.

The meats used in making stock should contain *gelatine*, *osmazome*, and a small amount of *fat*.

Gelatine is found in the bones, skin, tendinous and gristly portions of flesh, especially in veal. It is this which causes the stock to become a jelly. But a soup which forms a jelly, or is made principally from bones, is not the most nutritious. The jelly of bones and sinews boiled into soup can furnish only jelly for our bones and sinews. It is useful in convalescence, for then the portions of the system in which gelatine is needed have been wasted; but in other cases, though easily digested, it is unwholesome, for it loads the blood with disturbing products. It is entirely destitute of flavor, and therefore we need with it meat containing *osmazome.*

Osmazome is that part of meat which gives to each of the various kinds its distinctive flavor. It is more abundant in brown than in white meats, and in the meat of old rather than in that of young animals. It is found largely in lean beef, mutton, and fowls. Osmazome is more highly developed in roasted meats; therefore all the bones and remnants of roasts which cannot be utilized in *entrées,* should be put into the soup-kettle.

We need also the *alkaline* and *acid salts* found in the blood and juices of the flesh; therefore a small portion of *raw, lean meat* should form a part of all stock.

Fat is necessary, as an element of perfect food, and should always be used in making stock. It adds to the flavor, and all that is not absorbed in the stock may be removed when cold. The *marrow*, found in the shin bone, is the best form of fat. The browned fat of roast beef gives a fine flavor, and occasionally a bit of ham or bacon may be used. But all mutton fat should be avoided, because of its rankness.

These four kinds of meat — beef, mutton, veal, and poultry — may be used together or separately. It is better to use mutton, if in a large quantity, by itself, as the flavor is disagreeable to many. After having extracted all the nutriment from the meat in its juices, fat, albumen, and flavor, do not attempt to make further use of the worthless residue of muscular fibre. It is not only harmful, but dry, tasteless, and utterly useless as food. It needs the addition of many other materials to make it palatable even, and it is cheaper to get the fibrine we need from meat cooked in other ways, directions for which will be given under Boiling Meats and Stews. Therefore do not hesitate, as a matter of economy, to throw away this useless meat.

When fresh meat is bought expressly for stock, select a piece from the shin or lower part of the round of beef or veal. This has bone with marrow, a large proportion of gelatine, more or less osmazome, according to the amount of flesh, and costs less than other parts. In mutton, pieces from the neck and forequarter are the best. Fowls are better than chickens. With this fresh meat may be used the bones and trimmings from steak or chops, and the flank ends of roasting pieces, which yield more nutriment if added to the stock pot before being cooked. Add also any remnants of roasted or broiled meat, bone, fat, gristle, anything except mutton fat. In families where large roasts of beef and poultry are often used, there should be material enough for stock, without buying new meat, except for the nicest of clear soups, which the French call Consommé.

The proportions of bone and meat should be about equal by weight. When ready to begin the stock, wipe the fresh meat with a clean cloth wet in cold water. Never put the meat in a pan of cold water to soak. It takes out all the juices that you wish to save. *Wipe before cutting.* The inside is clean. But rinse the cloth and scrub the *outside* thoroughly. Cut away the parts that are tainted or discolored by rusty meat-hooks, etc. Examine all the odds and ends of cooked meat, and remove any smoked or burned parts from ham or broiled meat, also the stuffing and skin from roast poultry, if you wish to have the stock clear. Scrape the meat clean from the bones and cut into inch pieces. Break or saw the bones as small as you conveniently can. Remove the marrow (a soft, fatty substance, which you will find in the hollow of the bones) and put it in the soup kettle to keep the bones from sticking.

Put in the bones and pack the meat around them. Place your kettle on the back of the range before adding the water, so that there need be no heavy weight to lift. Allow one quart of fresh cold water to every pound of meat and bone ; one fourth less water if your stock is to be made altogether of cooked meats, or if you use a digester. Cover the kettle, and after the water is quite red, and the juices are well drawn out, draw the kettle forward and let it heat slowly, and *simmer*, or boil slowly, but *never boil hard.*

The scum, which soon rises on the surface, is the albumen and juices of the meat which have been drawn out and mixed with the cold water. They coagulate, or harden, as the water heats, and, being lighter than the water, rise to the surface in the form of scum. It has usually been considered essential, in making soup, to remove every particle of this scum ; but the practice is wholly unnecessary and wasteful. We learn, in the article on Boiling, the three distinct purposes and methods of cooking meat in water ; and yet in skimming a soup we act directly contrary to the general principle there explained. If the kettle be clean, the water pure, and the meat well cleansed from any impurities on its outer surface, what can there be in the meat not suitable to eat, any more than in roast beef, or steak, or boiled mutton ? In making beef tea we are directed by the highest scientific authorities to remove the fat, cut the meat small, soak it in cold water, heat gradually, and never skim, as the scum or thickened material in the water is the very thing desired. Soup is only another form of beef tea, and the fat which is objectionable can better be removed when the stock is cold. These juices and soluble parts of the meat should be retained ; they increase, rather than diminish, the flavor, and all the sediment which is fine enough to go through the strainer should be used. In any thickened soup it is so mingled with the other ingredients as not to be unpleasant to the eye. And for those who wish clear soups, which are *not* as nutritious, this sediment can easily be removed in the clearing.

In a criticism which so decidedly rejects a prevailing custom, it may be well to remark that the method of preparing soups which is recommended in the preceding paragraph has been successfully proved in the Boston Cooking School for the last three years. The French, who regard skimming as very important in making their *Pot-au-feu*, remove the meat as soon as tender, and serve it as *bouilli*, or *boiled beef*. As it has not been cut in small pieces, and is heated quickly, some of the juices are retained in the meat, and it is nourishing and palatable. Their *Pot-au-feu* is more like our beef stew than like soup stock.

In the preparation of the stock, the next step is to add the seasoning, which may be used in these proportions: For *every quart* of *water, one even teaspoonful* of *salt, two peppercorns* or *half a saltspoonful* of *ground pepper, two cloves, two allspice berries, one fourth* of *a saltspoonful* of *celery seed* or *a bit* of *celery root, a sprig* of *parsley, a teaspoonful* of *mixed herbs,* and *a tablespoonful* of *each vegetable.*

Herbs and spices are better whole than ground, as they may be more readily removed by straining. The French cooks use a bouquet of herbs, made with two leaves or blossoms of each herb wrapped in a sprig of parsley and tied securely so that it may be easily removed. A convenient and economical way is to strip off the leaves and blossoms, break the stalks in tiny pieces, mix them, and keep in a tin box. Use *sage, summer savory, thyme, marjoram,* and *bay leaves: a teaspoonful* of the *mixture* (not of each herb) for *every quart.* The vegetables generally used are *onion, carrot, turnip,* and *celery.* It is better to omit them entirely in warm weather, or if you wish to keep the stock more than a week, as the vegetable juices ferment quickly and sour the stock.

Wash, scrape, or pare the vegetables; cut them into small pieces for convenience in measuring. as one onion or one slice of carrot is rather indefinite. Keep them in cold water until the juices are drawn from the meat.

When old or strong, they may be blanched or parboiled first.

Onions, potatoes, and cabbage should always be scalded to draw out the indigestible qualities. Some object to the use of onions, particularly on account of the disagreeable odor; but when added with the other seasoning material, they are so completely absorbed in the stock that no trace of their presence can be detected. All or part of the vegetables may be fried first, if you like. One or two sour apples give a pleasant flavor to stock. Wines or catchups should be added just before serving, as boiling dissipates the flavor.

If you wish to have a *dark brown stock*, reserve part of the lean meat to brown with the onions. Fry the onions in a little fat, and when very brown remove them, to prevent burning, and brown the meat in the same fat. Add the onions and meat to the stock. Take a little water from the stock, and wash off all the browned glaze adhering to the frying-pan, as this is the best part. A tablespoonful of browned sugar or *caramel* (see page 134), which should always be kept on hand, will also give a rich dark color. After the seasoning is placed in the mixture, put the kettle where it will keep at a gentle, steady simmering. Do not let it boil furiously one half-hour and not at all the next, but find the place on the range where it will keep at just the right temperature, and then, if you have a steady fire, it will need no further attention until ready to strain. It is hot enough if the water just bubbles on one side of the kettle.

When the stock has simmered till the meat is in rags and the bones clean, strain at once. Do not let it stand, if in an iron kettle. If you have used a digester or steam-tight kettle, the water will not have lessened much. If boiled in an ordinary kettle, it will be reduced about one half by evaporation, and may be diluted when ready for the table. Strain in this way. Place a stone jar beside your kettle. It should be of a size suited to the amount of stock. Put a colander over the jar (it should fit inside it), and a strainer cloth over the colander. Then, with a ladle or dipper, dip the contents of the kettle and pour into the strainer. Never try to lift the kettle and pour it out, unless you have more strength and skill than most beginners. When you have only a pint left, you may try the pouring. Do not squeeze the cloth, but let the contents drain ten or fifteen minutes, then throw the scraps away. Remember that you have extracted all the nutriment, and have it in the water; so do not expect to have any virtue in the meat or vegetables. Set the jar in a cool place, uncovered, but not in the ice chest while hot. It keeps better to cool quickly. In cold weather, and if you have used a large proportion of bone, the stock will harden like jelly, with a cake of solid fat on the top. This fat, by excluding the air, helps to keep the stock, and should not be removed until the stock is needed. In winter stock will keep a week, and longer, if made without vegetables. It should be heated occasionally to the boiling-point, or after taking off any portion of it, that what remains may harden again in an unbroken form. A little fresh charcoal tied in a bag and boiled with the stock is said to restore it when only slightly changed.

In very warm weather, make only enough for each day, as sometimes it spoils in one night. If you wish to make a soup while the stock is still hot, put what portion you may need into a shallow pan and place the pan in ice water, with a larger pan of ice water over it. This will soon harden the fat; or if you have not time to do this, take off what fat you can with a spoon, and wipe off the remainder with soft tissue paper, or strain several times through a fine napkin. The grease will adhere to the napkin, which should be rinsed in cold water. That hardens the fat. Or you may let the soup boil gently, and nearly all can be taken off.

To remove the fat after the stock has jellied, run a knife around between the cake of fat and the jar. If the fat be solid, it will sometimes come off whole; but if soft, take off all you can without cutting into the jelly, then wring a cloth out of very hot water, and wipe the stock. The hot cloth w · absorb the fat readily. Remember, if the soup is to be served clear, not a pin-head of fat must be left; but if it is to be thickened with any starchy material, this will absorb what cannot be removed with a spoon. This fat must be saved and clarified according to directions on page 18.

With this stock for a foundation, you may make an endless variety of soups, each soup taking its name from the principal solid ingredient; and it is equally valuable to use, instead of water, in making gravies or sauces. No matter how little you have, one cupful is worth more than it costs to make it, as an addition to fricassees and braised meats. This stock, if properly made and strained, will be sufficiently clear for any common soups. But for clear sparkling soups and aspic jelly, it must be clarified with the white of an egg.

To clear Soup Stock.

Remove the fat, and allow the *white* and *shell* of *one egg* for *every quart* of stock. If you wish to flavor the stock more highly, add *half a saltspoonful* of *celery seed* and the *thinnest* possible *shavings* from the *rind* of *half a lemon*.[1] Add also the lemon juice, and more salt and pepper if needed. Mix celery seed, lemon, egg, etc. with the *cold* stock, and beat it well. If the stock be hot when the egg is added, the egg will harden before it has done its work. This is a point where many fail. Set it over the fire and stir it all the time, until it is hot, to keep the egg from settling. Then leave it, and let it boil ten minutes. By this time a thick scum will have formed, and as it breaks the liquid will be clear and sparkling, like wine, and darker than before. Draw it back on the stove, and add half a cup of cold water. Let it stand ten minutes, while you get your jar, colander, and fine napkin ready for straining. Wring your napkin out of hot water, and lay it over the colander. Put the finest wire strainer on the napkin and then pour it all through. This strainer will catch the scum

[1] Clear soup should be highly seasoned, as clearing destroys some of the strength.

and shells which would otherwise clog the napkin. Let it take its own time to drain ; but if you must h   ten it, raise the napkin first at one corner, and then at another, and let the liquid run down to a clean place. This is better than squeezing. This is all ready to serve as a clear soup by simply heating to the boiling-point. Serve with it, in the tureen, thin slices of lemon, a glass of sherry, yolks of hard-boiled eggs, or delicate flavored force-meat balls ; or put on each plate a poached egg, or a spoonful of grated Parmesan cheese.

In making soups from this stock, bear this fact in mind : Do not waste the stock by boiling in it any material which requires long boiling. Vegetables, rice, sago, tapioca, macaroni, vermicelli, etc., should be cooked separately and then added to the stock, which should be brought to the boiling-point.

The following are some of the principal varieties. These soups are all supposed to have no meat served with them. The broth is clear and thin, and every particle of vegetable or cereal should be distinct, except in the soups called Mixed Vegetable and Tomato.

Concise rules for Common Brown Stock and Consommé are given for the benefit of those who do not need to read all the preliminary remarks.

Brown Soup Stock.

6 pounds hind shin of beef.	1 large tablespoonful salt
6 quarts cold water.	3 small onions.
10 whole cloves.	1 carrot
10 whole peppercorns.	1 turnip.
10 allspice.	2 stalks celery.
Bouquet of sweet herbs.	2 sprigs parsley.

Wipe and cut the meat and bones into small pieces. Put the marrow, bones, half of the meat, and the cold water into the kettle. Soak half an hour before heating. Add spices and herbs. Brown the onions and the remainder of the meat, and add them to the stock ; add the vegetables cut fine. Simmer six or seven hours and strain.

Bouillon.

4 pounds beef, from the middle of the round.	1 tablespoonful salt.
	4 peppercorns.
2 pounds bone.	4 cloves.
2 quarts cold water.	1 tablespoonful mixed herbs.

Wipe and cut the meat and bones into small pieces; add the water, and heat slowly; add the seasoning, and simmer five hours. Boil down to three pints; strain, remove the fat, and season with salt and pepper. Serve in cups at luncheons, evening companies, etc. Boil one onion, half a carrot, and half a turnip with it if you like.

Clear, or Amber Soup, or Consommé.[1]

4 pounds shin of beef.	1 tablespoonful salt.
4 pounds knuckle of veal, or	3 onions.
3 pounds fowl.	1 carrot.
4 quarts cold water.	1 turnip.
2 ounces lean ham or bacon.	2 stalks celery.
6 cloves.	2 sprigs parsley.
6 peppercorns.	3 eggs, whites and shells
6 allspice.	1 saltspoonful celery seed.
Bouquet of herbs.	Rind and juice of one lemon.

Wipe and cut the meat and bones into small pieces. Put the marrow, bones, and part of the meat in the kettle with four quarts of cold water. Heat slowly; cut the onions and vegetables fine, and fry them in the ham fat or in drippings; then brown the remainder of the meat. Add onions, meat, herbs, spices, and vegetables. Simmer until the meat is in rags; it will take seven or eight hours. Strain, and when cold remove the fat; add the whites and shells of the eggs, celery seed, lemon, and salt and pepper if needed. When well mixed, heat it, and boil ten minutes. Strain through the finest strainer, and heat again to the boiling-point before serving. Add Kitchen Bouquet, lemon juice, or wine as preferred, to this, or any other brown stock. Clear soup should be perfectly transparent, of a light brown or straw color.

[1] *Consommé* means "consumed, boiled to rags."

Left-over Soup.

Bones and trimmings from a 6-pound roast of beef.	4 cloves.
	4 peppercorns.
2 cold mutton-chops.	1 cold fried egg.
The flank end of a sirloin steak, uncooked.	2 baked apples.
	1 cup cold boiled onions.
4 quarts cold water.	2 stalks celery.
1 tablespoonful salt.	1 tablespoonful parsley.

Cut up the meat and bones, and put them in the kettle with the cold water. Add all the other ingredients, and simmer till the bones are clean, the meat is in rags, and the water reduced one half. Strain, and the next morning remove the fat; when ready to serve, heat the stock to the boiling-point; warm with it one cup of cold macaroni or tomatoes left from yesterday's dinner. Add more salt if needed, and flavor with Kitchen Bouquet.

Julienne Soup.

1 quart stock.	½ teaspoonful salt.
1 pint mixed vegetables.	½ saltspoonful pepper.

Cut the celery into thin slices, the turnip into quarter-inch dice, and the carrot into three-quarters by one-eighth inch strips or straws, using only the orange part. Or cut carrot and turnip into quarter-inch slices, and then into fancy shapes with small vegetable cutters. Cover with boiling water, add half a teaspoonful of salt, and cook until soft, but not long enough to destroy their shapes. Let the quart of stock come to a boil; add the vegetables, the water, and more salt if necessary. Serve hot. In spring and summer use asparagus, peas, and string beans. It is quite important that the vegetables should be small and of uniform thickness; but if any require a longer time to cook, they should be cut into smaller pieces.

Macaroni Soup.

1 quart stock.	1 teaspoonful salt.
3 or 4 sticks macaroni.	½ saltspoonful pepper.

Cook the macaroni in boiling salted water, about half an hour, or until tender; drain, pour cold water through it, to keep it from sticking together. Lay the sticks close together on a board, and divide them into eighth-inch pieces, making tiny rings, or cut them into half-inch pieces. There should be about a pint of macaroni for a quart of stock. Bring the stock to a boil; add the macaroni, the salt, and the pepper; then pour all into the tureen.

Vermicelli Soup.

1 quart stock.	1 teaspoonful salt.
½ cup vermicelli.	½ saltspoonful pepper.

The vermicelli may be broken or not, as you please. Cook about ten minutes in boiling salted water. Drain, put it in the tureen, and pour over it the boiling stock. Spaghetti and Italian Paste may be used in the same way.

Rice, Tapioca, Sago, or Barley Soup.

1 quart stock.	1 teaspoonful salt.
2 tablespoonfuls either rice, barley, tapioca, or sago.	½ saltspoonful pepper.

Wash the grains, and cook until tender in boiling salted water; then add them to the boiling stock. Serve with croûtons. Barley should be soaked one hour, and boiled two hours or more. Vegetables and macaroni are better with beef stock; and rice, tapioca, and barley with mutton or chicken stock.

Tomato Soup with Stock.

1 quart stock.	1 can tomatoes.
1 teaspoonful sugar.	1 teaspoonful salt.
1 saltspoonful pepper.	

Stew the tomatoes until soft enough to strain. Rub all but the seeds through the strainer. Add the sugar, salt, and pepper. Add all to the boiling stock. Serve with croûtons.

Carrot, or Crecy Soup.

1 quart rich, brown stock.	1 teaspoonful salt.
1 pint carrot.	½ saltspoonful pepper.
1 teaspoonful sugar.	1 small onion, sliced.

Wash and scrape the carrot; shave off in thin slices a pint of the outer part. Do not use the yellow centre. Cook the carrot with the onion in boiling salted water to cover, till very tender. Rub the carrot through a squash strainer. Add the stock and heat again. Add the sugar, salt, and pepper, and when hot serve immediately with croûtons.

Mixed Vegetable Soup

1 quart stock.	1 cup strained tomatoes.
1 quart boiling water.	1 tablespoonful chopped parsley.
1 cup each chopped onion, carrot, and celery.	1 teaspoonful sugar.
½ cup each chopped turnip, parsnip, and cabbage.	1 teaspoonful salt.
	1 saltspoonful pepper.

Use all or as many varieties of vegetables as you wish, or if you have only a few, add macaroni, rice, or barley, having in all half the amount of vegetables that you have of liquid. Chop all the vegetables fine. Cabbage, cauliflower, parsnip, potatoes, or onions should be parboiled five minutes, and drained carefully. Fry the onions and carrot; then put all with the water and stock, and simmer until tender. Add the seasoning. Serve without straining. Always add sugar to all mixed vegetable soups.

The next division of soups includes those which are thickened in various ways, and in which the meat is served with the soup; also White Soups, and the materials to be served with soups.

Caramel, for coloring Soups, etc.

Melt *one cup* of *sugar* (either brown or white) with *one tablespoonful* of *water* in a frying-pan. Stir until it becomes of a dark brown color. Add *one cup* of *boiling water;* simmer ten minutes, and bottle when cool. It gives a rich, dark color to soups, coffee, and jelly; is more wholesome than browned butter in sauces, and is delicious as a flavoring in custards and pudding sauces. In many kitchens Tournade's Kitchen Bouquet is preferred for soups and meat sauces to give flavor and color.

Glaze.

Glaze is simply clear stock boiled down to one fourth of its original amount. Put two quarts of rich, strong stock into a saucepan, and boil it uncovered until reduced to one pint. It should have a gluey consistency, and will keep a month if put in a closely covered jar in a cool place. It is useful in browning meats which have not been colored by cooking, but which we wish to have the appearance of having been roasted or browned.

Thickening for Soups.

Soups are thickened with flour, cornstarch, or rice flour: one tablespoonful for a quart of soup, — heaping, if flour; scant, if rice flour or cornstarch. Flour is the cheapest, but cornstarch gives a smoother consistency. Mix the flour with a very little cold water or milk until it is a smooth paste; then add more liquid, until it can be poured easily into the *boiling* soup. Remember to boil the soup fifteen or twenty minutes after the thickening is added, that there may be no raw taste of the flour. Where butter and flour are used, the butter is rubbed to a cream, mixed or braided with the flour, and then made into a paste with a little of the soup.

A better way is to put the butter in a small saucepan, and when melted and bubbling stir in the flour quickly, until smooth (be careful not to brown butter for any white soup); then add gradually about a cup of the hot soup, letting it boil and thicken as you add the soup. It should be thin enough to pour. In vegetable soups or purées, as soon as the hot butter and flour are blended, they may be stirred at once into the soup. This is what is meant in many of the receipts by thickening with butter and flour which have been cooked together. The hot butter cooks the flour more thoroughly than it can be cooked in any other way. When a brown thickening is desired, as in Mock Turtle Soup, melt the butter and let it become as brown as it will without burning; then add all the flour at once and stir quickly, that every particle of it may be moistened in the hot butter; add the water or soup gradually.

Flour that is browned while dry, either in the oven or over the fire, colors, but does not thicken. A certain amount of moisture, of either fat or water, is necessary with the heat to thoroughly swell the grains of starch in the flour. Thickened soups should be about the consistency of good cream. Purées are thicker.

Material to be served with Soup.

Croûtons, or Fried Bread. No. 1. — Cut stale bread into half-inch slices, remove the crusts, and cut into half-inch cubes; put them in a frying-basket, plunge into fat hot enough to brown them while you count forty; drain and sprinkle with salt. They may be fried at any time and heated in the oven just before serving. They are especially nice with pea and bean soup.

No. 2. — Cut the bread into cubes, and brown in butter in an omelet pan; or butter first, then cut into cubes and brown in the oven. They are best when prepared after the first receipt.

Crisped Crackers. — Split butter crackers and spread with butter; put them, the buttered side up, into a pan, and brown in a hot oven. They are delicious with white or vegetable soups, and in fish chowder and oyster stews.

Egg Balls.

Boil *four eggs* twenty minutes; put them in cold water. When cool, cut carefully through the white, and remove the yolks whole. They may be served in the soup whole or cut into quarters. Or put the yolks in a small bowl and rub them to a paste with a wooden spoon. Season with *one saltspoonful* of *salt*, *one fourth* of a *sal'spoonful* of *pepper; one teaspoonful* of *melted butter.* Moisten it with the beaten yolk or white of *one raw egg*, using just enough to shape it easily into balls about the size of a walnut. Roll in flour and fry in butter; the same as force-meat balls. They are sometimes boiled five minutes in the soup, but are better fried.

Force-Meat Balls for Soup.

1 cup of any cooked meat.	Yolk of 1 raw egg.
1 saltsp. each of salt and thyme	A few drops onion juice.
½ saltspoonful pepper.	1 tablespoonful flour.
1 teaspoonful lemon juice.	1 tablespoonful butter.
1 teaspoonful chopped parsley.	

Chop the meat very fine; add the seasoning; beat the yolk of the egg, and add enough of it to moisten the meat; make it into balls the size of a nutmeg, put them in a soup plate, sprinkle them with flour, shake the plate until the balls are all floured; put the butter in an omelet pan, and when brown put in the balls, and shake the pan occasionally until the balls are browned.

Mock Turtle Soup.

1 calf's head.	1 carrot.
4 quarts cold water.	1 turnip.
1 tablespoonful salt.	Celery root.
6 cloves.	2 tablespoonfuls butter.
6 peppercorns.	2 tablespoonfuls flour.
6 allspice.	1 pint brown stock.
½ inch stick cinnamon.	3 eggs.
Bouquet of herbs.	1 lemon.
2 onions.	

Wash, scrape, and clean the head, and soak an hour in cold water. Remove the brains and tongue. Lay them in cold water, to be reserved for separate dishes. Cut the head into four or five pieces, and put it into the kettle with the skin side up, to prevent sticking. Add the cold water; heat slowly and skim thoroughly, as the meat is to be used again. Add the salt, and simmer two hours, or until the meat slips from the bones. Remove the meat, and put the face meat smoothly on a plate, so it can easily be cut into dice when cool. Reserve the remainder of the meat for force-meat balls. Put the bones on to boil again. Add the herbs, spices, and vegetables, and simmer until reduced to two quarts. Strain, and set away to cool. Half an hour before serving, remove the fat, put the stock on to boil, and season with one saltspoonful each of ground thyme or marjoram and pepper, and one teaspoonful of salt. Make a brown thickening with two tablespoonfuls of butter, browned, two tablespoonfuls of cornstarch or flour, and one pint of brown stock. Stir this into the stock. Add one cup of meat dice, made by cutting the face meat into half-inch cubes. Boil the three eggs twenty minutes, and make the yolks into egg balls, or cut the whole eggs in half-inch slices. Make force-meat balls with the reserved meat, according to directions on page 137. Put the meat balls and egg balls into the tureen, add the soup, and serve very hot with thin slices of lemon.

This is usually flavored with a glass of sherry wine, but is very good with only the lemon, or a tablespoonful of Worcestershire sauce. Or you may boil with it one pint of strained tomatoes.

If you have no brown stock, boil one pound of lean beef with the head, and use the head stock with the flour and butter thickening. This soup is often made from calf's feet, and one or two pounds of lean veal. The feet should be soaked and scalded, boiled in four quarts of water with the herbs, spices, and vegetables, until the water is reduced to two quarts. Strain, and use as directed in the first receipt, making force-meat balls of the veal, and meat dice from the gelatinous meat of the feet.

Ox-Tail Soup.

2 ox-tails.	1 tablespoonful salt.
1 large onion.	1 tablespoonful mixed herbs.
1 tablespoonful beef drippings.	4 cloves.
4 quarts cold water.	4 peppercorns.

Wash and cut up the ox-tails, separating them at the joints. Cut the onion fine and fry it in the hot beef drippings. When slightly browned, draw the onion to one side of the pan, and brown half of the ox-tails. Put the fried onion and ox-tails in the soup kettle, and cover with four quarts of cold water. Tie the cloves, peppercorns, and herbs in a small piece of strainer cloth, and add them to the soup. Add the salt, and simmer three or four hours, or until the meat separates from the bones, and the gristly portions are perfectly soft. Select some of the nicest joints to serve with the soup. Skim off the fat, and add more salt and pepper, if needed. Strain and serve very hot.

If vegetables are served with this soup, add one pint of mixed vegetables, — onion, carrot, turnip, and celery. Cut them into small pieces, or into fancy shapes with a vegetable cutter. Add them to the liquor after straining, and boil twenty minutes or until tender.

Mullagatawny Soup.

This is an Indian soup, and means " pepper pot." It can be made from veal, calf's head, chicken, or rabbit. Use one, or a mixture of two or more of these varieties of meat. Mullagatawny soup should always be very highly seasoned with onions, curry powder, and apples, or lemons, or some strong acid fruit. The best portions of the meat are usually removed as soon as tender, and served with the strained soup. Rice should also be served with this soup.

3 pounds chicken, or young fowl.	2 sour apples, or
1 pound veal bones.	The juice of 1 lemon.
2 onions.	4 quarts cold water.
1 tablespoonful beef drippings.	1 tablespoonful curry powder
4 cloves.	1 teaspoonful salt.
4 peppercorns.	1 teaspoonful sugar.

Clean the chicken, and cut it at the joints into nice pieces for serving. Put it in the soup kettle with the veal bones, or any pieces of veal you may have. Cover with four quarts of cold water. Slice the onions, and fry them brown in the beef drippings. Put the onions, cloves, peppercorns, and apples in the kettle. Mix the curry powder, salt, and sugar to a smooth paste with a little of the water; add it to the soup. Let the soup simmer until the chicken is tender. Remove the chicken and cut into small pieces. Put the bones back in the kettle, and simmer another hour. Strain the soup, remove the fat, and put the liquor on to boil again, with the pieces of chicken and three or four tablespoonfuls of boiled rice. When the chicken is hot, serve at once.

Scotch Broth.

½ cup pearl barley.	2 tablespoonfuls butter.
2 pounds neck of mutton.	1 tablespoonful flour.
2 quarts cold water.	2 teaspoonfuls salt.
¼ cup each of carrot, turnip, onion, and celery.	1 saltspoonful white pepper.
	1 tablespoonful chopped parsley.

Pick over, and soak the barley over night or several hours in cold water. Wipe the meat with a clean wet cloth. Remove the fat and skin. Scrape the meat from the bones and cut it into half-inch dice. Put the bones on to boil in one pint of cold water, and the meat in three pints of cold water. Let the latter boil quickly, and skim carefully just as it begins to boil. When the scum comes up white, add the barley and skim again. Cut the vegetables into quarter-inch dice, fry them five minutes in one tablespoonful of the butter, and add them to the meat. Simmer three or four hours, or until the meat and barley are tender. Strain the water in which the bones have simmered. Cook one tablespoonful of butter in a saucepan with one tablespoonful of flour. When smooth, add the strained water gradually, and stir into the broth. Add the salt, pepper, and parsley. Simmer ten minutes, and serve without straining. Many people have a prejudice against mutton in stews or broths. The strong, disagree-able flavor lies mostly in the skin. If this be removed together with the fat, it will repay one for the time and trouble. As this broth is not to be strained, it is always well to boil the bones separately. Care must be taken not to let the water boil away. This is a favorite dish among the Scotch. They often serve it with a larger proportion of vegetables. The carrots are sometimes grated, giving the broth a fine color, and sometimes the dice of meat are first browned in the butter. Rice may be used instead of bar-ley. Scotch broth made after this receipt has been tested by a native Scotchman, and pronounced more like the " auld countree " than any other dish eaten in America.

Mutton Broth.

Allow *one quart* of *cold water* to *each pound* of meat and bone. Break the bones and cut the meat (which should be lean) into small pieces. Cover with cold water and heat slowly. Add *one teaspoonful* of *salt* and *half a salt-spoonful* of *pepper*, and a small slice of *onion* and *turnip* if you like. Simmer until the meat is in shreds. Strain it, and when it is cool remove the fat. To *one quart* of the broth allow *two tablespoonfuls* of *rice*, washed and soaked half an hour. When the broth is boiling, add the rice; simmer until it is tender, being careful not to let the water boil away. Season, and serve at once. For seasoning, a little curry powder, used as you would use cayenne pepper, or a saltspoonful of celery salt, or a few leaves of fresh mint, are agreeable as a change.

When you have not time to cool the broth, a piece of soft tissue paper passed over the surface helps to take up any globules of fat which cannot be removed with a spoon. To make it quickly for a sick person, chop *one pound* of perfectly lean, juicy *mutton* very fine; pour over it *one pint* of *cold water*. Let it stand until the water is very red; then heat it slowly. Let it simmer ten minutes. Strain, and serve hot.

Chicken Broth.

Clean the chicken, and separate it at the joints. Remove all the skin and fat. Cover the chicken with cold water. Add *one tablespoonful* of *salt*, *one saltspoonful* of *pepper*, *one small onion*, sliced. Simmer until the chicken is tender. Remove the best part of the meat, and put the bones and gristle back and simmer until the bones are clean. Wash and soak *two tablespoonfuls* of *rice* half an hour. Strain the broth. Remove the fat. Put the broth on to boil again, and add to it the rice, and the nicest portions of meat cut into small pieces. Simmer until the rice is tender. Add seasoning to taste, and serve at once. A few spoonfuls of cream may be added if desired. Serve with toasted crackers.

Turkey Soup.

Take the bones and scraps left from roast turkey or chicken, or any kind of game. Scrape the meat from the bones, and lay aside any nice pieces, no matter how small. Remove all the stuffing, and keep that by itself. Break the bones, and pack them closely in a kettle. Cover with cold water. Add *one small onion*, sliced, *one teaspoonful* of *salt*, and *a little pepper*. Simmer two or three hours, or until the bones are clean. Strain, and remove the fat. Put the liquor on to boil again, and add for every quart of liquor, *one cup* of *cold meat*, cut into small pieces, and *half a cup* of the *stuffing*. Or omit the stuffing and thicken the soup with flour. Simmer till the meat is tender, and serve at once. If there be a much larger proportion of meat and stuffing left, use it in making scalloped turkey or croquettes. This is much better than to boil meat, bones, and stuffing together. In that case the stuffing absorbs the oil, and gives a very strong, disagreeable flavor to the soup.

White Soup Stock.

White soup stock is made from veal or chicken, seasoned with onion, celery salt, and white pepper, avoiding
anything which will give it color. White soups are thickened with rice, cornstarch, flour, eggs, or the white meat
of chicken chopped fine, and are made still richer by milk
or cream.

White Soup (from Veal).

4 pounds knuckle of veal.	1 pint milk.
3 quarts cold water.	1 tablespoonful butter.
1 even tablespoonful salt.	1 heaping tablespoonful flour.
6 peppercorns.	1 teaspoonful salt.
2 small onions.	1 saltspoonful celery salt.
2 stalks celery.	½ saltspoonful white pepper.

Wipe and cut the veal into small pieces. Put it into
the kettle with the cold water. Heat slowly and skim,
because we do not wish the soup colored. Add the salt,
peppercorns, onions, and celery. Simmer five hours,
strain, and when cool remove the fat. There should be
about three pints of stock. When ready to use it, put
the stock on to boil, and the milk into the double boiler.
Thicken the stock with one tablespoonful of butter and
one heaping tablespoonful of cornstarch, cooked together.
Add the boiling milk, the salt, and pepper. Beat two
eggs until light, put them in the tureen, and strain the
boiling soup over them. Many people prefer to use the
yolks of the eggs only. This makes a yellow soup.
Others vary it by boiling the eggs hard and rubbing the
yolks through a gravy strainer after the soup is in the
tureen.

This veal stock may be clarified with the white of an
egg, if you wish it transparent. But it is better with the
milk or cream, and should be highly seasoned, and reduced one half by boiling, as when made from veal alone
it is insipid. Serve with croûtons.

White Soup (from Chicken).

3 or 4 pounds fowl.	1 pint cream.
3 quarts cold water.	1 tablespoonful butter.
1 tablespoonful salt	1 tablespoonful cornstarch.
6 peppercorns.	1 teaspoonful salt.
1 tablespoonful chopped onion.	1 saltspoonful white pepper.
2 tablespoonfuls chopped celery.	2 eggs.

Singe, clean, and wipe the fowl. Cut off the legs and wings, and disjoint the body. Put it on to boil in cold water. Let it come to a boil *quickly*, because we wish to use the meat as well as the water, and skim thoroughly. The meat may be removed when tender, and the bones put on to boil again. (Use the meat for croquettes or other made dishes.) Add the salt and vegetables. Simmer until reduced one half. Strain, and when cool remove the fat. For one quart of stock allow one pint of cream or milk. If cream, use a little less flour for thickening. Boil the stock ; add the butter and flour, cooked together, and the seasoning. Strain it over the eggs, stirring as you pour, or the eggs will curdle. By substituting, for the eggs in this white soup, the white meat of the chicken, chopped fine and rubbed to a powder, we have *Potage à la Reine,* which many think too elaborate for any but a professional cook to undertake. The breast of a roast chicken may be used   Add it to the boiling stock, then thicken it with the flour and butter. Add the cream, and if not perfectly smooth, strain into the tureen. It should be quite thick like cream. Whole rice is sometimes served with clear chicken soup. If used as a thickening, boil the rice until soft enough to rub through a strainer. Add it to the chicken liquor, and unite them with butter and flour cooked together.

The liquor in which a fowl or chicken has been boiled, when not wanted for any other purpose, should be saved for white soup. If the vegetables and spices are not boiled with the fowl, fry them five minutes without burning, add them to the stock, and simmer fifteen minutes.

Strain before serving. Chicken stock clarified makes a pale straw-colored, transparent soup.

Potage à la Reine, No. 2. (*Queen Victoria's favorite Soup.*)

Remove the fat from *one quart* of the water in which *a chicken* has been boiled. Season highly with *salt*, *pepper*, and *celery salt*, and a little *onion* if desired, and put on to boil. Mash the yolks of *three hard-boiled eggs* fine, and mix them with *half a cup* of *bread* or *cracker crumbs*, soaked until soft in a little *milk*. Chop the white meat of the chicken until fine like meal, and stir it into the egg and bread paste. Add *one pint* of *hot cream* slowly, and then rub all into the hot chicken liquor. Boil five minutes; add more salt if needed, and if too thick add more cream, or if not thick enough add more fine cracker dust. It should be like a purée.

Cocoanut Soup.

Cook two pounds of veal bones in two quarts of cold water until the meat is tender and the stock reduced to one quart. Grate the cocoanut and let it simmer with the veal the last half hour. Strain out the bones and cocoanut, and add to it the milk of the cocoanut and one pint of cream. Put it on the fire again, and when boiling, thicken it with one tablespoon each of cornstarch and butter which must first be blended or cooked as for white sauce. Add salt and pepper, and just before serving add a little of the broth to two slightly beaten eggs, then stir it quickly into the broth and serve at once with dried dice of bread.

Quick Bouillon.

Combine the liquor from oysters and clams, stock from left overs, water from boiled vegetables (except potato) with water to make one quart. Boil, add salt, one teaspoon of beef extract and one of Kitchen Bouquet.

SOUPS WITHOUT STOCK.

ANY of the soups or purées in this division may be attempted before one has mastered the imaginary difficulties of stock-making. They are palatable, nutritious, inexpensive, and quickly prepared.

Potato Soup.

3 potatoes.	½ teaspoonful celery salt.
1 pint milk.	½ saltspoonful white pepper.
1 teaspoonful chopped onion.	¼ saltspoonful cayenne.
1 stalk celery.	½ tablespoonful flour.
1 teaspoonful salt.	1 tablespoonful butter.

Wash and pare the potatoes, and let them soak in cold water half an hour. Put them into boiling water, and cook until very soft. Cook the onion and celery with the milk in a double boiler. When the potatoes are soft, drain off the water and mash them. Add the boiling milk and seasoning. Rub through a strainer, and put it on to boil again. Put the butter in a small saucepan, and when melted and bubbling, add the flour, and when well mixed stir into the boiling soup ; let it boil five minutes, and serve very hot. This flour thickening keeps the potato and milk from separating, and gives a smoothness and consistency quite unlike the granular effect which is often noticed. If the soup be too thick, add more hot milk.

The celery salt may be omitted if you have the fresh celery, or, if you like, put *one tablespoonful* of fine chopped *parsley* into the soup just before serving.

When you wish a richer soup, use *a quart* of *milk*, making it much thinner, and add *two eggs*, well beaten, after you take it from the fire ; or put them in the tureen, and stir rapidly as you pour in the boiling soup. New raw potatoes, cut into small dice or balls and cooked till tender but not broken, are sometimes served in potato soup.

Celery Soup.

1 head celery.	1 tablespoonful butter.
1 pint water.	1 tablespoonful flour.
1 pint milk.	½ teaspoonful salt.
1 tablespoonful chopped onion.	½ saltspoonful pepper.

Wash and scrape the celery, cut into half-inch pieces, put it into one pint of boiling salted water, and cook until very soft. Mash in the water in which it was boiled. Cook the onion with the milk, in a double boiler, ten minutes, and add it to the celery. Rub all through a strainer, and put it on to boil again. Cook the butter and flour together in a small saucepan until smooth, but not brown, and stir it into the boiling soup. Add the salt and pepper; boil five minutes, and strain into the tureen. Serve very hot.

Tomato Soup.

1 quart can tomatoes.	1 saltspoonful white pepper.
1 pint hot water.	1 tablespoonful butter.
1 tablespoonful sugar.	1 tablespoonful chopped onion.
1 teaspoonful salt.	1 tablespoonful chopped parsley.
4 cloves.	1 tablespoonful cornstarch.
4 peppercorns, or	

Put the tomatoes, water, sugar, salt, cloves, and peppercorns on to boil in a porcelain stewpan. Put the butter in a small saucepan, and when it bubbles put in the onion and parsley. Fry five minutes, being careful not to burn it. Add the cornstarch, and when well mixed stir it into the tomato. Let it simmer ten minutes. Add more salt and pepper if needed. Strain, and serve with plain boiled rice, or croûtons, or toasted crackers.

Mock Bisque Soup.

½ can tomatoes.	1 tablespoonful cornstarch.
1 quart milk.	1 teaspoonful salt.
⅓ cup butter.	½ saltspoonful white pepper.

Stew the tomatoes until soft enough to strain easily. Boil the milk in a double boiler. Cook one tablespoonful of the butter and the cornstarch together in a small sauce-pan, adding enough of the hot milk to make it pour easily. Stir it carefully into the boiling milk, and boil ten minutes. Add the remainder of the butter in small pieces, and stir till well mixed. Add salt and pepper and the strained tomatoes. If the tomatoes be very acid, add *half a salt-spoonful* of *soda* before straining. Serve very hot. Many would use more tomatoes, but it is more delicate with a small quantity.

Black Bean Soup.

1 pint black beans.	1 saltspoonful mustard.
2 quarts cold water.	1 tablespoonful flour.
1 small onion	2 tablespoonfuls butter.
2 teaspoonfuls salt.	1 lemon.
1 saltspoonful pepper.	2 hard-boiled eggs.
¼ saltspoonful cayenne.	

Soak the beans over night. In the morning pour off the water, and put them on to boil in two quarts of cold water. Slice the onion and fry it in one tablespoonful of the butter. Put it with the beans. Add a bit of celery root, if you have it. Simmer four or five hours, or until the beans are soft. Add more cold water as it boils away, — about half a cup every half-hour, — to check the boiling and soften the beans, leaving about two quarts when done. Rub the beans through a strainer, put the soup on to boil again, and add the salt, pepper, and mustard. When boiling, thicken it with the flour and butter which have been cooked together. This will prevent the beans from settling. Season to taste. Cut the lemon and eggs into thin slices, put them into the tureen, and pour the hot soup over them. Serve with croûtons.

Many think tomatoes are an improvement. If that flavor be desired, add to the above half a can of tomatoes, before straining. Others think it is not just right unless a quarter of a pound of salt pork, or some bones and odds and ends of meat, have been boiled with it. The beans are sometimes boiled to quite a thick pulp, and after sifting made of the proper consistency by thinning with brown soup stock, and seasoned more highly with the addition of ground herbs, spices, force-meat balls, and wine. It is then not unlike Mock Turtle Soup.

A very good bean soup may be made from the remains of baked beans. Add one quart of water and a slice of onion to each pint of beans. Boil to a pulp, mash, and season. Or make the soup of equal parts of white beans and canned or dried sweet corn. If dried corn, soak it over night, chop it fine, and boil it with the beans. If canned corn, chop it, and add it to the beans after straining. But whichever way it is prepared, do not boil the beans in the water in which they were soaked, nor serve them without straining, to remove the hulls, which contain no nutriment and are indigestible.

Split Pea Soup.

1 cup dried split peas.	½ teaspoonful sugar.
3 pints cold water.	1 teaspoonful salt.
1 tablespoonful butter.	1 saltspoonful white pepper.
1 tablespoonful flour.	

Pick over and wash the peas. Soak over night, or for several hours in cold water. Put them on to boil in three pints of fresh cold water, and let them simmer until dissolved, adding enough more water, as it boils away, to keep three pints of liquid in the kettle. Keep it well scraped from the sides of the kettle. When soft, rub through a strainer and put on to boil again. Add either water, stock, milk, or cream to make the consistency you wish. It should be more like a purée than a soup. Cook one large tablespoonful of butter and one of flour together, and add to the strained soup when boiling. Add the salt and pepper, and when it has simmered ten minutes, serve at once with fried dice of bread.

This is delicious made in this simple way. It must always be strained, and thickened with the flour and butter, or it will separate as it cools. It will be smooth, perfectly free from grease; and those who like the natural taste of the peas prefer it to any other way of cooking. Do not think you must boil more or less salt pork with it, as most receipts advise. It may be varied in many ways, by adding half a can of tomatoes before straining, or by boiling with the peas a small onion which has first been cut fine and fried in a little butter, or by adding any remnants of bone or meat, being careful to remove them before straining. Always use the split peas, as the hulls have been removed, and they cook much more quickly than the whole peas.

Green Pea Soup.

1 quart green peas.	$\frac{1}{4}$ saltspoonful pepper.
1 quart water.	$\frac{1}{2}$ teaspoonful sugar.
1 pint milk.	1 tablespoonful butter.
$\frac{1}{2}$ teaspoonful salt.	1 tablespoonful flour.

Put the peas into one pint of boiling water, and cook until soft. Mash them in the water in which they were boiled, and rub through a strainer, gradually adding a pint of hot water, which will help to separate the pulp from the skins. Put on to boil again. Cook the butter and flour in a small saucepan, being careful not to brown it. Stir it into the boiling soup. Add the salt, sugar, pepper, and the milk, which should be hot, using enough milk to make it the consistency you prefer. This is a very good way to use peas that are old and hard, and unfit to serve as a vegetable, which is often the case with those that come from a market. When the pods are fresh, wash them thoroughly; allow more water, and boil them with the peas.

Green Corn Soup.

6 ears sweet corn, or enough to make 1 pint raw pulp.	$\frac{1}{2}$ saltspoonful white pepper.
Water to cover the ears.	1 teaspoonful sugar.
1 pint milk, or cream.	1 teaspoonful flour.
1 teaspoonful salt.	1 tablespoonful butter.

With a very sharp knife scrape the thinnest possible shaving from each row of kernels, and then, with the back of the knife, scrape out the pulp, leaving the hull on the cob. Break the cobs if long, and put them on to boil in enough cold water to cover them. Boil thirty minutes and strain. There should be about one pint of water after straining. Put the corn water on to boil again, and when boiling add the corn pulp. Cook fifteen minutes. Add the salt, pepper, sugar, and the boiling milk. Thicken it with one teaspoonful of flour and one tablespoonful of butter cooked together. Boil five minutes and serve at once.

Corn is better for soup when it is a little old for the table, and the pulp is *thick* rather than *milky.*

Vegetable Soup (Winter).

1 cup each of onion and carrot	1 teaspoonful sugar.
1 cup each of turnip and parsnip.	1 saltspoonful white pepper.
1 pint each of celery and potato.	¼ saltspoonful cayenne pepper.
¼ cup butter or drippings.	1 tablespoonful chopped parsley.
1 teaspoonful salt.	1 slice of bread crust toasted very
1 tablespoonful flour.	brown.

Cut the onion, carrot, turnip, parsnip, and celery into half-inch dice, reserving the onions to fry, and the potatoes to boil by themselves. Put the butter in a stewpan or soup kettle, and when hot add the onions. After frying them carefully until colored but not burned, add the flour, and when well mixed pour on gradually a pint of hot water. Add the salt, pepper, sugar, bread, vegetables (except the potatoes), and enough boiling water to cover all. Let them *simmer* two hours. Boil the potatoes ten minutes, drain, and add them to the soup. When the vegetables are soft, rub all through a strainer. Add more salt and pepper if desired, and keep over hot water until ready to serve.

A summer vegetable soup may be made in a similar manner, using young onions, turnips, carrots, and cauliflower. Cut fine and parboil; then cover with fresh boiling water, simmer until soft, mash, strain, season, make quite thin with hot cream or milk, and pour this over a small quantity of tender green peas and asparagus tips, previously boiled.

Fish Soup.

1 pound any boiled fish, — salmon, cod, or halibut.	1 tablespoonful butter.
	2 tablespoonfuls flour.
1 quart milk	1 teaspoonful salt.
1 slice onion.	1 saltspoonful pepper.

Cook the fish in boiling salted water, until it flakes easily. Drain it, remove the skin and bones, and rub through a coarse strainer. Cook the onion with one quart of milk ten minutes, remove the onion, and thicken the milk with the flour and butter cooked together. Add the seasoning and fish. Let it boil up once and serve.

Purée of Canned Salmon.

Remove the oil, bones, and skin from *half a can* of *salmon*. Chop the salmon very fine. Boil *one quart* of *milk*, and season and thicken it as for fish soup. Add the salmon, and when heated it is ready to serve.

Lobster Soup, or Bisque of Lobster.

2 pounds lobster.	1 teaspoonful salt.
1 quart milk.	1 saltspoonful white pepper.
1 tablespoonful butter.	¼ saltspoonful cayenne pepper.
2 tablesp. flour or cornstarch.	1 pint water.

Remove the meat of the lobster from the shell, and cut the tender pieces into quarter-inch dice. Put the ends of the claw meat and any other tough, hard parts, with the bones of the body, into one pint of cold water, and boil twenty minutes, adding more water as it boils away. Put the coral on a piece of paper, and dry it in the oven. Boil one quart of milk, and thicken it with one tablespoonful of butter and two of flour or cornstarch. Boil ten minutes. Strain the water from the bones and add it to the milk. Add the salt and pepper, using more if high seasoning be desired. Rub the dried coral through a strainer, using enough to give the soup a bright pink color. Put the green fat and lobster dice into the tureen, and strain the boiling soup over them. Serve immediately.

If you do not like so much of the lobster in the soup, chop it all very fine, boil it with the milk, and rub it through a squash or gravy strainer. Many like the additional thickening of *half a cup* of *fine cracker crumbs.*

This soup may also be varied by using *one pint* of *stock,* either chicken or veal, and *one pint* of *milk;* or by the addition of *force-meat balls* made in the following manner: Cut only half of the meat into dice; chop the remainder, and pound it to a fine paste with the *yolks* of *two hard-boiled eggs, one teaspoonful* of *butter, a little salt,* and *pepper;* beat *one raw egg,* and add enough of it to moisten the paste so that it may easily be made into balls the size of a nutmeg; let them simmer in the soup about five minutes, just enough to cook the egg.

Lobster Soup, No. 2.

The meat of *two small lobsters,* cut fine, *one pint* of *cream, one pint* of *milk.* Simmer twenty minutes. Add *one tablespoonful* of *flour* wet in *cold milk.* *Salt* and *cayenne pepper* to taste. Just before serving add *half a cup* of *butter,* cut into small pieces, and stir till it is entirely absorbed. Strain, and serve very hot.

Oyster Soup.

1 quart oysters.	2 tablespoonfuls flour.
1 pint milk.	Salt to taste.
1 tablespoonful butter.	½ saltspoonful pepper.

Put the milk on to boil in the double boiler, while you prepare the oysters. Place a colander over a pan. Put the oysters in a large bowl, and pour over them *one cup* of *water.* Take up each oyster with the fingers, to make sure no pieces of shell adhere to it, and drain in the colander. Strain the oyster liquor, which has drained from the colander, through the finest strainer. Put it on to boil. Remove the scum, and when clear put in the oysters. Let them simmer, but not boil, until they begin to grow plump and the edges to curl or separate. Strain the liquor into the milk, and put the oysters where they will keep hot, but not cook. Thicken the milk with the butter and flour, which have been cooked together; add salt and pepper to taste (the amount of salt depending upon the saltness of the oysters). Boil five minutes; add the oysters and serve at once. This receipt may be varied by boiling *one cup* of fine chopped *celery* and *a small slice* of *onion* with the milk ten minutes; then straining and thickening it with *half a cup* of *powdered cracker.* Add the butter, the seasoning, and the parboiled oysters. Serve at once.

Oyster Stew is made like oyster soup, without the thickening.

Clam Soup.

½ peck clams in the shell.	1 tablespoonful chopped parsley.
Salt to taste.	1 heaping tablespoonful butter.
1 saltspoonful pepper.	2 heaping tablespoonfuls flour.
¼ saltspoonful cayenne pepper.	1 pint milk or cream.
1 tablespoonful chopped onion.	

Prepare the clams by boiling in the shells, and cutting as directed for clam chowder, keeping the soft part separate from the hard. Pour off one quart of the clam liquor after it settles, being careful not to take any of the sediment; put it on to boil, and remove the scum. Add *one pint* of *hot water,* and season to taste with salt, pepper, cayenne, onion, and parsley. Put in the hard part of the clams. Simmer fifteen minutes, strain, and boil again, and when boiling thicken with the flour cooked in the butter. Add the hot milk or cream, and the soft part of the clams; serve at once, with crackers and pickles.

Another method of preparing clam soup, if needed quickly: Heat the clam broth to a boiling point; add the clams cut fine; season, and pour into the tureen over *two eggs* beaten up with the boiling milk.

The *clam broth* served hot with toasted crackers will often tempt a person with a capricious appetite.

Fish Chowder.

4 or 5 pounds cod or haddock or bass.	1 tablespoonful salt.
	½ teaspoonful white pepper.
6 potatoes.	1 tablespoonful butter.
A 2-inch cube of fat salt pork.	1 quart milk.
2 small onions.	6 butter crackers.

When buying a fish for a chowder, have the head left on but the skin removed ; or if you have to depend upon yourself, remove the skin according to directions on page 161. Then begin at the tail and cut the fish from the bone on one side, keeping the knife as close as possible to the bone ; remove the bone from the other side. Do not forget to take out the small bones near the head. Wipe the fish carefully with a damp cloth, cut it into pieces about two inches square, and put it away in a cool place. Break the bones and head, cover with cold water, and put them on to boil. Pare and slice the potatoes one eighth of an inch thick, using enough to make the same quantity by measurement as you have of fish. Soak them in cold water half an hour, and parboil or scald in boiling water five minutes ; then pour off the water. Cut the pork into quarter-inch dice, and fry it in an omelet pan. Cut the onions into thin slices and fry them in the pork fat, being careful that it does not burn. Pour the fat through a strainer into the kettle, leaving the pork scraps and onions in the strainer. Put the sliced potatoes into the kettle ; hold the strainer over the potatoes, and pour through it enough boiling water to cover them. This is easier than to fry in the kettle, and skim out the pork and onions, — which to a novice would be running the risk of burning the fat, cleaning the kettle, and beginning again. When the potatoes have boiled ten minutes, strain the water in which the bones were boiled, and pour it into the kettle. Add the salt and pepper, and when the chowder is boiling briskly, put in the fish, and set it back where it can sim-

mer ten minutes. Do not break the fish by stirring it.
Add the butter and the hot milk. Split the crackers, put
them in the tureen, and pour the chowder over them. Do
not soak the crackers in cold water. Butter crackers will
soften easily in the hot chowder. If you wish the broth
thicker, stir in one cup of fine cracker crumbs, or one
tablespoonful of flour cooked in one tablespoonful of butter.
More milk and a little more seasoning may be added to
this amount of fish and potato, if you wish to make a larger
quantity. When wanted richer, beat *two eggs*, mix them
with the hot milk, and put in the tureen before turning in
the chowder. If added while the chowder is in the hot
kettle, the eggs will curdle. Any firm white fish may be
used for a chowder, but cod and haddock are best. Many
use a cod's head with the haddock. The head is rich and
gelatinous, and it should always be boiled with the bones,
and the liquor added to the chowder. In this chowder you
have nothing but what the most dainty person may relish.
There are no bones, skin, or scraps of boiled pork. Fish,
potatoes, and crackers are all distinct in the creamy liquid,
instead of being a pasty mush, such as is often served.
For a change, the crackers may be buttered and browned.

If a highly seasoned dish be desired, boil an onion, cut
into thin slices, with the potatoes; add more pepper, and
either cayenne pepper, Worcestershire sauce, or curry
powder. Omit the boiling water, and use only that in
which the bones were boiled, when making a smaller
quantity.

Clam Chowder.

½ peck clams in the shells.
1 quart potatoes, sliced thin.
A 2-inch cube of fat salt pork.
1 or 2 onions.
1 teaspoonful salt.

½ teaspoonful white pepper.
1 large tablespoonful butter.
1 quart milk.
6 butter crackers.

Clam chowder is made in the same manner as fish
chowder, substituting half a peck of clams for the fish.
Clams in the shells are better, as you then have more
clam liquor. Wash with a small brush, and put them

in a large kettle with half a cupful of water, or just enough to keep the under ones from burning; set them over the fire. When the clams at the top have opened, take them out with a skimmer, and when cool enough to handle, take the clams from the shell; remove the thin skin; then with scissors cut off all the black end, cut the "leather straps" into small pieces, leaving the soft part whole. Let the clam liquor settle, and pour it off carefully. Use half water and half clam liquor. Fry the pork and onion the same as in fish chowder; add the potatoes, which have been soaked and scalded, and boiling water to cover. When the potatoes are soft, add the clam liquor, the seasoning, and the clams; when warmed through, add the hot milk and turn into the tureen. Do not put the clams into the chowder until the potatoes are nearly done, as prolonged boiling hardens them.

Corn Chowder.

1 quart raw sweet corn.	1 saltspoonful white pepper.
1 pint sliced potatoes.	1 large tablespoonful butter.
A 2-inch cube fat salt pork.	1 tablespoonful flour.
1 onion.	1 pint sliced tomatoes.
1 teaspoonful salt.	1 pint milk.

Scrape the raw corn from the cob. Boil the cobs twenty minutes in water enough to cover them; then skim them out. Pare, soak, and scald the potatoes. Fry the onion in the salt pork fat, and strain the fat into the kettle with the corn water. Add the potatoes, corn, salt, and pepper. Simmer fifteen minutes, or till the potatoes and corn are tender. Add the butter and milk, and serve very hot with crisped crackers.

Lobster Chowder.

1 pound lobster.	1 scant teaspoonful salt.
1 quart milk.	½ saltspoonful white pepper.
3 crackers.	¼ saltspoonful cayenne pepper.
¼ cup butter.	

Boil one quart of milk. Roll three crackers fine; mix with them one fourth of a cup of butter, and the green fat

of the lobster.   Season with one scant teaspoonful of
salt, half a saltspoonful of white pepper, and one fourth
of a saltspoonful of cayenne pepper.   Pour the boiling
milk gradually over the paste.   Put it back in the double
boiler ; add the lobster meat cut into dice ; let it boil up
once, and serve.

Purée of Clams.

One pint of *boiled clams ;* remove the dark substance
from the soft part, and chop the hard part very fine.
Thicken *one pint* of *hot cream* with *one tablespoonful* of *flour*
cooked in *one heaping tablespoonful* of *hot butter ;* add the
chopped clams, the soft parts, and salt and pepper.   Add
more hot cream or a little of the clam liquor if the purée
be too thick.   When hot, strain it into the tureen.

Courbouillon.

3 onions.	½ cup vinegar.
2 tablespoonfuls butter.	1 pint beef stock.
1 tablespoonful flour.	2 pounds fish, sliced.
1 cup claret, or	4 tomatoes.

Fry the sliced onions in the butter in the bottom of the
stewpan ; be careful not to burn them ; add the flour,
mix well ; add gradually the stock, and, when smooth,
put in half the fish, then half the tomatoes peeled and
sliced, and the wine or vinegar ; then another layer of
fish and tomatoes.   Simmer half an hour.   The fish
should be skinned and boned.

Cherry Soup.

Soups made from fruit juices only slightly sweetened,
thickened with arrowroot and served cold in bouillon cups
are quite acceptable in hot days.   Allow one pint of water
to a pint of fruit.   Stew, mash, and sift the fruit, sweeten
and thicken slightly, then boil till clear.   Some fruits require a little lemon juice or wine.   Add chipped ice and
serve with zwieback or toasted wafers.

FISH.

FISH, on account of its abundance, cheapness, and wholesomeness, is invaluable as an article of food. It is less nutritious and less stimulating than meat, as it contains less solid matter and more water. An exaggerated idea of the value of fish as brain food has prevailed; the latest authorities, however, state that there is no evidence to prove that fish is any richer than meat in phosphorus. But as it contains little fat, the white varieties particularly, it is easily digested, and as it has a large proportion of nitrogenous material, it is especially adapted to all those upon whom there are great demands for nervous energy.

Salmon heads the list " of whatsoever hath scales and fins," in nutritive qualities; and it is richer than meat. The next in value are fat halibut, shad, white-fish, mackerel, blue-fish, lean halibut, bass, flounder, trout, cod, haddock, cusk; etc.

Red-blooded fish, like salmon, mackerel, and blue-fish, have the oil distributed through the body. They are nutritious for those who can digest them, but are too rich and oily for invalids. White fish, like flounder, halibut, cod, and haddock, have the oil in the liver, and are more easily digested. Fish should be perfectly fresh and *thoroughly* cooked, or it will be very indigestible and sometimes poisonous. Broiling and baking are the best methods. Small pan-fish and fillets of large white dry fish are good if fried; but oily fish should never be fried. Salting draws out the nutritive part of fish the same as it does in meat; and either, when thus prepared, should be used as a relish, and not depended upon for nourishment. Fat fish are injured less than white fish, as the fat is not removed by salting.

All varieties of fish need an accompaniment of starchy foods, like bread and potatoes ; and white fish need beside to be cooked with butter or fat to make them desirable as food.   The juices of fish, shell-fish particularly, are of an alkaline nature ; and this renders lemon juice or vinegar a desirable condiment as a neutralizing agency.

The flesh of good, fresh fish is *firm* and *hard*, and will rise at once when pressed with the finger.   If the eyes be dull and sunken, the gills pale, and the flesh flabby or soft, the fish is not fresh.

Fish should be cleaned as soon as possible, in strongly salted water.   They should be washed (not soaked) by wiping with a cloth wet in salt water.   Then wrap them in a cloth which is sprinkled with salt, and put them in a cool place.   If put in the ice-chest, they will taint the butter and milk.   Put ice around them, if necessary ; but do not let them touch the ice, as fresh water and ice will soften them.   When once they lose their hard, firm consistency, they are considered unfit to eat by those who know what good fish really are.

Frozen fish should be thawed in cold water.   Fresh-water fish having a muddy taste or smell are improved by soaking in salt and water.   Salt fish should be soaked in fresh water, with the *skin side up*, to draw out the salt, and should be eaten only occasionally, for the reason before stated.

To Clean a Fish. — If the fish have scales, remove them before opening.   Scrape with a small, sharp knife from the tail to the head ; hold the knife flat and slanting, resting it on the fish, that the scales may be taken upon the knife ; scrape slowly, that the scales may not fly over everything near, and rinse the knife often in cold water.

When the fish is to be served *whole*, do not remove the *head* and *tail*.   Smelts and small fish served whole are opened under the gills, and the contents squeezed out by pressing from the middle with the thumb and finger.   Large fish are split open from the gills half-way down the lower part of the body, the entrails removed, and the inside scraped and cleaned. Open far enough to remove all the blood on the backbone. Many leave the sound, which is the white part adhering to the bone; but it is better to remove it.

To Skin a Fish. — Cut a thin, narrow strip down the backbone, taking off the dorsal fin. Then open the lower part half-way down. Slip the knife under and up through the bony part of the gills, and hold this bony part between the thumb and finger, and strip the skin off toward the tail. Then do the same on the other side.

Small fish, like mackerel and white-fish, when dressed for broiling, should be split through the back.

To Bone a Fish. — Clean, and strip off the skin; lay the fish flat on a board; begin at the tail, and run the knife in under the flesh close to the bone, and scrape it away clean from the bone, holding the flesh carefully, not to break the flakes. When the flesh on one side is removed, slip the knife under the bone on the other side, and raise the bone, leaving the flesh on the board; then pull out all the small bones left in the flesh, which you can easily feel with the fingers. Fish with many fine bones, like shad and herring, are not boned; but from cod, cusk, mackerel, white-fish, and haddock they may be easily removed.

Fillets of Fish are the flesh separated from the bone, and served whole or divided, as the case may require. Flounders or sole, chicken halibut, and bass, should have the fillets on each side divided lengthwise; making four long thin pieces, or fillets. Other fish are cut into thin slices or small squares. Very small fish may be split, the bone removed, and the whole fish rolled up from the tail to the head and fastened with a skewer.

Broiled Fish.

First clean the fish. Wash with a cloth wet in salt water, and dry on a clean fish towel, kept for no other purpose. Mackerel, white-fish, small blue-fish, trout, small cod, and shad should be split down the back, and if you prefer, cut off the head and tail. Halibut and salmon should be cut into inch slices, the skin and bone removed, and turned often while broiling. Cut flounder, bass, and chicken halibut into fillets. Oily fish need only *salt* and *pepper;* but dry white-fish should be spread with *soft butter* or *olive oil* before broili.· ;.

Use a double wire broiler, and grease well with *salt pork* rind. Put the thickest edge of the fish next the middle of the broiler, and always broil the flesh side first, as the skin burns easily. Cook the flesh side until it is brown. The time should vary with the thickness of the fish; move the broiler up and down, that all parts may be equally browned; then turn, and cook on the other side just enough to crisp the skin. Small fish require from five to ten minutes; thicker fish, fifteen or twenty minutes. The fire should be hot and clear. If the fish be very thick, hold it farther from the fire; or when nicely browned, put the broiler in the oven on a dripping-pan, and cook till the flesh separates easily from the bones. Mackerel, trout, and fresh herring are sometimes broiled whole. Clean without opening more than is necessary. Wipe and dry well. Gash through to the bone at intervals one inch apart on each side, and rub *salt, pepper,* and *butter* or *oil* in the incisions; wrap in buttered paper, and broil carefully from ten to twenty minutes. When ready to serve, loosen the fish from the broiler on each side, open the broiler, and, leaving the flesh side of the fish uppermost, slide it off without breaking. Or open the opposite way, hold a platter over the skin side, and invert platter and broiler together. Spread with *butter, salt,* and *pepper;* or add *chopped parsley* or *watercresses;* or serve with Maître d'hôtel, Tartare, Tomato, or Curry sauce. Garnish with *parsley* and slices of *lemon.*

Baked Fish.

Cod, haddock, cusk, blue-fish, small salmon, bass, and shad may be stuffed, and baked whole.

Stuffing for Baked Fish weighing from four to six Pounds.

1 cup cracker crumbs.	1 teaspoonful chopped parsley.
1 saltspoonful salt.	1 teaspoonful capers.
1 saltspoonful pepper.	1 teaspoonful pickles.
1 teaspoonful chopped onion.	¼ cup melted butter.

This makes a dry, crumbly stuffing. If a moist stuffing be desired, use *stale* (not dried) *bread crumbs*, and moisten with *one beaten egg* and the *butter;* or moisten the crackers with warm water.

Oyster Stuffing. — *One pint* of *oysters, one cup* of *seasoned* and *buttered cracker crumbs.* Drain and roll each oyster in the crumbs. Fill the fish with the oysters, and sprinkle the remainder of the crumbs over the oysters.

General Directions. — Fish bake through more evenly, brown better, and are more easily served, if placed upright in the pan instead of on one side. Fish that are broad and short, like shad, may be kept in place by propping with stale bread or pared potatoes. But all others that are narrow in proportion to the length may be skewered or tied into the shape of a letter Ṣ ; run a threaded trussing-needle through the head, middle of the body and tail in the direction indicated by the dotted line above ; then draw the string tight, and fasten the ends. Fish thus prepared will keep their shape after baking.

Have an iron sheet with rings at the ends for handles, and just large enough to fit into the dripping-pan. Rub the sheet well with salt pork, and put pieces of pork under the fish to keep it from sticking. This sheet will enable you to lift the fish from the pan and place it on the platter without breaking. If you have no sheet, put two broad strips of cotton cloth across the pan, before laying in the fish. When done, lift out on the cloth. Do not put water in the pan, unless you wish to steam instead of bake the fish. Put two or three slices of fat salt pork over and near the fish, and when the flour has browned, baste often with the pork fat. Bake till brown, and baste often.

No. 1. — Clean, wipe, and dry the fish; rub with *salt*; stuff and sew. Cut gashes two inches apart on each side. Skewer into shape of Ş, and put it on the fish sheet. Rub all over with *soft butter*, *salt*, and *pepper*. Put narrow strips of *fat salt pork* in the gashes. Dredge well with *flour*. Put it into a hot oven without water; baste when the flour is browned, and baste often afterwards. Remove it

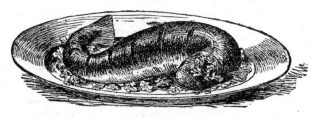

FIG. 7. Baked Fish.

carefully from the fish sheet, and place it on a hot platter. Draw out the strings or skewer, wipe off all the water or fat which runs from the fish, and remove the pieces of pork. Pour Hollandaise sauce around (not over) the fish, or serve a drawn butter sauce flavored with lemon, in a sauce-boat; and pile Saratoga potatoes lightly around the fish. Garnish the head of the fish with parsley or watercresses.

To serve the Fish. — Make an incision along the backbone the entire length of the fish; then draw the fish away from the bone on each side, cutting at right angles with the bone. Raise the bone to reach the stuffing, and serve a little of the fish, stuffing, and sauce to each person. The skeleton should be left entire on the platter.

No. 2. — Remove the head, tail, and skin. Rub well with *salt* and *lemon juice*. Stuff with *oyster stuffing*, and sew securely. Skewer it into shape, if long enough, or put it upright on a greased fish sheet, with bread to keep it in place. Or remove the bone, place the fish on a platter, and lay the prepared oysters between the layers of fish. Season *cracker crumbs* with *salt*, *pepper*, and *chopped parsley*, and moisten with *melted butter*. Brush the fish with *beaten egg*, then sprinkle with the crumbs. Set the platter in the oven over a pan of hot water to keep the platter from cracking. Bake from forty to sixty minutes. Serve with tomato or Hollandaise sauce poured around the fish.

No. 3. Baked Halibut. — Three or four pounds of halibut. Dip the dark skin in *boiling water*, and scrape clean. Rub well with *salt* and *pepper*. Put it into a clean pan, and pour *milk* over it till half an inch deep. Bake about an hour, basting with the milk. Remove the bone and skin, and arrange on the platter in the original form. Serve with plain drawn butter, egg sauce, or cream sauce, and garnish with slices of boiled eggs. The milk keeps the fish moist, is a good substitute for pork, and makes the fish brown better. Use just enough milk to baste, and let it cook away toward the last. Or sprinkle buttered crumbs over the top, when the fish is nearly done, and serve with tomato sauce.

A large cod, or any whole fish too large for a small family, may be cooked as follows: Remove the skin and bones from the middle and thickest part; stuff and bake. Use the bones and head for a chowder. Cut the tail piece into slices, *salt* well, and fry or broil them. Or crimp them by soaking in salted water; then simmer in water with *salt* and *lemon juice*, and serve cold with Tartare sauce.

Fried Fish.

Mackerel, salmon, blue-fish, and all oily fish should never be fried. Smelts, perch, and other small pan-fish may be fried whole. When fried smelts are used as a garnish, fry them in the shape of rings by pinning the tail in the mouth. Cod, halibut, etc., should be skinned and boned, and cut into slices one inch thick and two or three inches square. Flounder and bass may be cut in fillets, as described on page 161, and each fillet seasoned with salt and pepper, and fastened with a small wooden skewer. Small fish may be boned without parting in the middle.

and rolled from tail to head. Fish for frying should be thoroughly cleaned and dried, seasoned with salt and pepper, and covered first with flour or fine bread crumbs, then dipped in beaten egg, then in crumbs again. If this does not cover them completely, repeat the process.

When the fish has been kept on ice, let it become slightly warm before frying, as otherwise it will chill the fat and become greasy. Fry in deep, smoking hot fat. Observe the directions given for frying on page 15, testing the fat first with bread; and after the first plunge into the hot fat set the kettle back to keep from burning; then reheat before frying any more. Fry from two to five minutes. Drain and serve with tomato, or Tartare, or any acid sauce. Garnish with slices of pickle or lemon, and parsley.

Arrange small fish with heads and tails alternating;

FIG. 8.   Small Fish served whole.

or two or three on a skewer, one skewer for each person; or in a circle round a silver cup, placed in the centre of the platter and holding the sauce. Slices or rolled fillets may be arranged in a circle, with the sauce in the centre.

Boiled Fish.

Boiling is the most insipid and wasteful way of cooking fish. To make boiled fish palatable, a rich sauce, like lobster, oyster, or shrimp sauce, is needed for all kinds except salmon and blue-fish. Salmon is so much richer and more oily than other fish that boiling does not injure it. Hollandaise and sauce piquante are appropriate for salmon. A fish kettle with a drainer for lifting out the fish is quite essential. Or you may put a small piece of fish in a wire basket or on a plate; tie the plate in a square of cloth, and lift cloth, plate, and fish together. Never try to boil a fish whole, as nothing can be more unsightly than the head of a boiled fish. Clean the fish thoroughly, and remove the head, tail, and skin. Rub well with *salt* and *lemon juice.* Fish should be of uniform thickness, to boil nicely. A *small salmon* or the *middle cut* of a *large one,* or the thickest part of *cod* or *blue-fish,* or a thick piece of *halibut,* should be selected for boiling. Cod, haddock, and cusk, unless perfectly fresh, will break in boiling.

If fish be put into cold water, the juices are drawn out into the water. If cooked in rapidly boiling water, the fish breaks on the outside before the middle is done. The best and most economical way is to cook it in a steamer over boiling water. If that is not convenient, put the fish into boiling salted water, and simmer till done. Fish is cooked when the flesh separates easily from the bones, and should be taken up immediately, and well drained before serving. A very good way of boiling fish is to steep it for five minutes in strongly salted boiling water, with one or two tablespoonfuls of lemon juice, then plunge it into fresh boiling water without salt, and simmer till done. Less scum rises in the fresh water, and the fish looks whiter. Allow about six minutes to a pound for boiling; more if in a cubical form than for a thin narrow piece of the same weight.

Serve boiled fish on a folded napkin, and the sauce in a sauce-boat. Parisienne potatoes boiled or fried and piled like cannon balls, alternating with parsley and button mushrooms; or sliced pickles, fried oysters, Saratoga potatoes, slices of lemon, or hard-boiled eggs may be used as a garnish. If the fish break and look unsightly, remove the bones, and flake it; pile it lightly on a platter, and pour the sauce over the fish.

To boil Fish au Court Bouillon. — Fish are improved by cooking in water flavored with vegetables and spices. Mince *one onion, one stalk* of *celery,* and *two* or *three sprigs* of *parsley.* Fry them in a little butter; add *two tablespoonfuls* of *salt, six peppercorns, a bay leaf, three cloves, two quarts* of *boiling water,* and *one pint* of *vinegar* or *sour wine.* Boil fifteen minutes, skim well, strain, and keep to use in boiling fish. Rub the fish with *salt* and *lemon juice*, and put it into the boiling liquor, and simmer till the flesh separates from the bone.

Stewed Fish. — Any dry white fish or fresh-water fish may be stewed, and made into a very palatable and economical dish. Remove the skin, head, and bones from a *four-pound fish*. Cover the bones and head with cold water, and cook them for half an hour. Slice and scald *two small onions*. Drain, and fry them till yellow, in the fat obtained from a *two-inch cube* of *salt pork*. Pour it all into the kettle with the bones. Cut the fish into pieces two inches square, and season them with salt and pepper. Put them in a clean kettle with a little butter to keep them from sticking, and strain the boiling bone water over them, using just enough to cover. Add the juice of *half a lemon*, and when boiling thicken with *one heaping tablespoonful* of *butter* and *two* of *flour* cooked together. Simmer fifteen minutes. Add *salt* and *pepper* to taste, and *one tablespoonful* each of chopped *parsley*, and *tomato* or *mushroom catchup*, if desired ; or add *one quart* of *drained oysters*, and simmer till the oysters are plump. A *Matelote* of fish is the French name for fish stewed with wine.

Fish à la Crême.

Four to *six pounds* of *fish*, *one* to *one and a half pints* of *cream sauce*, and *one cup* of *cracker crumbs*, moistened in *one third* of a *cup* of *melted butter*.

This is one of the most attractive and convenient methods of serving any kind of dry white fish, — cod, haddock, or cusk. Clean the fish ; cook in boiling salted water with *one tablespoonful* of *vinegar* till the flesh separates easily. Drain, and when cool remove the skin and bones, and pick apart in flakes. Sprinkle well with *salt* and *pepper*. Make a rich white sauce. Put a layer of fish on a platter suitable for serving. Cover with the white sauce, letting the fish soak up all it will ; then arrange

another layer of fish and sauce. Moisten cracker crumbs
in melted butter, and spread over the top with a fork.
Set the platter in the oven over a pan of hot water, to
keep the platter from cracking, and bake till the crumbs
are brown. Garnish with *parsley.* The *whites* of *two* or
three eggs, beaten stiff and salted, are sometimes used in
the place of crumbs, but are not so palatable. *Two* or
three tablespoonfuls of *grated cheese* may be mixed with
the crumbs, if you like the flavor.

The sauce may be mixed with the fish; but be careful
not to mash the fish or get it too moist. Then the fish
may be piled on the platter, higher and broader at one
end and giving the outline of a flat fish; or arranged in
the form of a fish shaped like the letter S, and covered
with the crumbs. Or, if the fish be not broken in boiling,
take it up carefully on the drainer, remove the head, skin,
and small bones from one side, put a platter over the fish
and invert platter and fish together; then remove the
skin and the backbone from the other side, leaving the fish
as whole as possible. Cover with the sauce and crumbs,
and bake as above. This is not so desirable as the first
method, because some fine bones are liable to be over-
looked, and the sauce is not so well mixed with the fish.

Remnants of Cooked Fish.

Remnants of cold boiled or baked fish (using stuffing
and sauce also) may be freed from skin and bones, flaked,
and used in any of the following ways: —

Scalloped Fish. — Put *fish* and *stuffing* into a shallow dish
in alternate layers, with *cream sauce* to moisten; cover
with *buttered crumbs*, and bake till the crumbs are brown.

Fish in Potato Border. — Warm the *fish* slightly in a
white sauce, and put it in the centre of a dish with a border
of *mashed potatoes.* Or, if you have enough material for
a large platter, put the border on the edge and a higher
mound of *potatoes* in the centre, and fill the space between
with the *fish.* Sprinkle *buttered crumbs* lightly over the
whole and set in the oven till brown.

Chartreuse, or Casserole of Fish, No. 1. — *One cup* of any *cold fish*, flaked, seasoned, and moistened with a little *cream;* the same quantity of *mashed potatoes;* and *two hard-boiled eggs.* Butter a small mould and put in alternate layers of potatoes, fish, and slices of egg. Steam twenty minutes, turn out upon a hot platter, and garnish with *varsley.*

No. 2. — Mix *one cup* of *stale bread crumbs, one pint* of *cold fish,* flaked, and *two eggs.* Season to taste with *Worcestershire* or *tomato catchup, salt,* and *cayenne pepper.* Put into a buttered mould. Boil thirty minutes, and serve with any fish sauce.

Kedgeree. — Warm *cold flaked fish* slightly over hot water; and just before serving stir in *one egg,* beaten with *one* or *two tablespoonfuls* of *hot milk* and a bit of *butter,* and serve in a *rice* border. Steam the rice, *one cupful,* in *two cupfuls* of *highly seasoned stock,* in a double boiler thirty minutes, or till tender and dry.

Curried Fish. — Warm any *cold flaked fish* in *curry sauce,* page 190.

Creamed Fish with Oysters. — Add an equal amount of *oysters* to the *fish,* and cook in *white sauce* till the oysters are plump. Garnish with points of *toast.*

Spiced Fish. — Steep *six cloves, six allspice kernels, six peppercorns,* and *one tablespoonful* of *brown sugar* in *one cup* of *sharp vinegar* ten minutes, and pour it over *one pint* of any *cold flaked fish.*

Crimped Fish.

Soak slices of any firm white *fresh fish* in *very strongly salted water.* Put them into *boiling salted water* enough to cover, with *two tablespoonfuls* of *vinegar,* and boil about ten minutes. Drain; arrange on a platter; remove the skin and bones. Serve hot with *oyster* or *lobster sauce,* or cold with a *Mayonnaise* or *Tartare sauce* poured into the cavity left by the bone. Garnish with *water rresses.*

Potted Fish.

Three shad or *six small mackerel*, uncooked ; *one third* of *a cup* of *salt* with *half a saltspoonful* of *cayenne pepper* mixed with it, and *half a cup* of *whole spices,* — *cloves, peppercorns,* and *allspice* mixed in about equal proportions. *Vinegar* to cover. Clean, remove the skin, split in halves, cut each half into three pieces, and remove all the larger bones. Pack the fish in layers in a small stone jar. (Earthenware must not be used on account of the vinegar.) Sprinkle the salt and spices over each layer. Add *one onion* sliced thin, if you do not dislike the flavor. Add vinegar enough to completely cover the fish. Tie a thick paper over the top, or tie a cloth over and cover with a crust of dough to keep in all the steam. Bake in a very moderate oven five or six hours. Remove the dough-crust, and when cooled cover, and keep in a cool place.

This will keep some time, if the fish be kept under the vinegar ; the bones will be dissolved, and it makes an excellent relish for lunch or tea.

Rules for *Fish Salad, Croquettes,* and *Chowder* are given elsewhere.

Salt Fish Balls.

1 cup raw salt fish.	1 egg, well beaten.
1 pint potatoes.	¼ saltspoonful pepper.
1 teaspoonful butter.	More salt, if needed.

Wash the fish, pick in half-inch pieces, and free from bones. Pare the potatoes, and cut in quarters. Put the potatoes and fish in a stewpan, and cover with boiling water. Boil twenty-five minutes, or till the potatoes are soft. Be careful not to let them boil long enough to become soggy. Drain off all the water ; mash and beat the fish and potatoes till very light. Add the butter and pepper, and when slightly cooled add the egg and more salt, if needed. Shape in a tablespoon without smoothing much, slip them off into a basket, and fry in *smoking hot lard* one minute. Fry only five at a time, as more will cool the fat. The lard should be hot enough to brown a piece of bread while you count forty. Or, first dipping the spoon in the fat, take up a spoonful of the fish and plunge it into the hot fat. Drain on soft paper.

These fish balls should be mixed while the potatoes and fish are hot. If you wish to prepare them the night before, omit the egg, and in the morning warm the fish and potato in a double boiler, then add the egg. Keep the fish in a bowl of cold water while picking it apart, and it will need no further soaking.

Contrary to all old theories, boiling the fish with the potato does *not* harden it. When well mashed and beaten with a strong fork, the fish will only be recognized in the potato by the taste, and not by the presence of hard, lumpy pieces. Never chop salt fish. If picked apart into small pieces and then rubbed with a potato masher till it is reduced to fine threads, it will blend with any mixture better than it will when chopped. These are the most quickly prepared and the most delicious fish balls ever made, and are worthy the superlative adjectives which have been given them by enthusiastic pupils.

Fish Hash. — The same mixture as above, cooked in a little *salt pork fat* in a frying-pan till brown, and turned out like an omelet.

Fish Soufflé. — Prepare the fish as for fish balls ; add *two tablespoonfuls* of *cream* and *two eggs*, beaten separately ; and bake in a buttered dish.

To prepare Salt Fish for Cooking.

Soak over night in cold water with the *skin side up*, that the salt may be drawn out; or, if you can, strip the skin off before soaking. By changing the water often, less time will be required. *Salt mackerel* and other small corned fish should be broiled. *Salt codfish* should be put on the stove in fresh water and kept warm, but not boiling, till softened. Then remove the bones and skin, and flake in delicate pieces. Serve with *egg* or *cream sauce, potatoes, sweet beets, carrots*, and *onions*, and *crisp salt pork* scraps, and you have the old-fashioned *salt fish dinner.*

Creamed Salt Fish. — Serve *one cup* of the picked up *fish* in a rich *cream sauce* with *potato border* or on *toast.*

Mock Oyster Stew. (*Mrs. S. M. Bailey.*) — Prepare *one cup* of *salt fish* by washing, shredding, and simmering till soft; when ready to serve, put it in a shallow dish with *one pint* of *oyster crackers* or *three butter crackers* split and browned, and pour over it *one pint* of *hot milk.* Add *a tablespoonful* of *butter* and *half a saltspoonful* of *pepper*, and serve.

Scorched Salt Fish. — Pick a small piece of the *thickest part* of *salt fish* into long flakes. If very salt, soak a few minutes in cold water. Brown over hot coals. Spread with *butter*, and serve hot. Fish thus prepared is a nice relish with potatoes which have been roasted in the ashes. It will also tempt a convalescent. *Smoked salmon* or *halibut* may be prepared in the same manner.

Tongues and Sounds. — Soak them in warm water several hours, or till freshened; scrape off the skin. Cut them in small pieces and heat slowly in *milk* or *water.* Make a thin *white sauce* to pour over them, and serve on *toast* garnished with *hard-boiled eggs.*

Fish Roes, Fried.

Wash the roes and cook them ten minutes in *boiling salted water* with *one tablespoonful* of *vinegar.* Then plunge them into cold water. Drain, and roll in *beaten egg*, then in *seasoned crumbs*, and fry till brown in *smoking hot fat.*

Scalloped Roes. — Boil the roes as in the preceding receipt. Drain, and break up lightly with a fork. Sprinkle a layer of the roe in a shallow dish; then rub the *yolk* of *hard-boiled egg* through a fine strainer. Add a sprinkling of *parsley* and a little *lemon juice.* Moisten with a thin *white sauce.* Then another layer of *roe, egg, seasoning,* and *sauce.* Cover with *buttered crumbs* and bake till brown. If a larger dish be required, use with the roes any *cold flaked fish*, or a small quantity of *cooked rice.*

Small Fresh Fish Baked in a Crust.

Clean the fish, and wipe dry. Cut gashes one inch apart on each side; sprinkle with *salt* and *pepper.* Make a rich *biscuit crust* with baking-powder, or make a *pastry crust;* roll it out half an inch thick; wrap the fish in the crust, pinch the edges together, and bake about half an hour. Serve with *egg sauce.*

Table of the Cost, etc., of Fish.

	Cost.	*Weight.*	*How sold.*	*When in Season.*
Cod.	8 cts. per lb.	3 to 20 lbs.	Whole.	
Haddock.	6 to 8 cts. per lb.	5 to 8 lbs.	Whole.	
Cusk.	8 cts. per lb.	5 to 8 lbs.	Whole.	Winter.
Halibut.	12 to 20 cts. per lb.		By the lb.	
Flounders.	6 to 10 cts. per lb.	½ to 5 lbs.	Whole.	
Salmon.	25 to 50 cts. per lb.		By the lb.	May to Sept.
Shad.	$1.25 in March, 25 cts. in May.		Whole.	Spring.
Blue-fish.	7 to 15 cts. per lb.	4 to 10 lbs.	Whole.	June to Oct.
Tautog.	12 cts. per lb.		Whole.	July to Sept.
White-fish.	20 cts. per lb.	4 lbs.	Whole.	Winter.
Bass.	12 to 25 cts. per lb.	3 to 8 lbs.	Whole.	
Sword-fish.	15 cts. per lb.		By the lb.	July to Sept.
Smelts.	10 to 25 cts. per lb.	{ Average 8 to a lb.		Sept. to March.
Perch.	20 cts. per dozen.			Summer.
Pickerel.	15 cts. per lb.	1 to 4 lbs.	Whole.	
Trout, Brook.	75 cts. per lb.		Whole.	Spring.
Mackerel.	5 to 25 cts. each.		Whole.	April to Oct.
Eels.	15 cts. per lb.	½ to 1 lb.	Whole.	
Lobsters.	12 cts. per lb.	1 to 2 lbs.		
Oysters.	35 to 50 cts. per qt.			Sept. to May.
Clams.	20 cts. per qt.; 40 cts. per pk. in the shell.			
Crabs.	$1.25 to $1.50 per dozen.			Summer.
Herring.	20 cts. per dozen.			Mar. and Apr.
Salt Cod Fish.	10 cts. per lb., best.			
Smoked Fish.	20 to 35 cts. per lb.			

Where no time is specified the fish are always in season.

SHELL FISH.

Oysters, Clams, Scallops, Lobsters, Crabs, Shrimps, and *Prawns* are the principal varieties of shell fish used as food.

Oysters.

These shell fish are found in perfection in the cool waters of the Northern Atlantic coast. The Blue Points from Long Island are considered the best in the New York market. The Wareham and Providence River are equally esteemed in Boston. Oysters are neither healthful nor well flavored from May to September; at all other times they are used more extensively and are more highly prized than any other shell fish. They are nutritious, and are easily digested when fresh and eaten raw, or when only slightly cooked. When over-cooked, they are tough and leathery. Oysters should never be kept long after being taken from the shell; and if to be used raw, should not be opened till just before using.

Oysters cooked in the Shells. — Wash and scrub the shells, and put them in a pan with the round side down (to hold the juice), and cook either in a hot oven, on the top of a hot stove, on a gridiron over the coals, or in a steamer, ten to twenty minutes. When the shells open, the oysters are done. Remove the upper shell; season the oyster on the lower shell with *butter, pepper, salt,* and *vinegar,* and serve at once. Or take from the shells, put into a hot dish, season, and serve immediately. There is no other way of cooking the oyster in which the natural flavor is so fully developed.

Raw Oysters. — Open the oysters; look them over carefully; remove any fine pieces of shell which may adhere to them; then season slightly with *salt* and *pepper,* and let them stand half an hour in the ice chest. Serve on fancy oyster plates, or on the deep half-shell, with *slices* of *lemon.* Serve with small squares of buttered *brown bread.*

Oysters on Ice. — Put a rectangular block of *clear ice,* having smooth, regular surfaces, in a large pan. With a hot brick or flat-iron melt a cavity large enough to hold the desired number of oysters. Pour the water from the cavity, and fill with oysters, which should first be drained, and seasoned with *salt* and *pepper.* Place a thick napkin on a platter, put the ice upon this, cover the dish with *parsley* or *smilax,* and garnish with *lemon.* The ice is sometimes roughly chipped to resemble a rock. If the dinner be served from the sideboard, individual plates of ice are made.

To prepare Oysters for Cooking. — Pour half a cup of cold water over one quart of oysters; then with clean hands take out the oysters separately and remove any bits of shell or seaweed. Serious accidents have often resulted from the presence of pieces of shell. The crabs which are found among the oysters are considered a delicacy and should be saved. The oyster liquor is seldom used, as enough comes from the oysters in cooking; but, if desired, it should be strained before using. The oysters may then be cooked in any of the following ways.

To cook or parboil Oysters in their Liquor. — Put them in a saucepan without water; stir them, or shake the pan slightly; as soon as heated, sufficient liquor comes from them to keep them from burning. When the edges curl or ruffle, and the oysters look plump instead of flat, they are cooked. Season with *salt, pepper,* and *butter,* and serve as a *plain roast;* or pour on *toast,* and call it a *fancy roast.*

For *Oyster Stew,* see page 154.

Smothered Oysters. — Put *one tablespoonful* of *butter* in a covered saucepan with *half a saltspoonful* of *white pepper, one teaspoonful* of *salt,* and *a few grains* of *cayenne pepper.* When hot, add *one pint* of *oysters* carefully prepared. Cover closely, and shake the pan to keep the oysters from sticking; cook two or three minutes, or till plump. Serve on *toasted crackers.*

Creamed Oysters. — Make *one cup* of *thick cream sauce* (see page 190), and season with *salt, pepper, cayenne,* and *celery salt.* Wash and pick over *one pint* of *oysters,* and parboil until plump. Skim carefully; drain and add them to the sauce. Serve on *toast,* and garnish the dish with *points* of *toast;* or the toast may be omitted, and *bread crumbs* browned in *butter* sprinkled over the oysters. When served in *patty shells* or in a *vol-au-vent,* make the cream sauce thicker.

Fricasseed Oysters. — Cook *one pint* of *oysters* in *hot butter,* till plump, as directed for smothered oysters. Drain, and keep the oysters hot, and add enough *cream* to the oyster liquor to make *one cupful.* Cook *one tablespoonful* of *flour* in *one tablespoonful* of *hot butter.* Add slowly the hot cream and oyster liquor. Season with *one teaspoonful* of *lemon juice, salt,* and *pepper* to taste. Pour the sauce into *one well-beaten egg,* add the hot oysters, and heat one minute. Serve on *toast,* if for breakfast; or in *paper cases,* or *patties,* if for lunch or dinner.

Scalloped Oysters. — *One pint* of *solid oysters,* washed and drained; *one third* of *a cup* of *melted butter; one cup* of *cracker* or *stale bread crumbs,* moistened in the melted butter. Butter a shallow dish; put in a layer of crumbs, then a layer of oysters; season with *salt* and *pepper;* and, if you like, add *Worcestershire sauce, lemon juice, wine,* or *mace.* Then put in another layer of crumbs, then oysters and seasoning, with a thick layer of crumbs on the top. Bake in a hot oven about twenty minutes, until the crumbs are brown. Many prefer to heat the oyster liquor and the butter with an equal quantity of milk or cream, and use more cracker. Moisten each layer of cracker with the hot liquid. Reserve the larger part of the butter for the top layer of crumbs. In this way a larger dish may be prepared with the same quantity of oysters.

Oysters en Coquille. — Prepare as for scalloped oysters. Put one or two very large or several smaller oysters in

1

oyster or scallop shells; season, and cover with buttered crumbs. Bake till the crumbs are brown. Place the shells on small plates, and serve one to each person.

Large scallop shells may be obtained at the fish market, then cleaned and used several times. Tin, granite, or silver shells may also be used.

Oysters and Mushrooms in Crusts. — Bake *Parker-House-roll dough* in round pans, or as small round biscuit placed some distance apart. When cold, cut a slice from the top of each, and remove the soft inside without breaking through the crust. Fill with the following mixture: —

Parboil *half a pint* of *oysters*. Strain, and save the liquor. Cut the oysters fine, and mix with them *half a can* of *chopped mushrooms*. Mix the oyster liquor and mushroom juice with enough *cream* to make *one pint* in all. Pour this hot liquid slowly on *one tablespoonful* of *butter* and *three* of *flour* cooked together. Season highly with *salt, pepper, lemon juice,* and *cayenne*. Pour this into the crusts, and serve at once. This dish is acceptable to those who cannot eat oysters in puff-paste patties.

Pigs in Blankets, or Huîtres au Lit. — Season large oysters with *salt* and *pepper*. Cut very thin slices of *fat bacon;* wrap each oyster in a slice of bacon, and fasten with a wooden skewer. Put in a hot omelet pan, and cook just long enough to crisp the bacon. Serve on small pieces of delicate *toast*.

Fried Oysters. — Wash the oysters, drain, sprinkle with *salt* and *pepper*, and let them stand twenty minutes. Roll first in *seasoned crumbs*, then dip in *beaten egg* mixed with *one tablespoonful* of *milk;* roll in *crumbs* again, and fry one minute in *smoking hot lard*. Drain on paper, and garnish with *chopped* or *sliced pickle*, or *chowchow*. Serve with *cold slaw* or *celery salad*.

Fried oysters are much better, and spatter less in frying, if parboiled slightly and drained before rolling in the crumbs. When only a few are wanted, and those especially nice, select the large oysters, roll them in fine *crumbs*, then in *Mayonnaise dressing*, then in *crumbs* again, and fry.

Sautéd Oysters. — Prepare as for frying, and brown on each side in *hot butter;* or roll in the *cracker* only, and brown them.

Oysters in *Fritter Batter*, see page 107.

Broiled Oysters. — Pick over, and drain large oysters. Dip in *melted butter*, then in *fine cracker crumbs* seasoned with *salt* and *pepper.* Butter a fine wire gridiron; put the oysters in closely, and broil till the juice flows. Some prefer to broil them without the crumbs, but more juice is lost in this way.

Pickled Oysters. — Cook *one quart* of *oysters* in their liquor, till plump. Remove the oysters, and add to the liquor *half a cup* of good cider *vinegar.* Skim as it boils, and add *one teaspoonful* of *salt, two blades* of *mace, ten cloves, ten peppercorns, ten allspice berries,* and a few grains of *cayenne pepper.* Boil five minutes. Pour the liquor over the oysters, and when cold seal in glass jars, and put in a cool dark place. They will keep two weeks.

Clams.

Thin shell clams, and round shell clams, or quahaugs, furnish a delicious and wholesome form of food if eaten only when fresh. They are more easily opened and have a finer flavor when cooked in the shells.

Steamed Clams. — Wash and scrub the shells. Put them in a kettle without water, cover closely, and cook till the shells open. Take them out with a skimmer, pour the clam water into a pitcher, and let it settle. Straining is not sufficient, as the fine sand will go through the finest strainer; but the water will be clear if care be taken not to disturb the sediment. Remove the clams from the shells, peel off the thin skin around the edge, and cut off the whole of the black end. Scissors are better than a knife for this purpose. Rinse each clam in a little of the clam water, and if very large, cut the tough part into small pieces. When the water is clear, pour it into a saucepan, add the clams, and heat again till just hot, but do not let them boil. Serve with *brown bread*, or *toasted crackers;* and let each person season them to taste with *melted butter, pepper,* and *vinegar.*

Scalloped Clams. — Prepare the clams as in steamed clams. Make a *white sauce,* as for fish (see page 189); put the clams in a shallow dish or in clean shells; cover with the sauce and *buttered crumbs,* and bake till brown.

For *Clam Soup, Clam Chowder,* and *Clam Fritters,* see the Index.

A Clam Bake.

An impromptu clam bake may be had at any time at low tide along the coast where clams are found. If you wish to have genuine fun, and to know what an appetite one can have for the bivalves, make up a pleasant party and dig for the clams yourselves. A short thick dress, shade hat, rubber boots, — or, better still, no boots at all, if you can bring your mind to the comfort of bare feet, — a small garden trowel, a fork, and a basket, and you are ready. Let those who are not digging gather a large pile of driftwood and seaweed, always to be found along the shore. Select a dozen or more large stones, and of them make a level floor; pile the driftwood upon them, and make a good brisk fire to heat the stones thoroughly. When hot enough to crackle as you sprinkle water upon them, brush off the embers, letting them fall between the stones. Put a thin layer of seaweed on the hot stones, to keep the lower clams from burning. Rinse the clams in salt water by plunging the basket which contains them in the briny pools near by. Pile them over the hot stones, heaping them high in the centre. Cover with a thick layer of seaweed, and a piece of old canvas, blanket, carpet, or dry leaves, to keep in the steam. The time for baking will depend upon the size and quantity of the clams. Peep in occasionally at those around the edge. When the shells are open, the clams are done. They are delicious eaten from the shell, with no other sauce than their own briny sweetness. Melted butter, pepper, and vinegar should be ready for those who wish them; then all may "fall to." Fingers must be used. A Rhode Islander would laugh at any one trying to use a knife and fork. Pull off the thin skin, take them by the black end, dip them in the prepared butter, and bite off close to the end. If you swallow them whole, they will not hurt you. At a genuine Rhode Island clam bake, blue-fish, lobsters, crabs, sweet potatoes, and ears of sweet corn in their gauzy husks are baked with the clams. The clam steam gives them a delicious flavor. Brown bread is served with the clams, and watermelon for dessert completes the feast.

Scallops.

This shell fish has a round, deeply grooved shell. The muscle which unites the shell is the only part eaten. Scallops have a sweet flavor, and are in season during the fall and winter. They may be stewed like oysters, but are better fried.

Fried Scallops. — Pick over, and wash quickly; drain between towels; season *fine cracker crumbs* with *salt* and *pepper.* Dip the scallops in the crumbs, then in *beaten egg,* and again in crumbs. Fry in *smoking hot fat,* and serve at once.

Lobsters.

The markets are now so well supplied with these delicious shell fish, that they may be obtained in good condition all the year. The canned lobster is also convenient in an emergency, for use in soups and salads. Lobsters are put alive into boiling salted water, and cooked twenty minutes from the time the water boils. They should not be eaten until cold, and never be kept more than eighteen hours after boiling. Lobsters are difficult of digestion, and should be eaten with mustard, cayenne pepper, and lemon juice or vinegar.

To Choose a Lobster. — Select one of medium size, heavy in proportion to the size. Those with hard, solid shells, streaked with black, will be found full of meat; those with thin shells are watery. If the tail spring back quickly when straightened, the lobster is fresh.

To Open a Lobster. — Wipe the shell with a wet cloth. Break off the large claws, separate the tail from the body and the body from the shell, leaving the stomach, or lady, in the shell; then remove the small claws. Save the green liver and coral. Crush the tail by pressing the sides together, then pull it open on the under side, and take out the meat in one piece. Draw back the flesh on the upper end of this meat, and remove the intestinal canal, which runs the entire length. This is sometimes black, and sometimes the color of the meat. Break off all the gills on the body before picking the meat from the joints, as they are liable to drop off with the meat, and are too woolly to be palatable. The gills, stomach, and intestines are the only parts not eaten. Break the body in the middle, and pick the meat from the joints, being careful not to take any of the bones. When the shells of the large claws are thin, cut off a strip down the sharp edge, and remove the meat whole; or break them by hammering on the edge. Never pound them in the middle, as that crushes the meat. If the lobster shell is to be used for serving the meat, cut down the under side of the tail with a sharp knife, and remove the meat without breaking the outside shell. Trim the inside, and clean the shell. The body shell may be cleaned, split in halves, and trimmed with sharp scissors into the shape of clam shells.

Plain Lobster. — The simplest way of serving lobster is by many considered the best. Remove the meat from the shell, and arrange in a tasteful manner; or cut it into small pieces. Let each person season to taste with *salt, pepper, vinegar,* and *oil,* or *melted butter.*

Stewed Lobster. — Cut the lobster fine; put it in a stewpan, with a little *milk* or *cream.* Boil up once; add *one tablespoonful* of *butter,* a little *pepper,* and serve plain or on *toasted crackers.* Cook lobster just long enough to heat it, as a longer cooking renders it tough.

Creamed Lobster. — For *one pint* of *lobster meat* cut fine, make *one pint* of *white sauce* (see page 189). Season with *salt, cayenne,* and *lemon.* Heat the lobster in the sauce, but do not let it boil. Serve on *toast.*

Curried Lobster. — Make a *curry sauce* (see page 190). and warm the diced lobster in the sauce.

Fig. 9. Scalloped Lobster.

Scalloped Lobster. — Season *one pint* of *lobster,* cut into dice, with *salt, pepper,* and *cayenne.* Mix with *one cup* of *cream sauce* (see page 190) ; fill the lobster shells, using the tail shells of two lobsters. Cover the meat with *cracker crumbs,* moistened with *melted butter.* Bake till the crumbs are brown. Put the two shells together on a platter, with the tail ends out. to look like a long canoe. Lay the small claws over the side to represent oars. Garnish with *parsley.* The lobster may also be served in scallop shells.

Devilled Lobster. — The same as the preceding receipt, with the addition of more *salt, pepper,* and *cayenne ;* add, also, *chopped parsley, onion juice, mustard,* and *Worcestershire sauce.*

For *Lobster Soup, Chowder, Cutlets, Croquettes,* and *Salad,* see the Index.

Crabs.

These are found near the coast of the Southern and Middle States, and are considered such a luxury in Maryland that special means are taken for their propagation. They are usually quite expensive in Eastern markets.

Crabs, like lobsters, shed their shell annually. When the new shell is forming, they are called soft shell crabs, and are highly esteemed by epicures.

Soft Shell Crabs. — Use them only when freshly caught, as the shells harden after twenty-four hours. Pull off the sand bags, and the shaggy substance from the side; then wash, and wipe dry; sprinkle with *salt* and *pepper;* roll in *crumbs*, then in *egg*, again in *crumbs;* and fry in *smoking hot lard.*

Boiled Crabs. — These should be heavy, of medium size, and with stiff joints. Plunge them head first into boiling water, and cook fifteen minutes; then remove the outside shells and the shaggy substance, rinse in hot water, and arrange on a platter. They are eaten from the shell.

Scalloped Crabs. — Pick the meat from the shells, mince it, and mix with a *cream sauce;* season with *salt* and *pepper*, put the mixture in the crab shell or in scallop shells, cover with *buttered cracker crumbs*, and bake till brown.

Devilled Crabs. — Prepare as for scalloped crabs, adding *mustard*, *cayenne pepper*, and *lemon juice* to the seasoning.

Crab Salad. — Mix the meat with a *Mayonnaise dressing*, pack in the crab shells, and garnish with *sliced lemon* and *cresses.*

Shrimps.

Shrimps and *Prawns* are found in the summer season on the Southern coasts. They are similar in form to a lobster, but very small. They should be cooked in boiling salted water from five to eight minutes. Remove the shells and head; the part that is eaten resembles in shape the tail of a lobster. They are used in fish sauces, and are very effective as a garnish.

Shrimp Salad and *Shrimps en Coquille* may be prepared like lobster. Canned shrimps are generally used in Eastern markets.

Scalloped Shrimps. — Make a *tomato sauce* (see page 193). Pick over *one can* of *shrimps*, and heat them in the sauce;

add *one glass* of *wine*. Turn into a scallop dish, cover with *buttered crumbs*, and bake till the crumbs are brown.

Reptiles.

Fried Frogs. — Frogs are considered a delicacy by those who have cultivated a taste for them. If not already pre-pared for cooking, remove the skin from the *hind legs*, which is the only part used. Dip in *crumbs*, seasoned with *salt* and *pepper*, then in *egg*, and again in *crumbs*. Wipe the bone at the end; put in a basket, and fry one minute in *smoking hot fat*. Drain, and serve in a circle, around a centre of *green peas*. Some parboil them three minutes in *boiling salted water* and a little *lemon juice* before frying.

Frogs' legs may also be *broiled*, or they may be made into a *white* or *brown fricassee*, seasoned with *mushrooms* or *tomato catchup*.

Terrapin.

This expensive member of the turtle family is highly prized in Baltimore and Philadelphia, but seldom used in New England. Terrapin may be kept alive through the winter by putting them in a barrel, where they will not freeze, and feeding them occasionally with vegetable parings. Before cooking, soak them in strong salt water. Put them alive into boiling water, and boil rapidly ten or fifteen minutes. Remove the black outside skin from the shells, and the nails from the claws. Wash in warm water; then put them on again, in fresh boiling water; add a little salt, and boil about three quarters of an hour, or until the under shell cracks. Open them carefully over a bowl to save the gravy, remove the under shell, the sand bags, the head, and the gall bladder from the liver. If the gall bladder be broken in the process, the whole dish will be ruined by the escaping gall. Put the upper shells on to boil again in the same water, and boil until tender; watch them carefully, and take each out as soon as tender. Pick the liver and meat from the upper shell, and cut into several pieces. The intestines are used with the meat in winter, when the turtle is in a torpid condition; but in the summer they should be thrown away. Boil the intestines by themselves one hour. This should be prepared the day before. Heat the meat in the gravy. To each terrapin add *one wineglassful* of *cream, half a cup* of *butter,* a little *salt, cayenne,* and *one wineglassful* of *sherry.* Use the turtle eggs if there be any; if not, the *yolks* of *two hard-boiled eggs* to each terrapin. Rub smooth, mixing with raw yolk enough to make into balls the size of turtle eggs. Add these and the wine just as you send the dish to the table.

Green Turtle Soup.

The green turtle is highly prized on account of the delicious quality of its flesh; but as it is very large and expensive the canned turtle is more generally used.

One can of *green turtle, one quart* of *brown stock, two tablespoonfuls* each of *butter* and *flour, one lemon.* Cut the green fat into dice and lay it aside. Simmer the remainder of the turtle meat in the stock for half an hour. Brown the flour in the browned butter, add it to the soup, season highly with *salt* and *pepper.* Serve with *thin slices* of *lemon, egg balls,* and the reserved green fat.

Crab Olio — A Southern Recipe.

Scald and skin *six* large, smooth *tomatoes,* and drain on a sieve until the water is out. Chop fine the meat of *four* large *crabs* and the inside of *one egg-plant* which has been boiled, also the cold tomatoes. Add *three eggs,* slightly beaten, *salt* and *pepper* to taste, and *half a cup* of *bread crumbs.* Cook until warmed through in *a tablespoonful* of *butter,* but do not brown it. Put it into the crab shells, cover with buttered crumbs, place the shells in a pan, and bake until the crumbs are brown.

MEAT AND FISH SAUCES.

Drawn Butter, or water and melted butter thickened with flour, and seasoned, is the simplest form of a sauce.

When milk, or cream, or white stock is used in place of water, less butter is required, and the sauce is called *White*, or *Cream*, or *Béchamel sauce*.

By browning the butter, using brown stock, and adding different seasoning materials, we have all the varieties of *Brown sauces*.

Many people fail in making sauces by not cooking the flour sufficiently, and also by serving them with a mass of oily butter on the surface. Usually the flour is wet to a smooth paste and stirred into the boiling liquid. When made in this manner, the sauce should boil at least ten minutes to have the flour thoroughly cooked. But by cooking the dry flour in the hot butter the starch in the flour is more quickly cooked, and the butter is all absorbed and converted into an emulsion. Sauces made in this manner are perfectly smooth, free from grease, and have a fine flavor. Every one should learn how to make both white and brown sauces. They are adapted to nearly every form of food. Meats, fish, vegetables, eggs, macaroni, rice, toast, etc., are rendered more palatable by being served with an appropriate sauce.

Drawn Butter Sauce.

1 pint hot water or white stock.	2 tablespoonfuls flour.
	½ teaspoonful salt.
½ cup butter, scant.	⅛ saltspoonful pepper.

Put half the butter in a saucepan; be careful not to let it become brown; when melted, add the dry flour, and mix well. Add the hot water, a little at a time, and stir rapidly as it thickens. When perfectly smooth, add the remainder of the butter in small pieces, and stir till it is absorbed. Add the salt and pepper. When carefully made, this sauce should be free from lumps; but if not smooth, strain it before serving.

The following sauces may be made with one pint of this plain drawn butter as a foundation : —

Caper Sauce (for Boiled Mutton). — Add *six tablespoonfuls* of *capers*. *Pickled Nasturtium seeds* may be used in place of capers.

Egg Sauce (for Baked or Boiled Fish). — Add *two* or *three hard-boiled eggs*, sliced or chopped.

Parsley Sauce (for Boiled Fish or Fowls). — Add *two tablespoonfuls* of *chopped parsley*.

Lemon Sauce (for Boiled Fowl). — Add the juice and pulp of *one large lemon*, and the *chicken liver* boiled and mashed fine.

Shrimp Sauce (for Fish). — Add *half a pint* of *shrimps*, whole or chopped, *two teaspoonfuls* of *lemon juice*, and *a few grains* of *cayenne pepper*.

Acid Sauce. — Add *one tablespoonful* of *lemon juice* or *vinegar*, and *a few grains* of *cayenne pepper*.

Mustard Sauce (for Devilled Turkey, Salt Fish, etc.). — Add *three tablespoonfuls* of *mixed mustard* and *a little cayenne pepper*.

Lobster Sauce (for Boiled Fish). — *One pint* of *lobster meat*, cut into quarter-inch dice. Put the inner shells and scraggy parts in one and a half pints of cold water, and boil fifteen minutes. Strain and use the water in making one pint of drawn butter sauce. Add the *lobster dice*, the *dried* and *powdered coral*, a little *cayenne pepper*, and *two tablespoonfuls* of *lemon juice*.

Oyster Sauce (for Boiled Fish, Turkey, or Chicken). — Parboil *one pint* of *oysters ;* drain, and use the oyster liquor in making *one pint* of *drawn butter sauce*. Season with *celery salt* and *cayenne pepper*. Add the oysters ; cook one minute longer, and pour it over the fish or chicken. Add the beaten yolk of *one egg* or *one glass* of *claret wine*, if you wish a richer sauce.

Celery Sauce (for Boiled Fowl). — *One pint* of the tender part of *celery*, cut very fine. Cook in *boiling salted water*, enough to cover, till tender. Drain; add enough hot water to that in which the celery was cooked to make a pint, and use it in making one pint of drawn butter sauce. Add the cooked celery and the seasoning.

Richer Drawn Butter Sauce. — Make a plain *drawn butter sauce*, and when ready to serve, pour it boiling hot into the well-beaten *yolks* of *two eggs*. Stir thoroughly, season to taste, and serve at once.

Sauce Piquante. — Add *one tablespoonful* each of *vinegar* and *lemon juice*, two *tablespoonfuls* each of *chopped capers*, *pickles*, and *olives*, *half a teaspoonful* of *onion juice*, and *a few grains* of *cayenne pepper*, to *one pint* of *drawn butter*.

White Sauce (for Vegetables, Chicken, Eggs, etc.).

1 pint milk, or half milk and half white stock.	2 heaping tablespoonfuls flour.
	½ teaspoonful salt.
2 tablespoonfuls butter.	½ saltspoonful pepper.

Heat the milk over hot water. Put the butter in a granite saucepan, and stir till it melts and bubbles. Be careful not to brown it. Add the dry flour, and stir quickly till well mixed. Pour on one third of the milk. Let it boil, and stir well as it thickens; tip the saucepan slightly to keep the sauce from sticking. Add another third of the milk; let it boil up and thicken, and stir vigorously till perfectly smooth. Be sure that all the lumps are rubbed out while it is in this thick state. Then add the remainder of the milk; let it boil, and when smooth add the salt and pepper, using more if high seasoning be desired.

This white sauce may be used in place of drawn butter in any of the preceding rules.

Béchamel Sauce. — A white sauce made partly with cream and partly with rich white stock, either veal or chicken, according to directions for white sauce, is called Béchamel.

The water in which celery, oysters, or lobsters have been cooked may be mixed with milk in making sauces given under these names.

For *Fish à la crême* and other preparations of fish, boil *one slice* of *onion* with the milk, or add *half a teaspoonful* of *onion juice* and *one tablespoonful* of *chopped parsley.*

For *Oysters*, add *half a teaspoonful* of *celery salt, a few grains* of *cayenne pepper,* and *one tablespoonful* of *lemon juice.*

For *boiled Fowl,* add *half a can* of *mushrooms.*

A richer *white sauce* is made by *beating* the *yolks* of *two eggs,* and pouring the hot sauce into them just before serving.

Curry Sauce (for Curried Eggs, Chicken, etc.). — Cook *one tablespoonful* of *chopped onion* in *one tablespoonful* of *butter* five minutes. Be careful not to burn it. Mix *one tablespoonful* of *curry powder* with *two tablespoonfuls* of *flour,* and stir it into the butter. Add *one pint* of *hot milk* gradually, and stir as directed for white sauce.

Cream Sauce, No. 1.

1 pint hot cream.	½ teaspoonful salt.
1 heaping tablespoonful butter.	½ saltspoonful pepper.
2 heaping tablespoonfuls flour.	

Make in the same manner as white sauce, and vary the seasoning for the different dishes for which it is to be used, as directed in white sauce.

A *thicker Cream Sauce* is given under rules for Croquettes.

Cream Sauce, No. 2.

Warm *one cup* of *cream.* Beat the *yolks* of *two eggs,* strain them into the warm cream, and cook over hot water till the eggs thicken the cream like boiled custard. Stir all the time and when smooth and thickened remove from the fire, and add *salt* and *pepper* to taste. Serve with boiled celery, cauliflower, chicken, oysters, fish, etc.

Brown Sauce.

1 pint hot stock.	½ teaspoonful salt.
2 tablespoonfuls minced onion.	½ saltspoonful pepper.
2 tablespoonfuls butter.	1 tablespoonful lemon juice.
2 heaping tablespoonfuls flour.	Kitchen Bouquet to color.

Mince the onion and fry it in the butter five minutes. Be careful not to burn it. When the butter is brown, add the dry flour and stir well. Add the hot stock a little at a time, and stir rapidly as it thickens, until perfectly smooth. Add the salt and pepper, using more if high seasoning be desired. Simmer five minutes, and strain to remove the onion.

The stock for brown sauces may be made from bones and remnants of any kind of meat, by soaking them in cold water, and boiling until the nutriment is extracted. The onion may be omitted if the flavor be not desired; but the sauce is better with it if it be not burned.

By the addition of different seasoning materials to this brown sauce a great variety of sauces may be made. Half the quantity given is sufficient for most entrées, or to use for any purpose in a small family. Be very careful not to burn the butter, as the desired color can better be obtained by adding Kitchen Bouquet.

Brown Sauce Piquante (for Beef). — To *one cup* of *brown sauce* add *one tablespoonful* each of *chopped pickles* and *capers.*

Sauce Poivrade. — Make *one cup* of *brown sauce;* add *one teaspoonful* of *mixed herbs, thyme, parsley, bay leaf,* and *cloves.* Simmer ten minutes; add *two tablespoonfuls* of *claret,* and strain.

Sauce Robert. — To *one cup* of *brown sauce,* add *one teaspoonful* of *sugar, one teaspoonful* of made *mustard,* and *one tablespoonful* of *vinegar.*

Brown Mushroom Sauce (for Beef). — To *one cup* of *brown sauce* add *half a can* of *mushrooms,* whole or quartered,. and simmer five minutes.

Currant Jelly Sauce (for Mutton). — Make *one cup* of

brown sauce, strain it, and add *half a cup* of *melted currant jelly.* Heat till the jelly is well mixed, and serve very hot.

Olive Sauce (for Roast Duck). — Soak *twelve olives* in hot water enough to cover, thirty minutes, to extract the salt. Pare them round and round, close to the stone, leaving the pulp in a single piece, which should curl back into the natural shape after the stone is removed. Make *one cup* of *brown sauce,* add the olives, and simmer ten minutes.

Cumberland Sauce. — To *one cup* of *brown sauce* add *one teaspoonful* of made *mustard, two tablespoonfuls* of *currant ielly,* and *two tablespoonfuls* of *wine.*

Flemish Sauce (for Beef or Veal). — Cut *a cupful* of the *red part* of *carrot* into quarter-inch dice, and cook in *boiling salted water* till tender. Make *one cup* of *brown sauce,* add the cooked carrot, *half a tablespoonful* of *chopped parsley, one tablespoonful* each of *chopped pickles* and *grated horseradish.*

Sauce à la Italienne. — Fry *one tablespoonful* of *fine chopped shalots* in *one tablespoonful* of *salad oil* till yellow. Add *one bay leaf,* a *sprig* of *parsley, one tablespoonful* of *chopped mushrooms ;* fry five minutes. Remove the bay leaf, add *two tablespoonfuls* of *flour,* mix well, and add *one cup* of *stock.* When smooth, add *two tablespoonfuls* of *mushroom catchup,* and *one teaspoonful* of *essence of anchovy.* Serve without straining.

Chestnut Sauce (for Roast Turkey). — Remove the shells from *one pint* of *large chestnuts.* Scald or boil them three minutes to loosen the inner skin. Remove the skin ; break them in halves, and look them over carefully. Cook in *salted boiling water* or *stock* till very soft. Mash fine in the water in which they were boiled. Cook *one tablespoonful* of *flour* in *two tablespoonfuls* of *brown butter,* stir into the chestnuts and cook five minutes. Add *salt* and *pepper* to taste.

The boiled chestnuts may be added to the gravy made from the drippings of the poultry, or to *one cup* of *white sauce.* Common chestnuts are much sweeter and more highly flavored, but it takes a long time to prepare them.

Peanut Sauce may be made in the same manner.

Port Wine Sauce (for Venison). — *Half a cup of port wine, half a glass of melted currant jelly, one saltspoonful of salt,* a little *cayenne pepper,* one *teaspoonful* of *lemon juice, half a cup* of *thick brown stock,* or *half a cup* of the *drippings* from the *meat* freed from fat. Heat all together till very hot.

Espagnole Sauce. — Boil one quart of *strong consommé* or rich, highly seasoned brown stock, till reduced to one pint. Then use it as given under the rule for brown sauce, and flavor with *wine.*

Bread Sauce (for Game).

1 pint milk.	½ teaspoonful salt.
⅓ cup fine bread crumbs.	½ saltspoonful pepper.
2 tablespoonfuls chopped onion.	⅔ cup coarse bread crumbs.
1 tablespoonful butter.	1 tablespoonful butter.

Boil the fine bread crumbs and onion in the milk fifteen minutes, and add the butter, salt, and pepper. Fry the coarse bread crumbs in another tablespoonful of butter till brown. Pour the sauce around the birds, and sprinkle the brown crumbs over the whole.

Soubise Sauce (for Lamb or Mutton Chop).

Boil *three large onions* till very soft. Drain, and rub the onion through a sieve. Stir the onion pulp into *half a pint* of *white sauce* made with *milk* or *cream.*

Tomato Sauce (for Macaroni).

Stew *half a can* of *tomatoes* and *half a small onion* ten minutes. Rub all the tomato pulp through a strainer. Cook *one tablespoonful* of *butter* and *one heaping tablespoonful* of *flour* in a granite saucepan; add the strained tomatoes gradually, and *one saltspoonful* of *salt* and *a shake* of *white pepper.*

13

Tomato Sauce (for Chops or Fish).

½ can tomatoes.	2 sprigs parsley.
1 cup water.	1 tablespoonful chopped onion.
2 cloves.	1 tablespoonful butter.
2 allspice berries.	1 heaping tablesp. cornstarch.
2 peppercorns.	½ teaspoonful salt
1 teaspoonful mixed herbs.	½ saltspoonful pepper

Put the tomato, water, spices, herbs, and parsley on to boil in a granite saucepan. Fry the onion in the butter till yellow, add the cornstarch, and stir all into the tomato. Simmer ten minutes; add the salt and pepper, and a little cayenne pepper, and strain the sauce over boiled meat or fish.

Hollandaise Sauce (for Baked or Boiled Fish). (*Miss Parloa.*)

½ cup butter.	1 saltspoonful salt.
Yolks of 2 eggs.	¼ saltspoonful cayenne pepper.
Juice of ½ lemon.	½ cup boiling water.

Rub the butter to a cream in a small bowl with a wooden or silver spoon. Add the yolks, one at a time, and beat well; then add the lemon juice, salt, and pepper. About five minutes before serving, add the boiling water. Place the bowl in a saucepan of boiling water and stir rapidly until it thickens like boiled custard. Pour the sauce around the meat or fish.[1]

Tartar Sauce (Hot, for Broiled Fish).

1 tablespoonful vinegar.	1 tablespoonful Worcestershire
1 teaspoonful lemon juice.	sauce.
1 saltspoonful salt.	⅓ cup butter.

Mix the vinegar, lemon juice, salt, and Worcestershire sauce in a small bowl, and heat over hot water. Brown the butter in an omelet pan, and strain into the other mixture.

[1] Sprinkle chopped parsley and pickles over the sauce if you like.

Tartar Sauce (for Broiled or Devilled Chicken).

One tablespoonful each of *mustard, Chili vinegar, shalot vinegar,* and *claret wine,* and *two tablespoonfuls* of *Harvey sauce.* Heat in a bowl over hot water, and pour it over the chicken.

Horseradish Sauce (Hot, for Beef).

4 tablesp. grated horseradish.	1 teaspoonful salt.
4 tablesp. powdered cracker.	½ saltspoonful pepper.
½ cup cream.	1 teaspoonful made mustard.
1 teaspoonful powdered sugar.	2 tablespoonfuls vinegar.

Mix, and heat over hot water.

Horseradish Sauce (Cold).

Cream *one fourth* of *a cup* of *butter* till very light; add *two tablespoonfuls* of *grated horseradish, one tablespoonful* of very thick *cream,* and *half a teaspoonful* of *Tarragon vinegar.* Keep it on the ice till thick and cold.

Sauce Tartare (Cold, for Fried or Boiled Fish, Tongue, Fish Salad, or Broiled Chicken).

1 teaspoonful mustard.	3 tablespoonfuls vinegar.
½ saltspoonful pepper.	1 tablespoonful chopped olives.
1 teaspoonful powdered sugar.	1 tablespoonful chopped capers.
1 saltspoonful salt.	1 tablespoonful chopped cucumber pickles.
Few drops onion juice.	
Yolks 2 raw eggs.	1 tablespoonful chopped parsley.
½ cup oil.	

Mix in the order given; add the yolks, and stir well; add the oil slowly, then the vinegar and chopped ingredients. This will keep for several weeks.

Maître d'Hôtel Butter (Cold, for Beefsteak).

¼ cup butter.	1 tablespoonful chopped parsley.
½ teaspoonful salt.	1 tablespoonful lemon juice.
½ saltspoonful pepper.	

Rub the butter to a cream; add salt, pepper, parsley, and lemon juice. Spread it on hot beefsteak.

Maître d'Hôtel Sauce (Hot).

Add the beaten *yolks* of *two eggs* to the cold *Maître d' Hô-tel butter*, and when ready to serve add *one pint* of *drawn butter*, made with strong *white stock.*

Sauce for Fish Balls (Cold).

2 teaspoonfuls dry mustard.	1 teaspoonful flour.
1 teaspoonful salt.	1 teaspoonful soft butter.
1 teaspoonful sugar.	2 tablespoonfuls vinegar.

Mix in the order given, in a granite saucepan; add *half a cup* of *boiling water*, and stir over the fire till it thickens and is smooth. Serve it cold.

Mint Sauce (for Lamb).

1 cup fresh chopped mint.	½ cup vinegar.
¼ cup sugar.	

Use only the leaves and tender tips of the mint. Let it stand an hour before serving. Use more sugar if the vinegar be very strong.

Bearnaise Sauce.

Heat *two tablespoons* of *Tarragon vinegar* and *two* of *water*, and steep in it *a slice* of *onion*. Cream *four tablespoons* of *butter* very light. Beat the *yolks* of *four eggs* slightly, add *half a teaspoon salt* and *one salt-spoon paprika*. Remove the onion, and add the hot liquid to the egg. Cook over the fire, stirring constantly until it is thick and smooth. Lift it up frequently, and stir well from the bottom. Often the heat in the thickened portion is sufficient to cook the remainder. When all thickened, add the creamed butter, a fourth at a time, and stir each portion until well blended. Serve it on broiled steak or chops.

For fish, add *one tablespoon* each of fine chopped *pickles*, and *parsley*.

EGGS.

WHATEVER else you may economize in, do *not* limit your family in respect to eggs. They are nutritious, and even at four cents each are cheaper than meat. They should be used freely by all except those who *know* they cannot digest them. *Using freely* does not mean their unnecessary or extravagant use in rich cakes, custards, etc., nor in the indigestible form of fried or what is ordinarily called hard-boiled eggs; but it means the frequent use of them in any of the simple forms of boiling, baking, omelets, plain cake, and other wholesome combinations. It is very poor economy, especially for those who keep hens, to exchange eggs for corned beef or salt fish; or to use soda and cream of tartar as a substitute for eggs in sponge cake, or half-cooked flour in an omelet. They may be served in an unlimited variety of styles, are especially suitable for breakfast or lunch, attractive as a garnish, and when combined with sugar and milk make the most healthful puddings, desserts, or tea dishes.

But though a type of perfect food, eggs are not intended to be eaten exclusively, any more than other foods. They are one of the most highly concentrated forms of food, and, being wholly destitute of starch, should be eaten with bread or rice.

The white of the egg has but a trace of fat in it, and requires the addition of butter, milk, or fat meat, like bacon or ham. The white of egg contains water, mineral ingredients, and soluble albumen; the yolk has, in addition to these, oil and sulphur. The albumen is enclosed in layers of thin-walled cells. When beaten, these walls break, and the albumen, owing to its glutinous nature, catches and holds the air, and increases to many times its original bulk.

Do not use an egg till it has been laid ten hours, as the white does not become set or thick till then, and cannot be beaten stiff. Eggs for poaching or boiling are best when thirty-six hours old. Albumen, when heated, becomes a dense solid; if mixed and heated with a liquid, it hardens and entangles in its meshes any solids or impurities in the liquid, and rises to the surface with them as scum, or precipitates them. It is thus the white of egg clears soups, jellies, and coffee. Strong acids, corrosive sublimate, and creosote will also coagulate albumen; and therefore, if any of these poisons be taken into the system, the white of egg, swallowed quickly, will combine with the poison and protect the stomach.

The shells of newly laid eggs are almost full; but as the shells are porous, on exposure to the air, the water inside evaporates, and the eggs grow lighter, while air rushes in to fill the place of the water, and causes the nitrogenous elements to decompose, and the eggs soon spoil. This explains why a good egg is heavy, and will sink in water; and why a stale egg is lighter, has a rattling or gurgling sound, and floats in the water. Anything which will fill up the pores and thus exclude the air, when applied to perfectly fresh eggs, will preserve them indefinitely; a coating of liquid fat or gum, or a packing in bran or salt, with the small end downward, is effectual. Eggs should be kept in a cool, dark place, and handled carefully, as any rough motion may cause the white and yolk to become mixed, by rupturing the membrane which separates them, and then the egg spoils quickly.

Never buy eggs about the freshness of which you have any doubt, not even in winter. One can easily judge which is the better economy, — to pay twenty-five or thirty cents a dozen, and find none of them full and fresh, and perhaps half of them really rotten; or to pay fifty cents, and obtain them freshly laid, — not merely fresh from the country, — and all sound and good. Eggs with a dark shell are richer and have larger yolks. Eggs are of better flavor and more palatable in the spring, but are good and suitable, if perfectly fresh, at any season.

Boiled Eggs (the Best Way).

Put the eggs in a saucepan, cover with boiling water, and let them stand about ten minutes where the water will keep hot (180°), but not boiling. The white should be of a soft jelly-like consistency, and the yolk soft but not liquid. Experience will show the exact time to keep the eggs in the water to suit individual tastes. They should be served immediately, as they harden by being kept in the hot shell. An egg, to be cooked soft, should never be cooked in *boiling water*, as the white hardens unevenly before the heat reaches the yolk.

Hard-boiled Eggs. — Cook eggs for twenty minutes in water just below the boiling-point, for use in any receipt which specifies *hard-boiled* eggs. The yolk of an egg cooked ten minutes is tough and indigestible; twenty minutes will make the yolk dry and mealy; then it may be more easily rubbed smooth for salad or other mixtures, and more quickly penetrated by the gastric fluid. If the shell of an egg be cracked before boiling, pierce several small holes in the large end to keep the contents from bursting out at the crack.

Dropped or Poached Eggs on Toast.

Toast a slice of bread for each egg, and trim neatly, or cut with a round cutter before toasting. Have a very clean shallow pan nearly full of salted and boiling water. Remove all the scum, and let the water simmer. Break each egg carefully into a cup, and slip it gently into the water. Dip the water over them with a spoon, and when a film has formed on the yolk and the white is firm, take each up with a skimmer; drain, trim the edges, and place on the toast. Put a bit of *butter* and a little *salt* and *pepper* on each egg; or make a *thin cream sauce* and pour it around them. Put *a tablespoonful* of *lemon juice* in the water, or poach the eggs in muffin-rings to give them a better shape. An egg-poacher, something like a castor with perforated cups, is very convenient.

No. 2. — Spread the toast with *butter* and *anchovy paste* or *sardine paste*, and serve a poached egg on each slice; or spread the toast with *potted* or *finely minced boiled ham.*

Ham and Eggs. — Serve poached eggs on thin slices of *broiled* or *fried ham ;* when served on hot, highly seasoned boiled *rice,* they are called *Spanish Eggs.*

Eggs poached in Tomatoes, or à la Dauphine. (*M. L. Clarke.*) — Stew slowly for ten minutes *half a can of tomatoes* and *one small onion,* cut fine. Season highly with *salt* and *pepper* and *butter.* Break *six eggs* into a bowl without beating, and when everything else is ready to serve slip them into the hot tomatoes. Lift the white carefully with a fork, as it cooks, until it is all firm; then prick the yolks and let them mix with the tomato and white. It should be quite soft, but with the red tomatoes, the white and yellow of the egg, quite distinct. Serve at once on toast.

Scrambled Eggs. — Beat *four eggs* slightly with a fork; add *half a teaspoonful* of *salt,* *half a saltspoonful* of *pepper,* and *half a cup* of *milk.* Turn into a hot buttered omelet pan and cook quickly, stirring all the time till the egg is firm but soft. Serve on *toast* or with hot *minced ham* or *veal.* Any of the ingredients given in fancy omelets may be mixed with the beaten eggs before cooking.

No. 2. — Put *a tablespoonful* of *butter* in an omelet pan; when hot, add *three whole eggs ;* stir quickly till the mixture is firm but soft. Add a little *salt* and *pepper,* and serve at once.

Omelets.

Beat the *yolks* of *two eggs* till light-colored and thick; add *two tablespoonfuls* of *milk, one saltspoonful* of *salt,* and *one fourth* of a *saltspoonful* of *pepper.* Beat the *whites* of *two eggs* till stiff and dry. Cut and fold them lightly into the yolks till just covered. Have a clean, smooth omelet pan. When hot, rub it round the edge with *a teaspoonful* of *butter* on a broad knife; let the butter run all over the pan and when bubbling turn in the omelet quickly and spread it evenly on the pan. Lift the pan from the hottest part of the fire and cook carefully, until

slightly browned underneath; slip the knife under to keep it from burning in the middle. Put it on the oven grate to dry (not brown)

Fig. 10. Plain Omelet.

the top. When the whole centre is dry as you cut into it, run a knife round the edge, then under the half nearest the handle, and fold over to the right. Hold the edge of a hot platter against the lower edge of the pan, and invert the omelet upon the platter. Or add only half of the beaten whites to the yolks, and when nearly cooked spread the remainder over the top; let it heat through; fold over, and the white will burst out round the edge like a border of foam, making a *foam omelet*, or any fancy name you may choose to give it.

If you have no omelet pan, or no convenience for drying the omelet in the oven, use a smooth iron spider or frying-pan with a tin cover, and double the quantities given. Heat the pan and the cover very hot. Butter the pan, turn in the mixture, cover it, and place on the back of the stove for five minutes, or till firm. Fold as usual. Omelets should be only slightly browned, never burned, as the flavor of scorched egg is not agreeable.

One tablespoonful of *chopped parsley*, or *a teaspoonful* of *fine grated onion*, or *two* or *three tablespoonfuls* of *grated sweet corn* may be added to the yolks before cooking.

Thin slices of *cold ham*, or *three spoonfuls* of *chopped ham*, *veal*, or *chicken; stewed tomatoes* or *raw tomatoes sliced;* chopped *mushrooms, shrimps, oysters* which have been par boiled and drained; *cooked clams*, chopped fine; or *grated cheese*, — may be spread on the omelet before folding, giving all the varieties of *fancy omelets*, each variety taking the name of the additional ingredient.

No. 2. — Beat *six eggs* until light and foamy with a Dover egg-beater; add *half a teaspoonful* of *salt* and *one scant salt-spoonful* of *pepper*, and *one cup* of *milk*. Fry a large spoonful at a time in a hot pan or on a griddle, and roll over quickly like a French pancake. This is a convenient way where the family come irregularly to breakfast. The mixture may stand for some time if beaten again thoroughly before frying.

Creamy Omelet. (*Mrs. Ewing.*) — Beat *four eggs* slightly with a spoon till you can take up a spoonful. Add a scant *half-teaspoonful* of *salt*, *half a saltspoonful* of *pepper*, *four tablespoonfuls* of *milk* or *cream*, and mix well. Butter a hot omelet pan, and before the butter browns turn in the mixture. Then with the point of a fork pick or lift up the cooked egg from the centre and let the uncooked egg run under. This leaves the butter on the pan, and is better than stirring. Continue the lifting until the whole is of a soft creamy consistency; then place it over a hotter part of the fire to brown slightly; fold and turn out as usual.

Sweet or Jelly Omelet. — Allow *a teaspoonful* of *powdered sugar* to *each egg*, and omit the pepper. Mix and cook as in Omelet No. 1, and when ready to fold put *two* or *three tablespoonfuls* of any kind of *preserves, marmalade,* or *jelly* on the top. Fold and sprinkle with *sugar*.

FIG. 11. Orange Omelet.

Orange Omelet. — The *thinly grated rind* of *one orange* and *three tablespoonfuls* of the *juice, three eggs,* and *three teaspoonfuls* of *powdered sugar*. Beat the *yolks;* add the *sugar*, *rind*, and *juice;* fold in the *beaten whites*, and cook as in Omelet, No. 1. Fold, turn out, sprinkle thickly with powdered sugar, and score in diagonal lines with a clean red-hot poker. The burnt sugar gives to the omelet

a delicious flavor. Or cut the orange into sections, remove the seeds and tough inner skin; cut each section
into pieces, and mix with the yolks before cooking; or
spread part of the orange over the omelet before folding,
and sprinkle the remainder over the sugared top.

This is a convenient dessert for an emergency, and may
be prepared in ten minutes if one have the oranges.

Omelet Soufflé. — Allow *a heaping teaspoonful* of *powdered sugar, a few drops* of *lemon* or *vanilla* for flavoring,
and *two whites* to each yolk. To make a small omelet,
beat the *yolks* of *two eggs* till light and thick; add *two
heaping teaspoonfuls* of *powdered sugar* and *half a teaspoonful* of *lemon* or *vanilla.* Beat the *whites* of *four eggs* till
stiff and dry, and fold them lightly into the yolks. Put it
by the tablespoonfuls lightly into a well-buttered baking-
dish. Cook in a moderate oven about twelve minutes, or
till well puffed up and a straw comes out clean. Serve at
once, as it falls quickly.

Baked Eggs.

Small stone china dishes or egg-shirrers, holding one or
two eggs for each person, are convenient for this method
of serving eggs; or use a common platter placed over hot
water; or bake in the shells in a moderate oven ten minutes,
first pricking several holes with a large pin in the large end
of the egg, to keep the air within from bursting the shell
as it expands.

No. 1. — Break each egg into a cup, being careful not to
break the yolk, and put the eggs on a hot buttered dish
suitable for serving. Put a little *salt* on each egg. Bake
until the white is firm. Add a little *butter* and serve
at once. Garnish each egg with thin strips of *breakfast
bacon.*

No. 2.— Cover the buttered dish with *fine cracker crumbs.*
Put each egg carefully in the dish, and cover lightly with
seasoned and *buttered crumbs.* Bake till the crumbs are
brown.

No. 3. — Beat the whites of the eggs to a stiff froth, and salt slightly. Spread it roughly on a platter; make a nest or cavity for each yolk some distance apart. Season, and bake till the white is brown.

No. 4. — Cover the dish with any *poultry gravy* you may chance to have, or with *white sauce*, and have a slice of *toast* or *bread* sautéd for each egg. Set the platter in the oven over a pan of hot water, and when toast and gravy are hot drop the eggs on the toast, and bake till the eggs are set.

Eggs en Coquille. — Cut *slices* of *stale bread* in large rounds ; then with a smaller cutter cut half-way through and scoop out the centre, leaving them shaped like a *paté* shell, with the cavity large enough to hold one egg. Dip these bread shells in *raw egg*, beaten with a *little milk*, and sauté, or fry them in hot fat. Put them on a platter covered with hot *white sauce* or *poultry gravy*, and serve *a poached egg* in each shell ; or put *a raw egg* in each and bake till the eggs are set. *Half a cup* of *chopped* or *sliced mushrooms* may be cooked in the gravy. The shells may be toasted if you prefer.

No. 2. — Take *half a cup* of *soft bread crumbs*, an *equal amount* of *fine chopped ham* or *tongue*, and a little *pepper, salt, parsley, mustard*, and *melted butter*. Make it into a smooth paste with *hot milk* or *cream*. Spread the mixture on some scallop shells. Break the eggs carefully, and put one in the centre of each shell ; sprinkle with a little *salt* and *pepper*, and *fine cracker crumbs* moistened with *melted butter*. Set in the oven, and bake five or six minutes, or until the egg is firm. Or put the bread and meat mixture in a baking-dish, shaping it a little to hold *six* or *seven raw eggs ;* cover lightly with *buttered crumbs*, and bake till the whites of the eggs are firm.

Eggs and Minced Meat. — Chop *one pint* of *cold chicken, ham*, or *veal* fine, and rub it to a smooth paste ; add *one tablespoonful* of *melted butter, one tablespoonful* of *chopped parsley, salt* and *pepper* to taste, and *two beaten eggs*. If too dry, moisten with a little *cream* or *stock* or *gravy*, but do not

have it too soft to shape. Heat it in a frying-pan just
enough to warm through, letting it dry off if too moist.
Form it on a hot platter into a flat mound ; hollow the centre, leaving a ridge of the mixture round the edge. Keep
it hot, and put *three* or *four poached eggs* in the centre.

Fig. 12.   Eggs and Minced Meat.

Garnish with triangles of *toast* laid round the base of the
meat.   Or, if you have a larger quantity of meat, prepare
as above, and make a mound one inch deep on a round
dish and a smaller mound above that, and place eggs
baked in cups, or hard-boiled eggs cut in halves, or egg
baskets on the space between the mounds.   Garnish with
parsley.

Pannikins. — Warm *minced ham* or *tongue* or *veal* in a
thick cream sauce, and pile it in the centre of a platter.
Heat and butter some earthen cups, break an egg in each,
and bake till the egg is firm.   Turn them out and arrange
round the meat.

Various Ways of Serving Hard-boiled Eggs.

Curried Eggs. — Boil *six eggs* twenty minutes.   Remove
the shells and cut into halves or slices.   Fry *one teaspoonful* of *chopped onion* in *one tablespoonful* of *butter*, being
careful not to burn it ; add *one heaping tablespoonful* of
flour or *one even tablespoonful* of *cornstarch* mixed with *half
a tablespoonful* of *curry powder*.   Pour on slowly *one cup
and a half* of *white stock* or *milk* or *cream ;* add *salt* and
pepper to taste.   Simmer till the onions are soft.   Add

the eggs, and when warmed through serve in a shallow dish; or arrange the eggs on hot *toast*, and pour the sauce over them; or cover with *buttered crumbs* and bake till the crumbs are brown.

Egg Vermicelli. — Boil *three eggs* twenty minutes. Separate the yolks and chop the whites fine. Toast *four slices* of *bread;* cut half into small squares and half into points or triangles. Make *one cup* of *thin white sauce* with *one cup* of *cream* or *milk*, *one teaspoonful* of *butter*, *one heaping teaspoonful* of *flour*, *half a teaspoonful* of *salt*, and *half a saltspoonful* of *pepper.* Stir the whites into the sauce, and when hot pour it over the squares of toast. Rub the *yolks* through a fine strainer over the whole, and garnish with a border of toast points and a bit of *parsley* in the centre.

Or cut the bread into rounds before toasting. Pour the white sauce on the hot platter, and put the rounds of toast on the sauce some distance apart. Put a little of the chopped white on each slice, pile it high on the edge, rub the yolks through a fine strainer over the centre, and lay small sprigs of fine parsley between the toast.

Stuffed Eggs. — Boil *six eggs* twenty minutes. Remove the shells and cut carefully lengthwise. Remove the yolks, and put the two whites of each egg together,

that they may not become mixed. Mash the yolks, and add *one teaspoonful* of *soft butter*, *a few drops* of *onion juice*, and *half* the quantity of *potted* or *devilled ham* or *tongue.* Or, if *minced chicken, lamb*, or *veal*

Fig. 13. Stuffed Eggs garnished with Parsley.

be used, season to taste with *salt, pepper, mustard*, and *cayenne* or *chopped parsley.* Fill the whites with the mixture, smooth them, and press the two halves together, being careful to fit them just as they were cut. Spread the remainder of the yolk mixture on a shallow dish and place the eggs on it. Cover with a *thin white sauce*, or any *chicken* or *veal gravy;* sprinkle *buttered crumbs* over the whole, and bake till the crumbs are a delicate brown.

No. 2. — After the eggs are filled with the mixture and put together as above, roll each egg in *fine bread crumbs* and *beaten egg* and in *crumbs* again, then repeat the process, and fry in *smoking hot fat.* Drain, and serve hot with *tomato sauce* or garnished with *parsley.*

Scotch Eggs. — *One cup* of *lean cooked ham* chopped very fine; *six hard-boiled eggs.* Cook *one third* of *a cup* of *stale bread crumbs* in *one third* of *a cup* of *milk* to a smooth paste. Mix it with the ham; add *half a teaspoonful* of *mixed mustard, half a saltspoonful* of *cayenne,* and *one raw egg. Mix well,* remove the shells from the eggs, and cover with the mixture. Fry in *hot fat* two minutes. Drain, and serve hot or cold, for lunch or picnics. Cut them into halves lengthwise, and arrange each half on a bed of fine *parsley.* The contrast between the green, red, white, and yellow gives a very pretty effect.

No. 2. — Boil *six eggs* twenty minutes. Make a force-meat with *one cup* of any kind of *cold meat* finely chopped, *half a cup* of *soft bread crumbs* cooked to a paste, in *one third* of *a cup* of *milk* and *one raw egg,* beaten light, using just enough of the egg to unite the mixture, being careful not to have it too soft.

If *chicken* be used, season with chopped *parsley* and *a pinch* of *herbs;* season *ham* with *mustard* and *cayenne; veal,* with *lemon juice* or *horseradish;* and *salmon,* with *lemon* and *cayenne.*

Divide the eggs crosswise or lengthwise, or leave them whole. Cover each half or whole egg thickly with the force-meat, and place them on a buttered tin pan and bake in a hot oven till slightly browned. Arrange on a hot platter with a *white sauce* poured around (not over) them.

Scalloped Eggs. — Boil *six eggs* twenty minutes. Make *one pint* of *white sauce* with *stock* and *cream* or *milk,* and season to taste. Moisten *one cup* of *fine cracker crumbs* in *one fourth* of *a cup* of *melted butter* or *cream.* Chop fine *one cup* of *ham, tongue, poultry,* or *fish.* Remove the *yolks* of the eggs, and chop the *whites* fine. Put a layer of *buttered crumbs* in a buttered scallop dish, then a layer of *chopped whites, white sauce, minced meat, yolks* rubbed through a fine strainer, and so on, until the material is all used, having the buttered crumbs on the top. Bake till the crumbs are brown.

Egg Balls in Baskets. — Boil *three eggs* twenty minutes. Remove the shells, cut off a thin slice at each end, that the eggs may stand upright, and cut in halves crosswise. Remove the yolks, and stand the cups or baskets thus made around the edge of a platter. Rub the *yolks* to a smooth paste; add an equal amount of cooked *ham* or *tongue*, chopped fine, *one tablespoonful* of *melted butter, salt, pepper*, and *mustard* to taste. Make into balls the size of the original yolks, and fill the cups. Make *one cup* of *white sauce*, with *cream* or *milk* and *white stock*, seasoned with *salt* and *pepper*. Pour it in the centre of the eggs. Set the platter in the oven a few minutes, and when ready to serve put a tiny bit of *parsley* on each ball.

In place of the meat, you may use, if you prefer, *two tablespoonfuls* of *grated cheese, a speck* of *cayenne pepper*, and moisten with *vinegar* and *olive oil*.

Eggs à la Crême.

Boil *three eggs* twenty minutes. Cut off a slice at each end, and cut the eggs in halves crosswise. Remove the yolks, and cut them in thin slices. Mix with them an equal amount of small thin pieces of *cold chicken, ham, salmon*, or *lobster*, and season to taste. Fill the white

FIG. 14. Eggs à la Crême.

cups with the mixture. Place them on a shallow dish and pour *one cup* of *thick cream sauce* (page 190) around them. The sauce should come nearly to the top of the cups. Or cut the eggs in halves, and place them with the cut side down and serve in the sauce.

Eggs in a Nest.

Boil *six eggs* twenty minutes. Remove the shells. Separate the *yolks* without breaking; or rub them to a smooth paste with a little *olive oil* to moisten, and shape into *small* balls. Cut the *whites* in thin narrow slices, and mix with them an equal quantity of *fine shredded chicken, ham,* or *salmon,* and *a tablespoonful* of fine *sprigs* of *parsley.* Pile this mixture, which should be light and dry, on a platter in a circular or oval ring, and put the yolks in the centre. Set the platter in a steamer, to heat the mixture. Make *a pint* of *thick white sauce ;* pour enough of it round the edge of the dish to come half-way up the nest, and serve the remainder in a sauce-boat.

The same materials may be served cold as *Devilled Eggs.* Mix a little *cayenne pepper* and made *mustard* with the *yolks* and also with the *shredded meat;* add *a sprinkling* of *vinegar,* and garnish the dish with *parsley* or *watercresses.* Or serve as a salad, garnished with *cresses* or *lettuce,* and sprinkle a *French dressing* over the whole.

Egg Salad may be served in this form. Cut the *yolks* in dice, and mix them lightly with diced *chicken, salmon, fish,* or *lobster;* fill the *white cups* heaping with the mixture, and serve on a *bed* of *lettuce* or *cresses,* with *French* or *Mayonnaise dressing.*

Egg Timbales.

Beat *six eggs* lightly with fork till well mixed, add *one and one-half cups* of *milk, one teaspoonful* of *salt,* a little *pepper, one teaspoonful* of *minced parsley, one-fourth teaspoonful* of *onion juice;* stir all well, pour into well-buttered moulds, — set in pan of hot water, and cook in moderate oven till firm. Serve with either *cream* or *tomato sauce.*

Hot Eggs.

Into a hot bowl kept in very hot water break *two eggs,* add *one teaspoon* of *butter* and a dash of *salt* and *pepper,* beat them slightly, and when they taste *hot,* serve at once. Excellent when nourishment is needed quickly.

14

MEAT.

MEAT is a general term applied to the flesh of animals used for food. It includes the muscular flesh, sinews, fat, heart, liver, stomach, brains, and tongue. Meat is divided into three classes : —

Meat, including beef, veal, mutton, lamb, and pork.

Poultry, including chicken, turkey, geese, and ducks, or all domestic fowls.

Game, including partridges, grouse, pigeons, quail, or other birds, venison, and any wild meat that is hunted in the forest or field.

Meat consists of several substances, — *fibrine, albumen, gelatine, fat*, and the *juice of flesh*.

Fibrine exists in the blood and flesh. In the former it is soluble, owing to the alkaline nature of the blood ; it is deposited by the blood, made into flesh, and becomes .insoluble flesh-fibrine, and forms the basis or fibre of muscular tissue. It is separated into bundles by membranes, and into larger separate masses by cellular tissue, in which fat is deposited. Its true color is white; but the blood in the veins which penetrate every part of the fibre gives it a reddish tinge. This may be seen by washing a piece of lean meat in cold water. The red coloring matter is soon drawn into the water, and the meat is a mass of white fibre. Fibrine is hardened and contracted by intense heat, but softened by moderate and long-continued heat. Meat that has tough fibre should simmer and not boil.

Albumen exists in the flesh and in the blood. It is the soluble portion of the flesh. It dissolves in cold water, but hardens in hot water.

Gelatine is a peculiar substance found in the tendons

and gristly parts of flesh, the shin, and the sinewy parts about the joints, and in the nutritive parts of bones. It may be dissolved by soaking in cold water, and then boiling gently for several hours. The solution hardens when cold. Gelatine hardens in a dry heat, and such parts of meat as contain it in abundance should be stewed, rather than roasted or broiled.

Fat of meat is contained, a good measure of it, in the adipose tissue of almost all flesh which is used as food. It is liquefied by heat, and resolved into various acid and acrid bodies. It is a warmth-giver, and is therefore most appropriately used in cold seasons and climates.

The juice of the flesh consists of water, a small proportion of albumen, and a mixture of other compounds. It is not the blood, for it still exists after the blood has been withdrawn. It may be obtained by chopping lean meat fine, putting it in a closely covered jar without water, and heating it gradually. If heated above 160°, the albuminous matters in it harden and turn brown. The solid residue, consisting of fibres, tissue, etc., is white, tasteless, and inodorous. This separated juice is strongly acid, while the blood is always alkaline. It contains many substances which are very valuable as food, and the savory principle, or *ozmazome*, which gives flavor to the meat and causes it to differ in different animals. Meat should always be cooked in such a manner as to retain the largest proportion of this juice. The juice is drawn out into the brine in salting, and this renders salt meat less nutritious. The juice when the water has been separated from it by evaporation, is termed *extract of meat.*

The flesh of all young animals is more tender, but not so nutritious as that of maturer animals. Nearly all parts of an animal may be used as food.

Meat is in season all the year; but certain kinds are better at stated times. *Pork* is good only in autumn and winter; *veal*, in the spring and summer; *venison*, in the winter; *fowls*, in autumn and winter; *lamb*, in the summer and fall; *mutton* and *beef* at any time.

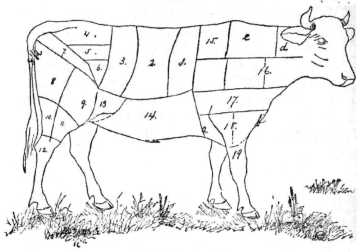

FIG. 15.   Diagram of Ox.

1. Tip of Sirloin.
2. Middle of Sirloin.
3. First Cut of Sirloin.
4. Back of Rump.
5. Middle of Rump.
6. Face of Rump.
7. Aitch Bone.
8. Lower Part of Round.
8½. Top of Round.
9. Vein.
10. Poorer Part of Round.
11. Poorer Part of Vein.

12. Shin.
13. Boneless Flank.
14. Thick Flank with Bone.
15. First Cut of Ribs.
c. Chuck Ribs.
d. Neck.
16. Rattle Rand.
17. Second Cut of Rattle Rand.
18. Brisket (a. the navel end; b the butt end).
19. Fore Shin.

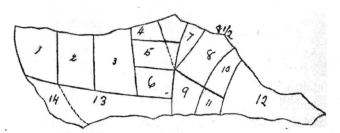

FIG. 16.   Hind Quarter of Beef.

The figures in the hind quarter correspond to those in the same section of the whole ox.

All meat should be removed from the brown paper in which it is wrapped as soon as it comes from the market, or it will taste of the paper and the paper will absorb the meat juices. Wipe all over with a clean wet cloth. Chops and steaks will keep sweet much longer if examined at once, and any parts that are not clean and sweet removed. In warm weather look at the meat often. Put it on a dish near, but never directly upon, the ice.

Cost of Meat and Game.

Shin of beef,	3 to 6 cts. per lb.	Lamb, leg,	14 to 30 cts. per lb.	
Middle cut of shin,	7 to 10 " "	Lamb, chops,	15 to 40 " "	
Lower part of round,	13 to 15 " "	Lamb, fore quarter,	10 to 25 " "	
Vein,	20 to 25 " "	Veal, knuckle,	12 to 17 " "	
Top of round,	20 to 25 " "	Veal, cutlet,	22 to 28 " "	
Aitch bone,	8 to 10 " "	Veal, breast,	9 to 14 " "	
Face of rump,	17 to 22 " "	Sweetbreads,	25 to 70 " whole.	
Middle, "	25 to 28 " "	Calf's liver,	25 to 70 " "	
Back, "	22 to 30 " "	Calf's heart,	5 to 8 " each.	
Sirloin,	28 to 33 " "	Calf's head,	25 to 60 " "	
Whole tenderloin,	75 c. to $1.00 "	Fresh pork,	9 to 15 " per lb.	
Small "	30 to 45 cts. "	Salt pork,	11 to 15 " "	
Tip of sirloin,	22 to 30 " "	Bacon, bag,	17 to 20 " "	
First cut of rib,	17 to 25 " "	Bacon, slices,	15 to 18 " "	
Second cut of rib,	15 to 20 " "	Ham, bag,	17 to 20 " "	
Chuck rib,	7 to 14 " "	Ham, sliced,	20 to 25 " "	
Second cut, rib corned,	12 to 15 " "	Lard,	11 to 15 " "	
Brisket,	8 to 12 " "	Leaf lard,	10 to 15 " "	
Boneless brisket,	15 " "	Sausage,	12 to 20 " "	
Flank,	6 to 11 " "	Turkeys,	20 to 35 " "	
Liver,	10 to 12 " "	Fowl,	12 to 30 " "	
Tripe, plain,	6 to 18 " "	Chickens,	18 to 75 " "	
Tripe, honey-comb,	15 " "	Ducks, wild,	25 c. to $1.50 each.	
Heart,	3 to 10 " "	Ducks, tame,	20 to 37 cts. per lb.	
Suet,	7 to 12 " "	Ducks, Canvas-back,	$1.50 to $2.00 each.	
Mutton, leg,	12 to 20 " "	Grouse,	75 c. to $1.25 "	
Mutton, loin,	14 to 20 " "	Partridge,	75 c. to $1.25 "	
Mutton, saddle,	15 to 20 " "	Pigeon, wild,	75 c. to $2.00 per d.	
Mutton, chops,	15 to 25 " "	Pigeon, tame,	12½ to 25 cts. each.	
Mutton, fore quarter,	8 to 12 " "	Squab,	$2.50 to $4.50 per d.	
Mutton, neck,	6 to 9 " "	Quail,	$1.50 to $3.00 "	

BEEF.

Good beef should be bright red, well marbled with yellowish-white fat, and with a thick outside layer of fat. The flesh must be firm, and when pressed with the finger no mark should be left. The suet should be dry, and crumble easily.

A side of beef is divided into the hind quarter and fore quarter. The *hind quarter* consists of the round, the rump, and the loin. The *fore quarter* is divided into the back half and the rattle rand. In cutting up a hind quarter, the flank is first removed. The cut should slant two or three inches toward the tip. The upper part of the flank has the ends of the short ribs, and is used for corning. The lower end of the flank has no bones. This may be stuffed, rolled, and boiled, either fresh or corned. The *round* is separated from the rump in the line

Fig. 17. Aitch Bone.

from 7 to 9. The aitch bone (7) lies between the back and middle cut of the rump and the top of the round. It is usually sold whole; it makes a good roast for a small family, considering the price (10 cents), and is the best piece for a beef stew.

The first cuts of the vein (9) which joins the face of the rump make good steak. The top of the round is the inside of the thickest part of the leg ($8\frac{1}{2}$, behind 8 in the diagram). As seen on the counter, it is above the bone. It consists of one large section or muscle with a thick edge of fat. The best round steaks lie between this point and the ridge of fat. The third slice is considered the best. After cutting beyond this ridge comes the beginning of another muscle, which is very tough. One may easily detect, by the separation of this narrow strip of meat along the top of the slice, whether the meat came from the best part of the top of the round. It may be the

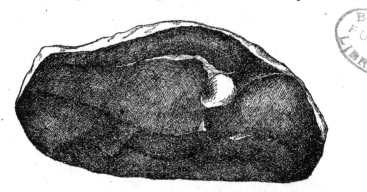

FIG. 18. Round, showing the beginning of the tough muscle on the top.

best the marketman has; but it is not the best cut, though often palmed off in place of the third slice. The under part of the round has two sections or muscles, the one nearest the bone being larger than the outside section. The skin is thin, with very little fat. Steaks from this cut are sometimes sold as good round steak to the ignorant buyer; but keep in mind that in the top cut there is one large muscle with thick fat, instead of two smaller muscles and thin fat, and you will not be deceived. This under cut of the round is excellent for braising. It is well shaped, requires no trimming, and is the cheapest cut, as every scrap of it may be eaten. Below this, as we follow down the leg, are nice pieces for stews, pie meat, etc.

The marrow bone, running through the round to the shin, contains the best marrow. The next best is in the foreshin. The hind shin differs from the fore shin in having a thick tendon, which separates entirely from the end of the leg, and unites again at the joint, forming a loop by which the hind quarter is hung on the meat hook. The

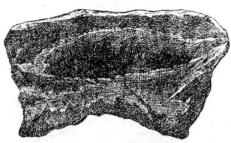

middle cut, of the shin may be used for stews and braising, and the lower part for soups.

The rump is usually separated from the loin, and divided into the back, middle, and face of the rump. The

FIG. 19. Back of Rump.

back of the rump, one of the best pieces for roasting, has part of the backbone and sometimes the rump bone, as some marketmen will not cut it out before weighing. The small end nearest the loin has the most tender meat.

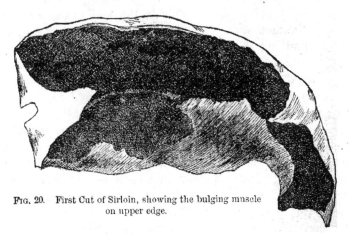

FIG. 20. First Cut of Sirloin, showing the bulging muscle on upper edge.

The middle cut has no bone, but it is not tender. It is better for braising than for roasting. Sometimes the rump is not divided, and is cut into steaks. If cut parallel with the backbone, it will be tough. If cut at right angles, and from the end nearest the loin, it makes the best steaks, and is well worth the extra price charged for cutting in this manner. The face of the rump has a thick piece of fat in the middle, often purposely covered by a thin cutting from the ten-derloin. This is a cheap piece for roasting, but not of the best quality.

The sirloin is separated from the rump in a slant-ing direction. Never buy the first slice, as it always has a small narrow bone near the top in addition to the rib, and a larger por-tion of tough flank and gristle than the middle or second cuts. As it lies on the counter you may easily

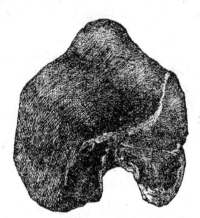

Fig. 21. Sirloin Roast, second Cut.

tell if it be the first slice by the small bone; and if you press on the top of the meat near the middle, a small sec-tion of meat bulges out. This is the end of the muscle forming the face of the rump and vein, and is very tough. The second cut of sirloin has the most tenderloin, and only a straight rib at right angles with the backbone. Any part after the first slice is taken off, until you come to the tip, is called the second cut, and is sold for roasts or steak. The tip is very juicy. The whole hind-quarter is hung up by the shin, the juices all flow down, and the tip holds a large portion. The muscles which are the least used have the most tender fibre and the least juice. These muscles, lying along the loin or middle of the backbone, above the ribs, and forming the top of the sirloin, are more tender, but less juicy, than those of the rump and round. The tenderloin, lying along the middle of the back under the sirloin, from below the tip to the face of the rump, is protected by its bed of suet below, and its roof of bones above. It is a muscle very little used, is very tender, but dry, and entirely without flavor. This is removed whole, and sold as the long fillet; or divided, and the smaller part, lying under the rump, sold as the short fillet.

In cold weather it is economy to buy a large sirloin. Remove the fillet, or tenderloin, and cook that first, as it

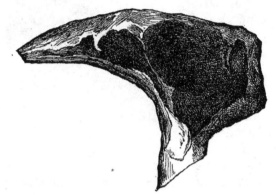

Fig. 22. Tip of Sirloin.

spoils easily; corn the flank, or use it for a stew; and roast the upper part. If very large, roast it slightly the first time, and it may be roasted again for a second dinner.

The Fore Quarter.

The back half of the fore quarter has the backbone on the upper edge. The best roasting piece is the first cut of the rib, which joins the tip of the sirloin, and is sometimes sold for the tip. The tip has only one thick muscle above the rib, and the bones are usually slanting. One side of the first cut of the rib looks just like the tip; the other side has the beginning of another tough muscle next to the skin, and the bones are straight. There are ten ribs in the fore quarter; three are left in the sirloin. This first cut may be one, two, three, or four ribs; but two are enough to roast for a small family. The shoulder blade begins in the fifth rib, and above this lie what are called the chuck ribs. The meat above the blade is tough, and only suitable for stews. The part underneath is cut into small steaks, and is often offered for sale as sirloin steaks. The shoulder of mutton, just above the fore shin, is good for braising and pie meat.

The rattle rand is divided into three long narrow strips, thick and lean at the upper end, and thin and fat at the lower end, all of which are usually corned. The upper part, called the rattle, is divided into three cuts. The

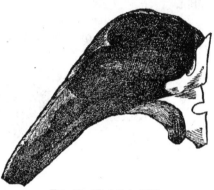

FIG. 23.   First Cut of Rib.

thick upper end is preferred by those who like lean corned beef. The second cut has straight ribs running through it, and three distinct layers of meat with fat, and is considered the choicest piece by those who like " a streak of fat and

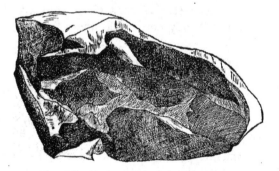

FIG. 24.   Chuck Rib, with six ribs removed.

a streak of lean." The middle strip has a thick layer of fat, and only one layer of lean, and the bones are slanting. This is not a desirable piece. The lower strip is the brisket, the upper end of which is thick; the lower end, toward the middle of the creature, is called the navel end. Brisket pieces always have what is called a selvedge on the lower side, and the breast bones running at right angles with the rib. After a little experience in marketing one may easily distinguish the various cuts of beef. It is well to know what you want, and to know whether you get what you have ordered.

Roast Sirloin of Beef.

Six or *eight pounds* from the *tip* or *second cut* of the *sirloin.* Wipe, trim, and tie or skewer into shape. If there be a large piece of the flank, cut it off, and use it for soups or stews. If you prefer to use it for this purpose after roasting, draw it round underneath and fasten it with a skewer. Lay the meat on a rack in a pan, and dredge all over with *salt, pepper,* and *flour.* Put it in a very hot oven with *two* or *three tablespoonfuls* of *drippings* or pieces of the beef fat placed in the pan. Place a rack under the pan, or turn the heat off from the bottom of the oven. Put the skin side down at first, that the heat may harden the juices in the lean part. When the flour is brown on the pan and the meat is seared, baste with the fat and reduce the heat. Baste often, and dredge twice with salt and flour. When seared all over, turn and bring the skin side up for the final basting and browning. Bake fifty or sixty minutes, if liked very rare ; an hour and a quarter to an hour and a half, if liked well done. If there be any danger of burning the fat in the pan, add a little hot water after the flour is browned. Meat may be roasted and carved better if placed in the pan and on the platter with the skin up instead of the flesh side.

Carve a sirloin roast by cutting several thin slices parallel with the ribs. Then cut down near the backbone and separate the slices. Cut out the tenderloin from under the bone, and slice it in the same manner. Many turn the sirloin over and remove the tenderloin first. Serve a little of the crisp fat on the flank to those who wish it.

Rib Roast. — Remove the backbone and ribs. Skewer or tie into a round shape, and prepare as for sirloin. Allow a longer time for roasting, as the meat is in a more compact form without the bones. Place it skin side up on the platter, and carve thin slices from the flesh side.

The Back of the Rump. — This is the best and cheapest piece for roasting, as the meat is all good and there is not as much bone as in other pieces. It is usually too large for a small family; but in cold weather it may be used to advantage, by cutting steaks from the thickest end, using the small end for a roast and the bones for soup.

In carving the rump, when the bone has not been taken out, a deep cut should be made at the base, to loosen the meat; then the slices may be cut lengthwise or crosswise. When the family is large and all the meat is to be used, it is well to cut it lengthwise. Should only a small quantity be needed, cut only from the small end, and save the tougher parts for a stew. Many think it more economical to serve the poorer parts the first day, as they are then more palatable,-reserving the tender meat to be served cold.

Roast from the Round. — A slice three inches thick, from the best part of the top of the round, may be dredged with *salt*, *pepper*, and *flour*, and roasted. Carve in thin slices, the same as steak. It is rather tough, but juicy and well flavored.

Yorkshire Pudding. — Beat *three eggs* very light. Add *one scant teaspoonful* of *salt* and *one pint* of *milk*. Pour *half a cup* of this mixture on *two thirds* of *a cup* of *flour*, and stir to a smooth paste. Add the remainder of the mixture and beat well. Bake in hot gem pans forty-five minutes. Baste with the drippings from the beef. This is a more convenient way than to bake in the pan under the beef, and gives more crust. Serve as a garnish for roast beef.

Gravy for Roast Beef. — When the meat is done, put it on a plate, and keep it hot while making the gravy. Hold the corner of the dripping-pan over a bowl; let the liquid in the pan settle; then pour off all the fat and save it.

When no water is used in baking and the oven is very hot, this liquid will be the fat from the meat. The brown flour will settle, and some will adhere to the pan. Pour *one pint* of *hot water* or *stock* into the pan, and scrape off all the sediment. Pour this water into a saucepan from which it may be poured easily, and place it on the stove to heat. Put *four tablespoonfuls* of the *hot fat* into a small frying-pan, and when browned stir in *two heaping tablespoonfuls* of *dry flour*, or enough to absorb all the fat. Stir until the flour is brown and well mixed; then add the hot liquid gradually, and stir as it thickens. Season with *salt* and *pepper*, and simmer five minutes. Strain if not perfectly smooth. Gravy can be made in the dripping-pan; but such pans are usually large, inconvenient to handle, and take up more space than can be spared on the top of the stove, and are much harder to wash when the gravy has been made in them. To make it in the pan, pour off nearly all the fat. Put the pan on the stove and add *dry flour* until the fat is all absorbed. Then add *hot water* or *hot stock*, and stir as it thickens. Cook five to eight minutes, and strain. It is well for those who like gravies to make a large quantity, as it is useful in warming over the remnants of the roast. But there is no sauce or made gravy equal to the natural juices contained in the meat, which should flow freely into the platter when the meat is carved.

FIG. 25.   Fillet of Beef.

Fillet of Beef. — Wipe, and remove the fat, veins, and tough tendinous portion in the middle. Trim into shape. Lard the upper side (see page 25). Dredge with *salt*, *pepper*, and *flour*. Put several pieces of pork in the pan under

the meat. Bake in a hot oven twenty or thirty minutes.
If you prefer, omit the pork and put the choice pieces of
beef fat over the meat. Serve with mushroom sauce. Or
brush the fillet with *beaten egg*, and sprinkle *seasoned and
buttered crumbs* all over it, and bake thirty minutes. Or
stuff the incisions left by the removal of the veins and
tendons with any *stuffing* or *force-meat*. Dredge with *salt*
and *flour*, and bake.

Broiled Steak.

Wipe, trim off the superfluous fat, and remove the bone.
Save the flank end for broiled meat cakes. Grease the
gridiron with some of the fat. Broil over a clear fire,
turning every ten seconds. Cook three or four minutes, if
liked rare ; longer, if well done. Serve on a hot platter.
Season with *butter, salt,* and *pepper,* or serve with *Maître
d'Hôtel butter.* Steaks should be cut at least an inch
thick. Many prefer them much thicker. Sirloin, cross
cut of the rump, and top of the round are all good steaks.
The round is juicy, but has a net work of tough white fibre,
which makes it difficult to masticate. If the steak be very
tough, pound it with a meat hammer (a hammer with sharp
teeth for cutting) or cut across it several times with a
sharp knife on each side. The intense heat will sear the
surface quickly, and prevent the escape of the juices.

Many prefer not to remove the bone in a sirloin steak ;
but it burns quickly, and is better for the soup kettle if
not cooked, and the steak is more easily carved when the
bone is removed. Carve in narrow slices, giving each
person a bit of tenderloin, fat, and upper part.

Broiled Fillet of Beef. — Cut slices from the tenderloin.
Wipe the meat ; grease the gridiron ; broil over a clear
fire, turning every ten counts, for three or five minutes.
Spread with *Maître d'Hôtel butter.*

Broiled Meat Cakes. — Chop *lean, raw beef* quite fine.
Season with *salt, pepper,* and a little *chopped onion,* or *onion
juice.* Make it into small flat cakes, and broil on a well-
greased gridiron or on a hot frying-pan. Serve very hot

with *butter* or *Maître d'Hôtel sauce*. The flank end of the sirloin is better when cooked in this manner than when broiled with the other part of the steak.

Hamburgh Steak. — Pound *a slice* of *round steak* enough to break the fibre. Fry *two* or *three onions*, minced fine, in *butter* until slightly browned. Spread the onions over the meat, fold the ends of the meat together, and pound again, to keep the onions in the middle. Broil two or three minutes. Spread with *butter, salt,* and *pepper.*

Braised Beef.

Four to *six pounds* of *beef* from the *lower part* of the *round* or *face* of the *rump*. Trim, and rub well with *salt, pepper,* and *flour*. Cut *two small onions* into dice, and fry them until light brown in salt pork fat or drippings. Skim them out into a braising-pan or large granite pan; then brown the meat all over, adding more fat if needed. Put the meat into the pan on skewers, to keep it from sticking, with the onions *around*, not under, the meat. Add *one quart* of *boiling water* and *one tablespoonful* of *mixed herbs*, which should be tied in a small piece of strainer cloth. Cover closely, putting a brick on the cover to keep it down, and cook in a moderate oven four hours, basting every twenty minutes. Turn over after two hours; add more water as it evaporates, so as to have one pint left for gravy. When tender, take up the meat, remove the fat and bag of herbs from the gravy; add more *salt* and *pepper*, and if desired add *lemon juice, tomato,* or *mushrooms;* thicken with *two tablespoonfuls* of *flour*, wet in *a little cold water*. Cook ten minutes, and pour the gravy over the meat. Garnish with *potato balls, boiled onions,* or with *vegetables à la Jardinière*. Horseradish sauce may be served with the meat. This is a very nutritious, palatable, and convenient way of cooking the cheaper parts of beef, a cushion of veal, tongues, fowls, liver, and some other kinds of meat. The meat is equally good cold or hot; there is no waste if care be taken not to let it become hard and dry by being exposed to the air. This method of cooking commends itself especially to those who " are tired of roasted, boiled, or fried meat."

Beef à la Mode.

Four to *six pounds* from the *under part* of the *round* of *beef*, cut thick. Wipe, and trim off the rough edges. Put it in a deep earthen dish, and pour over it spiced vinegar, made by boiling for five minutes *one cup* of *vinegar*, *one onion*, *chopped fine*, *three teaspoonfuls* of *salt*, and *half a teaspoonful* each of *mustard*, *pepper*, *cloves*, and *allspice*. Let the meat stand several hours, turning it often. Then daub it with *ten* or *twelve strips* of *salt pork*, cut *one third* of *an inch wide*, and as long as the meat is thick, inserting them with a larding-needle or carving-steel. Or make large incisions and stuff with *bread crumbs*, highly seasoned with *salt*, *pepper*, *onions*, *thyme*, *marjoram*, etc., moistened with *hot water*, *one tablespoonful* of *butter*, and *one well-beaten egg*. Tie it into good shape with a narrow strip of cotton cloth, to keep in the stuffing. Dredge with *flour*. Cut *two onions*, *half a carrot*, and *half a turnip* fine, and fry them in fat or drippings until brown. Put them in the stewpan. Then brown the meat all over in the fat; put it on a trivet in the pan, and half cover with *boiling water*. Add *one tablespoonful* of *mixed herbs*, tied in a small strainer cloth. Cover closely, and simmer four hours, or until tender. Take it up carefully, remove the strings, and put it on a large platter. Remove the fat from the gravy, add *more seasoning*, and thicken with *flour* wet in *a little cold water;* boil eight minutes, and strain it over the meat. Garnish with *potato balls* and *small onions*.

Beef Stew with Dumplings.

The aitch bone is the nicest piece for a beef stew. There is some very juicy meat on the upper side in the large muscle which lies next to the top of the round, and it will serve a small family for a roast, and then may be made

15

into a stew. The flavor obtained by roasting adds much to the stew; for this reason, when the meat has not been cooked, brown it in a little fat before stewing. The bones should never be chopped and splintered, but sawed carefully, and all the fine, crumbly pieces removed before cooking. Other good pieces for stews are *two* or *three pounds* from the *middle cut* of the *shin*, or the *flank end* of *a large sirloin* roast, or the upper part of the *chuck* rib. Any part that has bone and fat, as well as lean, either cooked or uncooked, makes the best-flavored stew. The fat and bones may be removed before serving, and such pieces are much better than dry, lean meat. Remove the meat from the bones, and put them with part of the fat into the stewpan. Cut the meat into small pieces, and if not previously cooked, dredge with *salt*, *pepper*, and *flour*, and brown all over in salt pork fat or drippings. Put it into the stewpan. Cut *two onions, one small white turnip,* and *half a small carrot* (if you like the flavor) into *half-inch dice.* Cook them slightly in the dripping, and add them to the stew. Add *boiling water* enough to cover, and simmer two or three hours, or till the meat is tender. Remove the bones, and skim off the fat. While the meat is cooking pare *six* or *eight small potatoes*, and soak them in cold water. When the meat is tender, pour boiling water over them, and boil five minutes to take out the acrid taste. Drain, and add them to the stew. Add *salt* and *pepper* to taste. When *dumplings* are to be served with the stew, add them when the potatoes are nearly done The liquor should come up just even with the potatoes, that the dumplings may rest on them. Cover closely to keep in the steam, and cook ten minutes without lifting the cover. Take out the dumplings, put the meat and potatoes in the centre of a hot platter, and the dumplings round the edge.

Remove the fat, and add more *salt* and *pepper*, if needed, to the broth; and if not thick enough, add *a little flour* wet smooth in *cold water*, and boil five minutes. Add *one cup* of *strained tomato* and *one teaspoonful* of *chopped parsley*

Pour the gravy over the meat, putting part of it in a sauce tureen if there be more than the platter will hold.

Dumplings. — *One pint* of *flour, half a teaspoonful* of *salt, one teaspoonful* of *cream of tartar,* and *half a teaspoonful* of *soda* (or *three level teaspoonfuls* of *baking-powder*). Mix with *one scant cup* of *sweet milk* into a dough soft enough to handle easily. Pat it out half an inch thick. Cut in small rounds, or mix softer and drop by the spoonful into the boiling stew. Cook ten minutes.

Rolled Flank of Beef.

Four or *five pounds* of the *flank.* Wipe, and remove the skin, membrane, and extra fat. Pound and trim until of uniform thickness. Make a stuffing with *one cup* of *cracker crumbs, two tablespoonfuls* of *fine chopped salt pork, half a teaspoonful* of *salt, one saltspoonful* each of *thyme, marjoram,* and *sage, half a saltspoonful* of *pepper, a few drops of onion juice,* or *one teaspoonful* of *chopped onion,* and *one egg.* Moisten with *hot water* until soft enough to spread over the meat. Roll over, and tie or sew securely. Wrap a cloth around it. Put it into boiling water, and simmer six hours or until tender. Remove the cloth, press it, and when cold remove the strings. Serve cold, cut in thin slices. Corned flank may be prepared in the same way. The stuffing may be omitted, and the meat covered with vinegar spiced and flavored with onion, and after remaining in the pickle several hours, rolled, and boiled as above.

Smothered Beef, or Pot Roast.

Four to *six pounds* from the *middle* or *face* of the *rump,* the *vein,* or the *round.* Wipe with a clean wet cloth. Sear all over by placing in a hot frying-pan and turning till all the surface is browned. Put in a kettle with *one cup* of *water,* and place it where it will keep just below the boiling-point. Do not let the water boil entirely away, but add only enough to keep the meat from burning

Have the cover fitting closely to keep in the steam. Cook until very tender, but do not let it break. Serve hot or cold. The meat when cold is delicious, cut in quarter-inch slices, and sautéd in *hot butter.*

Spiced Beef.

Four to six pounds from the *middle cut* of the *shin.* Wash the meat on the outside, and cut off any part of the skin which is not sweet and clean. Pick off all the fine fragments of bone. Cut the meat into several pieces; cover with *boiling water.* Skim carefully as it boils, and then simmer until the meat falls to pieces, and the liquor is reduced to *half a pint.* Remove the meat; season the liquor highly with *salt, pepper, sage,* and *thyme.* Add it to the meat, and mix with a fork till the meat is all broken. Pack in a brickloaf pan. When cold, cut in thin slices.

Corned Beef.

Select a piece of beef which has a fair proportion of fat, — the *brisket* or *second cut* of *rattle rund.* If very salt, soak in cold water half an hour. Put on to boil in fresh cold water, enough to cover it. If not very salt, wash it and use boiling water, but never let it boil fast. Skim carefully when it begins to boil, and cook slowly, simmering (not boiling) until so tender that you can pick it to pieces with a fork. Let the water boil away toward the last, and let the beef stand in the water until partially cooled. Lift it out of the water with a skimmer, and pack it in a brickloaf pan; let the long fibres run the length of the pan; mix in the fat so that it will be well marbled. Put a thin board, a trifle smaller than the inside of the pan, over the meat, and press by putting a heavy weight on the board. When cold, cut in thin slices. This is the most appetizing way of serving the fat of the meat, which in corned beef is a desirable part and is often untouched if offered in a mass on the edge of the lean.

An Old-fashioned Boiled Dinner. (*Mrs. Poor.*)

Notwithstanding that this dish has fallen into ill-repute with many people, it *may* be prepared so as to be both palatable and nutritious for those who exercise freely. It is more suitable for cold seasons. The most healthful and economical way, though perhaps not the old-fashioned way, is to boil the beef the day before.

Four pounds of *corned beef, two* or *three beets, a small cabbage, two small carrots, one small white French turnip, six* or *eight potatoes* of *uniform size,* and *one small crooked-neck squash.*

Wash and soak the corned beef in cold water, and put it on to boil in fresh cold water; skim, and simmer until tender, but not long enough for it to fall to pieces. Let it cool in the liquor in which it was boiled. Put it into a flat shallow dish, cover it with a board, and press it. Remove all the fat from the meat liquor, and save it to clarify for shortening. Save the meat liquor, but do not let it stand in an iron kettle or tin pan. Boil the beets the day before, also, and cover them with vinegar. The next day prepare the vegetables. Wash them all, scrape the carrots, and cut the cabbage into quarters; pare the turnip and squash, and cut into three-quarter-inch slices, and pare the potatoes. Put the meat liquor on to boil about two hours before dinner time; when boiling, put in the carrots, afterward the cabbage and turnip, and half an hour before dinner add the squash and potatoes. When tender, take the vegetables up carefully; drain the water from the cabbage by pressing it in a colander. Slice the carrots. Put the cold meat in the centre of a large dish, and serve the carrots, turnips, and potatoes round the edge, with the squash, cabbage, and pickled beets in separate dishes; or serve each vegetable in a dish by itself. This may all be done the same day if the meat be put on to boil very early, removed as soon as tender, the fat taken off, and the vegetables added to the boiling meat liquor, beginning with those which require the longest time to cook. This will depend very much upon their freshness. But whichever way the dish is prepared, boil the beets alone, remove the meat and fat before adding the vegetables, and serve each as whole and daintily as possible. The next morning use what remains of the vegetables as a vegetable hash.

Vegetable Hash. — *Equal parts* of *cabbage*, *beets*, and *turnips*, and as much *potato* as there is of all the other vegetables. Chop all very fine; add a little *salt* and *pepper;* put *a spoonful* of *drippings* in the frying-pan, and when hot add the hash, and cook slowly until warmed through.

Tongue in Jelly.

Wash a fresh tongue, and skewer the tip to the root. Cook until tender in boiling salted water; remove the skin; trim and tie it in good shape. Season *two quarts* of *soup stock* highly with *salt*, *pepper*, *herbs*, and *wine* or *lemon*. Clear it with *eggs*, and stiffen with the proportion of Cox's *gelatine*, as given for Aspic Jelly. Pour a little jelly into a mould; when cool, lay in the cold tongue, and add the remainder of the jelly slowly.

Smoked Tongue. — Smoked tongues are much more palatable, though not so economical as when fresh. Bend the tip of the tongue around, and tie it to the root. Put it in cold water and place over the fire. When the water boils, pour off the water, and put it on again in cold water. Boil until tender, or about two hours. Remove the skin, roots, and fat. Pour a *white sauce* over the tongue, and serve it hot; or serve it cold with a *salad dressing*. Tongues may also be braised (see Braised Beef, page 224) and served hot or cold.

Lyonnaise Tripe.

Tripe should always be boiled twenty to thirty minutes before cooking, or it will be tough.

Cut the tripe in small pieces; boil twenty-five minutes, and drain. Fry *one tablespoonful* of *chopped onion* in *one heaping tablespoonful* of *butter* till yellow. Add the tripe, *one tablespoonful* of *vinegar*, and *one tablespoonful* of *chopped parsley*, *salt* and *pepper* to taste. Simmer five minutes, and serve plain or on toast.

Broiled Tripe. — Boil the tripe twenty minutes; dry it, spread with *soft butter*, *salt*, and *pepper*, and broil until brown.

Tripe in Batter. — Boil the tripe twenty minutes. Cut in pieces two inches square, dip in *batter*, and fry in *salt pork fat* in a frying-pan.

Batter. — *One egg*, *one quarter* of *a cup* of *water*, *one tablespoonful* of *vinegar*, *one teaspoonful* of *salt*, and *flour* to make almost a drop batter.

Liver.

Soak ten minutes in boiling water to draw out the blood. Drain; remove the thin skin and veins. Cut into pieces for serving. Season with *salt* and *pepper;* roll in *flour*, and fry in *salt pork* or *bacon fat*. Drain, and serve with a *brown gravy*, seasoned with *onion*, *lemon juice*, or *vinegar*. Or spread with *butter*, and broil, and season with *salt*, *pepper*, and *butter*.

Kidneys.

Beef and sheep's kidneys are often recommended for food on account of their cheapness. Epicures are fond of them. The taste for them is an acquired taste, which it is not desirable to cultivate. The latest decision of physicians is that they are not suitable to eat; as "from their constant use in the animal system as excretory organs, — organs which separate from the blood that which, if it remained in the blood, would poison the system, — they are often liable to become diseased."

MUTTON AND LAMB.

MUTTON stands next to beef in nutritive qualities, and with many has even more value as food, because more easily digested. In mutton about one half the weight is in fat, while with beef it is only one third.

The choicest mutton comes from the mountainous re. gions of Pennsylvania, Virginia, and North Carolina. Good mutton should be large and heavy, the fat clear white and very hard, the flesh fine-grained and bright red. Poor mutton has but little fat, and little flesh as compared with the bone.

Mutton is cut at the market by splitting down the back, and dividing at the loin into the hind and fore quarters ; or the hind and fore quarters are separated without split-ting, and the loin is taken out whole and sold as the sad-dle of mutton. The leg, loin, and saddle are best for roasting, and are better if kept for some time before cook-ing. The leg, if to be boiled, should be fresh. The fore quarter is good boned and stuffed ; then steamed, and browned in the oven. The neck and bones are used for broths and stews. Chops are cut from the ribs and from the loin. The rib chops are sometimes cut long, with the flank on. The bone is removed and the meat rolled. These roll chops are not economical, as the flank forms the greater part. French chops are cut short from the rib, and the flesh is scraped clean from the end of the bone. The best-flavored, most tender, and cheapest in the end, are the chops from the loin. They have very little bone, and a piece of tenderloin.

Mutton has a strong flavor, disagreeable to many. It is said to be caused by the oil from the wool, which pen-etrates the skin. The pink skin above the fat should always be removed from chops, and wherever it is possible, scrape it off without cutting into the lean. The caul, or lining membrane of the abdomen, is fastened round the meat, particularly on the leg, partly to increase its weight. This is often left on in roasting to help baste the meat; but it gives a strong flavor, and should always be removed, and the kidney fat used if needed. If care be taken in selecting only the best mutton, and in cooking it in the best manner, many who have become prejudiced against it could eat it with as much relish as beef. Mutton may be cooked rare, but lamb should always be well cooked. The end of the bone in a leg of mutton is smooth and oval, and is separated at the joint; while lamb may be known from mutton by the flat, irregularly grooved end of the bone, which is broken off squarely, instead of separated at the joint. Sometimes the bone is cut off close to the second joint, and then you will have to depend upon the word of your butcher.

Saddle or Loin of Mutton or Lamb.

Trim off all the pink skin and superfluous fat. Remove the ends of the ribs, the cord, and veins along the back. Wipe, and rub the inside with salt. Roll the flank under on each side, and sew it across the middle. Dredge with *salt, pepper,* and *flour;* place it in the pan, with the inside up, in order to thoroughly cook the fat. Baste, and dredge often. When the fat is brown and crisp, turn, and cook the upper part till brown. Keep a buttered paper over it to prevent burning.

Carve long slices parallel with the backbone, then slip the knife under and separate the slices from the ribs. Divide the slices, and serve with some of the crisp fat.

A loin of mutton may be stuffed and rolled, having first removed the ends of the ribs. Bake, and serve in slices cut at right angles with the backbone.

· Leg of Mutton, Stuffed and Roasted.

Remove the bone; wipe inside and out with a wet cloth; sprinkle the inside with *salt;* stuff and sew. Put it on a rack in a dripping-pan, with some of the kidney suet on the meat and in the pan. Dredge with *salt*, *pepper*, and *flour*, and bake in a hot oven. Baste as soon as the flour is brown, and baste often. Bake one hour, if liked rare; one hour and a quarter, if well done.

Stuffing. — *One cup* of *cracker* or *stale bread crumbs.* Season with *one saltspoonful* each of *salt*, *pepper*, *thyme*, or *marjoram*, and moisten with *a quarter* of *a cup* of *melted butter.* Add *hot water* if a moist stuffing be desired.

Boiled Leg of Mutton or Lamb. — Wipe, remove the fat, and put into well-salted boiling water. Skim, and simmer twelve minutes for each pound of meat. *One quarter* of *a cup* of *rice* is sometimes boiled with the mutton, or the meat may be tied in a cloth to keep it from becoming discolored. Serve with a thick *caper sauce* poured over the mutton. Garnish with *parsley.* Serve with currant jelly.

Carve slices from the thickest part of the leg down to the bone; then slip the knife under and remove the slices from the bone. The thickest part of the leg should be toward the back of the platter.

What to do with a Fore Quarter of Mutton.

Mutton Duck. — Select a fore quarter of mutton with the whole length of the leg bone left on. Ask the butcher to cut off what is called a raised shoulder, that is, raised from the backbone and ribs, cutting it far up on the shoulder to take in the whole of the shoulder blade, bone, and gristle. You may cut it yourself by removing the neck, the back bones, the ribs, and breast bones, leaving the shoulder blade in the upper part. Then scrape the flesh from the shoulder blade, and separate the blade at the joint. Lay it aside for further use. Remove the meat from the leg bone, turning the meat over, as you would turn a glove over your hand. Be careful not to cut through the thin skin at the end of the leg. When within three inches of the lower joint, saw the bone off, and saw or trim the bone below the joint into the shape of a duck's bill. Bend the joint without breaking the skin. Wipe the meat and rub inside with *salt*. Make a *moist stuffing* and put it in between the layers of meat. With a coarse needle threaded with twine gather the edges of the meat, draw them together, fill the cavity with stuffing, and shape the meat into a long oval form like the body of a duck. Bend the leg at the lower joint to represent the duck's head and neck, and keep it in place with skewers. Run one skewer

Fig. 26. Mutton Duck.

through the side at the top of the body, and put one into the body on each side of the neck. Wind a string around the bill, and fasten it to the skewers. Scrape the shoulder blade clean, trim the bony end into a sharp point, and notch the gristle at the opposite end. Insert this in the body to represent the tail, and fasten with twine. Put the bones and scraps of meat in water in a steamer or kettle. Place the duck on a plate, and steam it over the bones one hour to make it tender. Dredge with *salt*, *pepper*, and *flour*, and bake one hour, or till brown; use the water in the kettle for basting if needed, or for a gravy. Tie paper over the head and tail to prevent burning. This may be made of lamb, and if tender will require no steaming. Garnish with *parsley* and *Scotch eggs*, or with any kind of *force-meat balls*, crumbed and fried, or with egg-shaped *potato croquettes*.

This Mock Duck is an attractive way of serving what is usually considered an inferior piece of meat, and solves the vexing problem, " how to carve a fore quarter of mutton."

The bones may be entirely removed, and the meat stuffed, and sewed in an oval shape, then steamed and browned; this will prove just as palatable to those who do not crave something new. In serving, cut it across in medium slices.

Braised Mutton. — Bone and stuff the leg or the fore quarter, as directed in the preceding receipts; cut the bone at the joints. Add oysters to the stuffing if preferred, and cook the same as braised beef. The breast of mutton may be boned and rolled without stuffing and then braised.

Lamb or Mutton Chops. — Wipe with a wet cloth; remove the skin and extra fat; have a frying-pan hissing hot, without any fat; put in the chops and cook one minute, turn, and sear the other side; cook more slowly until done, five minutes if liked rare. Stand them up on the fat edge to brown the fat, without over-cooking the meat. When nearly done, sprinkle a little *salt* on each side. Drain on paper, and serve hot, either plain or with *tomato* or *Soubise sauce.*

Mutton Cutlets, Breaded. — Trim the cutlets, and season with *salt* and *pepper.* Dip in *crumbs, beaten egg,* and *crumbs* again, and fry in *smoking hot fat,* four to six minutes if rare, eight to ten if well done. Arrange in the centre of a hot dish, and pour *tomato sauce* around them, or place them around a mound of *mashed potatoes* or *spinach.* Trim the bones with a *paper ruffle;* or arrange them with the bone end up, stacked like bayonets, and garnish with *stuffed tomatoes.*

FIG. 27.
Paper Ruffle.

Chops en Papillote. — Wipe, trim, wrap in buttered papers, and broil from three to five minutes; season, and serve plain or trimmed with paper ruffles. Or make a thick sauce with *one cup* of *boiling stock,* thickened with *one heaping tablespoonful* of *flour* and *one tablespoonful* of *butter,* cooked together and flavored with *mushrooms, parsley,* and *lemon juice.* Lay the cutlets on clean papers, spread the sauce over them, fold the edges, place in a pan in the oven for ten minutes. Serve in the papers. If the chops be tough, dip them in olive oil before broiling.

Fricassee of Mutton or Lamb with Peas. — Cut *two pounds* of the *breast* of *mutton* or *lamb* into square pieces. Dredge with *salt* and *flour*, and brown in *butter* or *drippings*. Put them in a stew-pan with *one onion* sliced, cover with *boiling water*, and simmer until the

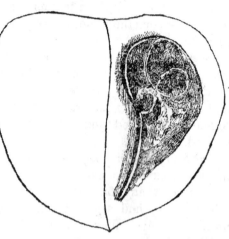

FIG 28. Chop.

bones slip out. Remove the bones, strain the liquor, skim off the fat, and when the liquor boils again, add the meat, salt, and *pepper*, and stew until nearly tender ; then add *one quart* of *peas*, or *one pint* of *boiled macaroni* cut into *half-inch* pieces, or *one pint* of *asparagus tips*, and simmer fifteen minutes.

Mutton Stew for Two. — *Two mutton chops*, cut from near the shoulder. Put them in a shallow pan having a tight cover. Pour on boiling water to the depth of one inch ; cover and simmer one hour ; add more water as it boils away, using only enough to keep the meat from burning. Add *two slices* of *French turnip*, *two small*

FIG. 29. Chop in Paper.

onions whole ; and when the meat and turnip are nearly tender, add *two common-sized potatoes*, having first soaked and scalded them. Add *one teaspoonful* of *salt* and *a little pepper.* Remove the vegetables without breaking; let the water boil nearly away, leaving enough for a gravy. Remove the fat, thicken the gravy with *flour*, and if needed add *salt* and *tomato catchup.* Pour it over the meat.

Curry of Mutton. — Fry *one large onion*, cut fine, in *one heaping tablespoonful* of *butter.* Mix *one tablespoonful* of *curry powder, one teaspoonful* of *salt, one tablespoonful* of *flour*, and stir it into the butter and onion. Add gradually *one pint* of *hot water* or *stock.* Cut *two pounds* of *lean mutton* into small pieces, and brown them in hot fat; add them to the sauce, and simmer until tender. Place the meat on a hot dish, and arrange a border of *boiled rice* or *Turkish pilaf* around the meat. Slices of cold cooked mutton may be used instead of the fresh meat. Veal curry is prepared in the same manner.

Ragout of Mutton, made from the fore quarter, or any cooked mutton, may be prepared as directed for beef stew, adding carrots and turnips cut small, and seasoning highly.

Sheep's Tongues, Braised.

Wash, dredge with *salt* and *flour*, and brown in salt pork fat, with *one* or *two minced onions.* Put them in a pan with *water* or *stock* to half cover; add *one sprig* of *parsley*, a little *salt* and *pepper;* cover and cook two hours, or until tender. Remove the skin, and trim neatly at the roots. Place a mound of *spinach* in the centre of the dish; arrange the tongues around the spinach, alternating with diamonds of *fried bread.*

Lambs' Tongues, Boiled. — Boil *six tongues* in salted water, with the *juice of half a lemon*, until tender. Serve cold with Tartar sauce. Or *pickle* them by covering with hot spiced vinegar.

VEAL.

VEAL is always in the market, but is better in the spring. The fat should be white and clear; and the lean, pink or flesh color. If the flesh be white, the calf has been bled before being killed, and the meat is unfit to eat. Veal contains less nitrogen, but more gelatine, than beef. It has very little flavor, and needs to be highly seasoned to make it even palatable. Veal stands lowest among heat-producing meats, and should be eaten with potatoes or rice, which stand highest, or with bacon and jelly, which furnish in their fat and sugar the carbon wanting in the flesh. It should always be thoroughly cooked, as under-done veal is not wholesome. At its lowest price veal is never a cheap food when we take into consideration the small amount of nutriment it contains, the large amount of fuel required to cook it, and the danger of being made ill by its use.

The lower part of the leg or knuckle and all the gristly portions are used for soups. Cutlets, or steaks, the fillet, fricandeau, or cushion, are cut from the thickest part of the leg. The loin is used for chops or roasts, the breast for roasts, and the neck for stews and soups. Calf's head and pluck includes the lights, heart, and liver. The head is used for soup, the heart and liver for braising. The lights are now seldom used.

Roast Veal.

The loin, breast, and fillet (a thick piece from the upper part of the leg) are the best pieces for roasting. The bone should be removed from the fillet, and the cavity filled with a *highly seasoned* and very *moist stuffing*. Tie or skewer into a round shape. Dredge with *salt, peppet,* and *flour.* Put strips of *pork* over the top, and bake. Allow half an hour to a pound. Cover with a buttered paper to keep the meat from burning. Add water, when the flour has browned, and baste often. Serve with *horseradish* or *tomato sauce.*

Fricandeau of Veal.—This is made of *a thick piece* of *lean meat* from the top of the *leg.* Trim it off high in the centre and thin on the edges, and lard the top. Braise it in *stock* highly seasoned with *bacon, onions,* and *herbs* (see Braised Beef). Serve it with *tomato* or *horseradish sauce.*

Veal Stew or Fricassee.

The *ends* of the *ribs,* the *neck,* and the *knuckle* may be utilized in a stew. Cut the meat—*two pounds*—in small pieces, and remove all the fine bones. Cover the meat with *boiling water ;* skim as it begins to boil ; add *two small onions, two teaspoonfuls* of *salt,* and *one saltspoonful* of *pepper.* Simmer until thoroughly tender. Cut *four potatoes* in halves ; soak in cold water, and parboil them five minutes ; add them to the stew. Add *one tablespoonful* of *flour* wet in cold water, and more seasoning if desired ; and just before serving add *one cup* of *cream,* or if *milk* be used add *one tablespoonful* of *butter.* Remove the bones before serving. To make *Veal Pot-Pie* add *dumplings,* as in Beef Stew. If intended for a *fricassee,* fry the veal in salt pork fat before stewing, and omit the potatoes. Add *one egg* to the liquor just before serving, if you wish it richer.

Veal Cutlets. (*Joanna Sweeny*)

One slice of *veal* from the *leg.* Wipe, and remove the bone, skin, and tough membranes. Pound and cut, or shape into pieces for serving. Sprinkle with *salt* and *pepper.* Roll in *fine crumbs,* then dip in *beaten egg,* then in *crumbs* again. Fry several slices of *salt pork,* and fry the cutlets brown in the pork fat. When brown, put the cutlets in a stewpan. Make a *brown gravy* with *one tablespoonful* of *butter,* or the fat remaining in the pan if it be not

burned, and *two heaping tablespoonfuls* of *flour.* Pour
on gradually *a cup and a half* of *stock* or *water.* Season
with *Worcestershire sauce* or *lemon* or *horseradish* or *tomato.*
Pour the gravy over the cutlets, and simmer forty-five minutes or till tender. Take them out on a platter, remove
the fat from the gravy, add more seasoning if needed, and
strain over the cutlets. Garnish with *lemon* and *parsley.*

Calf's Liver, Braised.

Wipe with a clean wet cloth. Lard the rounded side
with *bacon* or *salt pork.* Fry *one onion* in salt pork fat.
Put the liver and fried onion in a braising-pan; add *hot
water* or *stock* to half cover, *one teaspoonful* of *salt*, *one saltspoonful* of *pepper*, and *one tablespoonful* of *herbs.* Cover,
and cook in a moderate oven two hours, basting often.
When ready to serve, strain the liquor, season with *lemon
juice*, and pour it over the liver.

Calf's Heart, Braised. — Wash, remove the veins and
arteries, and stuff with *cracker crumbs*, seasoned with *onion
juice*, *salt*, *pepper*, and *herbs*, and moistened with *butter.*

FIG. 30. Calf's Heart.

Lard with *bacon* or *salt pork.* Dredge with *salt* and *flour.*
Fry *one onion* in *salt pork fat* or *dripping;* brown the meat
in the pork fat. Cook it as liver is cooked, by the preceding receipt.

Calf's Head.

Scrape and clean a calf's head. Take out the brains and
tongue, and put them in cold water. Remove all the dark
membrane from the inside, and the gristle around the nose

and eyes. Soak two hours in lukewarm water to whiten it. Put the head, tongue, and heart on to boil in cold water, and skim carefully. Add *one tablespoonful* of *herbs* tied in a piece of strainer cloth, *one tablespoonful* of *salt*, and *one saltspoonful* of *pepper*. Pour *boiling water* over the liver, let it stand ten minutes, and when the head is nearly done, add the liver. When done, take up the head; remove the skin in as nice pieces as possible. Put the pieces of head meat on the platter; lay the skin over them. Cut the heart, tongue, and liver in slices, and place them round the edge of the dish. If the head is to be served with the bones, tie it in a floured cloth, and boil it until tender, but not long enough for the skin to fall off. Serve it plain; or score the top, brush with *beaten egg*, sprinkle *buttered cracker crumbs* over it, and brown in the oven. Serve with it a *brown sauce piquante*, *tomato sauce*, or *brain sauce*.

Brain Sauce. — Clean the brains, remove the red membrane, and soak in cold water. Put them into *one pint* of *cold water* with *one tablespoonful* of *lemon juice* and *half a teaspoonful* of *salt*. Boil ten minutes; then plunge into cold water. Make *one pint* of *drawn butter sauce;* flavor with *lemon* and *parsley;* add the brains chopped fine, and when hot serve.

Calf's Head, Minced. — Chop what is left of the *head*, *tongue*, and *liver* very fine, and warm it in a sauce made with the *meat liquor;* season with *lemon* or *horseradish*, *salt*, and *pepper*.

Sweetbreads.

The sweetbreads found in veal are considered the best. They are two large glands lying along the back of the throat and in the breast. The lower one is round and compact, and called the heart sweetbread, because nearer the heart. The upper, or throat, sweetbread is long and narrow, and easily divided into sections. The connecting membrane is sometimes broken, and each gland sold as a whole sweetbread. But there should always be two. Sweetbreads were formerly thrown away as worthless; but the demand for them has increased so that now they are a luxury. They have a delicate flavor, and as they spoil quickly, should be put into cold water as soon as purchased, and parboiled before using in any form, to insure their being thoroughly cooked. They are sometimes left on the breast of veal, and may then be roasted with the meat.

To Prepare Sweetbreads. — Put them in cold water; remove the pipes and membranes. Cook them in boiling salted water, with *one tablespoonful* of *lemon juice*, twenty minutes, and plunge into cold water to harden. They may then be cooked in either of the following ways : —

Larded. — Lard, and bake until brown, basting with brown stock. Serve with peas.

Fried. — Roll in *fine bread crumbs*, *egg*, and a second time in *crumbs*, and fry in deep *fat*, or sauté in a little fat.

No. 2. — Cut in *half-inch slices*, roll in *seasoned crumbs*, *egg*, and *crumbs* again. Put *three slices* on a small skewer, alternating with *three thin slices* of *bacon one inch square*. Fry in

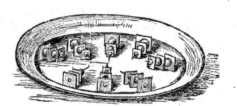

Fig. 31.   Sweetbreads and Bacon.

deep fat. Serve on the skewers, with *tomato sauce.*

Creamed. — Cut in small pieces, and serve in a *white sauce*, on *toast* or in *toast patties* or in *puff-paste shells* or as a *vol-au-vent.*

Broiled. — Rub with *butter*, *salt*, and *pepper;* wrap in buttered paper, and broil ten minutes. Serve with *Maître d'Hôtel butter.*

Scalloped or in Cases. — Cut or break the sweetbreads into small sections. Mix with a *rich cream sauce* made with *eggs* (see page 190). Put them in a scallop dish, in shells, or in paper cases. Cover with *buttered crumbs*, and bake until the crumbs are brown.

With Mushrooms. — Prepare as for *creamed* or *scalloped,* and add half or an equal amount of *mushrooms,* chopped or cut into quarters. Garnish with *toast points.*

Braised. — Lard with *bacon.* Put in a covered pan with fried *onions,* and *parsley,* and *a pinch* of *herbs,* tied in a cloth. Half cover with *stock.* Bake forty or fifty minutes.

Fritters. — Break into sections, and mix with a fritter batter (page 106). Fry by small spoonfuls in deep fat.

Sweetbread Croquettes, see Index.

To serve sweetbreads, either larded, broiled, or fried, arrange around a centre of tomato sauce, mushrooms, or

FIG. 32. Sweetbreads on Macaroni.

peas. Or put the sweetbreads in the centre on a nest of boiled macaroni. Sprinkle the macaroni with cheese, and pour white sauce or tomato sauce over it; or garnish the sweetbreads with stuffed tomatoes.

Garnish for Fried or Larded Sweetbreads. — Cut into strips the size of matches, part of the breast of a roasted or boiled *chicken,* some cold boiled *ham* and cooked *spaghetti,* about *a cup* of each. Keep them hot in a steamer until the sauce is ready. Stew *half a can* of *tomato* until soft. Rub all but the seeds through a purée strainer. Heat again and boil down till quite thick and reduced to *one cup.* Season with *one tablespoonful* of *butter,* *half a teaspoonful* of *salt,* *a bit* of *cayenne,* and *one tablespoonful* of *lemon juice.* Add *one tablespoonful* of *glaze* if you have it. When the sweetbreads are ready, arrange the mixture of ham, spaghetti, and chicken on a hot platter; pour the tomato over it and lay the sweetbreads on the top.

PORK.

Pork is an unwholesome meat, and should never be eaten by children, or people with weak digestion, nor, indeed, by any one except in cold weather. Salt pork, bacon, and ham are less objectionable than fresh pork. If fresh pork be desired, obtain it, if possible, from a source where you can be sure the animal has been kept in a cleanly manner and fattened on corn. Fresh pork should be young and firm, the fat white, the lean a pale red, and the skin white and clear. The fat, when salted, should be a delicate pink, and the rind should be thin. Soft, flabby flesh, and yellowish fat with kernels, indicate that the pork is not of the best quality. Unlike other meat, pork is divided into fat and lean. The flank and the thick layer of fat above the flesh are salted. The sides of very young pigs are smoked, as well as salted, and are called bacon. The hams and shoulders are salted and smoked. The head and feet are pickled or boiled, and made into souse or head cheese. After the fat is removed, the loin and ribs are used for roasting or for chops. The leaf fat from the kidneys is heated until melted, then strained, cooled, and used as lard. The trimmings of lean and fat, when chopped and highly seasoned; are called sausage meat.

Roast Pig.

Select a pig from three to five weeks old. Clean well, and stuff with hot *mashed potatoes*, or *stale bread*, highly seasoned with *sage, salt, pepper,* and *onions*. If bread be used, moisten with *warm water, melted butter,* and *one beaten egg*. Stuff and sew. Skewer the fore legs forward, and the hind legs backward. Rub all over with *butter, salt, pepper,* and *flour.* Put it into a pan with a little water; the oven should not be very hot at first, as it should be thoroughly warmed through before browning. Baste very often, and at first use *melted butter* to make the skin tender and soft. Be careful not to let it burn. Bake two and a half or three hours. Arrange in a bed of *parsley* and *celery leaves,* with a " tuft of *cauliflower* in the mouth and a garland of *parsley* round the neck." Serve with *apple sauce* or *pickles.* In carving, cut off the head, then the hams and shoulders; split down the back, and separate the ribs.

Roast Pork. — The chine, or loin, and the spare ribs are the best pieces for roasting. Rub well with *pepper,* or *sage, salt,* and *flour,* and bake twenty minutes for each pound. Baste often, and do not have the oven as hot as for other meat. Roast pork is more wholesome when eaten cold.

Pork Chops or Steaks. — If pork chops are to be broiled, they should be cut very thin, *salted,* and *peppered,* wrapped in greased paper, and broiled until thoroughly cooked, — from ten to fifteen minutes. To fry or sauté them, cook them in a hot frying-pan in a little *hot lard* or *salt pork fat.* Cook slowly after they are brown, and be careful not to burn them. If a gravy be desired, pour off nearly all the fat left in the frying-pan, add *two tablespoonfuls* of *flour,* and when brown add hot water until of the desired consistency. Season with *salt, pepper, vinegar,* and *chopped pickles.*

Breakfast Bacon. — Cut off the rind and smoked part; slice very thin; cook in a frying-pan till the fat is tried out and the bacon is dry and crisp, or fry in deep fat. Drain on paper, and serve alone or as a garnish for beefsteak.

Fried Salt Pork. — Cut *fat salt pork* in thin slices; pour hot water over them; drain, and fry in a pan until crisp; or roll in *egg* and *crumbs,* and fry in deep hot *fat.* Serve with *salt fish* or *fried mush* or *baked potatoes.*

Boiled Ham.

If very salt, let it soak over night. Scrub well; trim off the hard black part, cover with cold water, and let it simmer slowly, allowing half an hour to the pound. Take it from the fire; let it remain in the water until nearly cold; then peel off the skin and sprinkle *sugar* and *grated bread*, or *cracker crumbs*, over the top, and brown in the oven. Or boil until nearly tender; remove the skin and bake two hours; baste often with *vinegar*. Cover with crumbs, return to the oven, and brown. Or omit the crumbs and cover with a paste made with *one teaspoonful* of *brown flour* and *half a cup* of *brown sugar*, moistened with a little *port wine*. Spread this over the ham, and brown in the oven. Serve with a *brown sauce* flavored with *half a glass* of *champagne*. Trim the knuckle with a paper ruffle. In carving, cut in very thin slices. Old hams are improved by adding a *pint* of *vinegar* and *a tablespoonful* of *herbs* to the water in which they are boiled. If the ham is not to be served whole, boil till it is very tender; let it cool, and remove the skin and bones, and press it, with the fat well mixed with the lean. A boiled ham is done when the skin will peel easily.

To serve Cold Boiled Ham. — Cut in thin slices; season highly with *cayenne pepper*, or with *mustard* and *lemon juice*, and broil two minutes.

Melt *half a glass* of *currant jelly;* add *a teaspoonful* of *butter*, a little *pepper*, and when hot add several small thin slices of *ham*. Let it boil up and serve at once.

Fried Ham. — Cut the ham in thin slices, remove the outside, gash the fat, and cook in a frying-pan till the fat is crisp. If cooked too long, it will become hard and dry. Ham will fry quicker and be less dry if cooked in hot lard or some of the ham fat from a previous frying.

Broiled Ham. — Cut in very thin slices, and broil three or four minutes. Old or very salt ham should be parboiled five minutes before being broiled. Serve with *poached eggs.*

Sausages.

If you like to know what you are eating, have your sausage meat prepared at home or by some one whom you can trust. Of sweet *fresh pork* take *one third fat* and *two thirds lean*, and chop fine, or have it ground by your butcher. Season highly with *salt, pepper,* and *sage* (use the whole sage; dry, pound, and sift it). Mix thoroughly. Make cotton bags, one yard long and four inches wide. Dip them in strong salt and water, and dry before filling. Crowd the meat into the bags closely, pressing it with a pestle or potato-masher. Tie the bag tightly and keep in a cool place. When wanted for use, turn the end of the bag back, and cut off the meat in half-inch slices, and cook in a frying-pan till brown. Core and quarter several *apples*, and fry in the hot fat and serve with the sausages.

A safe rule in seasoning sausage meat is *one even table-spoonful* of *salt*, *one teaspoonful* of *sifted sage*, and *a scant half-teaspoonful* of *white pepper* to *each pound* of meat.

Souse.

Take the gristly part of the pig's head, but not the fat; also the ears and feet. Remove the hard part from the feet. Scald or singe the hairs, soak in warm water, and scrape thoroughly. Let them remain in salt and water for ten hours. Scrape, and clean again, and put them a second time in freshly salted water. With proper care they will be perfectly clean. Put them in a kettle and cover with cold water; skim when it begins to boil; set back and let it simmer till the bones slip out easily. Skim out the meat, and remove the hard gristle, bones, and any superfluous fat. Season with *salt, pepper,* and *vinegar,* and pack in stone jars. When hard, cut in slices, and brown in the oven.

Head Cheese. — Prepare the same as souse, omitting the *vinegar,* and season with *sage.* Put into a strainer cloth, and press out the fat. Pack it in jars or moulds. Serve cold, or brown slightly in a frying-pan.

Though seldom seen on modern tables, these dishes when carefully prepared are very acceptable to many who have pleasant recollections of them as served at "grand-mother's table."

To Try out Lard.

Cut the leaves into small pieces; remove all flesh and membrane; put a few pieces in a kettle on the back of the stove, and when they are heated through, put in the remainder. Cook slowly until the scraps are crisp; strain through a fine cloth into tin pails or pans, and press that obtained from the scraps into a separate pail. Never put water with the leaves, as the object is to expel that which they already contain, and there is no danger of burning if only a few pieces be put in at first, and the kettle be not over the hot fire. The kettle should not be covered until the scraps are crisp; then cover it, and if no steam condenses on the cover, the water is evaporated.

Baked Pork and Beans.

Soak *one quart* of *pea beans* in cold water over night. In the morning put them into fresh cold water, and simmer till soft enough to pierce with a pin, being careful not to let them boil enough to break. If you like, boil *one onion* with them. When soft, turn them into a colander, and pour cold water through them. Place them with the onion in a bean-pot. Pour boiling water over *one quarter* of *a pound* of *salt pork*, part fat and part lean; scrape the rind till white. Cut the rind in half-inch strips; bury the pork in the beans, leaving only the rind exposed. Mix *one teaspoonful* of *salt* — more, if the pork is not very salt — and *one teaspoonful* of *mustard* with *one quarter* of *a cup* of *molasses*. Fill the cup with hot water, and when well mixed pour it over the beans; add enough more water to cover them. Keep them covered with water until the last hour; then lift the pork to the surface and let it crisp. Bake eight hours in a moderate oven. Use more *salt* and *one third* of *a cup* of *butter* if you dislike pork, or use *half a pound* of fat and lean *corned beef*.

The mustard gives the beans a delicious flavor, and also renders them more wholesome. Many add *a teaspoonful* of *soda* to the water in which the beans are boiled, to destroy the acid in the skin of the beans. Yellow-eyed beans and Lima beans are also good when baked.

Much of the excellence of baked beans depends upon the bean-pot. It should be earthen, with a narrow mouth and bulging sides. This shape is seldom found outside of New England, and is said to have been modelled after the Assyrian pots. In spite of the slurs against "Boston Baked Beans" it is often remarked that strangers enjoy them as much as natives; and many a New England bean-pot has been carried to the extreme South and West, that people there might have "baked beans" in perfection. They afford a nutritious and cheap food for people who labor in the open air.

Parsnip and Pork Stew.

Clean and scrape the rind of *one quarter* of a *pound* of *fat salt pork*. Put it on to boil in *two quarts* of *cold water*. Put with it any remnants of *cold roast pork* or *pork chops*, first removing any burned parts; or you may use *one pound* of fresh, uncooked *pork*, or only the salt pork, if you prefer. After it has stewed for an hour, skim off the fat. Wash and scrape *two* large *parsnips*, cut then in inch slices, and add them to the stew; add, also, *one* small *onion*, sliced. Half an hour before dinner, add *four* or *five potatoes*, cut in small pieces, and parboiled five minutes. When done, skim out the meat and vegetables, thicken the liquor with flour and water, add more salt and pepper, if necessary, cook ten minutes longer, then pour it over the meat.

POULTRY AND GAME.

THE flesh of poultry and of game birds has less red blood than the flesh of animals; but as it abounds in phosphates, it is valuable food, particularly for invalids. The flesh is drier, and not marbled with fat as in that of quadrupeds. All game has a strong odor and flavor, which is by some mistaken for that of tainted meat. It should be kept till tender, but no longer, unless frozen.

White-fleshed game should be cooked till well done; that with dark flesh may be served underdone. The breast of all birds is the most juicy and nutritious part. "The wing of a walker and the leg of a flier are considered choice tidbits."

To Choose Poultry and Game. — The best *chickens* have soft yellow feet, short thick legs, smooth moist skin, plump breast; and the cartilage on the end of the breast bone is soft and pliable. This is sometimes broken in fowls to deceive purchasers; but the difference between a broken bone, that slips when moved, and a soft yielding cartilage may be very easily detected. Pin feathers always indicate a young bird; and long hairs, an older one. The bodies of *capons* are very plump and fat, and larger in proportion than those of fowls or chickens. The meat is of finer flavor.

. *Old fowls* have long thin necks and feet, and sharp scales; the flesh has a purplish tinge, and they usually have a large amount of fat.

The best *turkeys* have smooth black legs, with soft, loose spurs, full breasts, and white plump flesh.

Geese and *ducks* should be young, not more than a year old, have white soft fat, yellow feet, and tender wings, and be thick and hard on the breast. The windpipe should break when pressed with the thumb and finger. Wild ducks have reddish feet. Tame ducks have thick yellowish feet.

Young pigeons have light red flesh on the breast, and full flesh-colored legs. *Old pigeons* are thin, and the breast very dark. *Wild pigeons* are cheaper, but are dry and tough. Stall-fed pigeons are the best. *Squabs* are young tame pigeons, and always have pin feathers.

Grouse, partridge, and *quail* should have full heavy breasts, dark bills, and yellowish legs.

Young rabbits should have smooth, sharp claws, tender ears and paws, and short necks.

Venison should be dark red, with some white fat.

To Clean and Truss Poultry and Game. — The practice of sending poultry to market undressed is one that demands as earnest opposition from housekeepers as that of the adulteration of food. The meat is rendered unfit to eat, is sometimes infected with poison ; and the increase in weight makes poultry a very expensive food. All poultry should be dressed as soon as killed. The feathers come out more easily when the fowl is warm, and when stripped off toward the head. If the skin be very tender, pull the feathers out the opposite way. Use a knife to remove the pin feathers. Singe the hairs and down by holding the fowl over a gas jet, or over a roll of lighted paper held over the fire. Cut off the head, and if the fowl is to be roasted, slip the skin back from the neck and cut the neck off close to the body, leaving skin enough to fold over on the back. Remove the windpipe ; pull the crop away from the skin on the neck and breast, and cut off close to the opening into the body. Be careful not to tear the skin. Always pull the crop out from the end of the neck, rather than through a cut in the skin, which if made has to be sewed together. Cut through the skin about two inches below the leg joint ; bend the leg at the cut by pressing it on the edge of the table, and break off the bone. Then pull, not cut, out the tendons. If care be taken to cut only through the skin, these cords may be pulled out easily, one at a time, with the fingers. Or take them all out at once, by putting the foot of the fowl against the casing of a door, then shut the door tightly and pull on the leg. The tendons will come out with the foot; but if once cut they cannot be removed. The drumstick of a roast chicken or turkey is greatly improved by removing the tendons, which always become hard and bony in baking. There is a special advantage in cutting the leg below the joint, as the ends of the bones afford more length for tying, and after roasting this is easily broken off, leaving a clean, unburned joint for the table. Cut out the oil bag in the tail. It is better to dress a fowl for a fricassee first. Then you learn the position of the internal organs, and can tell better how to remove them when dressing for roasting, as with the whole fowl you work by feeling and not by sight.

To Cut up a Fowl for a Fricassee. — Cut through the loose skin between the legs and body, bend the leg over, and cut off at the joint; then cut off the wings. Make an incision in the skin near the vent, and cut the membrane lying between the breastbone and the tail, down to the backbone, on each side. Then you have the intestines, gizzard, liver, and heart exposed, and can easily remove them. Do not forget the kidneys, lying in the hollow of the backbone, and the lungs in the ribs. Cut the ribs through the cartilage, separate the collar bone, and break the backbone just below the ribs. Divide at the joints in the wings and legs; separate the side bones from the back, and remove the bone from the breast. Never chop the bones, but divide smoothly at the joints.

To Dress a Fowl for Roasting. — Make an incision near the vent; insert two fingers, loosen the fat from the skin, and separate the membranes lying close to the body. Keep the fingers up close to the breastbone, until you can reach in beyond the liver and heart, and loosen on either side down toward the back. The gall bladder lies under the lobe of the liver on the left side, and if the fingers be kept up, and everything loosened before drawing out, there will be no danger of its breaking. The kidneys and lungs are often left in by careless cooks; but everything that can be taken out must be removed. When the fowl has been cleaned carefully, it will not require much washing. Hold it under the faucet, or rinse out the inside quickly; then wipe dry.

If the breastbone protrude more than is desirable, put a small knife in at the opening, and cut through the cartilage in the ribs or through the breastbone. Or put a pestle in the inside, lay a towel over the breast, and pound slightly until the bone gives way.

To Stuff a Fowl. — Place the fowl in a bowl, and put the stuffing in at the neck; fill out the breast until plump and even. Then draw the neck skin together at the end, and sew it over on the back. Put the remainder of the stuffing into the body at the other opening, and if full, sew it with coarse thread or fine twine. If not full, sewing is unnecessary, except when the fowl is to be boiled.

To Truss a Fowl. — Draw the thighs up close to the body, and cross the legs over the tail, and tie firmly with twine. Put a long skewer through the thigh into the body and out through the opposite thigh, and another through the wings, drawing them close to the body. Wind a string from the tail to the skewer in the thigh, then up to the one in the wing, across the back to the other wing, then down to the opposite thigh, and tie firmly round the tail. If you have no skewers, the strings must be passed round the body, over the thighs and wings; and care must be taken, in removing them, not to tear the browned crust on the breast. Sometimes the feet are cut off in the joint, and the legs passed into the body and out through an opening under the sidebone near the tail, or left in the body and covered with the skin.

To Clean the Giblets. — Slip off the thin membrane round the heart, cut out the veins and arteries, remove the liver, and cut off all that looks green near the gall bladder. Trim the fat and membranes from the gizzard, cut through the thick part; open it, and remove the inner lining without breaking. Cut off all the white gristle, and use only

' the thick fleshy part. Wash, and put them in cold water, and simmer till tender. The neck and tips of the wings are often cooked with the giblets.

These directions apply to all kinds of poultry and game.

Wild ducks, coot, and geese should be washed thoroughly on the outside before being drawn. Scrub them with slightly warm water and soap. The skin is very thick and oily, and it is impossible to get it clean without soap.

The strong smell in old fowls may be removed by washing in warm soda water.

To dress Fowls or Birds for Broiling. — Singe, wipe, and split down the middle of the back; lay open, and then remove the contents from the inside. Cut the tendons in the thigh, or break the joints, and remove the breastbone to facilitate the carving.

To Carve Poultry — Place the fowl on the platter, with the head at the left. Put the fork in across the breastbone. Cut through the skin round the leg joint. Bend the leg over and cut off at the joint. Then cut off the wings, and divide wings and legs at the joints. Carve the breast in thin slices parallel with the breastbone. Some prefer to cut it at right angles with the bone. Take off the wish-bone; separate the collar-bone from the breast; slip the knife under the shoulder blade, and turn it over. Cut through the cartilage which divides the ribs, separating the breast from the back. Then turn the back over, place the knife midway, and with the fork lift up the tail end, separating the back from the body. Place the fork in the middle of the backbone, and cut close to the backbone, from one end to the other, freeing the side bone. As soon as the legs and wings are disjointed, begin to serve, offering white or dark meat and stuffing as each prefers. Do not remove the fork from the breastbone till the breast is separated from the back. Use an extra fork in serving. If all the fowl be not required, carve only from one side, leaving the opposite side whole for another meal.

Gravy for Roast Poultry and Game. — Put the *giblets*, or , neck, liver, gizzard, and heart, on to boil in *one quart* of *water*, and boil till tender, and the water reduced to *one pint*. Mash the liver, and if desired chop the gizzard, heart, and meat from the neck. Pour off the clear fat from the dripping-pan, and put the settlings into a sauce-pan; rinse out the pan with the water in which the giblets were boiled, and pour this water into the saucepan and put on to boil. Put *three* or *four tablespoonfuls* of the *fat* into a small frying-pan; add enough *dry flour* to absorb all the fat, and when brown add the giblet liquor gradually, and stir till it thickens. Season with *salt* and *pepper*. If not smooth, strain it; pour half of it into the gravy boat, and add the chopped giblets to the remaining half, and serve separately, as all may not care for the giblet gravy.

Roast Turkey.

Clean as directed on page 252. Stuff with *soft bread* or *cracker crumbs* highly seasoned with *sage, thyme, salt,* and *pepper*; moisten the stuffing with *half a cup* of *melted butter*, and *hot water* enough to make it quite moist. Add *one beaten egg*. Some use salt pork chopped fine, but stuffing is more wholesome without it. *Oysters, chestnuts, chopped celery, stoned raisins*, or *dates* make a pleasing variety.

For *Stuffing* and *Trussing*, see page 254. Put the turkey on a rack in a pan, rub well with butter, and dredge with *salt, pepper,* and *flour*. Put in a hot oven, and when the flour is browned reduce the heat, and add *a pint* of *water*. Baste with butter until nicely browned; then with the fat in the pan. Baste often, and dredge with *salt* and *flour* after every basting. Allow three hours for an eight-pound turkey. Cook till the legs will separate from the body. Prepare the gravy as directed above. Garnish the turkey with *parsley* or *celery leaves* and *sausages* or *force-meat balls*. Serve *cranberry sauce* or *currant jelly* with roast turkey.

If the giblets be not desired in the gravy, they may be boiled, chopped fine, and mixed with the stuffing; or make them into force-meat balls, with an equal amount of *soft bread crumbs*. Moisten, and season highly, and brown them in *hot butter*.

Boiled or Steamed Turkey or Fowl.

Clean; rub well with *salt*, *pepper*, and *lemon juice*, and stuff with *oyster* or *bread stuffing*. It is better without the stuffing, as the oysters are usually over-done, and the same flavor may be obtained from an oyster sauce served with the turkey. Truss the legs and wings close to the body; pin the fowl in a cloth to keep it whiter and preserve the shape. Put into boiling salted water. Allow twenty minutes to the pound. Cook slowly till tender, but not long enough for it to fall apart. Turkeys are much nicer steamed than boiled. Serve with *oyster*, *celery*, *lemon*, or *caper sauce*. Garnish with a border of *boiled rice* or *macaroni*, and pour part of the sauce over the fowl.

Fowls are sometimes stuffed with *boiled celery*, cut into pieces an inch long; or with *macaroni* which has been boiled and seasoned with *salt* and *pepper*.

Roast Chicken.

Singe; remove the pin feathers, oil bag, crop, entrails, legs, and tendons. Wipe, stuff, sew, and tie or skewer into shape. Place it on one side, on a rack in a dripping-pan, without water. Dredge, and rub all over with *salt*, *pepper*, *soft butter*, and *flour*. Put chicken fat or beef drippings over it and in the pan. Roast in a hot oven, with a rack under the pan. When the flour is brown, check the heat, baste with the fat, and afterwards with *one third* of a *cup* of *butter*, melted in *one cup* of *hot water*. When brown, turn the other side up; then place it on the back, that the breast may be browned. Baste often, and dredge with flour after basting. Add more water if needed. Bake a four-pound chicken an hour and a half, or till the

17

joints separate easily.　Lay buttered paper over it, if it brown too fast.

Stuffing. — Moisten *one cup* of *cracker* or *soft bread crumbs* with *one third* of *a cup* of *melted butter;* season highly with *salt, pepper,* and *thyme.*

Chestnut Stuffing — Shell *one quart* of large *chestnuts.* Pour on boiling water, and remove the inner brown skin. Boil in *salted water* or *stock* till soft.　Mash fine.　Take half for the stuffing, and mix with it *one cup* of *fine cracker crumbs;* season with *one teaspoonful* of *salt,* one *saltspoonful* of *pepper,* and *one teaspoonful* of *chopped parsley.* Moisten with *one third* of *a cup* of *melted butter.*　Professional cooks sometimes mix a little *apple sauce,* flavored with *wine, lemon,* and *sugar,* with a chestnut stuffing.

Chestnut Sauce. — Remove the fat from the dripping-pan; add nearly a *pint* of *hot water;* thicken with *flour* which has been cooked in *brown butter;* add *salt* and *pepper,* and the remainder of the *chestnuts.*

Braised Fowl.

Prepare the same as for roasting; dredge with *salt, pepper,* and *flour,* and brown slightly in *hot butter* or *chicken fat* in a frying-pan.　Put in a deep pan; half cover with water.　Add the *giblets, one onion,* and *one table-spoonful* of *herbs* tied in a bag.　Cover with a tightly fitting pan, and bake till tender, basting often.　Chop the giblets, thicken, season, and strain the gravy; add the giblets, and pour around the fowl.

Chicken Fricassee.

Singe, and cut the chicken at the joints, in pieces for serving　Cover with boiling water; add *one heaping teaspoonful* of *salt,* and *half a saltspoonful* of *pepper.*　Simmer one hour, or till tender, reducing the water to nearly a pint. Remove all the large bones, dredge with *salt, pepper,* and *flour,* and brown in *hot butter.*　Put the chicken on *toast* on a hot platter.　Strain the liquor and remove the fat.

Add to the liquor *one cup* of *cream* or *milk*, and heat it again. Melt *one large tablespoonful* of *butter* in a saucepan; add *two tablespoonfuls* of *flour*, and when well mixed pour on slowly the *cream* and *chicken liquor*. Add *salt, pepper, half a teaspoonful* of *celery salt, one teaspoonful* of *lemon juice*. Beat *one egg;* pour the sauce slowly on the egg; stir well, and pour over the chicken. The chicken may be browned before cooking, then stewed, and a brown gravy made by browning the butter before adding the flour. *Half a can* of *mushrooms* may be added to improve the flavor, letting them simmer in the sauce five minutes. Arrange the body of the chicken in the centre of the dish, with the wings at the top, the thighs below, and the ends of the drumsticks crossed at the tail.

If the chicken be not fried, it is simply a *chicken stew,* and dumplings may be added, or not, as you prefer. And if put into a deep dish with a rich gravy, made as for fricassee, but without the egg, and covered with a rich crust of pastry and baked, it is *chicken pie.*

Chicken Curry.

Cut the chicken at the joints, and remove the breast bones. Wipe, season with *salt* and *pepper*, dredge with *flour*, and brown lightly in *hot butter*. Put in a stewpan. Fry *one large onion*, cut in thin slices, in the butter left in the pan till colored, but not browned. Mix *one large tablespoonful* of *flour, one teaspoonful* of *sugar*, and *one tablespoonful* of *curry powder*, and brown them in the butter. Add slowly *one cup* of *water* or *stock* and *one cup* of *strained tomatoes*, or *one sour apple* chopped, and *salt* and *pepper* to taste. Pour this sauce over the chicken, and simmer one hour, or till tender. Add *one cup* of *hot milk* or *cream*. Boil one minute longer, and serve with a border of *boiled rice.*

Rabbit, veal, and lamb may be curried in the same way.

Broiled Chicken.

Singe, and split a young spring chicken down the back. Break the joints ; remove the breastbone, clean, and wipe with a wet cloth. Sprinkle with *salt* and *pepper*, and rub well with *soft butter*. Place in a double gridiron, and broil twenty minutes over a clear fire. Spread with *butter*, and serve very hot. Or cover with *fine bread crumbs* and bake in a hot oven half an hour. Serve with *Tartar sauce*.

To Carve. — Separate the legs and wings, and then separate the breast from the lower part.

Fried Chicken.

Singe ; cut at the joints ; remove the breast bones. Wipe each piece with a clean wet cloth ; dredge with *salt, pepper*, and *flour*, and sauté them in hot *salt pork fat* till brown and tender, but not burned. Arrange on a dish, with boiled *cauliflower* or *potato balls*, and pour a *white sauce* over them. Or dip in *egg* and *crumbs*, and fry in deep hot *fat*, and serve with *tomato sauce*.

Broiled Fillets of Chicken.

Remove the bone from the breast and thighs. Rub the meat with *butter* or *olive oil ;* season, and cover with *fine cracker dust*. Broil about ten minutes.

Devilled Chicken.

Boil a chicken until tender in boiling salted water. When cold, cut at the joints, baste with *soft butter,* and broil till brown. Or cut any cold boiled or roasted chicken at the joints, rub with *salt* and *butter*, and broil till warmed through. Pour hot *Tartar sauce* over them. Or make several incisions in the flesh, and rub with *mustard* and *cayenne pepper* before broiling.

Roast Goose.

Singe, remove the pin feathers, and before it is cut or drawn, wash and scrub thoroughly in warm soapsuds, to open and cleanse the pores, and render the oil more easy to be extracted. Then draw, as directed on page 253. Wash and rinse the inside in clear water, and wipe dry. Stuff with *mashed potatoes* highly seasoned with *onion, sage, salt,* and *pepper,* or with equal parts of *bread crumbs, chopped apples,* and *boiled onions,* seasoned with *salt, sage,* and *pepper.* Sew and truss; put on a rack in a pan, and cover the breast with slices of fat salt pork. Place in the oven for three quarters of an hour. The pork fat is quickly drawn out by the heat, flows over the goose, and aids in drawing out the oil. When considerable oil is extracted, take the pan from the oven, and pour off all the oil. Remove the pork, and dredge the goose with *flour,* and place again in the oven. When the flour is browned, add a little hot water, and baste often. Dredge with flour after basting. Cook until brown and tender. Make a gravy as on page 256. Garnish with *watercresses.* Serve with *apple sauce.*

Roast Ducks.

Pick, singe, and remove the crop, entrails, oil bag, legs, and pinions. Wipe, truss, dredge with *salt, pepper, butter,* and *flour.* Bake in a hot oven twenty minutes if liked rare, or thirty minutes if preferred well done. Serve with *olive sauce* and *green peas.* Geese and ducks have a strong flavor, and are improved by stuffing the craw and body with *apples* cored and quartered. The apples absorb the strong flavor, therefore should not be eaten. *Celery* and *onions* are also placed inside the duck, to improve its flavor.

Braised Ducks.

Ducks that are tough and unfit to roast are improved by being braised with *onions, carrots,* and *turnips.* Or they may be stewed, and served with canned *peas.*

Larded Grouse.

Clean, wipe, lard the breast and legs, and truss. Rub with *salt* and *soft butter*, and dredge with *flour*. Roast twenty minutes in a quick oven if liked rare, thirty minutes if well done. Serve with *bread sauce.*

Potted Pigeons.

Draw and clean. Break the legs just above the feet; leave enough below the joint to tie down to the tail. Wash and wipe. If old and tough, cover them with *vinegar*, spiced and flavored with *onion*, and let them stand several hours. This makes them tender. Drain and wipe; stuff, if you like, with *cracker crumbs* highly seasoned and moistened with *butter*. Dredge with *salt, pepper,* and *flour.* Fry several slices of *salt pork ;* cut *one large onion* fine, and fry in the salt pork fat. Put the crisp fat in the stewpan, add the fried onion, then brown the pigeons all over in the fat left in the pan. Put them in the stewpan ; add *boiling water* or *stock* enough to half cover them ; add *a pinch* of *herbs* tied in a bag. Simmer from one to three hours, or till the pigeons are tender. Remove the fat from the broth, season to taste, and thicken with *flour* and *butter* cooked together. Strain over the pigeons, and serve hot.

Braised Pigeons.

Prepare the pigeons as for potted pigeons, and cook in a braising-pan. Cook *spinach* (see page 296) ; chop it fine, and season. Spread the spinach on slices of *toast,* and lay the pigeons on the spinach one on each slice. Serve the gravy in a boat.

Pigeons Stuffed with Parsley. (*Miss Ward.*)

Allow *one pint* of *loose parsley* for each pigeon. Wash, remove the large stems, and chop very fine, adding *salt* and *pepper* and *two* or *three tablespoonfuls* of *water* while chopping. Stuff the pigeons with the parsley; add also the *heart* and a *half-inch cube* of *salt pork* for each pigeon. Add the water left in the tray to that in the stewpan, and cook as in the preceding rule.

Roast Birds.

Draw, and wash quickly; season with *salt* and *pepper*. Pin a thin slice of *salt pork* on the breast. Put on a shallow pan, and bake in a hot oven, fifteen or twenty minutes. Baste often. Serve on *toast* with *currant jelly* or with *bread sauce*. Small birds may be baked in *sweet potatoes*, or if large cut in halves, using the breast only. Cut the potatoes in halves lengthwise, make a cavity in each half, season the bird with *salt, pepper,* and *butter;* fit it into the potato, put the other half over it, and bake till the potatoes are soft. Remove the string, tie with a bright ribbon, and serve in the potatoes, garnished with *parsley.* An inviting dish to serve to an invalid.

Small birds are also *broiled* or *stewed*.

Quail.

Quail may be roasted, broiled, or braised; or the breasts only may be removed and broiled. Use the bones and trimmings to make stock for a rich sauce.

Woodcock.

Dress, and wipe clean. Dredge inside and out with *salt* and *pepper;* tie the legs close to the body, skin the head and neck, and tie the beak under the wings. Tie a piece of *bacon* over the breast, and fry in *boiling lard* two minutes; or roast in the oven, and serve on *toast*.

Venison.

Venison is one of the most easily digested meats. It may be cooked after the same rules as mutton or beef. It should be cooked rare, and served very hot with *currant jelly.* The saddle, or loin, is the choicest cut for roasting or for steaks. Steaks are also cut from the leg.

Venison steaks should be broiled the same as beefsteaks, and served with *Maître d'Hôtel butter*, made with *currant jelly* instead of *lemon juice.* The cheaper, tougher parts of venison may be stewed or braised. Venison should be wiped carefully before cooking, as the hairs are often found clinging to the meat.

Rabbits and Squirrels.

These may be cooked the same as chickens, — stewed, fricasseed, or larded and baked.

Fig. 83. Birds and Spinach on Toast.

Brunswick Stew.

Two squirrels, well skinned and cleaned, or *two* small *chickens.* Put them into a large kettle with *two quarts* of *cold water.* Add *one slice* of *bacon, two quarts* of *tomatoes, six* large *potatoes* sliced thin, *one quart* of *Lima beans, two* large *onions* sliced, *one tablespoon* of *salt,* and *half a teaspoon* of *pepper.* Let it stew until tender. Add more water as it boils away. Add *six* ears of *corn* cut from the cob, cook twenty minutes longer, being very careful not to let it burn.

ENTRÉES AND MEAT RÉCHAUFFÉ.

Boned Turkey or Chicken.

BONE the turkey as directed on page 27.

Stuffing for a Hen Turkey weighing Eight Pounds. — The meat from a *four-pound chicken, one pound* of *raw, lean veal, one cup* of *cracker crumbs, two eggs, boiling stock* enough to moisten, *salt, pepper,* and *thyme* to taste, and *one cup* of *potted ham* or *tongue.*

Disjoint the chicken; remove the skin, tough sinews, and bones. Cut the meat from the thighs and breast in

FIG. 34. Boned Turkey, browned and served like a Roast Turkey.

long thin strips, lay it aside, and chop all the remainder with the veal. Do not use any salt pork unless you wish the stuffing to taste like sausage meat. Add the cracker crumbs; make it quite moist with hot stock, and season to taste. Fill the legs and wings of the turkey with the force-meat. Put the fillets, which came out in boning, on the skin below the breast; then a layer of force-meat with a little of the tongue here and there; or you may use thin slices of boiled tongue or ham. Then a layer of the re-served meat from the chicken, and force-meat again. Sew and tie into the natural shape. Or, if for a galantine, turn the legs and wings inside before stuffing, and roll up. Sew tightly in a cloth. Put the bones of chicken and turkey and all the trimmings from the veal in a kettle, and cover with cold water. Steam the turkey over the bones three hours. Remove the cloth, dredge with *salt* and *flour*, and bake one hour or until nicely browned. Serve cold, and garnish with *parsley*, *sparkling jelly*, *carrots*, and *beets* cut into fancy shapes, or with *potato balls*. Carve in slices across the breast.

When the turkey is to be moulded in jelly, strain the liquor in which the bones were boiled; remove the fat, clear, and stiffen with gelatine as directed below. Make a brown aspic jelly with soup stock. Mould in the dark jelly and garnish with the light, or *vice versa*.

Stuffing for Boned Chicken. — Use more veal, omit the chicken, and vary the amount of the other ingredients

FIG. 35. Boned Chicken, larded and baked.

given in stuffing for turkey, according to the size of the fowl. Lardoons of pork may be inserted all over the top when the chicken is to be browned in the oven.

To Mould in Aspic Jelly. — Take enough *stock* to fill the mould, — *beef* if for dark jelly, and *veal* or *chicken*, if for light. Season highly with *salt*, *pepper*, *celery seed*, *herbs*, *lemon*, or *wine*. If a darker shade be desired, add a little *caramel*. For *three pints* of *stock* mix the *whites* and *shells* of *two eggs* with the cold stock; add *one box* of *Cox's gelatine* which has been soaked in *one cup* of *cold water*. Put all over the fire, and stir till hot. Boil till a thick scum has formed; remove that, and strain the liquor through a fine napkin.

Pack a mould in a pan of snow or broken ice, and pour in jelly to the depth of half an inch. When hard, garnish with *fancy vegetables* of *different colors*, *slices* of *hard-boiled eggs*, *Italian paste*, *rings* of *macaroni*, etc. Fasten each ornament in place with liquid jelly, and when hard add enough jelly to cover all. When this is hard, place the meat, or whatever you have to mould, in the centre, being careful not to let it break the jelly. Keep the meat in place with some of the liquid jelly, and when hard add enough jelly to fill the mould. If to be decorated on the side, dip

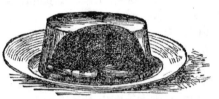

FIG. 36.   Chicken in Jelly.

the ornaments in the liquid jelly, and if the mould be icy cold, they will adhere. The jelly must be added slowly. Keep in the mould in a cool place till ready to serve. To remove it, dip the mould quickly in warm (not hot) water, put the dish over it, and invert dish and mould together. Garnish with *parsley* and *sparkling jelly*.

Tongue, boned turkey or *chicken, birds, moulds* of *different kinds* of *meat* and *fish*, etc., may be served in jelly.

Pressed Chicken.

An Easy Way of Preparing Boneless Chicken. — Boil a fowl in as little water as possible till the bones slip out and the gristly portions are soft. Remove the skin, pick the meat apart, and mix the dark and white meats. Remove the fat, and season the liquor highly with *salt* and *pepper;* also with *celery salt* and *lemon juice*, if you like. Boil down to *one cupful*, and mix with the meat. Butter a mould, and decorate the bottom and sides with slices of *hard-boiled eggs ;* also with thin slices of *tongue* or *ham* cut into round or fancy shapes. Pack the meat in, and set away to cool with a weight on the meat. When ready to serve, dip the mould in warm water, and turn out carefully. Garnish with *parsley, strips* of *lettuce* or *celery leaves,* and **radishes** or *beets.*

Blanquette of Chicken.

Make *one cup* of *cream sauce*, put it in a double boiler, and add *one pint* of *cooked chicken* cut in strips, and *one tablespoonful* of *chopped parsley*. When hot, beat the *yolks* of *two eggs;* add *two tablespoonfuls* of *milk*, and stir into the chicken. Cook two minutes. Serve in *rice* or *potato border*, or with a garnish of *toast points.*

Chicken Pilau.

Warm *one pint* of *canned chicken*, or *cold roast* or *boiled chicken*, in *one pint* of *water* till the meat is very tender. Skim out the meat, and add to the liquor *one pint* of *strained tomatoes*. Season highly with *salt, pepper, fine chopped onion*, and *curry* or *Chutney sauce*. When boiling, add *one cup* of well-washed *rice*, and cook twenty minutes, or till the rice is soft. Add the pieces of chicken and *half a cup* of *butter* or *cream*. When hot, turn out on a platter, and garnish with triangles of *toast.*

Scalloped Chicken.

Take *equal parts* of *cold chicken, boiled rice* or *macaroni*, and *tomato sauce.* Put in layers in a shallow dish, and cover with *buttered crumbs.* Bake till brown. Cold roast turkey, using stuffing and gravy, may be prepared in the same way.

Chicken Pie for Thanksgiving. (*Miss A. M. Towne.*)

Two chickens, three pints of *cream, one pound* of *butter, flour* enough to make a stiff crust. Cut the chicken at the joints, and cook in boiling salted water till tender.

Crust. — Three pints of *cream, one heaping teaspoonful* of *salt*, and *flour* to mix it hard enough to roll out easily.

Line a deep earthen dish having flaring sides with a thin layer of paste. Roll the remainder of the paste half an inch thick. Cut *three quarters* of *a pound* of *butter* into

small pieces, and put them on the dough quite close together. Sprinkle a little flour over the butter, and roll
the paste over and over. Roll out again half an inch thick
and roll up. Cut off from the ends of the roll, turn the
pieces over and roll out half an inch thick for rims. Wet
the paste in the dish with milk, and lay the rims round
the sides of the dish. Put on two, three, or four rims,
showing one above another, the inside rim the highest.
Wet each rim to make it adhere. Fill the centre with the
parboiled chicken. Take out some of the larger bones.
Season the chicken liquor with *salt* and *pepper*, and pour
it over the chicken ; use enough to nearly cover. Cut the
remaining *quarter* of *butter* into pieces the size of a chestnut, and put them over the meat. Roll the remainder of
the crust to fit the top. Make a curving cut in the crust
and turn it back, that the steam may escape. Bake three
hours in a brick oven. If baked in a stove oven, put on
only two rims of crust and bake two hours.

Chicken Terrapin. (*Miss Minot.*)

Chop *one cold roast chicken* and *one parboiled sweetbread* moderately fine. Make *one cup* of *rich cream sauce*,
with *one cup* of *hot cream*, *a quarter* of *a cup* of *butter*, and
two tablespoonfuls of *flour*. Then put in the chicken and
sweetbread. *Salt* and *pepper* to taste. Let it heat over
hot water fifteen minutes. Just before serving add the
yolks of *two eggs*, well beaten, and *one wineglass* of *sherry
wine*.

Calf's liver, parboiled till tender, and cut fine, may be
prepared in the same way, and used alone or with cold
chicken or veal.

Chicken Chartreuse.

Chop very fine *nine ounces*, or *a heaping cup*, of *cold
cooked chicken ;* add the inside of *two sausages*, or *two ounces*
of *lean, cooked ham*, chopped fine, *three tablespoonfuls* of
powdered bread crumbs, *one tablespoonful* of *capers*, or *one*

tablespoonful of *chopped parsley*, *two tablespoonfuls* of *lemon juice* or *vinegar*, *a speck* of *cayenne*, *two eggs*, well beaten, and enough *hot soup stock* to make it quite moist. Add *salt* and *pepper* to taste, the amount depending upon the seasoning in the sausages. The sausages may be omitted, and a larger amount of chicken used. Butter a small mould, and pack the meat in closely to within an inch of the top to allow for swelling. Put it on a trivet in a kettle, and steam three hours. If no uncooked meat be used, one hour will be sufficient. Cool it in the mould; when ready to serve, dip the mould quickly into warm water and loosen the meat around the edges with a thin knife and remove the mould. It may be served plain or moulded in jelly (see page 266).

Salmis of Game.

Cut the meat from *cold roasted game* into small pieces. Break up the bones and remnants, cover them with *stock* or with *cold water*, and add *a pinch* of *herbs*, *two cloves*, and *two peppercorns*. Boil down to *a cupful* for *a pint* of *meat*. Fry *two small onions*, cut fine, in *two tablespoonfuls* of *butter* till brown; add *two tablespoonfuls* of *flour*, and stir till dark brown. Strain the *liquor* in which the bones were boiled, and add it gradually to the butter and flour. Add more *salt* if needed, *one tablespoonful* of *lemon juice*, *two tablespoonfuls* of *Worcestershire sauce*, and the pieces of meat. Simmer fifteen minutes; add *six* or *eight mushrooms*, and *a glass* of *claret*, if you like, or the *juice* of *a sour orange*. Serve very hot on slices of *fried bread*, and garnish with *fried bread* and *parsley*. Or serve *canned peas* in the centre, with the meat on toast around the edge.

Beef Olives, or Beef Rolls.[1]

Cut thin slices from *cold roast beef*, two and a half by four inches. Chop the trimmings and fat, allowing *one*

---

[1] Olives is not an appropriate name, although in common use.

tablespoonful of the chopped mixture for each slice. Season highly with *salt, pepper,* and *herbs,* and mix with *one fourth* as much *cracker crumbs* as meat. Spread this on each slice, nearly to the edge. Roll and tie. Dredge with *salt, pepper,* and *flour,* and fry brown in *drippings* or *salt pork fat;* put in a stewpan, and make a brown gravy by adding *two tablespoonfuls* of *flour* to the fat left in the pan, and when brown pour on *one pint* of *hot water.* Season with *salt* and *pepper,* pour over the rolls and simmer till they are tender. Remove the strings, place the rolls on a platter, season the gravy and pour it over them.

Rolls may be made in the same way by using raw lean meat from the round, cut in small thin slices; pound it to break the fibre, and trim into shape. Rolls may be made of veal or thin slices of liver (parboil and remove the skin before using the liver). If there be any of the chopped mixture left, make it into round or oval balls, roll in *crumbs,* then in *egg,* and again in *crumbs;* and brown in the oven or fry in *fat.*

Beef Roulette. — Take a large thin slice of meat from the round, or any tough part; pound it enough to break the fibre, and trim into rectangular shape. Season and spread with a stuffing; roll, tie, and cook as directed for Beef Rolls. Serve hot with a gravy; or cold, cut into thin slices.

Fricadilloes, or Meat Balls, Sausages, or Rolls

Chop the meat fine; add *a slice* of *onion* chopped fine, and if the meat be lean, add *one* or *two slices* of *bacon;* season highly with *salt, pepper, sage, thyme, lemon juice,* and *parsley;* add *one fourth* as much *bread crumbs* or *boiled rice* as you have meat. Moisten with *beaten egg* and *hot water* or *stock* if needed; shape like a ball, egg, or cylinder. Brown them in *drippings* or *butter* in a frying-pan, or roll them in *crumbs, egg,* and *crumbs* again, and fry in hot deep *fat.*

Frizzled Beef.

Half a pound of *smoked beef*, cut in thin shavings. Pour boiling water over it, and let it stand ten minutes. Drain and heat it in *one tablespoonful* of *hot butter*, to curl or frizzle it. Add *one cup* of *hot cream*. Or make a cup of *thin white sauce* with *one cup* of *milk*, *one tablespoonful* of *butter*, and *one tablespoonful* of *flour*. Pour it over *one well-beaten egg*, add the beef and a little *pepper*, and serve at once. Or frizzle it, and mix it with *two* or *three poached eggs*.

Meat Pie.

Cut *cold cooked meat* into small thin slices or into half-inch cubes, remove all the gristle and fat except the crisped outside fat, put into a baking-dish, and cover with the *meat gravy* or with *tomato* or *brown sauce piquante*. Spread a crust of *mashed potatoes* over the meat, brush with *beaten egg* or sprinkle with *cracker crumbs*, and cook twenty minutes or till brown.

Meat Porcupine.

Chop fine some *lean cooked veal, chicken*, or *lamb;* add *one fourth* its amount of *cracker* or *bread crumbs*, or *mashed*

FIG. 37. Meat Porcupine.

potato, and a small quantity of *chopped bacon;* season highly with *salt, pepper, cayenne*, and *lemon juice;* moisten with *beaten egg* and *stock* or *water* enough to shape it. Mould it into an oval loaf, and put into a shallow pan well greased. Cut strips of *fat bacon*, one fourth of an inch wide and one inch long. Make holes in the loaf with a small skewer, insert the strips of bacon, leaving the ends out half an inch, and push the meat up firmly round the bacon. Bake till brown. The bacon will baste the meat sufficiently.

Ragout of Cooked Meat.

Cut *one pint* of *cold meat* into half-inch dice; remove the fat, bone, and gristle. Put the meat in a stewpan; cover with *boiling water*, and simmer slowly two or three hours, or till very tender; then add *half a can* of *mushrooms*, cut fine, *two tablespoonfuls* of *Madeira wine*, *salt* and *pepper* to taste. Wet *one tablespoonful* of *flour* to a smooth paste with a little *cold water;* stir it into the boiling liquor; add *a teaspoonful* of *caramel*, if not brown enough. Cook ten minutes, and serve plain or in a border of *mashed potatoes.* The seasoning may be varied by using *one teaspoonful* of *curry powder*, *a few grains* of *cayenne pepper*, or *half a tumbler* of *currant jelly*, and *salt* to taste.

Hash.

Equal parts of *meat* and *potatoes*, or *two* of *potatoes* to *one* of *meat.* Remove all the bone, gristle, and skin, and have only one-fourth part fat meat. Chop very fine, and mix well with the potatoes, which should be hot and well mashed. Season to taste with *pepper* and *salt.* Put in enough *hot water* to cover the bottom of the spider; add *one large tablespoonful* of *butter.* When the butter is melted, add the hash, and let it simmer till it has absorbed the water and formed a brown crust. Do not stir it. Fold like an omelet. Use corned meat or roast beef. If the potatoes be cold, chop them with the meat.

Sandwiches.

Chop very fine some *cooked ham* or *cold corned beef* or *tongue* with one-fourth part fat. Mix *one teaspoonful* of *dry mustard* and *one saltspoonful* of *salt* with *cold water* to a stiff paste; add to it *one fourth* of *a cup* of *butter* creamed. Cut *stale bread* in very thin slices; spread with the mustard and butter paste, then with the ham. Put two slices together, and cut into rectangular pieces.

18

Scalloped Mutton.

Remove the fat and skin from *cold roast mutton ;* cut the meat in small thin slices ; season it with *salt* and *pepper.* Butter a shallow dish, put in a layer of *bread* or *cracker crumbs,* then a layer of meat, then *oysters,* strained and seasoned, *tomato* or *brown gravy,* then crumbs, meat, etc., having on the top a thick layer of crumbs moistened in *one third* of *a cup* of *melted butter.* Cold *boiled macaroni,* cut into inch pieces, may be used in place of oysters.

Casserole of Rice and Meat.

Boil *one cup* of *rice* till tender. Chop very fine *half a pound* of any *cold meat ;* season highly with *half a teaspoonful* of *salt, half a saltspoonful* of *pepper, one saltspoonful* of *celery salt, one teaspoonful* of *finely chopped onion, one teaspoonful* of *chopped parsley,* and *one saltspoonful* each of *thyme* and *marjoram.* Add *one beaten egg, two tablespoonfuls* of *fine cracker crumbs,* and moisten with *hot water* or *stock* enough to pack it easily. Butter a small mould, line the bottom and sides half an inch deep with the rice, pack in the meat, cover closely with rice, and steam forty-five minutes. Loosen it around the edge of the mould ; turn it out upon a platter, and pour *tomato sauce* over it.

Casserole of Mock Sweetbreads with Potato Border.

One pound of uncooked *lean veal* cut into half-inch cubes, and cooked with *one slice* of *onion* in boiling salted water till tender, then put into cold water to whiten. Make *one cup* of *white sauce,* and season with *one saltspoonful* of *salt, one saltspoonful* of *celery salt,* and *half a saltspoonful* of *pepper.* Put the veal and *half a cup* of *mushrooms,* cut into quarters, into the sauce. Heat over hot water five minutes, or till the meat and mushrooms are hot. Remove from the fire ; add quickly *one teaspoonful* of *lemon juice* and *one well-beaten egg ;* serve inside a *potato border,* or on toast garnished with *toast points.*

Potato Border. — *One quart* of *mashed* and *seasoned potatoes* shaped into a mound like a wall on the edge of a platter. Brush over with *beaten white* or *yolk* of *an egg*, and brown slightly. Fill with any kind of cooked meat or fish warmed in a white or brown sauce.

Veal Birds.

Slices of *veal* from the *loin*, cut very thin. Wipe, re-move the bones, skin, and fat, and pound till one fourth of an inch thick. Trim into pieces two and a half by four inches. Chop the trimmings fine with *one square inch* of *fat salt pork* for each bird. Add *half* as much *fine cracker crumbs* as you have *meat;* season highly with *salt, pepper, thyme, lemon, cayenne,* and *onion.* Moisten with *one egg* and a little *hot water.* Spread the mixture on each slice nearly to the edge, roll up tightly, and tie or fasten with skewers. Dredge with *salt, pepper,* and *flour;* fry them slowly in *hot butter* till a golden brown, but not dark or burned. Then half cover with *cream,* and simmer fifteen or twenty minutes, or till tender. Remove the strings, and serve on *toast;* pour the cream over them; gar-nish with *points* of *toast* and *lemon.* If the veal be tough, dip in *olive oil* before spreading with the stuffing.

Melton Veal.

Take any *cold veal,* either roasted or boiled; chop it fine, and season with *salt, pepper,* and *lemon juice;* add *two* or *three tablespoonfuls* of *cracker crumbs,* and moisten with *soup stock* or *hot water.* Take one third as much *finely chopped ham* as of veal; season with *mustard* and *cayenne;* add *one tablespoonful* of *cracker crumbs,* and moisten with *hot stock* or *water.* Butter a mould, and line it with slices of *hard-boiled egg.* Put in the two mixtures irregularly, so that when cut it will have a mottled appearance; press in closely, and steam three-quarters of an hour. Set away to cool; remove from the mould, and slice before serving.

This is an excellent dish for lunch or tea, and is a con

venient way of using pieces of veal that would not otherwise be utilized.

Veal Loaf.

Parboil *two pounds* of *lean veal.* Chop fine with *one
fourth* of *a pound* of *salt pork* or *bacon ;* add *four butter
crackers*, pounded, *two eggs*, well beaten, *two teaspoonfuls
of salt, one saltspoonful* of *pepper*, and *half a saltspoonful* of
nutmeg or *mace.* Moisten with the meat liquor, mould
into an oval loaf, and put into a shallow tin pan. Add
a little of the water in which the meat was boiled. Bake
till quite brown, basting often. Serve hot or cold, cut in
slices. *Raw veal* may be used in the same way, baking
it two hours or more.

No. 2. — Select a *knuckle* of *veal*, or any bony piece that
has a *large proportion* of *gelatine.* Cut in small pieces, and
remove any fragments of bone. Cover with *cold water*,
boil quickly, skim, and add *one onion, one teaspoonful* of *salt*,
and *one saltspoonful of pepper.* Let it simmer till the meat
slips from the bones, the gristly portions are dissolved,
and the liquor reduced to *one cupful.* Remove the meat,
pick out all the bones, strain the liquor, and season highly
with *salt, lemon juice*, and *pepper*, and slightly with *sage* or
thyme. Chop or pick the meat apart; add *two* or *three
tablespoonfuls* of *powdered cracker* and the *meat liquor ;* mix
well and put into a bread pan. Put it in a cool place, and
when hard serve in thin slices. The gelatine in the meat
liquor will harden, and hold the meat together without
pressure.

Meat Soufflé.

Make *one cup* of *cream sauce*, and season with *chopped
parsley* and *onion juice.* Stir *one cup* of *chopped meat*
(chicken, fresh tongue, veal, or lamb) into the sauce.
When hot, add the beaten *yolks* of *two eggs ;* cook one minute, and set away to cool. When cool, stir in the *whites*,
beaten stiff. Bake in a buttered dish about twenty minutes, and serve immediately. If for lunch, serve with a
mushroom sauce.

Potting.

Chop and pound to a paste any fragments of cooked *ham, tongue, beef, poultry, game,* or *fish.* With ham use a quarter part fat. Remove all gristle and skin, and pound till free from any fibre and reduced to a paste. Season highly with *salt, pepper, cayenne,* and *made mustard,* and moisten with a little *melted butter* (except ham, which has fat enough). Pack closely in small stone or earthen jars. Put the jars in a steamer, and heat for half an hour. Then press the meat down again, and cover with hot melted butter. This will keep some time, and may be served in slices or used for sandwiches. Ham and tongue may be mixed with veal or chicken. Beef, game, and fish are better alone.

Potted Liver.

Braise a *calf's* or *lamb's liver* in rich, highly *seasoned stock.* When tender, cut fine and pound to a paste, adding enough of the *strained liquor* in which it was cooked to moisten it; add *half a cup* of *butter,* melted and strained. Rub all through a sieve; pack in jars and pour *melted butter* over the top.

Ragout of Lamb's or Calf's Liver.

Boil till tender. Cut in thin round slices. Make a rich brown sauce; season with *spices* and *wine.* Stew the liver in it till hot, and serve at once. Garnish with alternate slices of *lemon* and *hard-boiled eggs.*

Croquettes.

These may be made of any kind of cooked meat, fish, oysters, rice, hominy, and many kinds of vegetables, or from a mixture of several ingredients. When mixed with a thick white sauce (see page 278), which adds very much to the delicacy of meat or fish croquettes, less meat is required. The sauce is a stiff paste when cold, and being mixed with the meat or fish the croquettes may be handled and shaped perfectly, and when cooked will be soft and creamy inside.

To Shape a Croquette. — Croquettes may be shaped into rolls, or ovals, or like pears, with a bit of parsley or a clove in the end to represent the stem. Take *a tablespoonful* of the *cold mixture*, and shape into a smooth ball. If the mixture stick, wet the palms of the hands slightly. Give the ball a gentle, rolling pressure between the palms till slightly cylindrical; then roll it lightly in the crumbs, clasp it gently in the hand, and flatten one end on the board. Turn the hand over, and flatten the opposite end. Place the croquette on a broad knife, and roll it in beaten egg. With a spoon dip the egg over the croquette, drain on the knife, and roll again in the crumbs. Fry in deep hot fat (see page 15). Drain on paper.

In rolling any kind of croquettes, if the mixture be too soft to be handled easily, stir in enough fine cracker dust to stiffen it, but never add any uncooked material like flour, nor the dried bread crumbs used in rolling, as those will make the croquettes too stiff.

Thick Cream Sauce (for Croquettes and Patties).

1 pint hot cream.	½ teaspoonful salt.
2 even tablespoonfuls butter.	½ saltspoonful white pepper.
4 heaping tablespoonfuls flour, or	½ teaspoonful celery salt.
2 heaping tablesp. cornstarch.	A few grains of cayenne.

Scald the cream. Melt the butter in a granite saucepan. When bubbling, add the dry cornstarch. Stir till well mixed. Add one third of the cream, and stir as it boils and thickens. Add more cream, and boil again. When perfectly smooth, add the remainder of the cream. The sauce should be very thick, almost like a drop batter. Add the seasoning, and mix it while hot with the meat or fish. For croquettes, *one beaten egg* may be added just as the sauce is taken from the fire; but the croquettes are whiter and more creamy without the egg. For patties, warm the meat or fish in the sauce, and use the egg or not as you please.

Chicken Croquettes. — *Half a pound* of *chicken* chopped very fine, and seasoned with *half a teaspoonful* of *salt, half a teaspoonful* of *celery salt, a quarter* of *a saltspoonful* of *cayenne pepper, one saltspoonful* of *white pepper,* a few drops of *onion juice, one teaspoonful* of *chopped parsley,* and *one teaspoonful* of *lemon juice.* Make *one pint* of very *thick cream sauce* (see page 278). When thick, add *one beaten egg,* and mix the sauce with the chicken, us-ing only enough to make it as soft as can be handled. Spread on a shallow plate to cool. Shape into rolls. Roll in *fine bread crumbs,* then dip

Fig. 38.   Chicken Croquettes

in *beaten egg,* then in *crumbs* again, and fry one minute in *smoking hot fat.* Drain, and serve with a *thin cream sauce.* Many prefer to cut the chicken into small dice. If this be done, use less of the sauce, or the croquettes will be difficult to shape. The white meat of chicken will absorb more sauce than the dark. Mushrooms, boiled rice, sweetbreads, calf's brains, or veal may be mixed with chicken. Cold roast chicken, chopped fine, may be mixed with the stuffing, moistened with the gravy, and shaped into croquettes.

Veal Croquettes. — Chop *cold veal* fine; season highly with *salt, pepper, cayenne, onion juice, celery salt,* and *pars-ley.* If you like, add half the amount of *oysters,* parboiled and drained. Moisten with *beaten egg* and *white sauce.* Shape into rolls. Roll in *fine bread crumbs, egg,* and *crumbs* again, and fry in *smoking hot fat.*

Oyster Croquettes. — Parboil and drain *one pint* of *oysters.* Cut them into quarters, and mix with *cream sauce* enough to hold them together. Season with *salt* and *pepper.* Shape, roll in *crumbs,* then in *egg,* then in *crumbs* again, and fry.

Sweetbread Croquettes. — *One parboiled sweetbread, half a can* of *mushrooms,* chopped fine, and *half a cup* of *warm boiled rice.* Season to taste with *salt* and *pepper*, and moisten with *hot thick cream sauce* until soft enough to be handled. When cool, shape, roll in *crumbs*, then in *egg*, and again in *crumbs*, and fry. Calf's brains may be parboiled and mixed with sweetbreads or chicken for croquettes.

Lobster Croquettes. — *One pint* of *lobster meat*, cut fine. Season with *one saltspoonful* of *salt*, one *saltspoonful* of *mustard*, and a little *cayenne*, and moisten with *one cup* of *thick cream sauce*. Cool, and shape into rolls. Roll in *crumbs, egg*, and *crumbs* again, and fry in *smoking hot fat*. Drain on paper.

Lobster Cutlets. — Prepare the lobster as for croquettes, and spread it half an inch thick on a platter. Cut into the shape of cutlets. Roll in *crumbs, egg*, and *crumbs* again. Fry in *smoking hot fat*. Drain, and serve with a claw to represent the bone.

Salmon, or any fish croquettes or cutlets are made in the same way.

Clam Croquettes. — Steam the clams. Remove the shells, thin skin, black end, and the dark substance from the soft part. Cut the " leather straps," with the scissors, into small bits. Mix these and the soft part with a *thick cream sauce*, season with *salt* and *pepper*, and shape into rolls. Roll in *fine bread crumbs*, dip in *beaten egg*, then roll in *crumbs* again. Fry in *smoking hot lard*.

Potato Croquettes. — *One pint* of *hot mashed potatoes*, one *tablespoonful* of *butter*, *half a saltspoonful* of *white pepper*, a speck of *cayenne*, *half a teaspoonful* of *salt*, *half a teaspoonful* of *celery salt*, a few drops of *onion juice*, and the *yolk* of *one egg*. Mix all but the egg, and beat until very light. When slightly cool, add the yolk of the egg, and mix well. Rub through a sieve and add *one teaspoonful* of *chopped parsley*. Shape into smooth round balls, then into rolls. Roll in *fine bread crumbs*, then dip in *beaten egg*, then roll in *crumbs* again. Fry in *smoking hot lard* one minute. Drain and serve in the form of a pyramid.

Oyster Plant Croquettes. — Scrape, boil, mash, and season

the oyster plant. Shape into rolls. Roll in *crumbs*, dip in *egg*, and again in *crumbs*, and fry as usual.

Prepare parsnips in the same way.

Turkish Croquettes. — Stew *half a can* of *tomatoes* fifteen minutes with *one slice* each of *onion*, *carrot*, and *turnip*, *one teaspoonful* of *herbs*, *one sprig* of *parsley*, *two cloves*, *two peppercorns*, *one teaspoonful* of *salt*, and *one saltspoonful* of *pepper*. Rub through a strainer. Take *one cup* of the *strained tomatoes*, *one cup* of *brown soup stock*, season highly, and when boiling add *one scant cup* of *uncooked rice*. Cook till the liquor is absorbed. Add *a quarter* of *a cup* of *butter*, and steam it, or cook on the back of the stove until the rice is soft. Add *one beaten egg* and a little *cream sauce*, or *thick tomato sauce*, using enough to make it quite moist. When cool, shape into rolls. Roll in *fine bread crumbs*, then in *egg*, then in *crumbs* again, and fry in *smoking hot fat*. Sometimes it is better to parboil the rice for five minutes, as it is more difficult to soften it in stock than in clear water.

Sweet Rice Croquettes. — Steam *one scant cup* of *well-washed rice* in *one pint* of *boiling water*, or *milk* and *water*, thirty minutes, or till very soft. Add, while hot, *one teaspoonful* of *butter*, *two tablespoonfuls* of *sugar*, and the *well-beaten yolk* of *one egg*, and a little *hot milk*, if it need more moisture. When cool, shape into small ovals, roll in *crumbs*, dip in *egg*, roll in *crumbs* again, and fry. Or, after shaping, press the thumb into the centre of each, and put in *two boiled raisins* or *candied cherries*, or *half a teaspoonful* of *jelly* or *marmalade*. Close the rice over the centre, roll in *crumbs*, dip in *egg*, roll in *crumbs* again, and fry.

Savory Rice Croquettes. — *One pint* of *cold boiled rice* warmed in the double boiler with *two* or *three tablespoonfuls* of *milk*. When soft, add *one egg*, well beaten, *one tablespoonful* of *butter*, *half a teaspoonful* of *salt*, *one fourth* of *a saltspoonful* of *white pepper*, a few grains of *cayenne*, and *one heaping tablespoonful* of *fine chopped parsley*. Shape, roll, and fry as usual.

Rice or Macaroni Croquettes. — *One pint* of *cold boiled rice* or *macaroni* or *spaghetti.* Heat, and moisten with a little *thick white sauce;* add the *beaten yolk* of one egg, *two tablespoonfuls* of *grated cheese,* and *salt* and *pepper* to taste. Cool, shape, roll in *crumbs,* dip in *egg,* roll in *crumbs* again, and fry.

Hominy Croquettes. — Warm *one pint* of *cooked hominy* in one or *two tablespoonfuls* of *hot milk;* add the *beaten yolk* of one egg, and *salt* to taste. Cool, shape, roll, and fry.

Crême Frête. — Boil *one pint* of *milk* with *an inch stick* of *cinnamon.* Beat together *half a cup* of *sugar, two table-spoonfuls* of *cornstarch, one tablespoonful* of *flour,* the *yolks* of *three eggs,* a *quarter* of *a cup* of *cold milk,* and *one salt-spoonful* of *salt.* Pour the boiling milk on the mixture, and stir well. Strain into the double boiler, and cook fifteen minutes, stirring often. Add *one teaspoonful* of *butter* and *one teaspoonful* of *vanilla.* Pour into a buttered bread pan about one inch deep, and set away to cool. When very hard, sprinkle a bread board with *fine bread crumbs.* Turn the cream out on it, and cut into strips two and a half inches long and one inch wide, or in squares or diamonds. Roll these in *crumbs,* then dip in *beaten egg,* then in *crumbs,* and fry brown in boiling *lard.* Sprinkle *sugar* over them, and serve hot.

Welsh Rarebit.

¼ pound rich cream cheese.	A few grains of cayenne.
¼ cup cream or milk.	1 egg
1 teaspoonful mustard.	1 teaspoonful butter.
½ teaspoonful salt.	4 slices toast.

Break the cheese in small pieces, or if hard grate it. Put it with the milk in a double boiler. Toast the bread, and keep it hot Mix the mustard, salt, and pepper; add the egg, and beat well. When the cheese is melted, stir in the egg and butter, and cook two minutes, or until it thickens a little, but do not let it curdle Pour it over the toast. Many use ale instead of cream.

Cheese Soufflé. — Put *two tablespoonfuls* of *butter* in a saucepan; add *one heaping tablespoonful* of *flour;* when smooth, add *half a cup* of *milk*, *half a teaspoonful* of *salt*, and a *few grains* of *cayenne*. Cook two minutes. Add the *yolks* of *three eggs*, well beaten, and *one cup* of *grated cheese*. Set away to cool. When cold, add the *whites*, beaten to a stiff froth. Turn into a buttered dish and bake twenty-five or thirty minutes. Serve immediately.

Crackers à la Crême. — Split *butter crackers*, and spread with *butter*, *salt*, *pepper*, *mustard*, and *cheese* if you like. Put them in a buttered pudding-dish, cover with *milk*, and bake thirty minutes. Omit the *mustard*, *pepper*, and *cheese*, prepare in the same way, and it is called *Cracker Brewis*.

Sardine Canapes. — Mix the *yolks* of *hard-boiled eggs* with an equal amount of *sardines* rubbed to a paste ; season with *lemon juice*, and spread on thin slices of delicate *toast*. Put two pieces together, and cut in narrow strips.

Turkish Pilaf.

One cup of *stewed* and *strained tomatoes*, *one cup* of *stock*, seasoned highly with *salt*, *pepper*, and *minced onion*. When boiling, add *one cup* of well-washed *rice* ; stir lightly with a fork until the liquor is absorbed, then add *half a cup* of *butter*. Set on the back of the stove or in a double boiler, and steam twenty minutes. Remove the cover, stir it lightly, cover with a towel, and let the steam escape. Serve as a vegetable, or as a border for curry or fricassee.

No. 2. — Prepare as in the preceding receipt. Add with the butter *one cup* of cooked *meat* (lamb, veal, or chicken), cut into half-inch pieces and shredded very fine. Serve as an entrée.

Sour Milk Cheese (sometimes called Dutch, Curd, or Cottage Cheese).

1 quart thick sour milk.	1 saltspoonful salt.
1 teaspoonful butter.	1 tablespoonful cream.

Place the milk in a pan on the back of the stove, and scald it until the curd has separated from the whey.

Spread a strainer cloth over a bowl, pour in the milk, lift the edges of the cloth, and draw them together; drain or wring quite dry. There will be but *half* or *two thirds* of *a cup* of *curd*, but it is worth saving. It is the flesh-forming or nutritive part of the milk. Put it in a small bowl, with the butter, salt, and cream; mix it to a smooth paste with a spoon. Take a teaspoonful, and roll in the hand into a smooth ball. It should be quite moist, or the balls will crack If too soft to handle, put it in a cool place for an hour, and then it will shape easily. Or it may be served without shaping, just broken up lightly with a fork. If scalded too long, the curd becomes very hard and brittle. It is better when freshly made, and is delicious with warm gingerbread. An excellent lunch or tea dish. Season this cheese with *one tablespoonful* of finely powdered *sage*, if you like the flavor.

Forefathers' Dinner.

Succotash is the great dish in Plymouth at every celebration of Forefathers' Day, December 22. Tradition says it has been made in that town ever since the Pilgrims raised their first corn and beans, and it is supposed they learned to make it from the Indians.

Strangers are rather shy of this peculiar mixture; but it is a favorite dish with the natives, and to this day is made by some families many times through the winter season. Although the dish has never been made by the writer, it has been tested by her in that ancient town many times, and the excellence of the following receipt is unquestionable. It is given in the name of *Mrs. Barnabas Churchill*, of Plymouth, a lady who has made it for fifty years after the manner handed down through many generations.

One quart of *large white beans* (not the pea beans); *six quarts* of *hulled corn*, — the smutty white Southern corn; *six* to *eight pounds* of *corned beef*, from the second cut of the rattle rand; *one pound* of *salt pork*, fat and lean;

chicken weighing from *four* to *six pounds;* one large *white French turnip;* eight or ten medium-sized *potatoes.* Wash the beans, and soak over night in cold water. In the morning put them on in cold soft water. When boiling, change the water, and simmer until soft enough to mash to a pulp and the water is nearly all absorbed. Wash the salt pork and the corned beef, which should be corned only three or four days. Put them on about eight o'clock, in cold water, in a very large kettle, and skim as they begin to boil. Clean, and truss the chicken as for boiling, and put it with the meat about an hour and a quarter before dinner time. Allow a longer time if a fowl be used, and keep plenty of water in the kettle. Two hours before dinner time, put the beans, mashed to a pulp, and the hulled corn into another kettle, with some of the fat from the meat in the bottom to keep them from sticking. Take out enough liquor from the meat to cover the corn and beans, and let them simmer where they will not burn. Stir often, and add more liquor if needed. The mixture should be like a thick soup, and the beans should absorb all the liquor, yet it must not be too dry.

Pare, and cut the turnip into inch slices; add it about eleven o'clock, and the potatoes (pared) half an hour later. Take up the chicken as soon as tender, that it may be served whole. Serve the beef and pork together, the chicken, turnip, and potatoes each on separate dishes, and the beans and corn in a tureen. The meat usually salts the mixture sufficiently, and no other seasoning is necessary. Save the water left from the meat, to use in warming the corn and beans the next day, serving the meat cold. This will keep several days in cold weather; and, like many other dishes, it is better the oftener it is warmed over, so there is no objection to making a large quantity. The white Southern corn is considered the only kind suitable for this ancient dinner.

Hulled Corn.

Tie *a quart* of *oak wood ashes* in a flannel bag, and put it with *three gallons* of *cold water* into an iron kettle. Let it boil and become lye, or till the water is black. Put in *four quarts* of *corn*, and boil till the hulls have all started. Stir it well with a wooden spoon. Then pour it into a large pan of cold water, and rub with the hand thoroughly to loosen the hulls. Change the water five or six times, and wash and rub till the corn is white and clean. Keep in cold water over night; then put on in fresh cold water, and simmer four hours, or till soft and floury. Take off the hulls and scum from the water, and add fresh water several times during the simmering.

Indian Meal Pudding. (*Mrs. Barnabas Churchill.*)

Rub *a tablespoonful* of *butter* round the bottom and sides of a smooth iron kettle, — granite or porcelain will do; when melted, add *half a cup* of *boiling water*. This will prevent the milk from burning. Add *one quart* of *milk.* Let it boil up, and almost over the kettle; then sift in *one pint* of *fine yellow granulated corn meal*, sifting with the left hand, and holding the meal high, that every grain may be thoroughly scalded. Stir constantly; add *half a teaspoonful* of *salt*, and set away till cold. Then add *half a pint* of *New Orleans molasses* and *one quart* of *cold milk.* Put into a well-buttered deep pudding-dish, cover with a plate, and bake very slowly ten or twelve hours. Put it in a " Saturday afternoon oven," where the fire will keep low nearly all night. Let it remain over night, and serve for a Sunday breakfast.

Chickins forc'd with Oysters.

(*Taken from a receipt book written in* 1764.)

Take Oysters, parsley, Onions, butter, pepper, Salt, grated Bread, Mushrooms — if you can get y^m, & as many eggs as you think propper, fill them inside, & Cut y^m on the breast, if you have a mind to, & put some of the stuffing there, make gravy of Oysters, butter & mace, pepper, roast them well.

Bean Porridge. (*Mrs. C. M. Poor.*)

Five pounds of *corned beef*, not too salt, or *four pounds* of *beef* and *one* of *salt pork ; one pint* of dry *white beans, four tablespoonfuls* of *corn meal, pepper* and *salt* to taste, *one pint* of *hulled corn.* Soak the beans over night. In the morning parboil in fresh water with a pinch of *soda* till soft. Put the corned beef and pork in cold water; skim carefully, and simmer four or five hours, or till tender. Take out, and cut into two-inch pieces, and remove the bone and gristle ; also the fat from the liquor. Put the meat and beans into the meat liquor, and simmer very slowly three or four hours, or till most of the beans are broken. Half an hour before serving stir in the meal, first wetting it in cold water to a smooth paste. The meal should thicken the porridge to about the consistency of a thick soup. The meat should be cooked till it falls apart. Season to taste with *salt* and *pepper.* Add the hulled corn, and when hot serve with brown bread. Sometimes the vegetables usually served with a boiled dinner are cooked with the meat, then removed, and the beans cooked as above, in the meat liquor.

" This old-fashioned and very nutritious dish was one of the chief articles of winter food at my grandmother's farm in Northern New Hampshire eighty years ago. When cooked, it was poured into bowls or basins holding from a pint to two quarts. A nice tow string was laid in a loop over the edge, and the porridge was placed where it would freeze. By holding the dish in hot water it would cause the porridge to slip out; then it was hung up by the loops in the ' buttery,' and was considered ' best when nine days old.' At early dawn the ' men folks ' who went into the forest ' chopping ' would take the skillet, or a little three-legged iron kettle, some large slices of ' rye and

Indian' bread in their pockets to keep it from freezing. The porridge was hung, wrapped in a clean towel, upon the sled stakes. Their spoons were made of wood. The hay that lay on the floor of the ox sled was of use to keep their feet warm, and given to the oxen for 'bait' at noon. When it was twelve o'clock ' by the sun,' they kindled a fire by the aid of a ' tinder box,' warmed their porridge, and with their brown bread enjoyed this strong food as no modern epicure can his costly French dishes."

Smothered Chicken.   (*Adaline Miller.*)

Clean a chicken, too old for broiling ; split down the back, and put it breast upwards in a shallow pan ; pour over it *one cup* of *boiling water*, and cover tightly to keep in the steam.   Cook half an hour ; then baste with the hot water, rub all over with softened *butter*, and dredge with *salt* and *pepper*.   Baste often, keep closely covered, and cook till tender.   It should be yellow, not dark brown. Thicken the gravy ; add *chopped parsley, salt*, and *pepper*, and pour it over the chicken.

Steamed Apple and Indian Meal Pudding.   (*Mrs. Faunce.*)

Scald *two cups* of *corn meal* with boiling water.   Add *one teaspoonful* of *salt, one fourth* of *a cup* of *molasses*, and *two tart apples* cut into eighths and cored, but not pared.   Dissolve *half a teaspoonful* of *soda* in warm water, and add to the meal.   Add more warm water to make a batter thin enough to pour.   Pour into a greased pail, place it on a trivet in a kettle of boiling water. Cook three hours.   The water must not stop boiling.   To be eaten with roast meat.   The next day warm what is left in the meat gravy.

VEGETABLES.

VEGETABLE food, in its widest sense, includes some part of every form of plant growth, — herb, shrub, or tree, — used either as vegetables, fruits, grains, condiments, or beverages. Vegetables, as the term is generally used, are such plants as are cultivated for culinary purposes. They comprise a variety of the parts of the plant, — roots, stems, leaves, flowers, and fruit.

Before studying vegetables proper, it may be interesting for those who have never considered food from a botanical point of view to glance at the various forms of vegetable growth commonly used as food.

Beginning with *roots*, we find, among fleshy roots, the carrot, turnip, parsnip, beet, salsify, and radish, which are cooked in their natural state or used raw. Also from roots we get ginger, arrowroot, and tapioca. *Rootstocks*, or stems growing underground, consist of *tubers*, like the potato, yam, and artichoke, and of scaly *bulbs*, like the onion, chives, leek, and garlic. *Stems* we eat in asparagus; and whole *trunks* of trees are felled and used in making sago, which is the *pith* of a species of palm-tree.

Leaves include lettuce, endive, spinach, parsley, cabbage, and greens of various kinds. *Dried leaves* and *flowers* are used in the form of tea, sage, thyme, bay leaves, tobacco, marjoram, savory, and other herbs. *Leaf stalks* include celery and rhubarb; *flower stalks*, cauliflower and globe artichokes. The *juices* of vegetables furnish many forms of food, — sugar, acids, honey, oil, gum, and wines. The *bark* we use in cinnamon. *Unexpanded flower-buds* are pickled, as in capers, or dried, as in cloves. Ripe cloves have no aroma.

Many *seeds* or *berries* are gathered green, and are then dried for use. Allspice, or Jamaica pepper, cassia buds,

19

long peppers, and black pepper are of this class. Mustard and celery *seeds* are used as well as the leaves. Nutmegs are *seeds;* and mace is the *aril*, or covering, of the nutmeg. *Seed vessels* are used green, as in string beans, and also dried and ground, as in cayenne pepper. *Farinaceous seeds* or *grains* include wheat, rye, oats, corn, barley, rice, and buck-wheat. They have a thin seed vessel adhering closely to the whole surface of the seed. *Oleaginous seeds* contain oil and starch, like the cocoanut, walnut, chestnut, almond, etc. *Leguminous seeds* are enclosed in pods, as peas, beans, lentils, etc.

Under the general name of *fruit* we eat very different things. *Fleshy fruits*, like grapes, tomatoes, gooseberries, blueberries, cranberries, and currants, are *pulpy seed vessels.* Oranges and lemons are *pulpy seed vessels*, with a thick *leathery rind.* Squashes, melon, cucumbers, egg-plant, etc., are *fleshy fruits* with a *hard rind.* Chocolate is made from the seed of a *fleshy fruit.* In checkerberries, quinces, and in all parts of the apple and pear but the core, we eat a *fleshy, enlarged calyx.* In peaches, plums, apricots, cherries, and other stone fruits, we eat the *outer part* of a *pericarp* or *seed vessel.* Olives belong to this class, and are used green and in the form of oil expressed from the fleshy pericarp. Coffee is the *seed* of a *stone fruit.* In figs we eat a *hollow flower stalk*, grown pulpy, and the inside lined with a great number of flowers. Mulberries are clusters of the *pulpy flower leaves* and *stalk* of minute multiple flowers. Pineapples are mulberries on a large scale. The strawberry is the *receptacle* of a flower grown juicy and pulpy, and bearing many *one-seeded seed vessels* on its surface. Blackberries also are *receptacles*, though smaller, covered with clusters of *little stone fruits.* Raspberries are the *little stone fruits* in a cluster without the *receptacle.*

Many fruits, when dried, are called by different names. Dried currants are small grapes. Sultanas are larger grapes, and raisins are another and larger variety of the same fruit. Prunes and prunellas are dried plums.

Some of the lower orders of vegetation afford valuable food. Irish and Ceylon mosses are *seaweeds*. Iceland moss is a *lichen*. Truffles and mushrooms are a species of *fungi* of vegetable growth, but possessing a strong meaty or animal flavor.

We need a large variety of vegetables in our food to promote perfect health. Vegetables are rich in saline substances which counteract the evil effect of too much animal food. Some are rich in organic acids, and many abound in indigestible ligneous tissues which are useful in certain conditions. Those which contain starch and albumen and which can be stored for use during the winter months are considered the most valuable. All vegetables need the addition of salt and butter, or some form of fat, and many are rendered less indigestible by seasoning with pepper. Peas, beans, squashes, beets, turnips, etc., which contain sugar, should be slightly sweetened, as much of the natural sweetness is lost in cooking; and those containing potash salts, as cabbage and lettuce, need an acid condiment. Beans, peas, and other vegetables, which are difficult of digestion, are less indigestible if eaten in the form of purées.

Green vegetables should be freshly gathered, thoroughly washed in cold water, and cooked in freshly boiling salted water. It is impossible to give a definite time for cooking, as much depends upon their age and the time they have been gathered. Wilted vegetables require a much longer time than fresh. All vegetables should be cooked until soft and tender, and no longer. This is better ascertained by watching them carefully and piercing with a fork than by depending upon any time-table. Vegetables which are eaten raw and are liable to ferment in the stomach are usually dressed with some condiment, — oil, vinegar, salt, and pepper.

Every green vegetable keeps its color better if it be boiled rapidly and uncovered. Many use soda for the same purpose, but unwisely.

Potatoes.

The potato is more generally used than any other vegetable. It combines with other foods — meats particularly — to give the desired elements. But it should not be used alone, or in too great a proportion, as it gives very little flesh-forming material. When taken exclusively, such a large bulk of it is required for sustenance that it results in increased size and prominence of the stomach, which sometimes amounts to deformity.

Potatoes are three fourths water. The solid matter consists largely of starch, with a small quantity of albumen and mineral matter held in solution in the juices. The quantity of starch increases during the autumn, and remains stationary during the winter. In spring, when germination commences, the starch is changed to gum, and renders the potatoes mucilaginous. The sugar formed from this gum renders them sweeter. Potatoes which have been frozen and thawed suddenly are sweeter and more watery than before, because on exposure to the warmth and air the starch is changed to sugar. They should be kept frozen until ready to use, or used immediately after thawing in cold water. The sprouts on potatoes should be removed as soon as they appear, since, if they are allowed to grow, they exhaust the starch, and render the potatoes unfit for food. Potatoes should be kept in a dry, cool cellar.

Botanically, potatoes belong to the same poisonous order as tobacco and deadly nightshade, and contain an acid juice which is unpleasant to the taste and often renders them indigestible. This lies in and near the rind of the potato. It is drawn out by heat. When the potatoes are baked it escapes in the steam, if they are opened at once; and when they are boiled, it is absorbed by the water. It is not wasteful, therefore, to peel potatoes before cooking, or to take off quite a thick peel, as they are thus rendered more wholesome. Taste the water in which potatoes have been boiled, and you will have no desire to use it in your yeast, bread, or stews. Potatoes when first peeled are white, but turn brown on exposure to the air. For this reason they should be covered with cold water as soon as peeled. New potatoes are watery, as the starch is not fully formed. They have a very thin skin, which may be rubbed or scraped off.

Raw potatoes which are to be fried should be thinly sliced, and soaked in cold water to draw out all the starch, that they may be crisp and not mealy. The cells which hold the starch grains are of an albuminous nature. These cells are divided in slicing the potatoes, and the starch is drawn out into the water; the albuminous membrane hardens in frying, and makes the potatoes crisp.

Boiled potatoes should be drained the moment the heat bursts all the starch grains, which may easily be determined by their soft texture when pierced with a fork, else the starch will absorb water, and the potatoes become pasty and unwholesome.

Baked potatoes should be served as soon as soft, and the skin should be slightly ruptured by squeezing to let the steam within escape, else it will condense and make the potato watery and unwholesome. Potatoes which are cut or sliced for stews and chowders should be soaked and scalded to remove the greenness before adding them to the stew.

Boiled Potatoes. — Select potatoes of uniform size. Wash and scrub with a brush. Pare, and soak in cold water. Put them in boiling salted water, — *one quart* of *water* and *one tablespoonful* of *salt* for *six large potatoes.* Cook half an hour or until soft, but not until broken. Drain off every drop of the water. Place the kettle uncovered on the back of the stove to let the steam escape. Keep hot until ready to serve.

Potatoes à la Neige. — Prepare the potatoes as above, and when well drained and mealy beat them thoroughly with a fork, add salt to taste, and serve at once, piled lightly on the dish.

Rice Potato. — Rub the beaten potato through a squash

strainer into the dish in which it is to be served. Keep the dish in a pan of hot water, and use a potato masher or pestle to facilitate the rubbing. Mashed and riced potatoes may be browned by placing the dish in the oven a few minutes.

Mashed Potatoes. — To *one pint* of *hot boiled potatoes*, add *one tablespoonful* of *butter*, *half a teaspoonful* of *salt*, *half a saltspoonful* of *pepper*, and *hot milk* or *cream* to moisten. Mash in the kettle in which they were boiled, and beat with a fork until light and creamy, and turn out lightly on a dish. Never smooth it over, as that will make it heavy and compact.

Potato Balls. — *One pint* of *hot mashed potatoes* highly seasoned with *salt, pepper, celery salt, chopped parsley,* and *butter;* moisten, if needed, with a little *hot milk* or *cream.* Beat *one egg* light, and add part of it to the potatoes. Shape into smooth round balls. Brush over with the remainder of the egg, and bake on a buttered tin until brown. Be careful not to get them too moist.

Potato Puff. — Prepare as for potato balls, making it quite moist with *cream* or *milk.* Beat the *yolks* and *whites* of *two eggs* separately, and stir them into the potatoes when slightly cooled. Turn into a shallow baking-dish, pile it in a rocky form, and bake ten minutes, or until it is puffed and browned. Add *half a cup* of *finely chopped cooked meat,* to give a variety.

Lyonnaise Potatoes. — Cut *one pint* of *cold boiled potatoes* into dice, and season with *salt* and *pepper.* Fry *one scant tablespoonful* of *minced onion* in *one heaping tablespoonful* of *butter,* until yellow. Add the potatoes, and stir with a fork until they have absorbed all the butter, being careful not to break them. Add *one tablespoonful* of *chopped parsley,* and serve hot. *One tablespoonful* of *vinegar* heated with the butter gives the potatoes a nice flavor.

Creamed Potatoes. — Cut cold boiled potatoes into cubes measuring one third of an inch, or into thin slices. Put them in a small shallow pan, cover with *milk,* and cook until the potatoes have absorbed nearly all the milk. To *one pint* of *potatoes* add *one tablespoonful* of *butter, half a teaspoonful* of *salt, half a saltspoonful* of *pepper*, and a little *chopped parsley.*

Fried Potatoes. — Cut cold boiled potatoes into slices about a quarter of an inch thick. Have a frying-pan hot and well greased with *salt pork* or *bacon fat.* Cook the potatoes in the fat until brown, then turn, and brown the other side.

French Potatoes. — Fry as above, pour a *white sauce* on a platter, and arrange the fried potatoes on the sauce.

Potatoes à la Maître d'Hôtel. — Prepare the *Maître d'Hôtel butter;* mix *one tablespoonful* of *butter*, creamed, with the whole *yolk* of *one egg.* Add *one teaspoonful* of *lemon juice, one tablespoonful* of *chopped parsley, half a teaspoonful* of *salt*, and *half a saltspoonful* of *pepper.* Cut *one pint* of *cold boiled potatoes* in thin slices or dice, or cut raw potatoes into balls with a French cutter, and boil them ten minutes. Warm the potatoes in milk enough to barely cover them. When the milk is nearly absorbed, stir in quickly the Maître d'Hôtel butter, and serve at once.

Baked Potatoes. — Select smooth potatoes of uniform size. Wash, and scrub well. Bake in a hot oven about forty-five minutes, or until soft. Pinch them to break the skins, and let the steam escape. Serve at once, and never cover, as the steam causes them to become soggy.

Franconia Potatoes (Baked with Meat). — Wash, scrub, and pare potatoes of uniform size. Put them in the dripping-pan with the meat, and baste when the meat is basted. Or place them in a small tin pan beside the meat or on the grate, and baste with the dripping.

Potatoes in the Half-Shell, or Soufflé. — Wash, scrub, and bake *three smooth potatoes.* Cut in halves lengthwise, and without breaking the skin scoop out the potato into a hot bowl. Mash, and add *one even tablespoonful* of *butter, one* of *hot milk,* and *salt* and *pepper* to taste. Beat the *whites* of *two eggs* stiff, and mix it with the potato. Fill the skins with the potato mixture, heaping it lightly on the top. Brown slightly.

Stuffed Potatoes. — Bake potatoes of equal size ; when done, and still hot, cut off a small piece from the end of each potato. Scoop out the inside. Mash, and mix with it half the quantity of *cooked meat*, highly seasoned and finely chopped. Fill the skins a little above the edge. Set in the oven to brown the tops. Or omit the meat, and fill only with the mashed and seasoned potato. Replace the cover, and heat again.

FIG. 39. Stuffed Potatoes.

Fried Raw Potatoes. — Pare, wash, and cut into the desired shape. Soak in cold salted water, drain, and dry between towels. Fry in clear fat, hot enough to brown while counting sixty. Drain, and sprinkle with *salt*.

Saratoga Potatoes are shaved in thin slices. *Parisienne Potatoes* are cut in small balls with a French vegetable cutter. *Macaroni*, or *Shoo Fly*, *Potatoes* are cut in quarter-inch slices, then in quarter-inch strips. *Crescents* and other shapes may be cut with vegetable cutters.

These are all to be fried ; but some prefer to boil the Parisienne potatoes, and serve in a *cream sauce*, flavored with *parsley*.

Sweet Potatoes may be baked or boiled. They are better baked. Cold sweet potatoes may be cut in slices, warmed in *milk*, and seasoned with *butter* and *salt*, or browned in *butter*.

A Southern Dish. (*Adaline Miller.*) — Cut cold baked sweet potatoes into quarter-inch slices, and put them in an earthen dish. Spread each layer with *butter*, and sprinkle slightly with *sugar*, and bake until hot and slightly browned. Sweet potatoes are much richer when twice cooked.

Spinach.

Pick over, trim off the roots and decayed leaves ; wash thoroughly, lifting the spinach from one pan of water into another, that the sand may be left in the water, and changing the water until it is clear. Put the spinach in a large kettle without water. Place it on the stove where.it will cook slowly until the juice is drawn out, then boil until tender. Drain and chop fine. For *half a peck* of spinach add *one large tablespoonful* of *butter, half a teaspoonful* of *salt*, and *a quarter* of *a saltspoonful* of *pepper ;* or add a little thin *cream sauce.* Heat again and serve on *toast.* Garnish with *hard-boiled eggs* and *toast points*, or serve cold with *French dressing.*

Spinach is nearly all water, and a smaller portion of the potash salts — its most valuable constituent — is lost when it is cooked in its own juices.

Greens.

The leaves and stalks of young beets, milkweed, dandelions, and narrow dock are useful as food in the early spring, chiefly for the water and alkaline salts which they contain. They should be picked over, and washed carefully, cooked in boiling salted water until tender, then drained, and seasoned with *butter* and *salt.* *Vinegar* is often used with them as a desirable condiment. Many people consider it necessary to boil a piece of *salt pork* with greens, but they are more wholesome when seasoned with butter. Dandelions should be cooked in plenty of water; but other tender greens may be cooked, like spinach, in their own juices.

Asparagus.

Wash carefully and break (not cut) into inch pieces as far as each stalk can be broken. When it will not snap off quickly, the stalk is too tough to be used. Cook in boiling salted water, deep enough to cover, for fifteen minutes, or until tender. When the asparagus is not fresh and tender, it is well to boil the hardest part first, and add the tender heads after ten minutes. Drain, season with *butter* and *salt*, or pour *white sauce* over it, and serve on *toast.* Many people prefer to leave the stalks whole, and tie them into bundles before boiling. When served in this way, unless all the tough part be broken off before cooking, it is inconvenient, if not impossible, to cut the stalk afterward.

Green Peas.

Peas are fresh when the pods are green, crisp, and plump. The fresh pods are sweet, and full of flavor. Wash the pods before shelling, then the peas will require no washing. Put the peas into a colander, and sift out the fine particles. Boil the pods ten minutes, skim them out, and add the peas. Boil fifteen minutes, or till tender. When nearly done, add the *salt*. Let the water boil nearly away, and serve without draining, except when the peas are to be served as a garnish. Season with *butter, cream, salt*, and a little *sugar*.

Old peas should be cooked until tender, drained, mashed, and rubbed through a sieve, and served as a vegetable or made into a purée.

Peas are nutritious, but they are indigestible unless the hull be broken before they are swallowed.

Beans.

String Beans. — Remove the strings. The surest way to do that is to pare a thin strip from each edge of the pods. Many persons think this unnecessary ; but the beans are much more delicate, and two or three strings are enough to spoil the whole dish. Lay a handful of the pods on a board with the ends even, and cut them all at once into inch pieces. Wash, and cook in boiling salted water from one to three hours, the time varying with different varieties of beans. Drain ; season with *butter, salt,* and *cream,* and serve hot, or serve cold as a salad. When very young and tender, they may be cooked in just water enough to keep them from burning.

Shelled Beans. — Wash, and cook in boiling water ; always use soft water. Add salt after ten minutes, and boil until tender. Let the water boil nearly away, and serve without draining. Season with *butter* and *salt*. Lima beans and other white varieties are improved by adding a little *hot cream.*

Green or Sweet Corn.

Remove the husk, and every thread of the silky fibre. Put into boiling water, cover with the clean inner husks, and cook from five to fifteen minutes. Try a kernel, and take up the corn as soon as the milk has thickened and the raw taste is destroyed. Corn, if boiled a long time, is made hard and its flavor impaired.

Green Corn Fritters, or Mock Oysters. — Cut through each row of kernels with the point of a sharp knife. Then with the back of the knife press out the pulp, and leave the hull on the cob. This is better and easier than to shave or grate off the kernels. To *one pint* of *corn pulp* add *two well-beaten eggs, half a teaspoonful* of *salt, half a saltspoonful* of *pepper,* and *two tablespoonfuls* of *flour,* or just enough to keep the corn and egg together. Do not add milk, as then more flour will be required, and this destroys the flavor of the corn. Fry in small cakes on a buttered griddle, and brown well on each side; or add more flour, and drop by spoonfuls into deep fat. When highly seasoned with *salt* and *pepper,* these fritters have the flavor of oysters. Make in the same way with canned corn, finely chopped. Add *two tablespoonfuls* of *milk,* as the canned corn is less moist than the fresh.

Succotash. — This may be made by mixing equal quantities of *shelled beans* and *corn* cut from the cob, having first cooked and seasoned them separately. Or cut the raw corn from the cob, by scoring each row and pressing the pulp out with the back of the knife, leaving the hulls on the cob, and when the beans are nearly soft, add the corn, and cook fifteen minutes. Add *cream, butter, salt,* and *sugar* to taste.

In winter, when the vegetables are dry and hard, soak the corn and Lima beans over night. Put the beans on in cold water, changing it twice. As soon as it boils, add the corn, and cook slowly several hours, or till soft. Season with *butter, sugar,* and *salt.* Canned Lima beans and canned corn are also used.

Corn, beans, and peas are delicious and wholesome summer vegetables. Much of the prejudice against their use among children results from imperfect mastication, which renders them indigestible. Every row of kernels should be cut with a sharp knife if the corn be served on the cob, and every pea or bean should be mashed with a fork to insure their perfect digestion. Thus eaten, these vegetables are valuable food, and will cause no trouble.

Tomatoes.

Raw Tomatoes. — Scald and peel at least an hour before using. Keep them on the ice, and serve with *sugar, salt, vinegar*, or with *Mayonnaise dressing*. If very large, they may be sliced before serving.

Stewed Tomatoes. — Pour boiling water over them, remove the skins and the hard green stem. Cut them into quarters, and stew in a granite pan fifteen minutes, until the pulp is soft and the juice is partly boiled away. Add *salt, pepper, butter*, and *sugar* if desired. The tomato may be thickened with *cracker crumbs* or with *cornstarch* wet in a little cold water.

Scalloped Tomatoes. — Season *one quart* of *tomatoes* with *one teaspoonful* of *salt*, *one saltspoonful* of *pepper*, *half a cup* of *sugar*, and *a few drops* of *onion juice*. Butter a deep dish, and sprinkle with *fine crumbs*. Pour in the tomatoes. Moisten *one cup* of *cracker crumbs* with *half a cup* of *melted butter*. Spread over the top, and brown in the oven. Raw tomatoes sliced may be used in layers, alternating with crumbs and seasoning.

Stuffed Tomatoes. — Cut a thin slice from the stem end of *large, smooth tomatoes*. Remove the seeds and soft pulp, and mix with the pulp an equal amount of *buttered cracker crumbs*. Season to taste with *salt, pepper, sugar*, and *onion juice*. Fill the cavity with the mixture, heaping it in the centre, and sprinkle buttered crumbs over the top. Place the tomatoes in a granite pan, and bake until the crumbs are brown. Take them up carefully with a broad knife, and serve very hot. A small quantity of *cooked meat* finely chopped may be used with the crumbs.

Onions.

Pour boiling water over them, and remove the skins. Put them in boiling salted water. When they have boiled five minutes, change the water, and change again after ten minutes. Boil half an hour, or until tender, but not until broken. Drain off the water, add *milk* enough to cover, and cook five or ten minutes longer. Season with *butter*, *salt*, and *pepper*. Serve plain or as a garnish for beef. Or omit the seasoning, and pour *white sauce* over them.

Baked or *Scalloped Onions.* — Boil, and if large cut into quarters. Put into a shallow dish, cover with *white sauce* and *buttered crumbs*, and bake until the crumbs are brown.

Onions are rich in flesh-forming elements, are soothing to the mucous membrane, and are otherwise medicinal. They impart an agreeable flavor to many kinds of food.

Cauliflower.

The leaves should be green and fresh, and the heads creamy white. When there are dark spots, the cauliflower is wilted. Pick off the outside leaves, soak in cold salted water, top downwards, for one hour, to cleanse it thoroughly. Tie it in a twine bag, to prevent breaking. Cook in boiling salted water fifteen or twenty minutes, or until tender. If not boiled in a bag, remove the scum before it settles on the cauliflower. Serve in a shallow dish, and cover with a *cream* or *Hollandaise sauce*. Or add a little *grated cheese*, and cover with *cracker crumbs* moistened in *melted butter*, and bake until the crumbs are brown. Or when cold, serve as a *salad* with *Mayonnaise dressing*. Cauliflower may be cut in small pieces, and served as a garnish around broiled chicken or sweetbreads.

Cabbage.

Select a small heavy cabbage. Remove the outside leaves, cut into quarters, cut off the tough stalk, soak in cold salted water half an hour. Cook till tender in boiling salted water, changing the water twice. Drain, cut or chop fine, season with *salt* and *butter*, or cover with *white sauce* and *buttered crumbs*, and bake till the crumbs are brown.

The cauliflower and cabbage contain more gluten, and are therefore more nutritious, than any other vegetable food. They should be eaten with fat and oily food, and require an acid, like lemon juice or vinegar, as a condiment. Cabbage is considered indigestible, and many boil with it a small piece of red pepper to counteract this effect. If the water in which cabbage is boiled be changed two or three times, less of the strong odor and flavor is retained. With proper treatment this vegetable may be served as temptingly as any other. It is more wholesome when served in its raw state as a salad than when cooked.

Celery.

Scrape clean, and cut the stalks into inch pieces; cook in boiling salted water half an hour, or until tender. Drain and mix with a *white sauce;* or dip them in *fritter batter*, and fry in hot *fat*. Celery is usually eaten raw, as a salad, but is more digestible when cooked. Celery is particularly good for nervous or rheumatic people.

Egg Plant.

Cut the plant into slices one third of an inch thick, without removing the skin. Sprinkle salt over each slice, pile them, and cover with a weight to press out the juice. Drain, and dip each slice first in *fine crumbs*, then in *beaten egg*, and again in *crumbs*, and sauté them in hot *fat*. Egg plants belong to the same family as the potato and tobacco, all of which contain a bitter juice, more or less poisonous.

Egg Plant Fritters. (*Adaline Miller.*) — Put the egg plant whole into boiling salted water, mixed with *one tablespoonful* of *vinegar* or *lemon juice;* cook twenty minutes or until tender; mash and drain. To *one pint* of *egg plant* add *half a cup* of *flour, two eggs,* well beaten, and *salt* and *pepper* to taste. Fry in small cakes in hot *fat,* browning well on both sides.

Artichokes.

The *Jerusalem Artichoke* is a tuber, something like the potato; but as it contains no starch, it is not mealy. Peel and throw at once into cold water and vinegar to preserve the color. Cook in boiling salted water until tender, watch closely, and take them out as they become soft, for if left in longer they will harden again. Serve with a *white sauce.* Jerusalem artichokes may be used as a salad, or they may be pickled.

Globe Artichokes. — These are thick, fleshy-petalled flowers which grow on a plant that resembles the thistle. The thickened receptacle and scales of the involucre form the edible portion. Soak the artichokes, cut off the outside leaves, trim away the lower leaves and the ends of the others. Cook in boiling salted water, with the tops downward, half an hour, or until the leaves can be drawn out. Drain, remove the choke, and serve with *drawn butter.*

Mushrooms.

Peel the top and stalk, break in small pieces, place them in a stewpan, sprinkle slightly with *salt* and *pepper,* and let them stand half an hour, until the juice is drawn out. Stew the mushrooms in the juice and a little *butter* until tender, add *cream* to cover, and when the cream is hot serve on *toast.* Mushrooms are considered difficult of digestion. They are a fungous growth, and have a woody odor and a meaty flavor. They are used largely in sauces. Unless familiar with the difference between the edible and the poisonous mushrooms, it is safer to use the canned mushrooms, or to obtain the fresh at a reliable market.

The eatable mushroom first appears very small, and of a round button shape, on a short underground stalk. At this stage it is all white. It grows rapidly, and soon the skin breaks around the base of the button, which there spreads like an umbrella, and shows underneath a fringed fur of a fine salmon-color, which changes to a chocolate and then to a dark brown color, when the mushrooms have attained some size. They are in perfection before the last change. The skin should peel easily. Those with yellow or white fur, and which grow in low, damp shady places, should be avoided. The good mushrooms spring up in open sunny fields in August and September. Do not trust to any written description, but search the fields with some one who can unerringly distinguish them.

The common puff-ball, when white and hard, though not so delicate as the mushroom, makes a palatable dish. It should be peeled with a silver knife, cut in slices half an inch thick, dipped in *crumbs* and *egg*, or in a *batter*, and fried. Serve at once.

Winter Squash.

If the shell be soft, pare the squash, remove the seeds, and steam or cook in boiling salted water. If the shell be hard, split the squash, remove the seeds, and steam or boil until soft. Scrape out the soft part from the shell, mash, and season to taste. *A pint* of *squash* needs *one tablespoonful* of *butter*, *a few grains* of *pepper*, *half a teaspoonful* of *sugar*, and *salt* to taste. Squash may be baked in the shell, then mashed, and seasoned as above.

Summer Squashes are good only when young, fresh, and tender. Wash, and cut into quarters or small pieces. The skin and seeds need not be removed. Cook in boiling salted water twenty minutes, or until tender. Place the squash in a strainer cloth, mash it thoroughly, squeeze the cloth until the squash is dry. Add a little *cream* or *butter*, *salt* and *pepper*, and heat again before serving.

Carrots and Turnips.

Carrots and turnips contain, instead of starch, a gelatinous gummy substance, called pectine. They are useful in soups, giving them a fine flavor and color. Soups in which carrots are used are gelatinous when cold. Carrots are not a favorite vegetable for the table; but if young and tender, they are palatable when boiled, and served in a white sauce. They should be washed and scraped (not pared) before boiling. Old carrots are sometimes boiled, and served with corned beef and salt fish. Their rich color makes them effective as a garnish. The red, outside part is considered the best, as the inside is stringy.

Turnips contain but little nutriment. They are very watery, and having no starch are agreeable food to be eaten with potatoes. They contain no salt, and therefore need more than other vegetables. Being wholly deficient in starch and fat, they are good with fat meat, corned beef, roast pork, and mutton.

Turnips in White Sauce. — Wash and cut French turnips into half or three-quarter inch slices; pare and cut each slice into strips, and then into cubes. Boil in boiling salted water until tender. Drain and pour *white sauce* over them. Turnips may also be mashed, drained, and seasoned with *butter, pepper*, and *salt*.

Parsnips.

Parsnips contain starch and sugar, a small **portion** of gluten, and less water than carrots or turnips. They are eaten with salt fish and corned beef. Those which have remained in the ground through the winter are considered the best. They should be washed and scrubbed thoroughly, but are more easily peeled after boiling. Cut them into half-inch cubes, and serve in *white sauce.*

Parsnip Fritters. — After boiling the parsnips, plunge them into cold water and the skins will slip off easily, mash them,[1] and season to taste with *butter, salt*, and *pepper.* Flour the hands, and shape the mashed parsnip

---

[1] Parsnips are more digestible if mashed and rubbed through a purée sieve to remove the woody fibre.

into small, flat oval cakes. Roll them in flour, and fry them in *butter* until brown ; or dip them in *molasses*, and then fry.

Salsify, or Oyster Plant.

Scrape, and throw at once into cold water, with a little vinegar in it to keep them from turning black. Cook in boiling salted water one hour, or until tender. Drain, mash, and season, and fry like parsnip fritters ; or cut into inch lengths, and mix with a *white sauce ;* or dip the pieces in *fritter batter*, and fry in hot *fat*.

Beets.

Wash, but do not cut them, as that destroys the sweetness and color. Cook in boiling water until tender. Young beets will cook in one hour, old beets require a longer time ; and if tough, wilted, or stringy, they will never boil tender. When cooked, put them in a pan of cold water, and rub off the skin. Young beets are cut in slices, and served hot with *butter*, *salt*, and *pepper*, or cut in small cubes and served in a *white sauce*. They are often pickled in vinegar, spiced or plain, and served cold ; or they may be cut into dice, and mixed with other vegetables for a salad.

Rice.

Rice should be thoroughly washed. Turn the rice into a coarse strainer, and place the strainer in a deep dish of cold water. Rub the rice, and lift it in the strainer out of the water, changing the water till it is clear. It is important to observe all the steps of this process, for in this way all the grit is deposited in the water, leaving the rice thoroughly cleansed. Drain, and cook in either of the following ways, each of which, if followed carefully, will insure white, distinct kernels of thoroughly cooked rice.

Boiled Rice. — Have *two quarts* of *water* with *one table-spoonful* of *salt* boiling rapidly in an uncovered kettle. Throw in *one cup* of *well-washed rice*, and let it boil so fast that the kernels fairly dance in the water. Skim carefully, and stir with a fork, never with a spoon, as that mashes the kernels. Cook twelve, fifteen, or twenty minutes, according to the age of the rice, and add more boiling water if needed. Test the grains often, and the moment they are soft, and before the starch begins to dissolve and cloud the water, pour into a squash strainer. Drain, and place the rice — still in the strainer — in a pan in the hot closet or on the back of the stove. Stir it before serving, to let the steam escape and the kernels become dry. Be careful not to cook the rice enough to burst the grains, as then nothing can prevent them from sticking together.

Steamed Rice. — Pour *two cups* of *boiling water* on *one cup* of well-washed *rice;* add *half a teaspoonful* of *salt*. Cook in the double boiler thirty minutes, or till soft. Remove the cover, stir with a fork to let the steam escape, and dry off the rice. Rice will usually absorb twice its bulk of water; but when cooked in milk or stock a little more moisture will be required.

Some of the nitrogenous and mineral constituents, of which rice has but a small amount, are lost in the boiling water, and unless the water be used for soup, to boil rice is a wasteful process. Steaming is a much easier method, and is more economical. Many dishes may be prepared from combinations of rice and various seasoning materials.

Savory Rice. — Steam *one scant cup* of *rice* and *two cups* of *rich white* or *brown stock* highly seasoned with *salt, cayenne, chopped parsley*, and *ground herbs*. Stir in *one tablespoonful* of *butter* with a fork, just before serving.

No. 2. — Fry *one tablespoonful* of *chopped onion* in *one heaping tablespoonful* of *butter* until yellow; add *one scant cup* of *uncooked rice*, and stir until slightly colored; then add *one pint* of *chicken stock*, and pour all into the double boiler, and steam thirty minutes.

Salmon Rice. — Use *half stock* and *half strained tomatoes;* season highly with *curry*, and cook like Savory Rice.

Rice with Cheese. — Steam the rice after either of the preceding receipts, and put it in a shallow dish in layers, alternating with *grated cheese* and *tomato sauce*, or with slices of *hard-boiled eggs* and *thin cream sauce.* Heat in the oven with or without a crust of *buttered crumbs.*

Macaroni, Spaghetti, and Vermicelli.

These are thick pastes made from wheaten flour mixed with a small quantity of water. They are made to take various shapes by being forced through holes in metallic plates. These plates are arranged over a fire; and the macaroni, as it issues from the holes, is partially baked, and afterward hung to dry over rods. Vermicelli is used in soup and puddings; macaroni and spaghetti as vegetables.

Macaroni is a nutritious and economical food, and should be used more extensively than it is. Do not wash it, as the boiling water will better take off anything that needs to be removed. Always cook it in boiling salted water until tender, before serving it in any way. Drain, and pour cold water over it to keep it from becoming pasty. Macaroni, as frequently prepared, in long pieces, which utterly refuse to come out of the dish in a proper manner when served, is not attractive Nor is it palatable when it is only slightly seasoned, and is dried in the oven without a covering of sauce or crumbs.

Macaroni. — Break *one quarter* of *a pound* of *macaroni* in three-inch pieces, and put into *three pints* of *boiling salted water.* Boil twenty minutes, or until soft. Drain in a colander, and pour cold water through it to cleanse and keep it from sticking. Cut into inch pieces. Lay the strips on a board, parallel to each other, and cut through them all at once. Put in a shallow baking-dish and cover with a *white sauce*, made with *a cup and a half* of *hot milk, one tablespoonful* of *butter*, and *one tablespoonful* of *flour*, cooked according to directions for White Sauce (see page 189). Add *half a teaspoonful* of *salt.* Mix *two thirds* of *a cup* of *fine cracker crumbs* with *a third* of *a cup* of *melted butter*, and sprinkle over the top. Bake till the crumbs are brown.

If cheese be liked with it, use *half a cup* of *grated Parmesan* or any other dry *cheese*. Put part of it with the macaroni, and mix the remainder with the crumbs.

No. 2. — Mix *two hard-boiled eggs*, chopped fine, with the macaroni. Sprinkle each layer with *salt* and *pepper*, and add a little *made mustard*, if you wish. Cover with *milk* and *buttered crumbs*, and bake until the crumbs are brown.

No. 3. — Pour a rich *white sauce* over the macaroni, and serve *grated cheese* on a separate dish.

Macaroni and Tomatoes. — Boil as above, and cover with *tomato sauce*. Fry *one tablespoonful* of *chopped onion* in *one tablespoonful* of *butter*. Add *one large tablespoonful* of *flour*; when well mixed, add gradually *a cup and a half* of *strained tomato* and *half a teaspoonful* of *salt*. Pour over the macaroni, and warm in the oven; or cover with *buttered crumbs*, and bake until the crumbs are brown.

Spaghetti. — This is a variety of macaroni about one eighth of an inch in diameter. It is usually served unbroken. Take a handful of the long sticks, plunge the ends into rapidly boiling salted water. As they soften, bend and coil the spaghetti in the water, without breaking it, until it is all softened. Boil until tender. Drain, pour cold water through it, and serve without cutting, if you are skilled in the art of winding it around your fork, as the Italians do. Serve the same as macaroni, with *cream* or *tomato sauce*, *cheese*, and *crumbs*.

Salads.

Green vegetables which are eaten raw and dressed with oil, acids, salt, and pepper, are classed as salads. Potatoes, string beans, beets, asparagus, cauliflower, and many other vegetables which have been cooked, are eaten cold with a salad dressing. Lobster, oysters, salmon, and other kinds of cooked fish, eggs, chicken, and delicate meats are combined with lettuce, cresses, or celery, and salad dressing, and furnish many appetizing and refreshing varieties of this useful form of food.

There is a strong prejudice with many against the use of oil. It is not strange when we remember the rancid oil sometimes offered us. Pure olive oil is seldom to be obtained, if we are to believe all that the opposers of adulteration assert. No doubt much that is sold as olive oil is made from cotton seed; but if it were sold under its right name and at a reasonable price there would be no objection to its use. When properly purified, and sweet, it may be as wholesome as olive oil. They are both vegetable oils, which are always considered more nutritious than animal oils. Oil is one of the best forms of fat we can use, and aids in digestion. Oil, when taken only in lobster salad or at late suppers, as is often the case, is held accountable for the horrors and torment following such a use; but if used seasonably and moderately, there will be no ill effects.

French Dressing.

1 saltspoonful salt.	¼ teaspoonful onion juice.
½ saltspoonful pepper.	1 tablespoonful vinegar.
3 tablespoonfuls oil.	

Mix in the order given, adding oil slowly.

This dressing is suitable for vegetable and egg salads, and is also used to marinate, or pickle, a meat or fish salad. The onion may be omitted, and *lemon juice* may be used instead of vinegar. *A teaspoonful* of *made mustard* added to a French dressing is liked by many.

Boiled Dressing.

Yolks of 3 eggs beaten.	2 tablespoonfuls melted butter or oil.
1 teaspoonful mustard.	
2 teaspoonfuls salt	1 cup cream or milk.
¼ saltspoonful cayenne.	½ cup hot vinegar.
2 tablespoonfuls sugar	Whites of 3 eggs, beaten stiff.

Cook in the double boiler until it thickens like soft custard. Stir well. This will keep in a cool place two weeks, and is excellent for lettuce, celery, asparagus, string beans, and cauliflower.

Boiled Dressing for Cold Slaw. — Boil *half a cup* of *vinegar* with *two teaspoonfuls* of *sugar, half a teaspoonful* each of *salt* and *mustard,* and *half a saltspoonful* of *pepper.* Rub *a quarter* of *a cup* of *butter* to a cream, with *one teaspoonful* of *flour,* and pour the boiling vinegar on it. Cook five minutes, then pour it over *one well-beaten egg.* The yolk only may be used, and the white saved for clearing coffee. Mix this dressing, while hot, with *one pint* of *red cabbage,* shaved or chopped, or with a mixed vegetable salad. Cold slaw is delicious served with fried oysters or fish.

Mayonnaise Dressing.

1 teaspoonful mustard.
1 teaspoonful powdered sugar.
½ teaspoonful salt.
¼ saltspoonful cayenne.

Yolks of 2 raw eggs.
1 pint olive oil.
2 tablespoonfuls vinegar.
2 tablespoonfuls lemon juice.

Mix the first four ingredients in a small bowl. Add the *eggs.* Stir well with a small wooden spoon. Add the oil, a few drops at a time, stirring until it thickens. If by chance you add too much oil, do not attempt to stir it all in at once, but take it up gradually. When the dressing is thick, thin it with a little lemon, then add oil and lemon alternately, and lastly the vinegar. When ready to serve, add *half a cup* of *whipped cream,* if you like. The cream makes it whiter and thinner. The oil should thicken the egg almost immediately, and the mixture should be thick enough to be taken up in a ball on the spoon, before adding the vinegar. Should the egg not thicken quickly, and have a curdled appearance, *half a teaspoonful* of the unbeaten *white* of *egg* or a few drops of vinegar will often restore the smooth consistency. Be careful not to use too much, as it will make the dressing thin. The dressing liquefies as soon as mixed with vegetables or meat; therefore it should be made stiff enough to keep in shape until used. Many prefer to use a Dover egg-beater, and others succeed best with a fork. The mixture soon becomes too hard to use an egg-beater to advantage. Lobster coral, dried and pounded to a powder, will give a Mayonnaise a bright red color. Spinach green, green peas mashed, or chopped parsley will color it green. Never mix the Mayonnaise dressing with the meat or fish until ready to serve, and then only part of it, and spread the remainder over the top.

Mayonnaise Tartare is simply the addition of *chopped olives*, *pickles*, *parsley*, *capers*, and *onions* to the Mayonnaise.

Lettuce Salad. — Pick over and wash each leaf without breaking. Shake off the water and drain in a net. Keep the lettuce in a cool place until ready to serve. Just before serving, dry between two towels. Arrange the leaves in a salad bowl, the larger leaves around the edge and the light ones in the centre. Serve with *boiled dressing*, or *French dressing*, or *sugar*, *salt*, and *vinegar* to taste. Lettuce should be served cool, fresh, and crisp. Never cut it, as that causes the leaves to wilt quickly. Tear them apart.

Radishes or olives may be served with lettuce; and when a brilliant effect is desired, garnish with a few nasturtium blossoms. When lettuce is used with other materials, never mix them until ready to serve.

Dressed Celery. — Use only the white, crisp part of the celery stalks. The green parts may be made into a purée or used in soups. Scrape off the brown discolored part, and wash thoroughly. Keep in cold water, and when ready to serve, drain and arrange in a celery glass. Serve with *salt*. Or cut the celery in thin slices, moisten with *French* or *Mayonnaise dressing*, and garnish with *lettuce*, *cresses*, or *celery leaves*. Lettuce and celery may be served with the roast if desired.

Cucumber Salad. — Cut off an inch from each end of the cucumber, and pare off a thick paring, as a bitter juice lies near the skin. Cut in thin slices, or shave with a vegetable cutter. Keep in cold water until ready to serve.

Drain, and place in the bowl with ice. Serve with *salt,
pepper,* and *vinegar,* or with a *French dressing. Young
onions* thinly sliced are sometimes mixed with cucumbers.

Cucumber and Tomato Salad. — Place a bed of crisp
lettuce in a salad dish, then a layer of sliced *cucumbers,*
then sliced *tomatoes,* and pour a *French dressing,* or a
Mayonnaise, over the whole. Tomatoes peeled and cut
into halves, and served with *a spoonful* of *Mayonnaise*
on each half, make an attractive salad.

Potato Salad. — *One pint* of *cold boiled potatoes,* cut
in half-inch dice or shaved in thin slices, and seasoned
with *salt* and *pepper;* the *yolk* of *one hard-boiled egg,*
one heaping tablespoonful of *chopped parsley, half a cup*
of *cold beet dice,* and a *French dressing.* Put alternate
layers of potato, beet, yolk of egg, rubbed through a
fine strainer, parsley, and French dressing, until the
materials are all used. Have parsley and egg on the
top, and leave half of the dressing for the last layer.
Or arrange the potatoes, parsley, and egg in the centre
of the dish, then a circle of beets and lettuce around the
edge, with French dressing sprinkled over the whole.
Sliced *onions, red cabbage* chopped, *capers,* dice of
turnips, and *carrots* cut into fancy shapes or rubbed
through a strainer, may be used with potatoes for a
salad.

No. 2. — *One pint* of *hot potatoes,* mashed or cut in
slices, *half a cup* of *chopped cabbage, half a cup* of
chopped celery, one tablespoonful of *chopped parsley,*
one cucumber pickle, and *one hard-boiled egg,* chopped
fine. Mix well, and add enough of *Boiled Dressing
No. 2* to moisten. Keep on the ice until ready to serve.
Place *two tablespoonfuls* on a leaf of *lettuce,* and serve
in the leaf.

Many professional cooks prefer to mix a potato salad
while the potatoes are hot, as the salad looks more
appetizing, will keep longer, and have less of the soggy
peculiar taste than when made with cold potatoes.
Rubbing a cut *onion* or a little *garlic* round the salad

bowl is sufficient where only a slight flavor of onion is desired. Vegetable salads are suitable for lunch or tea, or may be served as a course at dinner.

Egg Salad. — Boil *six eggs* twenty minutes. Cut the whites in thin slices, or chop them very fine. Arrange a bed of *cresses* on a dish. Make nests of the whites, and put one whole yolk in the centre of each nest; or rub the yolks through a fine strainer over the whites. Sprinkle a *French dressing* over the whole. Serve small balls of *cottage cheese* with the salad.

Oyster Salad. — Steam or parboil *one pint* of *oysters*. Drain, cool, and marinate them with a *French dressing*. Serve with *cresses, celery,* or *lettuce,* and a Mayonnaise dressing.

Fish Salad. — *One quart* of any kind of *cold cooked fish*, flaked and freed from bones and skin, and placed on a bed of *lettuce.* Pound the *yolks* of *three hard-boiled eggs,* and *three sardines* (bones and skin removed) to a smooth paste. Mix this paste with the *Boiled* or the *Mayonnaise dressing,* and pour it over the fish. Garnish with slices of *lemon.*

Chicken Salad. — *One pint* each of *cold boiled* or *roasted chicken* and *celery*, or half as much celery as

Fig. 40. Chicken Salad.

chicken. Cut the chicken into quarter-inch dice. Scrape, wash, and cut the celery in dice. Mix and marinate with a *French dressing,* and keep on the ice until ready to serve. Make a *Mayonnaise dressing,* and mix part of it with the chicken; arrange the salad in a dish, pour the remainder of the dressing over it, and garnish with *celery leaves* and *capers,* or *lettuce,* and yolk of hard-boiled egg rubbed through a fine strainer.

Lobster Salad. — Cut *one pint* of *lobster meat* in dice, season with a *French dressing,* and keep it on ice until ready to serve, then mix with half of the *Mayonnaise dressing.* Make nests or cups of the crisp *lettuce* leaves.

Fɪɢ. 41. Lobster Salad.

Put *a large spoonful* of the lobster in each leaf, with *a tablespoonful* of the *Mayonnaise* on the top. Garnish with *capers* and *pounded coral,* sprinkled over the dressing, and with *lobster claws* and *parsley* round the edge.

Salmon Salad. — Prepare in the same way with cooked or canned salmon, freed from bones, skin, and oil.

Salad Sandwiches. — Mix a small quantity of *Mayonnaise dressing* with finely chopped *lobster* or *chicken.* Cover a small slice of *bread* with *lettuce,* then the salad, lettuce, and bread again. Wrap them in tin foil or oiled paper, and serve at picnics or when travelling.

Strawberry Salad.

Choose the heart leaves of nice head *lettuce,* and make cups of *two leaves,* stems crossed. Heap a few strawberries in the centre, dust lightly with *powdered sugar,* and put *a teaspoonful* of *Mayonnaise dressing* on each portion.

Sliced bananas may be served in the same way.

PASTRY AND PIES.

PUFF PASTE, when skilfully made, is light and tender, and so delicate that it cannot be touched without crushing. It should be thoroughly baked, and is therefore more suitable for tarts and patties and the upper crust of pies. Eat it sparingly ; unless you have a good digestion, and exercise freely, never eat it. It is, however, less injurious than the ordinary pastry seen on many tables, as it contains no more shortening than much of the pastry made with a " guess measure " of lard. It is not so much the amount of fat the paste contains that makes it indigestible, as the inferior quality of the fat, such as rancid butter or impure lard, or the soggy, greasy, half-cooked paste.

Pastry that is light, dry, and flaky is more easily separated by the gastric fluids than that which is heavy. Many housekeepers use lard in making pastry, as it is cheaper than butter, and makes a softer and more tender crust. Butter is more wholesome, and is preferable if you wish to make a brown crust. A mixture of half lard and half butter answers very well for common paste, but for puff paste butter alone should be used. In French receipts for puff paste eggs are considered essential, but there is no necessity for their use.

It requires practice to make puff paste well ; and as there are so many other dishes more easily made and vastly more important, it is better not to waste time and strength upon it. Let your ambition as a housekeeper soar higher than perfection in making puff paste. But those who *will* have it may observe the following directions.

Puff Paste. — *One pound* of the *best butter, one pound* of *pastry flour, one scant teaspoonful* of *salt*, about *one cup* of *ice water.* By measure, use *one quart* of *flour* and *one pint* of *butter.* Scald the bowl, then fill with cold water. Dip the hands into hot and then into cold water; this makes bowl and hands smooth, and keeps the butter from sticking. Wash the butter, by working it in the cold water, till soft and waxy. Divide into four parts; pat each part into a long and narrow piece, and wrap in a clean napkin.

Have three shallow oblong pans that will fit the one into the other. Fill the largest and smallest of the pans with broken ice. Put the butter, covered with the napkin, into the other, and place it between the two pans of ice to harden. Mix the salt with the flour, then break in one quarter of the butter. Rub with the tips of the fingers, and keep plenty of flour between the fingers and the butter. Many prefer to chop it, that the warmth of the hand may not soften the butter. When the butter and flour are well mixed, and fine and dry like meal, pour in the cup of ice water slowly. Mix with a knife, and cut, rather than stir. Wet only part of the flour at first and toss it to one side of the bowl, then wet another part; and when it is all of the proper consistency, cut and mix it together till it can be taken up clean from the bowl with the knife. Add the last of the water cautiously, wetting only the dry flour, and use less or more than the cupful as the flour may require. If the butter be softened by the heat in rubbing, it will moisten the flour, and less water will be required. But it should not be allowed to soften. The mixture should be light and dry, like separate minute crumbs of butter coated with flour.

Use a large smooth rolling-board and a glass rolling-pin. Put half a cup of flour in the dredger, and sprinkle the middle of the board with a light coating of flour. Toss the ball of paste in the flour with a knife until floured all over, then pat with the rolling-pin into a flat cake an inch thick. Have the end of the board next you, that you may roll the paste the required length. Hold the handles of the pin firmly, and roll with a light quick stroke as far as your arms will allow, — the whole length of the paste, if possible, at every stroke. Do not attempt to roll the paste when it is in a ball or a cubical form, but pat it lightly, to make as large and flat a surface as possible before rolling. Roll out to the thickness of one third of an inch, and to a rectangular form. Lay one of the quarters of butter in a little flour on the corner of the board, and roll quickly into a long thin piece ; scrape it up with a knife, and lay along the middle of the whole length of the paste. Fold over one side of the paste, then the other, letting the edges just meet in the middle of the butter. *Do not pat it down.* Then fold each end to the middle and double again. Pound into a flat cake and roll again one quarter of an inch thick. Roll another piece of butter thin, lay it on the paste, fold the sides over, then the ends over, and then together, and repeat the process with the remaining pieces of butter. When the butter is all rolled in, the paste may be folded, patted, and rolled out, two, three, or seven times, as your strength will permit. Twice is enough for pies, three or four times for patties ; but more are needed for a vol-au-vent.

When the butter is of the right texture, fine, smooth, and firm, not dry and crumbly, and the mixing and rolling are done so quickly and deftly that the butter does not soften, the paste will not stick, and very little flour will be required in rolling. Do not strike a hard blow in rolling, nor press the paste down to the board, but roll with a light gentle stroke. When the paste does not slip along the board, you may know it is sticking, and it must be lifted at once, the board scraped clean, and floured slightly.

Should the paste become soft and sticky, fold again, and pat it out to the size of the pan, and put it in the napkin between the two pans of ice. It will harden in ten minutes, and then may be rolled easily. After all the butter is in the dough, cut in two pieces, then roll and fold one, while the other is in the ice pan. Keep the board and pin wiped dry, and use only a little flour, but use enough to keep the paste from sticking.

Keep the edges even while rolling, and fold evenly, that there may be an equal number of layers in all parts. Each time the paste is folded over the butter a small amount of air is enclosed and is retained, unless the fold be patted down and allow the air to escape at the end. These bubbles of air may be plainly seen when the ball of dough is patted and rolled out, and care must be taken not to let the air escape. For this reason roll *lightly* and always *from you*, as a hard motion back and forth is more liable to break the bubbles. Roll with a fan-like sweep, a little to the right and left, to widen it and keep the rectangular shape; then roll gently on the edge nearest you, to make it of uniform thickness. The more of the bubbles you can retain in the paste, the lighter and more puffy it will be. The number of folds or layers of butter and paste makes the paste flaky, but the amount of air in it makes it rise and puff in baking.

The paste should be folded and rolled till no streaks of butter can be seen. After the last rolling, place it on the ice to harden, as it may then be cut and shaped more easily.

To Bake Puff Paste. — The dough should be icy cold when it is put into the oven. If the patties soften after being shaped, place them between the pans of ice till they are hard. The oven should be about as hot as for rolls, with the heat greater underneath, that the paste may rise nearly to its full height before browning; then quicken the fire to brown the tops, and turn the heat from underneath or put a pan or grate under to prevent burning. If the oven be too hot, the paste will burn before it is risen; if too slow, it will melt and spread.

Patty Shells, Tarts, Vol-au-vents, and other Forms of Puff Paste.

There are two ways of shaping the paste for patties and tarts. First, roll puff paste one eighth of an inch thick, and stamp out circular pieces with a cutter, two and

one half inches in diameter. With a smaller cutter stamp
out the centres from half of these pieces, leaving rings half
an inch wide. Dip the cutters in hot water, and cut
quickly, that the edges may not be pressed together or
cut unevenly Rub a little white of egg on the top of
the large rounds near the edge, put on the rings, and press
them lightly to make them adhere, but be careful not to
get any egg on the edges, as that will prevent them from
rising. Put round pieces of stale bread, cut half an inch
thick, in the centre, to keep the paste from rising and filling the cavity. Bake on shallow pans lined with paper,
and when done remove the bread and soft paste underneath. Bake the small pieces cut from the centre on a
pan by themselves, as they take less time for baking. In
serving place them on the top of the shells for a cover.

Another way is to roll the paste one fourth of an
inch thick, cut with a round cutter, and then with the
smaller cutter cut nearly through the centre of each round,
making a rim half an inch wide. After baking remove the
centre crust and soft part underneath, without breaking
through, as then the shell will not hold any liquid mixture.
Some persons prefer this method ; but there is less waste
when cut in the first way, as the parts cut out may be
baked for covers, and usually prove to be the most delicate
part of the paste. Or, if covers are not wanted, these centres may be rolled out thinner, and used as bottom pieces.

The paste for patties is usually rolled one fourth of an
inch thick and cut with a plain cutter. Two or three rims
may be put on when a deeper shell is desired. Any kind
of delicate cooked meat or fish (chicken, sweetbreads,
oysters, lobster, etc.) may be cut into small pieces, and
warmed in a thick cream sauce (see page 278), and served
hot in patty shells, with a cover of the paste.

Tarts are made thinner, and cut with a fluted cutter.
They are filled with jelly or preserves, and served cold
without a cover.

Cupid's Wells. — Cut the rounds of puff paste of three
or four different sizes ; use the largest one for the bottom,

and cut the centres from the others, leaving the rims of different widths, and put them on the whole round, with the narrowest at the top. Bake, and fill with jelly.

Vol-au-vent. — This is made from the lightest form of puff paste, cut to any size and shape desired, a large oval being generally preferred. Mark the outline with an oval mould or pan, and cut quickly with a knife dipped in hot water. Put on two or three rims, wetting the edge of each with white of egg. Make an oval hoop of stiff paper, two inches high, and slightly larger than the vol-au-vent, and place around it to prevent scorching. Bake a large vol-au-vent nearly an hour.

Cakes à la Polonaise. — Ro' puff paste very thin, cut into pieces three inches square, wet the centre, turn each corner over, press the point down in the centre, and put a very small round of paste on the centre. Bake, and when cool put dots of jelly on each corner.

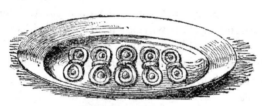

FIG. 42. Bow-Knots.

Bow-Knots. — Cut thin puff paste into half-inch strips, and shape them on the baking-pan into the form of a double bow-knot. When baked, put jelly on each loop of the bow.

Rissoles. — Roll the scraps of puff paste thin, and cut into rounds. Put a spoonful of whatever material is to be used in the centre of half of the number, wet the edges, and cover with the remaining rounds. first cutting a cross in the middle, or stamping out a small piece with a vegetable cutter or pastry tube. Any kind of cold meat may be cut fine, seasoned to taste, moistened with a white sauce, and used in the rissoles. Or they may be filled with stewed and sweetened fruit, or mince meat prepared

21

as for pies. They may be cut into larger rounds, the filling placed on one half, and the edges folded together like turnovers. Bake in a hot oven.

Plaits. — Roll very cold puff paste thin, and cut into half-inch strips. Braid them together, and bake quickly.

Cheese Straws. — Roll scraps of puff paste thin, sprinkle with grated cheese, and cayenne pepper if you like, fold, roll out, and sprinkle again, and repeat the

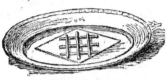

Fig. 43.   Cheese Straws.

process. Then place on the ice to harden. When cold, roll into rectangular shape one eighth of an inch thick; place it on a baking-pan, and with a pastry cutter dipped in hot water, cut into strips four or five inches long and less than a quarter of an inch wide. Bake, and serve piled cob-house fashion. Some-times, when the paste is very hard, they are cut as narrow as possible, laid on the pan in groups of five or six, with one straw laid over the middle to represent a bundle of straws, and baked in that form.

Pies.

For *Pies*, roll the puff paste out a quarter of an inch thick, then roll up, and cut from the end of the roll. Turn each piece on the side, so that the folds show in rings, and pat out flat, then roll to fit the plate. Keep the paste in a circular form, and roll evenly in every direction. Make slightly larger than the plate, as the paste shrinks when taken from the board, and should be fulled in rather than stretched to the required size. After a little practice it is just as easy to judge of the amount of paste required for one crust, and roll it in this way to fit the plate, as to roll so large a quantity that the edges have to be trimmed off and mixed with the remainder of the paste. Roll some of the paste, and cut into strips three quarters of an inch wide; wet the under crust and place the rim on the edge. Use one rim for pies which are to be covered, and two, if you

like, for pies without an upper crust. Fill the plate with
the material to be used. Roll the upper crust larger than
the plate, make a cut in the centre to let the steam escape,
wet the rims, put the crust on the edge even with the
rim and slightly fuller in the centre, to allow for shrinking
in baking; otherwise the crust, as it is forced up by the
steam within, will draw away from the edge.

Wet every spot of the rim and edge, and press closely
but lightly together, to keep the juices from boiling out.
All pies, meat pies especially, with a top crust should have
several holes cut in the crust to let the steam escape.
All fruit pies are better flavored if made with fresh, rather
than stewed, fruits. If to be filled with juicy fruit, or
cream, they are more wholesome prepared as follows:
Bake the two crusts separately, stew the fruit, fill, and put
the two together. Or fill with a mock filling of pieces of
clean cloth, bake, remove the cloth, and just before serving
fill with the prepared fruit.

Pies should bake from half to three quarters of an hour,
or till *brown.* Use tin plates, as pies bake better on the
bottom in them. No greasing is needed, and the pies
should be changed to earthen plates as soon as done.

Pastry for One Pie. — *One heaping cup* of *pastry
flour*, *one saltspoonful* of *baking-powder*, *one saltspoonful* of *salt*, and from *one third* to *one half* of *a cup of
butter* and *lard* mixed. Mix the baking-powder and salt
with the flour, and rub in the lard. Mix quite stiff with
cold water. Roll out, put the butter on the paste in little
pieces, and sprinkle with flour. Fold over, and roll out.
Roll up like a jelly roll. Divide in two parts, and roll to
fit the plate.

Cream Paste. — Mix *half a teaspoonful* of *salt* and
half a saltspoonful of *soda* with *one cup* of *cream*, and
stir in *flour* enough to mix to a stiff paste. Roll half
an inch thick. Cut half a cup of butter into small pieces,
and put it on the paste. Sprinkle with flour, fold and roll
out thin; roll up; cut a piece from the end, and roll to fit
the plate.

Plain Paste. (*Mrs. Tilton.*) — Beat the *white* of
one egg with *one tablespoonful* of *lard.* Work it into *one
quart* of *flour* with the hands, till fine as meal. Add
about *one cup* of *ice water.* Roll out, and put *half a
pound* of *butter* on the paste in little pieces, either all at
once or half of it at a time. Dredge lightly with *flour.*
Fold the edges over, roll up, pat, and roll out.

Lemon Pie, No. 1. — Mix *one heaping tablespoonful*
of *cornstarch* with *one cup* of *sugar ;* add *one scant cup*
of *boiling water*, and boil five minutes. Add *one teaspoonful* of *butter*, the *juice* of *one large lemon*, and *one
egg*, well beaten. Bake between two crusts.

No. 2. (*Miss M. L. Clarke.*) — Mix *three tablespoonfuls* of *cornstarch*, *one saltspoonful* of *salt*, and *one
cup and a half* of *sugar ;* add *one pint* of *boiling water*,
and boil five minutes. Add the *grated rind* and *juice* of
two large lemons. When slightly cooled, add the well-
beaten *yolks* of *four eggs*, then the *whites* beaten stiff.
Cut them in as for an omelet. Line the plate with crust
and rim, add the filling, and bake about twenty minutes. If desired, cover when cool with a méringue, made
with the *whites* of *three eggs* and *one third* of *a cup* of
sugar.

No. 3. (*Miss Hammond.*) — Mix *one cup and a half*
of *sugar* and *two heaping teaspoonfuls* of *flour ;* add the
well-beaten yolks of *six eggs* and the *whites* of *two eggs*,
beaten stiff, the *grated rind* of *one* and the *juice* of *two
lemons*, and *one cup* of *ice water.* Line two plates with
a crust and rim, fill, and bake in a moderate oven. Make
a méringue with the *whites* of *four eggs* and *one cup* of
powdered sugar.

Chess Pie. — Beat the *yolks* of *three eggs* until light
and thick ; add *half a cup* of fine *granulated sugar*, and
beat again ; add *one third* of a *cup* of *butter* rubbed to a
cream, and *half a teaspoonful* of *vanilla.* Bake on a plate
lined and bordered with puff paste. When done, cover
with the *whites* of *three eggs* beaten stiff, and mixed with
half a cup of *powdered sugar* and *one teaspoonful* of

lemon juice. Brown slightly, and cut while hot, but serve cold.

Apple Pie. — Cut sour apples in quarters, remove the cores and skins, and cut each quarter in two pieces lengthwise. Fill the plate, putting the pieces of apple round the edge in regular order, and piling slightly in the middle. They will cook as quickly as when sliced, though many are unwilling to believe it. When the apples are dry, add a little water. Cover with crust without wetting the edges, and bake about half an hour. When done, boil *three heaping tablespoonfuls* of *sugar* and *one* of *water* five minutes. Add the *grated rind* of *one quarter* of *a lemon*, or *one tablespoonful* of *lemon juice.* When the pie is done, remove to an earthen plate, pour this syrup through a cut in the top, or raise the upper crust and pour it over the fruit, or simply sprinkle with sugar and bits of butter. To sweeten before baking, sprinkle *half a cup* of *sugar*, mixed with a little *spice* or *grated lemon rind* over the apple. Bind the edge of the crusts with a narrow strip of wet cloth, to keep in the syrup. Or wet the edge of the lower crust, sprinkle with flour, put on a rim, wet and flour that also ; fill with fruit, sweeten, put on the upper crust, and press the edges firmly together.

Rhubarb Pie. — Peel the rhubarb, cut into inch pieces, pour boiling water over it, and let it stand ten minutes. Drain, fill the plate, sprinkle thickly with *one cup* of *sugar*, dot with bits of *butter*, cover with a crust, and bake.

Squash Pie. — *One cup and a half* of *stewed* and *sifted squash*, not watery, but dry and mealy, *one cup* of *boiling milk*, *half a cup* of *sugar*, *half a teaspoonful* of *salt, one saltspoonful* of *cinnamon*, and *one egg* beaten slightly. Mix in the order given. Line a plate with paste, put on a rim, and fill with the squash. Pumpkin pies are made in the same way.

Custard Pie. — Beat *three eggs* slightly, add *three tablespoonfuls* of *sugar, one saltspoonful* of *salt*, and *one saltspoonful* of *nutmeg*, if liked. Pour on *three cups* of *scalded milk;* strain into a deep plate, lined with paste. Bake slowly, and the moment it puffs and a knife blade comes out clean, it is done.

Berry Pies. — Pick over the berries and sprinkle slightly with *flour;* add *sugar* to taste, — about *one cup* for *a quart* of fruit. Do not spoil the fruit flavor by using spices. Bake in a deep plate, with two crusts.

Mince Meat for Pies.

1 cup chopped meat.	2 teaspoonfuls cinnamon.
1½ cup raisins.	½ teaspoonful mace.
1½ cup currants.	½ teaspoonful powdered cloves.
1½ cup brown sugar.	1 lemon (grated rind and juice).
⅓ cup molasses, or	¼ piece citron.
1 cup granulated sugar.	½ cup brandy.
3 cups chopped apples.	¼ cup wine.
1 cup meat liquor.	3 teaspoonfuls rose water.
2 teaspoonfuls salt.	

Mix in the order given. Use enough of the meat liquor to make quite moist. Substitute *one cup* of *cider* for the wine and brandy, if you prefer. Cook it in a porcelain kettle until the apple and raisins are soft. Do not add the wine, brandy, and rose water until the mixture is cooked. *One cup* of *chopped suet* or *half a cup* of *butter* may be added if preferred; but if the fat on the meat be used, or the pies are to be eaten cold, suet is not needed. Meat from the vein or the lower part of the round that has a little fat and no bone is the best for pie meat.

Plain Mince Pie. — *One cup* of *chopped meat* (cold steak or roast beef which has been simmered till tender), *two cups* of *chopped apple, one teaspoonful* each of *salt, allspice,* and *cinnamon, one cup* of *brown sugar, half a cup* of *small whole raisins, half a cup* of *currants,* moistened with *one cup* of *cider,* or *one cup* of *sweet pickle vinegar,* or *half a cup* of *water, juice* of *one lemon,* and *two* or *three spoonfuls* of any remnants of *jelly* or *preserve.*

Eccles Pie. (*Miss Barnes.*) — *Two cups* of *seedless raisins* and *half a pound* of *citron,* chopped very fine;

add *one cup* of *sugar*, the *juice* of *one lemon*, and a little *water*. Stew five minutes. Line small patty pans with puff paste, fill with the fruit mixture, cover, and bake.

Fanchonnettes. — Line small patty pans with puff paste, rolled very thin; fill them with lemon prepared as for Lemon Pie, No. 1; cover with a thin crust, and bake quickly. Or fill them as directed for Lemon Pie, No. 2, and bake without an upper crust.

Grandmother's Pumpkin Pies.

2 cups pumpkin.	¼ cup sugar.
2 cups milk.	¼ cup molasses.
1 egg or cracker.	½ teaspoonful salt
½ teaspoonful ginger.	2 tablespoonfuls raisins.

Bake the pumpkin; it will be drier than when stewed. Boil the raisins half an hour; let the water boil away, slip out the seeds, and add the pulp to the pumpkin. Scald the milk, and mix it with the pumpkin; add the seasoning, molasses, and egg last. Bake in a plate lined and bordered with crust.

Marlboro Pie.

2 cups hot apple sauce.	½ cup cracker crumbs.
2 tablespoonfuls butter.	Whites of 4 eggs.
Yolks of 4 eggs.	4 tablespoons powdered sugar.
1½ cups sugar.	Juice of ½ lemon.
1 lemon.	

Stew the apples and, if lumpy, sift them. Stir in the butter while the apples are hot. Add the sugar to the beaten yolks and beat well; mix with the cold apple, then stir in the lemon and half of the rind grated and the crumbs. Line and rim a plate with rich pastry, fill, and bake, and when done, cover with the meringue made with the whites, powdered sugar, and lemon juice. Color slightly, and serve cold.

PUDDING SAUCES.

Hard Sauce (for Hot Puddings).

¼ cup butter.
½ cup powdered sugar.

½ teaspoonful lemon or vanilla, or a little nutmeg.

Rub the butter to a cream in a warm bowl; add the sugar gradually, then the flavoring. Pack it smoothly in a small dish, and stamp it with a butter mould or the bottom of a figured glass. Keep it on ice till very hard. Or pile it lightly on a small fancy dish, and you may call it *Snowdrift Sauce.*

Lemon Sauce.

2 cups hot water.
1 cup sugar.
3 heaping teasp cornstarch.

Grated rind and juice of 1 lemon.
1 tablespoonful butter.

Boil the water and sugar five minutes, and add the cornstarch, wet in a little cold water.[1] Cook eight or ten minutes, stirring often, and add the lemon rind and juice and the butter. Stir until the butter is melted, and serve at once. If the water boil away and the sauce become too thick, add more hot water till of the right consistency.

Whipped Cream Sauce.

1 cup cream
1 teaspoonful lemon or vanilla.

½ cup powdered sugar.
White of 1 egg.

Mix the cream, vanilla, and sugar, and whip it without skimming off the froth. Add the beaten white of the egg and beat all together. Serve it on any pudding usually eaten with sugar and cream.

[1] Or mix the sugar well with the cornstarch and add the boiling water.

Apricot Sauce.

1 cup apricot juice.	1 teaspoonful cornstarch or
½ cup sugar.	flour.

Boil all together five minutes and strain. Use any kind of fruit juice or syrup in the same manner.

Creamy Sauce.

¼ cup butter.	2 tablespoonfuls wine,
½ cup powdered sugar, sifted.	2 tablespoonfuls cream.

Cream the butter; add the sugar slowly, then the wine and cream. Beat well, and just before serving place the bowl over hot water and stir till smooth and creamy, but not enough to melt the butter. When the wine and cream are added, the sauce has a curdled appearance. This is removed by thorough beating, and by heating just enough to blend the materials smoothly. It is not intended to be a hot sauce; and if the sauce become oily in heating, place the bowl in cold water and beat again until smooth like thick cream. Omit the wine if desired, and use *half a cup* of *cream*, and *one teaspoonful* of *lemon* or *vanilla.* Serve on any hot pudding.

Foamy Sauce, No. 1.

Whites of 2 eggs.	1 cup boiling milk.
1 cup sugar.	Juice of 1 lemon.

Beat the whites of the eggs till foamy, but not dry; add the sugar, beat well; add the milk and lemon juice.

Foamy Sauce, No. 2.

½ cup butter.	2 tablespoonfuls wine, or fruit
1 cup powdered sugar.	juice, or syrup.
1 teaspoonful vanilla.	¼ cup boiling water.
	White of 1 egg beaten to a foam.

Cream the butter; add the sugar, vanilla, and wine. Just before serving add the boiling water, stir well, then add the egg, and beat till foamy.

Half a cup of *jelly* melted in *one fourth* of *a cup* of *boiling water* and poured into the butter and sugar mixture, makes a pleasing variety.

Yellow Sauce. (*Mrs. Towne.*)

¼ pound butter.	1 gill brandy or wine.
¼ pound brown sugar.	A little nutmeg.
Yolk of 1 egg.	

Cream the butter, add the sugar, and stir over hot water till liquid, then add the yolk of the egg, beaten. Stir till it thickens; add brandy or wine and nutmeg, and serve.

Wine Sauce.

1 cup boiling water.	1 egg.
1 tablespoonful cornstarch.	1 saltspoonful grated nutmeg.
¼ cup butter.	½ cup wine.
1 cup powdered sugar.	

Wet the cornstarch in cold water, and stir into the boiling water. Boil ten minutes. Rub the butter to a cream; add the sugar gradually, then the egg, well beaten, and the nutmeg. When the cornstarch has cooked ten minutes, add the wine, and pour the whole into the butter, sugar, and egg, stirring until well mixed.

Caramel Sauce. (*Miss Parloa.*) — Put *half a cup* of *sugar* in an omelet pan, and stir over the fire till melted and light brown. Add *half a cup* of *boiling water* and simmer ten minutes.

Molasses Sauce. — Mix *one cup* of *molasses*, the *juice* of *one lemon* or *one tablespoonful* of *vinegar*, *half a saltspoonful* of *salt*, and *one tablespoonful* of *butter*. Boil ten minutes and serve with plain rice or apple pudding.

Plain Pudding Sauce. (*Miss Hammond.*) — Melt *one heaping tablespoonful* of *butter;* add *two tablespoonfuls* of *flour*, and *one cup and a half* of *hot water.* Cook as for drawn butter; then add *one cup and a half* of *brown sugar.* Stir till the sugar is melted, add *two teaspoonfuls* of *lemon juice* and a little *nutmeg.*

HOT PUDDINGS.

Cottage Pudding.

2 heaping cups flour.	¾ cup sugar.
3½ level teasp. baking-powder.	3 tablespoonfuls melted butter.
½ teaspoonful salt.	1 cup milk.
1 egg.	

Mix the salt and baking-powder with the flour. Beat the egg, add the sugar, melted butter, and milk, and stir into the flour. Bake in a shallow dish. Serve with *lemon, wine,* or *foamy sauce.*

Dutch Apple Cake.

This is used as a pudding (see page 86). It is easily prepared, attractive, and delicious, served with *lemon sauce.*

Scalloped Apple, or Apple Sandwich.

Mix *half a cup* of *sugar* and *half a saltspoonful* of *cinnamon* or the grated rind of *half a lemon.* Melt *half a cup* of *butter,* and stir it into *one pint* of *soft bread crumbs;* prepare *three pints* of *sliced apples.* Butter a pudding-dish, put in a layer of crumbs, then sliced apple, and sprinkle with sugar; then another layer of crumbs, apple, and sugar until the materials are used. Have a thick layer of crumbs on the top. When the apples are not juicy, add *half a cup* of *cold water;* and if not tart apples, add the *juice* of *half a lemon.* Bake about an hour. Cover at first, to prevent burning. Serve with *cream.* Ripe berries and other acid fruits may be used instead of apples, and oatmeal or cracked wheat mush in the place of bread crumbs.

Steamed Apple Pudding, or Dumpling. (*Mrs. S. M Bailey.*

Fill a *two-quart* granite pan two thirds full of *sour apples* cut into eighths, and add *half a cup* of *water*. Butter the edge of the pan and the inside of the cover. Cover with a biscuit crust, made of *one pint* of *flour*, *three level teasp.* of *baking-powder*, and *half a teaspoonful* of *salt ;* wet with *one scant cup* of *milk*, just stiff enough to roll out. Cover closely and steam one hour, or cook on top of the stove half an hour, with a trivet under the pan to keep the apple from burning. Serve at once with *lemon* or *molasses sauce*. Put a large round plate over the pan ; invert them, leaving the crust on the plate with the apples at the top. Cut like a pie.

The crust may be shortened, the apples sweetened with molasses, and then baked in the oven ; and it is called *Pandowdy*.

Steamed Carrot Pudding. (*Mr. Cole.*)

½ pound flour.	½ pound sugar.
½ pound chopped suet.	½ pound grated carrot.
½ pound currants.	½ teaspoonful salt.

Mix in the order given, and steam in a buttered mould three hours. Serve with *wine sauce*.

Bread and Fruit Pudding.

Soak *one cup* of *stale bread crumbs* in *one pint* of *hot milk ;* add *one tablespoonful* of *butter*, *one cup* of *sugar*, *one saltspoonful* of *salt*, and *one saltspoonful* of *spice*. When cool, add *three eggs*, well beaten. Add *two cups* of *fruit*, either chopped apples, raisins, currants, canned peaches, or apricots, — one, or a mixture of two or more varieties. When using canned fruit, drain it from the syrup, and use the latter in making a sauce. Vary the sugar according to the fruit. Turn into a buttered pudding-mould, and steam two hours.

No. 2. — Beat the *yolks* of *three eggs*, add *one cup and a half* of *sugar*, the grated *rind* and *juice* of *one lemon,* *one saltspoonful* of *salt*, *one cup* each of *chopped apples,* *currants*, and *grated bread crumbs.* Mix well, then add the *whites* of the *eggs*, beaten stiff. Boil in a buttered pudding-mould three hours, or bake two hours. Serve with *lemon* or *foamy sauce.*

Eve's Pudding. — Add *half a cup* of *butter* or *one cup* of *chopped suet* to the preceding rule.

Bird's-Nest Pudding.

Six or *seven apples*, cored and pared, and put into a buttered pudding-dish. Mix *five teaspoonfuls* of *flour* and *one teaspoonful* of *salt*, wet it to a smooth paste with *cold milk*, and add the *yolks* of *three eggs*, well beaten, then the *whites*, and more *milk*, using *one pint* in all. Pour it over the apples, and bake one hour. Serve with *hard* or *creamy sauce.*

Apple Tapioca Pudding.

Pick over and wash *three quarters* of *a cup* of *pearl tapioca.* Pour *one quart* of *boiling water* over it, and cook in the double boiler till transparent; stir often, and add *half a teaspoonful* of *salt.* Core and pare *seven apples.* Put them in a round baking-dish, and fill the cores with *sugar* and *lemon juice.* Pour the tapioca over them and bake till the apples are very soft. Serve hot or cold, with *sugar* and *cream.* A delicious variation may be made by using half pears, or canned quinces, and half apples.

Apple Méringue.

Core, pare, and bake *seven apples*, on a shallow plate, till soft, but not till broken. Beat the *yolks* of *three eggs;* add *three tablespoonfuls* of *sugar*, a little *salt*, and *one pint* of *scalded milk.* Pour it over the baked apples. Bake till the custard is firm. When cool, add a méringue made of the *whites* of *three eggs*, beaten till foamy; add *three tablespoonfuls* of *powdered sugar* gradually, flavor with *lemon*, and beat till stiff. Set the pudding-dish on a board in the oven, and brown the méringue. The whites of eggs for a méringue should be cool, and beaten till light and foamy, but not stiff; then add *sugar* gradually, in the proportion of *one tablespoonful* for *each egg*, and beat till stiff enough to keep its shape.

No. 2. — Pare and core the apples, fill the cavity with *sugar* and *spice* mixed, or with *sugar*, *butter*, and *lemon*. Bake the apples, cover with a méringue made with the *whites* of the *eggs;* make the *yolks* into a *boiled custard* for a sauce, or serve with *cream*. This may be served hot or cold. Brown the méringue by holding a hot stove cover over it.

Apple Porcupine.

Arrange *eight* or *ten apples* (baked as in the preceding rule, or cored, pared, and cooked carefully in syrup, see Compote of Apples) in a mound on a dish for serving. Put *quince jelly* among the apples. Cover with a méringue made of the *whites* of *four eggs* and *half a cup* of *powdered sugar*. Stick *blanched almonds* into the méringue. Put the dish on a board in the oven, and brown slightly, or hold a hot iron over it. Serve with *boiled custard sauce*.

Friar's Omelet.

Steam tart apples, mash, and drain quite dry. Take *one pint* of the *pulp*, and mix with it the *yolks* of *three well-beaten eggs*, *one cup* of *sugar*, and the *juice* of *half a lemon;* then add the *beaten whites*. Brown *one cup* of soft, fine *bread crumbs* in *one tablespoonful* of *butter* in an omelet pan. Butter a plain mould thickly with cold butter, and sprinkle over the bottom and sides as many of the browned crumbs as will adhere. Fill with the prepared apple; cover with buttered crumbs, and bake twenty minutes. When cold, turn out on a platter, and serve with *cream*. It may be baked in a pudding-dish, and eaten hot.

Apricots à la Neige.

Boil *one cup* of *rice* fifteen minutes, or steam till tender (see page 307). Wring small pudding-cloths (one third of a yard square) out of hot water, and lay them over a small half-pint bowl. Spread the rice one third of an inch thick over the cloth. Put an *apricot* in the centre, filling the cavity in each half-apricot with rice. Draw the cloth around till the apricot is covered smoothly with the rice. Tie tightly, and

FIG. 44. Apple Snowballs.

steam ten minutes. Remove the cloth carefully, and turn the balls out on a platter, and serve with *apricot sauce.* This amount of rice will make four or five balls. Apples, cored and pared, may be substituted for apricots. They should be steamed half an hour. These are more wholesome than apple or fruit dumplings, made with a flour crust. They are called *Apple Snowballs.*

Plain Rice Pudding.

Half a cup of well-washed *rice,* *half a cup* of *sugar,* a little *salt,* and *one quart* of *milk.* Soak half an hour. Bake about two hours, slowly at first till the rice has softened and thickened the milk; then let it brown slightly. This is creamy and delicious, though it is often called *Poor Man's Pudding.* Serve hot or cold.

No. 2. — *Three tablespoonfuls* of *rice,* a little *salt, three tablespoonfuls* of *sugar, one quart* of *milk,* and *three sour apples,* pared and quartered, or *one cup* of small, whole *raisins.* Put all into a deep pudding-dish, well buttered. Cover, and bake *slowly* four or five hours, till the milk is all absorbed and the rice is red or colored. Serve hot with *butter.*

Rice and Fruit Pudding.

Steam *one scant cup* of *rice* in *two cups* of *boiling water*, in the double boiler, thirty minutes. Add, while hot, *one tablespoonful* of *butter*, *one scant teaspoonful* of *salt*, *one beaten egg*, and *half a cup* of *sugar*. Cook five minutes. Butter a plain pudding-mould, sprinkle it with bread crumbs, or line with macaroons. Put in a layer of rice half an inch thick, then a layer of apricots or peaches or pineapple, then rice, fruit, etc., till the mould is full, having crumbs on the top. Bake twenty minutes in a moderate oven. Turn out on a platter, and serve with *boiled custard* flavored with *vanilla*, or with an *apricot sauce*.

Rice Soufflé.

Boil *half a cup* of *rice* in *one quart* of *boiling salted water* fifteen or twenty minutes, and drain it. Put the rice in the double boiler with *one pint* of *milk*, cook ten minutes; add the *yolks* of *four* or *six eggs* beaten with *four* or *six tablespoonfuls* of *powdered sugar* and *one tablespoonful* of *butter*. Cook five minutes, and set away to cool; add *half a teaspoonful* of *vanilla* or *lemon*. Half an hour before serving, beat the *whites* of the *eggs* stiff, and cut them lightly into the cooked mixture. Bake in a well-buttered pudding-dish half an hour. Serve immediately with *creamy sauce*.

Rice Custard.

Soak *half a cup* of *cold cooked rice* in *one pint* of *hot milk* till every grain is distinct. Add the *yolks* of *two eggs*, beaten with *a quarter* of *a cup* of *sugar* and a pinch of *salt*, and cook like soft custard. While still hot, stir in the *whites*, beaten stiff, and set away to cool. Or turn the hot custard into a dish, and when cool cover with a méringue of the whites. Brown slightly, and serve cold.

Custard Souffle. (*Miss Parloa.*)

Rub *two scant tablespoonfuls* of *butter* to a cream; add *two tablespoonfuls* of *flour*, and pour on gradually *one cup* of *hot milk*. Cook eight minutes in the double boiler, stirring often. Separate the *yolks* and *whites* of *four eggs*, and put the *whites* away in the ice-chest. Beat the *yolks*, add *two tablespoonfuls* of *sugar*, and add to the milk, and set away to cool. Half an hour before serving, beat the *whites stiff*, and cut them in lightly. Bake in a buttered pudding-dish in a moderate oven thirty minutes, and serve at once with *creamy sauce*. This mixture may be put into buttered paper cases, and baked ten or fifteen minutes. Serve in the papers.

Sponge Pudding. (*Miss Alice Walcott.*)

¼ cup sugar.	¼ cup butter.
½ cup flour.	Yolks of 5 eggs.
1 pint milk, boiled.	Whites of 5 eggs.

Mix the sugar and flour, wet with a little cold milk, and stir into the boiling milk. Cook until it thickens and is smooth; add the butter, and when well mixed stir it into the well-beaten yolks of the eggs, then add the whites beaten stiff. Bake in cups, or in a shallow dish, or in paper cases, in a hot oven. Place the dish in a pan of hot water while in the oven. Serve with *creamy sauce*.

Bread Pudding.

One pint of fine stale *bread crumbs*, soaked one hour in *one quart* of *milk*. Beat *two eggs*; mix *one quarter* of *a cup* of *sugar*, *one teaspoonful* of *salt*, *one saltspoonful* of *nutmeg* or *cinnamon*, and *one tablespoonful* of *softened butter*. Stir into the eggs, and then stir all into the milk. Bake one hour in a buttered pudding-dish.

Add *one cup* of *raisins*, and you have a *Plum Pudding*. The raisins should be first boiled, at least one hour, in water to cover, till plump and soft, as they will not cook sufficiently in the baking. *Four eggs* may be used when a richer pudding is desired. And this becomes the *Queen of Puddings* by leaving out the whites, and after baking spreading a layer of *jam* over the top, then a méringue of the whites, and browning slightly.

French Bread Pudding. — Butter small thin slices of nice *bread*, spread with *apple jelly*, and lay them loosely in a quart pudding-dish, filling it about half full. Pour over them *one quart* of *boiled custard*, and cover with a méringue. Brown the méringue and serve cold. Or put the prepared bread in a buttered mould lined with maca-roons, cover with the custard, steam one hour, and serve hot.

Plymouth Indian Meal Pudding. *(Mrs. Faunce.)*

Mix *one cup* of *yellow corn meal*, *one cup* of *molasses*, and *one teaspoonful* of *salt*. Pour on *one quart* of *boiling milk*, add *one tablespoonful* of *butter*, *three pints* of *cold milk*, and *one cup* of *cold water*, or *two eggs*. Bake in a deep, well-buttered pudding-dish, holding at least three quarts. Bake very slowly seven or eight hours. Do not stir, but cover with a plate if it bake too fast. *One cup* of *currants* may be used to give variety.

Baked Indian Meal Pudding (made quickly).

Boil *one quart* of *milk*. Pour it gradually on *three tablespoonfuls* of *granulated Indian meal*. Put it back in the double boiler, and boil one hour, stirring often. Then add *one heaping tablespoonful* of *butter*, *one tea-spoonful* of *salt*, *half a cup* of *molasses*, *two eggs*, and *one quart* of *cold milk*. Mix well, pour into a well-buttered dish, and bake one hour. Eat with *cream* or *butter*.

Whole-Wheat Pudding. *(Miss Helen Spaulding.)*

Mix *two cups* of *whole-wheat flour*, *half a'teaspoonful* of *soda*, and *half a teaspoonful* of *salt*. Add *one cup* of *milk*, *half a cup* of *molasses*, and *one cup* of stoned and chopped *raisins*, or *one cup* of ripe *berries*. Steam two hours and a half, and serve with *cream* or any plain pudding sauce. *One cup* of *dates, figs, stewed prunes,* or *chopped apple* makes a pleasing variety. This is an economical pudding, wholesome for children and invalids when served with *cream*, and rich enough to suit any one when served with *creamy* or *foamy sauce*.

Steamed Fruit Pudding.

1 pint flour.	2 eggs.
3 level teasp. baking-powder.	½ cup sugar.
½ teaspoonful salt	1 pint berries, or ripe fruit or cut
1 cup milk	small, or
2 tablespoonfuls melted butter.	1 cup raisins, stoned and halved

Mix the baking-powder and salt with the flour; add the milk and melted butter. Beat the yolks of the eggs, add the sugar, and beat them well into the dough. Then add the whites of the eggs, beaten stiff; and then the fruit, well rolled in flour. Steam two hours, and serve with *lemon* or *foamy sauce*.

Steamed Suet and Fruit Pudding.

2½ cups flour.	1 cup chopped suet, or
1 teaspoonful soda.	⅔ cup butter
½ teaspoonful salt.	1 cup chopped raisins or currants.
½ saltspoonful cinnamon.	1 cup water or milk.
½ saltspoonful nutmeg.	1 cup molasses.

Sift the soda, salt, and spice into the flour, rub in the butter, and add the raisins. Mix the milk with the molasses, and stir it into the dry mixture. Steam in a buttered pudding-mould three hours. Serve with *foamy sauce*.

If *water* and *butter* be used, *three cups* of *flour* will be required, as these thicken less than *milk* and *suet*. This pudding is sometimes steamed in small stone cups.

Cabinet Pudding.

Butter a melon mould, and decorate it with *candied fruit*, or with *raisins* boiled till soft and seeded; then put in a layer of *lady fingers* or *stale sponge cake*, then a few pieces of fruit, and repeat till the mould is nearly full. Pour *one pint* of *boiling milk* into the *yolks* of *three eggs*, beaten with *three tablespoonfuls* of *sugar* and *half a salt-spoonful* of *salt*. Pour over the cake in the mould. Set the mould in a pan of warm water on the back of the stove half an hour, then bake one hour, keeping it in the pan of hot water. Or steam it one hour. Serve hot with *wine* or *foamy sauce.*

Six macaroons or *six cocoanut cakes* may also be used, and the custard may be flavored with *wine.*

Christmas Plum Pudding. (*Mrs. J. M. Towne.*)

One pint and a half of *grated bread crumbs* (soft, not dried), *one pint* of *chopped suet*, *one pint and a half* of *currants* and *stoned raisins* mixed, *half a cup* of *citron* shaved thin, *one scant cup* of *sugar*, *half a teaspoonful* of *salt*, *half a teaspoonful* of *grated nutmeg, five eggs*, *two even tablespoonfuls* of *flour*, made into a thin batter with *milk*, and *half a glass* of *brandy.* Mix in the order given, and boil or steam four hours. Serve with *yellow sauce.*

Thanksgiving Plum Pudding. (*Mrs. S. M. Bailey.*)

Six butter crackers, rolled fine, and soaked in *three pints* of *milk.* Cream *one quarter* of *a cup* of *butter* with *one cup* of *sugar ;* add *half a teaspoonful* of *salt*, *one teaspoonful* of *mixed spice,* and *six well-beaten eggs.* Stir it all into the milk, and add *one pound* of the best *raisins.* Bake in a deep pudding-dish, well greased with cold butter. Bake very slowly in a moderate oven three or four hours. Stir several times during the first hour, to keep the raisins from settling. Make half of this receipt and steam it in a pudding-mould. Butter the mould, and line it with macaroons.

CUSTARDS, JELLIES, AND CREAMS.

Irish Moss Blanc-Mange.

½ cup Irish moss.
1 quart milk.

1 saltspoonful salt.
1 teaspoonful vanilla.

Soak the moss in cold water fifteen minutes; pick over, wash, tie in a lace bag, and put it into the double boiler with the milk. Boil until the milk thickens when dropped on a cool plate. Add the salt; strain and flavor. Mould in small cups or in egg-shells. Break off a piece as large as a ten-cent piece on one end of the egg-shell, pour out the egg, rinse the shells, stand them upright in a pan of meal, and fill with the blanc-mange. Serve blanc-mange with *sugar* and *cream*, also with *apple* or *grape jelly;* or put *half a peach* or any *candied fruit* in the bottom of the cup before filling.

Blanc-mange may be made by using *one tablespoonful* of *sea-moss farina.* Stir it into the boiling milk, and cook twenty minutes. Or use *three tablespoonfuls* of *Hecker's farina* in the same way. Cornstarch and gelatine are often used, but they are neither palatable nor nutritious without eggs.

Chocolate Pudding. — Use the same proportion of moss and milk as in the preceding rule. Put *one square* of *chocolate* in a saucepan with *two tablespoonfuls* each of *sugar* and *water.* Stir, and boil until smooth; add a little of the milk, until thin enough to pour easily, then mix it well with the remainder of the milk. Add the moss, and boil till thick.

Danish Pudding, or Fruit Tapioca.

¾ cup pearl tapioca.
1½ pint boiling water.
1 saltspoonful salt.

¼ cup sugar.
½ tumbler currant jelly.

Pick over and wash the tapioca. Put it in the double boiler with the boiling water, and cook one hour, or till soft and transparent, stirring often. Add the salt, sugar, and currant jelly. Stir till the jelly is all dissolved. Pour into a glass dish, and keep on ice. Serve very cold with *sugar* and *cream*. *Half a cup* of *lemon juice*, or any acid *fruit syrup*, or *one cup* of *canned apricot, peach,* or *quince,* may be used instead of the jelly. Or, in summer, use *one pint* of *ripe berries*, or any *small fruits*, adding more sugar as required.

Fruit Pudding. — Cook *one quart* of *ripe berries* or *canned peaches* or *apricots* with *one pint* of *water*, and *sugar* to taste, till the fruit is well scalded. Skim out the fruit into a dish for serving. Wet *one scant cupful* of *fine granulated wheat flour* in a little cold water, stir it into the boiling syrup; cook ten minutes, and pour it over the fruit. Serve very cold with *cream*.

Boiled Custard.

1 pint milk.
Yolks of 3 eggs.
3 tablespoonfuls sugar.

½ saltspoonful salt.
½ teaspoonful vanilla.

Scald the milk. Beat the yolks, add the sugar and salt, and beat well. Pour the hot milk slowly into the eggs, and when well mixed pour all back into the double boiler, and stir constantly till smooth and thick like cream. Strain, and when cool add the flavoring. Do not stir the egg into the hot milk, as there is danger of curdling, and a part of the egg will be left in the bowl. Scalding the milk hastens the process, so that less stirring is required. When nearly thick enough, the foam on the top disappears, and the custard coats the spoon; but the surest test is given by the sense of feeling. You are conscious that the custard is thicker by the way the spoon goes through it. Do not leave the custard an instant; take it off as soon as it is smooth, as it will thicken in cooling, and curdles quickly if cooked a moment too long or if left in the boiler. Have a fine strainer placed in a bowl or pitcher before you begin to cook the custard, that you may strain it quickly.

Boiled custard, when to be used as a sauce, should be thin enough to pour; when to be served as a custard, it should be cooked a moment longer, to make it thicker.

Four or even *five eggs* to a pint of milk may be used when a rich custard is desired. But *three* are sufficient for nearly all purposes.

Boiled custard is much smoother when only the yolks of the eggs are used. Many combinations may be made by adding the whites of the eggs after the custard is cold. Beat the whites stiff, put them on a sieve, and cook over steam, or pour boiling water through them. The water will cook and stiffen the egg, and when well drained it may be piled in rocky form on the custard. Or the white may be poached by dipping it by the spoonful into boiling milk. Serve the custard in a large glass dish, and pile the white in a mass, or put spoonfuls of it here and there on the custard, with bright-colored jelly on the white; or serve in small glass custard cups with the white and jelly on the top. Or pour the custard over slices of sponge cake (soaked in wine, if you prefer), and cover with a méringue of the whites sweetened and flavored. *Floating Island*, *Flummery*, *Tipsy Pudding*, and hosts of other dishes are only fancy names given to the different combinations of cake, boiled custard, and méringue.

Any of the following ingredients may be used as flavoring; this will give a variety of dishes, which want of space prevents us from giving as separate receipts : *half a square* of *chocolate*, melted ; the *three tablespoonfuls* of *sugar* melted to a caramel before mixing with the yolks ; *one cup* of *grated cocoanut*, or *cocoanut cakes* crumbled ; *six macaroons* soaked in *wine ; one cup* of *chopped almonds* or any of the varieties of *candied fruits;* *four oranges,* peeled, seeded, and cut fine ; *one pint* of any *canned fruit;* *one pint* of *lemon, wine,* or *orange jelly,* cut in cubes. Or color the méringue *pink* by beating *three tablespoonfuls* of bright-colored *jelly* with the whites ; or brown it with a salamander or hot poker, or by putting the dish on a board in the oven.

Baked or Steamed Custard.

1 quart milk.	6 tablespoonfuls sugar.
6 eggs.	1 saltspoonful salt.

Scald the milk. Beat the eggs ; add the sugar and salt, then the scalded milk. Strain, add a little nutmeg, and bake about twenty minutes in a deep dish or in cups set in a pan of warm water ; or steam in a bowl or in cups. Test the custard with a spoon ; if it come out clean, the custard is done.

Caramel Custard.

½ cup sugar.	6 eggs.
2 tablespoonfuls water.	½ teaspoonful salt.
1 quart milk.	1 teaspoonful vanilla.

Put the sugar in an omelet pan, and stir until it melts and is light brown ; add the water, and stir into the warm milk. Beat the eggs slightly, add the salt and vanilla and part of the milk. Strain into the remainder of the milk, and pour into a buttered two-quart mould. Set the mould in a pan of warm water, and bake thirty to forty minutes, or till firm. Cut into the middle with a knife ; if it come out clean, the custard is done. Serve cold with *caramel sauce.*

Delicate Pudding.

1 cup water.	½ saltspoonful salt.
1 cup fruit juice.	Sugar to taste.
3 tablespoonfuls cornstarch	3 eggs.

Boil the water and fruit juice (orange, lemon, or canned cherries, quince, or apricot). Wet the cornstarch in a little *cold water*, stir into the boiling syrup, and cook ten minutes. Add the salt and sugar to taste; the quantity depending upon the fruit. Beat the whites of the eggs till foamy, and stir into the starch. Turn at once into a mould. Serve cold with a *boiled custard sauce* made with the yolks of the eggs.

Apple Snow.

3 large tart apples.	½ cup powdered sugar.
3 eggs (whites).	½ cup jelly.

Stew or steam the apples (cored and quartered, but not pared), drain, and then rub them through a hair sieve. Beat the whites of the eggs stiff, add the sugar, beat again; add the apple, and beat till like snow. Pile lightly in a glass dish, garnish with jelly or *holly leaves*. Serve with *boiled custard*.

Tapioca Cream.

2 tablespoonfuls pearl tapioca.	½ saltspoonful salt.
1 pint milk.	Whites of 2 eggs.
Yolks of 2 eggs.	½ teaspoonful vanilla.
⅓ cup sugar.	

Soak the tapioca in *hot water* enough to cover it, in the top of the double boiler placed on the back of the stove. When the water is absorbed, add the milk, and cook until the tapioca is soft and transparent. Beat the yolks of the eggs, add the sugar and salt. Pour the boiling mixture on them, and cook two or three minutes, or till it thickens like boiled custard. Remove from the fire, add the whites of the eggs, beaten to a foam. Stir well, and when cool flavor. Do not try to mould it, as it is more delicate when soft.

Jellies and Fancy Dishes made with Gelatine, Custard, and Cream.

Gelatine, as now obtained, is refined and clarified during the process of manufacture, and this renders it unnecessary to use the white of egg in making jellies, as was required when using the old preparation of isinglass and gelatine. Much of the strength and flavor of jellies is lost in clearing them with eggs. Cox's gelatine makes a clear jelly, but it softens slowly and requires a strong flavoring like wine or lemon to disguise the fishy taste. Nelson's English gelatine is of fine quality, softens quickly, has an agreeable flavor, and is well adapted to creams and other delicate dishes. Granulated gelatines are convenient for accurate measurement and quick work.

Never cook gelatine. Soak (not dissolve) it in cold water, in the proportion of *one cup* of *cold water* to *one box* of *gelatine*. It will soften in fifteen minutes, if stirred often. Then dissolve in boiling liquid, — either water, milk, or custard, — and always strain through a fine strainer after it is dissolved.

Gelatine Pudding, or Spanish Cream.

¼ box gelatine.[1]	½ saltspoonful salt.
¼ cup cold water.	1 pint milk.
¾ cup boiling water.	Whites of 3 eggs.
Yolks of 3 eggs.	1 teaspoonful vanilla.
3 tablespoonfuls sugar.	

Soak the gelatine in the cold water till soft, then dissolve it in boiling water. Make a custard with the yolks of the eggs, beaten, and mixed with the sugar and salt. Pour on the hot milk, and cook in the double boiler till it thickens. Then add the strained gelatine water, the vanilla, and the whites of the eggs, beaten stiff. Mix all well, and turn into moulds wet in cold water. Place in ice water, and when hard and ready to serve turn out on a dish.

Italian Cream. — Use the same proportions as in the preceding receipt. Dissolve the soaked gelatine in the hot custard instead of in hot water, and strain the whole while hot into the beaten whites. When well mixed, add *lemon* or *vanilla*, and pour into a mould.

Quaking Custard. — The same proportions as in Span-

ish Cream. Dissolve the soaked gelatine in the hot custard, and strain into a mould. When ready to serve,
beat the whites of the eggs stiff, add *three heaping tablespoonfuls* of *powdered sugar*, and the *juice* of *one lemon.*
Turn the custard on a platter, and heap the méringue
around it.

Snow Pudding.

¼ box gelatine.[1]
¼ cup cold water.
1 cup boiling water.
1 cup sugar.
¼ cup lemon juice.
Whites of 3 eggs.

Yolks of 3 eggs.
3 tablespoonfuls sugar.
½ saltspoonful salt.
1 pint hot milk.
½ teaspoonful vanilla.

Soak the gelatine in the cold water fifteen minutes, or
until soft. Then dissolve it in the boiling water; add the
sugar and lemon juice. Stir till the sugar is dissolved.
Strain into a large bowl, and set in ice water to cool. Stir
occasionally. Beat the whites of the eggs to a stiff froth,
and when the gelatine begins to thicken, add the beaten
whites, and beat all together till very light. When nearly
stiff enough to drop, pour into a mould. Or beat until
stiff enough to hold its shape, if your strength will allow,
and pile lightly in a tall glass dish. Make a boiled custard
of the yolks of the eggs, the sugar, salt, and milk, and when
cool flavor with vanilla. Serve the sauce in a pitcher. Or,
if the snow be moulded, turn it out on a dish, and pour the
sauce around the pudding. The snow may be turned into
a shallow dish, two inches deep, to harden, and when ready
to serve cut into blocks and piled like a pyramid. Blocks
of *lemon* or *wine jelly,* mixed with the snow or sparkling
jelly (jelly broken up lightly with a fork), make a pleasing
variety. If the whites of the eggs be added to the gelatine
mixture before it becomes cold, as is directed in many receipts, more time will be required for the beating. Many
have never made the dish a second time on account of the
time and strength expended. Fifteen minutes is sufficient
when made according to this receipt.

[1] If granulated gelatine, use 1¼ tablespoons.

Orange Charlotte.

⅓ box gelatine.
⅓ cup cold water.
⅓ cup boiling water.
1 cup sugar.

Juice of 1 lemon.
1 cup orange juice and pulp.
3 eggs (whites).

Line a mould or bowl with lady fingers or sections of oranges. Soak the gelatine in cold water till soft. Pour on the boiling water, add the sugar and the lemon juice.

FIG. 45.   Orange Charlotte.

Strain and add the orange juice and pulp with a little of the grated rind. Cool in a pan of ice water. Beat the whites of the eggs stiff, and when the orange jelly begins to harden beat it till light. Add the beaten whites, and beat together till stiff enough to drop. Pour into the mould.

One pint of *whipped cream* may be used instead of the whites of the eggs, or it may be piled on the top after the Charlotte is removed from the mould.

Apple Charlotte. — *One cup* of cooked *sour apple* (steamed, drained, and sifted) may be used in place of the orange in the preceding receipt. Line the mould with lady fingers or sponge cake, and serve a *boiled custard*, made with the yolks of the eggs, as a sauce.

Or use *one cup* of *canned peach, pineapple,* or *apricot,* or *one pint* of *fresh strawberries* or *raspberries.* Mash and rub the fruit through a sieve before using.

Fruit Charlotte.

½ box gelatine.[1]
½ cup cold water.
1 cup sugar.
1½ cup water and
1 cup lemon juice, or

1 pint orange juice and
1 cup water.
Yolks of 4 eggs.
Whites of 4 eggs.
1 dozen lady fingers.

[1] If granulated gelatine, use 2 tablespoons.

Soak the gelatine in cold water till soft. Make a syrup with the sugar and fruit juice. When boiling, pour it into the beaten yolks of the eggs. Stir well, and cook in a double boiler till it thickens. Add the soaked gelatine, stir till dissolved, and strain at once into a granite pan placed in ice water. Beat occasionally till cold, but not hard. Beat the whites of the eggs to a stiff froth, and then beat all together till it thickens. When almost stiff enough to drop, pour at once into moulds lined with cake. Keep on ice, and serve with or without powdered sugar and cream. Vary the fruit by stewing *one pint* of *canned peaches, pineapple,* or *apricots* in *one cup* each of *sugar* and *water* till soft, then sift, add the yolks of the eggs, and cook till it thickens. Add the gelatine, strain, and when cool add the whites. Grated pineapple will not require sifting.

Velvet Cream. (*Miss Ward.*)

½ box gelatine.[1]	1½ cup sugar.
1½ cup sherry wine.	1½ pint cream.
1 lemon (grated rind and juice).	

Soak the gelatine in the wine, add the lemon and sugar, and heat all together till the gelatine is dissolved. Then strain and set it away to cool. When nearly cold, but before it begins to stiffen, add the cream. Beat till nearly stiff enough to drop, then pour it into moulds and set it on ice until stiff as blanc-mange.

Wine Jelly.

½ box gelatine.[1]	Juice of 1 lemon.
½ cup cold water.	1 cup sugar.
1 pint boiling water.	1 cup sherry or S. M. wine.

Soak the gelatine in cold water fifteen minutes, or until soft. Add the boiling water, lemon juice, sugar, and wine. Stir well, and strain through a fine napkin into a shallow dish. Keep in ice water till hard. When ready to serve, cut in cubes or diamonds, or break it up lightly

[1] If granulated gelatine, use 2½ tablespoons

with a fork. If you wish to mould it, or to use for moulding creams, add only *two thirds* of *a pint* of *boiling
water*.

Orange Jelly.

½ box gelatine.[1]	Juice of 1 lemon.
½ cup cold water.	1 cup sugar.
1 cup boiling water.	1 pint orange juice.

Soak the gelatine in cold water until soft. Add the
boiling water, the lemon juice, sugar, and orange juice.
Stir till the sugar is dissolved, and strain. Or use *one cup*
of *orange juice* and *one scant pint* of *boiling water*, *one
lemon*, *one scant cup* of *sugar*, and *two tablespoonfuls*
of *brandy*.

Lemon Jelly.

½ box gelatine.[1]	1 cup sugar.
1 scant cup cold water.	½ cup lemon juice (large).
1 pint boiling water.	1 square-inch stick cinnamon.

Soak the gelatine in the cold water till soft. Shave the
lemon rind thin, using none of the white. Steep it with
the cinnamon in the pint of boiling water ten minutes, then
add the soaked gelatine, sugar, and lemon juice, and when
dissolved strain.

Italian Jelly, or Fruit Moulded in Jelly.

½ box gelatine.[1]	1 cup sugar.
½ cup cold water.	1 pint orange juice.
Rind and juice of 1 lemon.	1 cup fruit.
1 scant cup boiling water.	

Soak the gelatine in the cold water till soft. Shave the
rind of the lemon, using only the yellow part, and soak with
the gelatine. Pour on the boiling water; add the sugar,
lemon juice, and orange juice. Strain through a fine
napkin into a pitcher, or something from which it can be
poured. Wet a mould in cold water, and pack it in a pan
of ice. Put in a layer of jelly half an inch deep and
harden it, then a layer of *candied fruit* or *sections* of

1 If granulated gelatine, use 2½ tablespoons.

oranges, fastening each piece of fruit in place with a little jelly before adding enough to cover the fruit, otherwise the fruit will float. Repeat till the mould is full. Place the pitcher where the jelly will keep liquid but not hot, and be sure that every piece of fruit is firmly in place before adding more. This may be made with *lemon* or *wine jelly*.

A variety of designs may be made by arranging different colors of fruit; and it well repays one for the trouble, which seems very slight after the first attempt. Do not devote your whole morning to it, but look at it occasionally while you are doing other things, adding fruit and jelly as required; and before you are conscious of it, the dish will be prepared.

Orange Baskets. — Cut as many oranges as will be required, leaving half the peel whole for the baskets, and a strip half an inch wide for the handle. Remove the pulp

FIG. 46.   Orange Baskets.

and juice, and use the juice in making orange jelly. Place the baskets in a pan of broken ice to keep upright. Fill with *orange jelly*. When ready to serve, put *a spoonful* of *whipped cream* over the jelly in each basket. Serve in a bed of *orange* or *laurel leaves*.

No. 2. — With a vegetable cutter cut out several small portions of the peel in the basket and handle, to give an open-work effect, and fill with a mixture of *orange, wine* and *lemon jelly*, cut into inch dice and piled lightly in the baskets. Or the baskets may be filled with Bavarian cream.

Orange Sections. — Cut off a small portion from the end of the orange, and scoop out the pulp and juice. Be careful not to break through the skin. Fill them with *orange jelly* which is thoroughly cold, but not hard, and place them upright in a pan of broken ice. When hard, cut each orange in quarters, and serve garnished with *green leaves.*

Imperial Cream.

Make the rule for Lemon Jelly (page 350), and color part of it pink with *cochineal* or *cranberry juice.* Harden it in a shallow pan. Make Snow Pudding (page 347), and when nearly stiff enough to drop, stir in small squares of the *pink* and *lemon jelly.* Mould, and when ready to serve, turn out on a dish, garnish the base and top with *macaroons* soaked in *wine.* Pour rich *boiled custard* round the dish, and put macaroons and cubes of the jellies in the custard.

Whipped Cream.

Many wholesome, delicious, and attractive dishes may be made with whipped cream. To those who can obtain plenty of cream, these dishes afford a cheaper, more easily prepared, and far more satisfactory course than pie and many forms of hot puddings. Many of them are equally suitable for tea. Very rich cream should be diluted and well mixed with an equal quantity of milk. The best quality of cream obtained from the milkman is usually of the proper consistency. Thin cream will become liquid after whipping, and thick cream will turn to butter. The cream should always be icy cold; when it is to be served as a garnish, or for cream whips, it should be sweetened and flavored before it is whipped.

A whip churn is the best utensil for whipping cream. This is a tin cylinder, perforated at the bottom and sides, and having a perforated dasher. When the churn is placed in a bowl of cream, and the dasher worked up and down, the air is forced from the cylinder into the cream, causing it to become light and frothy. A Dover egg-beater will make the cream light, but it has a different consistency from that obtained by churning.

To Whip Cream. — Place a bowl half filled with cream in a pan of broken ice. When very cold, put the churn into the cream, hold the cylinder firmly, and keep the cover in place with the left hand. Tip the churn slightly, that the cream may flow out at the bottom. Work the dasher with a *light short stroke up*, and a *hard, pushing stroke down.* When the froth appears, stir it down once or twice, as the first bubbles are too large; and when the bowl is full of froth, skim it off into a granite pan placed on ice. Take off the *froth* only, and do not take it off below the holes in the cylinder, as it whips better when they are covered. For this reason never whip a pint of cream in a three-quart bowl, and do not try to whip it all, as usually a little is left in the bowl which is too thin to whip.

One pint of cream should treble in whipping. If for a garnish, drain the whipped cream on a hair sieve placed over a pan, and keep it on ice till stiff enough to keep it shape. Creams that are to be moulded are made stiffer by the addition of gelatine

Cream Whips. (*Miss Ward.*)

1 pint rich cream.	½ cup sugar.
1 cup pale sherry wine.	Whites of 2 eggs, beaten light
1 lemon (grated rind and juice).	

Mix in the order given. Add more sugar if desired. Stir till the sugar is dissolved, then whip it and take off the froth as it rises, and put it on a hair sieve. Fill jelly glasses with the cream left in the bowl, and put the froth on the top.

Newport Whips. (*Mrs. Upham.*) — *One pint* of *cream,* sweet or sour, *one gill* of *sweet milk, half a lemon* sliced, *sugar* and *wine* to taste. Whip, and serve the whip only, in jelly glasses. If prepared in a covered bowl or tureen, the unwhipped cream may be kept for several days, adding more cream, sugar, and wine to taste, and whipping as required for use.

Charlotte Russe (Cream).

1 pint rich cream.	½ cup sugar.
1 teaspoonful vanilla.	Sponge cake.

Mix the cream, vanilla, and sugar. Place the bowl in ice water, and when chilled whip to a stiff froth, and skim off the froth into a sieve. Drain, and whip again that which has drained through. When nearly all whipped, line a glass dish with lady fingers or sponge cake, fill with the cream, put cubes of *wine jelly* or any bright jelly on the cream, and keep on ice till ready to serve.

Charlotte Russe, No. 2 (Cream and Eggs).

1 pint rich cream.	Whites of 2 eggs.
1 teaspoonful vanilla.	1 cup powdered sugar.
1 tablespoonful wine.	Sponge cake.

Flavor the cream with vanilla and wine, and whip to a stiff froth. Beat the whites of the eggs stiff, add the powdered sugar, and mix it lightly with the whipped cream. Keep it on ice till it stiffens. Line small cups or paper moulds with sponge cake, and fill with the cream. Or fill fancy paper cases with cream, and ornament each with thin triangles of sponge cake and a cube of *wine jelly*.

A small part of the cream may be colored with melted *chocolate* or *cochineal*, and used for decoration.

Charlotte Russe, No. 3 (with Gelatine). (*Miss Parloa.*)

¼ box gelatine.[1]	⅓ cup powdered sugar.
¼ cup cold water.	1 teaspoonful vanilla.
1 pint cream.	1 tablespoonful wine.
1 dozen lady fingers.	¼ cup boiling water

Soak the gelatine in the cold water till softened. Chill the cream. Line a three-pint mould with lady fingers or narrow slices of sponge cake, crust side out; leave a little space between the slices, and have the cake even at the top. Whip the cream, and skim off into a granite

[1] If granulated gelatine, use 1¼ tablespoons.

pan set in ice water. Sift the powdered sugar over the whipped cream, and add the vanilla and wine. Dissolve the gelatine in the boiling water, and strain through a fine strainer over the whipped cream. Then stir (not beat) rapidly with the bowl of the spoon resting on the bottom of the pan. Turn the pan with the left hand while stirring with the right. If it feel lumpy, lift the pan from the ice and place it in warm water to melt the gelatine. Stir till the gelatine is well mixed with the cream, and when nearly stiff enough to drop, turn it into the mould. Keep on ice, and when ready to serve, turn out and garnish the top with *jelly*.

This filling may be used in paper cases as directed in **No. 1.**

Plain Bavarian Cream.

¼ box gelatine.[1]	⅓ cup sugar.
¼ cup cold water.	1 teaspoonful **vanilla.**
1 pint cream.	

Soak the gelatine in cold water till soft. Chill and whip the cream till you have three pints of the whip. Boil the remainder of the cream (or if it be all whipped, use a cup of milk) with the sugar; and when boiling add the soaked gelatine. Stir till dissolved. Strain into a granite pan, add the vanilla or lemon, and wine if you wish; or flavor with *two tablespoonfuls* of *melted chocolate*, or *one quarter* of *a cup* of *strong coffee.* Place the pan in ice water, stir occasionally, and when the mixture is thoroughly cold and beginning to thicken, stir in lightly the whipped cream. When nearly stiff enough to drop, pour into the moulds.

This cream is sometimes moulded in small cups. Put *half* of a canned *apricot* or *peach*, or *three sections* of *orange*, or *several small cherries*, or *a candied plum*, in the bottom of the cup before filling with the cream. Or line a bowl with whole *strawberries* and fill with the cream. This is called a *Strawberry Charlotte. Red bananas* sliced may be used in the same manner.

[1] If granulated gelatine, use 1¼ tablespoons.

Riz à l'Impératrice. — Prepare the cream as for Bavarian Cream; put *one cup* of *cooked rice* in the *hot milk*, and stir till every grain is distinct, then proceed as directed in the preceding receipt.

Bavarian Cream, No. 2 (with Eggs).

½ box gelatine.[1]	½ cup sugar.
½ cup cold water.	½ saltspoonful salt.
1 pint cream.	1 teaspoonful vanilla
1 pint milk.	1 tablespoonful wine.
4 eggs (yolks).	

Soak the gelatine in cold water till soft. Chill and whip the cream till you have three pints. Keep the whipped cream on ice, and boil the remainder of the cream, adding enough milk to make a pint in all. Beat the yolks of the eggs, and add the sugar and salt. Pour the boiling milk on the eggs, and when well mixed put back in the double boiler and cook about two minutes, or just enough to scald the egg. Stir constantly, add the soaked gelatine, and strain at once into a pan set in ice water. When cool, add the vanilla and wine, or *half a cup* of *orange juice.* Stir till it begins to harden, then stir in quickly the whipped cream, and when nearly stiff enough to drop, pour into moulds wet in cold water.

Chocolate Bavarian Cream. — Melt *two sticks* of *sweetened chocolate,* and stir them into the custard before straining.

Coffee Bavarian Cream. — Add *one quarter* of *a cup* of *very clear, strong black coffee.* Or boil *half a cup* of *ground coffee* in the milk, before straining it over the eggs.

Bavarian Cream with Fruit.

1 quart berries.	½ cup cold water.
1 cup sugar.	½ cup boiling water.
½ box gelatine.[1]	1 pint cream.

Strawberries or Raspberries. — Mash the berries with the sugar; let them stand till the sugar is dissolved. Strain through a sieve fine enough to keep back the seeds. Soak

[1] If granulated gelatine, use 2½ tablespoons

the gelatine in the cold water, then dissolve in the boiling water, and strain it into the berry juice. Cool, and beat till slightly thickened ; add the cream (whipped), and mould it in a plain mould, or lined like a Charlotte.

Pineapple. — Stew *a can* of *grated pineapple* with *one cup* of *sugar* ten minutes, and use in the same manner without sifting.

Peaches and Apricots. — Mash and sift *one can* of *peaches* or *apricots* (use *juice* and *fruit*), and stew with *a heaping cup* of *sugar*, and use as above.

Norfolk Cream. — Line a mould with *one pound* of *candied plums*, having first removed the stones, and spread the plums out as thin as possible. Make the plain *Bavarian cream*, and when thick enough to drop, take out one third of it and color with *cochineal;* add *half a cup* of *candied cherries* cut in halves. Put a layer of the white

FIG. 47.   Mould of Bavarian Cream garnished with Whipped Cream and Fruit.

cream next to the plums, and fill the centre with the pink. When ready to serve, loosen the edges with a knife and invert carefully. Garnish with *whipped cream*.

Mock Canteloupe. — Mould the yellow *Bavarian cream* in a melon mould lined with *lady fingers*, and when ready to serve, turn out on a dish and sprinkle the top of the cream thickly with chopped *pistachio nuts*, or any green fruit, *plums*, or *angelica.* Garnish with *whipped cream* and *candied fruit.*

Prune Pudding. (*Mrs. A. A. Lincoln.*) — Make a small mould of *lemon jelly.* Boil large selected *prunes* slowly until very tender, taking care to keep the skins unbroken. Drain and place in a glass dish. Break up the jelly all about them, so that it will have the appearance of being made together. Pile *whipped cream*, prepared as for Charlotte Russe, No. 1, over the prunes and jelly.

Crême Diplomate. (*Miss M. L. Clarke.*)

½ box gelatine.[1]	4 eggs (whites)
½ cup cold water.	1 teaspoonful vanilla.
1 pint cream.	1 tablespoonful wine.
¾ cup sugar.	1 cup French fruit.

Soak the gelatine in the cold water. Chill and whip the cream. Boil the cream left in the bowl with milk enough to make a pint in all. Add the sugar, and when boiling add the soaked gelatine. Stir until dissolved, and strain it into the well-beaten whites of the eggs. Add the vanilla, and the wine, if you approve. Stir well, and when slightly thickened add the whipped cream. When stiff enough to drop, add the French fruit. Mould it, and garnish with *wine jelly, fruit,* and *green leaves.* Or add *one pint* of *blanched almonds* or *pistachio nuts,* chopped fine, instead of the fruit.

Combinations of Jelly, Cream, Custard, and Cake.

Royal Diplomatic Pudding. (*Miss Parloa.*) — Make *lemon, orange,* or *wine jelly,* using only *two thirds of a pint* of *boiling water,* that it may be stiff enough to mould.

FIG. 48. Royal Diplomatic Pudding.

Strain it into a pitcher. Place a two-quart mould in a pan of ice water; pour in jelly half an inch deep. When hard, put in *candied fruit* in some fanciful design. Cut cherries in halves, and cut plums to represent leaves, and arrange them like a cluster of cherries; or cut the cherries smaller, and design a branch of barberries. Fasten each piece of fruit in place

[1] If granulated gelatine. use 2½ tablespoons.

with a few drops of the liquid jelly, and when hard add jelly to cover the fruit. When this is hard, place a smaller mould in the centre on the jelly and fill with ice. Pour the remainder of the jelly between the two moulds, adding it slowly, and dropping in fruit here and there, if you choose, until the mould is full. When the jelly is all firm, remove the ice, and add *warm*, not *hot*, water to the smaller mould, and take it out carefully, without breaking the wall of jelly. Fill the space with a *Bavarian cream* (page 356). Make a rich soft custard with the *yolks* of *five eggs, half a cup* of *sugar*, and *a pint* of *milk;* strain, and flavor with *vanilla*. When ready to serve, dip the mould in warm water, put a dish over it, and invert dish and mould together. Remove the mould carefully, and pour the soft custard around the pudding. Make the soft custard while the jelly is hardening ; and do not put the materials for the Bavarian cream together until the small mould is removed from the jelly, and the cavity ready for the cream. Do not turn out of the mould until just before it goes to the table, as the slightest jarring breaks the jelly. A coffee cup within a quart bowl, and a small pail within a larger one, have been successfully used by those who had no moulds.

A variety of dishes may be made by using the different colored jellies and fruits ; and any of the creams stiff enough to mould can be used as filling. *Snow Pudding*, or *Crême Diplomate* and *Wine Jelly*, *Norfolk Cream* and *Lemon Jelly*, *Orange Sponge* and *Orange Jelly*, are attractive combinations. It may also be made in two sizes of small moulds, serving one mould to each person.

Gâteau St. Honoré. — Line a pie plate with thin *puff paste*, prick with a fork, and bake light brown. Make a *cream cake paste* (see Index), press it through a pastry bag round the edge of a jelly cake tin, and bake the remainder in balls the size of walnuts. Place the puff paste on a plate, and spread with *raspberry jam* or *orange marmalade*. Lay the border of cream cake paste on the edge, and press it into the marmalade. Fil' the centre with any kind of *Bavarian cream.* Garnish with the cream cake balls and *fruit.* Use *orange sections* with orange marmalade, and *candied cherries* and *plums* with raspberry jam.

Sponge cake or *feather cake,* baked thin in a round tin plate, is more delicate than puff paste as a foundation for the gâteau.

Gâteau de Princess Louise. — Bake *sponge drop mixture* or *feather cake* or *snow cake* in jelly cake tins. Cut the centre from one cake, leaving a rim one inch and a half wide. Put *jelly* on the remaining cake, lay the rim on the edge, and fill the centre with *Bavarian cream.* Garnish with *candied fruit.* Frost the rim if you prefer.

Chantilly Baskets. — Dip the edges of soft flexible *macaroons* in *syrup,* prepared as for crystallized fruit, and form them into a basket on a fancy plate, something as children shape a burr basket. A rim and handle of pasteboard aid in keeping the shape. When dry, fill with any fancy *Bavarian cream.*

Fig. 49   Strawberry Charlotte.

Andermatt Cream.

Cook *half a cup* of washed *rice* in *one cup* of *boiling water* until the water is absorbed; then turn it into the double boiler with *three cups* of boiling *milk.* Steam it until tender. Stir in *one heaped cup* of a mixture of *preserved fruits.* When cool, stir in *one pint* of *thick cream* whipped stiff, and turn it into a melon mould. When firm, turn out, and serve with *sponge cake.*

thin slices. Add a little *lemon juice* if the bananas lack flavor.

Baked Apple Ice-Cream. — Bake and sift *six sweet apples*. Add *one quart* of *rich cream*, and *sugar* to taste. When the sugar is dissolved, freeze.

Pistachio Ice-Cream. — *One cup* of *pistachio nuts*, and *one quarter* of *a cup* of *almonds*, blanched, chopped, and pounded to a paste. Add this to any receipt for ice-cream.

Macaroon, Almond, Walnut, Cocoanut, or *Brown Bread Ice-Cream* may be made by adding *one pint* of either of the above ingredients to any receipt for ice-cream. Crumble the macaroons and cocoanut cakes, and brown them slightly; dry, crumble, and sift the brown bread, and chop the nuts fine.

Fruit Ice-Cream. — Canned fruit, or ripe fruit sweetened to taste, and cut into small pieces, may be added to partly frozen cream, giving many delicious varieties. Use *peaches, strawberries, raspberries, pineapples, apricots,* or *cherries.*

Café Parfait. — *One pint* of *cream,* one cup of *sugar, half a cup* of *strong, clear coffee.* Mix, chill, and whip. Take the froth off into a freezer or into a mould. Pack the mould in ice and salt, and let it stand two hours without stirring.

Glacé Cream. — Boil *one cup* of *sugar* and *one scant cup* of *water* until the syrup forms into a ball when rubbed in water between the finger and thumb. Then pour this syrup in a fine stream into the *whites* of *three eggs* beaten stiff, and beat till stiff and cool. Stir it into any frozen cream, made with a little less than the usual amount of sugar.

Ice-Cream with Condensed Milk. — Mix *one can* of *condensed milk* with *three pints* of *scalded milk,* and use in making a rich custard, as directed in rule No. 2. Flavor highly, and add *a pound* of *candied fruit* if desired.

Tutti Frutti. — Make either of the receipts for ice-cream, and flavor with *two tablespoonfuls* of *Sicily Madeira wine* or *Maraschino.* When partly frozen, add *one pound* of *French candied fruit*, cut fine. Use a mixture of *cherries, plums, apricots, pineapples, pears, strawberries,* and *angelica root.* Or use *home-made preserves,* carefully drained from the syrup, and cut into dice.

Nesselrode Pudding. — Shell *one pint* of *chestnuts.* Blanch, and boil half an hour, then mash to a pulp, and stir into ice-cream made from rule No. 2. Strain, and when partly frozen add *one pint* of *mixed fruit*, cut fine.

Frozen Pudding. — Make ice-cream, No. 3 ; add *two tablespoonfuls* of soaked *gelatine*, flavor with *wine* and *vanilla*, and freeze. Cut *a pound* of *French fruit* or *brandy peaches* in small pieces ; or use *half a pound* of mixed *raisins, currants,* and *citron*, and *one cup* of *macaroons,* pounded, or *one cup* of mixed *almonds* and *pistachio nuts,* pounded fine. Wash, and soak the currants and raisins until swollen. Remove the seeds, drain and quarter the raisins, and shave the citron in small thin slices. Mix half the fruit and nuts with the frozen cream. Butter a melon mould slightly, and line with *lady fingers ;* then sprinkle over a layer of mixed fruit, pack in the frozen cream nearly to the top, then a layer of fruit, and cover with cake. Cover closely, and bind a strip of buttered cloth round the edge of the cover. Pack in ice and salt for two hours. When ready to serve, dip quickly in warm water, and turn out carefully. Sprinkle the remainder of the mixed nuts over the top, and garnish with *cream,* sweetened, flavored, and whipped. Some prefer to serve a rich *boiled custard sauce*, made with *one pint* of *cream,* the *yolks* of *four eggs,* *half a cup* of *sugar,* and *one teaspoonful* of *vanilla.*

Plombière. (*Miss Ward.*)

1 quart milk.	1½ cup sugar.
1 pint cream.	2 ounces each of preserved cit-
6 whole eggs.	ron, greengages, and pine-
3 egg yolks.	apple, cut fine.

Boil the milk and cream, and pour it on the beaten eggs and sugar. Cook slightly, and when cool add the fruit, and freeze.

Bombe Glacé. — Line a mould or the freezer with *one quart* of *raspberry* or *pomegranate sherbet.* Pack the sherbet round the bottom and sides of the mould one inch deep. Fill the centre with *Bavarian cream,* or *Charlotte Russe* cream, or *Crême Diplomate.* Cover with the sherbet, and pack in ice and salt one hour.

Biscuit Glacé. — Ice-cream and sherbet are often served in small, fancy paper cases, which may be obtained at a confectioner's. Make and freeze the cream, and fill the paper cases with two kinds, either sherbet and plain ice-cream, or sherbet and tutti frutti, or Charlotte Russe cream and sherbet, or ice-cream. Pack the cases in a freezer, and keep on ice and salt till very hard. Serve on a lace paper napkin laid on a fancy plate. Sometimes the biscuits are covered with a méringue, and colored slightly with a salamander just before serving.

Frozen Apricots. — Cut *one can* of *apricots* into small pieces, add *one pint* of *sugar* and *one quart* of *water.* When the sugar is dissolved, freeze. When partly frozen add, if you like, *one pint* of *whipped cream,* measured after whipping. This is delicious without the cream. Peaches, pineapples, cherries, and strawberries are delicious when frozen. Vary the amount of sugar as the fruit requires.

Sherbets, or Water Ices.

Sherbets, or water ices, are made with the juice of fruit, water, and sugar. With a supply of canned fruit, or fruit syrup always at hand, a variety of delicious desserts may be quickly prepared. *A tablespoonful* of *gelatine,* soaked and dissolved, gives a light and smooth consistency to water ices. Many prefer to boil the water and sugar to a clear syrup, remove the scum, and when cool add the fruit juice ; and others use the white of egg beaten stiff, adding it after the sherbet is partly frozen. The following are some of the most delicious water ices. Follow the directions given under Orange Sherbet, for all the other varieties.

Orange Sherbet.

1 tablespoonful gelatine.[1]	1 cup cold water.
½ cup cold water.	6 oranges, or
¼ cup boiling water.	1 pint of juice.
1 cup sugar.	

Soak the gelatine in the cold water ten minutes. Add the boiling water, and when dissolved add the sugar, another cup of cold water and the orange juice. Strain when the sugar is dissolved, and freeze.

Pomegranate Sherbet. — Make the same as Orange Sherbet, using the blood-red oranges.

Lemon Sherbet.

1 tablespoonful gelatine.[1]	1 pint sugar.
1 quart water.	Juice of 6 lemons.

The boiling water used in dissolving the gelatine should be part of the quart of water.

Pineapple Sherbet.

1 can grated, or	1 pint water.
1 pint fresh fruit.	1 tablespoonful gelatine.
1 pint sugar.	

In using fresh pineapple be careful to remove all the eyes.

Raspberry and Strawberry Sherbet.

1 pint berry juice.	Or, 1 pint preserved fruit.
1 pint sugar.	1 cup sugar.
1 pint water.	1 quart water.
Juice of 2 lemons.	2 lemons.
1 tablespoonful gelatine.[1]	1 tablespoonful gelatine.

When using preserved strawberries or raspberries, soak the fruit in part of the water and strain out the seeds.

[1] If granulated gelatine, use ½ teaspoon.

GENERAL DIRECTIONS FOR MAKING CAKE.

STUDY first the directions given under Measuring, Mixing, and Baking.

Cake is a mixture of part or all of the following materials : eggs, sugar or molasses, flour, butter or cream, milk or water, fruit, soda, cream of tartar, spices, etc.

An unlimited variety of cakes may be made by varying the proportions of these materials, and to the same proportions many different names are given. Many amusing experiences are known of the eagerness with which a newly named receipt for cake is received, which, after many trials, has been found to be an old receipt arranged in a different order. An analysis of the hundreds of receipts given in books devoted to cake-making would show that the general principles involved may be included under two divisions, namely, receipts for *sponge cakes*, made *without butter;* and *pound* or *cup cakes*, made *with butter.* Sponge cakes are made rich with eggs, the lightness depending wholly upon the amount of air beaten into the egg; or an inferior quality is sometimes made by substituting soda and cream of tartar for part of the eggs, and adding more flour and some liquid, usually water. They vary in color, according as the white or yolk of the egg is used. Butter cakes are varied in the same way, and also by the addition of fruit, or spices, or various coloring and flavoring materials.

There is no one department in cooking where so much depends upon the baking as in making cake. The fire should be rather low, but sufficient to last through the entire baking. In many stoves it is exceedingly difficult to bake cake by a morning fire ; as so much coal is put on,

24

the fire is too hot and cannot be checked sufficiently. The oven should be less hot than for bread. If too hot, leave the oven door open for ten minutes before putting in the cake, then watch it, and protect it by putting over it a covering of paper, or a pan on the grate above. Do not attempt to make cake unless you can have entire control of the fire.

Thin cakes require a hotter oven than those baked in thick loaves. If the oven be not hot enough at first, or be cooled too suddenly during the baking, the cake will not be light. Cakes with molasses in them burn more quickly than others. Thin cakes should bake from fifteen to twenty minutes, thicker cakes from thirty to forty minutes, very thick loaves about an hour, and fruit cake from two to three hours. Whichever kind you are baking, divide the time required into quarters. During the first quarter the heating is not manifested in appearance except by the rising; during the second the cake should continue to rise and begin to brown; then should become all over a rich golden brown; and in the last quarter settle a little, brown in the cracks, and shrink from the pan. Be careful not to take it out too soon. If necessary to move it, do it very gently, and never move it when it has risen to the full height, but is not browned or fixed in its shape.

If cake brown before rising, the oven is too hot. When it rises more in the centre, cracks open, and stays up, it is too stiff with flour. It should rise first on the edges, then in the middle, crack slightly, settle to a level again, when the cracks usually come together. Nothing is more suggestive of bakeshop cake, or inferior quality in material, than a loaf with an upper surface having sharp edges, then hollows, and a peaked centre, as if the inside of the cake had boiled up and run out over the top.

Line your cake tins with paper, to prevent burning the bottom and edges and to aid in removing the cake from the pans. Lay the paper over the outside of the pan, and crease it round the edge of the bottom. Allow it large enough to come above the top of the pan. Fold in the middle lengthwise and crosswise, and cut out the open corners to the crease made by the pan. Then fit it into the inside of the pan, and grease the paper, not the pan, with fresh butter or lard. Many use a rag tied on a stick; others grease with a brush. Nice brushes are very expensive (and no others are suitable), and unless carefully cleaned are quite objectionable. Rags and paper absorb the grease which should be put on the pan, and in any case the fingers should be washed after the process. So there is no quicker, easier, or more economical way of greasing a tin than to rub the butter on with the fingers.

Mix cake in an earthen bowl, and never in a tin pan. Use a wooden spoon, as iron spoons discolor the hand and the mixture. Use only the best materials. Go without cake rather than try to make it, or eat it when made, with what is called cooking butter and second-rate eggs. Such cake cannot be good or wholesome. Wash the butter, if very salt. Brown sugar is good for fruit cake, but for all other varieties use the finest granulated or powdered sugar. Very coarse granulated sugar makes heavy cake, with a hard and sticky crust. The flour should be dry. When it has been kept in a cool place it should be slightly warmed, and always sifted before using. St. Louis flour — or pastry flour, as it is sometimes called — is best for cake. When new-process flour is used, take one eighth less. Soda, cream of tartar, and baking-powders should be crushed and sifted into the flour, then sifted two or three times with the flour. Mix spices with the flour or with the sugar. Mix a little of the measure of flour with the fruit to keep it from sticking together or settling. If the sugar be lumpy, crush and sift before using. Eggs should be fresh, and cooled by keeping in cold water or in the ice-chest. The yolks and whites should be beaten separately. Break each egg on the edge of the cup, just enough to crack the middle of the shell, so the white will flow out, but not hard enough to break into the yolks. Then hold the egg over the cup, with the cracked side up, and break it apart. Let the white run into the cup, and keep the yolk in the half shell until all the white is drained off. Be careful not to break the yolk, as the smallest portion of it in the whites will prevent them from frothing. Beat the yolks in a bowl, and the whites in a platter if you use a fork or whisk, or in a bowl if you use a Dover beater. Never stop beating the whites until they are stiff and dry, as it is impossible to have them light if they become liquid again.

Measure all the ingredients, and have the fire and all utensils ready, before you begin to mix. Observe the following order in putting materials together.

Sponge Cake Mixtures. — Beat the yolks until light or lemon-colored and thick. Add the sugar gradually, and beat again. Add the lemon juice or flavoring, and water, if that is to be used. Beat the whites until stiff and dry, and cut or fold them in lightly, then sift in the flour, and fold in carefully without any stirring. Sponge cakes should not be beaten after adding the flour. Those made with soda and cream of tartar require less beating than those without, but they are a very poor substitute for genuine sponge cake.

Butter Cake Mixtures. — Warm the bowl with hot water, then wipe dry. Put in the butter, and rub with a wooden or silver spoon until light and creamy. Be careful not to have the bowl so hot as to melt the butter. Add the sugar and beat again. If the habit of rubbing the butter and sugar together with the hand be already formed, and you find it easier than to use a spoon, it is hardly worth while to change; but for those who are wholly inexperienced it is better to learn to use the spoon, and every lady would prefer to have her cook mix in that way. If the proportion of sugar be large for the butter, — more than double, — beat part of the sugar with the butter, and the remainder with the yolks of the eggs. Where a very small proportion of butter is to be used, it may be melted and mixed with the eggs and sugar. Beat the yolks till light and thick, then beat them well with the butter and sugar. Add the flavoring. Then add a little milk, then a little flour, and milk again, and continue until all the milk and flour are used. Lastly, add the beaten whites. All cakes made with butter require to be beaten long and vigorously after adding the flour, that they may be smooth and fine-grained. Fruit should be added last; cake with fruit should be a little stiffer with flour than that without fruit. Citron and large pieces of fruit may be put in in layers, or spread over the dough in the pan.

All cake should be baked as soon as possible after it is mixed. Put the scrapings from the bowl into small tins. If put into the loaf, they sometimes cause a heavy streak through the top.

Cake is baked when it shrinks from the pan and stops hissing, or when a straw inserted in the centre comes out clean. Remove the loaf from the pan as soon as baked, lifting it out by the paper; or, if not papered, loosen the edges with a knife, and turn the pan over upon a cloth laid over a bread-cooler. Remove the pan as soon as possible. Never let cake stand in the pan to become moist. When cake is baked too hard or burned, rub off the burned surface with a coarse grater.

Sponge Cake.

5 eggs.	1 saltspoonful salt.
1 cup sugar, powdered or fine granulated.	½ lemon (grated rind and juice). 1 cup pastry flour.

See general directions for putting together (page 372). The mixture should be stiff and spongy, of the consistency of Charlotte Russe filling, as it is poured into the pan. Bake in a deep bread pan, in a moderate oven, nearly an hour, — in a shallow pan, about forty minutes. If stirred instead of beaten, the bubbles of air will be broken and the mixture will become liquid. When baked, it will be tough and too close-grained. To make this cake well, requires strength in beating and judgment in baking; but when successful, it is one of the most satisfactory and perfect cakes made. Cut through the crust with a sharp pointed knife, then break apart.

Sponge Cake. (*Miss Josselyn.*) — Beat the *yolks* of *three eggs;* add *one cup* of *fine granulated sugar, one tablespoonful* of *lemon juice,* and *one tablespoonful* of *cold water,* or a lump of ice melted in the lemon juice to make two tablespoonfuls of liquid. Add the *whites,* beaten stiff, and *one cup* of *pastry flour.*

Lady Fingers and Sponge Drops. — *Four eggs, half a cup* of *powdered sugar, half a saltspoonful* of *salt, one teaspoonful* of *flavoring,* and *three quarters* of *a cup* of *pastry flour.* See general directions for mixing sponge cakes. Pour the mixture into a pastry bag, and press through it into shape, about three inches long and not quite one inch wide. Or drop by the spoonful on a buttered pan, and you have *Sponge Drops.* Sprinkle powdered sugar over them, and bake twelve or sixteen minutes in a very slow oven.

Miss Ward's Sponge Cake. — Break *ten eggs* into a bowl; add *one pound* of *powdered sugar,* and beat together for half an hour without stopping. Add *half a pound* of *flour,* the *grated rind* and *juice* of *one lemon,* and a *wineglassful* of *wine.* Bake in deep pans one hour; slowly at first, then quicken the fire the last half-hour. Sprinkle powdered sugar over the top before baking.

Angel Cake. — *One cup* of *flour,* measured after one sifting, and then mixed with *one teaspoonful* of *cream of tartar* and sifted four times. Beat the *whites* of *eleven eggs,* with a wire beater or perforated spoon, until stiff and flaky. Add *one cup and a half* of *fine granulated sugar,* and beat again; add *one teaspoonful* of *vanilla* or *almond,* then mix in the flour quickly and lightly. Line the bottom and funnel of a cake pan with paper not greased, pour in the mixture, and bake about forty minutes. When done, loosen the cake around the edge, and turn out at once. Some persons have been more successful with this cake by mixing the sugar with the flour and cream of tartar, and adding all at once to the beaten egg.

Sunshine Cake. — Make the same as Angel Cake, using *one teaspoonful* of *orange extract* instead of vanilla, and adding the well-beaten *yolks* of *six eggs* to the beaten whites and sugar before adding the flour.

Sponge Cake for Cream Pies, or Berwick Sponge Cake.

3 eggs, yolks.	1 teaspoonful cream of tartar and
1½ cup sugar.	½ teaspoonful soda, or
½ cup water.	2 level teasp. baking-powder.
1 teaspoonful lemon extract.	Whites of 3 eggs.
2 cups pastry flour.	

Beat the yolks of the eggs; add the sugar, lemon juice, and water; then the flour, mixed with the soda and cream of tartar, and, lastly, the whites of the eggs. Bake in round shallow pans. When cool, split and fill with cream.

When each part of the process of beating is done just two minutes by the clock, and baked in a loaf, it is called *Berwick Sponge Cake.*

Cream. — Boil *one pint* of *milk.* Beat *two eggs;* add *half a cup* of *sugar* and *one saltspoonful* of *salt.* Melt *one tablespoonful* of *butter* in a granite saucepan, and add *two tablespoonfuls* of *flour.* When well mixed, add the boiling milk gradually, pour it on the eggs and sugar, and cook in a double boiler five minutes, or till smooth. When cool, flavor with *lemon, vanilla,* or *almond.*

Sponge Cake with Fruit. — Make a *Sponge Cake,* bake in shallow pans, and put crushed and sweetened *strawberries* between the layers. Cover with *whipped cream.* Or put *one cup* of *candied fruit,* cut fine, in a *cream* prepared as above, and use in the same way.

Sponge Cake for Children. (*Miss M. L. Clarke.*) — Mix in a bowl *one cup and a half* of *pastry flour, one teaspoonful* of *cream of tartar* and *half a teaspoonful* of *soda,* or *two level teaspoons* of *baking-powder,* sifted with the flour, *one cup* of *sugar,* and *one teaspoonful* of *extract* of *lemon* or *orange; two eggs,* broken in a cup and the cup filled with *milk* or *cream.* Mix all in the order given, and beat very hard till light. Bake from twenty to thirty minutes in a moderate oven.

Roll Jelly Cake.

This is the simplest form of a butter cake. It is like a sponge cake, with the addition of a small amount of shortening. *Three eggs*, beaten separately till very light, then beaten together; add *one cup* of *sugar*, *three tablespoonfuls* of *cream*, or *one* of *melted butter*, *one cup pastry flour* mixed with *one teaspoonful* of *cream of tartar* and *half a teaspoonful* of *soda*, or *two level teaspoons* of *baking-powder*. Spread very thin on long shallow tins, and bake in a moderate oven. Spread with *jelly* while warm, trim the edges with a sharp knife, and roll up.

One Egg Cake.

½ cup butter, creamed	½ teaspoonful soda and
1 cup sugar.	1 teaspoonful cream of tartar, or
1 egg, beaten light.	2 level teasp baking-powder.
1 cup milk.	1 teaspoonful vanilla.
2 cups flour.	

Mix in the order given, and bake in a shallow pan, in a moderate oven, thirty minutes.

Park Street Cake.

½ cup butter.	½ teaspoonful soda.
1 cup milk.	1 teaspoonful cream of tartar.[1]
2 cups sugar.	1 teaspoonful vanilla or lemon
3 cups pastry flour.	extract.
4 eggs.	1 saltspoonful mace.

Contrary to our usual practice, this receipt is not given in the order in which the materials are to be put together, but in numerical order, as an aid in remembering the proportions. Rub the butter in a warm bowl, with a wooden spoon, until like cream, and add one cup of the sugar gradually; add the remaining cup of sugar to the beaten yolks of the eggs, beat until very light, and add to the butter. Add the flavoring. Then beat the whites stiff and dry, and let them stand while you add a little milk and flour alternately to the mixture. Add the whites last. This makes two loaves. Bake in a mod-

Macdonald Cake. (*Mrs. A. A. Lincoln.*)

1 cup butter, creamed.	1½ cup pastry flour.
1½ cup sugar.	1 teaspoonful cream of tartar and
4 eggs (yolks).	½ teaspoonful soda, or
1 teaspoonful lemon or vanilla.	2 level teasp. baking-powder.
½ cup milk.	Whites of the eggs.
½ cup cornstarch.	

Mix in the order given, and bake in two shallow pans in a moderate oven.

Cider Cake.

1 cup butter.	4 cups flour.
2 cups sugar.	1 teaspoonful soda, scant.
3 eggs, beaten separately.	1 teaspoonful spice.
¾ cup cider.	

Mix soda and spice with flour, then mix in the order given, and bake in two shallow pans.

Dominoes.

Bake *sponge* or *feather cake* in shallow pans; frost, cut in oblong pieces, and mark like dominoes.

Madelines.

Bake any *rich butter cake* mixture quarter of an inch thick. Cut in squares or rounds; ornament with *frosting* and *nuts*, or *candied fruits.*

Gold Cake.

½ cup butter.
1½ cup fine granulated sugar.
Yolks of 4 eggs.
1 whole egg.
½ cup milk.
½ teaspoonful mace.
¼ teaspoonful soda and
¾ teaspoonful cream of tartar.[1]
2½ cups flour.

Silver Cake.

½ cup butter.
1½ cup sugar.
½ teaspoonful almond.
½ cup milk.
¼ teaspoonful soda and
¾ teaspoonful cream of tartar, or
2 level teasp. baking-powder.
2¼ cups flour.
Whites of 5 eggs.

Mix in the order given, putting soda and cream of tartar in the flour, and adding milk and flour alternately.

[1] Or 2½ level teaspoons baking-powder.

Bake in a moderate oven, until the loaf shrinks from the pan.

Watermelon Cake may be made from this receipt by using red sugar in the gold cake, and adding *one cup* of *raisins,* seeded, quartered, and rolled in flour. Put the red cake in the centre of a round pan, and the white around the edge. Or put the red at the bottom, and the white on top. Bake in a large round pan, or two brickloaf pans.

Marble Cake. — Color *one cupful* of the yellow cake dough brown with *one tablespoonful* of *melted chocolate,* and mix the white, yellow, and brown in spots, or drop the brown in rings between the layers of white and yellow.

Cornstarch Cake.

½ cup butter, creamed.	1½ cup pastry flour.
1½ cup sugar.	½ teaspoonful soda.
½ cup milk.	1½ teaspoonful cream of tartar.
½ teaspoonful almond.	Whites of 6 eggs.
½ cup cornstarch.	

Mix in the order given, and bake in a moderate oven.

Snow Cake. (*Miss Alice Walcott.*)

¾ cup butter.	½ teaspoonful soda.
2 cups sugar.	1½ teaspoonful cream of tartar.
½ cup milk.	Whites of 8 eggs.
2½ cups pastry flour.	1 teaspoonful almond extract.

Mix the soda and cream of tartar with the flour. Be sure to use one teaspoonful and a half of cream of tartar, as the extra amount is intended to stiffen the whites of the eggs. Rub the butter to a cream, add the sugar, and beat again ; add the milk and flour alternately, a little at a time, and beat well. Lastly, add the beaten whites and the almond. Bake in two small pans in a moderate oven.

Dream Cake. — Bake the Snow Cake in three shallow pans. Make the Ornamental Frosting, and flavor one part with lemon, another with vanilla, and the third with rose. Frost each cake, put together, and sprinkle grated fresh cocoanut over the top.

Buttercup Cake. (*A. W.*)

¾ cup butter.
1½ cup sugar.
Yolks of 8 eggs.
1 whole egg.
½ cup milk.
2 cups flour.

½ teaspoonful soda and
·1½ teaspoonful cream of tartar,
or 2 level teasp. baking-powder
1 saltspoonful mace, or
1 teaspoonful lemon.

Mix in the order given,. and bake in two pans in a moderate oven till the loaf shrinks from the pan. Or bake in small round tins, and frost with *yellow frosting*, and decorate with *candied fruit*.

Harlequin Cake. (*Mrs. Williams.*)

1 cup butter, creamed.
2 cups sugar.
3 eggs (yolks).
1 cup milk.
3 cups pastry flour.

1 teaspoonful cream of tartar and
½ teaspoonful soda, or
3 teasp. baking-powder.
Whites of 3 eggs.

Mix in the order given, then divide the dough into four equal parts. Have two parts the color of the dough. Color the third with *two squares* of unsweetened *chocolate*, melted. Color the fourth part with *pink coloring*, and bake each part in a Washington pie plate. When all are done, lay first a light cake, then the chocolate, then another light, then the pink. Between the layers spread *lemon jelly*, and frost with *white frosting*.

Lemon Jelly for Cake. — Beat *one egg*, add *one cup* of *water*, the *grated rind* and *juice* of *one lemon*. Pour this slowly on *one cup* of *sugar*, mixed with *two tablespoonfuls* of *flour*. Cook in the double boiler till smooth, like cream.

Pink Coloring for Cake and Creams.

½ ounce cochineal.
½ ounce alum.
½ ounce cream of tartar.

½ ounce salts of tartar.
½ pint boiling water.
½ pound sugar.

To the first three ingredients add the boiling water, and put in a porcelain stewpan. Let it stand on the stove without boiling for twenty-five minutes. Add the salts of tartar very gradually, stirring all. the time. Add the sugar. Strain and bottle it. Use one or two teaspoonfuls, according to the shade desired.

Pokeberry Syrup for Coloring Pink. — Put the fruit in a porcelain kettle, and cover with water. Boil slowly till the skins break, then strain. Add *a pound* of *sugar* to *a quart* of *juice;* boil a few moments, bottle and seal.

Ribbon Cake.

1 cup butter.	3½ cups pastry flour.
2 cups sugar.	½ teaspoonful soda and
4 eggs, yolks and whites beaten separately.	1 teaspoonful cream of tartar, or 3½ level teasp. baking-powder.
1 cup milk.	

Have three long, shallow pans, of equal size. Divide the dough into three parts. Bake two parts as plain cake; add to the remaining dough,

½ cup raisins, stoned and chopped.	2 teaspoonfuls molasses.
1 cup currants	2 teaspoonfuls brandy or wine.
¼ pound sliced citron (the fruit all floured).	1 teaspoonful mixed mace and cinnamon.

Bake, and put the fruit cake between the two plain cakes, with *jelly* between. Press it lightly with the hand in putting together; trim the edges even, and frost.

Coffee Cake.

Use *one cup* of *strong, clear coffee* instead of *milk,* and make as in the preceding rule. Add the fruit and spices to the whole mixture. Bake it in one loaf.

Spice Cakes.

1 egg.	2½ cups flour.
⅔ cup molasses.	1 heaping teaspoonful soda.
⅔ cup sugar.	1 even teasp. cream of tartar.
⅔ cup melted butter.	1 tablespoonful mixed spice.
1 cup milk.	1 tablespoonful vinegar.

Mix in the order given, and bake in small tins. *One tablespoonful* of *lemon juice* and *one tablespoonful* of *ginger* may be substituted for the vinegar and spice.

Plum Cakes.

1 cup butter.
2 cups brown sugar.
Yolks of 3 eggs.
Whites of 2 eggs.
½ cup milk.
½ cup dark molasses.
½ teaspoonful soda.

½ teaspoonful cream of tartar.
½ pound raisins, stoned and chopped.
½ pound currants.
2 tablespoonfuls any fruit syrup.
4 cups flour.
2 teaspoonfuls mixed spices.

If not dark enough, add a little *melted chocolate.* Bake in small tins, and frost part of them with the remaining white of egg.

Pound Cake. (*Miss Ward.*)

1 pound butter.
1 pound sugar.
10 eggs.

1 pound flour.
½ wineglass wine.
½ wineglass brandy.

Cream the butter; add the sugar, yolks of the eggs, wine, brandy, whites of the eggs, and the flour. Put *currants* into one fourth of the dough, and *almonds,* blanched and pounded in *rose water,* into another part; leave the remainder plain. Fill very small round tins three quarters full. Into half of those containing the plain dough put small pieces of *citron,* three in each, inserting the citron upright a little way into the dough. Sift sugar over the tops of those containing the citron and almond before putting them into the oven. Bake twenty minutes. Frost the plain and currant cakes. Pound cake is lighter when baked in small cakes than in loaves.

Wedding Cake.

1 pound butter.
1 pound sugar.
12 eggs.
1 pound flour.
2 teaspoonfuls each of cinnamon and mace.
1 teaspoonful each of nutmeg and allspice.

½ teaspoonful cloves.
2 pounds raisins.
2 pounds currants.
1 pound citron.
1 pound almonds.
1 wineglass brandy.
1 lemon.
½ teaspoon salt

Line the pans with three thicknesses of paper; butter the top layer. Seed and chop the raisins; wash and dry the currants (see page 435) ; cut the citron in uniform slices, about one eighth of an inch thick ; blanch the almonds and chop fine. Mix all the fruit but the citron with enough of the flour to coat it thoroughly. Mix the spices with the sugar. Cream the butter; add the sugar, beaten yolks, beaten whites, lemon rind and juice, brandy, flour, and fruit, except the citron. Put a layer of dough half an inch deep in the pan, then spread evenly with the citron, then another layer of dough and citron ; repeat till the materials are all used. Have dough for the top layer. As this cake does not rise much in baking, the pans may be at least two thirds full. Bake in two large, deep, oblong pans three hours, in a moderate oven.

Frosting.

Plain Frosting. — *White* of *one egg, one teaspoonful* of *lemon juice,* and *one scant cup* of *powdered sugar.* Put the egg and lemon juice in a bowl, and stir the sugar in gradually. Then beat, not stir. all together five minutes.

Boiled Icing. — *One cup* of *granulated sugar, one third* of *a cup* of *boiling water, white* of *one egg,* and *one salt-spoonful* of *cream of tartar.* Boil the sugar and water without stirring, until the syrup taken up on a skewer will " thread " or " rope." When it is nearly at that point, beat the egg stiff, add the cream of tartar, and pour the boiling syrup over the egg in a fine stream, beating well. When it thickens and is perfectly smooth, pour it over the cake. It hardens quickly, and should be put on the cake before it stiffens enough to drop.

Golden Frosting. — Beat the *yolks* of *eggs* and stir in *powdered sugar* till stiff enough to spread, not to run. Flavor with *vanilla* or *wine.*

Ornamental Frosting. — *Whites* of *three eggs, three cups* of *confectioner's sugar,* sifted, and *three teaspoon-fuls* of *lemon juice.* Put the eggs in a large bowl; sprinkle with three teaspoonfuls of the sugar. · Beat with a perforated wooden spoon, adding three teaspoonfuls of sugar every five minutes. When it begins to thicken add the lemon juice and beat as before. It should thicken by the beating of the egg, and not by the addition of too much sugar. Do not use all the measure of sugar unless needed. Beat with a long flop, over and over, and *never* stir. When stiff enough to leave a " clean cut," or not to run together when cut with a knife, spread a thin layer of frosting on the cake, and when this is hard put on another layer a quarter of an inch thick. When this is firm, mark it for cutting. To the remainder of the frosting add sugar more rapidly, until it begins to harden on the spoon and bowl. Put a confectioner's tube into the end of a pastry bag, fill the bag with frosting, twist the end tightly, and press the frosting through the tube on the cake in any design you wish.

Pink Frosting. — Color a portion of the Ornamental Frosting with *cochineal*, adding it slowly till of the desired shade.

Chocolate Frosting. — Melt *a square* of *chocolate* in a saucepan, and add to the Ornamental Frosting, using enough to color light or dark as you prefer.

Orange Frosting. — Grate the thin *rind* of an *orange*, and soak it half an hour in *three* or *four teaspoonfuls* of the *orange juice*. Then squeeze the juice through a fine cloth, and use the same as lemon juice in Ornamental Frosting.

Cookies.

Plain Cookies.	*Richer Cookies.*
½ cup butter.	½ cup butter.
1 cup sugar.	1 cup sugar.
¼ cup milk.	1 tablespoonful milk.
1 egg.	2 eggs.
3 level teasp. baking-powder.	2 level teasp. baking-powder.
Flour to roll out thin.	Flour to roll out.

Cream the butter; add the sugar, milk, egg, beaten lightly, and the baking-powder mixed with two cups of flour, then enough more flour to roll out. Roll a little at a time. Cut out. Bake about ten minutes.

Cocoanut Cookies. — Add *one cup* of *grated cocoanut*, or *half a cup* of *cocoanut cakes*, crumbled, to either of these receipts before adding the flour.

Jumbles. — Roll either of these mixtures thicker, and cut with a doughnut cutter; sprinkle sugar over, and bake a delicate brown.

Hermits. — Add *half a cup* of *stoned* and *chopped raisins* to the receipt for *Richer Cookies*, and roll about a quarter of an inch thick. Cut into rounds.

New Year's Cookies. — Rub *three fourths* of *a cup* of *butter* into *six cups* of *flour*. Pour *half a cup* of *boiling water* over *one cup and a half* of *sugar*, add *a scant half-teaspoonful* of *soda*, and when the sugar is melted stir all into the flour. Roll out thin.

One-Two-Three-Four Cookies. (*Mrs. Whitney.*)

1 cup butter.	1 teaspoonful cream of tartar, or
2 cups sugar.	2 level teasp. baking-powder.
3 cups flour.	½ teaspoonful salt.
4 eggs.	1 teaspoonful spice, or
½ teaspoonful soda and	2 tablesp. carraway seed, or
	2 teaspoonfuls yellow ginger.

Cream the butter, and add half the sugar. Beat the yolks, add the remaining half of the sugar, and beat them

Fig. 50. Cookies.

with the butter, then add the beaten whites. Mix the soda, cream of tartar, spice, and salt with the flour, and stir into the butter mixture. Take *a teaspoonful* of the *dough*, make it into a ball with floured hands, place the balls in the pan some distance apart, then press or flatten into a round cake, and bake about ten minutes.

Thin Sugar Gingerbread. — Add to the preceding receipt *two teaspoonfuls* of *yellow ginger*, instead of *spice*, and spread the mixture thin on a tin sheet. Mark in squares or oblongs, and bake.

Superior Gingerbread. (*Mrs. Towne.*)

1¼ pound butter.
1½ pound sugar.
9 eggs, yolks and whites beaten separately.
1 wineglass wine.

1 wineglass brandy.
2 tablespoonfuls ginger and
1 nutmeg, grated, mixed with
2 pounds flour.

Mix as for cake in the order given, and spread very thin with a knife on tin sheets. Bake, and cut in squares while warm. This will keep six months.

Hard Gingerbread. (*Mrs. Dewey.*)

¾ pound butter.
1¼ pound sugar.
6 eggs.

1 teaspoonful soda, dissolved in
3 tablespoonfuls milk.
1 tablespoonful ginger.
2 pounds flour.

Cream the butter; add the sugar and beaten eggs, and beat well. Sift in the ginger, strain the soda, and add the flour. Roll half an inch thick, or thin as a wafer.

Hard Gingerbread. (*Miss A. M. Towne.*)

2 cups N. O. molasses.
1 cup butter.
1 tablespoonful ginger.

1 teaspoonful soda.
St. Louis flour to mix very stiff.

Heat (not boil) the molasses and butter; when the butter is melted, add the ginger, sifted, the soda dissolved in a little boiling water, and the flour. Roll very thin, and bake in a quick oven.

Soft Gingerbread.

1 cup molasses.
1 teaspoonful soda.
1 tablespoonful ginger.
½ teaspoonful salt.

⅓ to ½ cup butter or drippings, softened.
1 cup milk.
3 cups pastry flour.

Bake in shallow pans or gem pans in a moderate oven about thirty minutes.

Sugar Gingerbread.

½ cup butter.
½ cup cream.
1½ cup sugar.

2 teaspoonfuls ginger.
1 teaspoonful soda, scant.

Mix stiff with *flour*.   Roll thick or thin.

Hot Water Gingerbread.

1 cup molasses.
1 teaspoonful soda.
1 tablespoonful ginger.
1 tablespoonful butter, melted.

½ teaspoonful salt.
½ cup boiling water.
2 cups flour.

Mix in the order given, and beat well.   Bake in a deep cake pan.

Sour Milk Gingerbread.

½ cup molasses.
½ teaspoonful soda.
½ teaspoonful salt.
1 tablespoonful ginger.
½ cup sugar.

1 tablespoonful butter, softened.
1 cup sour milk.
2¼ cups pastry flour, with another
½ teaspoonful soda mixed with it.

Omit the butter when sour cream is used.   Bake in muffin pans.

Ginger Snaps.   (*Mrs. H. B. May.*)

1 cup molasses
½ cup sugar
1 tablespoonful ginger.

1 teaspoonful soda.
½ cup softened butter.
Flour to roll out very thin.

Heat the molasses, pour it over the sugar; add the ginger, soda, butter, and flour.   Cut, and bake quickly.

Ginger Drops (without Butter).

2 eggs, well beaten
1 cup brown sugar.
2 teaspoonfuls ginger.

1 cup N. O. molasses, boiled.
1 teaspoonful soda.
Flour to roll out.

Mix in the order given.   Roll thin, cut with a very small cutter, and bake in a quick oven.   If you like, add *one tablespoonful* of *vinegar* before adding the flour, and use *a heaping teaspoonful* of *soda*.

Soft Molasses Cookies. (*A. W.*)

1 cup molasses.	2 tablesp. warm water or milk.
1 tablespoonful ginger.	½ cup butter, softened.
1 teaspoonful soda.	Flour to mix soft.

Mix in the order given, dissolving the soda in the milk. Roll out one third of an inch thick. Cut in small rounds.

Cream Cakes.

1 cup hot water.	1½ cup pastry flour.
½ teaspoonful salt.	5 eggs, yolks and whites beaten
½ cup butter.	separately.

Boil the water, salt, and butter. When boiling, add the dry flour, stir well for five minutes, and when cool add the eggs. This is such a stiff mixture, many find it easier to mix with the hand, and some prefer to add the eggs whole, one at a time. When well mixed, drop, in tablespoonfuls, on a buttered baking-pan, some distance apart. Bake twenty to thirty minutes, or till brown and well puffed. Split when cool, and fill with cream.

Éclairs. — Bake the Cream Cake mixture in pieces four inches long and one and a half wide. When cool, split and fill with cream. Ice with *chocolate* or *vanilla frosting.*

Cream for Cream Cakes and Éclairs.

1 pint milk, boiled.	¾ cup sugar.
2 tablespoonfuls cornstarch.	1 saltspoonful salt, or
3 eggs, well beaten.	1 teaspoonful butter.

Wet the cornstarch in cold milk, and cook in the *boiling* milk ten minutes. Beat the eggs; add the sugar and the thickened milk. Cook in the double boiler five minutes. Add the salt or butter, and when cool, flavor with *lemon, vanilla,* or *almond.*

Kisses, or Cream Méringues.

Beat the *whites* of *three eggs* stiff and flaky; add *three quarters* of *a cup* of *powdered sugar*, sifting and cutting it in lightly. Drop by spoonfuls on paper placed on boards. Put in the hot closet or oven, with the door open for half an hour. Then brown slightly. Put two together; or put them on the paper in oblong shape, dry one hour, brown, remove the soft part, and fill with *whipped cream*.

To make these successfully, the steady, moderate heat of a confectioner's brick oven is essential. It is a waste of time and material to attempt them in an ordinary stove oven.

Macaroons.*

Half a pound of *almonds*, blanched, dried, and pounded to a paste, with *one teaspoonful* of *rose water*. Beat together the *whites* of *three eggs*, and *half a cup* of *powdered sugar*, adding the sugar by the teaspoonful. Add *half a teaspoonful* of *almond essence*, then add the pounded almonds and, if too soft to be shaped, add *one tablespoonful* of *flour*. Roll with wet hands into balls the size of walnuts, flatten them slightly, and place some distance apart on buttered paper. Bake slowly.

Almond paste, ready for use, may be obtained at a confectioner's. Break it up with a fork, add the beaten whites and sugar, using *four* or *five eggs* for *half a pound* of *paste*. Drop by teaspoonfuls on paper, and bake as above.

Cocoanut Cakes. (*Mrs. Richard Ward.*)

The *grated meat* of *two cocoanuts*, their weight in *loaf sugar*, *one cup* of *flour*, and *whites* of *two eggs*. Shape into balls, and bake twenty minutes.

Chocolate Caramels.

One cup of *molasses*, *half a cup* of *sugar*, *one quarter* of *a pound* of *chocolate*, cut fine, *half a cup* of *milk*, and *one heaping tablespoonful* of *butter*. Boil all together, stirring all the time. When it hardens in cold water, pour it into shallow pans, and as it cools cut in small squares.

FRUIT.

IT would be a great saving of time and work, give a pleasing variety to bills of fare, and be above all a great promoter of health, if people would use ripe fruit abundantly in its season at their tables (not between meals). With the markets bountifully supplied with many varieties of fruit, it is to be regretted that it cannot be found at every table at least once a day. Much of the money spent for some kinds of meat would be better expended for fruit. A simple course of fruit is all that is needed after a dinner, and is much more wholesome than pies. But it is so hard for some people to break away from old customs that it will be long before housekeepers generally will be content to serve the queen of all fruits, the apple, in its natural state instead of making it into the " persistent pie," over the preparation of which many women toil, for naught save the fear that they may be considered shiftless if they have n't a pie in the house.

Ripe fruit is especially appropriate at the breakfast-table, and may be taken before or after the principal dishes, according to individual needs and taste. Some people require the acid of oranges or grapes before they can eat anything substantial; others might be made ill by their use at that time, but be benefited by them afterwards.

All fruit should be served as fresh and cold as possible. A dish of fruit which has been kept from day to day in a warm room may answer for an ornament, but it is not tempting to the palate. Only sound, fresh fruit should appear at the table.

Apples for table use should have a pleasant spicy flavor, not too acid, and should be wiped clean, or polished if you prefer the street-vender's style.

Oranges may be served whole or cut. Many slice them across the sections ; but the presence of the seeds and tough inner skin is objectionable. A better way is to remove all the rind and white skin, divide into sections, then with the point of a silver fruit-knife cut off the inner skin in the middle, slip out the seeds, and cut each section into three pieces. Never serve with the seeds left in, nor sweeten until just before serving. A neat way to peel an orange is to cut the rind from the ends and leave a strip round the middle, then open, leaving the sections on the strip of peel. Or cut the oranges in halves crosswise without peeling, sprinkle with sugar, and eat with a spoon.

Grapes, Malagas especially, should be carefully rinsed in cold water, then drained. Fruit scissors should be used to divide the clusters.

Bananas may be served whole, or sliced and slightly sweetened or salted.

Peaches should have the wool wiped off, or if pared and quartered should be sprinkled with fine granulated sugar, and served at once.

Strawberries, if gritty, should be rinsed and drained, then hulled, and not sweetened till served. Large selected berries may be served with the stems on. Pass sugar with them, that those who prefer may roll them in it.

Currants should be sweetened, and large whole clusters may be served on the stem. Currants and *raspberries* are delicious when served together.

Watermelons should be served very cold. Cut off a slice at each end, that each half may stand upright. Serve the core only, taking it out with a tablespoon in cone-shaped pieces. Other *melons* should have the seeds removed before serving, be cut in halves, a lump of ice in each, and served with sugar or salt.

Pineapples. — Pare, remove the eyes, and cut in thin slices ; then remove the fibrous centre, and serve in slices, or cut the tender parts into small pieces and sweeten to taste. Or pare and pull off the tender part with a fork, as directed for *preserved pineapple.*

Iced Fruits. — Dip selected fruit into the white of egg slightly beaten, then roll in fine granulated sugar. Dry, and serve very cold.

Whole fruit should be served in a high dish, garnished with green leaves, flowers, or vines, and, with a tasteful combination of colors, arranged in a convenient way for serving.

Nuts should be cracked, and served with salt.

Almonds and other nuts having a tough inner skin should be blanched.

Raisins. — Use only choice varieties, and serve with nuts.

Tropical Snow.

8 sweet oranges.	1 glass sherry wine, or
1 cocoanut, grated.	¼ cup lemon juice.
6 red bananas.	Powdered sugar to taste.

Peel the oranges, divide into sections, and remove the seeds and tough membrane. Put a layer of orange in the bottom of a glass dish, pour over it a little wine or lemon juice, and strew with powdered sugar; add cocoanut, and then the banana cut in thin slices; repeat the process, using orange, cocoanut, banana, etc., as before. The top layer is to be heaped high in the centre, and sprinkled thickly with cocoanut and powdered sugar, and garnished around the base with slices of banana.

Other combinations of fruit may be arranged to suit the taste; and *cocoanut cakes* or *macaroons*, crumbled, or a méringue of *white* of *egg* and *sugar*, may take the place of the grated cocoanut.

Stewed and Baked Fruits.

The simplest forms of cooking fruit are stewing and baking. Only a small amount of sugar is needed, and it is not well to prepare a large quantity at a time, as stewed fruits do not keep long. In cooking fruit always use porce-lain or granite kettles, earthen dishes, wooden spoons, and

silver knives, and pare just before cooking. that the delicate flavor of the fruit may be preserved, and its attractive
appearance not impaired by discoloration.

Stewed Apple Sauce. — Pare, core, and quarter *six* or
eight tart apples. Make a syrup with *one cup* of *sugar,*
two thirds of *a cup* of *water,* and a little *lemon peel.*
When boiling, add the apples, and cook carefully two or
three minutes, till they are just tender, but not broken.
Remove them carefully, boil the syrup down a little, and
strain it over the apples. Cook them in granite or porcelain
pans, and use a wooden spoon.

Compote of Apples. — Make a syrup with *one cup* of
sugar, one cup of *water,* and *a square-inch* of *stick cin-*
namon. Boil slowly for ten minutes, skimming well.
Core and pare *eight* or *ten tart apples;* cook till nearly
done in the syrup. Drain, and cook them a few minutes
in the oven. Boil the syrup till almost like a jelly. Arrange the apples on a dish for serving. Fill the' core
cavities with *jelly* or *marmalade.* Pour the syrup over
them. Put *whipped cream* around the base, and garnish
the cream with *jelly.*

Baked Apples. — Core and pare sour apples. Put them
in a shallow earthen dish, fill the cavities with *sugar,*
mixed with grated *lemon rind;* add water to cover the
bottom of the dish. Bake in a very quick oven till soft,
basting often with the syrup.

Quinces may be baked in the same way, adding a little
more water, as they require a longer time for baking.
When eaten hot with *butter* and *sugar,* they are delicious.

No. 2. — Fill a deep pudding-dish with apples, pared,
cored, and quartered. For *two quarts* add *one cup* of
sugar and *one cup* of *water.* Bake, closely covered, in a
very moderate oven several hours, or till dark red.

Baked Pears. — Hard pears, or " windfalls," are delicious pared and baked as in the preceding receipt. When
done, and still hot, they may be sealed in Mason's jars,
and will keep indefinitely. By preparing one large dishful
every day during the pear season, a supply of wholesome

sauce may be easily obtained from fruit that is often left to waste on the ground.

Steamed Rhubarb. — Wash and cut the rhubarb into inch pieces without peeling. Put it into a granite double boiler, add *one cup* of *sugar* for *a pint* of *fruit,* and cook till the rhubarb is soft. Do *not* stir it. When the rhu-barb is very sour, steam it without sugar until the juice flows, then drain it, add the sugar, and steam again till the sugar is dissolved. Or pour boiling water over it and let it stand five minutes, then drain and steam.

Stewed Prunes. — Wash carefully, and if hard and dry soak an hour before cooking. Put them into a porcelain kettle, with boiling water to cover them. Boil, closely covered, from five to ten minutes, or until swollen and tender. Then add *one tablespoonful* of *sugar* for *one pint* of *prunes,* and boil a few moments longer, but not enough to break them. Use only the best selected prunes. If they lack flavor, add a little *lemon juice.*

Cranberries. — Put *three pints* of washed *cranberries* in a granite stewpan. On top of them put *three cups* of *gran-ulated sugar* and *three gills* of *water.* After they begin to boil cook them ten minutes, closely covered, and do *not* stir them. Remove the scum. They will jelly when cool, and the skins will be soft and tender.

No. 2. (*Miss Ward.*) — Equal measure of *cranberries* and *sugar.* Wash, drain, put in a porcelain kettle with cold water to just show among the berries when they are pressed down. When they boil add a quarter of the sugar. Sprinkle it over the berries without stirring. Let it boil again a minute, add another quarter, etc., till all the sugar is in. Boil up once more, and turn out. Boil slowly, and do not stir. This method is preferred by those who like a very rich sweet sauce.

Jellies.

Jellies are made of equal parts of clear fruit juice and sugar. *Apples, currants, quinces, grapes,* and *barberries* are the fruits usually used. *Low blackberries* and *swamp huckleberries* make delicious jelly. Crab apples and quinces will form jelly easily; but grapes are unreliable, and currants, if not gathered at the proper time, will sometimes fail. Cherries and some other fruits require the addition of gelatine. Berries, currants, and grapes require no water. Simply mash them in their own juice. Apples, peaches, and quinces should be stewed in as little water as possible, then mashed, and the juice strained. The juices of fruits contain a gelatinous substance called pectose, or pectic acid, which is soluble in the fruit juice, but has the property of coagulation when mixed with sugar, exposed to a slight heat, and then cooled. Sometimes the heat of the sun is sufficient, but usually a short but more intense heat is necessary. When the sugar has a bluish tinge, or when there is not enough sugar to absorb the water in the juice, or when the juice is unusually watery, as when the fruit is over-ripe, and the fruit is boiled a long time to evaporate this water, the mixture loses its gelatinous properties and becomes gummy, or, as disconsolate housekeepers say, " will not jelly."

Currant Jelly. — Currants should not be over-ripe, nor gathered after a rain, as then they are too watery. In New England currants are in the best condition about the 10th of July. Equal parts of *red* and *white currants*, or currants and raspberries, make a delicately colored and flavored jelly. Pick over and remove the leaves and poor fruit, and if gritty wash and drain them, but do not stem them. Mash them in a porcelain kettle with a wooden pestle, without heating, as that makes the jelly darker. Let them drain in a flannel bag over night. Do not squeeze them, or the jelly will be cloudy. In the morning measure a bowl of sugar for each bowl of juice, and heat the sugar carefully in an earthen dish in the oven. Stir it often to prevent burning. Boil the juice twenty minutes, and skim thoroughly. Add the hot sugar, and boil from three to five minutes, or till it thickens on a spoon when exposed to the air. Turn at once into glasses, and let them remain in the sun several days, then cover with paper dipped in brandy, and paste paper over the top of the glass.

One who is authority on this subject recommends covering 'with melted paraffine, or putting a lump of paraffine on the jelly while still hot; then no paper is needed. If one can be sure of several sunny days, and a perfectly dry place in which to keep jellies, they may be made without boiling. Mix the sugar with an equal weight of currant juice, and stir till dissolved. Fill the glasses and keep in the sun till dry.

After draining the juice the currants may be squeezed, and a second quality of jelly made. It may not be clear, but answers for some purposes.

Crab-Apple, Wild-Apple, or Porter-Apple Jelly. (*Miss Harriott T. Ward.*) — Wash the fruit; cut into pieces, but do not pare, nor remove the seeds; barely cover with cold water. Boil and mash them until soft. Then drain on a sieve. Use the juice only, and do not squeeze the fruit. Boil the juice with an equal quantity of sugar, until it jellies. *Peach jelly* is made in the same manner.

Quince Jelly. — Wipe the fruit carefully, and remove all the stems, and parts not fair and sound. Use the best parts of the fruit for canning or preserving, and the skin, cores, and hard parts for jelly. The seeds contain a large portion of gelatinous substance. Boil all together, in enough water to cover, till the pulp is soft. Mash, and drain. Use the juice only, and when boiling add an equal weight of hot sugar, and boil till it jellies in the spoon.

Grape Jelly. — Select the grapes when not fully ripe. Wash and drain, then put them in a preserving-kettle, mash well, and heat till all the skins are broken and the juice flows freely. Strain, and use the juice only with an equal weight of sugar, as for Currant Jelly.

Marmalade.

This is made of the pulp of fruits with the juice, unless that has been used for jelly. When fruit is not abundant, it is well to make marmalade at the same time with jellies, especially from peaches, quinces, and grapes. After draining, rub the fruit pulp through a sieve, add an equal weight of sugar, and boil very slowly half or three quarters of an hour. Stir often to prevent burning.

Preserves.

These are usually prepared with equal weights of sugar and fruit. Although too rich for daily use, there are many people who prefer them to the canned fruit, and there are some fruits which are better with the full weight of sugar. The fruit should be ripe, fresh, and perfectly sound. The following rules illustrate the best methods for the different varieties of fruit.

Peaches. — Pare the peaches ; or remove the skins by plunging the peaches into boiling lye (two gallons of water and one pint of wood ashes). When the skins will slip easily, take the peaches out with a skimmer and plunge them into cold water ; rinse in several waters, and there will be no taste of the lye. Weigh, and add *three fourths of a pound of sugar to each pound of fruit.* Halve them, and use some of the pits, or leave them whole as you please. The stones improve the flavor. Make a syrup by adding as little water as possible to the sugar, — about *one cupful* to *each pound* of *sugar.* When it boils, skim till clear, then add the peaches, and cook until transparent.

Brandy Peaches. — Prepare the peaches as above, and use *half a cup* of the best *brandy* to *every pound* of *fruit.* Add the brandy just as the syrup is taken from the fire. Some people prefer the yellow peaches, but white-fleshed freestone peaches have a delicious flavor.

Damsons and *Greengages* should be pricked in many places with a large needle, to prevent the skins from bursting. Or scald them and remove the skins, as sometimes they harden in cooking. Prepare the syrup as for peaches. Cook only a few at a time, that they may not be broken. On three successive mornings pour off the syrup, and boil it gently for ten minutes. This will thoroughly cook the fruit, without destroying the shape.

Preserved Quinces. — Use the orange quinces. Wipe, pare, quarter, and remove all the core and the hard part under the core. Take an equal weight of sugar. Cover the quinces with cold water. Let them come slowly to a boil. Skim, and when nearly soft put one quarter of the sugar on the top, but do not stir. When this boils, add another part of the sugar, and continue until all the sugar is in the kettle. Let them boil slowly until the color you like, either light or dark.

Another way is to cook the quinces in water till tender, drain, and put them in a stone jar in layers, with an equal weight of sugar. Cover closely. In a cold dry place they will keep perfectly. They are lighter-colored and more tender than when cooked in the syrup. Watch them during the first month, and if there be any signs of fermentation, set the jar in a kettle of hot water till the fruit is scalded. Reserve the broken or unshapely pieces of quince, cut them in small cubes, and use with *Strawberry Tomatoes.* Allow *three quarters* of *a pound* of *sugar* to *a pound* of *fruit.* Make the syrup, and cook the fruit in it till tender. Skim it out, and boil the syrup down for ten minutes. Fill the jars, and seal at once. Equal parts of *sweet apple*, cooked with the quince but with no extra sugar, can scarcely be distinguished from the quince.

Preserved Pineapple. — Remove the skin and all the eyes, take the pineapple in your left hand, and with a silver fork begin at the stem end of the fruit and fork out small bits. This will leave the core, which is juiceless and tasteless, in your hand. Weigh the pineapple after it is thus prepared, and sprinkle over it *three quarters* of *a pound* of *sugar* to *one pound* of *pineapple.* When a syrup is formed, cook the apple slowly in it until transparent, then remove the fruit and boil the syrup a little longer. Or slice the pineapple in half-inch slices, and cut out the core. Cook in the syrup, being careful not to break the slices.

Preserved Strawberries, Raspberries, Currants, Blackberries, and *Cherries.* — Measure a bowl of fruit and the same quantity of sugar. Put in a preserving-kettle, over night, a layer of fruit, and then one of sugar. In the morning cook slowly without stirring, until the liquid is clear and the fruit soft. Skim thoroughly before putting into the jars. Cherries should be stoned. The pits may be used if the flavor be desired.

No. 2. — Use only large and selected fruit, and allow *one cup* of *sugar* to *a pint jar* of fruit. Pick over the fruit, and put at once into the jars, with as little handling as possible, and sprinkle each layer with sugar. Place the jars in a boiler of water, and let the water boil ten minutes. Have a little syrup boiling, and fill each jar to the brim with the boiling syrup, and seal at once.

Jams.

Jams are made with whole small fruits, or large fruit cut fine, and cooked in an equal weight of sugar.

Grape Jam. — Wash the grapes, and squeeze or pinch the pulp from the skins. Boil the pulp until it separates from the seeds, and rub it through a sieve. Then add the skins to the pulp, and boil with an equal weight of sugar fifteen minutes. Put into small jars or tumblers, and cover with paper.

Currant, Raspberry, or *Blackberry Jam.* — Pick over and mash the fruit; allow *one pound* of *sugar* to *a pound* of *fruit.* Put the fruit and one quarter of the sugar into a granite or porcelain kettle; when boiling, add another quarter of the sugar; boil again, add more sugar, and when all is used, let it boil till it hardens on the spoon in the air.

Apples, pears, peaches, and *quinces* should be pared, cut small, and treated in the same way. Cooking in only a little sugar at a time prevents the fruit from becoming hard.

Canning.

Canning differs from preserving in that the fruit is kept, either with or without sugar, by sealing in air-tight jars or cans, and is not cooked long enough to destroy its natural flavor. Some authorities state that fruit may be kept by putting it in the jars, filling with cold water, and sealing immediately. But nearly all fruits are improved by the addition of more or less sugar. As a rule, all fruits that require sugar when fresh require it when canned.

The important points in canning are to have the fruit perfect in shape and quality; the syrup clear, rightly proportioned, and boiling hot; the jars hot and filled to overflowing, and sealed quickly and thoroughly, that no air may be left inside. Have all utensils in order and at hand, that there may be no needless delay. Large-mouthed glass jars with glass covers or porcelain-lined screw covers are the best. Pint jars are more convenient for a small family. They should be scalded, and the covers and rubbers clean and perfectly fitted. Keep the jars in hot water until ready to fill, or roll each one in hot water just before filling, or place them in a folded towel wrung out of hot water, and put a silver spoon or fork in the jar while filling. A clamp is a great convenience, as the jar may be held in the clamp directly over the kettle and filled very quickly. If without this, have a broad shallow pan, half filled with hot water, on the stove or on a table near by, and place the jars in it while filling them. A wide-mouthed tunnel aids in filling the jars. When the fruit is to be boiled in the jars, place a perforated tin or some flat stones or muffin rings in the boiler, to keep the jars from resting on the bottom. Then the water will be under as well as around the jar, and there will be no danger of breaking.

All ripe mellow fruit may be prepared and put at once into the jars. Place the jars in a boiler or kettle of warm water, with something underneath to avoid breaking. Make the syrup, using sugar according to taste, or in the proportion of *one cup* of *sugar* and *one cup* of *water* for

26

each jar of *small juicy berries*, and *one cup* of *sugar* and *two cups* of *water* for *pears* and *large fruits.* Pour the syrup boiling hot into the hot jars, boil five minutes, and seal at once.

Strawberries, plums, and *cherries* will require more sugar. *Cherries* should be stoned, but the stones may be used if liked.

Quinces, apples, hard peaches, pears, and fruits which require softening, should be cooked in *water* or in *syrup* until tender. Then fill the jars with boiling syrup, straining it if not clear.

Peaches may be canned whole, or if halved, a few of the pits removed and cooked in the syrup to give additional flavor.

Pears should be well ripened and of fine flavor. A tasteless, insipid pear is only suitable for sweet pickle.

Tomatoes should be peeled and cooked till well scalded, then salted and sealed at once.

Always fill to overflowing, using boiling water when there is not enough syrup. Run the handle of a silver tablespoon down the inside of the jar, that the syrup may completely surround the fruit. Fasten the covers on securely, and give the screw an extra turn every half-hour until the fruit is cold. If the jars be kept bottom up and in a dark place, there is hardly a chance of failure. The best quality of thick tin-foil may be used as a cover for any large-mouthed bottle or jar minus a cover. Fill the jar with the fruit and syrup, cover with a large piece of tin-foil, work it down over the rim until perfectly smooth and tight. If air-tight, there will be a depression in the cover as soon as the fruit is cold. Fruit thus covered should be kept away from mice, as they will eat the tin-foil.

Canned fruit should be opened some time before using, that it may be aerated and the flavor improved. There has been a strong feeling against the use of fruit prepared in tin cans. Chemists have examined canned fruit as soon as opened, and found it harmless; but if the fruit be left in the tin can, the action of the air causes the acid in the fruit to act upon the metal and form a poisonous compound. Care should be taken to remove the fruit from the can as soon as opened.

Sweet Pickles.

Eight pounds of *fruit, four pounds* of *best brown sugar, one quart* of *vinegar,* and *one cup* of *mixed whole spices,* — *stick cinnamon, cassia buds, allspice,* and *cloves ;* less of the latter than of the former. Tie the spices in a bag, and boil with the vinegar and sugar. Skim well; then add the fruit. Cook ten minutes, or till scalded and tender. Skim out the fruit, and put into stone jars. Boil the syrup five minutes longer, and pour over the fruit. The next day pour off the syrup and boil down again, and do this for three mornings. Keep the bag of spices in the syrup.

Tomatoes. — Scald, remove the skins, and cook without breaking if possible.

Peaches. — Scald or wipe off the "wool," and leave them whole. Do not stick them with cloves. If very ripe, merely pour the hot syrup over them on three successive mornings.

Pears. — Select sound fruit, not too ripe. Pare, and leave them whole with the stems on. Cook till tender.

Ripe Cucumber or Watermelon Rind. — Cut the pared rind into thick slices. Boil *one ounce* of *alum* in *one gallon* of *water,* pour it on the rinds, and let them stand in it several hours on the back of the stove. Take out into cold water, and when cold boil them half an hour in the sweet pickle.

Ripe Muskmelon or Canteloupe. — Pare, and cut into thick slices. Pour the boiling syrup over them. The next morning pour off the syrup, boil five minutes, and pour it boiling hot over the melon. Repeat this on three mornings.

Pineapple. — Slice it, or with a fork pick it off from the centre, in small pieces, and prepare as for melon.

Tomato Catchup. (*Mrs. Campbell.*)

Boil *one bushel* of *ripe tomatoes*, skins and all, and when
soft strain through a colander to remove the skins only.
Mix *one cup* of *salt*, *two pounds* of *brown sugar*, *half an
ounce* of *cayenne pepper*, *three ounces* each of *ground allspice*, *mace*, and *celery seed*, *two ounces* of *ground cinnamon*, and stir into the tomato. Add *two quarts* of best
cider vinegar, and when thoroughly mixed strain through
a sieve. Pour all that runs through into a large kettle, and
boil slowly till reduced one half. It is an improvement
to add *a pint* of *brandy* ten minutes before the catchup
is done, but many think it unnecessary. Put it in small
bottles, seal, and keep in a cool, dark place.

Piccallili, or Chow Chow.

1 peck green tomatoes.	1 teaspoonful white pepper.
1 cup salt	1 tablespoonful ground cinnamon.
6 small onions.	1 tablespoonful ground allspice.
1 large head celery.	1 tablespoonful mustard.
2 cups brown sugar.	2 quarts good, sharp vinegar.

Chop the tomatoes, mix the salt with them thoroughly,
and let them stand over night. In the morning pour off
the water, and chop the onion and celery. Mix the sugar,
pepper, cinnamon, and mustard. Put in a porcelain kettle
a layer of tomatoes, onion, celery, and spices, and so on
until all is used, and cover with the vinegar. Cook slowly
all day, or until the tomatoes are soft. *Cauliflower*, or
cabbage, or *one quart* of *cucumbers* may be used with the
tomatoes. Sliced or grated *horseradish* gives a pleasant
flavor.

Pickled Cucumbers. (*Miss Harriott Ward.*)

To *one hundred and fifty* small-sized *cucumbers* take
one pint of *salt*, dissolved in boiling water to cover them.
Let them remain in a covered vessel for forty-eight hours.
Then drain, and wipe each one carefully. Put them in a
pickle-pot or firkin with *one large onion*, peeled and

stuck full of cloves, *one green pepper*, some scraped *horse-radish*, and a small bit of *alum.* Boil *vinegar* enough to cover them. Fill a muslin bag with *one cup* of *mixed spices*, — *whole cloves, whole allspice, peppercorns, stick cinnamon, white mustard seed,* and a flake of *mace,* and boil ten minutes with the vinegar. Put this bag in the firkin when you pour on the boiling vinegar.

When cucumbers are gathered fresh from the vines every day, they may be kept in brine till wanted. Make the brine strong enough to float an egg, — *a pint* of *coarse salt* and *six quarts* of *boiling water,* boiled and skimmed clear. Pick the cucumbers as they ripen, wash carefully without removing the *prickles,* leave a bit of the stem on, and keep them covered with the brine. Soak, as required, in fresh cold water two days, and pour boiling spiced vinegar over them.

Mixed Pickles. (*Mrs. Poor.*)

150 small cucumbers.	1 tablespoonful stick cinnamon, broken into half-inch pieces.
1 quart small martinoes.	
1 quart small button onions.	1 tablespoonful whole cloves.
1 medium cauliflower.	½ tablespoonful peppercorns.
Rind of ½ watermelon.	½ tablespoonful allspice.
3 pints green string beans	½ tablespoonful whole mace.
3 cups salt.	1 teaspoonful celery seed.
4 quarts cold water.	2 quarts white wine vinegar.
¼ pound horseradish root.	1 ounce alum.
1 tablespoonful white mustard seed.	2 quarts boiling water.
	1 gill alcohol.

Wipe the cucumbers and martinoes with a damp cloth. Cut the cucumbers lengthwise into quarters, and the martinoes into halves. Scald and peel the onions; wash the cauliflower, watermelon rind, and beans; break the cauliflower into small pieces, and cut the melon rind about the size of the pieces of cucumber. Dissolve the salt in the cold water. Put the pickles in a large earthen or tight wooden vessel, and pour the brine over them; if they are not covered, add more cold water. Put a large earthen plate over them, with a clean brick or stone to keep them under the brine. Let them stand two days, remove them from the brine, and wash in cold water. Wash and scrape the horseradish root Pack the pickles in a stone jar or firkin. Put all the spices into a bag made of strainer cloth. Boil the vinegar, spices, and alum in a porcelain kettle ten minutes, skim carefully, add the boiling water, and pour immediately over the pickles. If a stronger spice be desired, leave the bag on the top of the pickles. Set them in a cold place, with the plate and weight over them to keep them under the vinegar. In about two weeks add the alcohol, and in four weeks they will be ready to use.

Mustard Pickles. (*Mrs. John Sheldon.*)

Equal quantities of *small cucumbers*, the largest ones sliced, *green tomatoes* sliced, *cauliflower* picked into flowerets, and small *button onions*. Keep them covered with strongly salted water twenty-four hours. In the morning scald the brine, and dissolve in it a bit of alum the size of a nutmeg. Pour the boiling brine over the pickles. When cold, drain thoroughly and prepare as much vinegar as there were quarts of brine. To *one quart* of *vinegar* use *one cup* of *brown sugar*, *half a cup* of *flour*, and *one fourth* of *a pound* of *ground mustard*. Boil the sugar and vinegar. Mix the flour and mustard, and stir the boiling vinegar into it, and when smooth pour it over the pickles.

Canned Fruit. (*Mrs. John Sheldon.*)

Put the prepared fruit in a jar, and cover with boiling syrup sweetened to taste. On three successive mornings drain off the syrup, boil again, and pour over the fruit. The last morning, let fruit and syrup come just to the boiling-point, but do not boil; then seal immediately. Fruit prepared in this way has been tested by the author and found perfect. Strawberries preserve their shape and never ferment.

GENERAL HINTS ON CARING AND COOKING FOR INVALIDS.

Ventilation. — The first condition of comfort and re-covery to the patient is that the room be perfectly ven-tilated, either directly or from fresh air in an adjoining room. A sunny exposure and an open fire, and in sum-mer an open fireplace, are essential aids. After all these points are secured, care must be taken that the air be not vitiated by anything in the room. Growing plants are more healthful than cut flowers ; unless the room be large and airy, the latter should not be allowed for any length of time, and even then should be removed as soon as their freshness is gone. If possible, avoid having a kerosene lamp in a sick-room. The odor is irritating to the mucous membrane, and in some conditions positively harmful. The wick should *never* be turned below the point of free combustion, either in the room of the sick or well. If you wish a dim light, place the lamp outside the door, or shade it by a screen. *Never* turn it down, as it will inevitably vitiate the atmosphere.

Avoid noise in replenishing the fire, by bringing the coal in a paper bag, and putting bag and all upon the fire. Keep all medicines and everything suggestive of a sick-room out of sight.

The Bed. — Arrange the bed so that the patient may be shielded from any draught. Neither sun nor lamp light should shine directly in the eyes. Whenever it is possible, change the position of the bed, furniture, and pictures, that the eye may have something new and inter-esting to dwell upon, if such changes interest instead of distress the invalid. Two small beds, that the patient may find relief in change, are desirable ; or, if possible, procure an invalid's bed, which admits of many changes of position and the airing and changing of the bed with no accompanying fatigue.

Cleanliness. — It is of the first importance that the bed linen and clothing of the patient should be kept fresh by frequent changes, and thoroughly dried and aired. Be careful to supply the needed warmth by light but not over-abundant clothing. The patient should be bathed freely ; avoid a chill by giving a sponge bath with alcohol and warm water, exposing only a part of the body at a time to the air, and rub till perfectly dry.

Wet a cotton-flannel bag, made with the nap side out, in cold water, wring it slightly, and tie it over the broom to use in sweeping. Be careful to wash it every time it is used. It is quite essential that the floor of a sick-room should be kept clean. Remove all dust with a damp cloth. The cleansing, drying, or airing of all objects should be done outside of the sick-room. Keep the room, the bed, the patient, and everything about yourself absolutely neat and clean.

Conversation. — In extreme sickness let no unnecessary word be spoken in a sick-room, and no needless, noisy, nor abrupt movements be made. Let the voice be calm and clear, neither loud nor whispering. In speaking to the patient do so in the way that requires the least effort in response, and never consult him about his food. Avoid all discussions of the disease, the medicine, and any excit-ing topic either with or before him. Do not excite the patient by needless conversation with the doctor outside of the sick-room. Never whisper, even when the patient is asleep or in delirium, because a whisper is more penetrat-ing than a low full tone. During convalescence do not weary with conversation ; let it always be bright and cheer-ful, and, as far as possible, of things outside the sick-room. Cultivate the power of talking to, rather than with, a sick person.

Conveniences in a Sick-Room. — " In severe sickness a glass tube is useful for feeding drinks and gruels ; and little white china boats with spouts are also good. A wooden tray with legs six or seven inches high, to stand upon the bed, is very convenient for serving meals."

To keep Ice for a Sick-Room. — Tie a square of coarse white flannel over a pitcher, leaving a cup-shaped depression of the flannel in the pitcher. Put broken ice in the flannel, and cover it tightly with a thicker flannel. The ice will keep all night, and the water may be poured off as wanted.

In applying hot bandages dip the flannel in boiling water, place it in the centre of a coarse towel, and twist and wring the ends of the towel ; or place the flannels in a steamer over hot water until penetrated with the steam ; they will then need no wringing.

Feeding the Patient. — When feeding the patient, do it gently and neatly. Anticipate his wants, and let the food be a surprise as far as practicable. In severe sickness give nourishment in a *small quantity often*, and never fail to give it immediately after a long sleep. During convalescence food should be given at longer, but regular intervals. If the patient be unable to use a toothbrush, wet a bit of soft cloth and wipe the teeth and gums, and give a little water or acid drink to soften the dry mucous membrane and destroy the bad taste in the mouth, before offering any food.

Let everything prepared for the invalid be arranged to please the eye as well as the palate. Serve less than you think the patient requires, and give as much variety as possible, serving in different forms or in different dishes if the material must be the same. Hot liquids should be *hot* when they reach the patient, not merely when they leave the kitchen. Serve them in a hot pitcher, and pour only a little into the hot cup or bowl, and so avoid its running over into the saucer or too rapid cooling. Never insult the patient by offering him a slice of dough covered with charcoal, under the name of toast. When the meal is over, remove immediately every trace of food from the room. Keep in the sick-room choice fruit or any delicacies which have been sent to the patient only long enough to gratify the eye, then remove to a cool place, and serve as fresh and daintily as possible.

Wines or liquors of any kind should never be given without the advice of a physician. Young persons do not need them, and, in any form of fever, stimulants are positively harmful. In some extreme cases, among very old people, or where there is a great lack of recuperative power, they may be given.

Visitors. — Visitors should never be admitted to a sick-room, except with the consent of the physician. Never visit a sick-room when in a violent perspiration or with an empty stomach, as then the system more readily receives contagion. If obliged to sit up all night with a patient, provide yourself with something to eat, if nothing more than a cake of chocolate, that there may be no needless exhaustion.

Not the least of the many qualifications desirable in a good nurse is a thorough knowledge of the nature, use, and digestibility, as well as the best methods of preparing different kinds of food, and of their adaptation to different forms of disease. Such knowledge is of still greater importance to every physician, and fully as essential as the study of drugs. Nurses, alas! are often wholly unqualified, or not to be obtained at all; and then that patient is fortunate, indeed, who has a physician who can in emergency fill the treble office of nurse, cook, and doctor.

Diet for the Invalid.

First Condition. — Sometimes the system from overtaxation, either mental or physical, needs a period of complete rest or comparative inaction; or, as in the commencement of many forms of sickness, the diet should be food which merely satisfies the hunger and which soothes and reduces inflammation and quenches thirst, but does not nourish nor stimulate. Foods proper at such times come under the head of starchy gruels, gelatinous soups and jellies, oranges, grapes, etc., and mucilaginous, acid, and aromatic drinks.

Flour or Arrowroot Gruel.

1 cup boiling water.	2 teaspoonfuls flour, wet in cold
1 saltspoonful salt.	water.

Cornstarch and rice-flour gruels are made in a similar manner. Use a little more of wheat flour than of the others.

Mix the flour and salt, and make into a smooth thin paste with cold water, then stir it into the boiling water. Cook five minutes, or until the desired consistency is obtained. Strain; then add *sugar*, if preferred, and thin with a little *milk*. If intended for a fever patient, a little *lemon juice* improves the flavor; if for a patient with summer complaint, boil with the gruel *half an inch stick* of *cinnamon* or a little *nutmeg*, — the spice will help to reduce the laxative condition. Sick people soon tire of sweets, and gruels should be sweetened only slightly, if at all. Flour and starchy gruels should not be given in typhoid fever, or when the disease is located in the intestines. Nor should they ever be used in excess, as, being rapidly swallowed, they are unaffected by the alkaline action of the saliva, and pass through the stomach unchanged and severely tax the intestines. They should be kept in the mouth and mingled with the saliva before swallowing.

Milk Porridge.

2 dozen raisins, quartered.	1 tablespoonful flour.
2 cups milk.	Salt to taste.

Boil the raisins in a little water twenty minutes. Let the water boil away, and add the milk. When boiling, add the flour rubbed to a thin paste with a little cold milk. Boil eight or ten minutes. Season with salt and strain. Or omit the raisins, and add *sugar* to taste; or add the *beaten white* of *one egg* after it comes from the stove.

Barley Gruel.

Boil *one ounce* of *pearl barley* a few minutes, to cleanse it. Pour off the water, add *one quart* of *cold water* and *half a teaspoonful* of *salt*, and simmer one hour, or until reduced one half. Strain it; sweeten to taste, and add a little *lemon* or *nutmeg*, if desired. Barley contains mucilage, and is soothing and refreshing in fevers and gastric inflammation.

Indian Meal Gruel.

1 tablespoonful flour.	1 teaspoonful salt.
2 tablespoonfuls corn meal.	1 quart boiling water.

Mix the flour, meal, and salt. Make into a thin paste with a little cold water, and stir into the boiling water. Boil thirty minutes, stirring often; thin with *milk* or *cream.* Milk may be used instead of water by making the gruel in a double boiler. Indian meal gruel requires longer time for cooking than any purely starchy gruels.

No. 2. — Wet *one heaping teaspoonful* of *meal* and *one saltspoonful* of *salt* in a little cold water, and stir into *one cup* of *boiling water.* Boil slowly thirty minutes.

Indian corn meal is heating in its nature, and should never be given where there is any inflammatory condition of the system. If given during convalescence after scarlet fever, it sometimes produces glandular swellings. When there is a deficiency of natural warmth, and no inflammation, it may be given without harm.

Oatmeal Gruel.

2 tablespoonfuls oatmeal.	1 quart boiling water.
¼ teaspoonful salt.	

Boil one hour. Strain, and serve with *milk* or *cream.*

No. 2. — Pound *half a cup* of *coarse oatmeal* until it is mealy. Put it in a tumbler, and fill the tumbler with cold water. Stir well; let it settle; then pour off the mealy water into a saucepan. Fill again, and pour off the water, and again repeat this, being careful each time not to disturb the sediment in the bottom of the tumbler. Then boil the water twenty minutes. Add *one saltspoonful* of *salt*. If very thick, add a little *cream* or *milk*. Strain and serve hot. *Beef essence* or *beef tea* may be used in place of cream. This is the most palatable and convenient way of making gruel from oatmeal.

Farina Gruel.

1 tablespoonful Hecker's farina.	1 cup boiling water.
1 saltspoonful salt.	1 cup milk.

Put all but the milk in the double boiler, and cook fifteen minutes, or until it thickens, then add the milk and boil again. Sweeten to taste.

Farina is a granulated preparation of the inner portion of the finest wheat, freed from bran and floury dust. It contains nitrogenous or flesh-forming material, is easily digested, and is a more nutritive food for invalids and children than cornstarch, sago, arrowroot, or tapioca, which contain only starch.

Cracker Gruel.

4 tablesp. powdered cracker.	1 cup milk.
1 cup boiling water.	½ teaspoonful salt.

Boil up once and serve.

Egg Gruel.

1 egg (yolk beaten well).	1 cup hot milk.
1 teaspoonful sugar.	White of egg, beaten till foamy.

Flavor with *nutmeg* or *lemon*. Good for a violent cold, if taken very hot after retiring.

Panada, No. 1.

1 cup stoned raisins.	1 cup bread crumbs.
1 quart water.	2 eggs.
2 slices toasted bread, or	1 tablespoonful sugar.

Boil the raisins one hour. Skim out the raisins, and add the bread to the boiling water; boil fifteen minutes, stirring well. Beat the eggs, add the sugar, and pour the panada over them, stirring all the time.

No. 2. — Split *two Boston* or *Graham crackers.* Put them into a bowl, sprinkle with *sugar* and *salt*, and cover with *boiling water.* Set the bowl in a pan of boiling water for half an hour, or until the crackers are clear. Slide them out into a hot saucer, and serve very hot with *sugar* and *cream.*

No. 3. — Boil *one tablespoonful* of *cracker crumbs* five minutes in *one cup* of *boiling water*, slightly *sweetened, salted*, and flavored with *lemon.*

Oatmeal Mush for Children or Invalids.

1 cup granulated oatmeal.	1 scant quart boiling water.
½ teaspoonful salt.	

Put the meal and salt in the double boiler, pour on the boiling water, and cook two or three hours. Remove the cover just before serving, and stir with a fork to let the steam escape. If the water in the lower boiler be strongly salted, the meal will cook more quickly. Serve with *sugar*, or *salt*, and *cream.* *Baked sour apples, apple sauce*, and *apple jelly* are delicious eaten with the oatmeal. They should be served with the mush, and the cream and sugar poured over the whole. They give the acid flavor which so many crave in the morning.

Coarse oatmeal is not suitable for any form of water brash, acidity, or bowel irritation. It often causes eruptions on the skin in warm weather.

Indian Meal Mush.

1 cup corn meal.	1 cup cold milk.
½ teaspoonful salt.	1 pint boiling water.

Mix the meal and salt with the cold milk. Stir this gradually into the boiling water. Cook half an hour in a double boiler, stirring often.

Graham Mush.

Mix *half a cup* of *Graham flour* and *half a teaspoonful* of *salt*. Make it into a thin smooth paste with a little *cold water*. Stir it into *one pint* of *boiling water*. Cook twenty minutes, stirring often. Serve with *cream*.

Rye Mush is made in the same manner, and sometimes served with *molasses*.

Gluten Mush. — Use *one cup* of *gluten* to *one pint* of *boiling water*, and cook as above. Being destitute of starch, it will not thicken like Rye Mush.

Brain Food. (*Health Food Co.*)

Wet *one cup* of *Brain Food* in a little *cold water*, and stir it into *one quart* of *salted boiling water*. Cook over hot water one to two hours. Eat, hot or cold, with *sugar* and *cream*.

Rice Water or Jelly.

2 tablespoonfuls rice.	Salt and sugar to taste.
1 quart cold water.	

Pick over and wash the rice, and cook in water one hour. or till the rice is dissolved. Add salt and sugar to taste. If intended for jelly, add *lemon juice* and strain into a mould. When cold, serve with *sugar* and *cream*. If to be used as a drink, add more hot water, enough to make a thin liquid, and boil longer. Add *half a square inch* of *stick cinnamon*, and strain. Serve hot or cold.

Rice is easily digested and almost wholly assimilated: it is good in diarrhœa or dysentery.

Tapioca Jelly.

¼ cup pearl tapioca.	1 tablespoonful lemon juice.
1 pint cold water.	1 heaping tablespoonful sugar.
1 saltspoonful salt.	

Pick over and wash the tapioca. Add the cold water, and cook in a double boiler until entirely dissolved. Then add the salt, lemon juice, and sugar. Turn into a mould. Serve with *sugar* and *cream. Half a cup* of *strawberry, raspberry,* or *blackberry jam* or *currant jelly* may be used in place of lemons.

Irish Moss Jelly.

½ cup Irish moss.	1 lemon
1 pint boiling water.	⅓ cup sugar.

Soak the moss in cold water until soft. Pick over and wash again. Then put it into the boiling water, and simmer until it is dissolved. Add the lemon juice and sugar. Strain into a mould. Use *currant jelly* in place of lemon, or steep *four* or *five figs* with the moss.

Sea mosses contain bromine and iodine, and are useful in rheumatic affections. Iceland moss may be used in the same manner. This, when dried, contains more starch than potatoes, and more flesh food than oatmeal or corn.

Restorative Jelly.

½ box gelatine.	2 tablespoonfuls lemon juice.
1 cup port wine.	3 tablespoonfuls sugar.
1 tablesp. powdered gum arabic.	2 cloves.

Put all together in a glass jar, and cover closely. Place the jar on a trivet in a kettle of cold water. Heat it slowly, and when the mixture is dissolved, stir well and strain. Pour into a shallow dish, and when cool cut it into small squares. This is good for an old person or a very weak patient.

Mutton Broth.

To make it quickly for an invalid, chop *one pound* of *lean juicy mutton* very fine; pour over it *one pint* of *cold water*. Let it stand until the water is very red, then heat it slowly. Let it simmer ten minutes. Strain, season, and add *two tablespoonfuls* of *soft-boiled rice*, or thicken it slightly with *rice flour* wet with *cold water*. Serve hot. When given to a person with a severe cold, or a consumptive, the fat should not be removed, as it is soothing to the chest, and when absorbed by the rice or some starchy material is not uninviting to the eye. For a fever patient, the fat should be removed. When you have not time to cool the broth, a piece of soft tissue paper passed over the surface helps to take up any globules of fat which will not come off with a spoon.

Barley Soup.

Remove the fat and bones from *one pound* of the *neck* of *mutton*. Cut the meat into dice, and add to it *one table-spoonful* of *well-washed barley* and *one pint* of *cold water*. Heat slowly, and simmer two hours. Put the bones into *one cup* of *cold water*, and boil gently half an hour. Then strain into the meat and barley. Season with *salt*. Skim off the fat, and serve with *whole-wheat* or *gluten wafers*.

Calves'-Foot Jelly or Broth.

4 calves' feet.	2 inch stick cinnamon.
4 quarts cold water.	1 inch blade mace.
1 cup sugar.	3 eggs (whites and shells).
2 lemons.	1 pint wine.

Scald the feet, and clean thoroughly. Split, break the bones, and put them into the cold water. Heat slowly, and simmer gently until reduced to three pints. Strain, and when cool remove the fat. Add the other ingredients except the wine. Put it over the fire, and stir until hot. Let it boil five minutes, or till a thick scum has formed. Set it back on the stove; skim, and add the wine. Strain through a fine napkin into a shallow dish. When ready to serve, cut it into blocks, or break it up lightly with a fork. If intended for broth, simply remove the fat, season to taste, and stir it into a *beaten egg;* or add *sago* or *tapi-oca,* having first soaked and boiled it till soft. Veal broth is not very palatable in itself; and as it does not contain the nutritive qualities of beef or mutton broth, it is not well to use it in the sick-room except for a variety.

Chicken Jelly or Broth.

Clean a *small chicken.* Disjoint and cut the meat into half-inch pieces. Remove all the fat. Break or pound the bones. Dip the feet into boiling water, and scald until the skin and nails will peel off. The feet contain gelatine, and when well cleaned may be used for jelly. Cover the meat, feet, and bones with cold water; heat very slowly, and simmer till the meat is tender. Strain, and when cool remove the fat. Season with *salt, pepper,* and *lemon,* and add the *shell* and *white* of *one egg.* Put it over the fire, and stir well until hot. Let it boil five minutes. Skim, and strain through a fine napkin. Pour it into small cups, and cool it if intended for jelly. When the patient can take it, small dice of the breast meat may be moulded in the jelly. Serve hot, without clearing, if intended for broth.

Beef Jelly or Broth.

Prepare the same as for Bouillon (page 131). If intended for jelly, clear it as directed for Clear Soup.

Barley Water.

1 tablespoonful pearl barley	½ lemon
3 blocks sugar.	1 quart boiling water.

Wash the barley in cold water, then pour off the water, and put the barley, sugar, and lemon into the boiling water, and let it stand covered and warm for three hours; then strain it. *Currant jelly* or *orange juice* may be used instead of lemon. This is a valuable demulcent in colds, affections of the chest, hectic fever, strangury and other diseases of the bladder or urinary organs.

Gum Water.

1 ounce clean gum arabic, and	1 pint boiling water.
½ ounce sugar, dissolved in	1 lemon (juice).

When dissolved, add the lemon juice, and strain through a fine strainer. This is soothing in inflammation of the mucous membrane.

Toast Water. — Toast *one pint* of *white* or *brown bread crusts* very brown, but be careful not to burn them; add *one pint* of *cold water;* let it stand for one hour, then strain, and add *cream* and *sugar* to taste. The nourishment in the bread is easily absorbed when taken in this liquid form.

Crust Coffee. — Pour *one pint* of *boiling water* over *two slices* of *brown toast.* Steep ten minutes, and strain. Add *sugar* and *cream* to taste.

Corn Tea and *Rice Coffee.* — Brown *one cup* of *dried sweet corn* or *rice.* Pound or grind it fine. Add *one pint* of *cold water*, and steep it one hour. Strain, and serve with *sugar* and *cream.* These are pleasant and nourishing beverages.

Slippery-Elm Tea. — Pour *one cup* of *boiling water* upon *one teaspoonful* of *slippery-elm powder* or a piece of the bark. When cool, strain and flavor with *lemon juice* and *sugar.* This is soothing in any inflammation of the mucous membrane.

Acid Fruit Drinks.

Pour *boiling water* on *mashed cranberries, barberries,* or *whortleberries.* When cold, strain, and sweeten to taste.

No. 2. — Stir *a tablespoonful* of any *acid jelly* or *fruit syrup* into *one tumbler* of *ice water.*

No. 3. — Dissolve *one tablespoonful* of *cream of tartar* in *one pint* of *water.* Sweeten to taste.

Apple Tea. — Roast *two large sour apples,* cover with *boiling water;* when cool, pour off the water and strain. Add *sugar* to taste.

Jelly and Ice. — With a large needle or pin, chip *half a cup* of *ice* into bits as large as a pea. Mix with it about the same quantity of *lemon, currant, blackberry,* or *barberry jelly.* Very refreshing in fevers.

Tamarind Water. — Boil *two ounces* of *tamarinds* with *four ounces* of *stoned raisins* in *three pints* of *water* for one hour. Strain and cool.

Baked Lemon. — Bake *a lemon* or *sour orange* twenty minutes in a moderate oven. When done, open at one end and take out the inside. Sweeten with *sugar* or *molasses.* This is excellent for hoarseness.

Lemonade. — Squeeze the *juice* from *one lemon* and add *one tablespoonful* of *sugar.* Pour on *one cup* of *boiling water,* and take hot for a cold, after retiring.

Flaxseed Lemonade. — Pour *one quart* of *boiling water* over *four tablespoonfuls* of *whole flaxseed,* and steep three hours. Strain and sweeten to taste, add the *juice* of *two lemons* and more water if too thick.

Irish-Moss Lemonade. — Soak, pick over, and wash *one quarter* of *a cup* of *Irish moss.* Pour on *one pint* of *boiling water* and cook in double boiler half an hour. Strain, add lemon juice and sugar to taste.

Whey. — Dissolve 1 junket tablet in 1 tablespoon cold water, warm one quart of pure unscalded milk to blood heat, add tablet, keep in warm room, when jellied stir till the curd separates, strain and sweeten the water, or not, and serve cold.

Wine Whey. — Boil *one cup* of *new milk,* and add *one cup* of *wine.* Let it stand on the back of the stove five minutes. Strain, and sweeten the whey.

The whey, or water, of milk contains the sugar, salt, and other saline bodies necessary for digestion and the repair of the mineral part of the body.

Herb Teas.

Pour *one cup* of *boiling water* over *one tablespoonful* of the *herbs.* Cover the bowl, set it over the teakettle, and steep ten minutes. Sweeten if desired. *Mullein tea* is good for inflammation of the lungs ; *Chamomile tea,* for sleeplessness ; *Calamus* and *Catnip tea,* for colds and infants' colic ; *Cinnamon tea,* for hemorrhages ; *Water-melon-seed* and *Pumpkin-seed tea,* for strangury and summer complaint. A few sprigs of *sage, burnet, balm,* and *sorrel, half a lemon,* sliced, and *three pints* of *boiling water,* sweetened to taste, and covered closely until cold, makes an agreeable drink for a fever patient.

Another Condition in sickness occurs when, after long-continued, prostrating, or rapidly wasting disease, the system demands immediate nourishment to supply that waste, or when there is a lack of nutrition from any cause. Food that contains the most nourishment in the most easily as-similated form is now needed ; but the physician should always be consulted as to the food suitable during the different diseases. *Liquid* food is most suitable, and should be *food* as well as drink. In nearly all cases of fever milk is given when the patient can take it. Two or three grains of pepsin in a cup of milk or broth facilitate its digestion. In typhoid fever milk has often proved of great value, and is now generally recommended by the medical faculty in all cases of scarlet fever, nervous disorder, and all diseases arising from imperfect nutrition. It keeps up the strength of the patient, acts well upon the stomach, soothes the in-testines, and promotes sleep. It should be taken slowly to prevent the curdling in a dense mass which may occur if too much be taken at once. A pint of hot milk taken slowly, every four hours, will often check the most violent diar-rhœa and dysentery. It should never be boiled, only scalded.

Eggnog or broth, meat broth, farina and oatmeal gruel, and port wine jelly, are all suitable at such times ; but beef juice and tea are most generally used by physicians. They afford a fluid and easily assimilated form of food, and have a remarkable power of restoring the vigorous action of the heart, and dissipating the sense of exhaustion following

severe, prolonged exertion. When taken alone, they are
stimulating rather than nutritive, and a patient would soon
starve if he did not have the addition of the fibrine of the
meat or of some farinaceous food, like bread crumbs or
oatmeal.

Beef Essence and Beef Tea.

Beef essence is the pure juice of the meat. This is given
where a patient needs much nourishment in a small compass. Beef tea is the juice of the meat diluted with water.
It is a mistake to think that any beef because it is lean
or cheap is good enough for beef tea. It will do for the
soup-kettle, but not for those who are ill. Meat for beef
tea should be lean, juicy, and of good flavor. Every particle of fat, skin, and membrane must be removed. The
top of the round and the back and middle of the rump contain the most and the best-flavored juice. It costs more
per pound than some other pieces; but as it yields nearly
double the amount of juice, it is really cheaper. The tenderloin is often recommended for sick persons. It should
never be used for beef tea, as it contains very little juice -
and lacks flavor. When the tender fibre of the meat is
desired, it may be broiled, and served with the juice from
some tougher steak.

Broiling is the quickest, and sometimes the most
palatable, way of preparing both essence and tea in an
emergency.

Drawing and *heating* the meat and juice is best where
a little nourishment is to be given often, and where all the
elements of the meat are needed. Soaking in cold water,
then straining, and heating the juice only, is the most
economical way, as more than twice the usual amount of
juice may be obtained by adding more water when the
meat has not been heated.

The albuminous juices of meat coagulate at 160°; if the
tea be allowed to boil, they become hard, and settle almost
immediately when served. Many make the mistake of
straining the tea, or leaving the sediment untouched. If

the tea be heated just enough to make it palatable, it will hold the juices in solution, not separated, and will be thick, and of the color of chocolate, and much more palatable and nutritious than when boiled.

Broiled Beef Essence. — Broil *half a pound* of *round steak* one or two minutes, or until the juice will flow. Cut it into small pieces. Squeeze the juice into a bowl placed over warm water. *Salt*, and serve without reheating. Or pour it over a slice of hot dry toast.

Broiled Beef Tea. — Add *half a cup* of *boiling water* to the meat after broiling as above.

Bottled Beef Essence. — Put *two pounds* of *round steak*, cut in small pieces, into a jar without water. Place the jar, covered closely, on a trivet in a kettle of cold water. Heat gradually, and keep it not quite at the boiling-point for two hours, or till the meat is white. Strain, pressing the meat to obtain all the juice; season with *salt*. Or place the jar in a moderate oven for three hours. The liquid thus obtained contains all the nutritive parts of the meat. It may be kept in the refrigerator, and a small portion heated (not boiled), as wanted. Or it may be made into beef tea by diluting with boiling water. Beef essence given ice cold is sometimes more agreeable to a fever patient.

Bottled Beef Tea. — Add *one cup* of *cold water* to the meat in the jar, and make as above. When the patient can take a little solid food, add *two tablespoonfuls* of *stale bread crumbs* to the beef tea, or mix with it *oatmeal gruel*, or add *one teaspoonful* of *finely chopped raw meat*.

Stewed Beef Essence. — Cut *half a pound* of *round steak* into small pieces, season with *one saltspoonful* of *salt*, press it with a pestle or potato-masher, and let it stand in a covered bowl half an hour. Pour off the juice, and heat, but do not boil it. Serve immediately, without straining.

As the salt without water will draw out only a small portion of the juice from the meat, a beef tea may be made from the scraps of meat left by adding *one cup* of *cold water* to the meat, and letting it stand two hours. Then strain and heat the liquid ; or the scraps of meat may be put in the soup-kettle.

Economical Beef Tea. — Cut *one pound* of *juicy rump steak* into small pieces, and add *one cup* of *cold water.* Let it stand in a covered bowl several hours. When ready to serve, squeeze the meat and put it into another bowl. Strain the juice already obtained, add *salt* to taste, and heat it just enough to be palatable, but not enough to curdle it. Serve at once, while hot. If it be heated over the fire, stir constantly, and take it off the moment it looks thick and is hot; or heat it carefully over hot water. Add another cup of cold water to the scraps of meat, and soak again. Often the third cup of tea may be obtained from the same meat. This is excellent for hard-working people to take, in times of great exhaustion, before a hearty meal. It is one of the best and most easily prepared forms of soup. or meat tea.

Dr. Mitchell's Beef Tea. — *One pound* of *lean beef,* cut fine ; add *one pint* of *cold water* and *five drops* of *muriatic acid.* Put into a glass jar. Place the jar in a pan of water at 110°, and keep it at that temperature for two hours. Then strain through thick muslin until the meat is dry, or press the juice out by squeezing. The acid makes the tea agreeable to a patient with fever, and also aids in drawing out the juices of the meat.

Raw Beef Sandwiches. — Scrape fine a small piece of fresh, juicy, tender, raw beef. Season highly with *salt* and *pepper.* Spread it on thin slices of bread, put them together like a sandwich, and cut into small squares or diamonds. This will often tempt a patient who could not otherwise take raw meat. The sandwiches are sometimes made more palatable by toasting them slightly.

Eggnog. — Beat the *yolk* of *one egg ;* add *one table- spoonful* of *sugar,* and beat to a cream. Add *one table- spoonful* of *wine* or *brandy,* and *half a cup* of *milk.* Beat the *white* of the egg to a froth, and stir in lightly. Omit the milk when more condensed nourishment is required, or the wine, if not approved by the physician. It is more palatable when made with the milk. Whipped cream may be substituted for the milk. In many cases it is desirable not to have the white beaten to a froth, as it causes wind in the stomach.

Portable Beef Tea. — *Two pounds* of *beef*, cut fine, and *half a box* of *gelatine.* Soak together in *one pint* of *cold water* one hour, squeezing often. Heat to nearly the boiling-point. Strain, pressing all the juice from the meat, fill a glass jar with the juice, place the jar in water, and heat till the water outside the jar boils. Seal while hot. Dissolve *two teaspoonfuls* of the above preparation in *half a cup* of *boiling water*, add a few grains of *salt*, and serve at once. A convenient form of food for travellers.

Broiled Beef Pulp. — Scrape raw beef to a pulp, make it into small cakes, and broil as steak. Season with *salt* and a few grains of *cayenne pepper*, and serve hot.

Egg Tea and Coffee. — Beat the *yolk* of *one egg;* add *one tablespoonful* of *sugar*, and beat to a cream; add *one cup* of *tea* or *coffee*, either hot or cold, and *half a cup* of *cream.* Stir in lightly the beaten *white* of the egg, and serve at once.

Egg and Beef Tea — Add *one cup* of *hot beef tea* to the egg, beaten as above.

Dishes for Convalescence.

When the crisis of disease is past, the system needs gradual but complete nutrition, and the appetite is clamorous, fickle, or perhaps altogether wanting. Then is the time most critical for the patient, and most trying to the tact, skill, and patience of the nurse. Many a person has been carried safely through a long and distressing illness, only to succumb at last to injudicious feeding, because of the nurse's ignorance or his own indiscretion. When solid food can be safely given, the patient may take it in any of the forms given in the preceding rules.

The following dishes may also be used : broiled squab, venison, chicken, chop, steak, salmon, chicken panada, boiled halibut, roast beef, mutton, cream toast, eggs, and oysters (except when especially forbidden by the physician), sweetbreads, baked potatoes, asparagus, onions, macaroni, custards, Charlotte Russe, snow pudding, ice-cream, sherbet, blanc-mange, Bavarian cream, sponge cake, simple puddings, stewed fruits, and many others, — receipts for which will be found as indicated in the table of lessons in the Nurse's Course.

Broiling for the Invalid (Broiled Steak or Venison). — Wipe with a clean wet cloth. Grease the gridiron with a bit of the fat. Broil over a clear fire, turning as often as you can count ten. Cook four minutes if the steak be about one inch thick ; not longer, as further cooking dries up the juices and destroys some of the nutritive qualities, Be careful to serve on a hot platter, and season with *salt*, and with *pepper* and *butter* if approved. Birds, chicken breasts, fish, and chops are better when seasoned, and wrapped in buttered paper, and then broiled, as this prevents them from burning or becoming too dry. Birds, fish, and chops are better, and more conveniently eaten, if boned before broiling.

Broiled Steak, No. 2. — Broil *half a pound* of *round steak* and *one slice* of *tenderloin.* With a meat or lemon squeezer squeeze the juice from the round over the tenderloin. Season, and serve hot.

Chicken Panada. — *One cup* of *cold roasted* or *boiled chicken*, pounded to a paste. Add *half a cup* of *stale bread crumbs*, and enough boiling chicken liquor to make it a thick gruel. Salt to taste. Boil one minute, and serve hot. When the chicken has been roasted, boil the bones to obtain the liquor.

Chicken Custard. — Scald together *one cup* of *strong chicken stock* and *one cup* of *cream.* Pour it over the well-beaten *yolks* of *three eggs*, and cook in a double boiler till slightly thickened. Salt to taste, and serve cool in custard cups.

Crackers and Orange Marmalade. — Toast *three crack-ers* slightly. Dip them quickly into *boiling salted water.* Spread with a little *butter*, and put a layer of *orange marmalade*, or any other jelly or preserve, between them. Set them in the oven a few minutes before serving.

Racahout des Arabes. (*Mrs. Devereux.*)

½ pound best French chocolate.	¼ pound arrowroot.
1 pound rice flour.	½ pound loaf sugar, sifted.

These materials are to be thoroughly mixed and rubbed together. A *dessert spoonful* of this mixture should be slightly wet with *milk* or *water*, then stirred into *one pint* of *boiling milk*, and boiled five minutes. This is excellent food for invalids or convalescents. Serve hot, as a beverage ; or make much thicker, to be eaten cold as a delicate pudding.

Laban. (*Miss Parloa.*) — *One quart* of *new milk*, into which stir *one tablespoonful* of *yeast.* Let it stand in a cool place to harden, which will take from three to twenty-four hours. When hard, take *a tablespoonful* of the mixture, and stir it into *a quart* of *new milk*, and set away to harden. This is " Laban." It should be eaten with *sugar* and *cream.* If a constant supply be needed, reserve *one tablespoonful* each day for the next preparation. This receipt is furnished by a lady who obtained it in Syria, and who advises a second or a third trial if the first attempt be unsuccessful. The dish is often palatable when the stomach is too weak for almost any other solid food. This is similar to Koumiss, or fermented mare's milk.

Ash Cake. (*Mrs. Henderson.*) — Wet *corn meal*, salted to taste, with enough *cold water* to make a soft dough. Let it stand half an hour, or longer. Mould into a cake one or two inches thick, as you prefer. Place it on a clean spot on the hearth, and cover with wood ashes. Bake from half to three quarters of an hour. Wipe before eating. The alkaline properties left by the ashes in the crust render it especially good for dyspeptics with an acid stomach.

Gluten Gems.

2 cups gluten.	2 tablespoonfuls sugar.
½ teaspoonful salt.	1 egg.
2 teaspoonfuls baking-powder.	2 cups water or milk.

Bake in very hot buttered gem pans, in a hot oven, half an hour.

Diet for Infants and Young Children.

Let very young children have mother's milk above everything else ; but if this be impossible, dissolve *one ounce* of *sugar of milk* or *loaf sugar* in *three fourths* of *a pint* of *boiling water*, and mix, as required for use, with an *equal quantity* of *fresh cow's milk.* Give it, slightly warm, from a sweet, clean bottle. Sugar of milk is quite expensive, but it is very much better for an infant than cane sugar.

Teething children should have the milk from but one cow ; the cow should not be fed on green corn nor sour apples, as these produce acidity in the milk. A little thin, well-boiled oatmeal, or farina gruel, may be added to the milk.

For *summer complaint,* use *scalded* (not boiled) milk, prepared flour, roasted rice, boiled, mashed, and thinned with milk ; also rice jelly or barley gruel. Avoid all purely starchy gruels, like arrowroot, sago, and cornstarch, upon which many children are fed to death.

For *constipation,* a little salt added to cow's milk is often beneficial ; also gruel made from prepared corn meal and wheat flour, and oatmeal gruel. For older children use oatmeal, hominy or farina mush, and ripe fruit.

Prepared Flour (for Infants). — Tie *one pint* of *flour* in a stout cloth, put it into boiling water, and let it boil three hours. Turn out the flour ball, and scrape off the gluten which will be found in a mass on the outside of the ball and is not desirable. The inside will prove a dry powder, which is very astringent. Grate *a tablespoonful* of this powder from the ball as wanted; wet it in *cold milk* or *water*, and stir it into *one cup* of *boiling milk.* Boil five minutes. Add a little *salt.*

This is excellent for teething children. If they be troubled with constipation, use *one quarter part corn meal* and *three quarters wheat flour*, boil as above, and stir some of the grated lump into *boiling cream* and *water*, using *one part cream* to *six parts water.* For an infant the preparation should be thin enough to be taken from a bottle. Flour, after being cooked in this way and then reduced to a finely divided form, loses its adhesive quality; and the particles are more easily separated and digested.

Children and *growing persons* need the most nutritious food, and plenty of it at regular intervals; but nothing stimulating nor exciting. They should be given, and compelled to take, sufficient time for eating; and should be taught to masticate everything slowly and thoroughly. They should eat milk; whole-wheat and cornmeal bread; oatmeal, farina, and hominy mush; plenty of ripe fruit raw, and stewed fruit sweetened; beef, mutton, venison, and poultry, either roasted, broiled, or boiled; baked potatoes, and asparagus; green peas, beans, and corn, if every hull be first broken or cut; eggs, omelets, and custards; plain sponge cake; ice-cream, if not too hard and cold, and eaten slowly; simple fruit and bread puddings; fruit, tapioca, and farina; plain gingerbread and molasses cookies; whole-wheat cookies and wafers. Children should avoid hot bread and griddle-cakes; fried meats or cakes or doughnuts; highly seasoned food; rich gravies; rich pastry and cake; pickles, preserves, all stimulants such as tea or coffee; raisins, unless cooked three hours and stoned; sago, arrowroot, and other purely starchy foods, except when combined with milk, eggs, or fruit, and eaten with sugar and cream; and especially veal and pork. Veal is an immature meat, lacking in nourishment; and of the free use of pork, apart from the question of the trichinæ, a majority of physicians believe that it is largely responsible for the forms of scrofulous disease that have so undermined the health of civilized nations.

What are termed the "fancies" of delicate persons, especially children, are often natural instincts, pointing out what is beneficial to the system, or the reverse. All children have a fondness for sugar, which should be gratified in moderation rather than repressed. Their desire for it is natural, else it would not have been placed in the milk which forms their only nourishment in infancy. But candy, rich preserves, and cake are not the best form of sweets for children. Pure block sugar or maple sugar is better than any form of candy. It should never be allowed between meals, but may be given occasionally as a part of the dessert. The habit of munching candy between meals destroys the appetite, disturbs the digestion, and is the cause of much illness among children. Children troubled with worms should avoid sugar, preserves, and green vegetables.

Milk should enter largely into the diet of children. It contains caseine, or flesh-forming material; cream and sugar, which are heat producers; mineral salts, for the bony structure; and water, as a solvent for all the other materials necessary in nutrition. It should be used with discretion, however; not drunk immoderately, but taken slowly as food after the pattern given by nature. Milk as taken is a fluid; but as soon as it meets the acid of the gastric juice, it is changed to a soft, curdy, cheese-like substance, and then must be digested, and the stomach is overtasked if too much be taken at once. A large glass of milk swallowed suddenly will form in the stomach a lump of dense, cheesy curd, which may even prove fatal to a weak stomach. Under the action of the stomach this cheesy mass will turn over and over like a heavy weight; and as the gastric juice can only attack its surface, it digests very slowly. But this same milk, taken slowly, or with dry toast, light rolls, or soft dry porridge, forms a porous lump through which the gastric juice can easily pass, and which breaks up every time the stomach turns it over. Milk should be slightly salted, and *eaten* with bread stuffs, or sipped by the spoonful.

Cow's milk produces less heat than human milk; a child would grow thin upon it unless a little sugar were added. Wheat flour has such an excess of heat-producing material as would fatten a child unduly, and should have cow's milk added to it to reduce its fattening power.

Hints on Diet for Invalids.

Vanilla should not be used as a flavoring in food for sick people. It is medicinal; and all medicines are more or less poisonous, and are not to be taken as food.

Pepper is allowable when a slight stimulant is needed. It should be white or cayenne pepper, as these are less irritating than black pepper.

Boiled onions are soothing to the mucous membrane. In inflammation of the stomach they are often helpful when a piece of white bread could not be digested.

Broiled or *roasted squab, venison, chicken, mutton,* and *beef,* in the order given, are the most easily assimilated meats.

Game, being rich in phosphates, is valuable for invalids.

Broiled bacon, dusted with *cayenne,* is an easily digested form of fat.

Tomatoes as an article of diet are considered by many physicians a remedy for dyspepsia and indigestion.

Watery, green, or *diseased potatoes* should never be eaten. If there be only a small spot of decay, it taints the whole potato. *Young potatoes* are very indigestible.

Eggs for sick people should be taken raw. When beaten with cold milk, they are more quickly absorbed. If cooked, they should be either very soft, or hard enough to be easily crumbled to a powder, as in any intermediate stage the albumen is tough instead of brittle, and being tough is insoluble by the gastric juice; these insoluble portions are often delayed in the stomach or intestines till they putrefy, and the sulphuretted hydrogen and ammonia evolved become poisonous to the intestinal canal.

Soups which have in them cream or milk are better for invalids than those rich in gelatine. *Cream of Celery* and *Potage à la Reine* are especially suitable. Strong *Bouillon* is adapted to those suffering from hemorrhoids or any disease of the rectum, as there is no solid waste.

Dyspeptics should avoid anything which *they* (not others) cannot digest. There are so many causes for and forms of dyspepsia, that it is impossible to prescribe one and the same diet for all. Nothing is more disagreeable or useless than to be cautioned against eating this or that, because your neighbor "So-and-so" cannot eat such things. If we would all study the nature and digestion of food, and remember that air and exercise are as essential as food in promoting good health, we could easily decide upon the diet best suited to our individual needs.

The *diabetic* should abstain from sugar and anything which is converted into sugar in digestion, such as all starchy foods, — fine wheat flour, rice, macaroni, tapioca, liver, potatoes, beets, carrots, turnips, parsnips, peas, beans, very old cheese, sweet omelets, custards, jellies, starchy nuts, sweet sauces, wine, and liquors. He may eat oysters, all kinds of fish, meat, poultry, and game, soups without any starchy thickening, lettuce, cucumbers, watercresses, dandelions, young onions, cold slaw, olives, cauliflower, spinach, cabbage, string beans, ripe fruit of all kinds without sugar, cream, butter, milk sparingly, gluten, flour, oily nuts freely salted, eggs, coffee, and cocoa.

The *corpulent* should abstain from fat as well as sugar and starch. A diet of whole-wheat, milk, vegetables, fruits, and lean meat will produce only a normal amount of fatness; while an excess of sweets, acids, spices, and shortening keeps the system in an unhealthful condition.

Those who can digest fine flour, pastry, sugar, and fats become loaded with fat, but are neither strong nor vigorous. Thin people with weak digestion should also avoid such food; for thin people are often kept thin by the same food which makes others fat. If they cannot digest the starch,

butter, and fine flour, the system is kept in a feverish, dys-
peptic state; they become nervous or go into consumption.
for no other reason than that life is burned out by a diet
which only feeds the fire and does not renew the tissues.
"Men dig their graves with their teeth; not only by
drinking whiskey and using tobacco, but by eating food
loaded down with inflammatory materials."

The *bilious* and *gouty* should eat sparingly of brown
meats, cheese, eggs, beans, peas, or food which is rich in
albuminoids. A certain amount of albuminoid or nitro-
genized food is requisite for tissue growth and repair;
more being required for growing persons and the convalescent than for healthy adults. Most Americans are inclined to eat more albuminoid food than is required. It
gives a sensation of energy, of being equal to work, which
is very pleasant. But when we have "too much of a good
thing," more than is needed for repair of tissue, this surplus of albuminous material is imperfectly oxidized, the
blood is laden with waste, and biliousness or gout is the
result. Fish gives less albuminoid waste than meat.

People who are inclined to *constipation* should eat
whole-wheat, rye, and corn bread and mushes, ripe fruit,
berries, green corn, vegetables, beef, mutton, poultry,
milk, cream, and butter; and should avoid fried or greasy
food, hot bread, rich cake, veal, pork, or anything which
has so much woody fibre or cellulose that it only irritates
the digestive canal, such as the outer bran of wheat, coarse
oatmeal, etc.

Those with *consumptive tendencies* should eat wholesome, easily digested and assimilated food, with plenty of
fat, — not in the indigestible form that it takes when
mixed with starch, but as in cream, sweet butter, fat of
roast or boiled meat, the fat, but not the lean, of ham and
corned beef, oil, salads, corn-meal, oatmeal, etc.

. The diet of people who are well should be governed
largely by their age, occupation, and exercise. Adults
should have a variety of wholesome food cooked in different
ways. Aged people should have a diet more like that of

children. If the occupation tax the *muscular strength*,
use muscle-making food ; not wholly meat, as many laboring people are inclined to think, but grains, peas, beans,
cabbage, milk, cheese, eggs, whole-wheat bread, and
chocolate, with a small amount of beef, mutton, and
poultry. *Students* and *brain-workers* need more of brain-
producing and less of muscle-making food. Brain food
must contain phosphorus, which is found largely in oysters,
eggs, fish, lean meat, wheat, peas, beans, and fruit. Those
who are engaged in *sedentary occupations,* who take
little exercise and live in close, confined rooms, should
eat only the most easily digested food.

People who engage in regular active labor, who take
plenty of exercise in the open air, cultivate a cheerful,
happy disposition, live temperately in every way, and have
naturally strong digestive organs, can eat any kind of
wholesome food that has been properly cooked, and have
no consciousness of a stomach or any visceral organs ; and
appetite, unless previously impaired, is their best guide.
If the digestive organs be not strong naturally, such a
mode of life as the above will tend to make them so, more
than any amount of drugs or quack medicines.

Junket. — Dissolve one junket tablet in one tablespoon
of cold water, and two tablespoons of fine granulated sugar
in one quart of pure unscalded milk. Heat the milk in
double boiler to 98°, or till warm all through but not hot.
Remove, flavor to taste by steeping stick cinnamon or
bay leaf in the milk and removing when hot ; add the
tablet, stir once all through, pour into small cups in a
shallow pan and let it stand undisturbed till jellied ; then
remove in the pan to a cool place If jarred it will
separate into curds and whey.

Serve with cream and powdered sugar. Many rich
combinations and fancy garnishings may be added, if
desired; such as custard, fruit juice and pulp, whipped
cream, etc., but this simple method is most satisfactory,
especially for children and the invalid conditions which it
is supposed to help.

MISCELLANEOUS HINTS.

To Chop Suet. — Cut into small pieces and remove the membrane. Sprinkle with flour, and chop in a cold place to prevent its becoming soft and sticky.

To Clean Currants. — Put them in a squash strainer, and sprinkle thickly with flour. Rub them well until they are separated, and the flour, grit, and fine stems have passed through the strainer. Then place the strainer and currants in a pan of water, and wash thoroughly. Lift the strainer and currants together, and change the water till clear. Drain between towels, and pick over carefully. Dry them in a sunny place or between towels, but do not harden them by putting them into the oven.

To Stone Raisins. — Pour boiling water over them, and let them stand in it five or ten minutes. Drain, and rub each raisin between the thumb and finger till the seeds come out clean, then cut or tear apart, or chop, if wanted very fine.

Core Apples before paring, and there is less danger of their breaking.

Egg Shells. — Wash eggs as soon as they come from the market, and then the shells may be used in clearing coffee, soup, etc.

To Boil a Pudding in a Cloth. — Wring strong cotton cloth out of boiling water, and spread over a bowl. Sprinkle with flour, fill with the pudding, draw the cloth together, and tie tightly, then flour near the opening. Plunge into boiling water, and keep the water boiling during the time for cooking. Add boiling water as needed, and replenish the fire often.

Meringues should be put on puddings after they are slightly cool, as, if the pudding be hot, the egg will liquefy.

Moulds should be greased for any steamed mixture
wet in cold water for jelly, creams, etc. ; and neither wet
nor greased if to be lined with cake. A mould of jelly
will cool quicker if placed in a pan of ice water or snow
than in the ice-chest.

Candied or Crystallized Fruit or Nuts. (*Mrs. Campbell.*) — Boil *one cup* of *granulated sugar* and *one cup* of
boiling water together for half an hour. Then dip the
point of a skewer into the syrup and then into cold water.
If the thread formed break off brittle, the syrup is ready.
The syrup must never be stirred, and must boil slowly,
not furiously. When done, set the saucepan in boiling
water, or pour the syrup into a bowl placed in hot water,
to keep the syrup from candying. Take the prepared
fruit or nuts on the point of a large needle or fine skewer,
dip them into the syrup, and then lay them on a dish,
which has been lightly buttered or oiled ; or string them
on a thread, and after dipping in the syrup suspend them
by the thread. When oranges are used, divide them into
eighths, and wipe all moisture. Cherries should be stoned.
English walnuts are especially nice prepared in this way.

To Blanch Almonds and other Nuts. — Remove the
shells, cover with boiling water, and let them stand till the
dark skin will rub off easily. Then put them in cold
water, rub off the skins, and dry between towels.

Corned Meat. — Fresh meat may be kept some time by
corning it slightly. Wipe carefully, and remove any parts
that are not sweet and fresh, then rub all over thickly
with salt. Or make a brine with rock salt and cold water ;
use salt enough to float the meat, then cover, and put
a heavy weight on the cover to keep the meat under the
brine. Three days' time is sufficient for corned meat.

To Make Paper Boxes. — These can be obtained, in a
variety of forms, from the confectioner ; but plain ones
may be made in this way. Take a piece of stiff white
paper, five inches square. Find the centre of the square
by folding two opposite corners together and creasing
lightly in the middle, then open and fold the other two in

the same way. Fold the two sides over till they meet in the centre, then fold the two ends. Open, and cut in the fold down to the line at each end, but not on the side. Fold the sides over on the outside about one quarter of an inch; then fold the middle part of the end in the same way. Then turn the ends of the side pieces round behind the end, and let them meet in the middle, and fold the edge of the end over them. Fasten the ends with a few stitches or with paste. A border of fancy perforated paper may be pasted on the edge.

A Pastry Bag. — One third of a yard of yard-wide rubber sheeting will make three bags one foot square. Fold two opposite corners together, stitch along the edge, and make a triangular bag. Cut off at the point to make an opening large enough to insert the end of a tin tube. It is convenient to have three bags, with openings of different sizes, — one for éclairs, one for lady fingers, and one for frosting. The tube for éclairs is three fourths of an inch wide at the small end; that for lady fingers, three eighths of an inch; and the frosting tubes, of various sizes, some of them quite small. Fit the tube into the opening, and fill the bag with the mixture. Draw the edges together, and twist the top tightly to keep out the air. Hold the bag in the left hand, with the tube close to the place where the mixture is to be spread; press with the right, and guide the mixture into any shape desired. A slight pressure is sufficient. When no longer needed, wash the bags in cold (never in hot) water, and dry carefully.

Vanilla Sugar. — *One pound* of *lump sugar* and *one ounce of Mexican vanilla beans.* Cut the beans in small pieces, and pound in a mortar, with the sugar, till fine like flour. Sift through a fine strainer, pound the remainder again, and sift till all is fine. Keep in a tightly corked bottle. Use *a tablespoonful* for *a quart* of *ice-cream.* Or cut the beans into small pieces, and split them that the seeds may be exposed. Put *an ounce* of the *beans* in a small jar with *a pound* of *sugar.* Sift the sugar as required, and use as above; add more sugar, keep closely covered, and use as long as there is any flavor in the sugar.

Canned Fruit Juices. — Fruit juices may be kept for a long time by canning the same as whole fruit. They are convenient for water ices and summer beverages. Mash the fruit, and rub the pulp through a fine sieve. Mix about *three pounds* of *sugar* with *one quart* of *fruit juice* and *pulp*. Fill Mason's jars with the syrup, cover, and place in a heater with cold water to come nearly to the top of the jar. Let the water boil half an hour, then fill each jar to the brim, seal, and cool in the water.

To Mould Ice Cream. — Ice cream is more attractive, when served, if moulded, and if one has no fancy moulds, the freezer can will always give the round shape. If moulds are used, the cream should be packed into them closely, filling every crevice. The cover should always fit *over* and not into the mould. Bind a buttered cloth round the edge of the cover, or lay a buttered paper over the top of the cream, or coat the edge with butter or melted suet to fill all the crevices and keep out the salt water. Bury the moulds in ice and salt; a little less salt than is used in freezing. Cover the ice with wet carpeting. The cream will keep hard several hours, but it is well to examine it occasionally, and when the mould floats, draw off the water and add more ice and salt. When ready to serve, wash off the butter and salt from the mould, lift off the cover and paper, and turn the mould over a platter. The warmth of the room will soon melt the cream sufficiently for the mould to be lifted; if not, then lay a hot cloth on the mould, or dip the mould quickly in warm water. Salt water cannot get into the mould if full, but often when cream is left over and you replace it in the mould only partially filled, the water will get in.

To keep Lettuce, Celery, Watercress, etc. — Wash them and nip off any part that shows signs of decay. Rinse each leaf separately to be sure it is free from grit, lay the inner leaves, such as may be used for a salad in regular order in a wet napkin, and put them away in a cold place. Break up the tough outside leaves, and cook them until tender in boiling water, as you do any greens.

THE DINING-ROOM.

The subjects of "The Arrangement of the Table," "Dinner-Giving," and "Bills of Fare" have been fully treated in other cook books, and it would be difficult to add to what has already been said. Hints on garnishing, carving, and appropriate combinations of dishes have been given in connection with many of these receipts; and want of space forbids anything more than some general rules.

Above all things, attempt nothing in style or expense beyond what you can well afford. There is no more paltry ambition, nothing that contains more certainly the seeds of unhappiness and disaster, than such a desire for "empty show," which all sensible people must despise.

Let your breakfasts be of wholesome and substantial food. The system needs nourishment in the morning after the long, unbroken fast of the night. The practice of taking only a cup of tea or coffee with hot biscuit, and possibly pie or doughnuts, gives a very poor foundation for the morning's labor, which is and should be the hard labor of the day. Milk, coffee, or chocolate, mushes, fruits, potatoes or bread, meat, fish, or eggs, in some of their simple and digestible combinations should form the basis of the breakfast. The morning meal should be taken as soon as possible after rising. Any prolonged bodily exertion or exposure to the early morning air, before the stomach is fortified by food, is now condemned by the majority of physicians.

The midday and evening meal may vary with the occupations and habits of the family; but a regular hour for eating should be observed, whether the more substantial meal come at noon or night; and if at night sufficient time should be allowed for digestion to be completed before sleeping. A supper of cold bread and cake or pie is neither appetizing nor satisfying for those who have been hard at work through the day. " Something warm or hearty, something for a relish," every man craves for supper. Toast, brewis, warm tea-cakes, cocoa, oatmeal, warmed-over potatoes, cold meat, made dishes, eggs, oysters, etc., are far better than the common supper of sweets.

Every one may have clean, if not fine, table linen. An under covering of cotton flannel or felt made to fit the table is desirable, as it prevents noise, and a linen cloth may be laid over it more smoothly than over the bare table. Thin tablecloths remain fresh longer if stiffened slightly with very thin starch, but heavy damask requires no stiffening. Keep the cloths in a drawer large enough to hold them without much folding. Avoid making many folds in ironing, and in handling them fold always in the creases. In laying the cloth, place the centre of it in the centre of the table, and have the folds straight with the edges of the table. Crease the cloth round the edge of the table, that it may drape smoothly.

Lay a plate, right side up, for each person. If the table be long, place one plate at each end, and those at the sides opposite each other. Place the napkin at the left of the plate, and at dinner place a piece of bread between the folds of the napkin. Place the knives, butter plate, and tumbler at the right of each plate, the forks at the left, and the soup and dessert spoons in front, the handles toward the right hand, — the number of each depending upon the number of courses. The fruit dish or flowers should occupy the centre of the table; the salt and pepper, butter, jelly, pickles, etc., at the corners. Place the various dishes on the table in regular order, straight with the table, or, if at an angle, let there be some uniformity, never helter-skelter. The cups, plates, and dishes for hot food should be heated in hot water or in a warming-oven. Use a spoon to place ice in delicate glasses or pitchers ; or put in the water first, and then the ice, to avoid breaking.

Do not let the table become disordered during the meal. The dishes, plates, etc., should be removed noiselessly, one by one; and never piled one upon another, after the hasty fashion of second-class hotels.

If the serving be done by the host and hostess, it is more convenient for them to sit at the sides of the table; the host serving the substantial dishes, and the hostess the tea or coffee, vegetables or entrées, puddings, and the dessert. Where there are servants to do the waiting, the host and hostess may sit at the ends of the table, as there they can command a better view of their guests, and see that they are properly served. The hostess should serve the soup, salad, dessert, and coffee; the host, the fish and meat; and the servants, the vegetables and entrées.

At a dinner served *à la Russe*, the fruit and flowers only are placed upon the table, the several courses being served from the side.

Many volumes have been written upon table etiquette. Some of the suggestions they contain are practical; others useless. What is considered proper at one place or time is not approved under other circumstances; and those desirous of observing the usages of good society are often sorely perplexed to keep pace with the variations of fashion. But if, instead of following mere arbitrary rules from the low standpoint of " style," we would take for our guidance the best definition of true politeness as given by Dr. Watts, — " Love manifested in an easy and graceful manner," — we need never be at a loss as to " what to do and what not to do." A moment's observation will show the strictness of etiquette maintained in the family in which you may be a guest, — for instance, whether the servants are expected to take entire charge of serving everything, or whether the family reserve to themselves something of the happy privilege of courtesy and thought for each other; and you may forget with them, in the mutual interchange of the proper attentions, that freezing formality which sometimes forbids that you should seem to know or care how your neighbor fares. " Think not of yourself, but of what will contribute most to another's comfort or convenience," remembering that for the time being utter deference should be paid to the evident arrangement of the house at which you are. This is the safest standard for table etiquette, as well as for good manners everywhere. No selfish person can ever be truly polite. Children should be carefully trained in table manners as soon as they are old enough to come to the table, and accustomed to perfect politeness; then there will be no fear of mishaps, nor special training needed for " company," nor any awkward habits to be overcome in later life.

After a meal brush up any crumbs that may have fallen, lest they be trodden into the carpet. Collect the knives, forks, and spoons by themselves. Put any food that may be used again on small dishes, never on the dishes used in serving. Scrape the dishes, empty and rinse the cups, and pack neatly near where they are to be washed. Brush the crumbs from the cloth, instead of shaking it, then fold and put it away carefully.

Never pile nice china or any other dishes in the dishpan. Begin with a pan half filled with hot soapy water. Keep the soap in a shaker made for that purpose, or in a tin cup; make a strong lather in the cup, and use as needed. Never leave the soap in the dishpan to waste and stick to the dishes. Wash glasses first. Slip them in sideways, so that the hot water will touch outside and inside at once, and then there will be no danger of breaking from unequal expansion. Wash one at a time, and wipe instantly without draining or rinsing. Wash the silver and wipe at once. as it keeps bright longer if wiped out of hot soapy water. Keep a cake of silver soap at hand, and rub each piece of silver as soon as discolored. Then wash the china, beginning with the cups, saucers, pitchers, and least greasy dishes, and changing the water as soon as cool or greasy. Place these dishes in the rinsing-pan with the cups inside up and plates resting on the edges, that they may be scalded inside as well as outside, and drain quickly. Scald and wipe immediately.

" Dave's " method of washing dishes, though not in general use, has been proved satisfactory. Place a pan of cold water between the washing and rinsing pans. After washing and wiping the glasses and silver, add more hot water, and wash the china first in the hot suds, then dip each dish instantly into the cold water, and stand it on the edge to drain in the rinsing-pan. The cold water rinses off the hot suds, and the sudden change of temperature dries the dishes almost instantly; and they require little or no wiping. They will be neither " sticky nor streaky."

Where there is only one woman for " cook, waitress, hostess, .and kitchen girl," it is well, after the table is cleared and the dishes neatly packed, to wash first the kitchen dishes, and pots and kettles; then with clean water and towels wash and wipe the table dishes. The hands will be left in much better condition than when the pots and kettles are washed last.

The Care of Kitchen Utensils.

A complete list of kitchen utensils is not given in this work, as the variety and number needed will be largely determined by circumstances. There are several utensils, which are not perhaps in general use, which lessen the labor of cooking, and add much to the attractiveness of food prepared by their aid.

There is nothing that makes so much difference between ordinary and delicate cooking as a *set of strainers.* There should be one of *very fine wire* for sifting soda, spices, etc., and for straining custards and jellies; others with meshes from *one sixteenth* to *one eighth* of *an inch* in diameter; also a *squash strainer* and a *colander.* *Extension wire strainers* are very convenient. Keep also a supply of *strainer cloths,* made from *coarse crash* or *cheese cloth,* and *fine napkin linen.*

A set of *oval tin moulds,* a *melon mould,* and one or two *fancy moulds* are convenient for entrées, puddings, and jellies.

Other useful articles are *Dover egg-beaters*, large and small; ordinary small *wooden spoons* and the larger perforated ones; a *whip churn;* *granite saucepans* and *stewpans*, holding from half a pint to six quarts; *double boilers;* a *wire basket* for frying; a *potato slicer;* a *fine wire broiler* for toast, and two coarser ones for steak and fish; a set of *pastry bags* and *frosting tubes;* *fancy vegetable cutters;* a *glass rolling-pin;* and, above all, a small sharp-pointed *knife*, made from the best steel, for paring potatoes. turnips, etc., and a set of *tin measuring-cups* holding half a pint, and divided into quarters and thirds.

It is a mistake to have many large, unwieldy dishes. Small saucepans and small bowls are more convenient, and granite or agate ware is much lighter to handle and more easily kept clean than ironware. Buckets are convenient for keeping sugar and small quantities of flour. Glass jars or wide-mouthed bottles are best for nearly all groceries, such as rice, tapioca, meal, raisins, etc. They are easily cleansed, and the contents are plainly seen. They may be kept air-tight, or, if that be unnecessary, old jars not suitable for canning may be utilized.

A refrigerator should be examined daily and kept thoroughly clean. If a suitable brush cannot be had, a long stiff wire with a bit of cloth on the end should be used to clean the drain pipe. Pour boiling washing-soda water through it every other day, and do not forget to wash off the slime that adheres to the water pan. Fish, onions, cheese, any strong vegetables, lemons, or meat not perfectly sweet, should not be kept in the same ice-box with milk or butter.

Do not become wedded to the idea that dishes can only be washed in a sink. If your pantry or cookroom be some distance from your sink, and have a broad shelf or table in it, take your dishpan to the pantry, wash and wipe your dishes there, and in this way save a few of the unnecessary steps which soon amount to miles with many weary housekeepers.

Never wash a bread-board in an iron sink. The iron

will leave a black mark on the board, which it is difficult
to remove. Wash the board on the table where you have
used it; use cold water, and scrub occasionally with sand
soap. In scraping dough from the board, scrape with the
grain of the wood, and hold the knife in a slanting direction, to prevent roughening the surface of the board.
Wash, and wipe dry, and never let dough accumulate in
the cracks. Have one board for bread and pastry, and
keep it smooth. Use a smaller board for rolling crumbs
and pounding and cleaning meat and fish.

A Dover egg-beater should never be left to soak in
water, as the oil will be washed out of the gears and the
beater be hard to turn; or, if used again before it be dry,
the oil and water will spatter into the beaten mixture.
Use it with clean hands, and then the handle will require
no washing. Wipe the wires with a damp cloth immediately after using, dry thoroughly, and keep it well oiled.

All dishes should be scraped before washing. A small
wooden knife is best for this purpose. Bread and cake
bowls, or any dishes in which flour or eggs have been
used, are more easily cleaned if placed in cold water after
using, or washed immediately.

Clear up as you work: it takes but a moment then, and
saves much time and fatigue afterward.

Never put pans and kettles half filled with water on the
stove to soak. It only hardens whatever may have adhered to the kettle, and makes it much more difficult to
clean. Keep them full of *cold* water, and soak them away
from the heat.

Kitchen knives and forks should never be placed in the
dish water. Many err in thinking it is only the handles
which should not be wet. The practice of putting the
blades into a pitcher of very hot water is wrong, as the
sudden expansion of the steel by the heat causes the handles to crack. Keep the knives out of the water, but wash
thoroughly with the dishcloth, rub them with mineral soap
or brick dust, and wipe them dry. Keep them bright, and
sharpen often on a sandstone. The disadvantage and

vexation of dull tools would be avoided if every woman would learn to use a whetstone, and where and when to apply a little oil.

Milk will sour quickly if put into dishes which have not been scalded. They should first be washed in clear cold water, then in hot soapy water, then rinsed in clear boiling water, and wiped with a dry fresh towel. Do not forget to scrape the seams and grooves of a double boiler.

Ironware should be washed, outside as well as inside, in hot soapy water, rinsed in clean hot water, and wiped dry, not with the dishcloth, but with a dry towel. Dripping-pans, Scotch bowls, and other greasy dishes should be scraped, and wiped with soft paper, which will absorb the grease. The paper will be found useful in kindling the fire, and is a great saving of water, which is sometimes an object A tablespoonful of soda added to the water will facilitate the cleaning.

Kitchen mineral soap or pumice stone may be used freely on all dishes. It will remove the stains from white knife handles, the brown substance that adheres to earthen or tin baking-dishes, and the soot which collects on pans and kettles used over a wood or kerosene fire. Tins should be washed in *clean*, hot soapy water. Rub them frequently with mineral soap, and they may be kept as bright as when new. Saucepans and other tin or granite dishes browned by use may be cleaned by letting them remain half an hour in boiling soda water, then rubbing with a wire dishcloth or stiff brush.

A new tin coffee-pot, if never washed on the inside with soap, may be kept much sweeter. Wash the outside, and rinse the inside thoroughly with clear water. Then put it on the stove to dry, and when dry rub the inside well with a clean, dry cloth. All the brown sediment may be wiped off in that way, but a soapy dishcloth should never be put inside.

Keep a granite pan near the sink to use in washing vegetables, and use the hand basin only for its legitimate purpose. Pare vegetables into the pan, and not into the sink. A strainer or any old quart tin pan with small holes in the bottom is a great help in keeping a sink clean. Pour the coffee and tea grounds, the dish water, and everything that is turned into the sink through the strainer first, and then empty the contents of the strainer into the refuse pail.

Never use a ragged or linty dishcloth. The lint collects round the sink spout, and often causes a serious obstruction. A dish mop is best for cups and cleanest dishes, but a strong linen cloth should be used for everything which requires hard rubbing. Wash the sink thoroughly, flush the drainpipe often with hot suds or soda water, wipe dry, and rub with a greased cloth or with kerosene. Keep it greased if you wish to prevent its rusting.

Cremation is the most satisfactory way of disposing of kitchen refuse, both as a matter of convenience and for sanitary reasons. But if there must be other disposition made of it, keep two pails and use them alternately, cleansing each as soon as emptied.

Wash dish towels in cold water, with plenty of soap, and rinse thoroughly in cold water, every time they are used. If left to dry without washing, they will be sticky to handle and have a disagreeable odor. If the dishes be well washed, rinsed, and drained, the dish towels will require no rubbing. It is easier to take care of three or four which have never been left to become grimy than to wash one after it is stained and saturated with grease. Towels used in this way may be kept sweet and clean without boiling or drying in the sun. This method has been proved by years of trial

With a little care in observing these hints, and always using clean, hot soapy water (and not a liquid fit only for the swill cart), changing it as soon as greasy, dish-washing would be robbed of half its terrors. And after the work is done, if the hands be carefully washed with *Castile* soap, not with strong washing-soap, and wiped dry, no unpleasant effect upon the skin will be felt. Some use a little vinegar to counteract the effect of the alkali in the soap.

A large apron made like a child's tire, high in the neck, with long sleeves, and buttoned in the back, is the best pattern for a work apron. It protects the entire dress, and can be easily removed when one is called from the kitchen. Print or cambric with a white ground and small black figures wears better than colored print.

New, white mosquito netting and cheese cloth are useful for draining lettuce and for putting around fish, chicken, or vegetables which require careful boiling; also for bags for herbs and spices. Small squares of new cotton cloth are useful for wiping meat or fish. Keep them clean, and use for nothing else.

Keep a good supply of small holders, large coarse towels to use about the oven, and fine crash towels for wiping dishes. Keep a damp towel on the table when cooking, for wiping the hands. Avoid the habit of working with sticky or floury fingers, or using your apron for a hand towel or oven holder, or using the dish towels about the stove.

These suggestions are given by one who has always liked to wash dishes, and who thinks it not beneath the dignity of any woman to learn to do such work in the very best manner, and that no apology is needed for acknowledging a taste for this much-abused portion of domestic work.

To remove Iron Rust. — Keep a bottle of strong solution of oxalic acid, plainly labelled " Poison," in a handy place for use on washing day. Gather up the cloth round the spot of rust, and dip the spot in cold water, then in the acid, and then in rapidly boiling water, holding it in the steam a few minutes. If the spot does not quickly disappear, repeat the process. The steam seems to be necessary with the acid. Then rinse thoroughly.

AN

OUTLINE OF STUDY FOR TEACHERS.

FOOD:

ITS USES, CLASSIFICATION, AND PROPORTION.

WEBSTER defines food as " anything that supports and nourishes life."

The kingdom of nature is divided into *organic* and *inorganic* bodies. Organic bodies have life; inorganic bodies are without life. Organic bodies are composed of several reciprocal parts, each of which is necessary to, and dependent upon, all the other parts. Organic bodies, therefore, include *plants* and *animals*, and inorganic bodies include *earths*, *metals*, and *minerals*. Organic bodies spring from some parent or immediate producing agent; they are supported by means of nourishment, and die without it; they increase in size by the addition of new particles of matter to all parts of their substances. Inorganic bodies are formed by some chemical law or union, and grow only by addition to their surfaces.

Organic and inorganic bodies are continually wasting away or wearing out. Waste takes place in all objects, animate and inanimate. The minutest change in position in any plant, animal, or rock cannot be effected without some loss of substance. It has always been beyond the power of man to make anything that would not wear out. But there is this important distinction between organic and inorganic bodies. Only organic bodies can repair their waste, and add to their substance; they alone have life, or vital force. When anything wears out in a stone or a steam-engine, there is no power in the stone or the engine to replace the lost matter; and when a plant or an animal dies, the power of repairing waste is gone from it forever. Hence it is with *animate* bodies, or bodies endowed with *life*, that we have to do in considering the subject of food.

29

Life is that form of energy in creation that results in de-velopment from within the object. The energy may be purely physical, as in plants; or it may involve mental and moral considerations, as in animals.

There are some essential distinctions between the various forms of organic life. Animals grow proportionally in all direc-tions, and, at a certain time of life, attain their average size. Plants grow upwards and downwards from a collet only, and continue to grow through a term of existence. Animals feed upon organic matter, consume oxygen from the air, and throw off carbonic acid; plants feed upon inorganic matter, consume carbonic acid, and restore oxygen to the air.

Living plants or vegetables are, with few exceptions, fixed to the spot of earth from which they spring, and receive their nourishment from external sources. It is furnished them by the soil, air, light, and heat by which they are surrounded; and they are every moment receiving all that is necessary for their sustenance. If one of these essential conditions be withdrawn, death follows. Living animals have the power of *locomotion*, and, being obliged to wander, they are not always directly in contact with their sources of nourishment. They have, there-fore, a storehouse in which they lay up at intervals a supply of material. The possession of this stomach, or storehouse, characterizes all animal beings.

The changes that occur in animal life are more rapid and variable than those in vegetable life. Not being, like vegeta-bles, always in connection with their food, animals need some monitor to warn them when to seek it. This is provided them in the *appetite*, or the sensations of *hunger* and *thirst*. There is also a pleasure in the regulated indulgence of these sensations, which never fails to insure attention to their demands.

The vegetable kingdom is the original source of all organic matter. All our food is derived directly from the vegetable world, or indirectly through animals which have been nourished on vegetable products. The ox and sheep, which are consumed in the form of beef and mutton, have not fed on flesh, but on grass, hay, oats, and other grains. It is only under exposure to the sun's rays that plants will grow. Hence to its influence we must refer the production of food in the first instance, and therefore the sustenance of all life.

Life and growth in human beings are dependent upon two conditions, — motion and warmth.

Motion. — Our bodies are constantly in motion. The heart

and lungs move with every breath. Every thought causes some change in the brain. Whenever any part of the body loses its power of motion, it dies. All this motion, whether voluntary or involuntary, results in the gradual wasting away of the flesh, blood, and bones of which the body is composed. "We begin to die as soon as we begin to live." If the worn-out materials be not replaced, we die. One great object of food is to supply this waste. The demand for building material is greatest when the body is in a state of activity. Until the human body has attained its complete growth, there should be a constant supply of material for *new growth*, as well as for repair. In maturity, or when, from bodily inactivity, there is less waste; a smaller supply will suffice. Food taken at regular intervals supplies means of growth, and repairs the worn-out tissues.

Warmth. — The temperature of the living human body is about 98°. In hot or cold climates, in summer or winter, though the temperature of the external parts may vary, the internal temperature is the same; and if not maintained within a few degrees of this point, death invariably follows. The source of this animal heat, so independent of outside circumstances, must be from within. To keep up this internal heat or fire, a constant supply of fuel is necessary. This fuel is supplied by our food. To furnish material for growth and repair, and to provide fuel for the warmth of the body, is the twofold object of food.

Animal Combustion. — The process by which food maintains the motion and warmth of the body is a kind of combustion, and has often been compared to the combustion carried on in the steam-engine (see Youmans's Chemistry). We can have no combustion without oxygen; therefore *oxygen* is the first important element of food. The air is our great source of supply of oxygen, and a volume might be written on the necessity for pure air and perfect ventilation. We breathe oxygen from the air into our lungs, and exhale carbonic acid. There must therefore have been some internal union of carbon or hydrogen with oxygen, and such a union always produces heat. The *carbon* and *hydrogen* are obtained from our food, and are important elements. They are necessary for animal combustion.

Food is taken in a natural or in a prepared state, and, after undergoing certain processes of digestion and assimilation, becomes a part of our bodies for a time, and then is burned in the body, the process resembling somewhat the burning of wood and coal in our grates. But this union of carbon and oxygen, "instead of taking place in one spot and so rapidly as to be accom-

panied by light, as in the case of the grate fire, takes place in
each drop of the blood, and so slowly and continuously as not to
be noticed." The force and heat absorbed from the sun by the
vegetable in growing, and stored in its starch and sugar, are set
free, by the decomposition of the vegetable, into carbonic acid
and water again. These are given out, partly as heat, keeping
the body temperature at 98°; and partly in other forms, — in
that of mechanical motion, etc.

All the external or internal work of the body is done by
the force and energy of the food which is burnt therein. The
greater the amount of work to be done, the greater must be the
supply of fuel. The fire is constantly burning. "The smoke
passes out in exhalation, inhalation is the bellows to furnish
more oxygen," and food supplies the fuel. The kidneys are
the grates through which the ashes are removed But if we
are "a house on fire," why are we not consumed? Because,
lest this internal fire burn too freely, the oxygen of the air is
diluted with nitrogen, which is incombustible. The blood,
bones, and muscles of the body are composed largely of nitrogen, sixteen per cent of that element being present; and this
prevents the complete burning up of the structure. "What the
iron is to the stove, the nitrogenous tissues are to the body."
But the stove wears out in time, and so our bodies are constantly wasting away; and these nitrogenous elements must be
supplied by our food.

Food, to accomplish its purpose fully, should consist of these
four elements: *oxygen*, to support combustion, — obtained from
the air; *carbon* and *hydrogen*, to furnish fuel, — obtained from
water and carbonaceous food; *nitrogen*, to build up and repair
the tissues of the body, — obtained from nitrogenous food.

Food, in the form in which it is eaten, cannot sustain life.
It must be converted into a fluid that can pass through very
small channels into the blood. Then it must be mixed with the
air, and undergo certain changes, before it can replace the worn-
out elements of the body. To prepare food so that it can most
readily be assimilated, that is, made like our bodies, should be
the chief purpose in cooking. To do this, three things are
essential: 1st. The food selected should be of the right material, and properly proportioned; 2d. It should be cooked in the
most digestible and attractive manner; 3d. It should be adapted
to the various circumstances of age, occupation, climate, and
state of health.

Food, to be of the right material, should contain all the elements that our bodies contain. It is of primary importance, then, in studying food, to understand first the composition of the human body.

THE COMPOSITION OF THE HUMAN BODY.

Our bodies are made up of different materials: skin, flesh, blood, bone, etc. These consist of a large number of substances, called compounds; the compounds contain two, three, or four elements, united chemically in definite proportion. Some of these compounds are: *water*, which forms more than two thirds of the whole body, and is the common carrier of food into and through the system; *fibrine*, which is the chief solid material of flesh, and forms one tenth of the body; *fat*, a mixture of three compounds, distributed all through the system; *albumen*, and other nitrogenous substances, of which *osseine* in bones, *keratin* in the hair, nails, and skin, *cartilagin* in cartilage, and *hemoglobin*, which contains iron and gives the red color to the blood, are the most important. *Chloride of sodium*, or common salt, and other mineral salts of *potassa*, *lime*, and *magnesia*, are found in all parts of the body. These compounds are made up . of two or more separate and distinct elements.

There are sixteen elements in the human body, — oxygen, carbon, hydrogen, nitrogen, phosphorus, sulphur, chlorine, fluorine, silicon, calcium, potassium, sodium, magnesium, iron, manganese, and copper. Compounds only, not the separate elements, are capable of nourishing the body. Oxygen only exists as an element. Its office is to support combustion.

Combinations of two or more of these elements are found in the various articles used as food. It is quite important that our food should consist of various materials, containing elements similar to, or capable of being changed into, the elements of our bodies, of which the most important are: water, to help digestion and assimilation of food, and to help carry away refuse material; *salts*, to renew the mineral parts and replenish certain tissues; *carbon*, to furnish fuel for warmth; *nitrogen*, to build up and repair the whole structure.

For convenience the elements are classified chemically into *Non-Combustibles*, or inorganic compounds, including *water* and *salts; Combustibles*, or organic compounds, including *carbonaceous* and *nitrogenous foods*. Some foods contain no carbon, some contain no nitrogen, and some have all the elements in various proportions. Food has been classified into gaseous, or air; liquid, or water; and solid, including animal and vegetable foods. But the division into carbonaceous, or heat-producing, and nitrogenous, or flesh-forming foods, answers every purpose.

NON-COMBUSTIBLE COMPOUNDS

Water and Salts.

Water forms more than two thirds of the whole body. It is especially abundant in the blood and secretions. It gives them the necessary fluidity, and enables them to dissolve the important materials they contain. It is contained in all kinds of solid food, as well as in the liquids drunk as beverages. It is most abundant in fruits and vegetables. Every pound of perfectly dry food should be accompanied with four pounds of water.

Pure water is composed of oxygen and hydrogen, one ninth hydrogen and eight ninths oxygen by weight. The usual test for pure drinking water is that it be " free from color, smell, or taste, be soft, bright, and aerated, and free from all deposit." But it is very seldom found in that condition, as its power of dissolving other substances is so great that it nearly always holds animal, vegetable, or mineral matters in solution, obtained from the earth through which it flows. It also absorbs gases and odors from the air. The animal and vegetable substances found in it render it impure. But the mineral matters, unless in excess, are not objectionable.

When water contains more than a few grains to the gallon of carbonate of lime, it is termed hard water. When water is hard or impure, it should be boiled before being used for drinking, as this destroys the vegetable and animal impurities.

Water evaporates at all temperatures, boils at 212°, and freezes at 32° Fahrenheit. In freezing, the substances dissolved in water are expelled. Water, as it approaches the freezing-point, expands, and often bursts the vessels in which it is contained. In ponds or rivers it expands, becomes lighter, freezes, and floats on the surface in the form of ice.

Water is perfectly neutral. It combines with acids and with bases. It becomes sweet, sour, salt, astringent, bitter, or poisonous, according to the nature of the bodies it holds in solution.

Salts and other Mineral Matters. — The chief purpose of mineral ingredients is to replenish certain tissues, and aid in the transferrence and absorption of the combustible nutrients, as a scaffolding aids in the construction of a building.

Chloride of sodium, or common salt, is essential to the life of the higher animals. It exists in all parts of the body. It is more abundant in the blood than any other inorganic ingredient except water; but it is an active poisonous irritant if taken in excess, causing diseases of the mucous membranes, as in catarrh, and stiffening of the muscles, as in rheumatism. We take it as a natural ingredient in many kinds of food, and as a condiment to increase the relish of many others.

The desire for salt is instinctive. There are people who do not use salt in food, but it is probable that they obtain sufficient sodium and chlorine in the brackish water they drink; or it may be, their habits of life render less salt necessary.

Salt must be added plentifully to all vegetable food. The bad effects of a salt-meat diet can be counteracted by the use of lemon juice and fresh green vegetables, which are rich in potash salts.

Salt taken with our food supplies two substances. Its chlorine supplies the hydrochloric acid of the gastric juice, that helps digest our food; and soda, which is an element of the bile, — a fluid which must be added to the dissolved or softened food before the nourishment can be extracted from it. People would very soon become ill if deprived of salt. A person requires from one fourth to half an ounce of salt daily. The attractive flavor which is developed by cooking and adding salt to our food excites the secretion of saliva and gastric juice, and therefore helps digestion. The Dutch used to condemn criminals to a diet of unsalted food. They suffered great physical torture, which soon ended in death.

Salt is one of the most abundant of all minerals. It is obtained from springs by evaporation, and from natural mines. It is readily soluble in hot or cold water. It is used for packing and preserving meats, as it prevents putrefaction by absorbing water from the flesh.

The other mineral ingredients needed in the system are combinations of *lime, soda, potash, magnesia, sulphur, phosphorus,* and *iron.* Phosphorus, lime, and magnesia are found in meat, fish, the cereals, and potatoes. Potash is found in meat, fish, milk, vegetables, and the dry seeds and fleshy parts of fruits, iron, in flesh, vegetables, and nearly all food, in very minute quantities.

Sulphur is in fibrine, albumen, and caseine. There is sufficient saline matter, except common salt, in all the ordinary food we eat and the water we drink.

These mineral matters become rearranged and combined before becoming part of the body, but they do not undergo any chemical change or decomposition. They are absorbed with the food, and form for a time part of the animal tissues, after which they are discharged with the secretions, and replaced by a fresh supply. They are absolutely indispensable to the nourishment of the body.

COMBUSTIBLE COMPOUNDS.

CARBONACEOUS FOODS.

The first division of combustible compounds is called *carbonaceous* because they all contain carbon; or *heat-producing*, because by their burning they generate heat. They consist of starch, sugar, fats and oils, gum, and the softer fibres of plants. They are found in vegetables, cereals, fruits, milk, eggs, and the fat of meat.

Starch.

Starch is one of the most important of vegetable foods; it is found in grains, seeds, and roots, and in the pith and bark of plants. When pure, it is a snow-white, glistening powder. It consists of exceedingly minute grains, varying in size and shape in the different kinds of starch. These grains are covered with an outer skin which is insoluble and unchanged by cold water; but in boiling, this membrane bursts and the interior of each grain dissolves in the water, forming a thick, gummy solution. When cool, it stiffens into a kind of pasty mass.

Starchy food is very unwholesome unless properly cooked. It must be mixed with a sufficient amount of liquid, and subjected to a great degree of heat, that the grains may swell and burst. This liquid is sometimes supplied by the boiling water in which certain starchy foods are cooked; and sometimes by fat which melts with the heat, as in pastry, or by boiling fat, as in anything fried. When flour or starchy food is mixed with fat, it should be finely and evenly mixed, that the fat may penetrate every part of the flour, or else it will cake, and all the grains will not burst. Anything that helps to make pastry lighter and the fat more evenly distributed, causes the starch grains to burst equally, and makes such food more wholesome.

Vegetables should be put into boiling water to burst the starch cells, and set free the confined air, of which there is a great deal in many kinds. They should be taken up as soon as they are soft, as they absorb water after the grains are fully burst.

Starch in its uncooked, insoluble state is not digested by the human stomach. Seeds and fruits which consist of starch, especially if it be combined with oil, as in many nuts, if eaten uncooked, are very difficult to digest.

All starchy articles of food should be masticated thoroughly, and mixed with the saliva. It is more necessary to chew bread and potatoes well than meat. Starch is changed by various means into sugar. If an acid be added to it in a watery solution, and boiled, it becomes clear and transparent, and after a time all the starch disappears, and sugar takes its place. The same change is caused by the saliva, and during digestion the starch is all changed into sugar, so that none of it is found in the fluids and secretions of the body. This is easily seen by chewing pure starch; after a while it will become sweet

Starch contains no albuminous substances, and therefore cannot supply any of the materials of which our bodies are formed. But it is the source of the warmth of our bodies, and the strength we exert. Taken alone, it would be useless as an article of food. It must have the addition of albuminoid and fatty substances, like milk or meat.

Starch is prepared by grinding some vegetable matter that contains it in abundance, and mixing it with cold water. The water is strained and allowed to stand; the starch settles at the bottom, and is then dried and powdered *Cornstarch* is obtained from Indian corn, by a chemical process. The glutinous, oily elements are freed from the seed by alkaline solutions, and the starchy parts are ground and dried. *Sago* is starch from the pith of a species of palm-tree *Tapioca* is from the root of a species of the cassava plant of South America. It is a coarsely granulated substance. *Cassava*, or *mandioc*, is a more finely granulated form of the same root. *Arrowroot* is from the rhizoma, or rootstalk, of a West Indian plant. The natives use the roots of a species of the plant in extracting the poison of arrows; hence the name.

Sugar.

Sugar is composed of oxygen, hydrogen, and carbon. There are three kinds, — cane sugar, or sucrose; grape sugar, or glucose; milk sugar, or lactose.

Cane sugar as an article of food closely resembles starch, but it is soluble and therefore more easily digested. It is readily distinguished by its sweet taste. It is found in many animal juices and also in fruits, but exists mainly in vegetable juices which have little or no acid in their sap, like sugar cane, rock maple, and beet-root. In its natural state it is dissolved in the vegetable fluids, mingled with many other substances. It is obtained by crushing the raw material; the fluids thus obtained are heated with a solution of lime, which causes the impurities to separate and rise in scum. These are removed, and the purified juice boiled down until it solidifies as a brownish deposit. This brown sugar is again dissolved, boiled, and filtered through charcoal, evaporated, and crystallized. Molasses is the drainage of the raw sugar. Brown sugar is the first product. Granulated sugar is brown sugar refined and re-crystallized. All brown and moist sugars are inferior in quality; they contain water and mineral matter, and are sometimes infested by a minute insect. Loaf sugar is the purest.

Sucrose, or cane sugar, is changed, by the acids of the gastric juice and the nitrogenous matter of the food, into grape sugar, or glucose. One of the most remarkable properties of sugar is that it can be decomposed and converted into other substances by fermentation. In its chemical relations sugar ranks with acids, and combines with bases, as in sugar of lead. It melts at 320°, and by cooling forms a transparent amber-colored solid known as barley sugar. If heated to 420°, it forms a brown mass, called caramel. Sugar has great preservative powers, and is used in preserving fruits, hams, bacon, etc.

Glucose, or grape sugar, is abundantly distributed throughout the vegetable kingdom. It is found in honey, figs, grapes, and other fruits which have acid juices. It is less sweet than cane sugar, and is immediately absorbed into the circulation when taken into the stomach. It is less soluble and less easily crystallized than sucrose.

Lactose, or milk sugar, is obtained only from the milk of mammalia. It has the composition of cane sugar, and is converted into grape sugar when taken as food.

Fats.

Fats, or oleaginous substances, are composed of carbon, hydrogen, and oxygen, — the two former elements preponderating, — and, having a very strong affinity for oxygen, are highly combustible.

Fats are solid; oils are liquid. Fats may be changed to oil by a slight accession of heat, and are obtained from both animal and vegetable tissues, — suet and dripping, from beef fat; lard, from the fat of pigs; butter, from the cream of milk; olive oil, from the fleshy pulp of the fruit of the olive tree. Oil is also found in nuts, seeds, cereals, and fruits. Croton oil, used for medicinal purposes, is from a plant, a native of India; cod liver oil, from the liver of cod fish; castor oil, from the seeds of the castor-oil plant.

Fats and oils contain three different oleaginous substances, known as stearine, margarine, and oleine. *Oleine* is that portion of oil that causes its fluidity. It is more abundant in oils than fats, and in the fat of swine than in the harder fat of sheep or beef. Lard is better than mutton fat or suet for frying, because, having more oleine, it can be converted into a liquid sooner. *Margarine* is harder than oleine. It exists in human fat, in butter, and olive oil. *Stearine* is the most solid substance of the three, and is most abundant in tallow and suet.

The peculiar odor some fats and oils possess is from the presence of an acid. In butter it is butyric acid. Glycerine is the base common to all the fats. In stearine, the hardest fat, it unites with stearic acid; in margarine, a less solid form, with margaric acid; in oleine, or oil, with oleic acid.

" Fat forms the chief material of adipose tissue. It serves to fill spaces and give rotundity and beauty to the form, to equalize external pressure, to diminish the friction of the parts, to give suppleness to the tissues, and, being a non-conductor of heat, to keep the body warm. An undue accumulation of fat is a species of disease."

Oils and fats will not mix with water; but if an alkaline substance, like potash or soda, be added, the oil becomes separated into fine particles, and is held suspended in the watery fluid. This is called an emulsion, and this is what takes place in intestinal digestion. The gastric juice, being acid, does not digest fat, but only separates it from these substances, that it may digest the albuminous portions with which it is mingled. But the pancreatic fluid, being alkaline, resolves the fat into an emulsion. This completes the digestion, then the fats are absorbed and received into the general circulation. Having a strong affinity for oxygen, these fatty particles in the venous blood, when they come in contact with the oxygen of the air, burn, and heat is evolved. The power of fat in maintaining heat and activity is two and a half times that of starch.

Oils which are used as food are *fixed* oils. *Volatile* oils are found in many condiments and perfumes. Volatile oils can be distilled, or changed to vapor, and recondensed into their original form; they leave no permanent stain on paper. Fixed or greasy oils cannot be distilled; before changing to vapor they recombine into new compounds.

Gum, Mucilage, Pectose, and Cellulose.

These are combustible compounds, but are neither starchy, saccharine, nor oily Gum is found in apple and plum trees. Gum arabic is from a species of acacia, and is soluble. Mucilage is found in onions, quinces, and flaxseed. It forms a jelly with water, but does nót dissolve like gum arabic. Pectose is found in many roots, like the turnip; also in the pear and peach. When boiled with water it changes to a vegetable jelly, called pectine. Currants, pears, peaches, plums, contain pectine, and this is what gives firmness to the preserves made from them. Cellulose is the woody fibre of stalks of grain, the membrane which envelops the grains, husks, and skin of seeds, rinds, cores, and stones of fruits It is the main and almost the sole constituent of linen, and of the paper which is made from linen.

NITROGENOUS FOODS.

The second division of the Combustible Compounds is called *nitrogenous*, or *flesh-forming foods*. Nitrogen is the flesh-forming element common to all foods. It enters largely into the composition of the body, forming sixteen per cent of the animal tissue. A liberal supply is necessary to form and repair tissue. Although the atmosphere is four fifths nitrogen, we get no supply from that source. It must be supplied in a state of combination, not as an element, from such compounds as have been produced under the influence of life. We require organic nitrogenous matter, and not pure nitrogen. This is sometimes derived from vegetable sources, but is most

abundant in animal substances. Animal food is richer and
more nutritious than vegetable food; but the latter, if taken in
large quantities, yields the same amount of flesh-forming material. Nitrogenous substances in plants and animals are identical
in composition; and, from whichever source they are taken, the
most important consideration is, to digest them and make them
into blood.

Nitrogen is an essential part of some of our most powerful
medicines, like quinine and morphine, and of our most dangerous
poisons, such as strychnine and prussic acid.

Nitrogenous foods are also called *albuminous*, because albumen
is their common element, though it is called by different names
in different things. *Albumen* is from *albus*, meaning white. The
principal varieties of albuminous food are lean meat, fish, eggs,
milk, cheese, peas, beans, oatmeal, flour, rye, and corn. These
are treated more fully in other parts of the book, in chapters on
Bread, Meats, Fish, Eggs, Milk, and Vegetables.

The albuminous portion of meat is the juice, or albumen, and
the fibre, or fibrine. In eggs it is the white. In milk it is the
caseine, or the curdy part that separates when milk has soured.
In peas and beans it is called vegetable caseine. In flour it
is gluten, — the sticky, glutinous substance which is left after
squeezing or washing out the starch.

Albumen exists in two states, — one soluble in water and one
insoluble. The soluble may be changed to insoluble by heating
to 120°, or by adding nitric acid. It is the most easily digested
of all flesh-forming foods.

Albuminous substances have the property of *coagulation;* but
all albuminoids do not coagulate in the same way. The albumen
of eggs and the juices of meat coagulate by heating to the boiling-
point. The fibrine of the blood coagulates when exposed to the
air. Milk coagulates by the addition of an acid.

Albuminous substances also have the property of *fermentation.*
This occurs principally in substances which are rich in sugar,
starch, and gluten, like flour, milk, etc. The fermentation in
flour and milk is explained in the chapter on Bread-Making.

Fermentation will not take place without air or moisture, and
a moderate degree of heat. Therefore, if albuminous substances
be excluded from air and moisture, and kept very hot or very
cold, they will not ferment. Fermentation is a change in the
elements of a body composed of oxygen, carbon, and hydrogen.
Sugar is composed of carbon, oxygen, and hydrogen in equal
parts; when sugar ferments, it decomposes and then reunites in

different proportions, forming different compounds, — alcohol, carbonic acid, and water.

Albuminous substances are the only substances which putrefy. *Putrefaction* resembles fermentation, and is due to the presence, in large proportion, of the fickle element, nitrogen, and also to the large number of elements combined in all albuminous substances. Complicated machinery is always more easily deranged than simple; and in all chemical combinations, the more complex they are, the more unstable. Nitrogen has a very weak affinity for other elements, and forms very unstable compounds. All substances rich in nitrogen, when exposed to the air, soon pass into a state of decomposition, or putrefaction. The oxygen of the air has a greater affinity than the nitrogen for the other elements, and unites with them very easily. In putrefaction the oxygen unites with the carbon to form carbonic acid, and with the hydrogen to form water. The hydrogen and nitrogen unite and form ammonia, and this occasions the peculiar, unpleasant odor of all putrefying bodies. In substances rich in sulphur and phosphorus, the hydrogen unites with them and forms sulphuretted and phosphoretted gases which are very offensive. Therefore, if we exclude the air or oxygen from such substances, we can arrest decomposition. This is done by keeping them in air-tight vessels, thus removing the oxygen from the outside; and by boiling or drying, to remove that which is diffused within. Freezing will have the same effect; also salting or preserving. The salt draws out the moisture, hardens the albumen, and prevents the access of oxygen. In preserving, by the use of a strong solution of sugar, the watery juices are drawn out and formed into a thick syrup which excludes the air.

There are some albuminous substances, such as isinglass and gelatine, which are taken as food ; but, strictly speaking, they are not *flesh-formers*. *Isinglass* is obtained from the sound, or swimming bladder, of the sturgeon, and is imported from Russia. It is not actually gelatine, but is transformed into it by boiling water. *Gelatine* is obtained from bones. *Ossein* is that part of the bones to which their strength and elasticity are due. It is insoluble in cold water, but is slowly dissolved and changed into gelatine by being boiled gently under a pressure sufficient to prevent the escape of steam. Gelatine is also obtained from tendons, calves' feet, fish scales, stag's horns, etc.

There are other varieties of nitrogenous food which are also carbonaceous. These are commonly included under the general term *Beverages;* namely, tea, coffee, cocoa, and chocolate. The nitrogenous principle of tea is theine; of coffee, caffeine; and of chocolate, theobromine. Tea also contains iron and manganese.

Drinks, Beverages, and *Liquid Foods* are classified as follows *water,* including rain, well, and mineral spring water; *mucilaginous, farinaceous,* or *saccharine* drinks, including toast water, Irish moss, and barley water, sago, tapioca, arrowroot, and other gruels; *aromatic* or *astringent* drinks, including, tea, coffee, chocolate, cocoa, and herb teas; *acidulous* drinks, including lemonade, raspberry vinegar, and other fruit syrups; *animal broths,* or drinks containing gelatine, including soups, broths, and beef tea; *emulsive* drinks, including milk; *alcoholic* and *intoxicating* drinks, including wines, cider, beer, ale, porter, brandy, and whiskey.

Water is discussed under Non-Combustible Foods. Receipts for mucilaginous and acidulous drinks, animal broths, and herb teas are given in the chapter on Cookery for the Sick. The aromatic drinks are included in a separate article under the head of Beverages. Alcoholic drinks will not be discussed for want of space. Milk is food as well as drink, and deserves especial consideration.

Milk.

Milk consists of three distinct substances, which separate from one another after standing awhile, — the cream, curd, and whey.

The *cream* is the carbonaceous part, and forms ten or twelve per cent of the whole. It consists of very small globules of fat, or butter, invisible to the naked eye, surrounded by a fine membrane of caseine or albuminous matter. These are dispersed in the milk at first; but as they are lighter than the other parts, they rise to the top of the milk in the form of cream. When the cream is churned, the membrane of each globule is ruptured, causing the butter to cohere in a separate mass. If all this caseine, or albuminous matter, be not removed, the butter soon becomes rancid. The butter has more margarine than oleine, and is therefore hard and firm instead of fluid. It contains butyric acid, which gives it its peculiar flavor.

The *curd* is the albuminous part of the milk, which separates in a solid form whenever milk sours or curdles. This separation is occasioned by the action of the oxygen in the air upon the nitrogen in the caseine, causing a portion of the caseine to ferment. This ferment acts upon the sugar of the milk, and converts it into lactic acid; and this acid acts as any other acid would, and causes the sourness of the milk. The caseine is insoluble in water, but in the milk it is combined with soda, and this compound is soluble. So, when the milk sours, and a sufficient quantity of acid is formed, it seizes upon the soda, takes it away from the caseine, and forms lactate of soda. The caseine, being thus set free, shrinks, and gathers into an insoluble curdy mass. This separation is spontaneous; but it is often caused artificially, by the use of an acid, — usually rennet, which is the lining membrane of a calf's stomach. The curd thus separated is pressed and prepared in various forms of cheese. It contains the nutritious elements of the milk in a condensed, but somewhat indigestible form. Cheese is more digestible when made from fresh than from skimmed milk.

The *whey* is the water of the milk that separates from the curd in souring, and contains dissolved in it the sugar of milk and the saline and mineral ingredients. It is much better to use milk in its natural state than to use the butter or cheese obtained from it. It is the cheapest form in which animal food can be obtained, and should be used freely, especially by the young or weak.

Condensed milk, when well prepared, is convenient and valuable as an article of diet, if fresh milk cannot be obtained. It can only be made from pure milk, and is therefore perfectly harmless.

CONDIMENTS.

There is another class of foods, called *condiments,* which should not pass unnoticed.

Food that " tastes good " is digested more readily, and assimilated more perfectly, so that we really derive more nourishment from it. We use many articles with our food to make it taste better, which are not in themselves valuable as food. But by stimulating the flow of saliva and gastric juice, and enhancing the fine flavor of food, they increase the pleasure of eating, and render digestion more complete. These are called condiments. They are not necessary to persons of sound digestion, and, with the exception of salt, should not be used by children, nor by any one in large quantities. In perfect digestion there is the first taste in the mouth and the after-taste of the digestive organs which require satisfaction. "Any cook may gratify the first, but the second requires a skilled chemist."

The principal condiments aie salt, pepper, mustard, and some herbs, including mint, thyme, parsley, sage, marjoram, summer savory, and bay leaves; spices, including ginger, nutmeg, cinnamon, clove, mace, and allspice; and flavorings or extracts of lemon, vanilla, orange, almond, pineapple, etc.

Salt is the only condiment actually necessary to health (see page 453).

Pepper is a stimulant when taken in small quantities, but irritating if taken in excess. It is the dried berry of a climbing plant of the *piper* family. The whole peppers are called *peppercorns*. These peppercorns are ground, and we have *black pepper*. The outer shells are sometimes removed before grinding, and these kernels ground give us *white pepper*, which has a different flavor and is less pungent than black pepper. *Red* or *Cayenne pepper* consists of seed-vessels or pods of different species of *capsicum* ground to powder. It is stimulating, and far more wholesome than the black pepper, though not as much used. It is valuable as a medicine.

Mustard is used as a condiment and medicine. It is made from seeds of black and white mustard, which are crushed between rollers, and then pounded in mortars. In small quantities it is good for digestion. Both red pepper and mustard, if used sparingly with indigestible food, like lobster and baked beans, are very useful.

The *herbs* are used dried or green, and when used judiciously, make meats, soups, and sauces more palatable.

Spices are used in cakes and articles of food containing sugar, and sometimes with meats. They are used whole, ground, and in the extract. Ginger is the most healthful, and is often used in sickness. It is a valuable stimulating tonic in hot weather. The other spices are better when mixed in small quantities, less of clove and more of cinnamon being used. When combined so that no one spice predominates, they are pleasant to the taste. Care should be taken lest they hide the natural flavor of the food.

Flavors are all good in small quantities. Almond, vanilla, lemon, and pineapple are often adulterated. They should never be added while the article is hot, as the heat wastes the strength of the flavor. Vanilla beans are better than the extract. It is always well, if possible, to use the fresh fruit juice.

Lemon juice and *vinegar*, used in moderation, increase the solvent properties of the gastric juice, and are useful with meats and vegetables which are difficult of digestion.

30

PROPER PROPORTION OF FOOD.

These different kinds of food, *water, salts, sugar, starch,* **fat,** and *albumen,* must be combined in our diet; for a simple substance which fulfils only one of the purposes required in our food will not support life. A man cannot live on water or salt, yet he would soon die without them. A diet composed exclusively of fats, starch, or sugar is equally incapable of supporting life. The albuminous foods, though they are considered the most nutritious, must be combined with the others to produce the desired result.

Milk is the only substance prepared by nature expressly as an article of food. Seeds grow, and produce plants and fruits after their kind; but milk is prepared as the natural food of the young of all mammalia. A baby fed on milk develops in every part; therefore milk must supply every requisite for the growth of the young body, and the proportions in woman's milk may be taken as the standard for human food. Milk analyzed is found to contain water, salt, fat, sugar, and caseine, — the five elements of food. It has enough of flesh-producing elements to restore the daily waste, and enough heat-giving elements to feed the oxygen in breathing. But when the teeth are formed, the child's system needs a greater proportion of some elements than are supplied by the milk, and other foods are gradually added to the diet.

Eggs also contain all the necessary elements: a diet of seven eggs per day furnishes all the nutrition a person needs. But the elements in eggs are too highly condensed, and are not properly proportioned for a continuous diet.

Many articles of food do not contain all these elements, and it is very important to proportion our food rightly, so that one kind will supply what another lacks. A certain bulk is also necessary in our food to stimulate a thorough action of the digestive fluids. If the quantity be not sufficient to distend the stomach, so that the churning motion of the muscular coats can affect every part of the food, the digestion is imperfect. Dyspepsia is often caused by lack of sufficient quantity of food, and by weakness of the muscles of the stomach. If this requisite quantity be wholly nutritious or highly condensed food, capable of entire absorption, the effect is too stimulating, and serious disorders of the alimentary canal are the result. To remedy this, it is necessary to have a certain amount of innutritious food, which furnishes the bulk required, and gives all parts of the digestive apparatus their proper amount of work to perform.

Many persons argue in favor of a vegetable diet, as we can obtain from vegetables all the necessary elements. There have been many cases known where people lived to an extreme age who used exclusively a vegetable diet, and others who lived equally as long upon animal food. But the general rule is, that we find the highest degree of bodily and mental vigor only among those who make use of a mixed diet. One of the strongest physiological arguments in favor of this rule is found in the structure and conformation of the teeth and alimentary canal. Part of the teeth are of the carnivorous, or flesh-eating kind, and part of the herbivorous, or vegetable-eating kind. The alimentary canal is equally well adapted to the digestion of animal or vegetable food, or an admixture of both. The proper proportion, by weight, is one third of animal, and two thirds of vegetable food.

"Nature has given us an unerring guide to a proper choice of diet. An unperverted appetite is the voice of the physical system making known its needs, and it may always be trusted to indicate the food necessary to the preservation of health. But as the voice of nature is often unheeded, it is necessary to exercise intelligence in selecting our food and adapting it to the circumstances of life. By a proper choice we can often counteract the effects of a violation of nature's laws."

ADAPTATION OF FOOD TO CLIMATE, AGE, OCCUPATION, AND STATE OF HEALTH.

In examining the foods adopted by different nations and classes of people, we find that many choose instinctively the kind best adapted to their individual needs. The climate, occupation, and water influence their choice.

Climate. — Animal food is better for cold than for hot climates. We breathe more rapidly, take in more oxygen in cold weather, and the internal fire burns up more of the food. We exercise more, and this causes more rapid wearing out of muscle and flesh. Fat meat is not digested easily unless exercise be taken freely; more oxygen must be mixed with it to produce heat than is required for sugar and starch. In summer, when we exercise less, the waste is less, and we need less warmth giving food. The starch and sugar obtained from fruits and vegetables are easily digested, and furnish sufficient warmth. The Esquimaux or Greenlander consumes a large quantity of *fat*, or *blubber oil*, the most condensed form of carbonaceous food. This gives him the amount of heat necessary in an extremely cold climate. With this blubber he mixes some indigestible substances to give the needed bulk for the perfect action of the stomach. The people of Norway, Sweden, and Russia use large quantities of *oily fish*. In China, India, and other extremely hot climates, *rice* is the universal food. Rice contains a very small amount of flesh-forming material, being mostly starch, which is changed into sugar by the action of the saliva. The natives of rice-eating countries owe much of their lack of spirit and energy to this defective diet. But when eaten with butter or olive oil, and made into curries, pilat, and pilau, with a small amount of flesh or fish, it supplies all the elements necessary for life in such climates. The Spaniard in his *olla podrida* — a stew of peas, bacon, or fowl, with red pepper — finds all the necessary elements. The red pepper, used so largely in the curries and other dishes common to hot climates, stimulates the liver, which is naturally weakened by the long-continued heat, and thus assists digestion. The Arab chooses *dates, parched grains, mare's* or *camel's milk*. The Turk adds to these *melons* and *cucumbers*. As we come northward again, we find more flesh-forming material in the *polenta* (a dish made of Indian corn) and the *chestnuts, macaroni*, and *cheese* used by the Italians. The *pot-au-feu* is the principal dish of every peasant in France. This furnishes the cheapest form of nutriment, and contains all the necessary elements of food.

The *waters* of a country sometimes determine the national food. In Ireland, where the waters are strongly impregnated with lime, they furnish what the potato, which is richer in potash and soda, lacks. When potatoes are combined with cabbage and pork, as in *kolcannon*, the flesh-forming element is supplied; and this, on account of the cost of meat, the laboring classes are unable to obtain in any other form. In England and Scotland, where the waters are soft, oats and wheat, which are rich in phosphates, are the staple diet. When combined with milk, eggs, rice, peas, beans, bacon, and cheese, their food is complete.

To satisfy the natural instinct to obtain these five elements, we all prefer our bread with butter or cream, our meat with potatoes, our rice with butter, milk, or eggs; our fish we cook in fat; we eat liver with bacon and ham, or bacon with eggs;

we eat cheese with crackers, butter with cauliflower or cabbage,
salt with all vegetables, oil with salad, and fresh vegetables with
salt meat. Fruits and foods intended to be eaten raw contain a
large proportion of water. • This is supplied, when lessened by
evaporation, by cooking and soaking in water. In cooking
meats, we endeavor to retain all the juices, which are largely
water. In spring we crave fresh green vegetables and salads,
that we may have the *potash salts* of which there has been a
deficiency in the winter diet.

Occupation affects our choice of diet. Persons engaged in sedentary occupations cannot digest as much nor as easily as those
who labor out of doors. They should have food that gives the
greatest amount of nourishment in the smallest compass, and it
should be served in the most digestible form. Those who tax
their brains severely should have animal food and the most
digestible forms of starchy and warmth-giving foods. Those
who exercise freely in the open air may take a larger quantity,
and it need not be the most digestible, as they require food that
will stay by them. The laborer instinctively prefers potatoes
underdone, or "with a bone in them;" and he chooses salt
meat, not only because it is cheaper, but because it stands by
him longer. The salt causes him to drink water freely, and
this supplies the waste caused by excessive perspiration. A
diet of vegetables, peas, beans, cheese, oatmeal, bacon, and
the cheaper, more indigestible parts of meat properly cooked,
is suitable for laboring people.

State of Health. — In selecting food with reference to health it
must be remembered that there are certain general rules which
have been established by the best authorities through many ages
and in a great variety of circumstances; there are, however,
some exceptions to these general rules. Milk is considered a
wholesome food, yet there are some persons who cannot take it.
Cheese is a cheap and nourishing food for laboring people, but
there are some persons to whom it is an active poison. This is
also true of oysters and strawberries. These exceptions are
owing to some idiosyncrasy of the palate or weakness of the
digestive organs, and should be regarded only as exceptions,
which do not affect the general principle.

The application of these general principles, given throughout
this book in connection with the various articles used as food,
must be left to each individual; but to those who have given
the subject no serious study a few hints may be helpful. They
will be found in the article treating of Cooking for the Invalid. .

NOURISHING AND STIMULATING FOOD.

There is another classification of food which it is well to consider briefly. In its effect upon the system food is nourishing
and stimulating, or the reverse.

Nourishing foods are those which serve to develop perfectly
every animal function, but do not increase the strength and
speed of organic action beyond the point of full nutrition.
Bread, vegetables, fruits, sugar, salt, and water are nourishing
foods.

Nourishing and Stimulating Food. — All food that nourishes
the body is in one sense stimulating, as it gives renewed energy
to the bodily functions. But there are foods which impart a
speed and energy to the organs above that necessary to perfect nutrition; these are termed stimulating foods. Animal
food is of this class.

Stimulants. — Alcoholic drinks and condiments are classed as
stimulants, because they impart no nourishment, but act simply
as excitants to preternatural activity.

Innutritious foods are those which are not assimilated; which
are by nature indigestible, or have been made so by improper
combinations and modes of cooking. The bran of wheat, fried
or greasy food, heavy bread, and rich soggy pastry are either
entirely unassimilated, and therefore not nourishing, or they
weaken the system by exciting particular organs to excessive
action

DIGESTION.

IN studying digestion, it is well to keep in mind the twofold division of food into nitrogenous, or flesh-forming, and carbonaceous, or heat-producing, elements. The process of digestion differs with the character of the food. The purpose of digestion is to change and combine all the elements of food into a fluid which will mingle with the blood, become assimilated, and furnish nutriment for the body.

Digestion is not confined to the stomach. It begins with *insalivation* in the mouth, and, after *deglutition*, is carried on in the stomach and intestines, the process continuing through the entire length of the alimentary canal, — a tube varying in diameter, and thirty-six feet in length.

The first process in digestion, as in any chemical analysis, is to crush the materials. The *teeth* are the grinders for reducing the food. If we bolt our food or swallow it in lumps, the soft coats of the stomach are made to do the tearing and grinding work of the teeth. A solvent being necessary, the *saliva* is secreted from the blood, and is poured through three pairs of glands into the mouth, each pair supplying a different saliva. This softens the starch and tender cellulose. Animals, like the beaver, which feed chiefly on woody matters, have very large salivary glands.

In health the saliva is always alkaline, especially during and after meals. It lubricates the mouth, and moistens the food so that it may assume a pasty condition. It is also necessary to the sense of taste, everything being tasteless that the saliva cannot dissolve. For this reason we cook and season our food so that it will excite the flow of the saliva.

'(This saliva is poured into the mouth *not to be cast out,* but to do a specific work, then pass into the stomach and be again absorbed. If the system be drained of the saliva by profuse spitting, as is the case with those who use tobacco freely, the order of bodily functions is reversed, and the mouth is made to do the work of the kidneys, which is to carry away a large amount of the superfluous water and all the waste salts."

The saliva consists mostly of water, with a very small amount of saline matter and about five parts in one thousand of *ptyalin*, an albuminous ingredient, or ferment, which has the power of converting the starchy portions of food into sugar, and sugar into lactic acid, but does *not* act upon nitrogenous food. The saliva froths easily, and aids in carrying air into the stomach.

This is the first step in digestion, and the most important, as any error in the beginning leads to evil consequences which affect the whole process. It is also important, because it is wholly a voluntary process. While the food is in the mouth, we may masticate it thoroughly or imperfectly, and swallow or reject it. But when deglutition has carried it into the stomach, it is wholly beyond our control, and we are not responsible for the remainder of the process, only so far as it may be affected by error in the first stages. Bread, potatoes, and all starchy foods should be thoroughly masticated, and mingled with the saliva. Meat may be swallowed hastily, or knives may be made to do the work of the teeth in masticating animal food; but no chemist can prepare an artificial saliva to be mixed with starchy food, to save the trouble of chewing it. If a piece of dry light bread be masticated thoroughly, it will crumble and be quickly mixed with the saliva, and become sweeter the longer it is kept in the mouth. The alkaline saliva changes the starch into sugar, and begins the digestion. Try to chew a piece of hot bread and it at once assumes a pasty condition, which neither teeth nor saliva can penetrate, and is swallowed involuntarily. A piece of putty would not be more indigestible. If this experiment be tried, no other argument would be needed against the use of hot bread.

The *stomach* carries on the second part of digestion. The presence of food excites the flow of a fluid called the *gastric juice*, which is secreted in large quantities in the mucous membrane of the stomach. At the same time the muscular coats of the stomach contract, and produce a sort of churning motion, which carries the food round and round and over and over, exposing all parts of it to the action of the fluid. This gastric juice is always decidedly *acid* in its nature, containing hydrochloric acid. The lactic acid formed from the sugar in the mouth is also present in the stomach. This acid arrests the work begun in the mouth on the starchy foods, renders the alkali neutral, and acts only on albuminous food. It contains an albuminous ingredient, or ferment, called *pepsin*, in about the same proportion as the ptyalin of the saliva. The pepsin mixed with the lactic acid is powerful enough to dissolve all the albumen and fibrine of flesh food into albuminose, and sets free the starch, sugar, and fat, melts the fat, but does not change either. When there is an excess or deficiency of acid in the stomach, the digestion is abnormal. Pepsin is sometimes used as a remedy for dyspepsia, and is obtained from the stomachs of young, healthy pigs which are kept hungry.

As all food which is to nourish the system must be converted into a fluid form, any substances which are taken in fluid form and afterward solidified in the stomach, as blood or juice of flesh, milk, and raw eggs, must be changed again to a permanent liquid form before they can be absorbed. All nitrogenous matters are not only dissolved by the gastric fluid, but are modified so as to remain dissolved. These changed albuminous matters are called *peptones*. Oil plays an important part in these changes, so that, although oil is not digested, it serves a useful purpose in passing through the stomach.

The stomach would digest itself were it not protected by a sheathing of mucus and by a continual forming of cells called *epithelium*, during the process of digestion. The liquid or watery portions of food enter at once into the circulation by absorption. If too much water be taken with food, it dilutes the gastric juice and retards the digestion; as all that is not needed must be absorbed before digestion can go on.

Digestion is also retarded by the presence of very hot or very cold food, as everything taken into the stomach has to be changed to the normal temperature of 100′. A large amount of food overloads the stomach, distends the muscular coats, and lessens the power of motion. Too little food is also a mistake, as the stomach needs a certain amount of bulk to work upon. Continual or irregular eating is wholly contrary to the intention of nature, since it does not allow the stomach time to rest and to form new cells to secrete digestive fluids. Flesh food that is finely minced, like hash, croquettes, and many entrées, passes rapidly through the stomach without being dissolved by the gastric juice; but when taken in larger pieces it remains long enough to be all digested.

The digestive power of the stomach is weakened when there is any undue action in any other part of the body, as in great muscular exertion or in powerful excitement of the brain. Therefore we should eat sparingly at first, when fatigued by exercise or study or when unduly excited, and should rest awhile after eating.

Lactic acid, small portions of sugar and digested nitrogenous substances, pass into the blood by absorption through the stomach veins. Thus the contents of the stomach leave it in two directions: a portion is absorbed through the coats of the stomach by the process of osmose, or the passage of fluids through animal membranes; the remainder passes through the pyloric opening into the duodenum and intestines for the completion of digestion. Food from the stomach enters the duodenum in an *acid* state, and in the intestines is mingled with three *alkaline* fluids, all containing soda.

The *pancreatic fluid*, secreted from the pancreas, digests the fatty matters. It breaks the large granules of oil and fat into a great many minute particles, and converts them into a milky liquid called *chyle*, which mixes freely with water and passes through the tissues of the intestines into the lacteals. It also changes the starch into sugar, and the sugar into lactic acid, but has very little action on albuminous substances.

The *bile*, secreted from the liver, plays an important part in intestinal digestion, the exact nature of which is unknown. Bile is a complex liquid, consisting of biliary acid in combination with soda. It certainly aids in the absorption of fat, and many suppose its purpose is to lubricate the walls of the intestinal canal; from its soapy consistency it effects a smooth, nonirritating passage of the contents. If there be any lack or surplus of the bile, it soon produces an injurious result in the system. The bile is in the intestines, and not in the stomach except when the action of the stomach is inverted, in nausea and vomiting; then the bile is forced up into the stomach instead of down into the intestines.

The *intestinal juice*, secreted in the mucous membrane the entire length of the intestine, combines the active and digestive powers of all the other secretions.

The lactic acid is formed so rapidly from the digestion of sugar that the contents of the intestine quickly becomes acidulous, and this completes the digestion of any portions of nitrogenous food not fully digested in the stomach. The combined amount of the salivary, gastric, pancreatic, biliary, and intestinal fluids secreted daily is twenty-one pints, of which the gastric juice forms more than one half. There are mechanical aids to intestinal as well as stomach digestion. The writhing, worm-like motion, or peristaltic movement, of the muscular coats of the intestines forces the food downward, and exposes all portions of it to the digestive fluids.

Notwithstanding all these powerful agents in digestion, a portion of useful matter passes through the intestines unchanged; and if there be a deficiency of either fluid, or a weakness of the muscular coats, or too great a quantity of irritating substance, like cellulose, woody fibre, bran, etc., the amount is increased. This is carried, with the innutritious portion, into the larger intestine, and forms a part of the excretions.

ABSORPTION.

The nutritive and perfectly digested portions of food are absorbed partly by the veins of the stomach, entering at once into the circulation, and partly by the intestines. The lining membrane of the intestines folds over and over upon itself, like a ruffle, along the entire edge; this is full of little tubes, or *villi*, which absorb the chyle.

The blood vessels absorb the nutritive elements from the villi and carry them to the veins in two ways: 1st. Through the portal vein into the liver, where it penetrates every part of the liver, then passes out through the hepatic vein into the veins near the heart; 2d. Through the lacteals, which are attached to the lining membrane of the intestines and empty into the thoracic duct, a tube extending along the spine, and then into the subclavian vein, which lies in the left side of the neck, under the collar bone. The veins also bring with them the lymph, — a thin colorless fluid which comes from the absorbent vessels situated all over the body, and which contains the worn-out particles.

Then the venous blood, supplied from the lacteals with new material, and from the lymphatic vessels with waste materials, enters the heart through the upper-door, or right auricle, passes through the valves down into the right ventricle; out through the pulmonary artery into the lungs, where, as purple venous blood, it penetrates to the most remote capillaries.

If the lungs be full of pure fresh air, the oxygen changes the purple blood into red blood, and burns up the impurities. The waste products of the combustion of carbon and hydrogen are expelled from the lungs at every breath in the form of carbonic acid and watery vapor; and not until now can the new elements in the blood, obtained from the food, become in reality food, or perfect blood.

This oxygenized or vitalized blood now returns from the lungs, and enters the heart through the left upper door, or left auricle; the valves open and allow it to pass into the left ventricle, then out through the aorta, or great artery, from which the arteries carry it to the capillaries all over the system.

In the capillaries the new material is deposited wherever needed, and changed by cell growth into new tissue. The lymphatic vessels take up all that is not needed, with the worn-out portions; and the veins then carry this impure blood back again to the lungs and heart.

Thus a continuous circulation is established, the blood coursing over the whole body once in every three to five minutes, the time varying with the amount of exercise and the state of health. During this circulation the combustible compounds are burned by the oxygen received into the blood in the lungs, the carbonaceous products of combustion are expelled through the lungs as carbonic acid gas and watery vapor, and the nitrogenous products through the kidneys in the form of urates.

" This process of digestion and absorption is really a kind of preliminary cooking process, going on from the mouth downwards all the way to the colon; and from every part of the long canal tiny lacteals and absorbing veinlets carry off contributions of food either to the general store of chyle, or to the venous blood which is hurrying back to the heart."

NUTRITION.

" Albumen is the basis of all animal nutrition. This is seen in the bird's egg during incubation. Under the influence of warmth and oxygen, all the tissues, membranes, and bones are developed from albumen."

In the human body a nutritious fluid is prepared from the food, and supplies materials for growth and repair. This fluid is the blood, and when examined under the microscope is found to consist of a clear colorless fluid, of a saline, alkaline, and albuminous nature, and an immense number of infinitely minute blood globules, or corpuscles. These corpuscles consist of an albuminous membrane called globulin, filled with a red coloring matter, hematine, in which there is much iron.

This liquid albuminous portion of the blood must be changed to fibrine before it can nourish the muscles of the body. The change of the gluten, caseine, and all the varieties of albuminous food into fibrine is a gradual process, begun in the lacteals, continued in the circulation of the blood, and completed in the lungs by the oxygen which they receive in breathing. This fibrine remains in the liquid state, owing to the alkaline nature of the blood, and is distributed by the circulation into all parts of the structure, where it gradually coagulates into a network of tough thread-like fibres, enclosing in its meshes the blood corpuscles, and is changed by cell growth into new tissue, solid flesh and bone.

The nervous system is also built and repaired from albumen. Nervous matter is about seven per cent albumen, and is the material by which we are put into relation with the external world. By it we see, hear, feel, taste, smell, and are conscious of existence.

Each elementary cell or particle of tissue, whether of bone, flesh, or nerves, seems to have a sort of gland-like power, not only of attracting materials from the blood, but of causing them to assume its structure and participate in its properties. The bones and teeth select and appropriate the phosphates of lime, and magnesia, also fluorine. The muscles and nerves take fibrine, phosphates of magnesia, and potash. The cartilages seek for soda; the hair, skin, and nails are made up of silica. Iron is needed in the coloring matter of the blood, the black pigment of the eye, and in the hair. Sulphur exists in the hair, and phosphorus in the brains. The glands of the mouth take the substances necessary to form saliva; those of the eye, the elements of tears; the coats of the stomach, gastric juice; and the liver, bile. Each part of the body has the power to select, from the common supply, the material which suits it best for building and growing.

If the conversion of albumen into fibrine be incomplete, the tissues are imperfectly nourished. The formation of tubercles in the lungs is caused by half-formed cells and coagulated albumen deposited in the lungs. This is caused by a deficiency of the oily matter, which is necessary for the perfect formation of cells and the growth of healthy tissue. Hence for these cases physicians prescribe cod-liver oil.

Distilled spirits coagulate the albumen which ought to go into the blood; this prevents the proper digestion of food, and causes one of the great evils resulting from their use. The nervous tissue is thus deprived of nourishment, which is one of the causes of delirium tremens.

Every twinge of pain in neuralgia is the nerves crying out for better blood. Imperfect digestion and assimilation of food are the chief causes of neuralgia.

Nutrition, though seemingly complex, is really a simple process; albumen is changed to fibrine, and fibrine to flesh. The relation of each to the other has been aptly compared to that of the raw cotton, the spun yarn, and the woven fabric.

The minute corpuscles in the blood are constantly building up the body, very much as the coral insect builds its structure. The work of each corpuscle is too small for our conception; but, taken in the aggregate, the result is the wonderful growth and renovation of the human body. And what is still more wonderful, every organ of the body is on the alert to keep the whole system in natural health. The activity of the vessels which remove the waste particles from the blood is untiring. The kidneys are the scavengers of the body, and stand next to the lungs in renovating it. If too much water be drunk, the kidneys, lungs, and skin carry it off, for fear that the blood should become too watery. We may cease to convey food into the body for days with no evil consequences; but let the removing organs cease operations for a single day, and disease ensues.

LIFE AND MOTION.[1]

Circulation of Water. — As a plant grows, water from the soil or air unites chemically with carbon, and forms the woody fibre of the stem, the sugar of the sap, and the starch of the seed. When the plant dies, the water is again set free from its structure and passes into the air. The starch and sugar, also, which the plant yields having been consumed by some animal, the water which they contain passes into the air through the lungs and skin. Thus the same water is caused to revolve in a circle of life-sustaining combinations. Within a single hour it may be in some vegetable structure in the form of sugar; then it may pass into and circulate through some animal system and be discharged as vapor from the lungs, and afterwards become

[1] This article is mainly an abstract of the chapters on the "Circulation of Matter," contained in "Johnston's Chemistry of Common Life." It is inserted here as bearing upon the general subject of food, and with the hope that all who read this will read the original.

absorbed by thirsty leaves and aid in the growth of flowers and fruits.

Circulation of Carbon. — Vegetables, which are largely starch and carbon, absorb carbonic-acid gas from the atmosphere, which contains thirty-three grains of carbon in every square inch. If the world were all dry land, and covered with dense vegetation, all the carbon would be extracted from the atmosphere in twenty-three years. This carbonic acid is restored to the atmosphere by the waste and decay of vegetable matter, by the exhalations from animals, and by combustion.

The leaf of a living plant draws in carbonic acid gas from the air, and gives off the oxygen contained in it, retaining only the carbon. The roots drink in moisture from the soil; and out of the carbon and water contained in it the plant forms starch, sugar, fat, and other substances.

The animal takes the starch, sugar, or fat into its stomach, and draws in oxygen through its lungs. New chemical combinations are thus formed, undoing the work of the plant, and sending back to the air, from the lungs and skin, both the starch and oxygen, in the form of carbonic-acid gas and water. The same material is constantly circulating, — now floating in invisible air, now forming the substance of the growing plant, now of the moving animal, and now diffusing itself through the air ready to go its round again. It forms part of a vegetable to-day; to-morrow it is in a man's backbone; a week hence it may have passed through another plant and into another animal.

In burning coal, we cause its carbon to unite with the oxygen of the air and to disappear as carbonic acid gas. The carbon returns to the atmosphere from which it may have been taken millions of years ago when it was appropriated by the growing plants, which, in the form of vegetable matter, were afterwards buried beneath the surface of the earth only to reappear ages subsequently in the form of fuel. The earth itself breathes out carbonic acid, sometimes with water, sometimes alone. It sparkles in the springs of Carlsbad and Seltzer; it kills man and beast in the terrible " Valley of Death " in the island of Java.

In this way is supplied the loss of that which is daily buried by the shell fish and coral insects in the limestone formations and coral growths. These rocks contain, chained down in seemingly everlasting imprisonment, two fifths of their weight of carbonic acid.

Circulation of Nitrogen. — Gluten and fibrine are distinguished from starch and fat by containing nitrogen. The nitrogen forms four fifths of the air. It exists also in ammonia, and in aqua fortis, or nitric acid. These two compound bodies exist and are found in the soil; and from the soil the nitrogen is taken up by the plants, and gluten is formed. When the animal consumes the gluten, it builds up and renews the waste of its several parts. The gluten of the plant is transformed into the flesh and tissues of the living animal. Thus the nitrogen of the soil through the plant has reached the dignity of being a part of breathing, intellectual man.

Having reached this form, this restless element, nitrogen, grows weary of inactivity and moves on. Not only the living body as a whole is in constant motion, but even its minutest parts are continually active. "They are like the population of a great city moving to and fro, coming and going continually, weeded out and removed every hour by deaths and departures, yet as unceasingly kept up in numbers by new in-comers, changing from day to day so insensibly as to escape observation, yet so evidently that after a few years scarcely a known face can be discovered among the congregated thousands." Scarcely has the gluten of the plant been fitted comfortably to its place in the muscle, the skin, or the hair of the animal, when it begins to be dissolved again and is removed.

The living animal absorbs much oxygen from the air by its lungs. One part of it converts the carbon of the food into carbonic acid; another portion is built into the substance of the body; a large part is employed in dissolving and removing the waste in urea, uric acid, etc. This urea and uric acid return to the soil from which the nitrogen they contain originally came, and where they are reconverted into ammonia, nitric acid, and other substances, and are now ready to enter into new roots and go the rounds again.

The undigested gluten is rejected in the animal droppings, mingles with the soil, and is changed to ammonia and nitric acid. The vegetables which die undergo natural decay, and again enter the soil and air as elements. Animal bodies themselves die at last, and the nitrogen they contain is made to assume the forms in which plants are able to take it up. The ammonia and volatile compounds of nitrogen, produced by animal and vegetable decay, rise in the form of gas or vapor, and escape into the air. The rains of heaven wash the ammonia out and bring it back to the earth. Part of it is, however, resolved into elementary nitrogen, and is thus lost to plants. To make up for this loss, nitric acid is formed in the air in small quantities.

Through the agency of the electric currents the oxygen and nitrogen of the air unite to form nitric acid. Ammonia is given off by volcanoes, and is returned to the earth by the rains and snows.

Circulation of Mineral Matter. — Everything which the animal body contains is derived, directly or indirectly, from vegetable foods; and the mineral or ash it leaves, when burned, must have come from the soil through the plant. When the animal dies, its body sooner or later returns to the soil. So we have another circle in which the earthy matter of animals and plants moves. It ascends from the soil to the plant, then to the animal, and back again to mother earth, so that it is really "dust to dust."

The plant does not absorb all mineral matters, but selects the rarer and more precious materials from the soil, and such as are held in solution by water. Phosphoric acid, lime, magnesia, and saline matter, of which common salt is a representative, are the principal substances chosen. The animal eating the vegetable, these substances enter its stomach, and are dissolved and enter the blood. The vessels provided for the purpose select the required material, and, like ships in commerce, sail away on the blood rivers to their destined havens. The saline portion is carried to the blood and tissues. The phosphate of lime goes to the bones, and phosphate of potash to the muscles After a time the animal, partly as it wastes and finally when it dies, returns to the soil all that the plant took from it. New plants receive it, and it goes the rounds again.

So, over and over again, as the modeller fashions his clay, plant and animal are formed out of the same material. Is all senseless matter to be constantly working, and are we intelligent beings to idle away a precious but limited existence? One should learn from this always to work for a definite purpose.

How lovely is the plant in its position of bond-servant of man! How willing and interesting! It serves till death, yet rises again rejoicing as ever, when spring returns, to renew its destined toil.

The least alteration in the natural constitution of things would insure the extinction of animal and vegetable life.

RECAPITULATION.

The Plant takes in, *water*, by its roots; *carbonic acid*, by its leaves; *nitrogen*, in the form of ammonia and nitric acid; *minerals*, in the form of phosphoric acid, lime, common and other salts, from the soil.

The Animal takes in, *water*, *starch*, *fat*, *gluten*, and *mineral matters*, in the form of vegetable and animal food, into its stomach; and *oxygen* into its lungs.

The Soil takes in, *urea* and other animal excretions, *dead animals* and *plants*.

The Plant produces, *oxygen*, from its leaves; *sugar, starch, gluten*, and *mineral matters*, in its sap and solid substances.

The Animal produces, *carbonic acid* and *water*, which are exhaled from the skin and lungs; *urea, phosphates*, and other salts, in the excretions; the *fat* in the body, which is in time breathed away in the form of carbonic acid; *water* and perfect *muscle, bone, blood*, and *tissues*, to build and repair the body.

The Soil produces, *carbon* in the form of wood and coal, and in spring water; *ammonia, nitric acid*, and other *nitrogenous compounds; phosphoric acid, lime, common salt*, and other *mineral matters*.

So the movement is circular; the beginning is the end. A marvellous commerce appears; soil, plant, and animal commingling; the elements of each being at different times the elements of all, and their interchange perpetual.

ADDITIONAL RECIPES.

Reception Chocolate.	2 qts. milk. 1 lb. cocoa powder. 3 rounded tbsp. white sugar.	1 pt. cream. 2 eggs. 3 tsp. vanilla extract.

Bring milk to boil, work the cocoa in a little of the cold milk, then stir into the boiling milk till smooth. Boil ten minutes, add the sugar and cream, and stir well while boiling. Turn into a double boiler and keep the water in lower boiler almost at boiling point for half an hour. Then beat the eggs very light, add them and remove immediately from the fire. When cool add the flavoring.

This can be made in the morning, and when ready to serve, put from one to two tablespoonfuls of the preparation into the cup and fill with boiling water.

By cooking the cocoa we have a much more delicious flavor than that obtained by pouring boiling water directly upon the raw cocoa in the cup. The eggs and cream give body and richness. It will serve from sixty to eighty people.

Church Sociable Coffee. — If we follow the proportion of *one rounded tablespoon* or *one-half ounce* of *coffee*, ground, for each half-pint cup water, we must allow one pound of coffee for eight quarts of water. This will make coffee of medium strength and will be sufficient for about thirty persons.

Soak the coffee one hour in two quarts of cold water in a tightly covered jar and then turn it into a cloth bag. Have the requisite amount of water in a large boiler with a tight cover, and when just ready to boil, put in the bag of coffee and the water in which it soaked, and let it boil ten minutes.

Handy Coffee. — Put *six rounded tablespoonfuls* of *coffee* in a hot coffee-pot or biggin, pour through it *one quart boiling water.* When all dripped through, pour the liquid through the grounds again, and after this second filtering let it come to the boiling point and then bottle tightly. When coffee is wanted, scald *three-fourths cup* of *milk,* heat *two tablespoons* of the *bottled coffee* and pour the two over the *sugar* in a hot cup.

Quick Rolls. — Dissolve *three yeast cakes* in *one cup* of *water,* add *one pint* of *milk* scalded and cooled, *one teaspoonful* of *salt,* *one tablespoonful* of *butter,* and *two teaspoonfuls* of *sugar.* Stir in flour enough to make a stiff dough, then knead it half an hour, being careful not to get it too stiff. Then without waiting for it to rise, divide it into equal portions for small rolls, and shape into balls and then into finger rolls, or press a small knife handle or roller through the middle, making cleft rolls, or it may be rolled with the hands into four long rolls. Put the rolls in a greased pan, cover with a cloth, let them rise about forty-five minutes. Then bake in a quick oven from twenty to forty minutes according to the size. Do not stop kneading until the time is up, or let the dough stand before shaping. If the dough is disturbed after it begins to rise, it will be difficult to avoid having very large air holes. The idea is to make the dough light quickly by the large amount of yeast, rather than to exhaust the strength and elasticity of the flour by slow rising. Thus in less than two hours you will have bread or rolls that will surprise you by their lightness, fine texture, and rich nutty flavor. Not a trace of the yeast in the bread; light, and yet unlike the extreme lightness of the usual yeast rolls, a rich crust that looks hard but proves to be soft and tender, and with none of the dry, chippy flavor common to bread raised over night.

Zwieback, No. 1. — Scald *one cup milk*, add *half a tea-spoon salt*, and when cool dissolve in it *half a cake* of *compressed yeast.* Stir in flour to make a batter that just drops from the spoon. Let the bowl stand in a pan of warm (not hot) water, and when the sponge is full of bubbles add the following mixture : *Two rounded tablespoons butter* creamed with *quarter cup sugar*, and *two well beaten eggs.*

Add more flour, and when stiff knead it until smooth and light. Let it rise until double its bulk, then shape it into finger rolls and place them close together in a shallow pan. Let them rise again until very light; then bake in a hot oven about half an hour. The next day, or when thoroughly cold, cut the loaf in half-inch slices and let them stand in a very slow oven until colored and dry all through.

Zwieback, No. 2. — Scald *one cup milk;* when luke-warm, dissolve in it *two yeast cakes, half a teaspoon salt*, and *flour* enough to make a soft dough. Let it rise until light, then stir in *quarter cup melted butter, quarter cup sugar*, and *two eggs* unbeaten. Mix thoroughly and add enough more flour to shape it into a loaf. Let it rise in the pan until very light; then bake in a quick oven, and when nearly done brush over with sugar dis-solved in milk. When cold cut in half-inch thick slices and let them color and dry in a moderate oven.

Gold Medal Corncake.	½ cup yellow gran corn meal. 1 cup flour. ½ tsp salt. 2 scant tsp. baking powder.	2 tbsp. sugar. 1 egg. 1 scant cup milk. 1 scant tbsp. butter melted.

Mix the corn meal, flour, salt, and baking powder thoroughly, beat the egg and add it to part of the milk, then add to the dry mixture, and add the butter last.

Bake in a hot oven twenty-five or thirty minutes.

Quick	1 pt new milk.	1 heaped cup coffee-
Raised	3 cakes Fleischman's	crushed sugar.
Doughnuts.	yeast.	½ cup butter.
(*E. E. Squire.*)	1 level teasp. salt.	½ a nutmeg.
		2 eggs.

Make a sponge of the milk warmed, the yeast and salt. When very light, add the butter and sugar creamed together with the thoroughly beaten eggs, also the nutmeg and sufficient bread flour to make a dough that will mould without added flour, but not too stiff. Mould one-half hour on a warm board, then roll out one-half inch thick, cut with a small biscuit cutter and arrange half an inch apart on the warm board and place near the range till light. Then fry slowly, roll in powdered sugar while hot if you prefer. This makes three dozen.

If a plainer rule is desired, omit one egg and use one-third cup of butter, the remainder of the rule the same as above. Be. careful that at any time before frying they do not get too warm.

Doughnuts. — Rub a *teaspoon* of *butter* into a generous *cup* of *sugar*, add *two unbeaten eggs* and stir thoroughly; add *one scant cup* of *milk.* Mix *four level teaspoons* of *baking powder* in *two cups* of *sifted flour*, and stir into the mixture. Then add more flour till soft as can be rolled out, one-third inch thick. Cut in rings and fry in clean hot fat. Test the fat by dropping in a piece of the dough, which should rise at once to the top with a good deal of ebullition and begin to brown at once. Turn only once.

Buckwheat Cakes. — Mix over night, *two cups buckwheat, one cup Graham flour*, and *one level teaspoon salt.* Stir in *warm water* for thick batter, *two tablespoons molasses*, and *one-half cake compressed yeast* dissolved in *water.* In morning, stir the batter down ; if too thick, thin with warm water, or if any sour odor, add *one-fourth teaspoon soda* dissolved in *water.* Rise again and fry on greased griddle as wanted.

Hors-d'œuvre. (*M. L. Clarke.*) — Remove the crust from a *loaf* of *rye bread*, cut into slices nearly two inches thick, remove crusts and hollow out the centre sufficiently to enable a lemon to stand upright in it. Cut the ends of the bread block into thin slices, not quite to the bottom. Cut a *lemon* in halves and scoop out the pulp from the sections, being careful to leave the membranous wall of every other section so there will be five distinct places in the cup thus formed. In these cavities put *minced olives*, *pickles*, the bits of *lemon*, pounded *sardines*, *caviare*, finely minced *ham*, *tongue*, *anchovies*, *capers*, or any other relish or combination you prefer. Have at least three varieties. Put the filled half lemon in the hollow of the bread. Put a dainty doily or paper on the plate, the bread on that, and an oyster fork across the plate. They may be placed beside the guest's plate and the various relishes nibbled as one fancies. The bread is broken from the cut end as needed.

Oyster Cocktail. — Use very small *oysters*, and allow from *four* to *eight* for each glass. Keep them on ice until wanted, and have the glasses thoroughly chilled before filling. Use the common claret glass if you have not the regular cocktail glass. When ready to serve, put the oysters in the glass and add either of the following mixtures, using from one to two teaspoonfuls according to taste.

No. 1.

Sauces for Oyster Cocktails.

1 tsp. grated horse-radish.
1 tsp. tomato catsup.
1 saltsp. salt.
½ saltsp. cayenne.

½ tsp. tabasco.
2 tbsp. lemon juice.
Mix thoroughly.
Enough for six cocktails.

No. 2.

1 tbsp. lemon juice.
1 tbsp. Worcestershire sauce.
1 tbsp. tomato catsup.
½ saltsp. paprika.

1 saltsp. salt.
5 drops tabasco.
Mix well and put one tsp. in each glass.

No. 3.

3 tsp. vinegar.	½ tsp. walnut catsup.
3 tsp. lemon juice.	1 saltsp. salt.
3 tsp. tomato catsup.	½ saltsp. paprika.
3 tsp. horseradish.	

Clam Cocktail. (*Lia Rand.*) — For every cocktail required, take one teaspoonful of lemon juice, one teaspoonful of vinegar, a quarter of a teaspoonful of walnut sauce, one-half teaspoonful of mushroom catsup, one-half teaspoonful of grated horseradish, one-half teaspoonful of tomato catsup, a pinch of salt, a dash of tabasco sauce: pour this mixture over eight little neck clams and serve in an ice cup, or in a glass which was set on ice for hours previous to serving. This cocktail finds great favor for luncheon, high teas, or suppers.

Caviare. — This is the roe of the sturgeon preserved in salt alone or in salt, pepper, and onions and left to ferment. The best caviare comes from the north of Europe; that made on the Volga, called caviare of Astrachan is preferred by some. It is regarded as a heavy food, difficult of digestion. The flavor is exceedingly disagreeable to an unaccustomed palate, and this has led to the expression, " Caviare to the general," for anything that cannot be appreciated or understood by the people. Caviare is highly esteemed by the Russians, and the most delicate species of the sturgeon are reserved for the royal family. It is classed among the hors-d'œuvres, or savouries, and is usually served on or with fried toast or croûtons, or brown bread, after the soup or fish. It should not be long exposed to the air. If you buy it in the little barrels, divide it into small bottles and cork them tightly, then open only as wanted. If it should become too hard, break it up and work in a little olive oil and lemon juice. This is often the only preparation given it at gentlemen's suppers, where a skilful host, if he prefers, can prepare it for each guest. Sometimes it is served on a side dish with slices of lemon around it, and sometimes with finely chopped scallions or other raw onions.

Caviare Canapes, No. 1. — Cut slices of *bread quarter* of an *inch* thick, then cut out with a two-inch cutter into rounds. Sauté or fry in hot butter on each side without burning, and set away to cool. Cream *quarter of a cup* of *fresh butter*, add *salt* and *paprika* to taste, and mix with it as much finely minced *water-cress* as will give it a fine flavor. Chop the cress very fine, then squeeze dry in a napkin and chop again until very fine and dry. Make the butter into balls, and let it become hard. When ready to serve, spread the croûtons with the *butter*, then spread a layer of *caviare* on top, and squeeze a little *lemon juice* over, and serve.

Caviare, No. 2. — Cut slices of *bread one inch* thick, then with a pattie cutter stamp them out into rounds. With a smaller cutter stamp the centre two-thirds of the way down. Fry them in hot deep fat until a delicate brown color, drain, and with a sharp knife remove the centre crust. Then fill the centres with a mixture made in the following proportions. *Two tablespoonfuls* of *caviare, one teaspoonful beef extract, one teaspoonful lemon juice, a saltspoonful curry powder*, and also of *paprika*. Put all into a sauce pan and stir over the fire until quite hot, then put it into the croûtons. This may be served hot or cold, one to each person on a plate with a paper doily.

Caviare, No. 3. — Prepare some croûtons from *quarter-inch slices* of *bread*, about *three* and a *half inches* long and *one* and a *half inches* wide, fry, cool, and spread with the *caviare* Pound together the *yolks* of *two hard boiled eggs, six boned anchovies, a teaspoonful* of *chopped capers, a saltspoonful* each of *mustard* and *paprika*, and *two tablespoonfuls butter*. Mix and pound until very fine, then press it through a purée strainer, and put it into a bag with a small frosting tube, and use as you would frosting. Use a paper cornucopia if you have no bag or tube. Chop some *parsley* or *water-cress* very fine

and put it on the corners of the croûton. Cut some *hard
boiled eggs* into halves, lengthwise, and place them in
the centre of the croûtons, then with the tube fill the egg
cavities with the purée.

Or, the egg whites may be sifted, and then the croûtons
decorated according to your taste, with fancy lines of the
purée, the white and the green salad.

Cheese Canapes. — Allow the beaten *white* of *one egg*
to each *cup* of finely crumbled or grated *cheese*, a *speck*
of *salt* and *cayenne*. Remove the crust from *inch-thick*
slices of *bread*, hollow out centre making a box, fill with
the cheese mixture heaped, bake about ten minutes, and
serve on napkin.

Thin Brown bread and Butter. — Trim off the crusts
from a loaf of brown bread, leaving it in rectangular
shape. Slice it very thin and spread with a thin coating
of butter. Put two slices together and cut each square
into triangles. Arrange them neatly on a plate and
serve them with raw oysters.

Halibut à La Conant. — In a baking pan put *three*
thin *slices* of *fat salt pork* about *two inches square*,
three slices of *onion* and a *bit* of *bay leaf*. On top of
these lay a *two-pound slice* of *halibut*, spread over it *one
tablespoonful butter* and *one tablespoonful flour* creamed
together. Cover with *buttered cracker crumbs* and small
strips of *salt pork* and bake twenty minutes. Take out
the fish with a fish spade or two long knives, and lay it on
a hot platter. Garnish with *lemon* and *parsley*. Cooked
in this way the halibut is delicious, moist inside with a
crisp brown crust, and so nicely flavored that no sauce
is required.

Broiled Shad. — Split the shad down the back, lay it
open, clean, remove the back bone and as many of the
fine bones as possible, and wipe dry. Brush all over
with *oil* or *melted butter*. Lay it on a greased broiler

and cook over coals or under gas, flesh side first, until brown, then turn and cook the skin side until crisp. Meanwhile have prepared *one large tablespoonful butter* creamed with *one level teaspoonful salt, one saltspoonful pepper* or *paprika, one tablespoon lemon juice* or *walnut catsup*, and *one tablespoon minced parsley*, and when the fish is on the platter spread this over the surface and make several incisions that it may penetrate the fish. Garnish with *lemon points* and *parsley*, and serve very hot.

Planked Fish. — Shad or bluefish are nice cooked in this way; indeed among camping parties along the shores of the Connecticut River planked shad is a favorite dish. Clean the fish, remove the head, and split entirely open. Nail it to a board, set in front of the fire and broil until the fish is browned and cooked through. Remove it from the plank, and spread with *butter, salt*, and *cayenne pepper*. If dishes are scarce, as they are very likely to be in camp, season the fish and serve upon the plank as a platter.

Turbot. — Select a turbot weighing from four to six pounds, and with yellowish-white flesh. Wash and soak it half an hour in *one quart cold water* with *two tablespoons salt* to remove the slime. Put again into fresh water, drain and wipe. Remove the skin, cut the fish away from the bone and divide through the centre lengthwise, making four fillets. Wipe, sprinkle with *salt* and *pepper*, brush over with *oil* or *melted butter*, and broil a delicate brown. Season with *butter, salt*, and *pepper*, garnish with *water-cress*, and serve with *cucumber sauce*.

Fried Pickerel or Pike. — This fish is especially nice for frying, as the flesh may be sliced into uniform pieces about one inch thick, giving round, shapely steaks. Of course, the fins, scales, and entrails are first removed, and the fish washed and wiped dry. Roll the slices lightly in *flour* or fine *white cornmeal*, and cook them quickly in hot fat, *half lard* and *half butter;* or use *salt pork fat.* Do not let the fat burn. Turn the fish when brown, and when the other side is cooked, remove them to a pan lined with soft paper, to absorb the grease, while you make a cream gravy. Scrape out any burned crumbs left in the pan, but if they are only browned they will do no harm. If pork has been used, remove the scraps and fat. Turn in *one-fourth cup* of *hot water,* and scrape off any brown glaze from the pan, then add *one cup* of *thick cream,* and let it boil a few minutes. Rub *one tablespoon* each of *butter* and *flour* together, stir it in, with *chopped parsley* and *salt* and *pepper.* Strain it on to a platter and lay the browned fish in the sauce. Serve the crisp pork as a relish for those who care for it. If the fish have been frozen, thaw them out in cold water.

Swordfish. — This valuable sea food has many friends among those who have eaten it at its best, and especially after the excitement of chasing it through the briny waves. But tastes differ, and some people dislike it exceedingly, and never include it in their summer menus. It has quite a strong, distinctive flavor, and in grain and texture is not unlike some meats. Some parts of the flesh are dark and oily, for it belongs to the red-blooded division of the finny tribe, but the lighter-colored portions, when perfectly fresh, are very rich and delicious. It is usually sold in thin steaks or slices after the manner of halibut, which it somewhat resembles in size. Swordfish steaks are cut about half an inch thick and are sometimes broiled over the coals, but more often they are parboiled in a hot spider slightly greased. As they are rich in fat, they need but little, and will take on a rich brown color without the aid of flour or crumbs, and will cook through without becoming hard and dry. A little *salt* and *pepper,* with *butter* and *lemon juice* is all the dressing required, but fried or broiled *tomatoes* are an excellent accompaniment.

Stuffed Smelts. — Chop *six* large *oysters*, add *one cup* of soft *bread crumbs*, one *tablespoonful* of *melted butter*, and *salt* and *pepper* to taste. Clean the smelts, fill with the mixture, sew the edges, roll in melted butter, then in soft bread crumbs, and bake in a moderate oven ten minutes. Serve with Maître d'Hotel butter. Cream *two tablespoonfuls butter*, add juice of *half* a *lemon* or *lime*, and a *teaspoonful* of *chopped parsley*.

Haddock Rarebit. — Have the haddock cut in slices or steaks about one inch thick and free from bone and skin. Lay them in a greased baking dish, and season with *salt* and *pepper*. Turn them over and spread on the top of each a cheese mixture prepared as for a rarebit. Have the *cheese* finely crumbled and seasoned with *salt*, *cayenne*, and a bit of *mustard*, and if you like you may bind the mixture with beaten *egg* or *cream*. Put into a very hot oven and cook until the cheese melts and browns, and the fish is firm. Take up carefully on a serving dish and pour over *one tablespoon* of *sherry* to each slice.

New	1 cup raw salt fish.	¼ teasp pepper.
Fish	1 pint potatoes.	Salt if needed.
Balls.	1 teasp. butter.	Whites of 2 eggs.

Wash the fish, pick in half-inch pieces, and free from bones. Pare the potatoes and cut in quarters, allowing a heaping pint measure to a level cup of fish. Put potatoes and fish in a stew pan and cover with boiling water. Boil twenty-five minutes, or till the potatoes are soft, but be careful not to let them boil long enough to become soggy. Drain off all the water; mash and beat the fish and potatoes with a wire beater till very light; add the butter and pepper, and when cooled add the stiffly beaten egg whites and more salt if needed.

While the fish and potatoes are cooking, try out several slices of sweet fat salt pork, being very careful that it does not burn, and when crisp remove the slices and keep them warm. Drop a large tablespoonful of the mixture on a floured board and shape it into a round cake about one and one-half inches thick, and floured on each side. When all are shaped, put them into the hot pork fat and brown them delicately on each side, but not on the edges. The white mixture should seem to be bursting out from the browned surfaces. Drain them on paper and serve them with hard-boiled eggs cut lengthwise and laid on each cake. Boil the eggs eight minutes, or just enough to set the yolks. Garnish with the crisp pork and pickles cut in fancy shapes.

Or you may omit the boiled egg garnish and make a sauce with the two yolks and pour it into the centre of the dish and lay the cakes around it. Or put the cakes in the centre, the yellow sauce at one end, and some sliced green tomato pickle at the other.

Hulled Corn Soup. — There is a distinctive flavor to hulled corn that is especially agreeable to many, particularly to those who have been accustomed to this dish in childhood. But often the corn is not quite tender, or one wishes to serve it in a more modern way, and a soup or purée will be found to be both novel and delicious. If the corn is tender, mash it until fine and sift it through a purée strainer; otherwise chop the corn fine before sifting. Then gradually stir in hot *milk* enough to make it the consistency of any cream vegetable soup. Put it on to boil and add *salt* and *pepper* to taste, and a generous *tablespoonful* of *butter*, for each *quart* of the *mixture*. Serve it with croûtons. It will have a slightly granular texture, and if this is not liked, you may add the usual flour thickening. *One tablespoonful* of *butter* and *one tablespoonful* of *flour* cooked together, and stirred into the hot soup. If a corn purée is desired, simply mash and sift the corn, heat and season to taste with *butter*, *salt*, and *pepper*, and serve as a vegetable, or as a garnish for sausage or pork chops.

Noodles. — Beat *two eggs* slightly, add *two tablespoon-fuls* of *milk*, and *half a teaspoonful* of *salt*. Stir in flour enough to make a very stiff dough. Knead it till stiff as possible. Roll it out into rectangular pieces and so thin you can see through it. Lay them on a napkin half an hour until they are dry, but not brittle. Rub over with a little flour so it will not stick. Roll up tight and hard, and then slice off from the end about one-eighth of an inch thick. Shake them out till long and straight. Put them into boiling salted water, stir them at first to prevent sticking, and cook until they swell and come to the top of the water. Skim them out into a dish for serving. Melt half a cup of butter in a frying pan, put half a slice of bread, crumbled finely, in the butter, stir until golden brown, then spoon up butter and bread and pour over the noodles. Pass sapsago cheese with the noodles.

If any be left over, warm it in butter until a delicate brown, and stir in three or four beaten eggs; serve as soon as firm. This makes a nice relish for supper.

Lentil Soup. — Lentils are rich in proteid material, and therefore are very suitable when a meat soup is not desired.

Pick over and wash *one cup* of *lentils*, and put them on to cook in *one quart* of boiling *water*. Let them cook very slowly until soft and the water reduced one-half. Rub the pulp through a strainer, add *one pint* of *milk*, and, when boiling, thicken with *one rounded tablespoon flour* cooked in *one rounded tablespoon butter*. Season with *paprika*, *salt*, and a *dash* of *sugar*, and serve with wafers or croûtons.

Cream of Onions. — Onions are usually used merely to flavor soups, but they may serve as the foundation or body of a soup the same as any other vegetable pulp. They are especially valuable in the spring, and by many are considered as almost a specific for some physical ills.

The large white Spanish and the Bermuda variety, having a mild flavor, are the best for soups. They should be peeled, sliced, and scalded for five minutes; then drain quite dry; this will remove much of the pungent oil. Then, for a *pint* of *sliced onion* put *one rounded tablespoonful* of *butter* in the stewpan, add the onions, and let them simmer very slowly for ten minutes. Put on boiling water to cover, and let them simmer until very soft — about an hour

Then rub them through a strainer, add *one cup* of *hot milk*, thickened with *one level teaspoonful* of *flour* cooked in *one rounded tablespoonful* of *butter*. Season with *one-fourth* of a *teaspoonful* of *white pepper*, *one-half teaspoon salt*.

Beat *yolks* of *two eggs*, add *one cup hot cream*, and put into the tureen. Turn the hot soup over the egg, stirring constantly, and serve at once.

Cream of	1 can peas		1 saltsp pepper.
Canned	1 pint hot water.		½ teasp sugar.
Peas.	1 qt. milk		1 tbsp. butter.
	1 teasp salt		1 tbsp flour.

Turn the peas from the can into a colander and pour cold water over them to remove the taste of the tin. Drain and heat slightly in quarter of a cup of water. Rub them through a purée strainer, gradually adding the pint of hot water, which will help to separate the pulp from the skins. Put the pea pulp and milk on to boil; add the seasoning; then the butter and flour, which have first been cooked together. Stir as it thickens, and, as the pea pulp will vary in thickening quality, it may be necessary to add more milk or water if too thick, or to let it cook longer if too thin. Remember that all vegetable cream soups become thicker as they cool, and should be served very hot.

Clam Bouillon. — Select clams in the shell, wash and scrub thoroughly and change the water until clean. Put them in a kettle with a pint of cold water for half a peck of clams. Cover tightly and let them cook until the shells open. Skim out the clams, pour off the liquor carefully into a pitcher, and let it stand until clear. Then pour off again from the sediment, and if too strong dilute it with water as desired, and to each quart of liquid, add the white and crumbled shell of one egg, and a little pepper.

Place over the fire and let it boil five minutes, constantly stirring until the egg has thickened. Draw it back, and when it is clear, strain it carefully. Serve hot or cold, in cups with whipped cream and wafers.

Gombo Soup. — Cut up a chicken as for a fricassee, and dredge it thickly with flour. Fry a sliced onion in bacon fat, remove the onion and brown the chicken; brown also one quart of sliced okra pods. Place the chicken, onion, and okra in a kettle, cover with boiling water, add one quart of sliced tomatoes. Simmer until the chicken is tender. Remove the larger bones and all the fat. Add salt, cayenne, and a very little sugar. Serve it without straining and with boiled rice.

Beef à La Russegue. — Select a piece of beef from the under part of the round, or the vein, weighing about three pounds. Put it on in boiling water to nearly cover, skim as it boils, and let it cook slowly three or four hours or until tender. When nearly done, add salt and pepper to taste. Remove it from the water and set away to cool In the water left in the kettle cook one dozen small onions. When nearly done, add the same amount of small potatoes pared into round shape, or cut with a large potato marble cutter. Remove these from the water when tender, and set away to cool.

Half an hour before serving time, cut the meat into quarter-inch slices and brown it quickly and delicately in hot butter. Use two spiders, so it may be done quickly. Put the onions and potatoes in the spider, adding more butter as needed, and let them color slightly. Then heat the water in which the meat was boiled, which should be about a pint, add one cup of cream, and thicken it slightly with flour wet in cold water. Add more seasoning, if needed, and one cup of canned mushrooms, and simmer until the mushrooms are hot. Arrange the potato balls around the meat, then a row of the onions around the potatoes, and dot here and there with the mushrooms. Pour the gravy over the meat, enough to cover and show under the vegetable garnish. Put a sprig of parsley at the corners.

This dish may seem to require considerable time in its preparation, but it is a very convenient dish for a six o'clock dinner, as the meat and vegetables may be boiled in the forenoon; then it takes but little time to reheat them at night. Do not think it can be served as soon as the meat and vegetables are cooked and be the same, for the flavor of the meat when cooled and then reheated is quite unlike that of the freshly boiled meat. And we all know how the potato changes in texture and flavor when warmed over, and while it may not be as wholesome for a delicate stomach, it would not harm others. It is an economical and appetizing dish.

Pepper Pot. — Cover two pounds of tripe and four calves' feet, or a knuckle of veal, with cold water and heat slowly, remove the scum, add one red pepper, and cook till the feet are tender, then remove the meat, let the liquor cool, skim off the fat, heat the liquor again and add seasoning to taste, salt, cayenne, and sweet herbs. Cut the tripe and the meat in small pieces, and slice about an equal amount of potatoes, add them and cook until the potatoes are done. When nearly done, add either egg balls or very small flour dumplings, and cook ten minutes.

Salisbury Steak. — Select the middle cut from the top of the best round steak. Free it from fat, skin, and fibre. Run it three times through a meat chopper. Make into a mass about one and one-fourth inch thick, and shape the edges even. Put it into a wire broiler and lay an iron band round it, which will help to keep the meat in shape. If the broiler shuts together too closely, bend it out in the middle slightly.

Put it over a Charcoal Broiler Stove and turn every ten seconds. Cook from four to six minutes. Lift the edge, and as soon as the meat is no longer raw, remove it to a hot plate. Sprinkle with salt. In serving, cut into thin strips, and let each person spread it with butter as desired.

In this way you have the full, sweet flavor of the butter without the injurious effect of melted butter.

Veal Chops. — These are cut from the loin and ribs, and correspond to the sirloin and rib steaks in beef, and to the chops in mutton. They are generally more tender than the cutlets from the leg, just as sirloin steak is more tender than that from the round.

Loin or kidney chops have quite a piece of fat with them which is very sweet and delicious, and sometimes the kidney is sold with the chop.

Trim off the fat and cook it slowly until crisp. Slice the kidney, season with salt and pepper, and cook it in the fat.

Trim the chops and remove the bone, if preferred. Press into compact shape and season slightly. Roll in fine cracker crumbs, then dip in beaten egg, then in seasoned crumbs, and cook carefully in the hot fat, adding more butter or salt pork fat, if needed. Do not let them become too brown. Drain and serve, garnished with the crisp fat and sliced kidney and a bit of parsley.

Braised Veal. — Chop *half a pound* of *fat pork* fine, and put half of it in the bottom of a broad pot; sprinkle with a *tablespoon* of chopped *carrot*, minced *onion*, a *bay leaf*, and a sprig of *thyme*. Lay a breast of veal on this bed, and cover with a similar layer. Pour in carefully a quart of stock, cover and set on back of the range; let simmer for two hours, remove the meat, rub over with butter, then dredge thickly with browned flour. Pour over the meat one cupful of the stock, then place in a hot oven and bake about half an hour, basting with the remaining gravy every few minutes. Serve the veal on a hot platter lined with buttered toast, and serve the gravy in a sauce boat. Plain boiled spaghetti, or home-made egg noodles should be served with it.

Brown Fricassee of Sweetbreads. — Parboil ten minutes. Remove fat and membranes, dredge with *flour*, and fry, till quite brown, in *butter*, with a minced *onion*. Add to the butter, *one cup* of *veal stock* and *two tablespoonfuls* of *mushroom ketchup*, or *half a cup* of *tomatoes* and *one tablespoonful* of *chopped parsley*. Season to taste with *salt* and *pepper*, cover, and stew slowly for half an hour. Strain the gravy, and pour it over the sweetbreads.

Shoulder of Mutton. — Remove the shoulder blade, back, and leg bones, any fine crumbs of bone or stringy membranes. Wipe with a wet cloth and rub slightly with salt. Roll or fold into shape and tie securely. Put it into boiling salted water to cover, remove the scum as soon as the water boils again, then turn the meat over and skim again. Let it cook gently. When it is nearly tender, remove it from the water, drain it, and place it in a baking pan. Dredge with salt, pepper, and flour, and set it in the oven. Bake until brown and crisp on the surface. Baste occasionally with some of the top of the water from the kettle, and dredge with flour after basting. The whole process will take from two and a half to three hours.

When the meat is sufficiently browned, remove it to a hot dish, put the pan on the stove, and let the water nearly boil out, leaving only fat in the pan. Stir into this fat about two tablespoonfuls of flour, and let them brown together. Scrape off all the glaze from the edges, and when well colored, add one pint of hot water from that used in boiling the lamb, or you may use half water and half strained tomato. Stir well as it thickens, and season to taste with salt and pepper. Serve in a gravy boat. Remove the strings from the meat, and in serving cut at right angles with the back edge.

After putting the lamb in the oven, put the bones and trimmings in the kettle with the water used in the boiling, add one onion, and a few bits of carrot and turnip, if you happen to have them, and let the whole simmer until the bones are clear of all gristle or meat. Then strain the liquor and set it away to cool, and the next day you may remove the fat, heat it again, and have a delicious lamb broth with boiled rice or curry.

Breaded Chops. — Remove the bone and tough portion from six chops cut from the loin or ribs. Pat them into shape. Make a dressing of stale *bread* crumbled, highly seasoned with *salt, pepper, cayenne,* and a little powdered *thyme,* moistened with melted *butter* and *one* well beaten *egg* and enough hot water to make it soft enough to spread easily. Lay the chops in a dripping pan with some of the surplus fat under them. Spread the dressing smoothly all over the top of each, place them in a hot oven, and bake about twenty minutes, or until brown.

Pork Chops. — It will be impossible to cook some pork chops, and have them juicy and tender. There is no meat that varies so much in quality, or that is so deceptive as fresh pork. The lean must be well marked with white lines of fat, or it will be dry and hard. It is often put into a very hot spider without any fat, and the surface quickly becomes very hard and brown.

Put in a tablespoonful of lard, and when hot lay in the chops, and then keep them turning constantly; reduce the heat as soon as they are browned on each side, and cook slowly until thoroughly done. Do not salt them until just before serving. They may be laid in a greased pan and baked quickly in a hot oven.

Bacon. — Do not buy bacon by the pound, nor have it cut in thick slices, if cut at the market, but purchase it by the whole strip, freshly cured. It will keep well if the paper and burlap cover are replaced whenever opened, and is as much a necessity in the storeroom as is a supply of flour, sugar, or any other staple article of food. It has no equal as an appetizer for breakfast, or in helping out when there is but a limited supply of other meat. Served with omelets, or some other forms of eggs, crisp curly bacon is all the meat necessary for a summer breakfast. It is invaluable to boil with greens or other vegetables. The fat of bacon is one of the most easily digested forms of fat, as the curing and smoking seem to have given it some qualities which render it less objectionable than when fresh. Many physicians prescribe it in place of cod liver oil.

Transparent Bacon. — Shave off the hard, lean strip from bacon, also the smoked edges and rind as far back on the strip as you require for one meal. Then with a very sharp knife shave off in slices not more than an eighth of an inch thick. Lay them in a hot frying pan, and turn as soon as transparent; cook a moment on the other side, tip the spider and let the fat drain away from the bacon. Then serve alone or with eggs, beefsteak, veal cutlets, liver, or oysters. The slices may be laid in a fine wire broiler and cooked over a clear hot fire, or the broiler laid in a pan and the whole placed in a hot oven until transparent.

Keep the bacon in a cold place, that it may be hard and firm before slicing, and if not ready to fry immediately, put the slices in the refrigerator until wanted.

Crisp Bacon. — Prepare as directed for Transparent Bacon, then shave in the thinnest possible slices; never mind if they are not entire slices so long as they are mere shavings. Take two or three tablespoonfuls of clear bacon fat from a previous frying, or use lard if you have no bacon fat; let it become quite hot in a small pan, then put the bacon in, stir it quickly with a fork for one minute, and skim it out as soon as it rattles. It should be only slightly colored, if dark brown, it has been over-cooked. Drain on paper. Should the bacon prove to be very salt, it may be soaked in milk over night after slicing, then drain, roll in very fine crumbs, or flour, and cook it quickly in hot fat.

With a gas stove bacon is readily made crisp by broil-ing. Then no additional fat is required.

Smothered Fowl. — Clean a fowl suitable only for boil-ing; stuff and truss as for roasting. Put it in a large deep kettle or jar. Parboil some white beans, season the same as for baking, and put them in the kettle with the fowl, — under, around, and over the fowl. Add water and a small piece of pork. Cover, and bake slowly about eight hours. Add water as it boils away, and treat the same as for beans alone. Pour the beans out, remove the fowl carefully, put it on a large platter, and garnish with the beans. If more convenient, the fowl may be cut as for a fricassee.

Hungarian Chicken or Paprika Huhn. — Put *one heaped tablespoonful butter* or *dripping* in a tight stew pan, add *two* good-sized *onions* sliced thin and left in long strips. When slightly colored, add *half teaspoonful* of *Hunga-rian pepper* or *paprika*, and mix well and let them brown. Then add the chicken cut in pieces, and salted and pep-pered. Brown well, turning often. Then add stock or water till nearly covered. Stew until tender. Just be-fore serving, take out the meat, put on a hot platter, and add a full *half cup* or more of thick *sour cream.* Just let it scald, but do not boil it, pour it over the chicken and serve at once.

Croustades of Chicken. — Cover the outside of small moulds or tin corn-cake cups with thin puff paste. Prick and bake, remove from the moulds and fill with mixture of mushrooms and chicken breasts chopped fine and moistened with highly-seasoned cream sauce.

Roast Mallard or Teal Ducks. — Singe, draw, and remove all the tiny pinfeathers Then wash very quickly, both inside and out, with cool water and wipe perfectly dry. For the stuffing, take *equal parts* of chopped *tart apples*, of *bread crumbs* which have been browned in the oven and sifted, and of *boiled onions*. Season highly with *salt* and *pepper*, and a little *sage*, and moisten with *two* or *three tablespoonfuls* of melted *butter*. Stuff the ducks, sew and truss. Put on a rack in a pan, sprinkle with salt, pepper, and a little flour. Cover with small slices of salt pork and put into a very hot oven. In about five minutes the ducks will be light brown. Now reduce the heat and pour into the pan a very little water. The dripping fat will burn unless a little hot water is added. Baste every four or five minutes. In forty minutes the ducks will be sufficiently cooked, if liked a trifle rare, but many prefer a longer cooking. When nearly done, the pork must be removed and the birds evenly browned on all sides. Serve with

Olive Sauce. — Skim off some of the fat in the dripping pan until only *four tablespoonfuls* remain. To this add *four tablespoonfuls* of *browned flour*, stir, then add slowly *one* and a *half cups* of *boiling water*. Let it boil until slightly thickened, stirring constantly, then add *four tablespoonfuls* of *olive pulp* cut in small pieces, *one teaspoonful* of *lemon juice* and *one teaspoonful* of *caramel*.

Roast Duck, No. 2. — Prepare as directed in first recipe, and stuff with stale *bread crumbs*, seasoned with a little melted *butter*, *salt*, *pepper*, and *three-fourths* of a *cup* of chopped *celery*. Place the duck on the bottom of the pan and not on the rack, and put close around it a *sweet potato*, a *carrot*, and a *parsnip*, each of them pared and cut in halves. When the duck is basted, baste the vegetables also, and when the duck has been taken from the pan, mash the vegetables in the drippings and press through the sieve. Add about *one* and a *half cups* of *boiling water*, season and serve in a gravy boat. The vegetables take the place of flour in thickening, help to flavor, and we think this is a very good everyday gravy for ducks. (*Miss Souther.*)

A Missouri Dainty.—Cut a carefully dressed young squirrel or rabbit into pieces for frying; rub each piece with *salt*, *pepper*, and dust with a trifle of *mace*; dredge well with flour, and fry to a rich brown in *half butter* and *half lard*. Remove the meat from the pan, add a heaping *tablespoonful* of *flour*, and when it is brown, enough seasoned *soup stock* to make a gravy as thick as cream. Next place the meat in a porcelain-lined pot, or earthenware "cooking-crock," pour over it the gravy, and a generous *cupful* of *tomatoes*, which have been well stewed down and seasoned with *salt*, *pepper*, and a grated *onion ;* place a tight-fitting lid on the vessel, stand it on a muffin ring in a moderate oven, and let it cook for three hours.

Rabbit Fricassee with Curry. — Select a fat, young, wild rabbit, which, if fresh, will have no unpleasant odor. Skin and clean it, and remove the head and neck, which are not to be used. Split it down the back, then disjoint it, or cut into convenient pieces. Wipe off with a clean wet cloth, and if you prefer you may soak it half an hour in salted water. Season with *salt* and *pepper*, dredge with *flour*, and brown slightly in hot *butter* or *salt pork* fat. Put the meat into a stewpan. In the fat left in the saucepan, put *one* sliced *onion* and cook until slightly colored. Mix *two teaspoonfuls* of *curry powder*, *one teaspoonful* of *sugar*, and *one heaping tablespoonful* of *flour*, and brown them in the *butter*. Add slowly one *pint* of *water, one cup* of strained *tomato, six raisins seeded, one cup* of *chopped sour apple, a dash* of *cay·*

enne, and *salt* to taste. Turn this sauce over the rabbit, and let it simmer until the flesh is very tender. When ready to serve, add *one cup* of hot *milk* and *quarter* of a *cup* of *chopped olives.* Have ready *one cup* of *rice*, cooked in boiling water until soft, turn the rabbit into a platter and pile the rice around the edge.

Brown Fricassee of Partridge. — Dress and clean a pair of partridges, split them through the back and breast as for broiling. Fry *two slices* of *salt pork* in a Scotch bowl or other deep iron kettle. Remove the scraps, lay the partridges in, and brown them carefully. Then add *one cup* of *boiling water;* cover the kettle closely and let it cook very slowly. Keep that amount of water in the kettle, adding a little as it boils away. Cook until very tender, about two hours. Then take out the meat, remove the fat from the gravy and pour in *half a cup* of *tomato ketchup;* thicken it with a little flour mixed with cold water. Add more salt if needed, put the meat in again, and when heated through, serve on a shallow dish with browned *sweet potatoes.* (*Mrs. Webster.*)

Baked Quail. — Pick, draw, and wipe the birds outside and inside with a wet cloth. Be careful to remove any shot in the flesh. Cut the wings and neck off close to the body, but leave the feet on. Take *two oysters* to each *bird*, dip them in *melted butter,* then in *cracker crumbs* seasoned with *salt* and *pepper.* Put them into the body, tie the feet and fasten them through the tail with a small wooden skewer so they will cover the opening. Rub the breasts with softened *butter* and dredge with *flour.* Pin a thin piece of fat salt pork on the breast, arrange them in a baking pan so they will keep breast up. Place them in a hot oven and bake twelve minutes. Baste with melted butter and water three times during the baking. They have a dry white meat, and should be well done and be basted frequently to make them delicious. Have ready a small slice of nicely toasted bread, no crusts, and moisten it slightly with hot salt water. Dish the birds on the toast without spilling any of the juice from the inside, as this is needed on the toast. Remove the skewers and pork, and garnish with cauliflower.

Broiled Squabs. — Remove the feathers, split down the back, remove the entrails, and wipe clean. Rub all over with soft *butter*, and dredge with *salt* and *pepper*. Lay them in a piece of buttered letter-paper, inside down, cross the legs over the outside, and fold the edges under to shape it well. Fold the paper over and fold the edges together. Broil over a clear fire about eight minutes. Spread *currant-jelly* on some hot buttered *toast;* lay a bird on each slice, with a little jelly on the breast. Pour over them the juice from the papers, and serve very hot.

ON THE CHAFING-DISH.

Scrambled Eggs. — Spread *four slices* of hot *toast* with a thin layer of *potted ham*. Beat *four eggs* slightly with a fork, season with *salt* and *pepper*, add *half a cupful* of *milk*. Turn into a hot buttered chafing-pan, and stir with a fork until the egg is slightly thickened. Turn at once on the toast, and serve quickly.

Tomato Omelet. — Fry *three slices* of *bacon* crisp, remove it, and in the same fat cook *one sliced onion* until light brown. Beat *three eggs* slightly, season with *cayenne*, add *three tablespoonfuls* of thick stewed *tomato*, the fried onions and the crisp bacon, finely crumbled. Turn into a greased chafing-pan, and pick it up with a fork as the egg thickens, then let it color slightly, roll over and turn out onto a hot platter.

Scotch Woodcock. — First toast and butter some bread on both sides, and spread on this some chopped *anchovies*. Beat the *yolks* of *four eggs* with *half a pint* of *cream*, and thicken this for a few moments in the chafing-dish without letting it come to a boil. Arrange the small pieces of toast into a little pyramid and pour the egg over it.

Deviled Eggs and Anchovy Toast. — Put a *walnut* of *butter* in the chafing-dish, *half* a *teaspoonful* of dry *mustard*, *two tablespoonfuls* of *tomato sauce*, *one tablespoonful* of *Worcestershire*, and *one* of *mushroom catsup*. Put into this *four* hard-boiled *eggs*, sliced, salted, and peppered. When heated, place the eggs on toast previously spread with anchovy paste.

Creamed Eggs. — Put into the chafing-dish *one teaspoonful butter* and place the pan over the bath. Beat *three eggs* slightly, add *half* a *cup* thin *cream* and a *saltspoonful pepper*. Turn into the butter and stir constantly as it thickens. Sprinkle with salt, and turn out while moist and soft.

Lobster Newberg. — Remove the meat from a large lobster and cut it into half-inch pieces. Have ready the *yolks* of *four eggs* beaten with *one pint* of rich *cream*. Put *two heaped tablespoons* of *butter* into a hot chafing-dish, remove the pan containing the hot water, and cover it while you put the blazer over the flame. Add to the lobster, *four tablespoons* of *sherry*, *one tablespoon* of *brandy*, and a *saltspoon* of *red pepper*, and let them cook five minutes. Place the pan of boiling water underneath, and then stir the cream and egg mixture in, and stir thoroughly. Remove as soon as the egg has thickened, that it may not curdle.

Lobster Newberg, No. 2. — Prepare *one pint lobster dice.* Beat *yolks* of *three eggs*, add *one pint* of *cream*, and *one glass* of *sherry*. Cook them in a double boiler, or in a chafing-dish over boiling water, and stir constantly until thick and smooth. Add *half* a *teaspoon* of *salt* and a *saltspoon* of *paprika*. Add the diced lobster, and merely let them get hot, and serve at once.

Lobster Newberg, No. 3. — Cook *one pint diced lobster* in *one rounded tablespoon butter* in a saucepan, add *one level teaspoon salt*, *one-quarter teaspoon paprika*, and *four tablespoons* of *Madeira* or *sherry wine.* Cook five minutes. Beat *yolks* of *two eggs*, add *half* a *cup* of *cream*, and stir in quickly and remove at once before the egg curdles.

Panned Oysters with Celery.— Put into the chafing-dish *one tablespoonful* of *butter*, and when melted add *one heaped tablespoonful* fine cut *celery*, *half* a *tablespoonful* of *paprika*, *half* a *teaspoonful* of *salt*, and the *juice* of *half* a *lemon.* When very hot, add *one pint* of *oysters*, previously picked over and drained. Cook until the edges curl. Add *one cup* of *cream*, and when this is hot serve on toast.

Oysters à la Demerara.— Put *one pint* of prepared *oysters* in the chafing-dish and cook until the edges curl. Drain off the water, add to the oysters *two tablespoonfuls* of *butter*, *half* a *teaspoonful* of *salt*, and *two tablespoonfuls* of *mango chutney sauce* and *two* of *A1 sauce.* Serve on Marguerite wafers.

Oysters à la Maître d'Hôtel. — Pick over one pint of large oysters, put them in the chafing-dish and heat quickly until the juice flows. Pour off the liquor. Then into the lower pan put *one tablespoonful* of *butter*, and, when hot and beginning to color, lay in the oysters and brown them slightly. Season with *salt* and *pepper;* turn, and, when brown, squeeze juice of half a lemon over and serve at once.

Creighton Oysters. — Put into the chafing-dish *one table-spoonful butter*, *one tablespoonful flour*, *one saltspoonful paprika*, *one saltspoonful salt*, *one tablespoonful mushroom catsup*, *one teaspoonful lemon juice*, and *one tablespoonful A1 sauce.* Cook five minutes, add *one pint oysters* picked over and drained, and cook until the edges curl. Serve on wafers or toast.

Curry of Scallops. — Put *one teaspoonful* of *butter* in the chafing-dish, and when melted add *one tablespoonful* of minced *onion.* After this is browned, stir in *one tea-spoonful* of *curry powder.* Cook for five minutes, then add *one pint* of *white stock* and let it simmer until reduced about one-half. Put in *one pint* of *scallops,* previously parboiled fifteen minutes, and cook from five to ten minutes. Add salt to taste.

Crab Terrapin. — *One pint* of *canned* or *fresh crab meat,* chopped fine. Boil *one* and a *half cups* of *cream.* Blend *two tablespoonfuls butter* and *two* of *flour* together, add the sifted *yolks* of *four* hard boiled *eggs.* Thin this with a little of the hot milk, then stir it into the remainder. Season with *salt* and *cayenne.* Add the crab meat and *quarter* of a *cup* of *sherry wine,* and when hot serve in bouillon cups.

Clams à la Newberg. — *One pint* raw *clams,* take out the soft part, remove the black end, and chop the tough parts very fine.

Put *one tablespoon* of *butter* in a stewpan with *one-half teaspoon salt* and a *saltspoon* of *paprika,* add the clams, and simmer ten minutes. Then add *two tablespoons* of *sherry* and the soft part. Beat *yolks* of *two eggs,* mix with *half* a *cup* of *cream,* and stir in quickly and remove as soon as the egg thickens.

Sardines à la Sterneau. — Drain off the oil from half a can of boneless sardines. Put them in the chafing-dish and mash with a silver fork. When hot, add *one tablespoonful lemon juice, one tablespoonful walnut catsup,* and *one tablespoonful A1 sauce.* Mix thoroughly, spread on wafers, and serve very hot.

Dried Beef and Celery. — Cut small *one cup celery,* and boil until tender in water enough to cover, adding a little more as it boils away. When soft, add *half* a *cup* sliced dried *beef* cut up very fine, and *one tablespoonful* of *flour,* mixed with the same amount of *butter, half* a *cup* of *milk,* and a little *salt* and *pepper.*

Sausages Sauted. — Cut large, thick sausages or the sausage cakes into thin slices. Brown them quickly in hot *butter* or *bacon fat* in the chafing-dish; add a little chopped *celery* and *paprika*, and serve on toast.

Welsh Rarebit, with Ale. — Put into the blazer over hot-water pan, *one tablespoon* of *butter*, a little *salt*, a few grains of *cayenne*, and *mustard*, if liked, and *one-half pound* of rich *cream cheese* crumbled fine. Stir as it melts, and add *ale* gradually till thin and smooth.

Welsh Rarebit, without Ale. — Have ready *one level tablespoon butter* creamed with *one level teaspoon corn-starch*, *one-fourth teaspoon salt*, and few grains *cayenne*, also *one-half pound cheese* grated or crumbled fine, *one-half teaspoon mushroom catsup*, and some *wafers, or squares* of delicate *toast*. Heat *one-half cup cream* in the blazer, and blend with it the butter mixture. When thick, set it over the hot water, add the cheese and catsup, stir till melted, then pour it over the wafers.

Roquefort Rarebit. — Take about *one-eighth pound* of *Roquefort cheese*, mash it with a silver fork on a plate until soft, stir in *half* a *teaspoonful salt* and the same of *mustard*, and *one inch cube* of soft *butter*. Add *ale* sufficient to blend the whole into a creamy mass. Spread it on wafers, and serve at once.

Mushrooms, Cream Saute. — Wipe or wash if needed, peel, cut stems fine, and if tough stew in a little milk. Slice or quarter the tops, cook them five minutes in plenty of *butter*, then add *cream* sufficient to make a sauce, sprinkle with *salt* and *pepper*, add the stems and simmer a few minutes, or till tender, adding more cream if needed. There should be sauce enough to moisten the toast. This is one of the simplest and most delicious ways of cooking mushrooms, especially the late varieties.

Panocha	4 cups brown sugar.	2 tbsp. vanilla.
M. E. Johnston.)	1 tsp. salt.	1 cup milk.
	1 tbsp. butter.	2 cups chopped walnuts.

Boil the sugar, butter, salt, and milk until it drops hard in cold water. When done, pour in the vanilla and walnuts, and stir constantly until well mixed. Pour on a buttered plate and cut into squares.

String	1 qt. butter beans.	1 saltsp. nutmeg.
Beans,	1 hpd. tbsp. butter.	1 tsp salt.
German	1 saltsp. pepper.	
Style.		

Break off the ends and strings, and if the latter do not come off readily, take a thin sharp paring knife and pare off the thickest string on the inside edge of the pod, taking as thin a strip as possible. Hold the bean with this edge toward you, and cut in thin slanting pieces not more than an inch and a half long, holding the back edge of the pod against the left forefinger. I give this minute direction because many of my pupils have found it difficult to get the knack of cutting them "on the bias," as we call it, and it does make a difference in the flavor if they are broken or snapped in the old way. It takes time to do this, but after you learn the art, it can be done as quickly as one shells peas. Beans prepared in this way require much less time for cooking, and housekeepers who often give up having a dinner of string beans because they could not get them on at nine o'clock, or do not want a hot fire all the morning, will do well to try this recipe. Do not be afraid to use the nutmeg. You will not recognize it, yet you will miss something if you omit it.

If the beans are not fresh from the vines, it may be well to put them in cold water before cutting, to make them more crisp and firm. After slicing, put them again into cold water, but do not prepare them more than half an hour before needed. Put the butter, salt, pepper, and nutmeg into a broad granite stewpan having a tight cover, and when the butter is melted, take the beans from the water in handfuls, with only the water that clings to them, and put them into the butter.

Add no more water. Cover tightly, and as soon as they are hot set them where they will cook very slowly. The butter and liquid that is drawn from the beans will make sufficient moisture to steam the beans, and they will be perfectly tender if cooked slowly and of finer flavor than when deluged with water. Stir them up from the bottom occasionally, and so long as there is barely liquid enough to cover the bottom of the pan they are safe. If they cook too rapidly, and become quite dry, you may add two or three tablespoonfuls of water. They should be quite dry except for the coating of butter, when done, and being already seasoned they are simply turned into the dish and sent at once to the table.

Small fresh-picked beans will cook in from thirty to forty minutes, larger or stale ones sometimes require nearly an hour. It will do no harm to let them stand some time in the kettle on the back of the stove or beyond the chance of burning, if they are tender before you are ready for them.

Purée of Green Beans. — One of the most wholesome, delicious, and convenient ways of using Lima or other shelled beans while in the green state is in a purée. Cook the beans in boiling water for ten minutes, then drain, rinse, and put again into boiling water. plenty of it, and cook until very tender. Turn into a purée strainer and press all the pulp through. Put on to boil again, and add milk or cream sufficient to make it the usual purée consistency. For each quart of the mixture, cook one tablespoonful each of butter and flour together as for white sauce, and stir it into the boiling liquid. Season with salt and pepper. Serve with wafers.

It is convenient to cook a quantity of the beans at once and sift them, then add milk and thickening only to whatever portion may be needed for that meal.

33

Cucumber Sauce. — Pare *two cucumbers.* Cut lengthwise in quarters, remove the seeds if large, chop fine and squeeze dry. Season with *salt, paprika,* and *vinegar,* and stir in *one-half cup* of *thick cream* whipped stiff. This is especially suitable for broiled fish.

Stewed Cucumbers. — Pare the large cucumbers, cut lengthwise into four parts, and remove the large seeds. Soak them half an hour in cold water. Cook in boiling salted water to cover until tender. Drain off the water; add a little butter, salt, and pepper, and, when well heated, serve on toast; or make a thin white sauce and pour over them. This is worth trying.

Heidelberg Carrots. — Wash and scrape three medium-sized carrots, cut into pieces about an inch and a half long, then into thin slices lengthwise, and then again into thin strips about like short matches. Put them into cold water for a few moments, and then cook in boiling salted water, barely enough to keep from burning. They will cook tender in from twenty to thirty minutes. For about *one pint* of the *carrot* allow *one heaping teaspoon* each of *butter* and *flour,* creamed together; stir it into the boiling liquid. There should be but a few spoonfuls, but by tipping the pan toward you they can be blended easily. Add *half* a *teaspoonful* of *salt* and a little *pepper,* let it boil about five minutes, then sprinkle over a little fine parsley; turn into the dish and sprinkle again with parsley, using about *one teaspoonful* in all.

Sweet Carrots. — The carrots are best cut in quarter inch dice. Boil them in salt water uncovered. When they are almost tender, pour off all but perhaps a quarter of a cup of the water, put them back on the stove, sprinkle with *two* or *three tablespoonfuls* of *sugar* and allow them to cook until the water has boiled away, shaking the pot occasionally and shifting the carrots from top to bottom with a fork that they may all come in contact with the sweetened water. They should be decidedly sweet. When the liquid is absorbed, melt a *tablespoon-ful* of *butter* in the carrots, and pour over a *teaspoonful* of *lemon juice*, and they are ready.

German Cabbage. — Cut a two inch cube of fat salt pork in dice and fry it slightly in the bottom of the stewpan, add *one cup* of boiling *water*, and *two quarts* of shredded *cabbage*, and *one* sour *apple* cut fine. Cook one hour very slowly. When it is half done, add *half* a cup of *vinegar*.

Summer Squash. — Use only very young, tender squashes. Wash and cut off the stem, lay them in a kettle with barely water enough to keep them from burning on, and cook until tender. Drain and let the water boil down to a thick syrup, add *butter*, *salt,* and *pepper*. Cut the squash in portions for serving, and pour the seasoned sauce over it. In this way the delicate flavor of the squash is retained.

Summer Squash, No. 2. — Steam the squash until tender. Then put into a cheese-cloth strainer and squeeze out some of the water. Mash and break up fine, and season with salt, pepper, and butter.

Fried Squash. — Cut young tender squash in half-inch slices, dip in flour seasoned with salt and pepper. Cook slowly in hot butter or salt pork fat, until browned.

Italian Chestnuts. (*Lia Rand.*) — *Two pounds* of large *chestnuts*, the shells taken clean off with a very sharp knife. Pour boiling water over them and the under skin will come off readily. Peel and cut up *four red onions*, stew them in butter until soft, but not brown. Add the peeled chestnuts, and pour over them enough soup stock to keep them moist without burning. Salt them but not too much. When the chestnuts are nearly done, add to them *four* large *apples* peeled, cored, and sliced. Add them to the chestnuts, and let them simmer until done. Then add sugar to taste.

This dish has a very rich flavor, and may be well worth trying by those who want a new combination.

Many poor families in Italy derive their principal sustenance from the fruit of the chestnut-trees. The nuts are peeled, dried in the sun, ground into flour, and made into bread. The chestnuts are used also in soups, sauces, purées, forcemeats, entrées, and sweet dishes for dessert.

Barley à la Strassburg. — Pour boiling water over *half* a *cup* of pearl *barley;* remove any specks or insects, and drain dry. Melt *one tablespoon butter* in a stewpan ; add the barley, and let it cook until slightly browned and it has absorbed the butter. Then add *one quart* of thin *stock* and let it boil until tender and dry. Season with salt and serve as a vegetable.

Lentil Hash. (*Dr. Alice B. Stockton.*) — Take *one pint* cooked *lentils, one-half pint* of cold *potatoes* chopped fine, *two tablespoonfuls* chopped *onions, one tablespoonful salt, one-half teaspoonful pepper, two tablespoonfuls butter, one-half cup milk,* cook slowly for an hour, then brown and turn.

The lentils used for the above should already have been cooked at least eight hours in a double boiler at a temperature of about 200°. When thus cooked they can be used for hash, croquettes, soup, and many other purposes.

B. B. B. Cakes. — A cupful more or less of cold baked beans may be left after the family are tired of seeing this dish for Saturday's supper, Sunday's breakfast, and washing day lunch, and yet it seems wasteful to throw them away. Sift them, and if very dry add a little hot water to moisten enough to shape them into small flat cakes. First season them with salt, if needed, and mustard. Cook *one tablespoonful* of chopped *onion* in a little *pork fat* or *butter,* and when slightly colored put in the cakes and brown on each side. Serve with toasted brown bread.

Baked Corn and Beans. — Take equal quantities of shelled beans and sweet corn cut from the cob, — put them into a bean-pot in layers, sprinkling salt and pepper between each layer. For *one pint* each of *corn* and *beans* take *one-half pound salt pork,* score the rind and place in the top of the bean-pot, letting the rind come up even with the corn and beans. Cover with boiling water and bake slowly seven or eight hours, adding more water as it cooks away.

A Rice Course for a Green-and-White Luncheon. — Put *one cup* of *rice* and *one cup* and a *half* of boiling *water* in a small tightly covered stewpan over the fire, and let it boil rapidly without raising the cover until the steam from the rice lifts the cover. When done, the rice will be full of steam holes. Season with *salt, pepper,* and *butter.* Drain the liquor from a *can* of *peas,* rinse them in cold water; put on to heat, with *one tablespoon* of *butter; salt, pepper,* and *sugar* to taste.

Arrange a portion of rice on a lettuce leaf, making a slight depression in the centre, into which pile a portion of the peas. Sprinkle a little grated cheese over the whole.

Mushrooms. Campestris. — Clean, peel the caps, and broil from six to ten minutes. Cook the gill side first. When done, spread at once with butter, creamed and flavored with lemon and parsley.

Baked Mushrooms.— Place the caps on toast, spread with prepared maître d'hôtel butter, and bake in a covered dish from twelve to fifteen minutes.

Fried Green Tomatoes.— Cut off both ends from nice, large, green tomatoes, cut in thin slices; roll them in flour, and cook them in hot butter in the frying-pan. Sprinkle with salt, pepper, and sugar, and cook until brown. Fry a sliced onion with them if you like the flavor. Serve them with fish-balls.

Potatoes au Gratin. — *One cup white sauce, one pint* cold boiled *potato* dice, *one-half cup cracker crumbs* moistened with *one tablespoon melted butter,* and *one-half cup cheese.* Put potatoes, cheese, and sauce, two layers of each, in buttered baking dish, cover with crumbs and bake fifteen minutes.

Potatoes Warmed in Stock. — Cut into half-inch dice, or into thin slices, enough cold boiled potatoes to make one pint. Season well with *salt, pepper*, fine-chopped *parsley*, and *one teaspoon* of *lemon juice*. Cook *one* sliced *onion* in *one tablespoon beef dripping* until you have a strong odor of the onion, but do not burn them. Add the potatoes, and cook a few minutes, or until slightly browned; toss them up and brown again, then add *one cup* of *corned beef liquor*, and let them simmer until the liquor is nearly absorbed. *One-fourth part* of *cold beet* and *vinegar* may take the place of the parsley and lemon, to make another variety.

Radishes. — The small, smooth, round, or slightly oval red radishes are generally preferred, although occasionally we find the long pointed varieties both red and white. The red skin is sometimes nearly removed by scraping, as it is objectionable to some tastes, but it adds so much to the attractive appearance of the table that it seems a pity to lose it. Trim off the fine roots and cut the leaves about an inch from the root. The delicate green will contrast prettily with the red, and the stems make a convenient handle. Put them in a pan of ice water till firm and crisp. With a small sharp knife begin at the point, and make several slight incisions through the skin merely, down about half-way and one-third inch or more apart. Slip the point of the knife under the skin at each point and separate it from the flesh. Press the points outward slightly, then let them remain in ice water, and when ready to serve you will find them open at the cut end like a flower. When the radishes are large, the point of each petal may be rounded off slightly to imitate a tulip. Use them as a garnish for meat or salads, or arrange them in a small glass dish, as a part of the table decoration, or serve two with two or three olives on fancy individual dishes at each plate. Salt is the only condiment needed.

Spring Salad. — In a salad bowl put first a layer of fresh crisp watercress, then a layer of thinly sliced cucumbers which have been soaked in cold water fifteen minutes, then a teaspoonful of minced chives, then another layer of cucumbers, and around the edge a light border of the cresses. When ready to serve, pour a French dressing over it and . toss it over until well mingled. This is appropriate to serve with a course of broiled fish.

Lincoln Salad.	1 quart oysters. 3 cucumbers. 1 tsp. salt.	1 saltsp. black pepper. 1 bunch watercresses. cream dressing to moisten.

Pick over the oysters and parboil until the edges curl, drain very dry, cool and cut into small uniform pieces. Pare the cucumbers and leave in cold water until needed. Then cut into quarters lengthwise (sixths, if very large), trim off the edge containing the seeds, then dry on a towel and cut into thin slices. Season them highly with salt and black pepper, and add them to the oysters. Moisten with cream dressing, turn into a salad bowl lined with cresses, put some of the best sprigs on the edge, and cover with the remainder of the dressing.

German Cucumber Salad. — The slightly acid juice of the cucumber is disagreeable to many delicate stomachs, and this is drawn out largely by this method of preparing them. We have been taught that cucumbers should be crisp and firm, and that if wilted or soft they were not suitable to serve. But I have eaten them frequently during the last season, prepared as below, and found them delicious and less likely to remind me of their presence in my internal economy than when served in our way.

This method also enables one to use cucumbers that are older than we generally like to have them, as the seeds which are the objectionable part when the fruit is too ripe, are not served.

Pare the cucumbers, and then cut them in half-inch slices. Then pare each slice as thinly as possible from the outside to the seed part, making a long, thin, curling strip. Cover them with cold water and add one round teaspoon of salt for each cucumber. Let them soak until soft, from one to two hours. Then drain off the water and squeeze them in a soft cloth until quite dry. Toss them up in a salad bowl and dress with cayenne, oil, and vinegar, and serve very cold.

Apple and Celery Salad.—Have the celery nicely cleaned and crisped by keeping it in a damp napkin on the ice until just before ready to use. Then cut it into thin crescent-shaped slices. With a silver knife pare and core some mildly tart apples, cut into eighths or narrower, if very large apples are used, and then cut across the sections into thin slices. Use equal parts of celery and apple. Mix in sufficient mayonnaise dressing to hold the pieces together. Arrange crisp cup-shaped lettuce leaves on a pretty shallow dish, put a portion of the mixture on each leaf, dot the top with a teaspoon of the mayonnaise, and serve quickly. Do not pare the apple until ready to put the mixture together. A simple French dressing may be used if preferred, and by many would be thought more suitable for a dinner salad.

No. 2. — Whip *one cup* of thick well-chilled *cream*, with an egg-beater or fork until thick, then add gradually sufficient lemon juice to thin it slightly, and season with *half* a *teaspoonful* of *celery salt* and a *spoonful* of *paprika*. Use a thin-skinned tart apple. Wipe, quarter, and core without paring, divide again lengthwise into two or three pieces, then slice very thin. For *two cups* of the *apple* use *one cup* of fine cut *celery*. Moisten with the cream dressing. Season to taste with salt and pepper. Arrange in a shallow glass dish and garnish with green celery tips and crescents of the red apples.

Chestnut, Apple, and Celery Salad. — Prepare the apple and celery as directed in the first recipe. Shell, parboil, and skin the large French chestnuts. Boil twelve minutes, or until soft, but not broken. Drain, and when cool cut them into thin slices. Use one cup of each measured after slicing. Season highly with a French dressing, and keep in a cold place. Serve in a salad bowl surrounded with crisp lettuce.

Apple and Onion Salad. — Boil *one cup* of *vinegar.* If strong, use half water. Mix *one teaspoonful mustard, one teaspoonful cornstarch, one-half teaspoonful salt,* and *one-half saltspoonful pepper* with *one* well-beaten *egg.* Stir this into the boiling vinegar and cook until creamy. Pour it over *two* mildly acid *apples* and *one onion* chopped fine. Serve it with lettuce cups.

Nut Salad. — Equal parts of apple, celery, and nuts. Cut the apple in eighths, pare and cut from the end in thin slices. Split the celery stalks if they are wide, and then lay several together and shave off in thin crescents.

Use almonds, peanuts, pecans, or walnuts. Salted almonds and peanuts may be chopped medium fine, pecans and walnuts crumbled, or chopped. Some prefer to parboil the walnuts and remove the skin; the slight cooking softens them somewhat. It is not necessary to have equal parts of each, for with almost any proportion that I have chanced to have, if the seasoning has been right, the salad has been good.

Mix with a mayonnaise dressing and serve with or without crisp lettuce. Salt and pepper the mixture well before adding the mayonnaise.

Fruit Salad. — Remove the sections of pineapple with a silver fork. Stone the cherries, being careful to save the juice. Hull the berries, mix all together, place on lettuce leaves and garnish with stars of mayonnaise dressing.

Another way: Make a bed of lettuce leaves on a glass dish, keeping the fruit separated one from the other; make three mounds, and garnish in the same way. Select the dark, almost black cherries, as it gives you three distinct colors. Use equal parts of pineapple, cherries, and strawberries.

Fruit Cups. — Cut oranges in halves and with a spoon scoop out the pulp and juice, then scrape out the white membrane and set the cups in a pan of ice. Cut Malaga grapes in halves and remove the seeds. If the skins are tough, peel them before cutting. Have equal parts of grapes and banana, cut in small pieces. Add the juice of one lemon to the juice of three oranges, and sweeten it quite sweet. Add also a dash of salt. Fill the orange cups with the mixture of fruits, pour the sweetened juice over the fruit, and put a spoonful of thick whipped cream on top. Serve very cold.

Tomato Jelly Salad. — Soak *one-half box* of *gelatine* in *one-half cup* of cold *water* fifteen minutes, or till soft. Stew *one can* of *tomatoes* till soft, cutting and mashing the pulp to hasten the process. For additional flavoring, stew with the tomato a *half inch* bit of *bay leaf, one-half teaspoon* of mixed whole *spices, one rounded tablespoon* of *celery salt*, and *one-half* a small *Bermuda onion.* Strain the tomato through a purée sieve, and if there is not enough to make three cups add boiling water. Heat again to boiling point, add the soaked gelatine, stir till dissolved, then pour it into small cups or fancy moulds, or into a ring mould, if individual forms are not desired. Chill, and when ready to serve, turn out and serve the small forms on lettuce leaves with mayonnaise on the top. Or turn the ring mould out on a salad dish, fill the centre with any salad mixture you prefer, and garnish with any appropriate border of green.

Salad in Tomato Jelly Cups. — Soak *one-half box* of *gelatine* in *one cup* of cold *water* in which some celery has been stewed. Put into a stewpan *one quart can* of *tomatoes, one tablespoon* of minced *parsley, one tablespoon* of *chives, one teaspoon* of *salt, one-fourth teaspoon* of *paprika, two tablespoons* of *lemon juice*, and *two carda-mom seeds.* Stew until the pulp is tender, then strain it, without pressure, heat again to a boiling point, add the soaked gelatine and strain it again into a pitcher. Have ready two sizes of small round moulds or cups. Put the larger moulds in a pan and surround them with broken ice. Pour in jelly to the depth of one-third inch. When firm, place the smaller mould inside and add a few spoonfuls of jelly between the moulds. When this is firm, add the remainder till the larger moulds are filled. Fill the smaller mould with broken ice to hasten the process. When the jelly is firm, remove the ice, add hot water to the smaller mould till it can be lifted out carefully. Fill the space with oyster salad, or any preferred salad, and when ready to serve, invert on a dish, and garnish with whipped cream dressing and watercress.

Salad of Remnants. — Mix *one cup* of cold boiled *celery* cut in bits, *one cup* of cooked *cauliflower*, and *one-half cup* of canned *butter beans*. If you have no mayonnaise dressing left over, or do not like the oil in the plain French dressing, make a cream dressing as follows: Mix *one-fourth teaspoon* of *mustard*, *one-fourth teaspoon* of *salt*, *one-half teaspoon* of *sugar*, and a few grains of *paprika*. Add the *yolk* of *one egg* and mix well, then the white beaten till foamy (not stiff), and *one tablespoon* of thick *cream*. Gradually add *one-fourth cup* of hot *vinegar*, and cook over boiling water till it thickens, stirring constantly. When cold pour it over the mixed vegetables. Or the vegetables may be arranged in groups, each kind by itself, and the dressing served separately.

Asparagus. — Break off the stalks where they are tender, wash, tie in a bundle, cook in boiling water till tender. Drain, cut into inch pieces, and pour white sauce over it, using only enough to moisten.

Asparagus Salad. — Use only about three inches of the tip end, and cook as directed above, and chill it thoroughly. Serve it on a platter, and pass with it a French dressing, served in small dishes, into which each stalk may be dipped as desired.

Potato Salad. — Boil potatoes without paring, and remove when not quite soft. Peel, and when cool slice thin, and season with salt and pepper. To *one quart*, allow *one* small *onion* sliced, and double the rule for French dressing. Mix thoroughly, and add more oil and vinegar if needed. Potatoes vary in the amount they will absorb. Chill thoroughly, and serve with a garnish of lettuce, parsley, celery, or boiled egg.

French Dressing. — *One-fourth teaspoon* of *salt, one-eighth teaspoon* of *pepper, three tablespoons* of *olive oil,* and *one tablespoon* of *vinegar,* tarragon vinegar preferred.

Sour Cream Dresssing, No. 1. — *Three-fourths cup* of sour *cream,* fill the cup with *vinegar,* stir in *half* a *teaspoonful salt* and *one saltspoonful paprika.*

No. 2. — *One pint* thick sour *cream, three tablespoonfuls sugar, one level teaspoonful salt, one saltspoonful paprika, half* a *saltspoonful black pepper two tablespoonfuls vinegar.*

No. 3. — *One cup* sour *cream, one tablespoonful sugar, half* a *teaspoonful salt, half* a *saltspoonful white pepper, one tablespoonful lemon juice.*

No. 4. — Make the usual mayonnaise with *yolk* of *one* raw *egg, half* a *teaspoonful salt, one saltspoonful paprika, one saltspoonful mustard, one cup oil* added in small portions until the mixture thickens, *two tablespoonfuls lemon juice,* and when ready to use, stir in *half* a *cup* of sour *cream.*

Cream Salad Dressing. — A small quantity of salad dressing may be made very quickly in an emergency, by simply mixing *two teaspoonfuls* of *vinegar* or *lemon juice* with *four tablespoonfuls* of sweet or sour *cream,* and seasoning with a speck of *cayenne* and *salt* and *pepper* to taste.

Whipped Cream Dressing. — Surround *one cup* of thick cream with broken ice, and whip it stiff with a wire whisk or egg-beater. Add gradually *three tablespoons* of *lemon juice, three* of grated *horse-radish, one-half teaspoon* of *salt,* and *one-fourth teaspoon* of *paprika.* It should be stiff enough to keep in shape when dropped from the spoon. Keep it very cold till ready to serve. Mix a small portion of it with the oysters and cucumbers, and use the remainder for a garnish. (See Lincoln Salad.)

Lettuce Salad with Claret Dressing. — Mix *one teaspoon* of *German mustard, one half teaspoon* of *salt, one-eighth teaspoon* of freshly-ground *pepper, four tablespoons* of *olive oil, one tablespoon* of *claret.* Have a head of lettuce washed and drained dry. Tear it into bits, put it in the bowl, pour the dressing over it, and toss about until well dressed.

Boiled Dressing. (*Mrs. Webster.*) — Heat *one-half cup* vinegar in the top of the double boiler. In a small bowl, mix thoroughly, *two* level *teaspoons* of *mustard, two* level *teaspoons* of *salt, three* level *tablespoons* of *sugar* (less if preferred), *one-fourth teaspoon* of *cayenne* or *paprika, two tablespoons* of melted *butter,* and *one cup* of rich *cream.* Break *four eggs* into a large bowl and beat them until very light and thick, add the mixture and pour all into the hot vinegar in the double boiler. Cook like boiled custard, stirring constantly, and be careful that it does not curdle.

Sorrento Sandwiches. — Boil the liver from a pair of chickens until very tender, rub through a strainer, and mix it with an equal amount of olives chopped very fine. Moisten with mayonnaise dressing, and put between two buttered rounds of bread.

Salmon and Brown Bread Sandwiches. — Use brown bread which has been steamed in half-pound baking-powder cans. Cut in thin slices. Flake *one cupful* of cold boiled *salmon* and mix it to a paste with *one tablespoonful mayonnaise dressing.* Add more *salt* and *cayenne* if desired. Spread it on the bread, cover with a layer of thin slices of *cucumber*, then another round of bread, press lightly, and arrange them in an overlapping circle around a few sprigs of *parsley.*

Sweetbread Sandwiches. — Break up one cold boiled sweetbread, remove the membranes and press through a potato-ricer. Moisten with half as much thick whipped cream, and season to taste with salt, cayenne, and lemon juice. Spread on thin slices of bread, cover with the leaves of watercress and another slice of buttered bread, press, and cut into triangles.

Lettuce Sandwiches. — Select nice tender, crisp lettuce, wash and dry well, but do not make the sandwiches until just before serving.

Butter the bread and cover with the lettuce, and spread a thin layer of salad dressing on the other slice, and press them together tightly. Cut in halves, or cut into rounds before filling. Tear the lettuce to fit the slices. When a rich mayonnaise is used, it is not necessary to spread with butter, although many recipes call for it.

Flower Sandwiches. — Sweet clover, sweet peas, violets, roses, cinnamon pinks, apple blossoms, nasturtiums, and heliotrope may be used, some for fragrance merely and some for a part of the filling.

Flavor the butter by cutting the desired quantity in small pieces, then lay it in thin cheese-cloth with the flowers all around it, and let it stand several hours in a close-covered jar.

Spread the bread with the fragrant butter, and, if you like, sprinkle a few petals over the butter, then roll over and press firmly. Put them back with the flowers and cover tightly, and when ready to serve arrange them in a dish with fresh flowers.

Cucumber Sandwiches. — Select cucumbers that are small and thin, that there may be no large seeds. Peel and slice as thinly as possible, into ice water, and let them stand ten minutes. Drain very dry, and place them between thin slices of bread which have been spread with mayonnaise dressing.

German Cucumber Sandwiches. — Peel the large cucumbers, cut in quarters lengthwise, and cut off the inside. Slice very thin, and let them stand in cold salted water until they are soft. Drain and press between towels to remove all the water. Butter thin rounds of brown bread, cover with a layer of the cucumber, season with a thick French dressing, and cover with another buttered round of bread.

Cheese and Nut Sandwiches. — Take equal parts of grated cheese and English walnuts pounded to a meal, or ground; moisten with thick sweet cream, and season to taste with salt. Spread between thin slices of buttered bread.

No. 2. — Chop fine or run through an almond grater *half* a *cup* of *pecans*. Melt *half* a *cup* of *Edam cheese*, and blend it thoroughly with the nuts. Add *half* a *saltspoon* of *paprika*, and salt to taste. Spread the paste on thin slices of bread, and cut in small squares or triangles.

Cherry Sandwiches. — Chop candied cherries fine, and moisten slightly with orange juice, or maraschino. Spread them on rounds of thin, lightly buttered bread, cover with another round, and serve on a dainty napkin.

Crab-Apple Sandwiches. — Use whole-wheat bread, cut in one-third inch slices. Spread with a thin coating of thick cream, a little salt, and thin slivers of crab-apple jelly. Serve these with lemonade.

Ginger Sandwiches. — Bake a plain gingerbread in a thin sheet, or make soft cookies, and when cold cut into oblong pieces and split carefully. Spread with cream cheese, and put a thin slice of preserved ginger in the middle, cover, press slightly, and arrange on a napkin.

Orange Marmalade Sandwiches. — Remove the crust from the end of a brick loaf of bread. Spread the end with creamed butter, and then cut off a thin even slice and repeat until you have sufficient.

Spread marmalade over the buttered side of one slice, being careful not to put it near the crust, lay another buttered slice on this, press them together with a broad knife, and trim off the crust. If the slices are large, divide them into triangles, or squares, or three long narrow pieces. Or you may roll them and press slightly. Arrange them neatly in a fringed napkin, cover and serve as soon as possible. For a luncheon course you may use bread one day old, and toast it slightly before filling, and serve hot.

Fig Sandwiches. — Use ripe figs that come in cans, or the delicious figs in cordial. Drain them from the syrup, then mash them to a paste, and spread on one part of the sandwich as directed for orange marmalade.

Dates and Nuts. — Remove the stones and scales from the dates and break them up with a fork. Take half as much in bulk of pecans chopped fine or run through a nut-grater, mix them with the dates and moisten with creamed butter. Add a dash of salt, and spread between two thin slices of bread.

Mushroom Sandwiches. — A popular sandwich for afternoon tea consists of thin slices of entire-wheat bread, with a layer of cooked mushrooms between. The mushrooms should be stewed until tender, and superfluous moisture allowed to evaporate, that the bread may not become soggy.

Deep Apple Pie. — Fill a deep earthen or granite dish with apples, pared, quartered, and cored. Sprinkle over them *half* a *cup* of *brown sugar* mixed with *one saltspoonful* of *allspice;* or you may use maple sugar, or half sugar and half molasses. Roll a strip of paste, one inch wide, wet the edge of the dish, put the paste on the edge, wet the rim of paste, then cover with a piece of paste a little larger than the dish, with the extra fulness thrown back into the centre. Press the cover to the rim, but not on the outer edge. Bake half an hour, or until the apples are soft.

Cherry Tarts — Into *one cup* of pastry *flour* mix *one scant half teaspoon* of *salt.* Add *one-fourth cup* of *lard,* and chop it fine, using a knife instead of the fingers to avoid softening the lard, which should have been kept on the ice till quite hard. Mix with cold water to a stiff dough. Toss it out on a floured board, and pound it flat half an inch thick. Put on butter in little dabs here and there, dredge it slightly with flour, roll up and pat it out again. Do this four times, using *one-fourth cup* in all. After the last patting out, put it on ice until chilled. Use small tin cups or corn-cake tins to shape the tarts. Sprinkle them with flour on the outside, shake off all that does not adhere, then cover the outside with a thin layer of the paste. Roll the paste very thin, and cut with a saucer or cutter which will give you just the size to fit the tin. Put the cups on a baking sheet and bake quickly. When done, remove the tin by turning the cup over, and fill the crust with the prepared cherries. Wash, stem, and stone the cherries. Allow about *one cup* of *sugar* to *one pint* of *cherries*, if the very sour variety, possibly more will be needed. Put the sugar and one-half cup of water on the fire, and when boiling add the fruit, and cook ten minutes. Stir in *one teaspoon* of *butter*, and if the syrup seems thin, wet *one teaspoon* of *cornstarch* in cold water, and stir in sufficient to thicken it slightly.

34

A Quick Dessert. — When an emergency arises where a dessert must be prepared quickly, open a can of peaches, apricots, raspberries, or any available fruit. Put it in a rather large kettle with a close-fitting cover. While it is heating, mix *one pint* of prepared *flour* with *one* beaten *egg* and *one* scant *cupful* of *milk*. Drop this like dumplings in a stew over the fruit, cover closely, and steam from ten to fifteen minutes. Unless the fruit is juicy, there is danger that it will burn on the kettle while the dumplings are cooking. Serve the dumplings and fruit together with sugar and cream, or with a hard sauce.

Noodles. (*A German Dessert.*) — Break *two eggs* into a bowl, and stir in as much *flour* as they will take up in making a very stiff dough. Knead well. Roll out thin as a wafer, and roll up and cut off in thin strips. Let them boil in sweetened milk ten or fifteen minutes, or until done; then skim them out. Rub *two tablespoons* of *butter* to a cream; add *four yolks* of *eggs* beaten; then stir in the noodles and enough of the milk to make them moist. Add the whites of the eggs, beaten stiff.

Put a layer of noodles in a baking dish, then a layer of any marmalade or jam, then another layer of each and another of noodles on top, and bake about twenty minutes, or until brown.

A friend who received her culinary education in Austria recommends the following as being a most delicious

Macaroon Pudding. — Take *eight zwieback*, remove the crusts and put them in melted butter to soften; then let them cool.

Put *half* a *pound* of *macaroons*, using part *butter* and part *suet*, into a bowl, and saturate them in *claret wine* thoroughly, or use syrup from whole *peaches* or *plums*, if you don't care for the wine. Remove the seeds from *quarter* of a *pound* of *raisins*, and cut the same amount of *citron* in small thin slices. Mix *one teaspoon* of *cinnamon* with *one teaspoon* of powdered *sugar*.

Butter a pudding mould, sprinkle with fine cracker or bread crumbs, and line it with the softened zwieback. Put in a layer of macaroons, then a layer of citron, spices, and raisins; then another layer of macaroons and another of zwieback. Mix half a cup of cream with four to six beaten eggs, and pour this over the pudding. Add also the wine or syrup left from the macaroons. Steam it one hour, and serve with creamy sauce.

Creamy	1 pt. milk.	1 rounded tbsp. butter.
Sponge	1 heaped cup flour.	3 eggs.
Pudding.	¼ cup sugar.	

Scald half of the milk in a double boiler. Mix the sugar and flour, add the cold milk, and stir into the boiling milk. Cook five minutes, stirring until it thickens. Stir the butter in and when well mixed remove from the fire, and when nearly cold stir in the well-beaten yolks of the eggs. Beat the whites of the eggs until stiff and dry, and fold them in lightly. Turn into a buttered pudding dish, place the dish in a pan of hot water, and bake half an hour in a hot oven. Serve immediately. This is a delicious pudding and convenient to make, as the materials are such as one would usually have on hand, and the first part of the process may be done in the early part of the day, leaving nothing to be done at dinner time except to beat the whites of the eggs. Plan to put it into the oven just half an hour before it will be served, as it is better if it be served directly from the oven to the table. When properly baked, it will not fall, and if any be left over it can be reheated for another meal, and will be good, even if not as nice as at first. Creamy sauce should be served with it.

Cherry Roly Poly. — Into *one pint* of *flour* mix *one-half teaspoon* of *salt* and *three* level *teaspoons* of *baking-powder*; rub in *one tablespoon* of *butter* and mix with milk into a stiff dough. Toss out on a floured board, and roll or pat out half an inch thick and in rectangular shape;

have ready some cherries stoned and well drained; lay
them on the surface, pressing them slightly into the
dough; dredge with flour and roll over into a loose roll;
pinch the ends together and wrap in a cloth; lay it on a
steamer and cook about one hour; make a sauce with the
juice of the cherries and as much water, add sugar to
taste, let the mixture boil, and thicken it with cornstarch;
stir in one heaped tablespoon of butter and serve at once.

Fig	1 cup butter.	1 lb figs, cut small.
Pudding	2 cups sugar.	½ cup milk.
(*Mrs. Morris*)	3 eggs	½ tsp nutmeg.
	3 cups bread crumbs.	1 tsp. cinnamon.

Cream the butter and sugar, add eggs beaten slightly,
then the bread crumbs, the figs cut in small pieces, the
milk and spice. Turn into a buttered mould or pail, and
steam three hours. Serve with a thin sauce, lemon, or
fruit-syrup sauce.

Eddington	2½ qts boiling milk.	½ tsp ginger.
Pudding.	1 cup cornmeal.	½ tsp cinnamon.
	1 cup water.	1 cup molasses.
	½ tsp salt	3 sweet apples.

Pour the boiling milk on the cornmeal, add the other
ingredients in order, and the apples cut into eighths.
Bake in a covered deep pudding dish four hours.

Coburg Pudding. — Heat *three cups* of *milk* in a double
boiler. Cook *half* a *cup* of well-washed *rice* in *one cup*
of boiling *water* five minutes, or until the water is all
absorbed. Turn it into the hot milk and cook until very
tender. Stir in *one teaspoonful* of *salt* and *one teaspoonful* of *butter*.

Beat *one egg* very light, add *two tablespoonfuls sugar*,
and stir this into the hot rice just as you take it from the
fire. When well mixed, and the egg is scalded, turn into
a dish for serving. Mix *two tablespoonfuls* of *sugar* and
one teaspoonful of *cinnamon*, sprinkle this evenly over
the top, dot with *one* heaping *teaspoonful* of *butter* in

little bits. Do this just before you are ready for dinner, and by the time the pudding should be served, the sugar, spice, and butter will have formed a delicious sauce over the surface of the pudding.

Sponge Cake Pudding. — Stale sponge cake, enough to fill a three-pint dish, when the cake is cut in slices ; between each layer place dates that have been cut length-wise to remove the stone, turn over this a custard made of *one pint milk, yolks* of *two eggs, half cup sugar, one spoonful wine* or *flavoring.*

Bake twenty minutes and cover with the whites beaten with one-half cup sugar and spread over the top and browned.

Dorchester Club Pudding.		
1 cup hot milk		½ teasp. salt.
½ cup stale sponge cake crumbs.		1 cup grated apple.
2 eggs, yolks.		½ cup whipped cream.
½ cup sugar.		2 eggs, whites
½ lemon, rind and juice.		2 tbsp. pd. sugar. }
		½ lemon, juice }

Soak the cake in the hot milk until soft. Beat yolks, add sugar, salt, grated rind and juice of half the lemon, and stir this into the milk. Whip the cream. Grate the apple quickly into the mixture, add the cream and turn into a buttered pudding dish, and bake about half an hour or until it puffs all over. When slightly cooled, cover with the meringue and brown in the oven.

Apricot Pudding.	
½ lb. dried apricots.	¼ lb. fine white hominy.
½ lb. sugar.	—

Wash the apricots in cold and then in hot water. Put them and the hominy in a scant quart of cold water and soak all day. Next day cook it two hours in a double boiler, then add sugar and cook two hours longer, stirring every half hour. Turn into wetted moulds and serve very cold with cream.

Iced Cherry Pudding. — Beat the *yolks* of *three eggs* slightly. Whip *one cup* thick *cream* and mix it with the yolks. Add *half* a *wineglass* of *rum* and the whites of the eggs, beaten stiff. Stir in *two tablespoons* of preserved *cherries*. Turn it into a mould which has been wet in cold water, and pack it in ice and salt for five hours.

Prune	1 pt. prune juice.	¼ cup cold water.
Cream.	¼ cup sugar.	¼ cup boiling water.
	1 tbsp. gian gelatine.	1 pt. cream

Measure the gelatine slightly more than level, or use one-fourth box of shredded, soak it in the cold water, then dissolve in the boiling water and strain it into the prune syrup. Add more or less sugar as the prunes require, but avoid having them too sweet. Some prunes are improved by the addition of lemon juice. Cool, and when it begins to thicken, beat in one cup of prunes stoned and cut small, and the whipped cream. Turn it into a plain mould or line the mould first with lady fingers. Use for this a thin cream whipped in a churn.

Prune Pudding. — Whip the *whites* of *five eggs* to a stiff froth, add slowly *five tablespoonfuls* powdered *sugar*, beating all the time. Then add *one cup* of cooked *prunes* chopped, and beat until very light. Put into a small pudding dish and bake about ten minutes; then set away to cool. Beat the *yolks* of *five eggs*, add *half* a *cup* of *sugar*, and beat until creamy. Add *one pint* of hot *milk* slowly, and cook in double boiler until thick like soft custard. Cool and serve as a sauce for the prune pudding.

Mist Pudding. — Steep the thin shavings of rind of *half* a *lemon* in *one pint water*. Mix *one cup sugar*, *one-half saltspoon salt*, and *three rounded tablespoons cornstarch*, and pour on them *two cups* of the strained boiling *lemon water*. Cook in double boiler ten minutes, stirring constantly. Add the juice of one lemon, and then stir in quickly the stiffly *beaten* whites of *three eggs.*

Mix well and turn into small cups or moulds.

Make a soft custard with the *yolks* of *three eggs, three tablespoons sugar,* and a *pinch* of *salt,* cook in double boiler till smooth. Strain, and when cool, flavor with vanilla. When ready to serve, turn out the puddings on individual dishes with the sauce around.

Coffee Jelly. — Soak *half box gelatine* in *half cup cold water,* then dissolve it in *one cup* boiling *water,* add *one-third cup sugar* and *one pint* clear boiled *coffee.* When sugar is dissolved, strain through fine cloth, pour into a ring mould which has been wet in cold water. When ready to serve, turn out and pour whipped cream into the centre. Sweeten the cream before whipping. Or you may serve it in a plain mould and pass thin cream and powdered sugar with it.

Coffee Cream with Junket. — Warm *one pint* of *milk* to blood heat. Dissolve in it *one tablespoon* of *sugar* and a *saltspoon* of *salt.* Flavor with *one teaspoon* of *coffee extract* or *one tablespoon* of *black* or very strong *coffee.* Remove from the fire and stir in quickly one junket tablet, then pour into a dish suitable for serving and place it on ice until ready to serve. To be eaten with sugar and cream.

Fruit Souffle with Junket. — Put into a bowl *one heaping cup* of fresh, whole *strawberries* or *raspberries*, those without any hard cores or spots are to be preferred. Sprinkle over them *one cup* of *powdered sugar* and add the unbeaten *white* of *one egg.* Beat with a perforated wooden spoon or a silver fork, slowly at first until the berries are broken and mixed with the egg and sugar, then rapidly and continuously until the mass is stiff enough to hold its shape. It takes about half an hour, so do not attempt it until you are blessed with the time and strength. When it is stiff, place it in the ice chest until ready to serve. Dissolve *one tablespoon* of *sugar* and *one saltspoon* of *salt* in *one pint* of fresh warm *milk*. Then stir in quickly one junket tablet and turn at once into a deep glass dish. When firm and cold, pile the fruit soufflé lightly on the surface.

Hot Chocolate Sauce, with Arrowroot. For Ice Cream. — Put into a saucepan *one cup* of *water*, *one-half cup* of *sugar*, *one-half inch* bit of stick *cinnamon*, and *one ounce* or *square* of *chocolate* melted over hot water and mixed with *one-half cup* of *milk*. When boiling, thicken with *one tablespoon* of *arrowroot* wet in *one-fourth cup* of *water*. Stir as it thickens, and cook five minutes. Remove the cinnamon, add *one teaspoon* of *vanilla*, a little *salt*, and serve it hot. Pour a small portion over each slice of ice cream.

Plain Chocolate Sauce, No. 2. — Melt *four squares* of *chocolate* over the teakettle, add *four tablespoons* of *sugar*, and stir till smooth. Add gradually *one scant cup* of hot *water*, and boil it slowly ten minutes. Then add *one-half cup* of *cream*.

Hot Chocolate Sauce, No. 3 with Eggs. — Scald *one pint* of *milk*. Mix *one-half cup* of *sugar*, *one slightly rounding tablespoon* of *cornstarch*, and a dash of *salt*, and stir them into the hot milk. Cook in a double boiler about ten minutes. Melt *one square* of *chocolate* over hot water, add *two tablespoons* of powdered *sugar* and *two tablespoons* of hot *water*, stir till smooth, then combine it with the milk. Beat the *yolks* of *two eggs* with *one-half cup* of powdered *sugar*, and when well mixed, stir them into the cooked mixture, cook one minute, add *one tablespoon* of *vanilla*, and serve hot. This should be smooth and about as thick as cream, and if necessary add more hot milk and strain it before serving.

Chocolate Sauce, No. 4. — Mix *two cups* of granulated *sugar* and *two ounces* of *Ceylon chocolate*, add *four tablespoons* of *cream, one-half cup* of *water*, and boil without stirring till it forms a soft ball in cold water. Pour it hot over the ice cream, and it will candy immediately.

Grandmother's Pound Cake. — For many years I tried in vain to make a pound cake that would have the soft, velvety texture which I remembered in that eaten at the table of a dear friend in my girlhood. The recipes which I tried made a fairly good cake, light and fine flavor, but the texture was never what I desired.

Soon after my Boston Cook Book was completed a friend gave me her mother's recipe for pound cake, and it was as definite as most of the old style formulas. *One and one-half teacups butter, two blue cups sugar, five* unbeaten *eggs*, added one at a time, and *five handfuls* of unsifted *flour*. Fortunately, my friend could show me by actual measurement just what she meant by handfuls of flour, and how she packed the butter in the teacup. The recipe then, as it stands, after a careful weighing and measurement by our standard half-pint cup, reads thus: *One cup butter* packed solid, *one and two-thirds cups* granulated *sugar, one-half teaspoon mace, five* unbeaten *eggs, two cups* sifted pastry *flour*. Have a round pan, greased and floured, the oven ready and ingredients measured, as the mixing must all be done by the hand. Cream the butter, add sugar, and work until very light, add spice and one egg at a time, and stir with the hand until you do not see any of the egg yolk, then another egg, and so on until all are used. Then mix in the flour, and turn at once into the pan, and bake slowly, about an hour.

The grain of the cake should be fine and close, with not a suspicion of any toughness or heaviness, not porous like a cake made light with gas from soda and cream of tartar or by long beating, and yet soft, light, and velvety. This texture is obtained by the thorough blending of the butter and sugar, and not over beating the eggs.

Boswell	3 cups butter.	1 nutmeg.
Cake.	6 cups sugar	1 teasp mace.
(*Mrs. Gould.*)	8 eggs.	1 teasp soda
	3 cups milk.	1 wine glass St. Croix
	10 cups flour.	rum.
	2 lbs. raisins	

Pick over and seed the raisins, and flour them with part of the measure of flour.

Mix the spice with one cup of the flour.

Measure the butter easy, in pieces about like walnuts packed in lightly, cream it with the sugar, and beat into it the well-beaten yolks of eggs.

Reserve one-fourth cup of milk to wet the soda. Warm the remainder of milk with the rum.

Then add the spiced flour to the butter mixture, then a little of the milk, and beaten whites of eggs, then alternate flour, milk, and egg white, until all are used. Stir in the fruit before the last portion of flour is added, and, if stiff enough, do not use all the flour. Add the soda dissolved in the milk last.

Bake in several small round pans, frost, and serve in the whole loaf, dividing it as needed.

White Mountain Cake. — The distinguishing feature of this cake is that it has a soft frosting, or cream, instead of jelly, between the layers. This cream is sometimes flavored and enriched with chopped nuts, or fruits. The cake is baked in pans which are much deeper than jelly cake tins, and in most stores they are known as White Mountain cake pans.

White	¾ cup butter.	1 cup milk.
Mountain	2 cups sugar.	3½ cups flour.
Cake,	2 eggs.	3 tsps. baking-powder.
No. 1.		

Mix in the order given and beat thoroughly. Bake in White Mountain cake tins, which are about one inch deep. Spread each cake with the prepared filling, and make two or three layers, as you prefer.

Filling for White Mountain Cake. — Put *half a cup boiling water* and *one cup granulated sugar* in a smooth saucepan over the teakettle, and stir until sugar melts. Place it over the fire, and boil without stirring. Dip a silver fork in occasionally, and when the syrup forms a fine thread as the fork is withdrawn, it is done. Meanwhile, have the *whites* of *two eggs* beaten stiff, and slowly pour the syrup onto it, beating as you pour. Beat until thick enough to spread easily, then flavor with *two teaspoons lemon juice*, and spread it over the cake. Add *half a cup* of *pineapple* chopped and drained, or any fine French candied fruit, or raisins, figs, nuts, in any combination you please. Mix them with a part of the frosting for the middle layers, and save a few larger pieces of the fruit or nuts for the top, pressing them into the icing before it hardens.

White Mountain Cake, No. 2.		
1 cup butter.	2½ cups pastry flour.	
2 cups fine gran. sugar.	2½ tbsp. baking powder.	
5 egg yolks.	½ tbsp. mace.	
1 scant cup milk.	3 egg whites.	

Reserve two whites for the frosting. Mix baking-powder and spice with the flour, then cream, butter, and sugar, and add beaten yolks; then milk and flour alternately, and whites last. Beat vigorously at the last, and bake in three round, shallow cake pans. Put boiled frosting between the layers, and caramel frosting on the top.

Snow-Flake Cake.		
½ cup butter.	1¾ cups flour.	
1½ cup sugar.	1 tsp. baking-powder.	
¼ cup milk.	½ tsp. rosewater.	
5 eggs (whites).	1 grated cocoanut.	

Bake in jelly-cake tins. Frost each cake, and sprinkle the cocoanut between each layer, and over the top and sides.

Caramel	½ cup butter.	3 cups pastry flour.
Cake.	2 cups sugar.	3 tsps baking-powder.
	4 eggs	1 saltsp. mace.
	1 cup milk.	1 cup walnuts (chop'd).

Cream the butter with one cup sugar. Beat yolks of eggs with the other cup. Combine the two, and add milk and flour (mixed with baking-powder, spice, and nuts), alternately. Measure baking-powder level. Bake half of it in a long cake pan and the remainder in two round pans. Frost the long loaf with caramel frosting and decorate with halved walnuts. Put caramel frosting on top of one of the round cakes, lay the other on this, pressing it slightly, and pour the remainder of the frosting over the whole.

Caramel	3 cups of C. C. sugar.	1 cup cream.
Frosting.	1 heaping tbsp. butter	

Boil them in a granite saucepan without stirring, until when dropped in cold water it is hard enough to be waxy. Stir only on the bottom, to keep from burning. Then set the pan in cold water, as it hardens, spread it on the cake while it is still soft enough to spread. It will settle into a smooth surface almost instantly.

Frosting. — *One cup powdered sugar, one tablespoonful cornstarch,* slightly rounding, *two tablespoonfuls water* or *milk,* flavor as desired. Spread with a wet knife.
This is simply mixed and requires no cooking.

Sponge Cream Cake. (*E. E. Squire.*) — This recipe is desirable when one is limited for time. It may be made, baked, filled, and decorated in just twenty-five minutes.
Two eggs and *three-fourths of a cup* of *granulated sugar* beaten together very light. Add *five tablespoonfuls* of *boiling water* (be sure the water is boiling) as quickly as possible, beat slightly, then add *one cup flour* sifted twice with *one teaspoonful baking powder* and a *saltspoonful* of *salt.* Flavor slightly with *lemon* or *vanilla* or *nutmeg.*

Beat until the flour is absorbed, no longer. Bake in two jelly-cake pans twelve minutes in a quick oven. The batter is so thin the whole process of mixing can be done with the egg-beater.

Whip *one cup* of *cream* stiff, sweeten with *pulverized sugar*, adding it a spoonful at a time while you are beating, until you have it sweet enough. Flavor to taste. Put part of it on the bottom of one cake, lay the other cake on with the top up, and put the remainder of the cream in a pastry bag containing a star tube in the end, and decorate the surface with dots of the cream.

Marshmallow Cake.	½ cup butter.	3 level teaspoons baking-powder.
	½ cup sugar.	
	½ cup milk.	½ teaspoon cream of tartar.
	1 teaspoon vanilla.	
	½ cup cornstarch.	Whites of 6 eggs.
	½ cup pastry flour	

Mix the starch, flour, baking powder, and cream of tartar. Cream the butter and sugar, add the flavoring, then a little of the flour mixture, then milk and flour alternately, and lastly the stiffly beaten whites of the eggs. If preferred, use two cups of flour and omit the cornstarch. Bake in two shallow pans, and when done, frost and mark in squares and ornament with marshmallows which have been slightly toasted, or kept in the oven until puffed. Or spread the cake with a

Marshmallow Frosting. — Cut *half a pound* of *marshmallows* in small pieces, put them in the double boiler with *four tablespoons* of *hot water* and stir till melted and smooth.

Boil *one cup* of *sugar* and *one-third of a cup* of *hot water*, without stirring, till the syrup threads when dropped from the spoon. Have the *white* of *one* large *egg* beaten stiff, and pour the syrup gradually into the egg while beating, then add the melted marshmallows gradually, flavor with *one teaspoon* of *vanilla* and *a few drops* of *lemon juice*, beat until cool and thick enough to spread

Put it on back of cake, and if you like a thick loaf, lay one on top of the other. The peculiar flavor which is noticeable in many marshmallow cakes, especially those made by Germans, is obtained from the extract of *anise seed.* Add it in small portions to the frosting till flavored to your liking; *a half teaspoonful* is usually sufficient.

Marshmallow Cake, for Dessert. (*Miss Kate E. Whittaker.*) — Bake angel cake in a square pan, and when quite two days old, cut in slices and spread a marshmallow filling between, *à la* layer cake. Ice the top and sides with a soft icing of a pale violet tint. Serve with whipped cream around and candied violets scattered on the cake.

Marshmallow Filling. — Put *one ounce* of *granulated gum arabic* with *four tablespoons* of *cold water* and soak it one hour. Then stir it over boiling water until melted. Strain it into a double boiler, add *half a cup* of *sugar* and cook thirty minutes. Then add the *whites* of *three eggs* beaten very stiff and *one teaspoon* of *vanilla.* Beat until the mixture is stiff and white.

Pistachio	½ cup butter.	2¾ cups flour.
Cream	2 cups sugar, scant	2 tsps. baking-powder.
Cake.	1 cup milk.	½ tsp almond.
	Whites of 3 eggs.	

Cream the butter, add the sugar, milk, eggs beaten till foamy, almond and flour mixed with the baking-powder. Bake in shallow pans, and fill with one cup rich cream, half cup powdered sugar, half cup pistachio-nuts, half cup almonds. Whip the cream stiff with a Dover beater; add the sugar, and the nuts chopped and pounded fine.

Cheese Cakes. — Line little patty pans with pastry, puff paste, or that which is quite rich. Make a cake after the recipe for Park Street cake, put a dessert spoonful of the cake batter on the paste, and then a teaspoonful of any kind of jelly, jam, or marmalade, with another dessert spoonful of the cake batter on the top. Bake in a quick oven

and frost when done. This is a convenient way to use up any remnants of paste, cake batter, and jelly, when one does not care to make a large quantity of the cakes.

Fig Cake. 1½ cups sugar. ½ cup butter. ½ cup sweet milk. 1½ cups flour. | 1 tsp. baking-powder. ½ cup cornstarch. 6 eggs, whites.

Bake in two layers, and fill with fig filling.

Fig Filling. 1 lb figs. ½ cup sugar. | 1 cup water.

Chop the figs, add the sugar and water, and stew until soft and smooth. Spread between the layers, and ice the whole cake with boiled icing.

Sour-Cream Cake. 3 eggs. 2 cups sugar. ½ tsp. salt. 1 tsp. lemon. | 1 scant tsp. soda. 1 cup rich sour cream. 3 cups flour.

Beat the yolks until light and thick; add the sugar, the whites beaten stiff, the salt and lemon. Dissolve the soda in the cream, add the flour, and bake in a shallow pan.

Half and Half Cake. ½ cup sugar. ½ cup butter. 1 egg. ½ cup molasses. ½ cup sour milk. | 2 cups flour. ½ tsp. soda. ½ tsp. salt. ½ tbsp. mixed spice

Mix soda, salt, and spice with the flour, cream the butter and sugar, add the beaten egg, the molasses, and sour milk, and then stir in the flour. Bake in a shallow pan about half an hour.

Black-Cap Cake. 1 cup butter creamed. 1½ cups sugar. 2 tbsp. molasses. 2 eggs. ½ cup sour milk. | 2½ cups flour. 1 tsp. soda. ½ tsp. each cinnamon and cloves. 1 cup each raisins and walnuts.

Mix in the order given, and bake in two shallow pans. Half lard and half butter may be used instead of all butter, in any cake with molasses.

Sponge	1 cup sour milk.	1 egg.
Gingerbread.	1 cup dark rich mo-	1 tsp soda.
	lasses.	1 tbsp. ginger.
	½ cup butter.	2 cups bread flour.
	½ cup sugar.	

Warm the butter, molasses, and ginger together, add the milk, flour, and egg and a pinch of salt, and last the soda dissolved in one tablespoon of warm water. Bake in shallow pans.

Grandmother's	½ cup sugar.	½ tsp. ginger.
Hard	½ cup butter.	¼ tsp. salt
Gingerbread.	½ cup molasses.	1 even tsp. soda.
	½ cup milk.	Flour for stiff dough.

Mix in the order given, dissolving the soda in the milk and mixing the salt and ginger in a little of the flour. Mix quite stiff, then knead till smooth and light; roll out one-third of an inch thick and to fit long shallow pans. Mark in half inch strips with a pastry jagger, and bake about fifteen minutes.

Anise-Seed Wafers. — Rub *half a cup* of *butter* till creamy, add *one cup* of fine *granulated sugar*, and when light beat in the *yolks* of *three small eggs*, one at a time. Beat the whites stiff, and add them with *two cups* of *flour* in alternation. Stir in *one teaspoon* of *anise seed* and enough more *flour* to enable you to roll it very thin. Cut into rounds and bake quickly. Anise seeds are used by the Germans and the Chinese as a flavoring in cake and sweet dishes. They are the fruit of seed of a small annual of the parsley family. A cordial or liquor is also prepared from them. They have an aromatic, agreeable odor and a warm sweetish taste.

Hermits.	1½ cups sugar.	1 teasp soda.
	½ cup butter.	1 teasp. each of spices,
	2 eggs.	cinnamon, nutmeg, and
	2 cups seedless raisins	clove.
	3 tbsp. milk	Flour to roll.

Cream the butter and sugar, add the eggs well beaten, then the milk. Mix the soda and spices (cinnamon, nutmeg, and clove) with one cup of flour; add the raisins, which must be washed, boiled until tender in water to cover, and drained, cut in halves or chopped, and floured. Then add flour to roll about a quarter of an inch thick, cut out in fancy shapes and bake quickly.

Walnut Wafers. — Cream *one-fourth* of a *cup* (two ounces) of *butter* gradually, add *half a cup* of *powdered sugar*, and almost drop by drop *four tablespoonfuls* of *milk*. Next mix in *a scant cupful* of *bread flour*, a few drops of any flavoring extract preferred, and *one-fourth* of a *cupful* of *chopped walnuts*. Spread on the bottom of an inverted dripping pan as thin as possible. The pan should be buttered unless it is very smooth. Because it is difficult to spread unless the nut meats are very finely chopped, many prefer to sprinkle them over the top of the dough after it is spread on the pan. *Almond paste* may be creamed in with the butter.

Mark in squares, then sprinkle with the nuts, and bake in a moderate oven. In five minutes they should be ready to roll, and this must be done at the oven door before they have a chance to cool a particle. With a wafer iron the process is slower, but the shape can be made more uniform.

Sand Cakes. — Cream *one scant cup* of *butter* with *one cup and a half* of *light brown sugar*. Beat *two eggs*, reserving part of *one white*, and beat them into the butter. Mix *half a teaspoon* of *cinnamon*, *two level teaspoons* of *baking-powder*, with *three and a half cups* of *flour*, stir this into the butter; add another *half cup* of *flour* if needed to roll thin as a wafer. Use fancy cutters, hearts, diamonds, etc.; lay the cakes in a greased baking pan. Brush the top with the *remaining egg white*. Split *blanched almonds* and put *three* or *four* on each cake in corners or radiating from the centre. Mix *one-fourth* of a *teaspoon cinnamon* with *one-fourth* of a *cup coarse granulated sugar* and sprinkle it over the cakes. Bake in a quick oven six or eight minutes.

Fancy Ice Creams. — Fancy ice creams depend largely for their right to this name, upon the moulding. Any good recipe for a cream ice or water ice may be used, but it is not advisable to attempt much in this line unless you have two freezers and a variety of fancy moulds. Plain brick moulds, melon moulds, brown bread moulds, pails, baking-powder cans, or fruit cans, if they are water tight, may all be utilized. Individual fancy moulds are quite expensive, but if one can afford their first cost, and is likely to use them often, it is cheaper in the end than to depend upon the confectioner.

Café Parfait, No. 1. — Mix *half a cup* of strong clear *coffee* with *one pint* of medium *cream*. Sweeten to taste and stir until the sugar is dissolved. Place the bowl of cream in a pan of ice. When the cream is chilled, whip it with a whip-churn and skim off the froth into a strainer placed over a granite pan, which should be in another pan of ice to keep the whipped portion cold. Pack a mould in ice and salt, and when the whipped cream is drained, pack it into the mould. The liquid cream which drains through may be whipped again. Be careful not to have any liquid cream in the mould. Cover the mould and let it stand in the ice from two to three hours.

Café Parfait, No. 2. — Make *half a cup* clear strong *coffee*. Beat the *yolks* of *three eggs*, add *half a saltspoon* of *salt* and *half a cup* of *sugar*, and when well mixed stir it into the coffee and cook in a double boiler till thick and smooth, stirring constantly. Strain, and when cold add *one quart* of *cream*, whipped. Beat until well blended, and add more sugar if needed. Turn into the freezer can, packed in ice and salt, and freeze without turning the crank.

Line a melon mould with an inch-thick layer of vanilla or plain coffee ice cream, then fill the centre with the whipped cream as in No. 1, and cover with ice cream. Pack in ice and salt, and let it stand for three hours.

lumps of loaf sugar which are afterward dissolved in the juice. Mix the lemon syrup with the ice-cold milk, and freeze as usual. When the milk is very cold, there is little danger that it will curdle.

Ice Cream with Fruit Syrup. — Fill punch glasses half full with vanilla ice cream. Crush strawberries and sweeten to taste with sugar dissolved in a little water boiled and cooled. Pour the fruit over the ice cream, nearly filling the glass.

Banana Ice Cream. — Select *eight* large nice *bananas*, ripe, but free from all blemish on the skin. Wipe them, and carefully peel off the flat strip of skin. Remove the pulp, scrape out the fibrous portion from the skins, and put them in the ice chest until the cream is ready. Mash the pulp of half of the bananas, mix with it *two cups* of *sugar* and *one quart* of *cream* of medium thickness, add *one saltspoon* of *salt*, and *two* of *lemon juice*. Press it through a fine sieve and freeze. Chop fine some *French candied fruit*, *cherries*, *green plums*, and *angelica* enough to make *eight* rounded *tablespoonfuls*. When the cream is nearly frozen, put a layer of it in the banana skins, sprinkle a tablespoonful of the fruit over the cream, add enough more cream to fill the skins, lay back the strip, and tie them with narrow green ribbons. Put them into a clean freezer, and let them stand surrounded with ice and salt, for an hour or two to ripen. Serve them on plates lined with lace paper.

Sultana Roll. — Wash and soak *one-fourth* of *a cup* of *Sultanas* in *brandy* or *wine* to cover. Mix *one scant tablespoon* of *flour* and *a speck* of *salt* with *one cup* of *sugar ;* add *one egg*, and beat well. Pour on slowly *one pint* of *hot milk*. Turn into the double boiler, and cook twenty minutes. Cool and stir in *one quart* of *cream*, a *few drops* of *almond* and a *tablespoon* of *vanilla*. Color a delicate green with *green color paste*. Freeze it, and

then use it to line baking-powder cans, pound size. Scatter the drained Sultanas through the cream, fill the centre
with *thick cream*, sweetened, flavored with *vanilla* and
whipped stiff. Cover, and let the cans stand in ice and
salt one or two hours. Turn out, cut in slices, and serve
with

Claret Sauce. — Boil *one cup* of *sugar* with *one-fourth
of a cup* of *water;* when slightly thickened, cool and add
one-half of a *cup* of *claret.*

Frozen	1 quart milk	4 eggs, whites.
Pudding.	1 hpd tbsp. arrowroot.	1 tbsp vanilla.
(*E. E. Squire.*)	2 cups sugar.	½ lb. French fruit.
	½ level tsp. salt.	2 oz pistachio nuts.
	3 cups cream	Color and flavor to taste.

Scald the milk in a double boiler. Mix the arrowroot,
sugar, and salt thoroughly, turn them into the boiling milk
and stir constantly until it thickens and is smooth. Cook
for twenty minutes. Or if you prefer you may wet the
arrowroot with a little cold milk and stir it, into the boiling milk and then add the sugar.

Let this mixture become very cold, and when ready to
freeze it, whip the cream to a light froth, beat the eggs
until light, but not stiff, and stir them into the cold mixture. Should there be any doubt as to the sweetness of
the cream, scald and cool it, before whipping. Add the
vanilla, using enough to give a strong flavor. If you like,
you may color it a delicate tint with yellow, pink, or green
color paste.

Turn it into the freezer and when partly frozen stir in
the French fruit and nuts. The fruit should be cut into
small bits. Candied cherries, apricots, and green plums
make an agreeable combination. Blanch the nuts in
boiling water until the skins loosen easily, remove them,
and cut into thin slices.

Frozen pudding as usually served at first-class hotels
is flavored with a fine quality of Santa Cruz or Jamaica

Rum, about two tablespoonfuls put in with the fruit.
Those who approve of and are accustomed to this flavor
would doubtless consider a frozen pudding made without
it, as not worthy of the name, but when made after this
recipe it is delicious with only the vanilla flavoring, and
although more expensive than the usual formula, it is
well worth an occasional trial.

Strawberry Ice Cream. — Sprinkle *two cups* of *sugar*
over *two quarts* of *strawberries*. Mash them, and let
them stand half an hour, or until the sugar is dissolved;
and meanwhile prepare the ice, and pack the freezer.
Turn the berries into a large square of cheese-cloth,
placed over a bowl, and squeeze as long as any juice or
pulp will come. Then empty the pulp and seeds left in
the cloth into a pan, and pour on gradually about *a pint*
of *milk;* mix it well with the pulp, until the pulp is separated from the seeds. Squeeze again until perfectly
dry. There should be nothing left in the cloth save a
ball of seeds. Add to the juice as much *cream* as you
may have, from *one cup* to *three pints*, and *sugar* to
make it very sweet. Freeze as usual. After tasting
this, you will never want any other strawberry ice
cream.

Stewed Green Apple Sauce. — The first green apples
that are found in the market usually awaken an appetite
for apple sauce and apple pie. The former is seldom
seen in perfection. Try this method.

With a sharp silver knife cut the apples in quarters,
remove the cores and skin and put them, as fast as pared,
into a bowl of cold water. When all are ready, skim them
out into a porcelain-lined or agate kettle with a large
surface, so there will not be much depth to the apples.
Add boiling water, just to show among the pieces, cover
tightly to keep in the steam, and let them cook quickly.
Shake the pan occasionally, and as soon as soft, mash
them with a silver fork, sprinkle over sugar to taste,

cover again and cook until the sugar is dissolved, and serve hot or cold. It should be free from lumps, white or about the shade of the inside of a lemon, and not too sweet. When eaten hot for breakfast, sometimes a pat of butter is an improvement. When cooked in this careful way, it will be far more appetizing than if of a dingy-brown color, of half cooked, and there will be no occasion for sifting it.

Bananas with Fruit Sauce. — Pick over *one quart* of *currants;* wash, drain, and mash them. Sprinkle over them *one cup* of *sugar*, and let them stand until the sugar is dissolved. Stir occasionally, then squeeze through coarse cheese-cloth, or press through a strainer fine enough to keep back the seeds. Peel *four bananas*, remove all the stringy membranes, cut them in halves lengthwise and crosswise. Arrange them in a shallow glass dish, and pour the currant juice over them. Keep it in a cold place until ready to serve. The flavor of the currant juice improves the bananas, and the color gives a pretty effect. Do not use the currants without sifting, for the seeds will be quite objectionable in the sauce. Blackberry juice may be used in the same way. A cool, simple dessert like this is more acceptable on a summer day than a hot starchy pudding served with meringue or whipped cream.

Stewed Prunes. — It would appear that so simple a thing as a dish of stewed prunes might always be acceptably served, but they are usually too sweet or insufficiently cooked. All dried fruits — that is, fruits that have been deprived of their natural juices by quick evaporation, or sun drying — need to have this juice or water replaced by a long soaking in cool water before being subjected to heat. This softens the cellular tissues so that they can absorb the water, the fruit swells out to nearly its natural condition; and then by the heat applied in cooking, the softening process is continued until every particle of the skin is, or should be, perfectly soft.

Just enough water to cover them, so that all may be equally softened, is all that is necessary, and when the prunes are sufficiently cooked this should boil down to a thick syrup. Except in some of the most acid varieties, no sugar is needed. In fact, many prunes are so rich in sugar that a little lemon juice seems to be an improvement. It is understood, of course, that the prunes should be well washed in tepid water before they are soaked.

Preserved Strawberries. — Select the choicest berries and lay aside not necessarily very large ones, but perfect, firm, and of even size they must be. Press the remainder of the fruit for juice, taking only what drips easily. These berries can be used later for a jam.

To a pound of juice allow a pound of sugar, and make as one does any jelly. Boil fully twenty minutes until surely jellied. Meantime weigh the fruit selected and an equal amount of sugar. Add these then to the jelly and boil carefully a few minutes more. No exact time can be given. It would not keep with raw strawberries dropped in, neither must they be allowed to shrivel like preserved ones. Occasionally try it on a saucer, keeping the kettle at a simmer only. Do not do much at a time. It is better to repeat the operation. When it grows firm in the saucer, put in a cold place, remove it from the fire (and seal, as usual, when cold), dipping it with care into glasses soon after taking from the fire.

It will not be a jelly that moulds like gooseberry or like quince and sustains its weight. It is apt to fall in luscious masses, catching the light in its clear red depths and showing the imprisoned berries.

A very little apple juice prepared as for jelly — and carefully strained — added at the beginning, with the same allowance of sugar, pound for pound or fractions thereof, would help it to form or " set " as old housekeepers say, and the flavor would not be detected. This is frequently done for making pear, cherry, and peach jellies, for the same reason that they do not form jelly well alone. A flannel jelly bag is very nice for a second straining, using the usual linen cheese-cloth for the first pressing. *Cincinnati Recipe.*

Pot-Pourri. — Put *a pint* of *alcohol* or *white preserving brandy* into a large stone jar that has a tightly fitting cover; then, as the summer fruits come on, put them into the alcohol with an equal amount of sugar; thus *a cup* of *sugar* and *a cup* of *fruit.* Stir every day with a clean wooden spoon. Use strawberries, pineapples, raspberries, currants, blackberries, apricots, cherries, peaches, plums, and grapes. Plums and peaches should be peeled, stoned, and cut fine. Cherries should be stoned, and grapes should be seeded. The alcohol is enough for the jarful of fruit, and will cook and keep the fruit perfectly. About a month after putting in the last fruit, it will be ready to use.

As the seeds of small fruits become hard by the brandy, it is better to mash them and use only the juice, particularly with currants, blackberries, and raspberries.

Rhubarb Jelly. — September, or not earlier than the middle of August, is the best time to make rhubarb jelly, as it is almost impossible for it to thicken when made of the spring rhubarb.

Wash the rhubarb, but do not peel it, simply cut it into small pieces and never mind if it be stringy. To every pound of rhubarb add *half a cup* of *water* and let it stew slowly in a granite or porcelain pan until it is all in shreds. Then strain through a fine cloth. Measure the juice and allow *one pound* of *sugar* to *one pint* of *juice.* Let the juice simmer ten minutes, or until it begins to thicken on the edge, then add the sugar and let it simmer till it jellies on the spoon or when dropped on a cool plate. Remove the scum carefully when done, turn into glasses which have been rolled in hot water and are still standing in it, and when cold and firm, pour melted paraffine over the top. Cover with paper and keep in a cool, dark closet.

Wild Unripe Grape Sauce. — Wash the grapes and remove the stems. Cut through the middle with a sharp knife and remove the seeds. Then weigh the fruit and allow an equal weight of sugar. Put the cut fruit in a kettle with cold water to show just to the top of the fruit. Let it boil, remove the scum, then sprinkle over it one quarter of the sugar. Boil again and press the grapes down, but do not stir to break them. Then add another quarter of the sugar, and when it has boiled five or eight minutes, repeat until all the sugar is used. Cook slowly until the syrup is thick or will jelly. Turn into small jars or glasses and seal with paper. When cold, the grapes should be quite distinct in the clear jelly.

Grape Jelly. — The wild grapes, gathered just as they begin to turn, are the best for jelly. Cultivated grapes, if fully ripe, are quite likely to disappoint one, if used for jelly; the color is dark and unattractive, and the compound is often a syrup rather than a jelly, but they make delicious marmalade.

Wash the grapes and free them from the stems. Put them in the kettle, and mash them until all broken. Heat slowly, and cook until the juice is well drawn out. Then place a square of cheese-cloth over a colander, and set the colander over a bowl. Turn in the grapes, and let it drip without any pressure. Measure the juice, and allow an equal measure of sugar. If wild grapes are used, allow a little more than an equal portion of sugar. Boil the juice fifteen minutes. Skim, and strain again, then add the sugar, and boil until the surface looks wrinkled, and the liquid jellies on the edge. Skim well, and turn into glasses.

Preserved Citron. — Cut the citron melon in halves each way, then cut each quarter in three quarter-inch slices from the stem and blossom ends to the middle. In this way you cut across the seeds, and they can be more easily removed than if the melon be cut in the same direction that the seeds lie.

Pick out all the seeds, and cut the slices in squares, stars, triangles, or any shape preferred. Put the harder outside pieces by themselves. Weigh the fruit and allow an equal weight of sugar or a little less if you prefer. Cook the citron in clear water until tender and transparent, the harder pieces first. As the fruit softens, take it out into another kettle or deep dish and sprinkle each layer with sugar. When it is all cooked, let it stand until the sugar is nearly dissolved and some of the citron juice is drawn out. Then put it over the fire again, and let it heat slowly until the fruit is heated through. Remove the fruit into the jars, which should be near at hand, in a pan of hot water. Boil the syrup down until it seems thick and rich, then pour it into the jars and seal quickly. If the fruit seems dry after standing in the sugar, you may add a little water when it is put on to boil. If you like, you may use the thinly shaved rind and juice of one lemon to each jar of fruit. Be sure that the lemon is not bitter. One tablespoonful of crystallized ginger cut fine gives a flavor preferred by many.

Strawberry Tomato Preserve. — For *one pound* of *strawberry tomatoes* allow *one-half pound* of *sugar* and *one lemon.*

Remove the husks. Make a syrup with the sugar and water enough to dissolve it, bring it to a boil and remove the scum. Add the tomatoes and let them stew until heated through, then skim them out and boil the syrup down until quite thick. Cook the sliced lemon in boiling water until the rind is tender, then add it to the syrup.

Tutti Frutti for Tarts. — Take equal parts of stoned cherries, currants, red raspberries, and large gooseberries. Mash the currants, squeeze out the juice, and use that to dissolve the sugar. Allow one pound of sugar to each pound of fruit. Mix and boil until thick like jam. Delicious for tarts

Lemon Butter. — The juice and grated rind of *three lemons, three eggs* well beaten, *one pound* of *sugar*, *one small cup* of *water*, *one level teaspoonful* of *butter*. Beat well together and boil five minutes or until thick. Keep . it in covered jelly-glasses. This is an English recipe.

Mangoes. — These are made from small, green water or muskmelons, green tomatoes, peppers, peaches, large cucumbers, or any fruit from which the seeds, stone, or inside portion can be removed, the cavity filled with a highly-seasoned mixture, and the opening closed again in such a way as to give the appearance of whole fruit. In using peppers and green tomatoes, cut a circular piece from the stem end, remove the seeds, and put the pieces in place again, or beside the one from which they were taken. If melons are used, cut out a piece one inch wide and three long, then scoop out the seeds and soft portion. When the fruit is prepared, let it soak over night in strongly-salted water. In the morning drain, and be careful to have the cut portions kept where they belong. Prepare the following mixture to use as stuffing : Chop enough firm, white *cabbage* to fill the cavities, it is impossible to give the exact amount. You may use with it, if you prefer, *one-fourth part* of *chopped celery*, or *green tomatoes*, or *cucumbers*. Sprinkle well with salt and let it stand two hours. Allow *one* small *onion, two* or *three nasturtium-seeds*, and *half a teaspoonful* of *whole mustard-seed* to each pint of chopped vegetables. Season to taste with *ground cloves, cinnamon, allspice, ginger, pepper*, and *salt*. Mix thoroughly, and then fill the cavities; press it in well, fit in the pieces that were removed, and then tie them firmly with fine twine. Put the mangoes in a preserving kettle, cover with cold vinegar and let them remain over night. The next morning heat all together and simmer gently half an hour. Take them out carefully and put in a stone jar and cover with cold vinegar. The next morning pour off the vinegar, add *half a cup* of *sugar* to *each quart* of *vinegar*, bring to a boil, and pour it over the mangoes. Repeat this for three or four mornings, and after the last scalding, cover when cool, and put away in a dry place. The latter part of this process applies only to mangoes made from melons and cucumbers. Pepper and tomato mangoes are simply covered. with cold vinegar after stuffing, then put away, and in a month they will be ready for the table.

Orange Marmalade. —*One dozen* of large navel *oranges.* Cut in halves, and scoop out the juice. Boil the peels two or three hours in plenty of water until you can run a broom corn through them. Drain, and when cool enough to handle, scrape out all the white, leaving only the yellow outside. Cut into straws. Weigh the pulp free from membrane and add an equal weight of *sugar.* Boil pulp, sugar, and straws for two hours, and then turn into glasses. It makes six one-pint jelly tumblers.

Vegetable Jelly Salad.

One quart of sliced cucumbers, or one pint of. sliced celery. Add one slice of onion, one quart of cold water, salt and pepper, and stew till soft and reduced to three cups of liquid. Add one-half box of Crystal gelatine soaked in one-half cup of cold water, stir well, strain without pressure, and again through fine cloth if not clear. Mould it in a ring; or small cups; or make cups of the jelly by moulding it in two of different size. Serve as a border for fresh cucumbers, or to hold celery and apple salad.

Junket Ice Cream.

Sweeten fresh strawberries, mash well; when sugar is dissolved, strain through fine cheese cloth; to one cup of the juice add one cup of thin cream and one quart of pure unscalded milk. Heat over boiling water till blood warm, remove, stir in two junket tablets dissolved in two tablespoons of cold water, and turn at once into the freezer can. Let it stand in a warm place till jellied, then pack the freezer with ice and salt and freeze as usual. The milk will jelly without heating if it stands several hours.

EXPLANATION OF TERMS USED IN COOKERY.

Abatis. Giblets.

Agneau. Lamb.

À la, au, aux. With; as *huîtres aux champignons*, oysters with mushrooms. Dressed in a certain style; as *Smelts à la Tartare*, with Tartare sauce.

À l'Aurore. A white sauce colored pink with the spawn of lobster.

À la bonne Femme. Of the good housewife.

À l'Estragon. With tarragon.

À la Neige. In the style of snow.

À la Poulette. Meat or fish warmed in a white sauce with yolks of eggs.

À la Reine. Of the queen.

Allemande. A thick white sauce made with cream and the yolks of eggs, and seasoned with nutmeg and lemon juice.

Almond. A nut grown in Southern Europe. It consists of a stone fruit, the fleshy pericarp of which dries in ripening, and forms a hard tough covering to the stone. Bitter almonds are obtained from Morocco. They contain prussic acid, and are poisonous. The sweet almonds include the Jordan and Valencia varieties. The Jordan almonds, imported from Malaga, are long and narrow, and are considered the best.

Angelica. A plant, the stems of which are preserved in syrup, and used for decorating pastry, etc.

Anguilles. Eels.

Apricot. A stone fruit cultivated in temperate and tropical climates. The skin has a highly perfumed flavor.

Asperges. Asparagus.

Aspic Jelly. A transparent jelly made with stock, and used for garnishing.

Au Beurre roux. With browned butter.

Au vert Pie. With sweet herbs.

Aux Cressons. With watercresses.

Aux Rognons. With kidneys.

Avena. Oats.

Baba. A very light yeast cake soaked in rum.

Bain Marie. A shallow open vessel filled with hot water, in which smaller dishes containing soups and sauces may be placed and kept warm without further cooking until serving-time.

Bannock. Primitive cake without yeast, cooked on a griddle, in Scotland made of pease, barley, and oatmeal, in America of cornmeal.

Barbecue. To roast any animal whole, usually in the open air.

Barm. The scum from fermented malt liquors, used as yeast.

Baron of Beef. The two sirloins not cut down the back. Formerly a favorite dish in England.

Baron of Lamb. The entire loin, not divided at the backbone, with the upper part of both legs.

Basil. An herb having a perfume like that of cloves, used as seasoning.

Bavaroise. Bavarian.

Bay Leaves. The leaves of the cherry-laurel tree.

Bearnaise. A rich egg sauce flavored with tarragon, named from Bearn, birthplace of Henry IV. of France.

Bécasses. Woodcock.

Béchamel. A white sauce made with stock and cream, named from a celebrated cook.

Beignet. A fritter.

Beurre noir. Browned butter.

Bisque. A shell-fish soup.

Blanch. To parboil, to scald vegetables, nuts, etc., in order to remove their hulls or skins.

Blanquette. Any white meat warmed in a white sauce thickened with eggs.

Bouchées. Very small Patties.

Bœuf. Beef.

Bouillabasse. Several kinds of fish boiled quickly, and highly seasoned

36

with onion, orange peel, saffron, oil, etc

Bouille. Broth made from beef.

Bouilli. Beef stewed, generally in one large piece, and served with a sauce

Bouquet, or *Fagot of Herbs.* A sprig of each of the herbs used in seasoning, rolled up in a spray of parsley and tied securely

Braising Stewing in a covered pan, with heat applied both below and above.

Brawm. Head cheese.

Bretonne. A purée of red onions.

Brioche Paste. Cakes made with yeast.

Broché A spit

Brochette A skewer

Brunoise. A brown soup or sauce.

Bubble and Squeak A dish of vegetable hash and meat

Buttock. A round of beef.

Café au Lait Coffee with hot milk.

Café noir. Black coffee.

Caille. Quail.

Calipash. The glutinous meat of the upper shell of the turtle

Calipee The glutinous meat of the under shell of the turtle

Canard. Duck.

Canellons. Puff paste baked round a form of cardboard, shaped like a cane

Cannelon of Meat. Minced and highly seasoned meat, baked in the form of a large roll.

Capers Unopened buds of a low trailing shrub grown in Southern Europe. Pickled and used in sauces.

Capon. A chicken castrated for the purpose of improving the quality of the flesh.

Caramel. A syrup of burnt sugar, named after Count Caramel, who discovered what is called the seventh degree of cooking sugar

Cardoon. A vegetable resembling the artichoke.

Casserole. A mould formed of rice or potato, and filled with a réchauffé

Champignons Mushrooms.

Charlotte. A preparation of cream or fruit, formed in a mould, lined with cake or fruit

Chartreuse. A preparation of game, fillets, etc, moulded in jelly and surrounded by vegetables. Invented by the monks of the monastery of Chartreuse as a convenient way of disguising meat.

Chervil. The leaf of a European plant used as a salad.

Chillies. Red peppers.

Chine. A piece of the backbone of an animal, with the adjoining parts cut for cooking Usually applied to pork.

Chives. An herb allied to the onion family

Chou-fleur. Cauliflower.

Chutney. A hot acid sauce made from apples, tomatoes, raisins, cayenne, ginger, garlic, shalots, salt, sugar, lemons, and vinegar.

Citric Acid. The acid of the citron family, lemons, oranges, etc.

Citron The rind of a fruit of the lemon species preserved in sugar.

Cochineal. Coloring matter made from the dried bodies of insects found in Mexico, where they feed on a species of the cactus

Cock-a-leekie. A soup used in Wales, made from fowls and leeks.

To Collar. To cure meat in a spiced brine.

Collops Meat cut in small pieces.

Compote Fruit stewed in syrup.

Confitures Preserves

Consommé. Very rich stock.

Coriander. A plant cultivated for its tender leaves, which are used in soups and salads and in making curry powder.

Cornichons Pickles.

Côtelettes. Cutlets.

Coulis. A rich brown gravy.

Crème Brulée Browned sugar or caramel with cream

Créole, À la With tomatoes.

Crévettes Shrimp.

Crimp. To cause to contract, or render more crisp, as the flesh of a fish by gashing it, while living, with a knife.

Croquettes. A preparation of mince with a bread-crumbed coating, and cooked till crisp.

Croustade A kind of patty of bread or prepared rice.

Croûton A sippet of fried or toasted bread.

Crumpet. Raised muffins baked on a griddle.

Cuen de Bœuf Ox-tails.

Currants. Dried currants are small black grapes, named from Corinth where they are grown.

Curries. Stews of meat or fish, seasoned with curry powder and served with rice.

Curry Powder. A mixture of turmeric, coriander seed, pepper, ginger, cardamoms, cumin seed, caraway, and cayenne.

De, d'. Of; as, *filet de bœuf*, fillet of beef.

Désosser. To bone.

Devilled. Seasoned hotly.

Dinde. Turkey.

En Coquille. Served in shells.

En Papillote. In papers

Endive. A plant of the Composite family, used as a salad.

Entrées. Small made dishes served with the first course at an elaborate dinner.

Entremets. Second-course side dishes, including vegetables, eggs, and sweets.

Epigrammes. Small fillets of poultry, game, and lamb prepared as an entrée

Espagnole. A rich brown sauce, the foundation of most brown sauces.

Épinards. Spinach.

Éperlans. Smelts.

Faisan. Pheasant.

Fanchonnettes and *Florentines.* Small pastries covered with a méringue.

Farcie. A kind of force-meat or stuffing.

Fausse Tortue. Mock Turtle.

Feuilletage. Puff paste.

Fillets. Long thin pieces of meat or fish, generally rolled and tied

Financière A rich brown sauce, with wine and mushroom catchup.

Finnan Haddock. Haddock smoked and dried, named from Findhorn in Scotland, where they are obtained in perfection.

Flaus, Darioles, and *Mirlitons.* French cheese cakes.

Foie. Liver.

Fondant. Melting. Boiled sugar, basis of French candy.

Fondue A preparation of melted cheese.

Fowl à la Marengo. A fowl browned in oil, and stewed in rich stock, seasoned with wine. Eaten and approved by Napoleon after the battle of Marengo.

Fraise. Strawberry.

Fricandeau. A thick piece of meat larded and browned, and stewed in stock, or baked and covered with glaze.

Fricassee. A stew in which the meat is first fried slightly.

Fromage. Cheese.

Galantine. Boned meat or poultry.

Gâteau. A cake.

Gaufres Waffles.

Gelée. Jelly.

Genevese Sauce. A white sauce made with white stock, highly seasoned with herbs, spices, mushrooms, lemon, and wine, and served with salmon or trout.

Glacé. Covered with icing

Glaze. Stock boiled down to a thin paste.

Gnocchi A light savory dough boiled, served with Parmesan.

Goulasch. A Hungarian beef stew, highly seasoned.

Gratins. Served in a rich sauce with browned crumbs.

Grilled. Broiled.

Groseilles Currants.

Gumbo A dish of food made of young capsules of okra, with salt and pepper, stewed and served with melted butter.

Gumbo Filet Powder Made from the tender young leaves of the sassafras, picked in the spring, and dried carefully in the shade like any herb. Powdered fine and bottled tight. Used in New Orleans

Haggis. A preparation of the heart, tongue, and liver of sheep.

Haricot A small bean ; a bit A stew in which the meat and vegetables are finely divided.

Hodge-podge. A Scotch meat stew.

Homard. Lobster.

Hors-d'œuvres. Relishes.

Huîtres. Oysters.

Jambon. Ham

Jardinière. A mixed preparation of vegetables stewed in their own sauce ; a garnish of various vegetables.

Julienne. A clear soup with shredded vegetables.

Kabobs. A dish of meat with India curry.

Kirsch-kuchen. German cherry cake.

Kippered. Dried or smoked.

Kohl Cannon. Boiled potatoes and cabbage, minced together, and seasoned with butter, pepper, and salt.

Koumiss. Milk fermented with yeast.

Kromeskies. Minces of meat or fish dipped in fritter batter, and fried crisp.

Laitue. Lettuce.

Lardoon The piece of salt pork or bacon used in larding.

Lentils. A variety of the bean tribe used in soups, etc.

Liaison. The mixture of egg yolks, cream, etc used for thickening

Lit. A layer. Articles in thin slices placed in layers, with seasoning or sauce between.

Macedoine. A mixture of fruit moulded in jelly, or of vegetables.

Madeline. A kind of pound cake.

Maigre. Dishes for fast days, made without flesh

Maître d'Hôtel Master of the hotel

Malic Acid The acid of apples, partially changed to sugar as apples ripen and into a bitter principle as they decay.

Mango. A kidney-shaped, sub-tropical fruit of variable quality, used green for pickles, and ripe for dessert.

Manna Kroup A flour made from wheat and rice, sometimes mixed with saffron and yolk of egg

Maraschino A kind of brandy.

Marinade. A pickle for boiling meat or fish in.

Marinate. To pickle or to sprinkle with a French dressing.

Marrons. Chestnuts.

Matelote. A rich stew, made of fish, and flavored with wine

Mayonnaise. Cold sauce, or salad dressing, of raw eggs and oil.

Menu. A bill of fare

Méringue. A kind of icing made of white of egg and sugar well beaten.

Mi-Carême. Dishes used in mid-Lent.

Mignonnette Pepper. Peppercorns ground coarsely.

Mirepoix. A rich brown broth used in braising meat.

Miroton. Pieces of meat cut larger than collops, for a stew or ragout.

Morel. A species of mushroom.

Morue. Codfish.

Mouton. Mutton.

Nectarine. A variety of the peach, having a smooth skin.

Nougat A mixture of almonds and sugar

Nouilles A kind of vermicelli.

Noyau. A cordial.

Œufs Eggs.

Ognon Onions.

Okra The green mucilaginous pods of an annual plant, used in the South for soups and pickles.

Oxalic Acid. The acid in sorrel and rhubarb.

Panais. Parsnips.

Paner. To cover with bread crumbs.

Panure. Any entrée that is bread-crumbed.

Pâté aux Choux. Cream-cake paste, so called because when baked it resembles a head of cabbage.

Pâté de Foie gras A pie of fat livers.

Perdreux. Partridge

Persillade of Fish With parsley.

Petits Panis. Little bread.

Petits Pois Pease.

Pigeonnaux. Squab.

Pimento. Allspice or Jamaica pepper.

Pistachio. A pale greenish nut resembling the almond.

Poêlée. Stock used instead of water for boiling poultry, sweetbreads, etc.

Poisson. Fish

Pommes. Apples

Pommes de Terre. Potatoes

Pot-au-feu. The stock pot.

Potage. A soup.

Pot-Pourri. A mixture of minced cooked meat and vegetables. A mixture of fruits and sugar.

Poulet. A chicken

Praline. Flavor with burnt almond.

Printanier (à la). With young spring vegetables.

Purée. A thick soup rubbed through a sieve.

Quenelle. A delicate force-meat used in entrées.

Ragout. A highly seasoned stew flavored with wine.

Ramakins. A preparation of cheese and puff paste or toast, baked or browned.

Ratifias. Almond cakes. A kind of liquor flavored with nuts.

Ravigote. A highly flavored green herb sauce.

Réchauffé. Anything warmed over.

Removes, or *Relèves.* The roasts or principal dishes

Ris de Veau Sweetbread

Rissoles. Small shapes of puff paste filled with some mixture, and fried or baked. Or balls of minced meat, egged and crumbed, and fried till crisp.

Risotto. An Italian dish of rice and cheese

Rizotta. Italian rice and cheese.

Rognons Kidneys

Roux. Thickening made with butter and flour.

Salmi. A stew or hash of game.

Salpicon. A mince of poultry, ham, and other meats used for entrees

Savoy Cakes, or *Naples Biscuits.* Lady Fingers.

Sauce Piquante. An acid sauce.

Sauté. Fried and tossed over in a little fat

Scones. Scotch cakes of meal or flour.

Semona, or *Semolina* Same as Manna Kroup

Shalot. A variety of onion.

Soubise Sauce. A purée of white onions named after Prince Soubise.

Soufflé. A very light pudding or omelet. The name means " puffed up."

Soy. A Japanese sauce prepared from the seeds of *Dolichos Soja* It has an agreeeble flavor and a clear brown color. Used to color soups and sauces.

Stock. The essence extracted from meat.

Sultanas. White or yellow seedless grapes, grown in Corinth.

Tamis. A sieve or fine strainer cloth

Tarragon An herb, the leaves of which are used as seasoning and in flavoring vinegar

Tendrons de Veau The gristles from the breast of veal stewed in stock, and served as an entrée

Timbale. A drum-like shell of rice or macaroni filled with force-meat or ragout.

Toad in the Hole. A dish of cold meat baked in a batter of milk, eggs, and flour.

Tourte. A tart.

Truffles. A species of fungi growing in clusters some inches below the soil, and having an agreeable perfume, which is easily scented by pigs, who are fond of them, and by dogs trained to find them. They are found abundantly in France, but are not subject to cultivation. Used in seasoning and garniture.

Truite. Trout.

Turbans Ornamental drum-shaped cases containing entrées made of force-meat and fillets of game, etc.

Vanilla. The fruit of a Mexican plant. Pure vanilla beans are from seven to nine inches long, soft, oily, flexible, can easily be wound over the finger, and when cut have a frosted appearance. The seeds are so fine as to be hardly discernible An ounce contains seven or eight beans, and costs $1.50.

Veau Veal.

Velouté. A smooth white sauce.

Vin (Au) With wine.

Vinaigrette Sauce. With acid wine or vinegar.

Vol-au-vent. A crust of very light puff paste, filled with oysters or chickens, warmed in a cream sauce, or filled with fruit.

Zest of lemon. The grated or shaved yellow layer of oil cells.

Zwieback. Bread toasted twice.

ADDENDA.

Alaska, Baked. Ice cream covered with meringue and slightly baked.

Anise The aromatic seed of one of the Umbelliferae ; a favorite flavoring for bread and cakes with Germans

Bordelaise. A sauce of rich brown stock, with marrow.

Boudins An entrée of forcemeat and fillets, or forcemeat with a salpicon inside

Boulettes Croquettes the size of small marbles

Casserole, En. Meat or game cooked in an earthen dish with a cover in a rich stock.

Chapon. A bit of bread flavored with garlic used beneath a salad.

Chaudfroid Dishes dressed with a hot gelatinized sauce and served cold

Chiffonade Salad herbs finely shredded and sautéd, or used in salad

Cummin. A seed used to flavor cheese, by the Dutch

Dariole. Shallow cups of puff paste with a sweet cream, or custard filling.

Dill. A seed used for flavoring pickles

Escarole A broad-leaved kind of Endive

Flageolet. A flat green bean used in France.

Fontage. A cup, of batter cooked on an iron, same as Swedish Timbale

Junket. Milk jellied by means of rennet.

Liaison Egg yolks and cream used for thickening soups, sauces, etc

Meunière. Flour made into thin batter with water used for thickening.

Mirlitons. Fancy tartlets

Mousse A rich finely minced mixture of meat, game, eggs, etc , made very light with egg whites and whipped cream, and served cold Or whipped cream frozen without motion.

Mousseline A thimble shaped mould for forcemeats, etc

Printanière. With mixed vegetables

Profiteroles Tiny balls, filbert size, of cream cake mixture, sometimes filled with forcemeat and heated again, and served with soup.

Roulettes Bread balls highly seasoned and fried.

Savarin. A kind of cake with yeast, similar to Baba, or Brioche.

Scones. Scotch cakes similar to our baking powder biscuit

Talmouse. Like a Dariole, with cheese in the custard.

To despumate. Remove all the skin or fat forming on the surface while boiling

To reduce. Cook until liquid has evaporated or made less

To tammy To put through a sieve or strainer.

ALPHABETICAL INDEX.

ADDENDA.